SMALL BUSINESS CONSIDERATIONS, ECONOMICS AND RESEARCH

SMALL BUSINESS ADMINISTRATION PROGRAMS

OVERVIEW AND CONSIDERATIONS

SMALL BUSINESS CONSIDERATIONS, ECONOMICS AND RESEARCH

Additional books in this series can be found on Nova's website under the Series tab.

Additional E-books in this series can be found on Nova's website under the E-book tab.

BUSINESS ISSUES, COMPETITION AND ENTREPRENEURSHIP

Additional books in this series can be found on Nova's website under the Series tab.

Additional E-books in this series can be found on Nova's website under the E-book tab.

SMALL BUSINESS CONSIDERATIONS, ECONOMICS AND RESEARCH

SMALL BUSINESS ADMINISTRATION PROGRAMS

OVERVIEW AND CONSIDERATIONS

WALTER JANIKOWSKI
EDITOR

New York

Copyright © 2013 by Nova Science Publishers, Inc.

All rights reserved. No part of this book may be reproduced, stored in a retrieval system or transmitted in any form or by any means: electronic, electrostatic, magnetic, tape, mechanical photocopying, recording or otherwise without the written permission of the Publisher.

For permission to use material from this book please contact us:
Telephone 631-231-7269; Fax 631-231-8175
Web Site: http://www.novapublishers.com

NOTICE TO THE READER

The Publisher has taken reasonable care in the preparation of this book, but makes no expressed or implied warranty of any kind and assumes no responsibility for any errors or omissions. No liability is assumed for incidental or consequential damages in connection with or arising out of information contained in this book. The Publisher shall not be liable for any special, consequential, or exemplary damages resulting, in whole or in part, from the readers' use of, or reliance upon, this material. Any parts of this book based on government reports are so indicated and copyright is claimed for those parts to the extent applicable to compilations of such works.

Independent verification should be sought for any data, advice or recommendations contained in this book. In addition, no responsibility is assumed by the publisher for any injury and/or damage to persons or property arising from any methods, products, instructions, ideas or otherwise contained in this publication.

This publication is designed to provide accurate and authoritative information with regard to the subject matter covered herein. It is sold with the clear understanding that the Publisher is not engaged in rendering legal or any other professional services. If legal or any other expert assistance is required, the services of a competent person should be sought. FROM A DECLARATION OF PARTICIPANTS JOINTLY ADOPTED BY A COMMITTEE OF THE AMERICAN BAR ASSOCIATION AND A COMMITTEE OF PUBLISHERS.

Additional color graphics may be available in the e-book version of this book.

Library of Congress Cataloging-in-Publication Data

ISBN: 978-1-62417-992-1

Published by Nova Science Publishers, Inc. † New York

CONTENTS

Preface		**vii**
Chapter 1	Small Business Administration: A Primer on Programs *Robert Jay Dilger and Sean Lowry*	**1**
Chapter 2	The SBA Disaster Loan Program: Overview and Possible Issues for Congress *Bruce R. Lindsay*	**29**
Chapter 3	Small Business Administration 7(a) Loan Guaranty Program *Robert Jay Dilger*	**53**
Chapter 4	Small Business Administration 504/CDC Loan Guaranty Program *Robert Jay Dilger*	**87**
Chapter 5	Small Business Administration Microloan Program *Robert Jay Dilger*	**117**
Chapter 6	SBA Small Business Investment Company Program *Robert Jay Dilger*	**137**
Chapter 7	Small Business Management and Technical Assistance Training Programs *Robert Jay Dilger*	**173**
Chapter 8	The "8(a) Program" for Small Businesses Owned and Controlled by the Socially and Economically Disadvantaged: Legal Requirements and Issues *Kate M. Manuel and John R. Luckey*	**207**
Chapter 9	Small Business Administration HUBZone Program *Robert Jay Dilger*	**239**
Chapter 10	SBA Surety Bond Guarantee Program *Robert Jay Dilger*	**271**
Chapter 11	Small Business Innovation Research (SBIR) Program *Wendy H. Schacht*	**301**

Chapter 12	SBA New Markets Venture Capital Program *Robert Jay Dilger*	**311**
Chapter 13	SBA Veterans Assistance Programs: An Analysis of Contemporary Issues *Robert Jay Dilger and Sean Lowry*	**335**
Index		**363**

PREFACE

The Small Business Administration (SBA) administers several programs to support small businesses, including loan guarantee programs to enhance small business access to capital; contracting programs to increase small business opportunities in federal contracting; direct loan programs for businesses, homeowners, and renters to assist their recovery from natural disasters; and small business management and technical assistance training programs to assist business formation and expansion. This book provides an overview of these programs, with a focus on stimulating economic activity, creating jobs, and assisting in the national economic recovery.

Chapter 1 - The Small Business Administration (SBA) administers several programs to support small businesses, including loan guarantee programs to enhance small business access to capital; contracting programs to increase small business opportunities in federal contracting; direct loan programs for businesses, homeowners, and renters to assist their recovery from natural disasters; and small business management and technical assistance training programs to assist business formation and expansion. Congressional interest in the SBA's loan and contracting programs has increased in recent years, primarily because small businesses are viewed as a means to stimulate economic activity, create jobs, and assist in the national economic recovery. Many Members of Congress also regularly receive constituent inquiries about SBA disaster loans, the loan guarantee programs, and contracting programs. This report provides an overview of these programs, including changes made by P.L. 111-5, the American Recovery and Reinvestment Act of 2009, and P.L. 111-240, the Small Business Jobs Act of 2010. It also provides an overview of the SBA's budget.

Chapter 2 - Through its Office of Disaster Assistance (ODA), the Small Business Administration (SBA) has been a major source of assistance for the restoration of commerce and households in areas stricken by natural and human-caused disasters since the agency's creation in 1953. SBA offers low-interest, long-term loans for physical and economic damages to businesses to help repair, rebuild, and recover from economic losses after a declared disaster. However, the majority of the agency's approved disaster loans (approximately 80%) are made to individuals and households (renters and property owners) to help repair and replace homes and personal property.

The three main types of loans for disaster-related losses include (1) Home and Personal Property Loans, (2) Business Physical Disaster Loans, and (3) Economic Injury Disaster Loans (EIDL). Home Disaster Loans are used to repair or replace disaster-damaged primary residences. Personal Property Loans are used to replace personal items such as furniture and clothing. SBA regulations limit Home Physical Disaster Loans to $200,000 and Personal

Property Loans to $40,000. Business Physical Disaster Loans help businesses of all sizes and nonprofit organizations repair or replace disaster-damaged property, including inventory and supplies. EIDLs provide financial assistance to businesses located in a disaster area that have suffered economic injury as a result of a declared disaster (regardless if there has been physical damage to the business). EIDLs are used to meet financial obligations it could have met if the disaster had not occurred. Both Business Physical Disaster Loans and EIDLs are limited by law to $2 million per applicant. Business Physical Disaster Loans and EIDLs also provide assistance to small businesses, small agricultural cooperatives (but not enterprises), and certain private, nonprofit organizations that have suffered substantial economic injury resulting from a physical disaster or an agricultural production disaster. Since 1953, SBA has approved roughly 1.9 million disaster loans for a total of more than $47 billion (nominal dollars).

Congressional interest in the Disaster Loan Program has increased in recent years primarily because of concerns about the program's performance in responding to the 2005 and 2008 hurricane disasters. Supporters of the Disaster Loan Program argue that it is an important form of assistance to help victims recover from disasters. Critics argue that the responsibility for disaster recovery should be borne by homeowners through the purchase of private insurance. Supporters reply that by covering individuals and households unable to afford private insurance, the program fills a need not met by traditional market mechanisms.

This report describes the SBA Disaster Loan Program, including the types of loans available to individuals, households, businesses, and nonprofit organizations and highlights issues that may be of potential congressional concern: (1) the pace of implementation of the Small Business Disaster Response and Loan Improvement Act of 2008 (P.L. 110-246), (2) SBA's loan processing procedures, (3) the funding of the Disaster Loan Program, (4) the potential need for loan forgiveness and waivers, (5) decline rates for SBA disaster loans, (6) the use of disaster loans to replace allegedly toxic drywall, (7) the transfer of the Disaster Loan Program to FEMA, (8) the perceived increase in federal spending for disasters, and (9) interest rates for SBA disaster loans.

Chapter 3 - The Small Business Administration (SBA) administers several programs to support small businesses, including loan guaranty programs designed to encourage lenders to provide loans to small businesses "that might not otherwise obtain financing on reasonable terms and conditions." The SBA's 7(a) loan guaranty program is considered the agency's flagship loan guaranty program. It is named from Section 7(a) of the Small Business Act of 1953 (P.L. 83-163, as amended), which authorized the SBA to provide business loans and loan guaranties to American small businesses.

In FY2012, the SBA approved 44,377 7(a) loans amounting to more than $15.1 billion. Proceeds from 7(a) loans may be used to establish a new business or to assist in the operation, acquisition, or expansion of an existing business.

Congressional interest in the 7(a) loan guaranty program has increased in recent years because of concerns that small businesses might be prevented from accessing sufficient capital to enable them to assist in the economic recovery. Some, including President Obama, argue that the SBA should be provided additional resources to assist small businesses in acquiring capital necessary to start, continue, or expand operations with the expectation that in so doing small businesses will create jobs. Others worry about the long-term adverse economic effects of spending programs that increase the federal deficit. They advocate

Preface ix

business tax reduction, reform of financial credit market regulation, and federal fiscal restraint as the best means to assist small business economic growth and job creation.

This report discusses the rationale provided for the 7(a) program; the program's borrower and lender eligibility standards and program requirements; and program statistics, including loan volume, loss rates, use of the proceeds, borrower satisfaction, and borrower demographics. It examines issues raised concerning the SBA's administration of the 7(a) program, including the oversight of 7(a) lenders and the program's lack of outcome-based performance measures.

It also examines congressional action taken during the 111th Congress to help small businesses gain greater access to capital. For example, P.L. 111-5, the American Recovery and Reinvestment Act of 2009 (ARRA), provided $375 million to temporarily subsidize the 7(a) and 504/CDC loan guaranty programs' fees and to temporarily increase the 7(a) program's maximum loan guaranty percentage to 90%. P.L. 111-240, the Small Business Jobs Act of 2010, provided $505 million to extend the fee subsidies and 90% loan guaranty percentage through December 31, 2010; increased the 7(a) program's gross loan limit from $2 million to $5 million; and established an alternative size standard for the 7(a) and 504/CDC loan programs. P.L. 111-322, the Continuing Appropriations and Surface Transportation Extensions Act, 2011, authorized the SBA to continue the fee subsidies and 90% loan guaranty percentage through March 4, 2011, or until available funding was exhausted (which occurred on January 3, 2011).

This report also examines three bills introduced during the 112th Congress that would affect the 7(a) program. S. 1828, a bill to increase small business lending, and for other purposes, would reinstate for a year following the date of its enactment ARRA's fee subsidies and 90% loan guaranty percentage for the 7(a) program. H.R. 2936, the Small Business Administration Express Loan Extension Act of 2011, would extend a one-year increase in the maximum loan amount for the SBAExpress program from $350,000 to $1 million for an additional year. That temporary increase expired on September 26, 2011. S. 532, the Patriot Express Authorization Act of 2011, would provide statutory authorization for the Patriot Express Pilot Program and increase its loan guaranty percentages and its maximum loan amount from $500,000 to $1 million. Information concerning the 7(a) program's SBAExpress, Patriot Express, Small Loan Advantage, and Community Advantage programs is also provided.

Chapter 4 - The Small Business Administration (SBA) administers programs to support small businesses, including several loan guaranty programs designed to encourage lenders to provide loans to small businesses "that might not otherwise obtain financing on reasonable terms and conditions."

The SBA's 504 Certified Development Company (504/CDC) loan guaranty program is administered through non-profit Certified Development Companies (CDC). It provides long-term fixed rate financing for major fixed assets, such as land, buildings, equipment, and machinery. Of the total project costs, a third-party lender must provide at least 50% of the financing, the CDC provides up to 40% of the financing through a 100% SBA-guaranteed debenture, and the applicant provides at least 10% of the financing.

It is named from Section 504 of the Small Business Investment Act of 1958 (P.L. 85-699, as amended), which authorized the program. In FY2012, the SBA approved 9,471 504/CDC loans amounting to about $6.7 billion.

Congressional interest in the SBA's 504/CDC program has increased in recent years because of concern that small businesses might be prevented from accessing sufficient capital to assist in the economic recovery. During the 111th Congress, P.L. 111-240, the Small Business Jobs Act of 2010, increased the 504/CDC program's loan guaranty limits from $1.5 million to $5 million for "regular" borrowers, from $2 million to $5 million if the loan proceeds are directed toward one or more specified public policy goals, and from $4 million to $5.5 million for manufacturers. It also temporarily expanded, for two years, the types of projects eligible for 504/CDC program refinancing of existing debt, created an alternative 504/CDC size standard to increase the number of businesses eligible for assistance, and provided $510 million to extend temporary fee subsidies for the 504/CDC and 7(a) loan guaranty programs and a temporary increase in the 7(a) program's maximum loan guaranty percentage to 90%.

The temporary fee subsidies and 90% loan guaranty percentage ended on January 3, 2011, and the temporary expansion of the projects eligible for 504/CDC program refinancing of existing debt expired on September 27, 2012.

This report opens with a discussion of the rationale provided for the 504/CDC program, the program's borrower and lender eligibility standards, program requirements, and program statistics, including loan volume, loss rates, use of the proceeds, borrower satisfaction, and borrower demographics.

It then examines congressional action taken during the 111th Congress to help small businesses gain greater access to capital, including the enactment of P.L. 111-5, the American Recovery and Reinvestment Act of 2009 (ARRA), and P.L. 111-240, the Small Business Jobs Act of 2010. It also discusses congressional efforts during the 112th Congress to extend the temporary expansion of the projects eligible for 504/CDC program refinancing of existing debt, which expired on September 27, 2012. For example, H.R. 2950, the Small Business Administration 504 Loan Refinancing Extension Act of 2011, would extend that expiration date another year and S. 3572, the Restoring Tax and Regulatory Certainty to Small Businesses Act of 2012, would extend that expiration date another year and a half. S. 1828, a bill to increase small business lending, and for other purposes, is also discussed. It would reinstate for a year following the date of its enactment the temporary fee subsidies for the 504/CDC and 7(a) programs and the 90% loan guaranty percentage for the 7(a) program, which ended on January 3, 2011. Issues raised concerning the SBA's administration of the program, including the oversight of 504/CDC lenders, are also discussed.

Chapter 5 - The Small Business Administration's (SBA's) Microloan program provides direct loans to qualified non-profit intermediary Microloan lenders who, in turn, provide "microloans" of up to $50,000 to small business owners, entrepreneurs, and non-profit child care centers. It also provides marketing, management, and technical assistance to Microloan borrowers and potential borrowers. The program was authorized in 1991 as a five-year demonstration project and became operational in 1992. It was made permanent, subject to reauthorization, in 1997. The SBA's Microloan program is designed to assist women, low-income, veteran, and minority entrepreneurs and small business owners and other individuals possessing the capability to operate successful business concerns by providing them small-scale loans for working capital or the acquisition of materials, supplies, or equipment. In FY2012, Microloan intermediaries provided 3,973 Microloans amounting to $44.7 million. The average Microloan was $11,254 and had a 8.18% interest rate. Critics of the SBA's Microloan program argue that it is expensive relative to alternative programs, duplicative of the SBA's 7(a) loan guaranty program, and subject to administrative shortfalls. The program's advocates argue that it provides assistance that reaches many who otherwise would not be served by the private sector and is an important source of capital and training assistance for low-income women and minority business owners. Congressional interest in the Microloan program has increased in recent years, primarily because microloans are viewed as a means to assist very small businesses, especially women- and minority-owned startups, to get loans that enable them to create and retain jobs. Job creation, always a congressional interest, has taken on increased importance given the nation's current economic difficulties.

This report opens with a discussion of the rationale provided for having a Microloan program, describes the program's eligibility standards and operating requirements for lenders and borrowers, and examines the arguments presented by the program's critics and by its advocates. It concludes with an examination of changes to the program authorized by P.L. 111-240, the Small Business Jobs Act of 2010. The Small Business Jobs Act increased the Microloan program's loan limit for borrowers from $35,000 to $50,000, and for intermediaries after their first year of participation in the program from $3.5 million to $5 million. It also authorized the SBA to waive, in whole or in part through FY2012, the non-federal share requirement for loans to the Microloan program's intermediaries and for grants made to Microloan intermediaries for small business marketing, management, and technical assistance for up to a fiscal year.

Chapter 6 - The Small Business Administration's (SBA's) Small Business Investment Company (SBIC) Program is designed to enhance small business access to venture capital by stimulating and supplementing "the flow of private equity capital and long term loan funds which small business concerns need for the sound financing of their business operations and for their growth, expansion, and modernization, and which are not available in adequate supply." Facilitating the flow of capital to small businesses to stimulate the national economy was, and remains, the SBIC program's primary objective.

At the end of FY2012, there were 301 privately owned and managed SBICs licensed by the SBA, providing financing to small businesses with private capital the SBIC has raised (called regulatory capital) and funds the SBIC borrows at favorable rates (called leverage) because the SBA guarantees the debenture (loan obligation). SBICs pursue investments in a broad range of industries, geographic areas, and stages of investment. Some SBICs specialize in a particular field or industry, while others invest more generally. Most SBICs concentrate on a particular stage of investment (i.e., startup, expansion, or turnaround) and geographic area.

The SBA is authorized to provide up to $3 billion in leverage to SBICs annually. The SBIC program has invested or committed about $18.2 billion in small businesses, with the SBA's share of capital at risk about $8.8 billion. In FY2012, the SBA committed to guarantee $1.9 billion in SBIC small business investments, and SBICs provided another $1.3 billion in investments from private capital, for a total of more than $3.2 billion in financing for 1,094 small businesses.

Some Members of Congress, the Obama Administration, and small business advocates argue that the program should be expanded as a means to stimulate economic activity, create jobs, and assist in the national economic recovery. For example, S. 3442, the SUCCESS Act of 2012, and S. 3572, the Restoring Tax and Regulatory Certainty to Small Businesses Act of 2012, would, among other provisions, increase the program's authorization amount to $4 billion from $3 billion, increase the program's family of funds limit (the amount of outstanding leverage allowed for two or more SBIC licenses under common control) to $350 million from $225 million, and annually adjust the maximum outstanding leverage amount available to both individual SBICs and SBICs under common control to account for inflation. Also, H.R. 6504, the Small Business Investment Company Modernization Act of 2012, would increase the program's family of funds limit (the amount of outstanding leverage allowed for two or more SBIC licenses under common control) to $350 million from $225 million.

Others worry that an expanded SBIC program could result in loses and increase the federal deficit. In their view, the best means to assist small business, promote economic growth, and create jobs is to reduce business taxes and exercise federal fiscal restraint.

Some Members have also proposed that the program target additional assistance to startup and early stage small businesses, which are generally viewed as relatively risky investments but also as having a relatively high potential for job creation. In an effort to target additional assistance to newer businesses, the SBA has established, as part of the Obama Administration's Startup America Initiative, a $1 billion early stage debenture SBIC initiative (up to $150 million in leverage in FY2012, and up to $200 million in leverage per fiscal year thereafter until the limit is reached). Early stage debenture SBICs are required to invest at least 50% of their investments in early stage small businesses, defined as small businesses that have never achieved positive cash flow from operations in any fiscal year.

This report describes the SBIC program's structure and operations, including two recent SBA initiatives, one targeting early stage small businesses and one targeting underserved markets. It also examines several legislative proposals to increase the leverage available to SBICs and to increase the SBIC program's authorization amount to $4 billion.

Chapter 7 - The Small Business Administration (SBA) has provided "technical and managerial aides to small-business concerns, by advising and counseling on matters in connection with government procurement and on policies, principles and practices of good management" since it began operations in 1953. Initially, the SBA provided its own small business management and technical assistance training programs. However, over time, the SBA has relied increasingly on third parties to provide that training. In FY2012, the SBA will provide nearly $170 million to about "14,000 resource partners," including more than 900 small business development centers, 108 women's business centers, and 364 chapters of the mentoring program, SCORE. The SBA reports that more than 1 million aspiring entrepreneurs and small business owners receive training from an SBA-supported resource partner each year. The SBA has argued that these programs contribute "to the long-term success of these businesses and their ability to grow and create jobs." The Department of Commerce also provides management and technical assistance training for small businesses. For example, its Minority Business Development Agency provides training to minority business owners to assist them in becoming suppliers to private corporations and the federal government.

A recurring theme at congressional hearings concerning the SBA's management and technical assistance training programs has been the perceived need to improve program efficiency by eliminating duplication of services and increasing cooperation and coordination both within and among SCORE, women's business centers (WBCs), and small business development centers (SBDCs). For example, on March 15, 2011, the House Committee on Small Business recommended that several SBA training programs be defunded "because they duplicate existing programs at the SBA or at other agencies." Congress has also explored ways to improve the SBA's measurement of the programs' effectiveness and to address the impact of national economic conditions on WBC and SBDC finances and their capacity to maintain client service levels and meet federal matching requirements. This report examines the historical development of federal small business management and technical assistance training programs; describes their current structures, operations, and budgets; and assesses their administration and oversight, the measures used to determine their effectiveness, and WBC and SBDC finances and their capacity to maintain client service levels and meet federal matching requirements. This report also discusses P.L. 111-240, the Small Business Jobs Act of 2010. It authorized $50 million in additional funds for SBDCs to provide targeted technical assistance to small businesses for various specified activities, such as seeking access to capital or credit; guaranteed each state not less than $325,000 of these additional funds; and waived the non-federal matching requirement for these funds. The act also authorizes the SBA to temporarily waive, in whole or in part, for successive fiscal years, the non-federal share matching requirement relating to "technical assistance and counseling" for WBCs. Two bills introduced during the 111th Congress, H.R. 2352, the Job Creation Through Entrepreneurship Act of 2009, and S. 3967, the Small Business Investment and Innovation Act of 2010, are also examined. They would have authorized several changes to the SBA's management and technical assistance training programs in an effort to improve their performance and oversight.

Chapter 8 - Commonly known as the "8(a) Program," the Minority Small Business and Capital Ownership Development Program is one of several federal contracting programs for small businesses. The 8(a) Program provides participating small businesses with training, technical assistance, and contracting opportunities in the form of set-asides and sole-source awards. A "set-aside" is an acquisition in which only certain contractors may compete, while a sole-source award is a contract awarded, or proposed for award, without competition. In FY2011, the federal government spent $16.7 billion on contracts and subcontracts with 8(a) firms. Other programs provide similar assistance to other types of small businesses (e.g., women-owned, HUBZone).

Eligibility for the 8(a) Program is generally limited to small businesses "unconditionally owned and controlled by one or more socially and economically disadvantaged individuals who are of good character and citizens of the United States" that demonstrate "potential for success." Each of these terms is further defined by the Small Business Act, regulations promulgated by the Small Business Administration (SBA), and judicial and administrative decisions.

A "business" is generally a for-profit entity that has a place of business located in the United States and operates primarily within the United States or makes a significant contribution to the U.S. economy by paying taxes or using American products, materials, or labor. A business is "small" if it is independently owned and operated; is not dominant in its field of operations; and meets any definitions or standards established by the Administrator of Small Business. Ownership is "unconditional" when it is not subject to any conditions precedent or subsequent, executory agreements, or similar limitations. "Control" is not the same as ownership and includes both strategic policy setting and day-to-day administration of business operations.

Members of certain racial and ethnic groups are presumed to be socially disadvantaged, although individuals who do not belong to these groups may prove they are also socially disadvantaged. To be economically disadvantaged, an individual must have a net worth of less than $250,000 (excluding ownership in the 8(a) firm and equity in one's primary residence) at the time of entry into the 8(a) Program. This amount increases to $750,000 for continuing eligibility. In determining whether an applicant has good character, SBA looks for criminal conduct, violations of SBA regulations, or current debarment or suspension from federal contracting. For a firm to have demonstrated "potential for success," it generally must have been in business in the field of its primary industry classification for at least two years immediately prior to applying to the 8(a) Program. However, small businesses owned by Indian tribes, Alaska Native Corporations (ANCs), Native Hawaiian Organizations (NHOs), and Community Development Corporations (CDCs) are eligible for the 8(a) Program under somewhat different terms.

The 8(a) Program has periodically been challenged on the grounds that the presumption that members of certain racial and ethnic groups are disadvantaged violates the constitutional guarantee of equal protection. The outcomes in early challenges to the program varied, with some courts finding that plaintiffs lacked standing because they were not economically disadvantaged. Most recently, a federal district court found that the program is not unconstitutional on its face because "breaking down barriers to minority business development created by discrimination" constituted a compelling government interest, and the government had a strong basis in evidence for concluding that race-based action was necessary to further this interest. However, the court found that the program was unconstitutional as applied in the military simulation and training industry because there was no evidence of public- or private-sector discrimination in this industry.

Chapter 9 - The Small Business Administration (SBA) administers several programs to support small businesses, including the Historically Underutilized Business Zone Empowerment Contracting (HUBZone) program. The HUBZone program is a small business federal contracting assistance program "whose primary objective is job creation and increasing capital investment in distressed communities." It provides participating small businesses located in areas with low income, high poverty rates, or high unemployment rates with contracting opportunities in the form of "set-asides," sole-source awards, and price-evaluation preferences. Firms must be certified by the SBA to participate in the HUBZone program. On December 4, 2012, there were 5,667 certified HUBZone small businesses.

In FY2011, the federal government awarded 91,864 contracts valued at $9.9 billion to HUBZonecertified businesses, with about $2.75 billion of that amount awarded through a HUBZone set-aside, sole source, or price-evaluation preference award. The program's FY2011 administrative cost was about $15.6 million. Its FY2013 appropriation is just over $2.5 million, with the additional cost of administering the program provided by the SBA's appropriation for general administrative expenses.

Congressional interest in the HUBZone program has increased in recent years, primarily due to reports of fraud in the program. Some Members have called for the program's termination. Others have recommended that the SBA continue its efforts to improve its administration of the program, especially its efforts to prevent fraud.

This report examines the arguments presented both for and against targeting assistance to geographic areas with specified characteristics, such as low income, high poverty, or high unemployment, as opposed to providing assistance to people or businesses with specified characteristics. It then assesses the arguments presented both for and against the continuation of the HUBZone program.

Preface

The report also discusses the HUBZone program's structure and operation, focusing on the definitions of HUBZone areas and HUBZone small businesses and the program's performance relative to federal contracting goals. The report includes an analysis of (1) the SBA's administration of the program, (2) the SBA's performance measures, and (3) the effect of the release of economic date from the 2010 decennial census on which areas qualify as a HUBZone.

This report also examines congressional action on P.L. 111-240, the Small Business Jobs Act of 2010, which amended the Small Business Act to remove certain language that had prompted federal courts and the Government Accountability Office (GAO) to find that HUBZone set-asides have "precedence" over other small business set-asides. It also discusses several bills introduced during the 112th Congress to extend the eligibility for firms that lost their HUBZone redesignated eligibility status due to the release of economic data from the 2010 decennial census, including H.R. 2131, the Protect HUBZones Act of 2011; S. 1756, the HUBZone Protection Act of 2011; S. 633, the Small Business Contracting Fraud Prevention Act of 2011; and S. 3572, the Restoring Tax and Regulatory Certainty to Small Businesses Act of 2012. S. 633 and S. 3572 would also require the SBA to implement several GAO recommendations designed to improve the SBA's administration of the program. Also, S. 3254, the National Defense Authorization Act for Fiscal Year 2013, as amended, would extend HUBZone eligibility for BRAC base closures for an additional five years.

Chapter 10 - The Small Business Administration's (SBA's) Surety Bond Guarantee Program is designed to increase small businesses' access to federal, state, and local government contracting, as well as private-sector contracts, by guaranteeing bid, performance, and payment bonds for individual contracts of $2 million or less for small businesses that cannot obtain surety bonds through regular commercial channels. The SBA's guarantee ranges from 70% to 90% of the surety's loss if a default occurs. In FY2012, the SBA guaranteed 9,503 bid and final surety bonds with a total contract value of about $3.9 billion. A surety bond is a three-party instrument between a surety (who agrees to be responsible for the debt or obligation of another), a contractor, and a project owner. The agreement binds the contractor to comply with the contract's terms and conditions. If the contractor is unable to successfully perform the contract, the surety assumes the contractor's responsibilities and ensures that the project is completed. Surety bonds are viewed as a means to encourage project owners to contract with small businesses that may not have the credit history or prior experience of larger businesses and are considered to be at greater risk of failing to comply with the contract's terms and conditions. P.L. 111-5, the American Recovery and Reinvestment Act of 2009 (ARRA), temporarily increased, from February 17, 2009, through September 30, 2010, the program's bond limit to $5 million, and up to $10 million if a federal contracting officer certifies in writing that a guarantee over $5 million is necessary. The Obama Administration has recommended that the bond limit be increased to $5 million, most recently as part of its request for supplemental assistance for damages caused by Hurricane Sandy. During the 112th Congress, several bills were introduced to increase the program's bond limit, including S. 1334, the Expanding Opportunities for Main Street Act of 2011, and its companion bill in the House, H.R. 2424. They would reinstate and make permanent ARRA's higher limits. Also, H.R. 4310, the National Defense Authorization Act for Fiscal Year 2013, passed by the House on May 18, 2012, would increase the program's bond limit to $6.5 million, and up to $10 million if a federal contracting officer certifies that such a guarantee is necessary. Also, on December 12, 2012, the Senate

Committee on Appropriations released its draft of the Hurricane Sandy Emergency Assistance Supplemental bill. It includes a provision to increase the program's bond limit to $5 million. Advocates of raising the program's bond limit argue that doing so would increase contracting opportunities for small businesses and bring the limit more in line with limits of other small business programs, such as the 8(a) Minority Small Business and Capital Ownership Development Program and the Historically Underutilized Business Zone (HUBZone) Program. Opponents argue that raising the limit could lead to higher amounts being guaranteed by the SBA and, as a result, an increase in the risk of program losses. This report examines the program's origin and development, including the decision to supplement the original Prior Approval Program with the Preferred Surety Bond Guarantee Program that provides a lower guarantee rate (70%) than the Prior Approval Program (80% or 90%) in exchange for allowing preferred sureties to issue SBA-guaranteed surety bonds without the SBA's prior approval. It also examines the program's eligibility standards and requirements, provides performance statistics, and concludes with a discussion of proposals to increase the program's $2 million bond limit and to merge the Prior Approval Program and the Preferred Surety Bond Guarantee Program while retaining the Preferred Program's more flexible operating requirements.

Chapter 11 - In 1982, the Small Business Innovation Development Act (P.L. 97-219) established Small Business Innovation Research (SBIR) programs within the major federal research and development (R&D) agencies designed to increase participation of small innovative companies in federally funded R&D. Government agencies with R&D budgets of $100 million or more are required to set aside a portion of these funds to finance the SBIR activity. Through FY2009, over 112,500 awards have been made totaling more than $26.9 billion.

Reauthorized several times over the years, the SBIR program was scheduled to terminate on September 30, 2008. A companion pilot activity, the Small Business Technology Transfer (STTR) program, was scheduled to end the following year. A series of temporary extensions kept both programs in operation until the SBIR/STTR Reauthorization Act of 2011 was enacted as Title LI of the National Defense Authorization Act for Fiscal Year 2012, P.L. 112-81.

In general, the new legislation reauthorizes the SBIR and STTR programs through September 30, 2017; incrementally increases the set aside for the SBIR effort to 3.2% by FY2017 and beyond; incrementally expands the set aside for the STTR activity to 0.45% in FY2016 and beyond; increases the amount of Phase I and Phase II awards; allows the National Institutes of Health, the Department of Energy, and the National Science Foundation to award up to 25% of SBIR funds to small businesses that are majority-owned by venture capital companies, hedge funds, or private equity firms and other agencies to award up to 15% of SBIR funds to such firms; creates commercialization pilot programs; and expands oversight activities, among other things.

Chapter 12 - Authorized by P.L. 106-554, the Consolidated Appropriations Act, 2001 (Appendix H — the New Markets Venture Capital Program Act of 2000), the New Markets Venture Capital (NMVC) program is designed to promote economic development and the creation of wealth and job opportunities in low-income geographic areas by addressing the unmet equity investments needs of small businesses located in those areas. Modeled on the SBA's Small Business Investment Company (SBIC) program, SBA-selected, privately owned and managed NMVC companies provide funding and operational training assistance to small businesses using private capital the NMVC company has raised (called regulatory capital) and up to 150% of that amount (called leverage) from the sale of SBA-guaranteed 10-year debentures (loan obligations) to third parties, subject to the availability of funds. Because the SBA guarantees the debenture, the SBA is able to obtain favorable interest rates. NMVC companies are responsible for meeting the terms and conditions set forth in the debenture. At least 80% of the investments must be in small businesses located in a low-income area.

Specialized Small Business Investment Companies (SSBICs) established under the SBIC program are also eligible for NMVC operational assistance training grants, which are awarded on a dollar-to-dollar matching basis. There are currently six NMVC companies participating in the program.

The NMVC program was appropriated $21.952 million in FY2001 to support up to $150 million in SBA guaranteed debentures and $30 million for operational assistance training grants for FY2001 through FY2006. The funds were provided in a lump sum in FY2001 and were to remain available until expended. In 2003, the unobligated balances of $10.5 million for the NMVC debenture subsidies and $13.75 million for operational assistance grants were rescinded. The program continues to operate, with the number and amount of financing declining in recent years as the program's initial investments expire and NMVC companies engage only in additional follow-on financings with the small businesses in their portfolio.

More than 30 bills have been introduced in recent Congresses to either expand or amend the NMVC program. Many of these bills would increase the program's funding. For example, during the 112th Congress, H.R. 2872, the Job Creation and Urban Revitalization Act of 2011, was introduced on September 8, 2011. The bill would provide the NMVC program such subsidy budget authority as may be necessary to guarantee $75 million of debentures and $15 million for operational assistance training grants for FY2012 through FY2013. The bill was referred to the House Committee on Small Business on September 8, 2011, and is awaiting further action.

This report examines the NMVC program's legislative origins and describes the program's eligibility and performance requirements for NMVC companies, eligibility requirements for small businesses seeking financing, and the definition of low-income areas. It also reviews regulations governing the SBA's financial assistance to NMVC companies and provides program statistics. The report concludes with an examination of (1) efforts to eliminate the program based on concerns that it duplicates other SBA programs and is relatively expensive, (2) the rescission of the program's unobligated funding in 2003, and (3) recent congressional efforts to provide the program additional funds.

Chapter 13 - Several federal agencies, including the Small Business Administration (SBA), provide training and other assistance to veterans seeking civilian employment. For example, the Department of Labor, in cooperation with the Department of Defense and the Department of Veterans Affairs, operates the Transition Assistance Program (TAP) and the Disabled Transition Assistance Program (DTAP). Both programs provide employment information and training to service members within 180 days of their separation from military service, or retirement, to assist them in transitioning from the military to the civilian labor force.

In recent years, the SBA has focused increased attention on meeting the needs of veteran small business owners and veterans interested in starting a small business, especially veterans who are transitioning from military to civilian life. In FY2011, the SBA provided management and technical assistance services to more than 100,000 veterans through its various management and technical assistance training partners (e.g., Small Business Development Centers, Women Business Centers, Service Corps of Retired Executives (SCORE), and Veteran Business Outreach Centers). The SBA also responded to more than 85,000 veteran inquires through its SBA district offices. In addition, the SBA's Office of Veterans Business Development administers several programs to assist veteran-owned small businesses.

Congressional interest in the SBA's veterans assistance programs has increased in recent years primarily due to reports by veterans organizations that veterans were experiencing difficulty accessing the SBA's programs, especially the SBA's Patriot Express loan guarantee program. There is also a continuing congressional interest in assisting veterans, especially those returning from overseas in recent years, in their transition from military into civilian life. Although the unemployment rate (as of September 2012) among veterans as a whole (6.7%) was lower than for non-veterans 18 years and older (7.4%), the unemployment rate of veterans who have left the military since September 2001 (9.7%) was higher than the unemployment rate for non-veterans 18 years and older.

The expansion of federal employment training programs targeted at specific populations, such as women and veterans, has also led some Members and organizations to ask if these programs should be consolidated. In their view, eliminating program duplication among federal business assistance programs across federal agencies, and within the SBA, would result in lower costs and improved services. Others argue that keeping these business assistance programs separate enables them to offer services that match the unique needs of various underserved populations, such as veterans. In their view, instead of considering program consolidation as a policy option, the focus should be on improving communication and cooperation among the federal agencies providing assistance to entrepreneurs.

This report opens with an examination of the current economic circumstances of veteran-owned businesses drawn from the Bureau of the Census 2007 Survey of Business Owners, which was administered in 2008 and 2009, and released on the Internet on May 17, 2011. It then provides a brief overview of veteran employment experiences, comparing unemployment and labor force participation rates for veterans, veterans who have left the military since September 2001, and non-veterans. The report then describes the employment assistance programs offered by several federal agencies to assist veterans in their transition from the military to the civilian labor force, and examines, in greater detail, the SBA's veteran business development programs, the SBA's Patriot Express loan guarantee program, and veteran contracting programs. The SBA's Military Reservist Economic Injury Disaster Loan program is also discussed.

In: Small Business Administration Programs
Editor: Walter Janikowski

ISBN: 978-1-62417-992-1
© 2013 Nova Science Publishers, Inc.

Chapter 1

SMALL BUSINESS ADMINISTRATION: A PRIMER ON PROGRAMS[*]

Robert Jay Dilger and Sean Lowry

SUMMARY

The Small Business Administration (SBA) administers several programs to support small businesses, including loan guarantee programs to enhance small business access to capital; contracting programs to increase small business opportunities in federal contracting; direct loan programs for businesses, homeowners, and renters to assist their recovery from natural disasters; and small business management and technical assistance training programs to assist business formation and expansion. Congressional interest in the SBA's loan and contracting programs has increased in recent years, primarily because small businesses are viewed as a means to stimulate economic activity, create jobs, and assist in the national economic recovery. Many Members of Congress also regularly receive constituent inquiries about SBA disaster loans, the loan guarantee programs, and contracting programs. This report provides an overview of these programs, including changes made by P.L. 111-5, the American Recovery and Reinvestment Act of 2009, and P.L. 111-240, the Small Business Jobs Act of 2010. It also provides an overview of the SBA's budget.

INTRODUCTION

The Small Business Administration's (SBA's) origins can be traced to the Great Depression of the 1930s and World War II, when concerns about unemployment and war production were paramount. The SBA assumed some of the functions of the Reconstruction Finance Corporation (RFC), which had been created by the federal government in 1932 to provide funding for businesses of all sizes during the Depression and later financed war

---

[*] This is an edited, reformatted and augmented version of Congressional Research Service, Publication No. RL33243, dated October 1, 2012.

production. During the early 1950s, the RFC was disbanded following charges of political favoritism in the granting of loans and contracts.[1]

In 1953, Congress passed the Small Business Act (P.L. 83-163), which authorized the SBA. The act specifies that the SBA's mission is to promote the interests of small businesses to enhance competition in the private marketplace:

> It is the declared policy of the Congress that the Government should aid, counsel, assist, and protect, insofar as is possible, the interests of small-business concerns in order to preserve free competitive enterprise, to insure that a fair proportion of the total purchases and contracts or subcontracts for property and services for the Government (including but not limited to contracts or subcontracts for maintenance, repair, and construction) be placed with small-business enterprises, to insure that a fair proportion of the total sales of Government property be made to such enterprises, and to maintain and strengthen the overall economy of the Nation.[2]

The SBA currently administers several programs to support small businesses, including loan guarantee programs to enhance small business access to capital; contracting programs to increase small business opportunities in federal contracting; direct loan programs for businesses, homeowners, and renters to assist their recovery from natural disasters; and small business management and technical assistance training programs to assist business formation and expansion. Congressional interest in these programs has increased in recent years, primarily because small businesses are viewed as a means to stimulate economic activity, create jobs, and assist in the national economic recovery. Many Members of Congress also regularly receive constituent inquiries about SBA disaster loans, the loan guarantee programs, and contracting programs. This report provides an overview of the SBA's programs, including changes made by P.L. 111-5, the American Recovery and Reinvestment Act of 2009, and P.L. 111-240, the Small Business Jobs Act of 2010. It also provides an overview of the SBA's budget and references other CRS reports that examine the SBA's programs in greater detail.[3] The SBA's FY2013 congressional budget justification document includes funding and program costs for the following programs and offices:

1) disaster assistance;
2) business loan guarantee programs (including the 7(a) program, the 504/Certified Development Company program, the Microloan program, and the Small Business Investment Company program);
3) entrepreneurial development programs (including Small Business Development Centers, Women's Business Centers, and SCORE, among others);
4) government contracting and business development programs (including the 8(a) Minority Small Business and Capital Ownership Development Program, the Historically Underutilized Business Zones (HUBZones) program, the Service-Disabled Veteran-Owned Small Business Program, and the Women-Owned Small Business (WOSB) Federal Contract program);
5) capital access programs (including international trade programs, the new market venture capital program, and the surety bond guarantee program);
6) the SBA Office of Inspector General (OIG);
7) the SBA Office of Advocacy;

8) executive direction programs (National Women's Business Council, Ombudsman, and Veteran's Business Development); and
9) other programs, including regional and district office programs.

Table 1 shows the SBA's estimated costs in FY2012 for these program areas.

Table 1. Major SBA Program Areas, Estimated Program Costs, FY2012

Program Category	Estimated Costs
Disaster loan program	$249,129,000
Business loan guarantee programs	$194,018,000
Entrepreneurial development programs	$163,258,000
Government contracting and business development programs	$109,992,000
Capital access programs	$13,085,000
SBA Office of Inspector General	$24,765,000
SBA Office of Advocacy	$12,810,000
Executive direction programs	$12,560,000
Other programs, including regional and district office programs	$27,337,000
Total	$806,954,000

Source: U.S. Small Business Administration, *FY2013 Congressional Budget Justification and FY2011 Annual Performance Report*, Washington, DC, 2011, pp. 21-22.

Notes: Program costs often differ from program appropriations as appropriations may be carried over from previous fiscal years. The SBA also has limited, specified authority to shift appropriations among various programs.

SBA DISASTER LOANS

Overview[4]

SBA disaster assistance is provided in the form of loans, not grants, and therefore must be repaid to the federal government. The SBA's disaster loans are unique in two respects: (1) they are the only loans made by the SBA that go directly to the ultimate borrower and (2) they are the only loans made by the SBA that are not limited to small businesses.[5]

SBA disaster loans are available to individuals, businesses, and nonprofit organizations in declared disaster areas.[6] About 80% of the SBA's direct disaster loans are issued to individuals and households (renters and property owners) to repair and replace homes and personal property. In recent years, the SBA disaster loan programs have been the subject of regular congressional and media attention because of concerns expressed about the time it takes the SBA to process disaster loan applications.

Types of Disaster Loans

The SBA Disaster Loan Program includes the following categories of loans for disaster-related losses: home disaster loans, business physical disaster loans, economic injury disaster loans, and pre-disaster mitigation loans.[7]

Disaster Loans to Homeowners, Renters, and Personal Property Owners

Homeowners, renters, and personal property owners located in a declared disaster area (and in contiguous counties) may apply to the SBA for loans to help recover losses from a declared disaster. Only victims located in a declared disaster area (and contiguous counties) are eligible to apply for disaster loans. Disaster declarations are "official notices recognizing that specific geographic areas have been damaged by floods and other acts of nature, riots, civil disorders, or industrial accidents such as oil spills."[8] Five categories of declarations put the SBA Disaster Loan Program into effect. These include two types of presidential major disaster declarations as authorized by the Robert T. Stafford Disaster Relief and Emergency Assistance Act (the Stafford Act),[9] and three types of SBA declarations.[10]

The SBA's Home Disaster Loan Program falls into two categories: personal property loans and real property loans. These loans are limited to uninsured losses. The maximum term for SBA disaster loans is 30 years, but the law restricts businesses with credit available elsewhere to a maximum seven-year term. The SBA sets the installment payment amount and corresponding maturity based upon each borrower's ability to repay.

Personal Property Loans

A personal property loan provides a creditworthy homeowner or renter with up to $40,000 to repair or replace personal property items, such as furniture, clothing, or automobiles damaged or lost in a disaster. These loans cover only uninsured or underinsured property and primary residences and cannot be used to replace extraordinarily expensive or irreplaceable items, such as antiques or recreational vehicles. Interest rates vary depending on whether applicants are able or unable to obtain credit elsewhere. For applicants who can obtain credit without SBA assistance, the interest rate may not exceed 8% per year. For applicants who cannot obtain credit without SBA assistance, the interest rate may not exceed 4% per year.[11]

Real Property Loans

A creditworthy homeowner may apply for a "real property loan" of up to $200,000 to repair or restore the homeowner's primary residence to its pre-disaster condition.[12] The loans may not be used to upgrade homes or build additions, unless upgrades or changes are required by city or county building codes. The interest rate for real property loans is determined in the same way as it is determined for personal property loans.

Disaster Loans to Businesses and Nonprofit Organizations

Several types of loans, discussed below, are available to businesses and nonprofit organizations located in counties covered by a presidential disaster declaration. In certain circumstances, the SBA will also make these loans available when a governor, the Secretary of Agriculture, or the Secretary of Commerce makes a disaster declaration. Physical disaster loans are available to almost any nonprofit organization or business. The other business disaster loans are limited to small businesses.

Physical Disaster Loan

Any business or nonprofit organization, regardless of size, can apply for a physical disaster business loan of up to $2 million for repairs and replacements to real property, machinery, equipment, fixtures, inventory, and leasehold improvements that are not covered by insurance. Physical disaster loans for businesses may use up to 20% of the verified loss amount for mitigation measures in an effort to prevent loss from a similar disaster in the future. Nonprofit organizations that are rejected or are approved by the SBA for less than the requested amount for a physical disaster loan are in some circumstances eligible for grants from the Federal Emergency Management Agency (FEMA). For applicants who can obtain credit without SBA assistance, the interest rate may not exceed 8% per year. For applicants who cannot obtain credit without SBA assistance, the interest rate may not exceed 4% per year.[13]

Economic Injury Disaster Loans

Economic injury disaster loans (EIDLs) are limited to small businesses as defined by the SBA's size regulations, which vary from industry to industry.[14] If the Secretary of Agriculture designates an agriculture production disaster, small farms and small cooperatives are eligible. EIDLs are available in the counties included in a presidential disaster declaration and contiguous counties.

The loans are designed to provide small businesses with operating funds until the business recovers. The maximum loan is $2 million and the terms are the same as personal and physical disaster business loans. The loan can have a maturity of up to 30 years and has an interest rate of 4% or less.[15]

Pre-Disaster Mitigation Loan Program

To support FEMA's Pre-Disaster Mitigation Program, SBA may make low-interest, fixed-rate loans to small businesses to finance measures to protect commercial property, leasehold improvements, or contents from disaster-related damages that may occur in the future.[16]

A business that participates in the program may borrow up to $50,000 each fiscal year. The business applying for the loan must be located in a Special Flood Hazard Area (SFHA).[17] The interest rate for a pre-disaster mitigation loan is fixed at 4% per annum or less.[18]

SBA FINANCIAL PROGRAMS

Overview

The SBA has the authority to make direct loans to small businesses, but, with the exception of disaster loans, has not exercised that authority since 1994. The SBA indicated that it stopped issuing direct business loans primarily because the subsidy rate was "10 to 15 times higher" than the subsidy rate for its loan guaranty programs.[19] Instead of making direct loans, it guarantees loans issued by approved lenders to encourage those lenders to provide loans to small businesses "that might not otherwise obtain financing on reasonable terms and conditions."[20] With few exceptions, to qualify for SBA assistance, an organization must be both a business and small.[21]

What Is a Business?

To participate in any of the SBA programs, a business must meet the SBA's definition of "small business."

This is a business that

- is organized for profit;
- has a place of business in the United States;
- operates primarily within the United States or makes a significant contribution to the U.S. economy through payment of taxes or use of American products, materials, or labor;
- is independently owned and operated; and
- is not dominant in its field on a national basis.[22]

The business may be a sole proprietorship, partnership, corporation, or any other legal form.

What Is Small?[23]

The SBA uses two measures to determine if a business is small: SBA-derived industry specific size standards or a combination of the business's net worth and net income. For example, businesses participating in the SBA's 7(a) loan guarantee program, including its express programs, are deemed small if they meet the SBA's industry-specific size standards for firms in 1,141 industrial classifications and 18 sub-industry activities described in the North American Industry Classification System (NAICS) or if they do not have more than $15 million in tangible net worth and not more than $5 million in average net income after federal taxes (excluding any carry-over losses) for the two full fiscal years before the date of the application.

All of the company's subsidiaries, parent companies, and affiliates are considered in determining if it meets the size standard.[24]

The SBA's industry size standards vary by industry, are designed to encourage competition within the industry, and are based on one of the following four measures: the firm's (1) average annual receipts in the previous three years, (2) number of employees, (3) asset size, or (4) for electrical power industries, the extent of its power generation. Historically, the SBA has used the number of employees to determine if manufacturing and mining companies are small and average annual receipts for most other industries.

As a starting point, the SBA presumes $7.0 million in average annual receipts in the previous three years as an appropriate size standard for the services, retail trade, construction, and other industries with receipts based size standards; 500 employees for the manufacturing, mining, and other industries with employee-based size standards; and 100 employees for the wholesale trade industries.

These three levels, referred to as "anchor size standards," are used by the SBA as benchmarks or starting points when establishing its size standards. To the extent an industry displays "differing industry characteristics" necessary to enable small businesses to compete successfully with larger businesses within that industry, the SBA will consider a size standard higher, or in some cases lower, than an anchor size standard.[25] Overall, more than 97% of all businesses are considered small by the SBA.[26]

These firms account for approximately half of the nation's gross domestic product, just under half of the nation's total private sector employment, and about 40% of the nation's private sector payroll.[27]

Loan Guarantee Programs

Overview

The SBA provides loan guarantees for small businesses that cannot obtain credit elsewhere. Its four largest loan guarantee programs are the 7(a) loan guaranty program, the 504/Certified Development Company loan guaranty program, the Microloan program, and the Small Business Investment Company program.

The SBA requires personal guarantees from borrowers and shares the risk of default with the lender by making the guarantee less than 100%. In the event of a default, the borrower owes the amount contracted less the value of any collateral liquidated. The SBA can attempt to recover the unpaid debt through administrative offset, salary offset, or IRS tax refund offset. Most types of business are eligible for loan guarantees, but a few are not. A list of ineligible businesses (such as insurance companies, real estate investment firms, firms involved in financial speculation or pyramid sales, businesses involved in illegal activities, and businesses deriving more than one-third of gross annual revenue from legal gambling activities) is contained in 13 C.F.R. Section 120.110.[28] With one exception, nonprofit and charitable organizations are also ineligible.[29]

Also, as shown in the following tables, most of these programs charge fees to help offset program costs, including costs related to loan defaults. In most instances, the SBA's fees are set in statute. For example, for 7(a) loans with a maturity exceeding 12 months the SBA is authorized to charge lenders a guarantee fee of up to 2% for the SBA guaranteed portion of loans of $150,000 or less, up to 3% for the SBA guaranteed portion of loans exceeding $150,000 but not more than $700,000, and up to 3.5% for the SBA guaranteed portion of loans exceeding $700,000. Also, lenders with a 7(a) loan which has a SBA guaranteed portion in excess of $1 million can be charged an additional fee not to exceed 0.25% of the guaranteed amount in excess of $1 million. These loans are also subject to an ongoing servicing fee not to exceed 0.55% of the outstanding balance of the guaranteed portion of the loan.[30] Lenders are also authorized to collect fees from borrowers to offset their administrative expenses.

From 2005 to 2009, the SBA recommended that the fees achieve a zero subsidy rate, meaning that the loan guarantee program does not require annual appropriations of budget authority for new loan guaranties. However, in recent years, the fees have not generated enough revenue to cover loan losses, resulting in the need for additional appropriations to account for the shortfall. In FY2010 and FY2011, the SBA was provided an additional $80 million for the cost of guaranteed loans. The SBA was provided $207.1 million for this purpose in FY2012, and $333.6 million for FY2013.[31]

7(a) Loan Guaranty Program[32]

The 7(a) loan guaranty program is named after the section of the Small Business Act that authorizes it. These are loans made by SBA partners (mostly banks, but also some other financial institutions) and partially guaranteed by the SBA. The 7(a) program's current guaranty rate is 85% for loans of $150,000 or less and 75% for loans greater than $150,000 (up to a maximum guaranty of $3.75 million—75% of $5 million). Although the SBA's offer to guarantee a loan provides an incentive for lenders to make the loan, lenders are not required to do so. Table 2 provides information on the 7(a) program's key features, including its eligible uses, maximum loan amount, loan maturity, interest rates, and guarantee fees.

Table 2. Summary of the 7(a) Loan Guaranty Program's Key Features

Key Feature	Program Summary
Use of Proceeds	Fixed assets, working capital, financing of start-ups or to purchase an existing business; some debt payment allowed, but lender's loan exposure may not be reduced with the Express products. Lines of credit are offered with the Express programs.
Maximum Loan Amount	$5 million.
Maturity	5 to 7 years for working capital, up to 25 years for equipment & real estate. All other loan purposes have a maximum term of 10 years.
Maximum Interest Rates	Base rate plus 2.25% for maturities under 7 years. Base rate plus 2.75% for maturities of 7 years or longer. Loans of $50,000 or less may add an additional 1% and loans under $25,000 may add an additional 2%. There is a prepayment penalty for loans with maturities of 15 years or more if prepaid during the first 3 years.
Guarantee Fees	A fee of 0.25% of the guaranteed portion of the loan is charged for loans with maturities of 12 months or less. For loans with maturities over 12 months, the fees are 2% for loans of $150,000 or less; 3% for loans of $150,001 to $700,000; 3.5% for loans over $700,000; and 3.75% for the guaranty portion over $1 million. There is an on-going servicing fee of 0.55%.
Job Creation	No job creation requirements.

Source: Table compiled by CRS from data from the Small Business Administration.

Note: In 2009 and 2010, Congress provided $962.5 million to temporarily eliminate some of the SBA's fees. For example, the Small Business Jobs Act of 2010 (P.L. 111-240) provided $510 million to subsidize fees in the SBA's 7(a) and 504/CDC loan guarantee programs from its date of enactment (September 27, 2010) through December 31, 2010.

Variable-rate loans can be pegged to either the prime rate or the SBA optional peg rate, which is a weighted average of rates that the federal government pays for loans with maturities similar to the guaranteed loan. The spread over the prime rate or SBA optional peg rate is negotiable between the borrower and the lender, but no more than 6%. The adjustment period can be no more than monthly and cannot change over the life of the loan.

Variations on the 7(a) Program

The 7(a) program has four specialized programs that offer streamlined and expedited loan procedures for particular groups of borrowers, the SBAExpress program, the Small Loan Advantage program, Community Advantage program, and the Patriot Express program.

Lenders must be approved by the SBA for participation in these programs. For example, the SBAExpress program was established as a pilot program by the SBA on February 27, 1995, and made permanent through legislation, subject to reauthorization, in 2004 (P.L. 108-447, the Consolidated Appropriations Act, 2005).

The program is designed to increase the availability of credit to small businesses by permitting lenders to use their existing documentation and procedures in return for receiving a reduced SBA guarantee on loans. It provides a 50% loan guarantee on loan amounts up to $350,000.[33]

The loan proceeds can be used for the same purposes as the 7(a) program except participant debt restructuring cannot exceed 50% of the project and may be used for revolving credit. The loan terms are the same as the 7(a) program, except that the term for a revolving line of credit cannot exceed seven years.

Special Purpose Loan Guarantees

In addition to the 7(a) loan guaranty program, the SBA has special purpose loan guaranty programs for small businesses adjusting to the North American Free Trade Agreement (NAFTA), to support Employee Stock Ownership Program trusts, pollution control facilities, and working capital.

Community Adjustment and Investment Program

The Community Adjustment and Investment Program (CAIP) uses federal funds to pay the fees on 7(a) and 504/CDC loans to businesses located in communities that have been adversely affected by NAFTA.

Employee Trusts

The SBA will guarantee loans to Employee Stock Ownership Plans (ESOPs) that are used either to lend money to the employer or to purchase control from the owner. ESOPs must meet regulations established by the IRS, Department of the Treasury, and Department of Labor. These are 7(a) loans.

Pollution Control

In 1976, the SBA was provided authorization to guarantee the payment of rentals or other amounts due under qualified contracts for pollution control facilities. P.L. 100- 590, the Small Business Reauthorization and Amendment Act of 1988, eliminated the revolving fund for pollution control guaranteed loans and transferred its remaining funds to the SBA's business loan and investment revolving fund. Since 1989, loans for pollution control have been guaranteed under the 7(a) loan guaranty program.

CAPLines

CAPLines are five special 7(a) loan guaranty programs designed to meet the requirements of small businesses for short-term or cyclical working capital. The maximum term is five years.

The 504/CDC Loan Guaranty Program[34]

The 504/CDC loan guarantee program uses Certified Development Companies (CDCs), which are private, nonprofit corporations established to contribute to economic development within its communities. Each CDC has its own geographic territory.

The program provides long-term, fixed-rate loans for major fixed assets such as land, structures, machinery, and equipment. Program loans cannot be used for working capital, inventory, or repaying debt.

A commercial lender provides up to 50% of the financing package, which is secured by a senior lien. The CDC's loan of up to 40% is secured by a junior lien. The SBA backs the CDC with a guaranteed debenture.[35] The small business must contribute at least 10% as equity.

To participate in the program, small businesses can not exceed $15 million in tangible net worth and can not have average net income over $5 million for two full fiscal years before the date of application. Table 3 summarizes the 504/CDC loan guarantee program's key features.

Table 3. Summary of the 504/Certified Development Company Loan Guaranty Program's Key Features

Key Feature	Program Summary
Use of Proceeds	Fixed assets only—no working capital.
Maximum Loan Amount	Maximum CDC/504 participation in a single project is $5 million, and $5.5 million for manufacturers; minimum is $50,000. There is no limit on the project size.
Maturity	10 years for equipment; 20 years for real estate.
Maximum Interest Rates	Based on current market rate for 5 and 10 year Treasury Bonds.
Participation	504/CDC projects generally have three main participants: a third-party lender provides
Requirements	50% or more of the financing; a CDC provides up to 40% of the financing through a 504/CDC debenture, which is guaranteed 100% by the SBA; and the borrower contributes at least 10% of the financing. No more than 50% of eligible costs can be from federal sources.
Guarantee Fees	There is a 0.5% fee on the lender's share, plus the CDC may charge up to 1.5% on their share. CDC charges a monthly servicing fee of 0.625% to 1.5% on the unpaid balance. There is an on-going guaranty fee of 0.749% of the principal outstanding.
Job Creation	Must intend to create or retain one job for every $65,000 of the debenture ($100,000
Requirements	for small manufacturers) or meet an alternative job creation standard if it meets any one of 15 Community or Public Policy Goals. A minimum down payment of 10% is required.

Source: Table compiled by CRS from data from the Small Business Administration.

Notes: The maximum loan amount is the total financial package including the commercial loan and the CDC loan. It does not include the owner's minimum 10% equity contribution. It assumes that the CDC loan is 40% of the total package.

The Microloan Program[36]

The Microloan program provides direct loans to qualified non-profit intermediary Microloan lenders who, in turn, provide "microloans" of up to $50,000 to small businesses and non-profit child care centers. It also provides marketing, management, and technical assistance to Microloan borrowers and potential borrowers. The program was authorized in 1991 as a five-year demonstration project and became operational in 1992. It was made permanent, subject to reauthorization, by P.L. 105-135, the Small Business Reauthorization Act of 1997. Although the program is open to all small businesses, it targets new and early-stage businesses in underserved markets, including borrowers with little to no credit history, low-income borrowers, and women and minority entrepreneurs in both rural and urban areas who generally do not qualify for conventional loans, or other, larger SBA guaranteed loans. Table 4 summarizes the Microloan program's key features.

The Small Business Investment Company Program[37]

The Small Business Investment Company (SBIC) program enhances small business access to venture capital by stimulating and supplementing "the flow of private equity capital and long term loan funds which small business concerns need for the sound financing of their business operations and for their growth, expansion, and modernization, and which are not available in adequate supply."[38]

Table 4. Summary of the Microloan Program's Key Features

Key Feature	Program Summary
Use of proceeds	Working capital and acquisition of materials, supplies, furniture, fixtures, and equipment. Loans cannot be made to acquire land or property.
Maximum Loan Amount	$50,000.
Maturity	Up to six years.
Maximum Interest Rates	The interest rate charged to the intermediary is based on the five-year Treasury rate, adjusted to the nearest one-eighth percent, less 1.25%. The SBA's interest rate is updated on a monthly basis. In addition, intermediaries that maintain an average loan size of $10,000 or less are charged an interest rate based on the five-year Treasury rate, adjusted to the nearest one-eighth percent, less 2.0%. Portfolios are evaluated annually to determine the applicable rate.
	On loans of more than $7,500, the maximum interest rate that can be charged to the borrower is the interest rate charged by the SBA on the loan to the intermediary, plus 7.75%. On loans of $7,500 or less, the maximum interest rate that can be charged to the borrower is the interest charged by the SBA on the loan to the intermediary, plus 8.5%. Rates are negotiated between the borrower and the intermediary, and typically range from 8% to 10%.
Guarantee Fees	The SBA does not charge intermediaries upfront or on-going service fees under the Microloan program.
Job Creation Requirements	No job creation requirements.

Source: Table compiled by CRS from data from the Small Business Administration.

The SBA works with nearly 300 privately owned and managed SBICs licensed by the SBA to provide financing to small businesses with private capital the SBIC has raised and with funds the SBIC borrows at favorable rates because the SBA guarantees the debenture (loan obligation). SBICs provide equity capital to small businesses in various ways, including by

- purchasing small business equity securities (e.g., stock, stock options, warrants, limited partnership interests, membership interests in a limited liability company, or joint venture interests);[39]
- making loans to small businesses, either independently or in cooperation with other private or public lenders, that have a maturity of no more than 20 years;[40]
- purchasing debt securities from small businesses, which may be convertible into, or have rights to purchase, equity in the small business;[41] and
- subject to limitations, providing small businesses a guarantee of their monetary obligations to creditors not associated with the SBIC.[42]

Table 5. Summary of Small Business Investment Company Program's Key Features

Key Feature	Program Summary
Use of Proceeds	To purchase small business equity securities, make loans to small businesses, purchase debt securities from small businesses, and provide, subject to limitations, small businesses a guarantee of their monetary obligations to creditors not associated with the SBIC.
Maximum Leverage Amount	A licensed SBIC in good standing, with a demonstrated need for funds, may apply to the SBA for financial assistance (called leverage) of up to 300% of its private capital. However, most SBICs are approved for a maximum of 200% of its private capital and no fund management team may exceed the allowable maximum amount of leverage, currently $150 million per SBIC and $225 million for two or more licenses under common control. SBICs licensed on or after October 1, 2009, may elect to have a maximum leverage amount of $175 million per SBIC and $250 million for two or more licenses under common control if it has invested at least 50% of its financings in low-income geographic areas and certifies that at least 50% of its future investments will be in low-income geographic areas.
Maturity	SBA-guaranteed debenture participation certificates can have a term of up to 15 years, although currently only one outstanding SBA-guaranteed debenture participation certificate has a term exceeding 10 years and all recent public offerings have specified a term of 10 years. SBA-guaranteed debentures provide for semi-annual interest payments and a lump sum principal payment to investors at maturity. SBICs are allowed to prepay SBA-guaranteed debentures without penalty. However, a SBA-guaranteed debenture must be prepaid in whole and not in part, and can only be prepaid on a semi-annual payment date. Also, low-to-moderate income area (LMI) debentures are available in two maturities, for 5 years and 10 years (plus the stub period).
Maximum Interest Rates	The debenture's coupon (interest) rate is determined by market conditions and the interest rate of 10-year treasury securities at the time of the sale.
Guarantee Fees	The SBA requires the SBIC to pay a 3% origination fee for each debenture issued (1% at commitment and 2% at draw), an annual fee on the leverage drawn which is fixed at the time of the leverage commitment, and other administrative and underwriting fees which are adjusted annually.
Job Creation Requirements	No job creation requirements.

Source: Table compiled by CRS from data from the Small Business Administration.

Entrepreneurial Development Programs[43]

The SBA's entrepreneurial development programs provide technical and managerial training to small businesses. Some of this training is free and other training is at low cost and includes services provided by the Service Corps of Retired Executives (SCORE), Small Business Development Centers (SBDCs), Women's Business Centers (WBCs), Veteran Business Outreach Centers, and Native American Outreach programs, among others.

SCORE was established on October 5, 1964, by then-SBA Administrator Eugene P. Foley, as a national, volunteer organization, uniting more than 50 independent nonprofit organizations into a single, national nonprofit organization. SCORE's 364 chapters and more than 800 branch offices are located throughout the United States and partner with nearly

13,000 volunteer counselors, who are working or retired business owners, executives, and corporate leaders, to provide management and training assistance to small businesses.

SBDCs provide free or low-cost assistance to small businesses using programs customized to local conditions. SBDCs support small business in marketing and business strategy, finance, technology transfer, government contracting, management, manufacturing, engineering, sales, accounting, exporting, and other topics. SBDCs are funded by grants from the SBA and matching funds. There are more than 900 SBDCs and at least one in every state and territory.

WBCs are similar to SBDCs, except they concentrate on assisting women entrepreneurs. There are currently 108 WBCs, with at least one WBC in most states and territories.

The SBA's Veterans Business Outreach Centers Program provides "outreach, assessment, long term counseling, training, coordinated service delivery referrals, mentoring and network building, procurement assistance and E-based assistance to benefit Small Business concerns and potential concerns owned and controlled by Veterans, Service Disabled Veterans and Members of Reserve Components of the U.S. Military."[44] There are currently 16 Veterans Business Outreach Centers.[45]

The SBA's Office of Native American Affairs provides management and technical educational assistance to Native Americans (American Indians, Alaska Natives, Native Hawaiians and the indigenous people of Guam and American Samoa) to start and expand small businesses.

Small Business Contracting Programs[46]

A number of programs assist small businesses in obtaining and performing federal contracts and subcontracts. These include various prime contracting programs; subcontracting programs; and other assistance (e.g., the federal goaling program and federal Offices of Small and Disadvantaged Business Utilization).

Prime Contracting Programs

Several contracting programs allow small businesses to compete only with similar firms for government contracts, or receive sole-source awards in circumstances when such awards could not be made to other firms. These programs, which give small businesses a chance to win government contracts without having to compete against larger and more experienced companies, include the following:

- **8(a) Program:**[47] The 8(a) Minority Small Business and Capital Ownership Development Program (named for the section of the Small Business Act from which it derives its authority) is for businesses owned by persons who are socially and economically disadvantaged.[48] A firm that is certified by SBA as an 8(a) firm is eligible for set-aside and sole-source contracts. The SBA also provides technical assistance and training to 8(a) firms. Firms may participate in the 8(a) Program for no more than nine years. As of October 1, 2012, there were 8,459 firms with active certifications in the 8(a) program.[49]
- **Historically Underutilized Business Zone Program:**[50] This program assists small businesses located in Historically Underutilized Business Zones (HUBZones)

through set-asides, sole source awards, and price evaluation preferences in full and open competitions.[51] The determination of whether or not an area is a HUBZone is based on criteria specified in 13 C.F.R. Section 126.103. To be certified as a HUBZone small business, at least 35% of the small business's employees must generally reside in a HUBZone. As of October 1, 2012, there were 5,878 firms with active HUBZone certifications.[52]

- **Service-Disabled Veteran-Owned Small Business Program:** This program assists service-disabled veteran-owned small businesses through set-asides and sole-source awards. For purposes of this program, veterans and service-related disabilities are defined as they are under the statutes governing veterans affairs.[53]
- **Women-Owned Small Business Program:** Under this program, contracts may be set aside for economically disadvantaged women-owned small businesses in industries in which they are underrepresented, and women-owned small businesses in which they are substantially underrepresented.
- **Other small businesses:** Agencies may also set-aside contracts or make sole-source awards to small businesses not participating in any other program under certain conditions.

Subcontracting Programs for Small Disadvantaged Businesses

Other federal programs promote subcontracting with small disadvantaged businesses (SDBs). Agencies must negotiate "subcontracting plans" with the apparently successful bidder or offeror on eligible prime contracts prior to awarding the contract. Subcontracting plans set goals for the percentage of subcontract dollars to be awarded to SDBs, among others, and describe efforts that will be made to ensure that SDBs "have an equitable opportunity to compete for subcontracts." Federal agencies may also consider the extent of subcontracting with SDBs in determining to whom to award a contract, or give contractors "monetary incentives" to subcontract with SDBs. All 8(a) firms qualify as SDBs, but firms that are not participants in the 8(a) Program can also qualify as SDBs. As of October 1, 2012, there were 8,541 certified SDBs.[54]

Goaling Program

Since 1978, federal agency heads have been required to establish federal procurement contracting goals, in consultation with the SBA, "that realistically reflect the potential of small business concerns" to participate in federal procurement. Each agency is required, at the conclusion of each fiscal year, to report its progress in meeting the goals to the SBA.[55]

In 1988, Congress authorized the President to annually establish government-wide minimum participation goals for procurement contracts awarded to small businesses and small businesses owned and controlled by socially and economically disadvantaged individuals. Congress required the government-wide minimum participation goal for small businesses to be "not less than 20% of the total value of all prime contract awards for each fiscal year" and "not less than 5% of the total value of all prime contract and subcontract awards for each fiscal year" for small businesses owned and controlled by socially and economically disadvantaged individuals.[56]

Each federal agency was also directed to "have an annual goal that presents, for that agency, the maximum practicable opportunity for small business concerns and small business concerns owned and controlled by socially and economically disadvantaged individuals to participate in the performance of contracts let by such agency."[57] The SBA was also required to report to the President annually on the attainment of the goals and to include the information in an annual report to the Congress.[58] The SBA negotiates the goals with each federal agency and establishes a "small business eligible" baseline for evaluating the agency's performance.

The small business eligible baseline excludes certain contracts that the SBA has determined do not realistically reflect the potential for small business participation in federal procurement (such as contracts awarded to mandatory and directed sources), contracts awarded and performed overseas, contracts funded predominately from agency-generated sources, contracts not covered by Federal Acquisition Regulations, and contracts not reported in the Federal Procurement Data System (such as contracts or government procurement card purchases valued less than $3,000).[59] These exclusions typically account for 18% to 20% of all federal prime contracts each year. The SBA then evaluates the agencies' performance against their negotiated goals annually, using data from the Federal Procurement Data System—Next Generation, managed by the U.S. General Services Administration, to generate the small business eligible baseline. This information is compiled into the official Small Business Goaling Report, which the SBA releases annually. Over the years, federal government-wide procurement contracting goals have been established for small businesses generally (P.L. 100-656, the Business Opportunity Development Reform Act of 1988, and P.L. 105-135, the HUBZone Act of 1997 − Title VI of the Small Business Reauthorization Act of 1997), small businesses owned and controlled by socially and economically disadvantaged individuals (P.L. 100-656, the Business Opportunity Development Reform Act of 1988), women (P.L. 103-355, the Federal Acquisition Streamlining Act of 1994), small businesses located within a HUBZone (P.L. 105-135, the HUBZone Act of 1997 − Title VI of the Small Business Reauthorization Act of 1997), and small businesses owned and controlled by a service disabled veteran (P.L. 106-50, the Veterans Entrepreneurship and Small Business Development Act of 1999).

The current federal small business contracting goals are

- at least 23% of the total value of all small business eligible prime contract awards to small businesses for each fiscal year,
- 5% of the total value of all small business eligible prime contract awards and subcontract awards to small disadvantaged businesses for each fiscal year,
- 5% of the total value of all small business eligible prime contract awards and subcontract awards to women-owned small businesses,
- 3% of the total value of all small business eligible prime contract awards and subcontract awards to HUBZone small businesses, and
- 3% of the total value of all small business eligible prime contract awards and subcontract awards to service-disabled veteran-owned small businesses.[60]

There are no punitive consequences for not meeting the small business procurement goals. However, the SBA's Small Business Goaling Report is distributed widely, receives media attention, and serves to heighten public awareness of the issue of small business contracting. For example, agency performance as reported in the SBA's Small Business Goaling Report is often cited by Members during their questioning of federal agency witnesses during congressional hearings. As shown in Table 6, in FY2011, federal agencies met the federal contracting goal for small disadvantaged businesses, but not the other goals. Federal agencies awarded 21.65% of the value of their small business eligible contracts to small businesses, 7.67% to small disadvantaged businesses, 3.98% to women-owned small businesses, 2.35% to HUBZone small businesses, and 2.65% to service-disabled veteran-owned small businesses.[61] The percentage of total reported federal contracts (without exclusions) awarded to small businesses, small disadvantaged businesses, women-owned small businesses, HUBZone small businesses, and service-disabled veteran-owned small businesses in FY2011 is also provided in the table for comparative purposes.

Table 6. Federal Contracting Goals and Percentage of FY2011 Federal Contract Dollars Awarded to Small Businesses, by Type

Business Type	Federal Goal	Percentage of FY2011 Federal Contracts (small business eligible)	Percentage of FY2011 Federal Contracts (all reported contracts)
Small Businesses	23.0%	21.65%	17.0%
Small Disadvantaged Businesses	5.0%	7.67%	6.0%
Women-Owned Small Businesses	5.0%	3.98%	3.1%
HUBZone Small Businesses	3.0%	2.35%	1.8%
Service-Disabled Veteran-Owned Small Businesses	3.0%	2.65%	2.1%

Source: U.S. Small Business Administration, "Statutory Guidelines," Washington, DC, at http://www.sba.gov/ content/goaling-guidelines-0 (federal goals); U.S. General Services Administration, Federal Procurement Data System—Next Generation, "Small Business Goaling Report: Fiscal Year 2011," Washington, DC, at https://www.fpds.gov/downloads/top_ requests/FPDSNG_SB_Goaling_FY_2011.pdf; and U.S. General Services Administration, Federal Procurement Data System—Next Generation, Washington, DC, at https://www.fpds.gov/fpdsng/ (contract dollars).

Notes: The total amount of federal contracts awarded in FY2011, as reported in the FPDS, was $536.8 billion; $422.5 billion of this amount was deemed by the SBA to be small business eligible. Of the total amount reported, $91.5 billion was awarded to small businesses, $32.4 billion to small disadvantaged businesses, $16.8 billion to women owned small businesses, $9.9 billion to SBA-certified HUBZone small businesses, and $11.2 billion to service-disabled veteran-owned small businesses.

Office of Small and Disadvantaged Business Utilization

Government agencies with procurement authority have an Office of Small and Disadvantaged Business Utilization (OSDBU) to advocate within the agency for small businesses, as well as assist small businesses in their dealings with federal agencies (e.g., obtaining payment).

Capital Access Programs

The SBA has several programs to improve small businesses access to capital markets, including the Surety Bond Guarantee Program, two special high technology contracting programs (the Small Business Innovative Research and Small Business Technology Transfer programs), and the New Market Venture Capital program. In addition, the previously discussed Small Business Investment Company program is also designed to improve access to capital markets.

Surety Bond Guarantee Program[62]

The SBA's Surety Bond Guarantee Program is designed to increase small businesses' access to federal, state, and local government contracting, as well as private sector contracts, by guaranteeing bid, performance, and payment bonds for individual contracts of $2 million or less for small businesses that cannot obtain surety bonds through regular commercial channels.[63] The SBA's guarantee ranges from 70% to 90% of the surety's loss if a default occurs.

A surety bond is a three-party instrument between a surety (someone who agrees to be responsible for the debt or obligation of another), a contractor, and a project owner. The agreement binds the contractor to comply with the terms and conditions of a contract. If the contractor is unable to successfully perform the contract, the surety assumes the contractor's responsibilities and ensures that the project is completed. The surety bond reduces the risk of contracting.[64]

Surety bonds are viewed as a means to encourage project owners to contract with small businesses that may not have the credit history or prior experience of larger businesses and are considered to be at greater risk of failing to comply with the contract's terms and conditions.[65]

Small Business Innovation Research Program[66]

The Small Business Innovation Research (SBIR) program is designed to increase the participation of small, high technology firms in federal research and development (R&D) endeavors, provide additional opportunities for the involvement of minority and disadvantaged individuals in the R&D process, and result in the expanded commercialization of the results of federally funded R&D.[67] Current law requires that every federal department with an R&D budget of $100 million or more establish and operate an SBIR program. A set percentage of that agency's applicable extramural research and development budget—originally set at not less than 0.2% in FY1983, and currently not less than 2.7 in FY2013—is to be used to support mission-related work in small businesses.[68]

Agency SBIR efforts involve a three-phase process. First, phase I awards of up to $150,000 for six months are made to evaluate a concept's scientific or technical merit and feasibility. The project must be of interest to and coincide with the mission of the supporting organization. Projects that demonstrate potential after the initial endeavor may compete for Phase II awards of up to $1 million, lasting one to two years. Phase II awards are for the performance of the principal R&D by the small business. Phase III funding, directed at the commercialization of the product or process, is expected to be generated in the private sector. Federal dollars may be used if the government perceives that the final technology or technique will meet public needs.

Eleven departments currently have SBIR programs, including the Departments of Agriculture, Commerce, Defense (DOD), Education, Energy, Health and Human Services, Homeland Security, and Transportation; the Environmental Protection Agency; the National Aeronautics and Space Administration (NASA); and the National Science Foundation (NSF). Each agency's SBIR activity reflects that organization's management style. Individual departments select R&D interests, administer program operations, and control financial support. Funding can be disbursed in the form of contracts, grants, or cooperative agreements. Separate agency solicitations are issued at established times.

The SBA is responsible for establishing the broad policy and guidelines under which individual departments operate their SBIR programs. The SBA monitors and reports to Congress on the conduct of the separate departmental activities.

Small Business Technology Transfer Program

The Small Business Technology Transfer program (STTR) provides funding for research proposals that are developed and executed cooperatively between a small firm and a scientist in a nonprofit research organization and fall under the mission requirements of the federal funding agency.[69] Up to $150,000 in Phase I financing is available for approximately one year to fund the exploration of the scientific, technical, and commercial feasibility of an idea or technology. Phase II awards of up to $1 million may be made for two years. During this period, the R&D work is performed and the developer begins to consider commercial potential. Only Phase I award winners are considered for Phase II. Phase III funding, directed at the commercialization of the product or process, is expected to be generated in the private sector. The small business must find funding in the private sector or other non-STTR federal agency. The STTR program is funded by a set-aside, initially set at not less than 0.05% in FY1994 and now at not less than 0.35%, of the extramural R&D budget of departments that spend over $1 billion per year on this effort.[70] The Departments of Energy, Defense, and Health and Human Services, NASA, and NSF participate in the STTR program.

The SBA is responsible for establishing the broad policy and guidelines under which individual departments operate their STTR programs. The SBA monitors and reports to Congress on the conduct of the separate departmental activities.

New Market Venture Capital Program[71]

The New Market Venture Capital (NMVC) program encourages equity investments in small businesses in low-income areas that meet specific statistical criteria established by regulation. The program operates through public-private partnerships between the SBA and newly formed NMVC investment companies and existing Specialized Small Business Investment Companies (SSBICs) that operate under the Small Business Investment Company program. The NMVC program's objective is to serve the unmet equity needs of local entrepreneurs in low-income areas by providing them developmental venture capital investments and technical assistance, create quality employment opportunities for low-income area residents, and build wealth within those areas. The SBA's role is essentially the same as with the SBIC program. The SBA selects participants for the NMVC program, provides funding for their investments and operational assistance activities, and regulates their operations to ensure that public policy objectives are being met. The SBA requires the companies to provide regular performance reports and have annual financial examinations by the SBA.

Office of Inspector General

The Office of Inspector General's (OIG's) mission is "to improve SBA management and effectiveness, and to detect and deter fraud in the Agency's programs."[72] It serves as "an independent and objective oversight office created within the SBA by the Inspector General Act of 1978 (P.L. 95-452 as amended)."[73] The Inspector General, who is nominated by the President and confirmed by the Senate, directs the office. The Inspector General Act provides the OIG with the following responsibilities:

- promote economy, efficiency, and effectiveness in the management of SBA programs and supporting operations;
- conduct and supervise audits, investigations, and reviews relating to the SBA's programs and support operations;
- detect and prevent fraud and abuse;
- review existing and proposed legislation and regulations and make appropriate recommendations;
- maintain effective working relationships with other governmental agencies, and non-governmental entities, regarding the Inspector General's mandated duties;
- keep the SBA Administrator and Congress informed of serious problems and recommend corrective actions and implementation measures;
- comply with the Comptroller General's audit standards;
- avoid duplication of Government Accountability Office (GAO) activities; and
- report violations of law to the U.S. Attorney General.[74]

Office of Advocacy

The SBA's Office of Advocacy is "an independent voice for small business within the federal government."[75] The Chief Counsel for Advocacy, who is nominated by the President and confirmed by the Senate, directs the office. The Office of Advocacy's mission is to "encourage policies that support the development and growth of American small businesses" by

- intervening early in federal agencies' regulatory development process on proposals that affect small businesses and providing Regulatory Flexibility Act compliance training to federal agency policymakers and regulatory development officials;
- producing research to inform policymakers and other stakeholders on the impact of federal regulatory burdens on small businesses, to document the vital role of small businesses in the economy, and to explore and explain the wide variety of issues of concern to the small business community; and
- fostering a two-way communication between federal agencies and the small business community.[76]

Executive Direction Programs

The SBA's executive direction programs consist of the National Women's Business Council, the Office of Ombudsman, and the Office of Veteran's Business Development.

The National Women's Business Council

The National Women's Business Council is a bi-partisan federal advisory council created to serve as an independent source of advice and counsel to the President, Congress, and the SBA on economic issues of importance to women business owners. The council's mission "is to promote bold initiatives, policies, and programs designed to support women's business enterprises at all stages of development in the public and private sector marketplaces—from start-up to success to significance."[77]

Office of Ombudsman

The National Ombudsman's mission "is to assist small businesses when they experience excessive or unfair federal regulatory enforcement actions, such as repetitive audits or investigations, excessive fines, penalties, threats, retaliation or other unfair enforcement action by a federal agency."[78] It works with federal agencies that have regulatory authority over small businesses to provide a means for entrepreneurs to comment about enforcement activities and encourage agencies to address those concerns promptly. It also receives comments from small businesses about unfair federal compliance or enforcement activities and refers those comments to the Inspector General of the affected agency in appropriate circumstances. It also files an annual report with Congress and affected federal agencies that rates federal agencies based on substantiated comments received from small business owners. Affected agencies are provided an opportunity to comment on the draft version of the annual report to Congress before it is submitted.[79]

Office of Veterans Business Development[80]

In recent years, the SBA has provided management and technical assistance training services to more than 100,000 veterans annually through its various management and technical assistance training partners (e.g., Small Business Development Centers, Women Business Centers, Service Corps of Retired Executives [SCORE], and Veteran Business Outreach Centers) and has responded to more than 85,000 veteran inquires annually through its SBA district offices.[81] In addition, the Office of Veterans Business Development (OVBD) administers several programs to assist veteran-owned businesses, including the Veterans Business Outreach Center program, which provides veterans and their spouses management and technical assistance training at 16 locations. The training includes assistance with the development and maintenance of a five-year business plan and referrals to other SBA resource partners when appropriate for additional training or mentoring services.[82]

OVBD also sponsors (1) the Entrepreneurial Boot Camp for Veterans with Disabilities Consortium of Universities, which provides, at eight universities, management and experiential training in entrepreneurship to post-9/11 veterans with disabilities;[83] (2) the Veteran Women Igniting the Spirit of Entrepreneurship (V-WISE) program at Syracuse University, which offers women veterans a 15-day, online course focused "on the basic skills of entrepreneurship and the 'language of business,'" followed by a three-day conference featuring "accomplished entrepreneurs and entrepreneurship educators from across the United States" and "courses on business planning, marketing, accounting/finance, operations/production, human resources and work life balance";[84] and (3) the Operation Endure and Grow Program, also at Syracuse University, which is an eight-week online training program focused on how to start and expand a small business and is available to National Guard and Reservists and their family members.[85]

LEGISLATIVE ACTIVITY

Most of the legislative activity concerning the SBA during the 112th Congress involved oversight of the agencies programs and measures concerning the agency's funding and authorization status. Congressional oversight focused on ways to minimize program fraud, especially in the small business contracting programs, improve program efficiency, and explore options for measuring program impact. The SBA's funding is discussed under the "Appropriations" section of this report. The SBA's statutory authorization expired on July 31, 2011.[86] Since then, the SBA has been operating under authority provided by annual appropriations acts. Prior to July 31, 2011, the SBA's authorization had been temporarily extended 15 times since 2006.

During the 111th Congress, several laws were enacted that made major changes to the SBA's programs, primarily to enhance small business access to capital. For example, P.L. 111-5, the American Recovery and Reinvestment Act of 2009 (ARRA), provided the SBA an additional $730 million, including

- $375 million to subsidize fees for the SBA's 7(a) and 504/CDC loan guaranty programs and to increase the 7(a) program's maximum loan guaranty percentage from up to 85% of loans of $150,000 or less and up to 75% of loans exceeding $150,000 to 90% for all regular 7(a) loans through September 30, 2010, or when appropriated funding for the subsidies and loan modification was exhausted (after several extensions, the subsidies and loan modification ended on January 3, 2011);
- $255 million for a temporary, two-year small business stabilization program to guarantee loans of $35,000 or less to small businesses for qualified debt consolidation, later named the America's Recovery Capital (ARC) Loan program (the program ceased issuing new loan guarantees on September 30, 2010);
- an additional $15 million for the SBA's surety bond program and a temporary increase in that program's maximum bond amount from $2 million to $5 million, and up to $10 million under certain conditions (the higher maximum bond amounts ended on September 30, 2010);
- an additional $6 million for the SBA's Microloan program's lending program and an additional $24 million for the Microloan program's technical assistance program; and
- increased the funds ("leverage") available to SBA-licensed Small Business Investment Companies (SBICs) to no more than 300% of the company's private capital or $150 million, whichever is less.[87]

More recently, P.L. 111-240, the Small Business Jobs Act of 2010, authorized the Secretary of the Treasury to establish a $30 billion Small Business Lending Fund (SBLF) to encourage community banks with less than $10 billion in assets to increase their lending to small businesses (about $4.0 billion was issued), a $1.5 billion State Small Business Credit Initiative to provide funding to participating states with small business capital access programs, numerous changes to the SBA's loan guaranty and contracting programs, funding to continue the SBA's fee subsidies and the 7(a) program's 90% maximum loan guaranty percentage through December 31, 2010, and about $12 billion in tax relief for small businesses.[88] P.L. 111-322, the Continuing Appropriations and Surface Transportation

Extensions Act, 2011, authorized the SBA to continue its fee subsidies and the 7(a) program's 90% maximum loan guaranty percentage through March 4, 2011, or until available funding was exhausted, which occurred on January 3, 2011. The following provides a summary of the Small Business Jobs Act's provisions relating to the SBA's loan guaranty programs.

Small Business Jobs Act of 2010[89]

P.L. 111-240, the Small Business Jobs Act of 2010, made several changes relating to SBA's loan guaranty programs. The legislation increased the loan limits for the 7(a) program from $2 million to $5 million. The act increased the 504/CDC Program's loan limits from $2 million to $5 million for standard borrowers, and from $4 million to $5.5 million for manufacturers; and temporarily expanded for two years the eligibility for low-interest refinancing under the SBA's 504/CDC program for qualified debt. The law also amended the SBA Express Program, the SBA Microloan Program, the SBA secondary market program, the SBA size standards, and the SBA International Trade Finance Program. These changes are summarized in Table 7.

Table 7. Selected Provisions, the Small Business Jobs Act of 2010

Issue/Program	Program Change
SBA 7(a) Program	increased the 7(a) Program's loan limit from $2 million to $5 million.
SBA 504/CDC Program	increased the 504/CDC Program's loan limits from $2 million to $5 million for standard borrowers, and from $4 million to $5.5 million for manufacturers; and temporarily expanded for two years the eligibility for low-interest refinancing under the SBA's 504/CDC program for qualified debt.
SBA Express Program	temporarily increased for one year the Express Program's loan limit from $350,000 to $1 million (expired on September 27, 2011).
SBA Microloan Program	increased the Microloan Program's loan limit for borrowers from $35,000 to $50,000; and increased the loan limits for Microloan intermediaries after their first year in the program from $3.5 million to $5 million.
Temporary SBA fee subsidies and loan modifications	temporarily increased the SBA's guarantee on 7(a) loans to 90% and provided for the elimination of selected fees on the SBA's 7(a) and 504 loans through December 31, 2010 (after several extensions, expired on January 3, 2011).
SBA secondary market	extended the SBA's secondary market lending authority under ARRA from two years from enactment to two years from the first sale of a pool of first lien position 504 loans guaranteed under this authority (which took place on September 24, 2010).
SBA size standards	authorized the SBA to establish an alternative size standard for the SBA's 7(a) and 504 programs that would use maximum tangible net worth and average net income; and established an interim alternative size standard of not more than $15 million in tangible net worth and not more than $5 million in average net income for the two full fiscal years before the date of the application.
SBA International Trade Finance Program	increased the International Trade Finance Program's loan guaranty to up to 90% and increased the program's loan limit from $2 million (up to $1.75 million guaranteed) to $5 million (up to $4.5 million guaranteed).

Source: P.L. 111-240, the Small Business Jobs Act of 2010.

Discontinued Programs

Over the years, the SBA has discontinued many programs. Some of these cancellations were done administratively, others at the direction of Congress. In many cases key features of the programs were incorporated in other programs. In recent years, the small loans FA$TRAK loan program (now called SBAExpress, which continues), LowDoc loan program, handicapped assistance loan program, disabled assistance loan program, and community express pilot program have been discontinued. The SBA has also ended its support of the veterans franchise program (VETFRAN), but the Department of Veterans Affairs continues its support. Also, during the 112th Congress, both the House and Senate Committees on Small Business have considered legislation to legislatively terminate several smaller SBA programs, such as the Drug-Free Workplace Program, and several authorized but inactive programs, such as the lease guarantee loan program, the pollution control loan program, and the small business telecommuting pilot program.[90]

APPROPRIATIONS[91]

P.L. 112-175, the Continuing Appropriations Resolution, 2013, which provides funding for federal agencies through March 27, 2013, provided the SBA a projected appropriation of $1.049 billion for FY2013, an increase of $130.9 million over its FY2012 appropriation of $918.8 million. The SBA received an appropriation of $729.7 million in FY2011.[92]

The SBA was provided a projected appropriation of $419.9 million for salaries and expenses for FY2013. Included in that amount is $173.4 million for non-credit programs, such as HUBZones, Microloan Technical Assistance, SCORE, SBDCs, Veteran's Business Development, and WBCs. The SBA was provided a projected appropriation of $118.0 million for its disaster loan program, $148.9 million for administrative expenses related to the SBA's business loan programs, $333.6 million for business loan guaranty credit subsidies, and $29.3 million for all other SBA programs.[93]

The Obama Administration had requested $1.115 billion for the SBA in FY2013, an increase of $196.6 million over the SBA's FY2012 appropriation of $918.8 million. The Administration requested $423.6 million for salaries and expenses. Included in that amount was $159.1 million for non-credit programs, such as HUBZones, Microloan Technical Assistance, SCORE, SBDCs, Veteran's Business Development, and WBCs. The Administration also requested $167.0 million for the SBA's disaster loan program, $145.1 million for administrative expenses related to the SBA's business loan programs, $348.6 million for business loan guaranty credit subsidies, and $31.1 million for all other SBA programs.[94]

End Notes

[1] U.S. Congress, Senate Committee on Expenditures, Subcommittee on Investigations, Influence in Government Procurement, 82nd Cong., 1st sess., September 13-15, 17, 19-21, 24-28, October 3-5, 1951 (Washington: GPO, 1951); and U.S. Congress, Senate Banking and Currency, *RFC Act Amendments of 1951*, hearing on bills to

amend the Reconstruction Finance Corporation Act, 82nd Cong., 1st sess., April 27, 30, May 1, 2, 22, 23, 1951 (Washington: GPO, 1951).

[2] P.L. 83-163, the Small Business Act of 1953 (as amended), see http://statutes.legcoun.house. gov/PDF/Small%20 Business%20Act.pdf.

[3] The SBA's programs have detailed rules on program requirements and administration that are not covered in this report. More detailed information concerning the SBA's programs is available in the CRS reports referenced later in this report, on the SBA's website at http://www.sba.gov, in 15 U.S.C. §631 et seq., and in Title 13 of the Code of Federal Regulations.

[4] For additional information and analysis, see CRS Report R41309, *The SBA Disaster Loan Program: Overview and Possible Issues for Congress*, by Bruce R. Lindsay.

[5] 13 C.F.R. §123.

[6] 13 C.F.R. §123.105 and 13 §123.203.

[7] The SBA also offers military reservist economic injury disaster loans. These loans are available when economic injury is incurred as a direct result of a business owner or an essential employee being called to active duty. Generally, these loans are not associated with disasters.

[8] 13 C.F.R. §123.2.

[9] P.L. 93-288, Disaster Relief Act Amendments; and 42 U.S.C. §5721 et seq.

[10] Disaster declarations are published in the *Federal Register* and can also be found on the SBA website at http://www.sba.gov/content/current-disaster-declarations.

[11] 13 C.F.R. §123.105(a)(1).

[12] 13 C.F.R. §123.105(a)(2). For mitigation measures implemented after a disaster has occurred to protect the damaged property from a similar disaster in the future, a homeowner can request that the approved loan amount be increased by the lesser of the cost of the mitigation measure, or up to 20% of the verified loss (before deducting compensation from other sources), to a maximum of $200,000. 13 C.F.R. §127.

[13] 13 C.F.R. §123.203.

[14] See 13 C.F.R. §123.300 for eligibility requirements. Size standards vary according to a variety of factors, including industry type, average firm size, and start-up costs and entry barriers. Size standards can be located in 13 C.F.R. 121. For further information and analysis, see CRS Report R40860, *Small Business Size Standards: A Historical Analysis of Contemporary Issues*, by Robert Jay Dilger.

[15] 13 C.F.R. §123.302.

[16] For further information and analysis concerning FEMA's Pre-Disaster Mitigation Program see CRS Report RL34537, *FEMA's Pre-Disaster Mitigation Program: Overview and Issues*, by Francis X. McCarthy and Natalie Keegan.

[17] 13 C.F.R. §123.403(a).

[18] 13 C.F.R. §123.406.

[19] U.S. Congress, Senate Committee on Small Business, *Hearing on the Proposed Fiscal Year 1995 Budget for the Small Business Administration*, 103rd Cong., 2nd sess., February 22, 1994, S. Hrg. 103-583 (Washington: GPO, 1994), p. 20.

[20] U.S. Small Business Administration, *Fiscal Year 2010 Congressional Budget Justification,* Washington, DC, p. 30.

[21] The SBA provides financial assistance to nonprofit organizations to provide training to small business owners, and to provide loans to small businesses through the SBA Microloan program. Also, nonprofit childcare centers are eligible to participate in SBA's Microloan program.

[22] 13 C.F.R. §121.105.

[23] For additional information and analysis, see CRS Report R40860, *Small Business Size Standards: A Historical Analysis of Contemporary Issues*, by Robert Jay Dilger.

[24] 13 C.F.R. §121.201; and P.L. 111-240, the Small Business Act of 2010, §1116. Alternative Size Standards.

[25] U.S. Small Business Administration, Office of Government Contracting and Business Development, "SBA Size Standards Methodology," Washington, DC, April 2009, pp. 1-8, at http://www.sba.gov/idc/groups/public /documents/sba_homepage/size_standards_ metho dology.pdf.

[26] U.S. Small Business Administration, "Table of Small Business Size Standards Matched to North American Industry Classification System Codes," Washington, DC, at http://www.sba.gov/idc/groups /public /documents/sba_homepage/ serv_sstd_tablepdf.pdf; and U.S. Small Business Administration, "SBA's Size Standards Analysis: An Overview on Methodology and Comprehensive Size Standards Review," power point presentation, Khem R. Sharma, SBA Office of Size Standards, July 13, 2011, p. 4, at http://www.actgov.org

/sigcom/SIGs/SIGs/SBSIG/Documents/2011%20-%20Documents%20and%20Presentations/Size%20Stds%20Presentation_SIG%20Meeting.pdf.

[27] U.S. Census Bureau, *Statistics of U.S. Businesses: 2009*, Washington, DC, http://www.census. gov/econ/susb/.

[28] Title 13 of the Code of Federal Regulations can be viewed at http://www.gpo.gov/fdsys/browse /collectionCfr.action?collectionCode=CFR&searchPath=Title+13%2FChapter+I&oldPath =Title+13&isCollapsed=true&selectedYearFrom= 2010&ycord=510.

[29] P.L. 105-135, the Small Business Reauthorization Act of 1997, expanded the SBA's Microloan program's eligibility to include borrowers establishing a nonprofit childcare business.

[30] 15 U.S.C. §636(a)(23)(a).

[31] H.Rept. 112-136, Financial Services and General Government Appropriations Bill, 2012; S.Rept. 112-79, Financial Services and General Government Appropriations Bill, 2012; U.S. Office of Management and Budget, *The Appendix, Budget of the United States Government, Fiscal Year 2013*, Washington, DC, p. 1267, at http://www.whitehouse.gov/ sites/default/files/omb/budget/fy2013/assets/sba.pdf; and P.L. 112-175, the Continuing Appropriations Resolution, 2013.

[32] For further information and analysis, see CRS Report R41146, *Small Business Administration 7(a) Loan Guaranty Program*, by Robert Jay Dilger.

[33] P.L. 111-240, the Small Business Jobs Act of 2010, temporarily increased the SBAExpress program's loan limit to $1 million for one year following enactment (through September 26, 2011).

[34] For further information and analysis, see CRS Report R41184, *Small Business Administration 504/CDC Loan Guaranty Program*, by Robert Jay Dilger.

[35] A debenture is a bond that is not secured by a lien on specific collateral.

[36] For further information and analysis, see CRS Report R41057, *Small Business Administration Microloan Program*, by Robert Jay Dilger.

[37] For further information and analysis, see CRS Report R41456, *SBA Small Business Investment Company Program*, by Robert Jay Dilger.

[38] 15 U.S.C. §661.

[39] 13 CFR §107.800. The SBIC is not allowed to become a general partner in any unincorporated business or become jointly or severally liable for any obligations of an unincorporated business.

[40] 13 CFR §107.810; and 13 CFR §107.840

[41] 13 CFR §107.815. Debt securities are instruments evidencing a loan with an option or any other right to acquire equity securities in a small business or its affiliates, or a loan which by its terms is convertible into an equity position, or a loan with a right to receive royalties that are excluded form the cost of money.

[42] 13 CFR §107.820.

[43] For further information and analysis, see CRS Report R41352, *Small Business Management and Technical Assistance Training Programs*, by Robert Jay Dilger.

[44] U.S. Small Business Administration, Office of Veterans Business Development, "Special Program Announcement: Veterans Business Outreach Center Program," Washington, DC, April 2010, p. 1, at http://archive.sba.gov/idc/groups/public/documents/sba_program_office/ovbd_vboc_prgm_announce2010. pdf.

[45] U.S. Small Business Administration, "Veterans Business Outreach Centers," Washington, DC, http://www.sba.gov/ content/veterans-business-outreach-centers. There were eight veterans business outreach centers in FY2009.

[46] These programs apply government-wide, but are implemented under the authority of the Small Business Act pursuant to regulations promulgated by the SBA that determine, in part, eligibility for the programs.

[47] For further information and analysis, see CRS Report R40744, *The "8(a) Program" for Small Businesses Owned and Controlled by the Socially and Economically Disadvantaged: Legal Requirements and Issues*, by Kate M. Manuel and John R. Luckey.

[48] Section 8(a) of the Small Business Act, P.L. 85-536, as amended, can be found at 15 U.S.C 637(a). Regulations are in 13 C.F.R. §124. For recent legal developments, see CRS Report R40987, *"Disadvantaged" Small Businesses: Definitions and Designations for Purposes of Federal and Federally Funded Contracting Programs*, by Kate M. Manuel, and CRS Report RL33284, *Minority Contracting and Affirmative Action for Disadvantaged Small Businesses: Legal Issues*, by Jody Feder.

[49] U.S. Small Business Administration, "Dynamic Small Business Search," Washington, DC, at http://dsbs.sba.gov/ dsbs/search/dsp_dsbs.cfm.

[50] For additional information and analysis, see CRS Report R41268, *Small Business Administration HUBZone Program*, by Robert Jay Dilger.

[51] For recent legal developments relating to the priority given to the HUBZone program, see CRS Report R40591, *Set-Asides for Small Businesses: Recent Developments in the Law Regarding Precedence Among the Set-Aside Programs and Set-Asides Under Indefinite-Delivery/Indefinite-Quantity Contracts*, by Kate M. Manuel.

[52] U.S. Small Business Administration, "Dynamic Small Business Search," Washington, DC, at http://dsbs.sba.gov/dsbs/search/dsp_dsbs.cfm.

[53] It should be noted that veteran-owned small businesses and service-disabled veteran-owned small businesses are eligible for separate preferences in procurements conducted by the Department of Veterans Affairs under the authority of the Veterans Benefits, Health Care, and Information Technology Act, as amended by the Veterans' Benefits Improvements Act of 2008.

[54] U.S. Small Business Administration, "Dynamic Small Business Search," Washington, DC, at http://dsbs.sba.gov/dsbs/search/dsp_dsbs.cfm.

[55] P.L. 95-507, a bill to amend the Small Business Act and the Small Business Investment Act of 1958.

[56] P.L. 100-656, the Business Opportunity Development Reform Act of 1988.

[57] Ibid.

[58] Ibid.

[59] See U.S. General Services Administration, Federal Procurement Data System—Next Generation, "Small Business Goaling Report: Fiscal Year 2011," Washington, DC, at https://www.fpds.gov/downloads/top_requests/FPDSNG_SB_Goaling_FY_2011.pdf.

[60] 15 U.S.C. §644(g)(1)-(2).

[61] U.S. General Services Administration, Federal Procurement Data System—Next Generation, "Small Business Goaling Report: Fiscal Year 2011," Washington, DC, at https://www.fpds.gov/downloads/top_requests/FPDSNG_SB_Goaling_FY_2011.pdf.

[62] For additional information and analysis, see CRS Report R42037, *SBA Surety Bond Guarantee Program*, by Robert Jay Dilger.

[63] Ancillary bonds are also eligible if they are incidental and essential to a contract for which SBA has guaranteed a final bond. A reclamation bond is eligible if it is issued to reclaim an abandoned mine site, and for a project undertaken for a specific period of time.

[64] U.S. Small Business Administration, "Surety Bonds," Washington, DC, at http://www.sba.gov/category/navigationstructure/loans-grants/bonds/surety-bonds.

[65] Ibid.

[66] For further information and analysis of the SBIR program, see CRS Report 96-402, *Small Business Innovation Research (SBIR) Program*, by Wendy H. Schacht.

[67] See P.L. 97-219, the Small Business Innovation Development Act of 1982; and 15 U.S.C. §638.

[68] The percentage of each designated agency's applicable extramural research and development budget to be used to support mission-related work in small businesses is scheduled to increase to: not less than 2.7% in FY2013, not less than 2.8% in FY2014, not less than 2.9% in FY2015, not less than 3.0% in FY2016, and not less than 3.2% in FY2017 and each fiscal year thereafter. See P.L. 112-81, the National Defense Authorization Act for Fiscal Year 2012; and U.S. Small Business Administration, "Small Business Innovation Research Program Policy Directive," 77 *Federal Register* 46806-46855.

[69] See P.L. 102-564, the Small Business Research and Development Enhancement Act of 1992; and 15 U.S.C. §638.

[70] The STTR program's set-aside is scheduled to increase to: 0.4% in FY2014 and 0.45% in FY2016 and each fiscal year thereafter. See P.L. 112-81, the National Defense Authorization Act for Fiscal Year 2012; and U.S. Small Business Administration, "Small Business Technology Transfer Program Policy Directive," 77 *Federal Register* 46855 – 46908.

[71] For further information and analysis of the New Markets Venture Capital program, see CRS Report R42565, *SBA New Markets Venture Capital Program*, by Robert Jay Dilger.

[72] U.S. Small Business Administration, "Office of Inspector General," Washington, DC, at http://www.sba.gov/officeof-inspector-general.

[73] U.S. Small Business Administration, "Office of the Inspector General Strategic Plan for FY 2006 – 2011," Washington, DC, at http://www.sba.gov/office-of-inspector-general/860 /4753#Mission.

[74] Ibid.

[75] U.S. Small Business Administration, "Office of Advocacy: About Us," Washington, DC, at http://www.sba.gov/category/advocacy-navigation-structure/about-us.

[76] U.S. Small Business Administration, Office of Advocacy, "FY 2013 Congressional Budget Justification," Washington, DC, p. 2, at http://www.sba.gov/about-sba-info/46741.

[77] The National Women's Business Council, "About the Council," Washington, DC, at http://www.nwbc.gov/aboutus/ ABOUT_THE_COUNCIL.html.

[78] U.S. Small Business Administration, "Office of the National Ombudsman and Assistant Administrator for Regulatory Enforcement Fairness," Washington, DC, at http://www.sba.gov/ombudsman.

[79] U.S. Small Business Administration, "2010 Fiscal Year National Ombudsman Annual Report to Congress," Washington, DC, at http://www.sba.gov/ombudsman/886/13145.

[80] For further information and analysis see CRS Report R42695, *SBA Veterans Assistance Programs: An Analysis of Contemporary Issues*, by Robert Jay Dilger and Sean Lowry.

[81] Interagency Task Force on Veterans Small Business Development, "Report to the President: Empowering Veterans Through Entrepreneurship," November 1, 2011, p. 15, at http://www.sba.gov/sites /default/files /FY2012- Final%20Veterans%20TF%20Report%20to%20President.pdf.

[82] U.S. Small Business Administration, "Veterans Business Outreach Centers," at http://www.sba.gov/content /veteransbusiness-outreach-centers/. Each Veterans Business Outreach Center is funded on an annual basis, with funding not to exceed $150,000 each year. Awards "may vary, depending upon location, staff size, project objectives, performance and agency priorities, and additional special initiatives initiated by the Office of Veterans Business Development." See U.S. Small Business Administration, Office of Veterans Business Development, "Special Program Announcement: Veterans Business Outreach Center Program," April 2010, p. 2, at http://archive.sba.gov/idc/groups /public/documents/sba_program_office/ovbd_vboc_prgm_announce 2010.pdf. Also, existing centers may receive additional funding for special outreach or other initiatives. The initial grant award is for 12 months, with the possibility of four additional (option) years. In FY2011, the Veterans Business Outreach Centers Program conducted its seventh annual "Customer Satisfaction Survey." The FY2011 survey found that 91% of the clients using the centers were satisfied or highly satisfied with the quality, relevance, and timeliness of the assistance provided. See U.S. Small Business Administration, "FY2013 Congressional Budget Justification and FY2011 Annual Performance Report," 2012, p. 62, at http://www.sba.gov/sites/default/files/files/FY%202013%20CBJ%20FY%202011% 20 APR.pdf.

[83] Syracuse University, "About the EBV," Syracuse, NY, at http://whitman.syr.edu/ebv/.

[84] Syracuse University, "Women Veterans Igniting the Spirit of Entrepreneurship (V-WISE)," Syracuse, NY, at http://www.whitman.syr.edu/vwise/index.asp.

[85] Syracuse University, "About Operation Endure and Grow," Syracuse, NY, at http://www.whitman.syr.edu/ EndureAndGrow/About/.

[86] P.L. 112-17, the Small Business Additional Temporary Extension Act of 2011.

[87] For further information and analysis, see CRS Report R40241, *Overview and Analysis of Small Business Provisions in the American Recovery and Reinvestment Act of 2009*, by Oscar R. Gonzales and N. Eric Weiss.

[88] For further information and analysis concerning the Small Business Lending Fund, see CRS Report R42045, *The Small Business Lending Fund*, by Robert Jay Dilger; for further information and analysis concerning the State Small Business Credit Initiative see CRS Report R42581, *State Small Business Credit Initiative: Implementation and Funding Issues*, by Robert Jay Dilger.

[89] For further information and analysis concerning P.L. 111-240, the Small Business Jobs Act of 2010, see CRS Report R41385, *Small Business Legislation During the 111th Congress*, by Robert Jay Dilger and Gary Guenther; and CRS Report R40985, *Small Business: Access to Capital and Job Creation*, by Robert Jay Dilger.

[90] See the legislative history of H.R. 2608, the Continuing Appropriations Act, 2012. Before becoming the legislative vehicle for the continuing appropriations bill, the bill contained the Small Business Program Extension and Reform Act of 2011.

[91] For further information concerning appropriations for the Small Business Administration and other independent agencies, see CRS Report R42476, *Financial Services and General Government: A Summary of the President's FY2013 Budget Request*, by Garrett Hatch.

[92] P.L. 111-117, the Consolidated Appropriations Act, 2010; P.L. 111-242, the Continuing Appropriations Act, 2011; P.L. 112-4, the Further Continuing Appropriations Amendments, 2011; P.L. 112-8, the Further Additional Continuing Appropriations Amendments, 2011; P.L. 112-10, the Department of Defense and Full-Year Continuing Appropriations Act, 2011; P.L. 112-74, the Consolidated Appropriations Act, 2012; and P.L. 112-175, the Continuing Appropriations Resolution, 2013. If sequestration should occur on January 2, 2013, as prescribed by P.L. 112-25, the Budget Control Act of 2011, the SBA's budget would be reduced by $75.194 million. See U.S. Office of Management and Budget, "OMB Report Pursuant to the Sequestration Transparency Act of 2012 (P.L. 112-155)," pp. 204, 205 at http://www.whitehouse.gov/sites/default/files /omb/assets/legislative_reports/sta report.pdf.

[93] P.L. 112-74, the Consolidated Appropriations Act, 2012; and P.L. 112-175, the Continuing Appropriations Resolution, 2013.

[94] U.S. Office of Management and Budget, *The Appendix, Budget of the United States Government, Fiscal Year 2013*, Washington, DC, pp. 1265-1275.

In: Small Business Administration Programs
Editor: Walter Janikowski

ISBN: 978-1-62417-992-1
© 2013 Nova Science Publishers, Inc.

Chapter 2

THE SBA DISASTER LOAN PROGRAM: OVERVIEW AND POSSIBLE ISSUES FOR CONGRESS[*]

Bruce R. Lindsay

SUMMARY

Through its Office of Disaster Assistance (ODA), the Small Business Administration (SBA) has been a major source of assistance for the restoration of commerce and households in areas stricken by natural and human-caused disasters since the agency's creation in 1953. SBA offers low-interest, long-term loans for physical and economic damages to businesses to help repair, rebuild, and recover from economic losses after a declared disaster. However, the majority of the agency's approved disaster loans (approximately 80%) are made to individuals and households (renters and property owners) to help repair and replace homes and personal property.

The three main types of loans for disaster-related losses include (1) Home and Personal Property Loans, (2) Business Physical Disaster Loans, and (3) Economic Injury Disaster Loans (EIDL). Home Disaster Loans are used to repair or replace disaster-damaged primary residences. Personal Property Loans are used to replace personal items such as furniture and clothing. SBA regulations limit Home Physical Disaster Loans to $200,000 and Personal Property Loans to $40,000. Business Physical Disaster Loans help businesses of all sizes and nonprofit organizations repair or replace disaster-damaged property, including inventory and supplies. EIDLs provide financial assistance to businesses located in a disaster area that have suffered economic injury as a result of a declared disaster (regardless if there has been physical damage to the business). EIDLs are used to meet financial obligations it could have met if the disaster had not occurred. Both Business Physical Disaster Loans and EIDLs are limited by law to $2 million per applicant. Business Physical Disaster Loans and EIDLs also provide assistance to small businesses, small agricultural cooperatives (but not enterprises), and certain private, nonprofit organizations that have suffered substantial economic injury resulting from a physical disaster or an agricultural production disaster. Since 1953, SBA has approved roughly 1.9 million disaster loans for a total of more than $47 billion (nominal dollars).

---

[*] This is an edited, reformatted and augmented version of Congressional Research Service, Publication No. R41309, dated August 8, 2012.

Congressional interest in the Disaster Loan Program has increased in recent years primarily because of concerns about the program's performance in responding to the 2005 and 2008 hurricane disasters. Supporters of the Disaster Loan Program argue that it is an important form of assistance to help victims recover from disasters. Critics argue that the responsibility for disaster recovery should be borne by homeowners through the purchase of private insurance. Supporters reply that by covering individuals and households unable to afford private insurance, the program fills a need not met by traditional market mechanisms.

This report describes the SBA Disaster Loan Program, including the types of loans available to individuals, households, businesses, and nonprofit organizations and highlights issues that may be of potential congressional concern: (1) the pace of implementation of the Small Business Disaster Response and Loan Improvement Act of 2008 (P.L. 110-246), (2) SBA's loan processing procedures, (3) the funding of the Disaster Loan Program, (4) the potential need for loan forgiveness and waivers, (5) decline rates for SBA disaster loans, (6) the use of disaster loans to replace allegedly toxic drywall, (7) the transfer of the Disaster Loan Program to FEMA, (8) the perceived increase in federal spending for disasters, and (9) interest rates for SBA disaster loans.

INTRODUCTION

For more than 50 years, the Small Business Administration (SBA) Disaster Loan Program has been a source of economic assistance to areas stricken by disasters.[1] Authorized by the Small Business Act,[2] it is the only SBA program that provides *direct loans* to help businesses, nonprofit organizations, homeowners, and renters repair or replace property damaged or destroyed in a federally declared or certified disaster.

The SBA Disaster Loan Program is also designed to help small agricultural cooperatives recover from economic injury resulting from a disaster. SBA disaster loans include (1) Home Physical Disaster Loans, (2) Business Physical Disaster Loans, and (3) Economic Injury Disaster Loans (EIDL).

Since 1953, SBA has approved roughly 1.9 million applications for disaster loans of all types, amounting to approximately $47 billion.[3] Most direct disaster loans (approximately 80%) are awarded to individuals and households rather than small businesses.[4] The program generally offers low-interest disaster loans at a fixed rate.[5]

This report provides an overview of the Disaster Loan Program, discusses how disaster declarations trigger the SBA loan process, explains the different types of loans potentially available to disaster victims, and discusses terms and restrictions related to each type of loan. The report also explains the SBA disaster loan application process and provides national data on SBA loans from 2000 to 2011, including data related to the Gulf Coast hurricanes since 2005.[6]

This report also examines issues that may be of potential interest to Congress, such as SBA compliance with the Small Business Disaster Response and Loan Improvement Act of 2008 (P.L. 110-246), decline rates for SBA disaster loans, the use of SBA disaster loans to replace allegedly toxic drywall, and the SBA process for conducting credit checks, and interest rates for SBA disaster loans.

TYPES OF SBA DISASTER LOANS

The following section provides a description of the types of disaster loans available to homeowners, renters, and businesses. Each description explains loan limits, eligible recipients and loan activities, and loan maturities.

SBA Disaster Loans Available to Homeowners and Renters

As mentioned elsewhere in this report, 80% of SBA disaster assistance is made available to individuals and households rather than businesses. SBA disaster assistance is provided in the form of loans, not grants, and therefore must be repaid to the federal government.

Homeowners, renters, and personal property owners located in a declared disaster area (and in contiguous counties) may apply to SBA for loans to help recover losses from the disaster. Home loans provided by SBA fall into two categories: personal property loans and real property loans.[7]

Personal Property Loans
A Personal Property Loan provides a creditworthy homeowner or renter with up to $40,000 to repair or replace personal property items such as furniture, clothing, or automobiles damaged or lost in a disaster.[8] These loans cover only uninsured or underinsured property and primary residences and cannot be used to replace extraordinarily expensive or irreplaceable items such as antiques, recreational vehicles, or furs. Interest rates for Personal Property Loans cannot exceed 8% per annum.

However, the interest rate cannot exceed 4% if the applicant is unable to obtain credit elsewhere. Loan maturities may be up to 30 years.

Real Property Loans
A creditworthy homeowner may apply for a "real property loan" of up to $200,000 to repair or restore the homeowner's primary residence to its pre-disaster condition.[9] The loans may not be used to upgrade a home or build additions, unless the upgrade or addition is required by city or county building codes. A homeowner may borrow the lesser of a mitigation measure or up to 20% of the approved loan amount for repairs to protect the damaged property from similar incidents in the future.[10]

As with Personal Property Loans, interest rates for Personal Property Loans cannot exceed 8% per annum or 4% if the applicant is unable to obtain credit elsewhere. Loan maturities may be up to 30 years.

SBA Disaster Loans Available to Businesses

SBA disaster assistance for businesses is also in the form of loans rather than grants and must be repaid.

SBA offers loans to help businesses repair and replace damaged property and financial assistance to businesses that have suffered economic loss as a result of a disaster. The following sections briefly describe each of these loans.

Business Physical Disaster Loans

Any business, regardless of size, located in a declared disaster area may be eligible for a Business Physical Disaster Loan. Business Physical Disaster Loans are made available to repair or replace damaged physical property. The maximum loan amount is $2 million.[11]

Physical Disaster Loans may be used for repairs and replacements to real property, machinery, equipment, fixtures, inventory, and leasehold improvements that are not covered by insurance.[12] Physical Disaster Loans for businesses may utilize up to 20% of the verified loss amount for mitigation measures in an effort to prevent loss should a similar disaster occur in the future.

Interest rates for Business Physical Disaster Loans for businesses must be no higher than 8%, and no higher than 4% if the business does not have credit elsewhere.[13] Loan maturities may be up to 30 years.

Economic Injury Disaster Loans

EIDLs are available only to small businesses as defined by SBA size regulations, which vary from industry to industry.[14] For example, to be considered small, most manufacturing firms must have no more than 500 employees and most retail trade firms must have no more than $7 million in average annual sales. Small agricultural cooperatives and most private and nonprofit organizations that have suffered economic losses as the result of a declared disaster are also eligible for EIDLs. The maximum loan amount for an EIDL is $2 million. The loan can have a maturity of up to 30 years and has an interest rate of 4% or less.[15]

DECLARED DISASTERS AS DEFINED BY SBA

Only victims located in a declared disaster area (and contiguous counties) are eligible to apply for disaster loans. Disaster declarations are "official notices recognizing that specific geographic areas have been damaged by floods and other acts of nature, riots, civil disorders, or industrial accidents such as oil spills."[16] Usually, the incident must be sudden and cause severe physical damage or substantial economic injury. For example, the contamination of food supplies or natural events that cause the sudden displacement or closure of fishing waters may result in a disaster declaration and eligibility for SBA assistance. In contrast, some slow-onset events such as shoreline erosion or gradual land settling are not viewed by SBA as declarable disasters. Droughts and below-average water levels in lakes, reservoirs, and other bodies of water may, however, warrant declarations.[17]

Types of Declarations

There are five ways in which the SBA Disaster Loan Program can be put into effect. These include two types of presidential major disaster declarations as authorized by the

Robert T. Stafford Disaster Relief and Emergency Assistance Act (the Stafford Act),[18] and three types of SBA declarations.[19]

While the type of declaration may determine the types of loans that are available, declaration type has no bearing on loan terms or loan caps. The following describes each type of declaration:

1) The President declares a major disaster, or an emergency, and authorizes both Individual Assistance (IA) and Public Assistance (PA).[20] When the President issues such a declaration, SBA Disaster Loan loans become available to affected homeowners, renters, businesses of all sizes, and nonprofit organizations.

2) The President makes a major disaster declaration that only provides the state with PA. In such a case, a private nonprofit entity that provides noncritical services may be eligible for an SBA loan.

   The entity must first have applied for an SBA loan and must have been deemed ineligible or must have received the maximum amount of assistance from SBA before seeking grant assistance from FEMA.[21] Home and physical property loans are not provided if the declaration only provides PA.

3) The SBA administrator issues an SBA physical disaster declaration.[22] In other cases, the governor of a state may submit a written request to the SBA administrator to issue a physical disaster declaration.[23]

   When the SBA administrator makes such a declaration, disaster loans become available for homeowners, renters, businesses of all sizes, and nonprofit organizations in primary and contiguous counties.

4) The SBA administrator may make an EIDL declaration when SBA receives a certification from a state governor that at least five small businesses have suffered substantial economic injury as a result of a disaster. This declaration is offered only when other viable forms of financial assistance are unavailable. EIDL declarations provide Economic Injury Disaster Loans to small businesses, small agricultural cooperatives, and most private nonprofit organizations.

5) The SBA administrator may issue a declaration for EIDL loans based on the determination of a natural disaster by the Secretary of Agriculture.[24] These loans are available to small businesses, small agricultural cooperatives, and most private nonprofit organizations in primary and contiguous counties. Additionally, the SBA administrator may issue a declaration based on the determination of the Secretary of Commerce that a fishery resource disaster or commercial fishery failure has occurred.[25]

Frequency of Declarations

As shown in Table 1 (also see Figure 1), 5,032 declarations were issued from 1990 through 2012—an average of 219 a year. The greatest number of declarations, an average of 123 a year, originated from the Secretary of Agriculture.

In contrast, the fewest declarations, averaging less than one per year, came from the Secretary of Commerce.

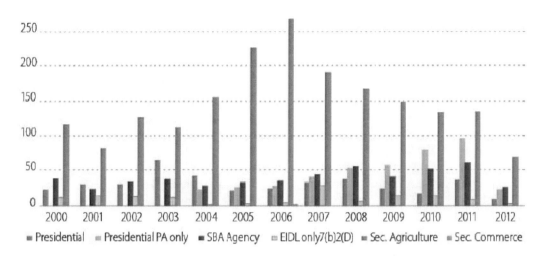

Figure 1. Declaration by Type; 1990 to 2012.

Table 1. Declaration by Type 1990 to 2012

Year	Presidential	Presidential (PA Only)	SBA	EIDL Only-7(b)2(D)	Secretary of Agriculture	Secretary of Commerce	Total
1990	30	28		11	53	0	122
1991	21	31		10	61	0	123
1992	33	28		17	84	0	162
1993	31	38		14	84	0	167
1994	12	31		11	76	0	130
1995	19	36		8	93	0	156
1996	36	34		4	128	0	202
1997	38	31		8	129	0	206
1998	45	48		12	85	0	190
1999	40	29		9	112	0	190
2000	22	38		12	116	0	188
2001	30	24		15	82	0	151
2002	30	34		13	126	0	203
2003	64		37	12	112	0	225
2004	41	22	28	2	154	0	247
2005	21	26	32	3	226	0	308
2006	25	28	35	5	268	2	363
2007	33	40	44	29	190	0	336
2008	37	53	55	7	167	0	319
2009	25	57	40	15	149	0	286
2010	17	80	51	15	133	0	296
2011	36	95	60	9	134	0	334
2012	9	22	26	3	68	0	128
Total	695	423	838	244	2830	2	5,032

Source: Data provided by SBA and available from the CRS author upon request.

SBA Disaster Loan Program and Statistics

Not all applicants approved for a disaster loan accept them. As shown in Table 2, SBA approved 465,244 applications for home, business, and EIDLs from 2000 to 2011.[26] However, 338,192 loans (roughly 73% of the loans approved) amounting to roughly $14 billion in disaster loans were actually disbursed to disaster survivors.

As shown in Figure 2, 82% of disbursed loans were home disaster loans (including physical and personal property loans), 11% were for Business Physical Disaster Loans, and 6% were EIDLs.[27]

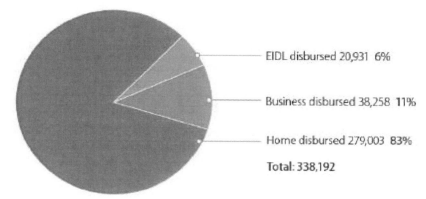

Source: Data provided by SBA and available from the CRS author upon request.

Figure 2. Disbursed SBA Disaster Loans by Type; FY2000-FY2011.

The following describes disaster loan approvals and disbursements for each type of loan between 2000 and 2011.

Home Disaster Loans

SBA approved 387,938 home disaster loans between fiscal years 2000 and 2011. Of this amount, 279,003 home disaster loans were disbursed for a total of $8.6 billion. The yearly average number of approved home disaster loans between fiscal years 2000 and 2011 was 32,328. In contrast, the yearly average number of disbursed loans was 23,250.

Business Disaster Loans

SBA approved 53,897 applications for Business Physical Disaster Loans—a yearly average of 4,491. The number of disbursed Business Physical Disaster Loans was 38,258 for $3.3 billion in loans. The yearly average number of Business Physical Disaster Loans disbursed by SBA was 3,188.

Economic Injury Disaster Loans

SBA approved 23,409 applications for EIDLs between 2000 and 2011—a yearly average of 1,951. The total number of EIDLs disbursed by SBA was 20,931 for $1.9 billion. The average number of disbursed EIDLs per year is 1,744 per year.

Table 2. SBA Home, Business and Economic Disaster Loans FY2000 to FY2011

Fiscal Year	EIDL Number Approved	EIDL Percentage of Combined Total	Home Disaster Loans Number Approved	Home Disaster Loans Percentage of Combined Total	Business Disaster Loans Number Approved	Business Disaster Loans Percentage of Combined Total	Combined Total
2000	912	3.2%	23,070	81.8%	4,236	15.0%	28,218
2001	1,156	2.4%	43,519	89.1%	4,177	8.6%	48,852
2002	9,548	43.7%	10,114	46.3%	2,167	9.9%	21,829
2003	2,803	10.8%	20,235	78.3%	2,818	10.9%	25,856
2004	624	2.2%	25,024	87.8%	2,862	10.0%	28,510
2005	1,480	2.4%	52,677	84.9%	7,918	12.8%	62,075
2006	4,302	2.5%	145,164	85.4%	20,517	12.1%	169,983
2007	499	3.6%	11,760	83.9%	1,755	12.5%	14,014
2008	517	3.4%	12,755	84.2%	1,856	12.3%	15,128
2009	647	3.0%	18,408	84.4%	2,725	12.5%	21,780
2010	609	4.0%	13,286	86.5	1,461	9.5%	15,356
2011	312	2.3%	11,926	87.4	1,405	10.3%	13,643
Total	23,409	5.0%	387,938	83.4%	53,897	11.6%	465,244
Average	1,951		32,328		3,188		38,770

Source: Data provided by SBA and available from the CRS author upon request.
Notes: Numbers have been rounded. Numbers shown in this table represent the numbers of approved disaster loans. A large number of Home Disaster Loans were approved in 2001 due mainly to the Nisqually Earthquake on February 28, 2001. Other noticeable increases in approved applications occurred in 2005 and especially in 2006, following the Gulf Coast hurricanes.

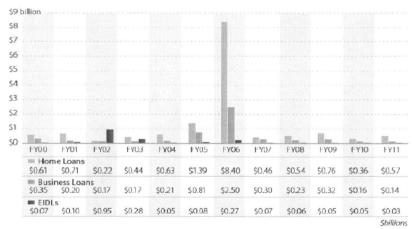

Source: Data provided by SBA and available from the CRS author upon request.
Notes: Amounts shown in this figure reflect approved disaster loans. Not all approved loans are accepted by disaster victims and businesses. Therefore, actual loan acceptance and accepted amounts may be smaller than the amounts shown here.

Figure 3. SBA Home, Business, and Economic Disaster Loans; FY2000 to FY2011.

As shown in Figure 3, SBA usually approves larger dollar amounts for Home Disaster Loans than for Business Disaster Loans. However, because of the September 11, 2001, terrorist attacks, dollar amounts for business loans in 2002 and 2003 exceeded those for home loans.

POTENTIAL ISSUES FOR CONGRESS

Several issues related to the SBA Disaster Loan Program may be of interest to Congress. Some of these key matters are discussed below including (1) the pace of implementation of the Small Business Disaster Response and Loan Improvement Act of 2008 (P.L. 110-246), (2) SBA's loan processing procedures, (3) the funding of the Disaster Loan Program, (4) the potential need for loan forgiveness and waivers, (5) decline rates for SBA disaster loans, (6) the use of disaster loans to replace allegedly toxic drywall, (7) the transfer of the Disaster Loan Program to FEMA, (8) the perceived increase in federal spending for disasters, and (9) interest rates for home and business disaster loans.

COMPLIANCE WITH THE SMALL BUSINESS DISASTER RESPONSE AND LOAN IMPROVEMENTS ACT OF 2008

In response to criticism of SBA's disaster loan processing, and in an effort to improve SBA's Disaster Loan Program, Congress passed the Small Business Disaster Response and Loan Improvements Act of 2008(P.L. 110-246).[28] Among the act's 26 new program requirements for SBA are provisions designed to improve coordination efforts with FEMA, ensure that SBA has an adequate number of full-time-equivalent employees, update or develop a disaster response plan, and keep Congress better informed concerning the agency's progress on meeting the act's requirements through annual reports. The act is divided into three parts as follows:

- **Part I, Disaster Planning and Response:** Part 1 of the act includes a number of measures intended to improve SBA's coordination with other agencies when responding to disasters. For instance, Section 12062(a)(5) requires the SBA administrator to ensure that the agency's disaster assistance programs are coordinated, to the maximum extent practicable, with FEMA's disaster assistance programs. Section 12063(5) requires that the administrator make every effort to communicate, through radio, television, print, and internet-based outlets, all relevant information needed by disaster loan applicants. Section 12069(a) requires that if SBA's primary facility for disaster loan processing becomes unavailable, another disaster loan processing facility must be made available within two days.
- **Part II, Disaster Lending:** Part 2 of the act provides additional loan amounts in certain circumstances, reforms some of SBA's loan processes, and grants SBA authority to defer payments of loans made to homeowners and businesses affected by the 2005 Gulf Coast hurricanes. For example, Section 12081 grants the SBA administrator authority to provide additional disaster assistance for events that cause

significant loss of life or damage, Section 12085 establishes an Expedited Disaster Assistance Loan Program, and Section 12086 allows the SBA administrator to carry out a program to refinance Gulf Coast disaster loans.

- **Part III, Miscellaneous:** Part 3 of the act pertains to reporting requirements for SBA disaster assistance programs. Section 12091 requires, after a major disaster, the SBA administrator to submit to the Senate Committee on Small Business and Entrepreneurship, the Senate Committee on Appropriations, the House Committee on Small Business, and the House Committee on Appropriations a report on the operation of the Disaster Loan Program not later than the fifth business day of each month during the applicable period for a major disaster. The reports must include the daily average lending volume (in number of loans and dollars), the percentage by which each category has increased or decreased since the previous report, the amount of funding available for loans, and an estimate of how long the available funding for salaries and expenses will last, based on SBA's spending rate.

A GAO report released in July 2009 found that SBA met 13 of the 26 requirements of the act, partially addressed 8, and did not take action on 5.

Among the critical issues the 2008 act aims to address is the need to inform affected businesses and persons about types of assistance available from SBA and how to access such assistance, and the need for SBA to process high volumes of applications effectively and efficiently while coordinating assistance with other agencies.

One of the requirements GAO found to be only partially addressed was that SBA develop a region-specific marketing and outreach program to make information readily available to regional entities. GAO also reported that SBA had only partially met the act's requirement to fully develop a disaster recovery plan. The plan must include

- an assessment of the various types of disasters likely to occur in each SBA region;
- an assessment of the likely demand for SBA assistance;
- an assessment of SBA's resource needs related to information technology, telecommunications, human resources, and office space; and
- guidelines on how SBA intends to coordinate with other agencies.

In response to the report, SBA officials acknowledged that the agency had not yet completely addressed some of the reforms because implementing new programs and changing existing programs would require it to make extensive changes that would take time.[29] The SBA response, paraphrased by GAO, was as follows:

> SBA generally agreed with our recommendations and stated the agency's plan to incorporate them into its ongoing efforts to implement the Act and improve the application process. Specifically, SBA said that the agency has plans to expand its outreach efforts to ensure the public in all regions of the country are more aware of SBA disaster assistance programs before a disaster strikes. SBA is also planning to submit both the required annual report, and the 2009 revision to its DRP [Disaster Recovery Program] to Congress by November 15, 2009. Additionally, SBA officials said the agency has plans to develop an implementation plan for completion of the remaining provisions. Finally, in response to our recommendation on the application process, the officials cited the electronic loan application as an example of its efforts to improve the application

process and said the agency has plans to continue its improvement efforts and make such improvements an ongoing priority.[30]

On September 25, 2009, Manuel Gonzalez, Director of the SBA Houston District Office,[31] testified before the Senate Committee on Small Business and Entrepreneurship that the agency's 2008 response to Hurricane Ike demonstrated programmatic improvements. For example, loan processing times had decreased and better interagency cooperation had been achieved. Gonzalez conceded, however, that there was still room for improvement. According to Gonzalez, SBA learned a number of lessons from the Gulf Coast hurricanes that have led to improved disaster assistance. These reforms included

- implementing new programs such as bridge loans or private disaster loans following catastrophic disasters;[32]
- working to improve coordination efforts with FEMA and the Internal Revenue Service (IRS);
- extending eligibility of the SBA Economic Injury Disaster Loan program to nonprofit groups; and
- significantly shortening the time taken to process loans.

On November 30, 2011, James Rivera, Administrator of SBA's Office of Disaster Assistance testified before the House Committee on Small Business that SBA had made "dramatic improvements" in its loan operations since the 2005 Gulf Coast hurricanes. Among the improvements, Rivera stated that SBA provided better quality customer service to disaster survivors.[33] One newly implemented strategy cited by Rivera as evidence of better customer service was in SBA's response to Hurricane Irene and Tropical Storm Lee in which 900 additional employees were trained and deployed to help with disaster loan processing.[34]

However, William Shear, GAO Director of Financial Markets and Community Investment, testified at the same hearing that while SBA had taken steps to implement three of the five recommendations from GAO's 2009 report, SBA did provide evidence it was developing an implementation plan that identifies problems in the disaster loan application process in order to make improvements for future applicants.[35] In addition, GAO had recommended to SBA that it implement a process to address identified problems in the application process. However, GAO interviewed and surveyed disaster survivors in 2009 and found some responses reported concerns with the amount of paperwork required to complete applications and the timeliness of loan disbursements.[36] Despite the reported improvements discussed above, SBA may be behind schedule in executing reforms and streamlining loan processes. Among the oversight questions that might arise from the GAO findings are what circumstances have impeded the reform requirements of the act thus far and what additional efforts are needed to overcome such impediments.

IMPROVED TIME FRAME FOR LOAN PROCESSING

At the September 25, 2009, hearing, Director Gonzalez stated that revised procedures that were established before Hurricane Ike reduced the amount of time needed to process an average loan. Senator Mary Landrieu—chairman of the Senate Committee on Small Business and Entrepreneurship and the Senate Committee on Homeland Security and Governmental Affairs, Subcommittee on Disaster Recovery—agreed with Gonzalez, noting that local officials in southwest Louisiana reported that SBA was better prepared and more responsive following Hurricanes Gustav and Ike. For example, SBA took five days to process a home loan following Ike, compared to the 90 days it had taken after Hurricanes Katrina and Rita. The processing time for business loans also improved, averaging just over a week, compared to the 70-day average following Hurricanes Katrina and Rita.[37]

At the previously mentioned November 30, 2011, hearing before the House Committee on Small Business Rivera testified that loan processing times in response to Hurricane Irene and Tropical Storm Lee had exceeded SBA processing goals by approving or declining homeowner requests within 8 days and business requests within 10 days.[38]

Although processing times appear to have decreased, Members may continue to be concerned about the timeliness of the disaster loan decisions. Congress may also be concerned that small businesses with limited resources may have difficulty filling out loan applications and providing business related documents. If so, Congress could conduct oversight hearings on methods for reducing processing time while guarding against the unintended consequence of an increased potential for loan fraud and abuse.

DECLINE RATES FOR SBA DISASTER LOANS

On July 25, 2011, the Senate Committee on Small Business and Entrepreneurship sent a letter to Karen Mills, the SBA Administrator, regarding reports of high decline rates for disaster rates and the reasons behind them.[39] The letter provided examples of disaster loan decline rates of recent disasters including decline rates of 73% and 68% for Louisiana and Florida respectively after the Deepwater Horizon oil spill. The committee stated they were concerned that the high decline rates, coupled with negative media coverage, may serve as a deterrent for businesses that may want to apply for a disaster loan, but are discouraged to do so. The letter also requested information from SBA, including an update of disaster operations in Joplin, MS, and northern Alabama, to determine whether SBA policy changes to the disaster loan program since the 2005 hurricanes have influenced the declined rates among applicants. The committee asked why decline rates are so high immediately following an incident. If Members are concerned that high decline rates may discourage disaster survivors from applying for SBA disaster loans, or want to inquire whether the high decline rates are advantageous (such as decreasing default rates on loans), a congressional oversight hearing might be considered.

CONSUMER PRODUCT SAFETY

Drywall imported from China was used to repair and replace some of the structures damaged in the 2005 and 2008 Gulf Coast hurricanes. Chinese drywall is generally less expensive, making its use arguably desirable as a cost-saving measure over more expensive, domestically produced drywall. Some of the imported drywall, however, was alleged to be contaminated with sulfuric acid. According to Representative Mario Diaz-Balart:

Recent reports are that about 100,000 homes could be affected. This imported drywall from China contains sulfuric gas, which actually has corroded copper electrical wiring. It's corroded air conditioning units and copper pipes, including to the point where there have been fire hazards. It's also a health issue. It has created sinus problems, created bloody noses, and headaches. It has created bronchitis and pneumonia in children, and now we hear that it's also harmful to pregnant women. As a matter of fact, Mr. Chairman, on April 17, the *Wall Street Journal* stated that the University of Southern California's School of Medicine, a professor there, stated "that sulfur compound gasses, even at low levels, have been found to cause respiratory problems such as asthma.[40]

To eliminate the problem, observers have called for the drywall to be removed and replaced. To some, the toxic drywall has constituted a second disaster. Concern over the product prompted Senators Bill Nelson, Mary Landrieu, Mark Warner, and Jim Webb to request that economic assistance from FEMA be given to homeowners affected by toxic drywall.[41]

Many of the owners of structures that have been replaced or repaired using the drywall received SBA disaster loans; however, SBA views the toxic drywall as a consumer product problem.[42] Hence, the agency does not plan to extend the amount of current loans or provide additional or new loans to replace the drywall.

Even if the loans were to be extended, it is unclear how many households would be approved for an extension because numerous homeowners (particularly in Louisiana) have defaulted on their SBA disaster loans and are therefore unlikely to be approved for second loans. It is also unclear who would fund the removal and replacement of the drywall in foreclosed homes. Unless the drywall is removed, resale of the home will be difficult.

Congressional attempts have been made to address the issue. For example, in the 110th Congress, H.R. 3854, the Small Business Financing and Investment Act of 2009, passed the House on October 29, 2009, and was referred to the Senate Committee on Small Business and Entrepreneurship. The bill would authorize the SBA administrator to make disaster loans available to homeowners "for the repair and replacement" of toxic drywall manufactured in China.

In addition to authorizing the SBA administrator to make disaster loans available to replace the drywall, another policy option that might help owners of affected properties is loan forgiveness, or a loan waiver.

As a general rule, SBA does not offer loan forgiveness unless Congress intervenes. One exception was granted after Hurricane Betsy, when President Lyndon B. Johnson signed the Southeast Hurricane Disaster Relief Act of 1965.[43] Section 3 of the act authorized the SBA administrator to grant disaster loan forgiveness or issue waivers for property lost or damaged in Florida, Louisiana, and Mississippi as a result of Hurricane Betsy. The act stated that SBA

> ... to the extent such loss or damage is not compensated for by insurance or otherwise, (1) shall at the borrower's option on that part of any loan in excess of $500, (A) cancel up to $1,800 of the loan, or (B) waive interest due on the loan in a total amount of not more than $1,800 over a period not to exceed three years; and (2) may lend to a privately owned school, college, or university without regard to whether the required financial assistance is otherwise available from private sources, and may waive interest payments and defer principal payments on such a loan for the first three years of the term of the loan.[44]

CREDIT CHECKS FOR SBA DISASTER LOANS

On March 28, 2008, the SBA Office of Inspector General (OIG) raised an issue of potential congressional concern when it released a study that was critical of the agency's Office of Disaster Administration (ODA).

The report indicated that ODA (1) did not perform annual credit reviews, as required by SBA's standard operating procedures, before making distributions of disaster loan proceeds; (2) did not obtain updated financial information; and (3) failed to cancel loans in instances where the borrower had no repayment ability. As a result, the Office of Inspector General stated that the ODA inappropriately extended credit reviews, first from 12 to 16 months, and later to 24 months.

According to the Office of Inspector General, the extensions arguably eliminated credit reviews for 10,100 disaster loans totaling over $1 billion in disbursements without assurance that borrowers had the ability to repay the loans.[45]

The OIG further concluded that the ODA circumvented a critical management control by disbursing additional funds on these loans without first determining whether adverse changes had occurred in the borrowers' financial condition that could have compromised their ability to repay the additional loan proceeds. The OIG reported that both extensions were made outside the normal process for amending standard operating procedures, which require clearance by senior agency executives who are external to the ODA.[46]

The ODA responded to the study, stating that the OIG report failed to recognize the devastating effects of the Gulf Coast hurricanes on the financial condition of borrowers and the need for SBA to adjust its lending policies accordingly.

The ODA argued that because the hurricanes negatively affected borrowers' credit, SBA needed to grant the borrowers additional opportunities to explain poor credit history and credit bureau reports.

The ODA further claimed that disaster-related poor credit may have been beyond the borrowers' control (because of the disaster) and that continuing to enforce the standard credit review policies would have created additional hardships for borrowers.[47]

Although the OIG conceded that the damage caused by the 2005[48] hurricanes was extensive, it concluded that ODA lacked the authority to circumvent the regulatory requirement that loan disbursements be made only to individuals who have the ability to repay their loans. The OIG further argued that Congress intends for the loans to be repaid and that the Disaster Loan Program is not a grant program, indicating that the OIG suspected that some of the loans would not be repaid.[49]

POSSIBLE REFORMS TO THE DISASTER LOAN PROGRAM

Critics of SBA's Disaster Loan Program argue that it should be terminated and the responsibility for disaster assistance transferred to businesses and individuals through private insurance. Other critics argue that the federal share of disaster and emergency costs is disproportionately high when compared to state, local, and individual spending on disaster relief. They add that reforms are needed to contain the costs of federal disaster assistance.[50] They point to an OMB report[51] that federal spending on disasters is predicted to rise from

$3.6 billion for FY2010 to $225.5 billion in FY2019 as evidence of the need to contain costs.[52] Bills to terminate the Disaster Loan Program have been introduced a number of times in the past. For example, H.R. 3728, the Disaster Relief Partnership Act, in the 105th Congress, would have terminated the SBA Disaster Loan Program and amended the Stafford Act to establish a national insurance program. If it had been enacted, individuals would have become responsible for insuring their property against disasters without any federal assistance.

The following sections provide (1) SBA data on the funding of disaster loans for the Gulf Coast, and (2) a national comparison of SBA loans and insurance losses for disasters from the years 2000 to 2009. The data show the amount of money loaned through the SBA Disaster Loan Program.

Comparing disaster loan amounts to catastrophic insurance losses could help frame a debate about shifting some or all of the responsibility for funding recovery from the federal government to individuals by privatizing disaster loss through the use of insurance.

National SBA Data: 2000 to 2011

Nationally, from 2000 to 2011, SBA disbursed 279,003 disaster loans to help homeowners repair and replace property damaged by disasters, representing a yearly average of 23,250 disbursed loans. During the same period, the average annual amount disbursed for home disaster loans was $716 million.[53] With regard to Business Physical Disaster Loans, SBA disbursed 38,258 applications, for a total of $3.3 billion, during the period. The average number of Business Physical Disaster Loans disbursed each year was 7,352, and the average annual amount approved was $273 million. The devastation caused by the 2005 hurricanes pushed the average number of applications and loans higher.

As previously noted, the loan activity due to the 2005 hurricanes produced outlying figures that skewed the data results (see Table 2). If the data exclude 2005 and 2006, the national average of SBA disbursed disaster loans for homes drops to 135,665. The average annual amount falls to $269 million. When these years are excluded, the number of disbursed Business Physical Disaster Loans drops to 18,793, producing an average annual loan amount of $128 million.

Private Insurance Disaster Losses: 2000 to 2011

SBA disaster loan amounts are generally less than the catastrophic loss amounts paid out by the insurance industry. In 2006, however, SBA Home Disaster Loans and Business Disaster Loans (because of Hurricane Katrina) exceeded the private insurance industry's expenditures by roughly $2 billion. (See Figure 4 for comparisons.)

Private insurance companies paid out a total of $244 billion for disaster-related losses from 2000 to 2010, a yearly average of about $22 billion per year. If the year 2005 is removed, the total cost to private insurance companies decreases to $155 billion, with a yearly average of $17 billion per year.[54]

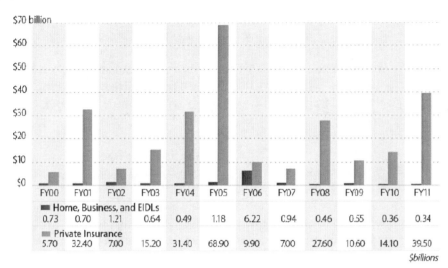

Source: Data provided by SBA and available from the CRS author upon request. Insurance data are derived from Property Claims Service/ISO; Insurance Information Institute.

Notes: Amounts shown in this figure represent the number of approved disaster loans. Not all approved loans are accepted by disaster victims and businesses. Therefore, actual loan acceptance and amounts may be less than the amounts shown here. Insurance data for 2009 were available only as a rounded number. Amounts shown in this figure present SBA loans in aggregate form. Disaggregated SBA amounts can be found in Appendix A.

Figure 4. National Comparison of SBA Loans to Private Insurance Disaster Losses; FY2000 to FY2011.

SBA Assistance Provided after the Gulf Coast Hurricanes of 2005 and 2008

According to SBA, since the summer of 2005, the largest distributions of disaster loans (in terms of number of applications and dollar amounts) have been for recovery efforts after the Gulf Coast hurricanes. As of June 2012, SBA had approved roughly 150,000 loans for homeowners, 22,000 for Business Physical Disaster Loans, and 3,400 EIDLs to applicants in the Gulf Coast region (see Table 3). The total amounts for these loans include $8.9 billion in Home Disaster Loans, $2.9 billion in business loans, and $215 million in EIDLs (see Table 4 and Figure B-1 and Figure B-2).

Prior to FY2005, SBA's Disaster Loan Program had an outstanding loan balance of $4 billion. The balance increased to $9 billion by FY2007. In FY2008, the balance decreased to $8.6 billion. According to SBA, two-thirds of the $8.6 billion in outstanding loans pertained to Gulf Coast states, including approximately $3 billion for Business Disaster Loans or Home Disaster Loans in Louisiana, more than $2 billion for Florida and Mississippi, and roughly $7 million for Texas. Most of the loans resulted from the hurricanes that occurred in 2005.[55] Figure 5 displays the unpaid principal balances for SBA disaster loans as of September 30, 2008. More than half (58%) of the unpaid loans were associated with Hurricanes Katrina, Rita, and Wilma. Of these, 44% were for Home Disaster Loans and 14% for Business Disaster Loans. According to SBA, defaulted loans increased the purchase rates by 60% in FY2007 and 80% in FY2008.[56]

**Table 3. SBA Disaster Loans by Type of Approved Application
Number of approved applications for the Gulf Coast as of June 26, 2012**

Program	Alabama	Florida	Louisiana	Mississippi	Texas	Total
Home Disaster Loans	2,497	14,021	86,206	31,243	15,935	149,902
Business Disaster Loans	360	2,578	12,921	4,388	2,545	22,792
Economic Injury Disaster Loans	82	812	1,801	335	410	3,440
Total	2,939	17,411	100,928	35,966	18,890	176,134

Source: Data provided by SBA and available from the CRS author upon request. For graphic representations, see Figure B-1.

Notes: SBA provided disaster loans to Alabama and Florida for Hurricanes Katrina, Rita, and Wilma. Alabama and Florida did not receive loans for Hurricanes Gustav and Ike. SBA provided disaster loans to Mississippi for Hurricanes Katrina, Rita, Wilma, and Gustav. Mississippi did not receive loans for Hurricane Ike. SBA provided disaster loans to Texas for Hurricanes Katrina, Rita, Wilma, and Ike. Texas did not receive loans for Hurricane Gustav. Louisiana received assistance for all five hurricanes.

Table 4. SBA Disaster Loans by Gulf Coast State Cumulative loan amounts for the Gulf Coast as of July 2009; dollars in thousands

Program	Alabama	Florida	Louisiana	Mississippi	Texas	Total
Home Disaster Loans	96,244	450,170	5,445,887	2,069,160	686,533	8,895,399
Business Disaster Loans	47,052	412,085	1,526,241	546,417	324,016	2,878,243
Economic Injury Disaster Loans	7,221	48,917	111,486	19,267	24,277	214,525
Total	150,517	911,172	7,083,615	2,634,844	1,034,826	11,988,168

Source: Data provided by SBA and available from the CRS author upon request. For a graphic representation, see Figure B-2.

Notes: See Table 3 notes.

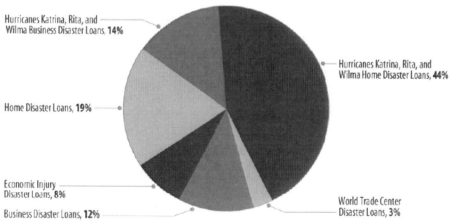

Source: U.S. Small Business Administration, *Financial Report: FY2008*, November 17, 2008.
Notes: More recent data have not been reported by SBA.

Figure 5. Disaster Loan Unpaid Principal Balance by Category; As of September 30, 2008.

PRIVATIZING DISASTER LOANS

As previously mentioned, several policy scholars have argued that federal disaster assistance should be privatized. Their primary argument is that government programs are overly generous to disaster victims. Hence, federal disaster assistance functions as a disincentive because individuals and households expect to rely on it after a disaster instead of investing in mitigation, preparedness, and other resiliency practices. One way to shift the responsibility for recovery from the federal government to citizens would be to privatize federal disaster assistance programs, such as the Disaster Loan Program. Proponents maintain that some of the benefits associated with privatization might include

- reducing federal costs for disaster assistance;
- rewarding behaviors that protect against future disasters through insurance deductibles; and
- preventing development in hazard prone areas because insuring properties in these areas might be cost prohibitive.

Other observers, however, could note some potential negative aspects and questions about privatizing the Disaster Loan Program. Among them are the following:

- Some individuals might not be able to afford insurance, so they might risk going without it. The National Flood Insurance Program (NFIP) was put into place to make flood insurance more affordable. The utility and success of the NFIP has been subject to debate. Would another program similar to the NFIP need to be put into place? What resources would be available to individuals and households who could not afford to purchase insurance? Would the federal government refuse to help them?
- What would happen if only affluent households could afford to purchase hazard insurance? How would one determine that an individual or household could have purchased insurance, but chose not to?
- Would individuals be required to purchase disaster insurance? If so, how would this requirement be enforced? Would all Americans be required to purchase disaster coverage, or just those in hazardous areas? Moreover, who would be responsible for determining what hazards are specific to what areas?
- What if the private insurance industry decided not to cover a certain area or type of hazard? Would this be considered a market failure? Would there be a need for federal insurance to fill the void?
- Would the private insurance industry be able to cover the costs associated with a catastrophic disaster? Would a disaster the size and scope of Hurricane Katrina bankrupt the industry?
- Would the private insurance industry continue to fund recovery projects that took as long as a decade to complete?
- Could the nation recover from an incident as large as Hurricane Katrina without the use of federal disaster assistance?

CONCLUSION

Supporters of the SBA Disaster Loan Program might argue that the criticisms aimed at SBA's handling of its disaster loan processing in 2005 and 2006 have been addressed. They contend that loan processing times have been reduced, interagency coordination has improved, and new mechanisms such as bridge loans have improved the program. On the other hand, some critics might be troubled by SBA's perceived slow progress in implementing some of the requirements set forth in the Small Business Disaster Response and Loan Improvements Act of 2008 (P.L. 110- 246).

While SBA's response to Hurricane Ike has been generally regarded as competent, some might argue that if the requirements in the act had been implemented, such as compliance with reporting, the agency's response could have been more successful. In addition, comparing SBA's performance after Hurricane Ike with its performance after Hurricane Katrina might not be a good indicator of improved disaster response because of the more devastating economic damage inflicted by Hurricane Katrina.

APPENDIX A. WHY DOES SBA INSTEAD OF FEMA ISSUE DISASTER LOANS?

In 1978, President Jimmy Carter signed Executive Order 12127. The order merged many of the disaster-related responsibilities of separate federal agencies into the Federal Emergency Management Agency (FEMA). During FEMA's formation, it was determined that SBA would continue to provide disaster loans through the Disaster Loan Program rather than transfer that function to FEMA.

At the 1978 hearing before a Subcommittee of the Committee on Government Operations, Chairman Jack Brooks questioned the rationale for keeping the loan program outside of FEMA.[57] According to James T. McIntyre, Director, Office of Management and Budget (OMB), the rationale was as follows:

> [O]ne of the fundamental principles underlying this proposal is that whenever possible emergency responsibilities should be an extension of the regular missions of federal agencies. I believe the Congress also subscribed to this principle in considering disaster legislation in the past.
> The Disaster Relief Act of 1974 provides for the direction and coordination, in disaster situations, of agencies which have programs which can be applied to meeting disaster needs. It does not provide that the coordinating agency should exercise direct operational control.... [I]f the programs ... were incorporated in the new agency we would be required to create duplicate sets of skills and resources.... [S]ince the Small Business Administration administers loan programs other than those just for disaster victims, both the SBA and the new agency [FEMA] would have to maintain separate staffs of loan officers and portfolio managers if the disaster loan function were transferred to the new Agency.... [O]ne of our basic purposes for reorganization ... would be thwarted if we were to have to maintain a duplicate staff function in two or more agencies.

McIntyre added, "We believe we have achieved a balance in this new agency [FEMA] between operational activities and planning and coordination functions." He further stated that "we can provide better service to the disaster victims if oversight of disaster response and recovery operations is vested in an agency which can adopt a much broader prospective than would be possible if this agency [FEMA] had operational responsibilities as well." Additionally, a clause in the Stafford Act that prohibits recipients of disaster aid from receiving similar types of aid from other federal sources is often cited as a rationale for keeping the entities distinct.[58] Section 312 of the act states:

> The President, in consultation with the head of each Federal agency administering any program providing financial assistance to persons, business concerns, or other entities suffering losses as a result of a major disaster or emergency, shall assure that no such person, business concern, or other entity will receive such assistance with respect to any part of such loss as to which he has received financial assistance under any other program or from insurance or any other source.[59]

APPENDIX B. SBA DISASTER LOAN APPROVALS FOR APPLICANTS IN GULF COAST STATES

The following figures are provided to help frame discussions concerning SBA Loan Program activity in the Gulf Coast in response to the 2005 and 2008 hurricane seasons.

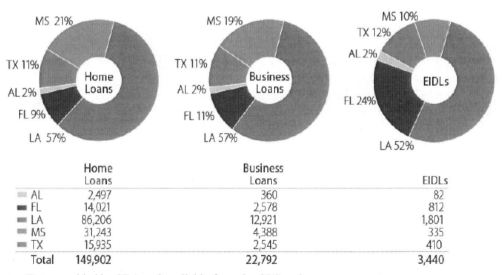

Source: Data provided by SBA and available from the CRS author upon request.
Notes: Numbers shown in this figure refer to approved disaster loans. Not all approved loans are accepted by disaster victims and businesses. Therefore, actual loan acceptance and accepted numbers of loans may be smaller than the numbers shown here.

Figure B-1. Number of Approved Applications for Home, Business, and EIDLs by Gulf Coast State; As of June 2012.

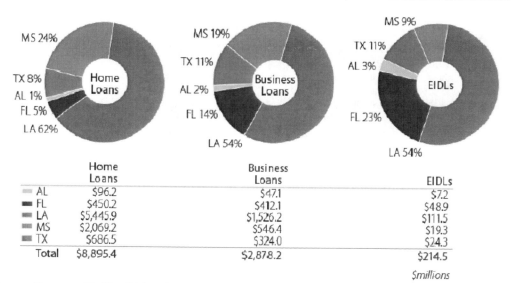

Source: Data provided by SBA and available from the CRS author upon request.
Notes: SBA amounts shown in this figure refer to approved disaster loans. Not all approved loans are accepted by disaster victims and businesses. Therefore, actual loan acceptance and amounts may be smaller than the amounts shown here.

Figure B-2. Disaster Assistance Loans by SBA; As of June 2012.

End Notes

[1] Declarations and certifications that can trigger SBA's Disaster Loan Program assistance are discussed later in this report under the heading "Types of Declarations." SBA also offers Military Reservist Economic Injury Disaster Loans. These loans are available when economic injury is incurred as a direct result of a business owner or an essential employee being called to active duty. Generally, these loans are not associated with disasters. The policies and regulations of the Disaster Loan Program are contained in Title 13, part 123, of the *Code of Federal Regulations* (C.F.R.) and may be accessed at http://ecfr.gpoaccess. gov/cgi/t/text/text-idx?sid=a6359c887c16327c658d80667dd78f04&c=ecfr&tpl= /ecfrbrowse/Title13/13tab_02.tpl.

[2] P.L. 85-536, Section 7(b) 72 Stat. 387, as amended.

[3] Testimony of Manuel Gonzalez, director, Houston District Office, Small Business Administration, in U.S. Congress, Senate Committee on Small Business and Entrepreneurship, *Disaster Recovery in Galveston*, hearing, 111th Cong., 1st sess., September 25, 2009.

[4] Small Business Administration, *Disaster Recovery: Introduction*, Washington, DC, p. 2, Notes, http://training.sba.gov:8000/response. See also Table 2 of this CRS report for annual data on Home Disaster Loans and Business Disaster Loans. Based on discussions with SBA, the ratio of home loans to business loans is most likely due to the composition of most communities which are generally comprised of more homes than businesses.

[5] The rationale for disbursing disaster loans through SBA rather than FEMA is explained in Appendix A of this report.

[6] These are Hurricanes Katrina (August 29, 2005), Rita (September 24, 2005), Wilma (October 24, 2005), Gustav (September 1, 2008), and Ike (September 13, 2008).

[7] Federal regulations on the SBA Disaster Loan Program can be located at 13 C.F.R. §123.

[8] 13 C.F.R. §123.105(a)(1).

[9] 13 C.F.R. §123.105(a)(2).

[10] 13 C.F.R. §123.107.

[11] P.L. 110-246, the Food, Conservation, and Energy Act of 2008 (subtitle: Small Business Disaster Response and Loan Improvements Act of 2008) Note: At the time of this report, the *Code of Federal Regulations* had not been updated to reflect this amount.

[12] Leasehold is a fixed asset and gives the right to hold or use property for a fixed period of time at a given price, without transfer of ownership, on the basis of a lease contract.

[13] 13 C.F.R. §123.203(a).

[14] See 13 C.F.R. §123.300 for eligibility requirements. Size standards vary according to a variety of factors, including industry type, average firm size, and start-up costs and entry barriers. Size standards can be located in 13 C.F.R. 121. For further analysis, see CRS Report R40860, *Small Business Size Standards: A Historical Analysis of Contemporary Issues*, by Robert Jay Dilger.

[15] 13 C.F.R. §123.302.

[16] 13 C.F.R. §123.2.

[17] Ibid. Areas affected by droughts and below-average water levels are only eligible for Economic Injury Disaster Loans, which are discussed later in this report.

[18] P.L. 93-288, 42 U.S.C. 5721 et seq.

[19] Disaster declarations are published in the *Federal Register* and can also be found on the SBA website at http://www.sba.gov/services/disasterassistance/basics/recentdisaster /SERV_ RECENT_WV_11750.html.

[20] Administered by FEMA, Individual Assistance (IA) includes various forms of help for families and individuals following a disaster event. The assistance authorized by the Stafford Act can include housing assistance, disaster unemployment assistance, crisis counseling, and other programs intended to address people's needs. Public Assistance (PA) provides various categories of assistance to state and local governments and nonprofit organizations. Principally, PA covers the repair or replacement of infrastructure (roads, bridges, public buildings, etc.), but it also includes debris removal and emergency protective measures, which cover additional costs incurred by local public safety groups through their actions in responding to the disaster. FEMA's PA program provides assistance only to public and nonprofit entities. For further analysis of Stafford Act declarations, see CRS Report RL34146, *FEMA's Disaster Declaration Process: A Primer*, by Francis X. McCarthy.

[21] 13 C.F.R. §123.3(2). See also 42 U.S.C. §5172(a)(3).

[22] Some SBA declarations are based on criteria such as the occurrence of at least a minimum amount of uninsured physical damage to buildings, machinery, inventory, homes, and other property. Generally, this minimum is at least 25 homes or businesses (or some combination of the two) that have sustained uninsured losses of 40% or more in any county or other smaller political subdivision of a state or U.S. possession. See 13 C.F.R. §123.3(3)(ii).

[23] 13 C.F.R. §123.3(3)(iii).

[24] 13 C.F.R. §123.3(4).

[25] 15 U.S.C. §632(k)(1).

[26] The total includes physical and real property loans.

[27] Figures have been rounded.

[28] Subtitle B of P.L. 110-246, §12051.

[29] U.S. Government Accountability Office, *Small Business Administration: Additional Steps Should Be Taken to Address Reforms to the Disaster Loan Program and Improve the Application Process for Future Disasters*, July 29, 2009, http://www.house.gov /smbiz/hearings/hearing-7-29-09-SBA-oversight/GAO-Report.pdf. According to SBA, the five provisions require no action by SBA at this time because they are discretionary, or require additional appropriations to satisfy the act's requirements.

[30] Ibid., p. 32.

[31] Testimony of Manuel Gonzalez, Director, Houston District Office, Small Business Administration, in U.S. Congress, Senate Committee on Small Business and Entrepreneurship, *Disaster Recovery in Galveston*, hearing, 111th Cong., 1st sess., September 25, 2009.

[32] Bridge loans are part of the SBA's America's Recovery Capital (ARC) Loan Program. They provide up to $35,000 in short-term relief for viable small businesses facing immediate financial hardship to help them endure uncertain economic times and return to profitability. Created under the American Recovery and Reinvestment Act of 2009 (P.L. 111-5), the temporary ARC program offers interest-free loans that carry a 100% guaranty from SBA to the lender and require no fees to be paid to SBA. Loan proceeds are provided over a six-month period, and repayment of the ARC loan principal is to be deferred for 12 months after the last disbursement of the proceeds. Repayment can extend up to five years. Each small business is limited to one ARC loan.

[33] U.S. Congress, House Committee on Small Business, *Disaster Assistance: Is SBA Meeting the Recovery Needs of Disaster Victims?*, 112th Cong., 1st sess., November 30, 2011, H. Hrg. 112-046 (Washington: GPO, 2011), p. 3.

[34] Ibid, p. 4.

[35] U.S. Congress, House Committee on Small Business, *Disaster Assistance: Is SBA Meeting the Recovery Needs of Disaster Victims?*, 112th Cong., 1st sess., November 30, 2011, GAO-12-253T, p. 1. http://smbiz.house.gov/UploadedFiles/Shear_Testimony.pdf

[36] Ibid, p. 7.

[37] Opening Statement of Senator Mary Landrieu, in U.S. Congress, Senate Committee on Small Business and Entrepreneurship, *A Year Later: Lessons Learned, Progress Made, and Challenges that Remain from Hurricane Ike,* hearing, 111th Cong., 1st sess., September 25, 2009.

[38] U.S. Congress, House Committee on Small Business, *Disaster Assistance: Is SBA Meeting the Recovery Needs of Disaster Victims?*, 112th Cong., 1st sess., November 30, 2011, H. Hrg. 112-046 (Washington: GPO, 2011), p. 4.

[39] Letter from Mary L. Landrieu, United States Senator, Claire McCaskill, United States Senator, and Roy Blunt, United States Senator, to Karen Mills, Administer, Small Business Administration, July 7, 2011, http://www.sbc.senate.gov/public/index.cfm?a =Files.Serve& File_id=3a2e8429-c31c-4767-a411-a04df1c61c78.

[40] Representative Mario Diaz-Balart, "Study of Effect of Drywall Presence on Foreclosures," remarks in the House, *Congressional Record*, daily edition, May 7, 2009, p. H5363.

[41] Bill Nelson, Mary Landrieu, Mark Warner, et al., "Letter to Craig Fugate, Administrator, Federal Emergency Management Agency," October 1, 2009, http://billnelson.senate.gov /news/details.cfm?id=318788&.

[42] In an email exchange on November 5, 2009, between the author and the SBA legislative liaison.

[43] H.R. 11539 was signed into law November 8, 1965. Hurricane Betsy made landfall on August 27, 1965.

[44] P.L. 89-339, 79 Stat. 1301.

[45] Debra S. Ritt, Assistant Inspector General for Auditing, *Annual Credit Reviews for Gulf Coast Hurricane Disaster Loan Disbursements*, U.S. Small Business Administration, Office of Inspector General, 08-10, Washington, DC, March 28, 2008, p. 8, http://www.sba.gov/idc /groups/public/documents/sba/oig_dl_8-10.pdf.

[46] Ibid., p. 3.

[47] Ibid., p. 6.

[48] The response did not cover the 2008 hurricane season.

[49] Ibid., p. 4.

[50] For example, see James F. Miskel, *Disaster Response and Homeland Security: What Works, What Doesn't* (Westport, CT: Westport Press, 2006), pp. 126-127.

[51] Office of Management and Budget, *A New Era of Responsibility: Renewing America's Promise*, Washington, DC, 2009, p. 121, http://www.gpoaccess.gov/usbudget/fy10/pdf /fy10-newera.pdf.

[52] Figures were based on the statistical probability of other large-scale disasters in the future. The OMB report did not discuss the methodology used to derive these figures. (The Senate explored alternative funding options for disaster assistance in the 1980s. See Task Force Report on the Environmental Protection Agency, the Small Business Administration, and the Federal Emergency Management Agency, *President's Private Sector Survey on Cost Control,* Washington, DC, April 15, 1983, pp. 39-45.)

[53] Nominal dollars.

[54] 2010 dollars. Some of the figures in this section have been rounded.

[55] U.S. Small Business Administration, *Agency Financial Report: FY2008*, November 17, 2008, pp. 16-17, http://www.sba.gov/idc/groups/public/documents/sba_homepage /serv_abtsba_ 2008_afr_001-030.pdf.

[56] Ibid., p. 16. The dollar volume of loan guaranties purchased by SBA divided by the dollar amount of the guarantied loan portfolio outstanding each month.

[57] U.S. Congress, House Subcommittee on Legislation and National Security, Committee on Government Operations, *Reorganization Plan No. 3 of 1978 (Federal Emergency Management Agency)*, hearing, 95th Cong., 2nd sess., June 26 and 29, 1978, p. 13.

[58] P.L. 93-288, 42 U.S.C. §5121 et seq. For further analysis of the Stafford Act, see CRS Report RL33053, *Federal Stafford Act Disaster Assistance: Presidential Declarations, Eligible Activities, and Funding*, by Francis X. McCarthy.

[59] P.L. 93-288, 15 U.S.C. §5155(a).

In: Small Business Administration Programs
Editor: Walter Janikowski

ISBN: 978-1-62417-992-1
© 2013 Nova Science Publishers, Inc.

Chapter 3

SMALL BUSINESS ADMINISTRATION 7(A) LOAN GUARANTY PROGRAM[*]

Robert Jay Dilger

SUMMARY

The Small Business Administration (SBA) administers several programs to support small businesses, including loan guaranty programs designed to encourage lenders to provide loans to small businesses "that might not otherwise obtain financing on reasonable terms and conditions." The SBA's 7(a) loan guaranty program is considered the agency's flagship loan guaranty program. It is named from Section 7(a) of the Small Business Act of 1953 (P.L. 83-163, as amended), which authorized the SBA to provide business loans and loan guaranties to American small businesses.

In FY2012, the SBA approved 44,377 7(a) loans amounting to more than $15.1 billion. Proceeds from 7(a) loans may be used to establish a new business or to assist in the operation, acquisition, or expansion of an existing business.

Congressional interest in the 7(a) loan guaranty program has increased in recent years because of concerns that small businesses might be prevented from accessing sufficient capital to enable them to assist in the economic recovery. Some, including President Obama, argue that the SBA should be provided additional resources to assist small businesses in acquiring capital necessary to start, continue, or expand operations with the expectation that in so doing small businesses will create jobs. Others worry about the long-term adverse economic effects of spending programs that increase the federal deficit. They advocate business tax reduction, reform of financial credit market regulation, and federal fiscal restraint as the best means to assist small business economic growth and job creation.

This report discusses the rationale provided for the 7(a) program; the program's borrower and lender eligibility standards and program requirements; and program statistics, including loan volume, loss rates, use of the proceeds, borrower satisfaction, and borrower demographics. It examines issues raised concerning the SBA's

---

[*] This is an edited, reformatted and augmented version of a Congressional Research Service publication, CRS Report for Congress R41146, prepared for Members and Committees of Congress, from www.crs.gov, dated October 11, 2012.

administration of the 7(a) program, including the oversight of 7(a) lenders and the program's lack of outcome-based performance measures.

It also examines congressional action taken during the 111th Congress to help small businesses gain greater access to capital. For example, P.L. 111-5, the American Recovery and Reinvestment Act of 2009 (ARRA), provided $375 million to temporarily subsidize the 7(a) and 504/CDC loan guaranty programs' fees and to temporarily increase the 7(a) program's maximum loan guaranty percentage to 90%. P.L. 111-240, the Small Business Jobs Act of 2010, provided $505 million to extend the fee subsidies and 90% loan guaranty percentage through December 31, 2010; increased the 7(a) program's gross loan limit from $2 million to $5 million; and established an alternative size standard for the 7(a) and 504/CDC loan programs. P.L. 111-322, the Continuing Appropriations and Surface Transportation Extensions Act, 2011, authorized the SBA to continue the fee subsidies and 90% loan guaranty percentage through March 4, 2011, or until available funding was exhausted (which occurred on January 3, 2011).

This report also examines three bills introduced during the 112th Congress that would affect the 7(a) program. S. 1828, a bill to increase small business lending, and for other purposes, would reinstate for a year following the date of its enactment ARRA's fee subsidies and 90% loan guaranty percentage for the 7(a) program. H.R. 2936, the Small Business Administration Express Loan Extension Act of 2011, would extend a one-year increase in the maximum loan amount for the SBAExpress program from $350,000 to $1 million for an additional year. That temporary increase expired on September 26, 2011. S. 532, the Patriot Express Authorization Act of 2011, would provide statutory authorization for the Patriot Express Pilot Program and increase its loan guaranty percentages and its maximum loan amount from $500,000 to $1 million.

Information concerning the 7(a) program's SBAExpress, Patriot Express, Small Loan Advantage, and Community Advantage programs is also provided.

SMALL BUSINESS ADMINISTRATION LOAN GUARANTY PROGRAMS

The Small Business Administration (SBA) administers programs to support small businesses, including loan guaranty programs to encourage lenders to provide loans to small businesses "that might not otherwise obtain financing on reasonable terms and conditions."[1] The SBA's 7(a) loan guaranty program is considered the agency's flagship loan program.[2] It is named from Section 7(a) of the Small Business Act of 1953 (P.L. 83-163, as amended), which authorizes the SBA to provide business loans to American small businesses.

The SBA also administers several 7(a) subprograms that offer streamlined and expedited loan procedures for particular groups of borrowers, including the SBAExpress, Patriot Express, Small Loan Advantage, and Community Advantage Pilot programs (see the Appendix for additional details). Although these subprograms have their own distinguishing eligibility requirements, terms, and benefits, they operate under the 7(a) program's authorization.[3]

Proceeds from 7(a) loans may be used to establish a new business or to assist in the operation, acquisition, or expansion of an existing business. Specific uses include to acquire land (by purchase or lease); improve a site (e.g., grading, streets, parking lots, and landscaping); purchase, convert, expand, or renovate one or more existing buildings; construct one or more new buildings; acquire (by purchase or lease) and install fixed assets;

purchase inventory, supplies, and raw materials; finance working capital; and refinance certain outstanding debts.[4]

In FY2012, the SBA approved 44,377 7(a) loans amounting to more than $15.1 billion.5 As will be discussed, the total number and amount of SBA 7(a) loans approved declined in FY2008 and FY2009, increased during FY2010 and FY2011, and then declined somewhat in FY2012.

The SBA attributed the decreased number and amount of 7(a) loans approved in FY2008 and FY2009 to a reduction in the demand for small business loans resulting from the economic uncertainty of the recession (December 2007 - June 2009) and to tightened loan standards imposed by lenders concerned about the possibility of higher loan default rates resulting from the economic slowdown. The SBA attributed the increased number and amount of 7(a) loans approved in FY2010 and FY2011 to legislation that provided funding to temporarily reduce the 7(a) program's loan fees and temporarily increase the 7(a) program's loan guaranty percentage to 90% for all standard 7(a) loans from up to 85% of loans of $150,000 or less and up to 75% of loans exceeding $150,000.[6] The fee subsidies and 90% loan guaranty percentage were in place during most of FY2010 and the first quarter of FY2011.[7]

Historically, one of the justifications presented for funding the SBA's loan guaranty programs has been that small businesses can be at a disadvantage, compared with other businesses, when trying to obtain access to sufficient capital and credit.[8] Congressional interest in the 7(a) loan program has increased in recent years because of concerns that small businesses might be prevented from accessing sufficient capital to enable them to assist in the economic recovery.

Some, including President Obama, argue that the SBA should be provided additional resources to assist small businesses in acquiring capital necessary to start, continue, or expand operations with the expectation that in so doing small businesses will create jobs.

Others worry about the longterm adverse economic effects of spending programs that increase the federal deficit. They advocate business tax reduction, reform of financial credit market regulation, and federal fiscal restraint as the best means to assist small business economic growth and job creation.

This report discusses the rationale provided for the 7(a) program; the program's borrower and lender eligibility standards and program requirements; and program statistics, including loan volume, loss rates, use of the proceeds, borrower satisfaction, and borrower demographics. It also examines issues raised concerning the SBA's administration of the 7(a) program, including the oversight of 7(a) lenders and the program's lack of outcome-based performance measures.

It then examines congressional action taken during the 111th Congress to help small businesses gain greater access to capital. For example, P.L. 111-5, the American Recovery and Reinvestment Act of 2009 (ARRA), provided $375 million to temporarily subsidize the 7(a) and 504/CDC loan guaranty programs' fees and to temporarily increase the 7(a) program's maximum loan guaranty percentage to 90%. P.L. 111-240, the Small Business Jobs Act of 2010, provided $505 million to extend the fee subsidies and 90% loan guaranty percentage through December 31, 2010; increased the 7(a) program's gross loan limit from $2 million to $5 million; and established an alternative size standard for the 7(a) and 504/CDC loan programs to enable more small businesses to qualify for assistance.

Also, P.L. 111-322, the Continuing Appropriations and Surface Transportation Extensions Act, 2011, authorized the SBA to continue the fee subsidies and the 7(a) program's 90% maximum loan guaranty percentage through March 4, 2011, or until available funding was exhausted (which occurred on January 3, 2011).

This report also examines three bills introduced during the 112th Congress that would affect the 7(a) program. S. 1828, a bill to increase small business lending, and for other purposes, would reinstate for a year following the date of its enactment the fee subsidies and 90% loan guaranty percentage for the 7(a) program, which were originally authorized by ARRA. H.R. 2936, the Small Business Administration Express Loan Extension Act of 2011, would extend a one-year increase in the maximum loan amount for the SBAExpress program from $350,000 to $1 million for an additional year. That temporary increase was authorized by P.L. 111-240 and expired on September 26, 2011. S. 532, the Patriot Express Authorization Act of 2011, would provide statutory authorization for the Patriot Express Pilot Program and increase its loan guaranty percentages and its maximum loan amount from $500,000 to $1 million.

Information concerning the SBAExpress, Patriot Express, Small Loan Advantage, and Community Advantage programs is also provided.

BORROWER ELIGIBILITY STANDARDS AND PROGRAM REQUIREMENTS

Borrower Eligibility Standards

To be eligible for an SBA business loan, a small business applicant must

- be located in the United States;
- be a for-profit operating business (except for loans to eligible passive companies);
- qualify as small under the SBA's size requirements;[9]
- demonstrate a need for the desired credit; and
- be certified by a lender that the desired credit is unavailable to the applicant on reasonable terms and conditions from non-Federal sources without SBA assistance.[10]

To qualify for an SBA 7(a) loan, applicants must be creditworthy and able to reasonably assure repayment. SBA requires lenders to consider the applicant's

- character, reputation, and credit history;
- experience and depth of management;
- strength of the business;
- past earnings, projected cash flow, and future prospects;
- ability to repay the loan with earnings from the business;
- sufficient invested equity to operate on a sound financial basis;
- potential for long-term success;

Small Business Administration 7(a) Loan Guaranty Program

- nature and value of collateral (although inadequate collateral will not be the sole reason for denial of a loan request); and
- affiliates' effect on the applicant's repayment ability.[11]

Borrower Program Requirements

Use of Proceeds

Borrowers may use 7(a) loan proceeds to establish a new business or to assist in the operation, acquisition, or expansion of an existing business. 7(a) loan proceeds may be used to

- acquire land (by purchase or lease);
- improve a site (e.g., grading, streets, parking lots, landscaping), including up to 5% for community improvements such as curbs and sidewalks;
- purchase one or more existing buildings;
- convert, expand, or renovate one or more existing buildings;
- construct one or more new buildings;
- acquire (by purchase or lease) and install fixed assets;
- purchase inventory, supplies, and raw materials;
- finance working capital; and
- refinance certain outstanding debts.[12]

Borrowers are prohibited from using 7(a) loan proceeds to

- refinance existing debt where the lender is in a position to sustain a loss and the SBA would take over that loss through refinancing;
- effect a partial change of business ownership or a change that will not benefit the business;
- permit the reimbursement of funds owed to any owner, including any equity injection or injection of capital for the business's continuance until the loan supported by the SBA is disbursed;
- repay delinquent state or federal withholding taxes or other funds that should be held in trust or escrow; or
- pay for a non-sound business purpose.[13]

Loan Amounts

As mentioned previously, P.L. 111-240 increased the 7(a) program's maximum gross loan amount for any one 7(a) loan from $2 million to $5 million (up to $3.75 million maximum guaranty). In FY2012, the average loan amount was about $340,000.[14]

Loan Terms, Interest Rate, and Collateral Loan Terms

7(a) loans are required to have the shortest appropriate term, depending upon the borrower's ability to repay. The maximum term is 10 years, unless the loan finances or refinances real estate or equipment with a useful life exceeding 10 years. In that case, the loan term can be up to 25 years, including extensions.[15]

Interest Rate

Lenders are allowed to charge borrowers "a reasonable fixed interest rate" or, with the SBA's approval, a variable interest rate.[16]

The SBA uses a multi-step formula to determine the maximum allowable fixed interest rate and periodically publishes that rate and the maximum allowable variable interest rate in the *Federal Register.*[17]

The maximum allowable fixed interest rates in October 2012 for 7(a) loans with maturities less than seven years are 6.7% for loans greater than $50,000, 7.7% for loans over $25,000 but not exceeding $50,000, and 8.7% for loans of $25,000 or less. The maximum allowable fixed interest rates in October 2012 for 7(a) loans with maturities of seven years or more are 7.2% for loans greater than $50,000, 8.2% for loans over $25,000 but not exceeding $50,000, and 9.2% for loans of $25,000 or less.[18]

The 7(a) program's maximum allowable variable interest rate may be pegged to the lowest prime rate (3.25% in October 2012), the 30 day LIBOR rate plus 300 basis points (3.21% in October 2012), or the SBA optional peg rate (2.125% in the first quarter of FY2013).[19]

The optional peg rate is a weighted average of rates the federal government pays for loans with maturities similar to the average SBA loan.[20]

Collateral

The SBA requires lenders to collateralize the loan to the maximum extent possible up to the loan amount. If business assets do not fully secure the loan, the lender must take available personal assets of the principals as collateral. Loans are considered "fully secured" if the lender has taken security interests in all available assets with a combined "liquidation value" up to the loan amount.[21]

LENDER ELIGIBILITY STANDARDS AND PROGRAM REQUIREMENTS

Lender Eligibility Standards

Lenders must have a continuing ability to evaluate, process, close, disburse, service, and liquidate small business loans; be open to the public for the making of such loans (and not be a financing subsidiary, engaged primarily in financing the operations of an affiliate); have continuing good character and reputation; and be supervised and examined by a state or federal regulatory authority, satisfactory to SBA.

They must also maintain satisfactory performance, as determined by SBA through on-site review/examination assessments, historical performance measures (such as default rate, purchase rate, and loss rate), and loan volume to the extent that it affects performance measures.[22] There are currently about 3,500 active lenders providing SBA loans.[23]

Lender Program Requirements

The Application Process

Borrowers submit applications for a 7(a) business loan to private lenders. The lender reviews the application and decides if it merits a loan on its own or if it has some weaknesses which, in the lender's opinion, do not meet standard, conventional underwriting guidelines and requires additional support in the form of an SBA guaranty. The SBA guaranty assures the lender that if the borrower does not repay the loan and the lender has adhered to all applicable regulations concerning the loan, the SBA will reimburse the lender for its loss, up to the percentage of the SBA's guaranty. The small business borrowing the money remains obligated for the full amount due.[24]

If the lender determines that it is willing to provide the loan, but only with an SBA guaranty, it submits the application for approval through the mail, website, or e-mail to the Standard 7(a) Loan Guaranty Processing Center operating out of two locations: Citrus Heights, CA, and Hazard, KY.[25] This center has responsibility for processing 7(a) loan guaranty applications for lenders who do not have delegated authority to make 7(a) loans without the SBA's final approval.[26] The application must include the following documentation and forms:

- SBA Form 4, Application for Loan, which includes specific requirements for providing financial assistance to a small business located in a floodplain or a wetland, the use of lead-based paint, seismic safety of federal and federally assisted or regulated new building construction, coastal barrier protections, laws prohibiting discrimination on the grounds of race, color, national origin, religion, sex, marital status, disability or age, and rights under the Financial Privacy Act of 1978 (P.L. 95-630);
- SBA Form 4, Schedule A—Schedule of Collateral, or the lender may use their own form to list collateral and label it "Exhibit A";
- SBA Form 912, Statement of Personal History—required of all principals, officers, directors and owners of 20% or more of the small business applicant;
- 7(a) Eligibility Questionnaire;
- Personal Financial Statement, dated within 90 days of submission to the SBA, on all owners of 20% or more (including the assets of the owner's spouse and any minor children), and proposed guarantors. SBA Form 413 is available. However, lenders may use their own form;
- Business Financial Statements dated within 90 days of submission to the SBA, consisting of (1) year end balance sheets for the last three years, (2) year-end profit and loss statements for the last three years, (3) reconciliation of net worth, (4) interim balance sheet, (5) interim profit and loss statements, (6) affiliate and subsidiary financial statement requirements, and (7) cash flow projection— month-by-month for one year if less than three fiscal years provided and for all loans with a term of 18 months or less;
- history of the business, résumés of principals, and copy of lease, if applicable;
- detailed listing of machinery and equipment to be purchased with loan proceeds and cost quotes;

- if real estate is to be purchased with loan proceeds an appraisal, lender's environmental questionnaire, cost breakdown, and copy of purchase agreement;
- if purchasing an existing business with loan proceeds a (1) copy of buy-sell agreement, (2) copy of business valuation, (3) pro forma balance sheet for the business being purchased as of the date of transfer, (4) copy of seller's financial statements for the last three complete fiscal years or for the number of years in business if less than three years; (5) interim statements no older than 90 days from date of submission to SBA, and (6) if seller's financial statements are not available the seller must provide an alternate source of verifying revenues;
- Equity Injection Form—explanation of type and source of applicant's equity injection;
- Franchise Form—if listed on www.franchiseregistry.com a certification of material change or certification of no change or non-material change is required. If not listed on the registry, a copy of the Franchise Agreement and Federal Trade Commission Disclosure Report of Franchisor must be submitted;
- SBA Form 159 (7a), Fee Disclosure and Compensation Agreement, must be completed for each agent compensated by the applicant or lender and retained in lender's loan file;
- a copy of Internal Revenue Service (IRS) Form 4506-T, Request for Copy of Tax Return—lender must identify the date IRS Form 4506-T was sent to IRS;
- for non-citizens, a copy of the U.S. Citizenship and Immigration Services (USCIS) Form G-845, Document Verification Request—prior to disbursement, lenders must verify the USCIS status of each alien who is required to submit USCIS documents to determine eligibility. The lender must document the findings in the loan file;
- SBA Form 4-I, Lender's Application for Guaranty—must be completed in its entirety, including pro forma balance sheet and submitted with (1) explanation of use of proceeds and benefits of the loan, (2) lender's internal credit
- memorandum, (3) justification for new business, including change of ownership. For new businesses and change of ownership where historical repayment ability is not demonstrated, lender must provide a narrative addressing the business plan and cite any areas of concern and justification to overcome them, and (4) business valuation must be supplied by lender for change of ownerships;
- SBA Form 1846, Statement Regarding Lobbying, must be signed and dated by lender; and
- SBA National 7(a) Authorization Boilerplate language on-line "wizard" must be completed.[27]

The SBA established the Certified Lenders Program (CLP) on February 26, 1979, initially on a six-month pilot basis.[28] It is designed to provide expeditious service on 7(a) loan applications received from lenders who have a successful SBA lending track record and a thorough understanding of SBA policies and procedures. In recent years, CLP lenders have approved about 4.8% of the number of 7(a) loans approved each year and 7.4% of the amount of 7(a) loans approved each year.[29] For loan applications of $350,000 or less, CLP lenders must submit all forms and exhibits listed above for a standard 7(a) loan application and a draft authorization. For loan applications greater than $350,000, in addition to all of the standard

7(a) forms and exhibits, CLP lenders must submit a copy of its written credit analysis and must discuss SBA eligibility issues.[30]

The SBA started the Preferred Lenders Program (PLP) on March 1, 1983, initially on a pilot basis.[31] It is designed to streamline the procedures necessary to provide financial assistance to small businesses by delegating the final credit decision and most servicing and liquidation authority and responsibility to carefully selected PLP lenders.[32] In recent years, PLP lenders have approved about 22.5% of the number of 7(a) loans approved each year and about 55% of the amount of 7(a) loans approved each year.[33] PLP lenders must complete and retain in the lender's file all forms and exhibits listed above for the Standard 7(a) application. They must submit the following forms to the SBA for review: (1) a copy of page 1 of SBA Form 4, Application for Business Loan, (2) a copy of page 1 of SBA Form 4-I, Lender's Application for Guaranty or Participation (signed by two authorized officials of the lender), (3) a copy of Form 1920SX (Part B) "Supplemental Information for PLP/SBA Express Processing," and (4) a copy of Form 7, "Eligibility Information for Preferred Lender Participation (PLP) Loans." If the PLP loan is to refinance debt (not same institution debt), a fully completed business indebtedness schedule must be attached. If the PLP loan is to finance change of ownership and a business valuation is performed by the lender, a synopsis of the analysis must be submitted.[34]

SBA Guaranty and Servicing Fees

To offset its costs, the SBA charges lenders an upfront, one-time guaranty fee and an annual, ongoing servicing fee for each loan approved and disbursed. The maximum guaranty fee for 7(a) loans with maturities exceeding 12 months is set by statute. Also, the servicing fee cannot exceed 0.55% per year of the outstanding balance of the SBA's share of the loan.

The 7(a) program's guaranty fee is based on loan maturity and the amount of the guaranty portion of the loan.

For loans with a maturity of 12 months or less, the SBA charges the lender a 0.25% guaranty fee, which the lender is required to submit with the application. The lender may charge the borrower for the fee when the loan is approved by the SBA.[35]

For loans with a maturity exceeding 12 months, the SBA charges the lender a 2% guaranty fee for the SBA guaranteed portion of loans of $150,000 or less, a 3% guaranty fee for the SBA guaranteed portion of loans exceeding $150,000 but not more than $700,000, and a 3.5% guaranty fee for the SBA guaranteed portion of loans exceeding $700,000. Loans with an SBA guaranteed portion in excess of $1 million are charged an additional 0.25% guaranty fee on the guaranteed amount in excess of $1 million.[36] These fees are the maximum allowed by law.[37]

The lender must pay the SBA guaranty fee within 90 days of the date of loan's approval and may charge the borrower for the fee after the lender has made the first disbursement of the loan. Lenders are permitted to retain 25% of the up-front guaranty fee on loans with a gross amount of $150,000 or less.[38]

The annual ongoing servicing fee for all 7(a) loans is required to be no more than the "rate necessary to reduce to zero the cost to the Administration" of making guaranties and, as mentioned previously, cannot exceed 0.55% of the outstanding balance of the guaranteed portion of the loan.[39] The current rate is the maximum allowed by law—0.55% of the outstanding balance of the guaranteed portion of the loan.[40] The lender's annual service fee to the SBA cannot be charged to the borrower.[41]

Lender Packaging, Servicing and Other Fees

The lender may charge an applicant "reasonable fees" customary for similar lenders in the geographic area where the loan is being made for packaging and other services. The lender must advise the applicant in writing that the applicant is not required to obtain or pay for unwanted services. These fees are subject to SBA review at any time, and the lender must refund any such fee considered unreasonable by the SBA.[42]

The lender may also charge an applicant an additional fee if, subject to prior written SBA approval, all or part of a loan will have extraordinary servicing needs. The additional fee can not exceed 2% per year on the outstanding balance of the part requiring special servicing (e.g., field inspections for construction projects). The lender may also collect from the applicant necessary out-of-pocket expenses, including filing or recording fees, photocopying, delivery charges, collateral appraisals, environmental impact reports that are obtained in compliance with SBA policy, and other direct charges related to loan closing.[43] The lender is prohibited from requiring the borrower to pay any fees for goods and services, including insurance, as a condition for obtaining an SBA guaranteed loan, and from imposing on SBA loan applicants processing fees, origination fees, application fees, points, brokerage fees, bonus points, and referral or similar fees.[44]

The lender is also allowed to charge the borrower a late payment fee not to exceed 5% of the regular loan payment when the borrower is more than 10 days delinquent on its regularly scheduled payment. The lender may not charge a fee for full or partial prepayment of a loan.[45]

For loans with a maturity of 15 years or longer, the borrower must pay to the SBA a subsidy recoupment fee when the borrower voluntarily prepays 25% or more of its loan in any one year during the first three years after first disbursement. The fee is 5% of the prepayment amount during the first year, 3% the second year, and 1% in the third year.[46]

PROGRAM STATISTICS

Loan Volume

The SBA generally uses the number and amount of loans approved each fiscal year, as opposed to the number and amount of loans disbursed, for making comparisons of lending volume among its loan guaranty programs. Although loan disbursement data can be useful, loan disbursements in one fiscal year typically include significant amounts approved in previous fiscal years. For example, in FY2012, 38% of 7(a) loan disbursements were from loans approved prior to FY2012.[47]

The number of 7(a) loans approved annually is typically about 10% to 20% higher than the number of loans disbursed (e.g., some borrowers decide not to accept the loan or there is a change in business ownership.).

The amount of 7(a) loans approved annually is typically about 10% to 15% higher than the amount disbursed.[48]

As shown in *Table 1*, the total number and amount of SBA 7(a) loans approved declined in FY2008 and FY2009, increased during FY2010 and FY2011, and then declined somewhat in FY2012.

Table 1. 7(a) Loan Guaranty Program, Loan Volume, FY2007-FY2012

FY	Number of Loans Approved	Amount Approved	Total Unpaid Principal Balance
2007	99,606	$14. 3 billion	$46.1 billion
2008	69,434	$12.7 billion	$47.7 billion
2009	41,289	$9.2 billion	$48.6 billion
2010	47,002	$12.4 billion	$50.8 billion
2011	53,706	$19.6 billion	$56.4 billion
2012	44,377	$15.2 billion	$59.4 billion

Sources: U.S. Small Business Administration, Agency Financial Report Fiscal Year 2010, Washington, DC, November 15, 2010, p. 7; U.S. Small Business Administration, Fiscal Year 2011 Congressional Budget Justification and FY 2009 Annual Performance Report, Washington, DC, pp. 36, 125; U.S. Small Business Administration, "SBA Lending Statistics for Major Programs (as of 9/30/2012)," at http://www.sba.gov/about-sba-info/317721; and U.S. Small Business Administration, "Table 1 — Unpaid Principal Balance By Program," Washington, DC, http://www.sba.gov/sites/default/files/files/WDS_UPB_Report_2011Q3.pdf.

Notes: The number of 7(a) loans approved annually is typically about 10% to 20% higher than the number of loans disbursed (e.g., some borrowers decide not to accept the loan, there is a change in business ownership, etc.). The amount of 7(a) loans approved annually is typically about 10% to 15% higher than the amount disbursed. U.S. Small Business Administration, Office of Congressional and Legislative Affairs, correspondence with the author, September 17, 2012.

As mentioned previously, the SBA attributed the decreased number and amount of 7(a) loans approved in FY2008 and FY2009 to a reduction in the demand for small business loans resulting from the economic uncertainty of the recession (December 2007 - June 2009) and to tightened loan standards imposed by lenders concerned about the possibility of higher loan default rates resulting from the economic slowdown. The SBA attributed the increased number of loans approved in FY2010 and FY2011 to legislation that provided funding to temporarily reduce the 7(a) program's loan fees and temporarily increase the 7(a) program's loan guaranty percentage to 90% for all standard 7(a) loans from up to 85% of loans of $150,000 or less and up to 75% of loans exceeding $150,000.[49] The fee subsidies and 90% loan guaranty percentage were in place during most of FY2010 and the first quarter of FY2011.[50]

Table 1 also provides, for comparison purposes, the total amount of the 7(a) program's unpaid principal balance. Precise measurements of the total credit market for small businesses is not available. However, the SBA has estimated that the credit market for small businesses (outstanding bank loans of $1 million or less, plus credit extended by finance companies) is roughly $1.0 trillion.[51] The SBA's 7(a) program's unpaid principal balance of $59.4 billion is about 5.9% of that amount.

Loss Rate and Appropriations for Subsidy Costs

Since its inception in 1953 through 2008, the 7(a) program (including subprograms) experienced a 5.83% loss rate (ratio of actual losses to disbursements).[52] In recent years, the loss rate for both 7(a) and 504/CDC programs has exceeded historical averages. As of June 30, 2012, the 7(a) program's loss rate since the program's inception in 1953 was 6.36%.[53]

One of the SBA's goals is to achieve a zero subsidy rate for its loan guaranty programs. A zero subsidy rate means that the SBA's loan guaranty programs do not require annual appropriations of budget authority for the issuance of new loan guarantees. From 2005 to 2009, the SBA did not request appropriations to subsidize the cost of any of its loan guaranty programs, including the 7(a) program. However, in recent years, SBA loan guaranty fees and loan liquidation recoveries, especially in the 7(a) loan guaranty program, have not generated enough revenue to cover loan losses, resulting in the need for additional appropriations to account for the shortfall.

In FY2010 and in FY2011, the SBA was provided $80.0 million to subsidize the cost of SBA guaranteed loans. In FY2012, the SBA was provided $207.1 million for that purpose, and P.L. 112-175, the Continuing Appropriations Resolution, 2013 (which provides appropriations through March 27, 2013), provided a projected $333.6 billion for the cost of SBA loan guaranty program subsidies for FY2013.

The SBA reports that most of the agency's loan losses have occurred in the SBA's 7(a) loan guaranty program. For example, the SBA applied all of the FY2010 and FY2011 subsidy amounts ($80.0 million each year) to the 7(a) program, anticipates applying 67.3% ($139.4 million) of the FY2012 subsidy amount ($207.1 million) to the 7(a) program, and 67.6% ($224.5 million) of the FY2013 subsidy ($333.6 million) to the 7(a) program.[54]

Administrative Expenses

In FY2011, the SBA's spent $88.0 million on the 7(a) program for administrative expenses, including $44.2 million for loan making, $4.0 million for loan servicing, $26.8 million for loan liquidation, and $13.0 million for lender oversight. The SBA anticipates that the administrative costs for the 7(a) loan will be $89.5 million in FY2012 and $93.8 million in FY2013.[55]

Use of Proceeds and Borrower Satisfaction

In 2008, the Urban Institute released the results of an SBA-commissioned study of the SBA's loan guaranty programs. As part of its analysis, the Urban Institute surveyed a random sample of SBA loan guaranty borrowers. The survey indicated that borrowers used 7(a) loan proceeds to

- purchase or install new equipment (34%);
- finance working capital (23%);
- acquire original business (21%);
- other (19%);
- expand or renovate current building (14%);
- purchase new building (10%);
- refinance existing debt (8%);
- hire additional staff (6%);
- build new building (4%);

- purchase new land (3%); and
- improve land (2%).[56]

The Urban Institute also reported that most of the 7(a) borrowers responding to their survey rated their overall satisfaction with their 7(a) loan and loan terms as either excellent (18%) or good (50%). One out of every five 7(a) borrowers (20%) rated their overall satisfaction with their 7(a) loan and loan terms as fair, and 6% rated their overall satisfaction with their 7(a) loan and loan terms as poor (7% reported don't know or did not respond).[57] In addition, 90% of the survey's respondents reported that the 7(a) loan was either very important (62%) or somewhat important (28%) to their business success (2% reported somewhat unimportant, 3% reported very unimportant, and 4% reported don't know or did not respond).[58]

Borrower Demographics

The Urban Institute found that about 9.9% of conventional small business loans are issued to minority-owned small businesses and about 16% of conventional small business loans are issued to women-owned businesses.[59] In FY2012, 22.5% of 7(a) loan recipients were minority-owned businesses (12.1% Asian, 7.1% Hispanic, 2.4% African-American, and 0.9% other minority) and 16.6% were women-owned businesses.[60] Based on its comparative analysis of conventional small business loans and the SBA's loan guaranty programs, the Urban Institute concluded:

> SBA's loan programs are designed to enable private lenders to make loans to creditworthy borrowers who would otherwise not be able to qualify for a loan. As a result, there should be differences in the types of borrowers and loan terms associated with SBA-guaranteed and conventional small business loans.
>
> Our comparative analysis shows such differences. Overall, loans under the 7(a) and 504 programs were more likely to be made to minority-owned, women-owned, and start-up businesses (firms that have historically faced capital gaps) as compared to conventional small business loans. Moreover, the average amounts for loans made under the 7(a) and 504 programs to these types of firms were substantially greater than conventional small business loans to such firms. These findings suggest that the 7(a) and 504 programs are being used by lenders in a manner that is consistent with SBA's objective of making credit available to firms that face a capital opportunity gap.[61]

CONGRESSIONAL ISSUES

Access to Capital

Congressional interest in the 7(a) loan program has increased in recent years largely because of concerns that small businesses might be prevented from accessing sufficient capital to enable them to assist in the economic recovery. During the 111th Congress, several laws were enacted to increase the supply and demand for capital for both large and small businesses.[62] For example, in 2008, Congress adopted P.L. 110-343, the Emergency

Economic Stabilization Act of 2008, which authorized the Troubled Asset Relief Program (TARP). Under TARP, the U.S. Department of the Treasury was authorized to purchase or insure up to $700 billion in troubled assets, including small business loans, from banks and other financial institutions. The law's intent was "to restore liquidity and stability to the financial system of the United States."[63] P.L. 111-203, the Dodd-Frank Wall Street Reform and Consumer Protection Act, reduced total TARP purchase authority from $700 billion to $475 billion. The Treasury Department's authority to make new financial commitments under TARP ended on October 3, 2010. The Department of the Treasury has disbursed approximately $389 billion in TARP funds, including $337 million to purchase SBA 7(a) loan guaranty program securities.[64]

In addition, as mentioned previously, in 2009, ARRA provided an additional $730 million for SBA programs, including $375 million to temporarily reduce fees in the SBA's 7(a) and 504/CDC loan guaranty programs and increase the 7(a) program's maximum loan guaranty percentage from up to 85% of loans of $150,000 or less and up to 75% of loans exceeding $150,000 to 90% for all standard 7(a) loans. Congress subsequently provided another $265 million, and authorized the SBA to reprogram another $40 million, to extend the fee reductions and loan modification through May 31, 2010, and the Small Business Jobs Act of 2010 provided another $510 million to extend the fee reductions and loan modification from September 27, 2010, through December 31, 2010. Also, P.L. 111-322, the Continuing Appropriations and Surface Transportation Extensions Act, 2011, authorized the use of any funding remaining from the Small Business Jobs Act of 2010 to extend the fee subsidies and 90% maximum loan guaranty percentage through March 4, 2011, or until the available funding was exhausted.[65] Funding for these purposes were exhausted on January 3, 2011.

The Obama Administration argued that TARP and the additional funding for the SBA's loan guaranty programs helped to improve the small business lending environment and supported "the retention and creation of hundreds of thousands of jobs."[66] Critics argued that small business tax reduction, reform of financial credit market regulation, and federal fiscal restraint are the best means to assist small business economic growth and job creation.[67]

Program Administration

The SBA's Office of Inspector General (OIG) and the U.S. Government Accountability Office (GAO) have independently reviewed the SBA's administration of the agency's loan guaranty programs. Both agencies have reported deficiencies in the SBA's administration of its loan guaranty programs that they argue need to be addressed, including issues involving the oversight of 7(a) lenders and the lack of outcome-based performance measures.

Oversight of 7(a) Lenders
The SBA's OIG has argued that the 7(a) loan guaranty program "is vulnerable to fraud and unnecessary losses because it relies on numerous third parties (e.g., borrowers, loan agents, and lenders)" to complete loan transactions for about 80% of the loans guaranteed annually by the SBA.[68] It has argued that the SBA needs to strengthen oversight of 7(a) lenders to "establish more robust controls to prevent waste, fraud, abuse, and inefficiencies."[69]

The SBA OIG has argued that the results of its review of the 7(a) program's FY2008 lending indicate the need for strengthened lender oversight. The SBA OIG found that the SBA's estimate of improper payments for FY2008 significantly understated the level of erroneous payments in the program. The SBA reported that improper payments were 0.53% of FY2008 program outlays, whereas the SBA's OIG estimated the improper payment rate to be 29% (approximately $248 million) of the $869 million in loan guaranties purchased between April 1, 2007, and March 31, 2008.[70] In addition, the SBA OIG's review of a sample of 30 7(a) loans issued in FY2008 found that 14 of the loans lacked evidence to support lender compliance with SBA origination, servicing, or liquidation requirements, resulting in improper payments totaling $723,293. In contrast, the SBA reported improper payments of $4,468 on two of the sampled loans.[71]

In 2009, GAO also recommended that the SBA strengthen its oversight of 7(a) program lenders. GAO argued that although the SBA's "lender risk rating system has enabled the agency to conduct some off-site monitoring of lenders, the agency does not use the system to target lenders for on-site reviews or to inform the scope of the reviews."[72] It also noted that

> the SBA targets for review those lenders with the largest SBA-guaranteed loan portfolios. As a result of this approach, 97 percent of the lenders that SBA's risk rating system identified as high risk in 2008 were not reviewed. Further, GAO found that the scope of the on-site reviews that SBA performs is not informed by the lenders' risk ratings, and the reviews do not include an assessment of lenders' credit decisions.[73]

GAO argued that although the SBA "has made improvements to its off-site monitoring of lenders, the agency will not be able to substantially improve its lender oversight efforts unless it improves its on-site review process."[74]

In a separate report concerning the SBA's administration of the 7(a) program, GAO also argued in 2009 that the SBA needs to "improve its oversight of lenders' compliance with the credit elsewhere requirement."[75] The Small Business Act specifies that "no financial assistance shall be extended pursuant to this subsection if the applicant can obtain credit elsewhere."[76] The SBA provides lenders the following six reasons for certifying in its application that the borrower meets the credit elsewhere requirement:

- the business needs a longer maturity than the lender's policy permits (for example, the business needs a loan that is not on a demand basis);
- the requested loan exceeds either the lender's legal lending limit or policy limit regarding the amount that it can lend to one customer;
- the lender's liquidity depends upon selling the guaranteed portion of the loan on the secondary market;
- the collateral does not meet the lender's policy requirements;
- the lender's policy normally does not allow loans to new businesses or businesses in the applicant's industry; or
- any other factors relating to the credit that, in the lender's opinion, cannot be overcome except for the guaranty. These other factors must be specifically documented in the loan file.[77]

GAO argued that "SBA's guidance to lenders on documenting compliance with the credit elsewhere requirement is limited" because it "does not specify the amount of detail lenders should include in their explanations."[78] GAO noted that "even with the lack of detail required," the SBA's own on-site reviews of 7(a) lenders over a recent six-quarter period indicated that nearly a third of the lenders reviewed had not consistently documented that borrowers met the credit elsewhere requirement.[79]

The SBA has argued that it currently "conducts a continuous risk-based, off-site analysis of lending partners through the Loan/Lender Monitoring System (L/LMS), a state-of-the-art portfolio monitoring system that incorporates credit scoring metrics for portfolio management purposes."[80] According to the SBA:

> The Loan/Lender Monitoring System focuses on 7(a) lenders, certified development companies and microloan intermediaries that pose the most risk to the SBA. In addition to overseeing lenders, the L/LMS provides policy, portfolio and program analysis. The Office of Credit Risk Management (OCRM) is divided into four teams: large lender oversight, small lender oversight, lender transaction, and program and policy analysis. The differentiation of lender oversight by lender size reflects the different forms of oversight needed for large lenders versus small lenders.[81]

The SBA asserts that

> The OCRM is continually enhancing and updating oversight programs and practices to provide a more robust and responsive system. Enhancements include: (1) better integration of delegated lending decisions into oversight practices; (2) addition of different types of lender reviews (targeted, desk, agreed upon procedures, etc.) to provide more options to obtain information in the most timely and efficient manner possible; (3) assessment of current on-site review practices to customize them based on risk factors and consider credit decisions made by lenders; (4) development of a lender certification program (particularly for community lenders); (5) quarterly reporting for non-bank lenders; (6) identification/ monitoring of risk related red flags and triggers; and (7) training for OCA staff, district office staff and lenders in the new process.[82]

In addition, in its FY2012 congressional budget request, the SBA reported that it had "created a more robust risk rating system, with more transparency in portfolios, and "best practices" for lender oversight (including more on-site and off-site lender monitoring)."[83]

Outcome-Oriented Performance Measures

GAO has argued that the 7(a) program's performance measures (e.g., number of loans approved, loans funded, and firms assisted across the subgroups of small businesses) provide limited information about the impact of the loans on participating small businesses:

> The program's performance measures focus on indicators that are primarily output measures–for instance, they report on the number of loans approved and funded. But none of the measures looks at how well firms do after receiving 7(a) loans, so no information is available on outcomes. As a result, the current measures do not indicate how well the agency is meeting its strategic goal of helping small businesses succeed.[84]

The SBA OIG has made a similar argument concerning the SBA's Microloan program's performance measures. Because the SBA uses similar program performance measures for its Microloan and 7(a) programs, the SBA OIG's recommendations could also be applied to the SBA's 7(a) program.

Specifically, as part of its audit of the SBA Microloan program's use of ARRA funds, the SBA OIG found that the SBA's performance measures for the Microloan program are based on the number of microloans funded, the number of small businesses assisted, and program's loan loss rate.

It argued that these "performance metrics ... do not ensure the ultimate program beneficiaries, the microloan borrowers, are truly assisted by the program" and "without appropriate metrics, SBA cannot ensure the Microloan program is meeting policy goals."[85] It noted that the SBA does not track the number of microloan borrowers who remain in business after receiving a microloan to measure the extent to which the loans contributed to the success of borrowers and does not determine the effect that technical training assistance may have on the success of microloan borrowers and their ability to repay loans.[86] It recommended that the SBA "develop additional performance metrics to measure the program's achievement in assisting microloan borrowers in establishing and maintaining successful small businesses."[87]

In its response to GAO's recommendation to develop additional performance measures for the 7(a) program, the SBA indicated that there are legal constraints and cost considerations associated with tracking the success or failure of SBA borrowers and that it had, at that time, "a new administrator who may make changes to the agency's performance measures and goals."[88]

In response to the SBA OIG's recommendation to develop additional performance metrics for the Microloan program, the SBA reported that it has "contracted with the Aspen Institute to advise on appropriate program and performance metrics for both microloans and technical assistance grants."[89]

It also indicated that the program metrics developed will be used to assist the agency in measuring the Microloan program's effectiveness. Given that the Microloan program and 7(a) program use similar performance measures, it could be argued that the program metrics developed for the Microloan program may be applied to the 7(a) program as well.

LEGISLATIVE ACTIVITY DURING THE 111TH CONGRESS

Congress authorized several changes to the 7(a) program during the 111th Congress in an effort to increase the number, and amount, of 7(a) loans, including provisions contained in ARRA and the Small Business Jobs Act of 2010. Congress has not approved any changes to the 7(a) program during the 112th Congress.

The Obama Administration's Proposals

During the 111th Congress, the Obama Administration supported congressional efforts to temporarily subsidize fees for the 7(a) and 504/CDC loan guaranty programs and to increase the 7(a) program's loan guaranty percentage from up to 85% of loans of $150,000 or less and up to 75% of loans exceeding $150,000 to 90%. As mentioned previously, Congress subsequently provided more than $1.1 billion to subsidize fees for the 7(a) and 504/CDC loan guaranty programs and to increase the 7(a) program's maximum loan guaranty percentage to 90% for all standard 7(a) loans.

The Obama Administration also proposed the following modifications to several SBA programs, including the 7(a) program:

- increase the maximum loan size for 7(a) loans from $2 million to $5 million;
- increase the maximum loan size for the 504/CDC program from $2 million to $5 million for regular projects and from $4 million to $5.5 million for manufacturing projects;
- increase the maximum loan size for microloans to small business concerns from $35,000 to $50,000;
- increase the maximum loan limits for lenders in their first year of participation in the Microloan program, from $750,000 to $1 million, and from $3.5 million to $5 million in the subsequent years;
- temporarily increase the cap on SBAExpress loans from $350,000 to $1 million; and
- temporarily allow in FY2010 and FY2011, with an option to extend into FY2012, the refinancing of owner-occupied commercial real estate loans within one year of maturity under the SBA's 504/CDC program.[90]

Arguments for Increasing the SBA's Maximum Loan Limits

The Obama Administration argued that increasing the maximum loan limits for the 7(a), 504/CDC, Microloan, and SBAExpress programs would allow the SBA to "support larger projects," which will "allow the SBA to help America's small businesses drive long-term economic growth and the creation of jobs in communities across the country."[91] The Administration also argued that increasing the maximum loan limits for these programs will be "budget neutral" over the long run and "help improve the availability of smaller loans."[92]

Arguments Against Increasing the SBA's Maximum Loan Limits

Critics of the Obama Administration's proposals to increase the SBA's maximum loan limits argued that it might increase the risk of defaults, resulting in higher guaranty fees or the need to provide the SBA additional funding, especially for the SBAExpress program, which has experienced somewhat higher default rates than other SBA loan guaranty programs.[93] Others advocated a more modest increase in the maximum loan limits to ensure that the 7(a) program "remains focused on startup and early-stage small firms, businesses that have historically encountered the greatest difficulties in accessing credit" and "avoids making small borrowers carry a disproportionate share of the risk associated with larger loans."[94]

Others argued that creating a small business direct lending program within the SBA would reduce paperwork requirements and be more efficient in providing small businesses access to capital than modifying existing SBA programs that rely on private lenders to determine if they will issue the loans.[95]

Also, as mentioned previously, others argued that providing additional resources to the SBA or modifying the SBA's loan programs as a means to augment small business access to capital is ill-advised.

In their view, the SBA has limited impact on small access to capital.

They argued that the best means to assist small business economic growth and job creation is to focus on small business tax reduction, reform of financial credit market regulation, and federal fiscal restraint.[96]

H.R. 3854, the Small Business Financing and Investment Act of 2009

H.R. 3854 would have authorized several new SBA programs and change several existing SBA programs, including the 7(a) program, in an effort to enhance job creation by increasing the availability of credit to small businesses.

The bill was passed by the House, 389-32, on October 29, 2009. The Senate did not act on the bill.[97]

It would have

- increased the maximum loan size for 7(a) loans from $2 million to $3 million;
- increased the maximum loan size for 504/CDC loans from $1.5 million to $3 million for regular projects, from $2 million to $4 million for projects located in a low-income community, from $4 million to $8 million for manufacturers, and for up to $10 million for projects that constitute "a major source of employment" as determined by the Administration;
- extended ARRA's fee reductions and the 7(a) program's 90% loan guaranty limit through September 30, 2011;
- authorized the SBA to establish an alternative size standard for the 7(a) program that uses maximum tangible net worth and average net income as an alternative to the use of industry standards and established an interim size standard of a maximum tangible net worth of not more than $15 million and an average net income after federal taxes (excluding any carryover losses) for the preceding two fiscal years of not more than $5 million;
- extended, with modifications, ARRA's America's Recovery Capital Loan Program (ARC) which temporarily provides small businesses loan assistance for debt relief, through the end of FY2011;[98] and
- provided a 100% loan guaranty for small business concerns owned and controlled by veterans, and expanded and made permanent the SBA's secondary market lending authority.[99]

The bill would have also created a temporary SBA direct lending program following enactment that would be available to creditworthy small business borrowers that are unable to find credit elsewhere.[100]

S. 2869, the Small Business Job Creation and Access to Capital Act of 2009

S. 2869 was ordered to be reported by the Senate Committee on Small Business and Entrepreneurship on December 10, 2009. The Senate did not take further action on the bill, but many of its provisions were later included in P.L. 111-240.

It would have authorized changes to several SBA programs, including the 7(a) program, and was designed to enhance job creation by increasing the availability of credit to small businesses.

It would have

- increased the maximum loan size for 7(a) loans from $2 million to $5 million;
- increased the maximum loan size for the 504/CDC loans from $1.5 million to $5 million for regular projects, from $2 million to $5 million for projects meeting one of the program's specified public policy goals, and from $4 million to $5.5 million for manufacturers;
- increased the maximum loan size for the Microloan program from $35,000 to $50,000;
- extended ARRA's fee reductions and the 7(a) program's 90% loan guaranty limit through December 31, 2010;
- authorized the SBA to establish an alternative size standard for the 7(a) and 504/CDC programs that uses maximum tangible net worth and average net income as an alternative to the use of industry standards and established an interim size standard of a maximum tangible net worth of not more than $15 million and an average net income after federal taxes (excluding any carryover losses) for the preceding two fiscal years of not more than $5 million; and
- allowed 504/CDC loans to be used to refinance up to $4 billion in short-term commercial real estate debt each fiscal year for two years after enactment into long-term fixed rate loans.[101]

P.L. 111-240, the Small Business Jobs Act of 2010

P.L. 111-240 was signed into law by President Obama on September 27, 2010. It increased the 7(a) program's loan guaranty limit from $2 million to $5 million, provided $510 million to extend the 7(a) program's 90% maximum loan guaranty percentage and 7(a) and 504/CDC loan guaranty programs' fee subsidies through December 31, 2010 (later extended to March 4, 2011), or until available funding was exhausted (which occurred on January 3, 2011).

The act also includes all of the provisions listed above in S. 2869, the Small Business Job Creation and Access to Capital Act of 2009, except that it would allow 504/CDC loans to be used to refinance up to $7.5 billion in short-term commercial real estate debt each fiscal year for two years after enactment into longterm fixed rate loans instead of up to $4 billion each fiscal year.[102]

The act also authorizes the Secretary of the Treasury to establish a $30 billion Small Business Lending Fund (SBLF) to encourage community banks to provide small business loans ($4 billion was issued), a $1.5 billion State Small Business Credit Initiative to provide funding to participating states with small business capital access programs, and about $12 billion in tax relief for small businesses.[103]

It also contains revenue raising provisions to offset the act's cost and authorizes a number of changes to other SBA loan and contracting programs.

LEGISLATIVE ACTIVITY DURING THE 112TH CONGRESS

As mentioned previously, Congress has not approved any changes to the 7(a) program during the 112th Congress. However, several bills have been introduced during the 112th Congress that would affect the 7(a) program.

S. 1828, a bill to increase small business lending, and for other purposes, was introduced on November 8, 2011 and referred to the Senate Committee on Small Business and Entrepreneurship. The bill would reinstate for a year following the date of its enactment the temporary fee subsidies for the 7(a) and 504/CDC loan guaranty programs and the 90% loan guaranty for standard 7(a) loans, which were originally authorized by ARRA and later extended by several laws, including the Small Business Jobs Act of 2010.

H.R. 2936, the Small Business Administration Express Loan Extension Act of 2011, introduced on September 15, 2011, and referred to the House Committee on Small Business, would extend a one-year increase in the maximum loan amount for the SBAExpress program from $350,000 to $1 million for an additional year. The temporary increase in that program's maximum loan amount was authorized by P.L. 111-240, the Small Business Jobs Act of 2010, and expired on September 26, 2011 (see *Appendix*).

S. 532, the Patriot Express Authorization Act of 2011, introduced on March 9, 2011, and referred to the Senate Committee on Small Business and Entrepreneurship, would provide statutory authorization for the Patriot Express Pilot Program (see *Appendix*). The bill would also increase the program's maximum loan amount from $500,000 to $1 million, and it would increase the guaranty percentage from up to 85% of loans of $150,000 or less and up to 75% of loans exceeding $150,000 to up to 85% of loans of $500,000 or less and up to 80% of loans exceeding $500,000.

CONCLUSION

The congressional debate concerning the SBA's 7(a) program during the 111th Congress was not whether the federal government should act, but which federal policies would most likely enhance small business access to capital and result in job retention and creation. As a general proposition, some, including President Obama, argued that the SBA should be provided additional resources to assist small businesses in acquiring capital necessary to start, continue, or expand operations with the expectation that in so doing small businesses will create jobs.[104] Others worried about the long-term adverse economic effects of spending programs that increase the federal deficit. They advocated business tax reduction, reform of financial credit market regulation, and federal fiscal restraint as the best means to assist small business economic growth and job creation.[105]

In terms of specific program changes, increasing the 7(a) program's loan limit, extending the 7(a) program's temporary fee subsidies and 90% maximum loan guaranty percentage, and establishing an alternative size standard for the 7(a) program were all designed to achieve the same goal: to enhance job creation by increasing the ability of 7(a) borrowers to access credit at affordable rates. However, determining how specific changes in federal policy are most likely to enhance job creation is a challenging question. For example, a 2008 Urban Institute study concluded that differences in the term, interest rate, and amount of SBA financing "was not significantly associated with increasing sales or employment among firms receiving SBA financing."[106] However, they also reported that their analysis accounted for less than 10% of the variation in firm performance. The Urban Institute suggested that local economic conditions, local zoning regulations, state and local tax rates, state and local business assistance programs, and the business owner's charisma or business acumen also "may play a role in determining how well a business performs after receipt of SBA financing."[107]

As the Urban Institute study suggests, given the many factors that influence business success, measuring the SBA's 7(a) program's effect on job retention and creation is complicated. That task is made even more challenging by the absence of performance-oriented measures that could serve as a guide. Both GAO and the SBA's OIG have recommended that the SBA adopt outcome performance oriented measures for its loan guaranty programs, such as tracking the number of borrowers who remain in business after receiving a loan to measure the extent to which the program contributed to their ability to stay in business.[108] Other performance-oriented measures that Congress might also consider include requiring the SBA to survey 7(a) borrowers to measure the difficulty they experienced in obtaining a loan from the private sector and the extent to which the 7(a) loan or technical assistance received contributed to their ability to create jobs or expand their scope of operations.

APPENDIX. 7(A) SPECIALIZED PROGRAMS

The 7(a) program has four specialized programs that offer streamlined and expedited loan procedures for particular groups of borrowers, the SBAExpress, Patriot Express, Small Loan Advantage, and Community Advantage programs. Lenders must be approved by the SBA for participation in these programs.

SBAExpress Program

The SBAExpress program was established as a pilot program by the SBA on February 27, 1995, and made permanent through legislation, subject to reauthorization, in 2004 (P.L. 108-447, the Consolidated Appropriations Act, 2005). The program was designed to increase the availability of credit to small businesses by permitting lenders to use their existing documentation and procedures in return for receiving a reduced SBA guaranty on loans.[109] It provides a 50% loan guaranty on loan amounts up to $350,000.

In FY2012, the SBA approved 23,146 SBAExpress loans (52.2% of total 7(a) program loan approvals) amounting to $1.78 billion (11.8% of total 7(a) program amount approvals).[110]

The SBA approved 26,838 SBAExpress loans amounting to $2.87 billion in FY2011 and 20,452 SBAExpress loans amounting to $1.55 billion in FY2010.[111] The program's higher loan volume in FY2011 was due, at least in part, to a provision in P.L. 111-240, the Small Business Jobs Act of 2010, which temporarily increased the SBAExpress program's loan limit to $1 million for one year following enactment (through September 26, 2011).

H.R. 2936, the Small Business Administration Express Loan Extension Act of 2011, was introduced on September 9, 2011, and referred to House Committee on Small Business. As mentioned previously, the bill would have extended the higher loan limit for an additional year (through September 26, 2012).

SBAExpress loan proceeds can be used for the same purposes as the 7(a) program (expansion, renovation, new construction, the purchase of land or buildings, the purchase of equipment, fixtures, and lease-hold improvements, working capital, to refinance debt for compelling reasons, seasonal line of credit, and inventory) except participant debt restructure cannot exceed 50% of the project and may be used for revolving credit. The program's loan terms are the same as the 7(a) program (the loan maturity for working capital, machinery, and equipment (not to exceed the life of the equipment) is typically 5 to 10 years and the loan maturity for real estate is up to 25 years), except that the term for a revolving line of credit cannot exceed 7 years.

The SBAExpress loan's interest rates are negotiable with the lender, subject to maximums. Rates can be fixed or variable. Fixed rates may not exceed prime plus 6.5% on loans of $50,000 or less and prime plus 4.5% on loans over $50,000. Variable interest rates are based on either the prime rate (as published in The Wall Street Journal), the 30-day LIBOR plus 3.0%, or the SBA's optional peg rate (published quarterly in the Federal Register) plus 6.5% on loans of $50,000 or less and plus 4.5% on loans over $50,000.[112] The program's fees are the same as the 7(a) program. To account for the program's lower guaranty rate of 50%, lenders are allowed to perform their own loan analysis and procedures and receive SBA approval with a targeted 36- hour maximum turnaround time.[113] Also, collateral is not required for loans of $25,000 or less. Lenders are allowed to use their own established collateral policy for loans over $25,000.

Patriot Express Pilot Program

In 2007, the SBA created the Patriot Express Pilot Program "to support the entrepreneur segment of the Nation's military community (including spouses)."[114] Eligible businesses must be owned and controlled (51% or more) by one or more of the following groups: veteran, active duty military participating in the military's Transition Assistance Program, reservist or national guard member or a spouse of any of these groups, a widowed spouse of a service member who died while in service, or a widowed spouse of a veteran who died of a service-connected disability.[115] The SBA announced on December 10, 2010, that it will continue to operate the program for at least three more years.[116]

S. 532, the Patriot Express Authorization Act of 2011, was introduced on March 9, 2011, and referred to the Senate Committee on Small Business and Entrepreneurship. The bill would provide the Patriot Express program statutory authorization. Also, S.Amdt. 229, to establish the Patriot Express Loan Program, was introduced as an amendment to S. 493, the SBIR/STTR Reauthorization Act of 2011, on March 16, 2011. The Senate did not vote on the amendment as cloture on the base bill (S. 493) was not invoked.

The Patriot Express Pilot Program provides the same loan guaranty as the 7(a) program on loan amounts up to $500,000 (up to 85% of loans of $150,000 or less and up to 75% of loans exceeding $150,000). The loan proceeds can be used for the same purposes as the 7(a) program (expansion, renovation, new construction, the purchase of land or buildings, the purchase of equipment, fixtures, and lease-hold improvements, working capital, to refinance debt for compelling reasons, seasonal line of credit, and inventory) except participant debt restructure cannot exceed 15-25% of the project and may be used for revolving lines of credit. The loan terms are the same as the 7(a) program (the loan maturity for working capital, machinery, and equipment (not to exceed the life of the equipment) is typically 5 to 10 years and the loan maturity for real estate is up to 25 years), except that the term for a revolving line of credit cannot exceed 7 years. Also, collateral is not required for loans of $25,000 or less. Lenders are allowed to use their own established collateral policy for loans over $25,000 and up to $350,000. For loans exceeding $350,000, lenders must follow the SBA's regulations on collateral for standard 7(a) loans.[117]

The Patriot Express Pilot Program features streamlined documentation and processing features similar to the SBAExpress program, with a targeted SBA processing time of one business day. The program's interest rates are negotiable with the lender, subject to the same maximum rate limitations as the 7(a) program. It also has the same fees as the 7(a) program.[118]

The SBA has indicated in both testimony at congressional hearings and in press releases that it views the Patriot Express Program as a success. For example, in 2007, William Elmore, Associate Director of the SBA's Office of Veterans Business Development, testified at a congressional hearing shortly after the Patriot Express program's rollout that

> so far, the results have been good. The number of loans made to veterans increased from 4,800 in fiscal year 2000 to approximately 8,000 loans in fiscal year 2006.[119]

In 2010, Joseph Jordan, SBA's Associate Administrator for Contracting and Business Development, testified at a congressional hearing that

> SBA is committed to assisting veteran-owned small businesses access the capital they need. All of SBA's loan programs are available to veterans. In FY2009, veteran-owned small businesses received 8.00% of all 7(a) loans, totaling approximately $523 million, and 4.56% of all 504 development company loans, or $176 million. Additionally, veteran-owned small businesses received 4.33% of all microloans, totaling approximately $1.9 million. In total, SBA has supported more than $2 billion in recovery lending to veteran-owned small businesses. SBA also has a loan program dedicated to the military community—Patriot Express.... It features our lowest interest rates and fastest turnaround times, often within days.... In FY2009, we approved more than 2,300 Patriot Express loans and are on track to increase those numbers in FY2010.[120]

More recently, when the SBA announced in a December 10, 2010, press release that it was extending the Patriot Express Loan Program for another three years, the SBA characterized the program as "a very popular initiative that in just three-and-a-half years has provided more than $560 million in loan guarantees to nearly 7,000 veterans to start or expand their small businesses."[121]

Congressional testimony provided by various veteran service organizations provides a different perspective. For example, a representative of the American Legion testified at a congressional hearing in 2010 that being turned down for a SBA Patriot Express loan "is probably the largest, most frequent complaint that we receive from our business owners."[122]

At that same congressional hearing, a representative of the Vietnam Veterans of America testified in response to that statement that

> I would have to concur ... in talking with some of the veterans with regard to the Patriot Express Loan, they are having difficulties also to acquire that capital. The rationale seems to be ... the banks in general seem to be tightening the credit, their lending practices, so that is ... what we are hearing.[123]

There are no empirical assessments of veterans' experiences with the SBA Patriot Express Loan program that would be useful for determining the relative ease or difficulty of veteran-owned small business owners accessing capital through the program.[124] The SBA does not conduct annual surveys of veteran-owned small businesses applying for SBA Patriot Express Loans similar to the annual survey the SBA currently sponsors for small businesses receiving services from the SBA's management and training programs.[125]

Small Loan Advantage and Community Advantage Programs

The Small Loan Advantage and Community Advantage programs became operational on February 15, 2011.[126] They are designed to increase lending to underserved low- and moderate-income communities. Both programs offer a streamlined application process for loans up to $250,000. The two programs replaced the Community Express Pilot Program, which was also designed to increase lending to underserved communities. It was created by the SBA in May 1999, and ended on April 30, 2011.[127]

The Small Loan Advantage program "is structured to encourage larger, existing SBA lenders to make lower-dollar loans, which often benefit businesses in underserved markets."[128] It provides the same loan guaranty as the 7(a) program on loan amounts up to $250,000 (85% for loans up to $150,000 and 75% for those greater than $150,000). The loan proceeds can be used for the same purposes as the 7(a) program (expansion, renovation, new construction, the purchase of land or buildings, the purchase of equipment, fixtures, and lease-hold improvements, working capital, to refinance debt for compelling reasons, seasonal line of credit, and inventory). The loan terms and guaranty fees are also the same as the 7(a) program.[129] The program's interest rates are negotiable with the lender, subject to the same maximum rate limitations as the 7(a) program.[130]

The program is available to lenders participating in the SBA's Preferred Lender Program (about 545 lenders, including most of the SBA's highest volume lenders). These lenders are authorized to use expedited loan processing procedures, which include a two-page application for borrowers and allow lenders to use their own note and guaranty agreements. Most Small Loan Advantage loans are expected "to be approved in a matter of minutes through electronic submission" or "within 5 to 10 days" otherwise.[131]

The Community Advantage pilot program is designed to increase lending in underserved communities by increasing "the number of SBA 7(a) lenders who reach underserved communities, targeting community-based, mission-focused financial institutions which were previously not able to offer SBA loan."[132] These mission-focused financial institutions include "Community Development Financial Institutions, SBA's Certified Development Companies and SBA's nonprofit microlending intermediaries."[133] They are expected "to maintain at least 60% of their SBA loan portfolio in underserved markets, including loans to small businesses in, or that have more than 50% of their workforce residing in, low-to-moderate income (LMI) communities; in Empowerment Zones and Enterprise Communities; in HUBZones; start-ups (firms in business less than 2 years); and veteran-owned businesses and those that would be eligible for Patriot Express."[134]

The Community Advantage program is a three-year pilot program that provides the same loan guaranty as the 7(a) program on loan amounts up to $250,000 (85% for loans up to $150,000 and 75% for those greater than $150,000). The loan proceeds can be used for the same purposes as the 7(a) program (expansion, renovation, new construction, the purchase of land or buildings, the purchase of equipment, fixtures, and lease-hold improvements, working capital, to refinance debt for compelling reasons, seasonal line of credit, and inventory). The loan terms and guaranty fees are also the same as the 7(a) program.[135] The loan's maximum interest rate is prime, plus 6%.[136] The program has an expedited approval process which includes a two-page application for borrowers and a goal of completing the loan approval process within 5 to 10 days.[137]

The SBA has indicated that the Community Advantage program's goal is to "leverage the experience these institutions already have in lending to minority, women-owned and start-up companies in economically challenged markets, along with their management and technical assistance expertise, to help make their borrowers successful."[138]

End Notes

[1] U.S. Small Business Administration, Fiscal Year 2010 Congressional Budget Justification, p. 30.

[2] U.S. Congress, House Committee on Small Business, Subcommittee on Finance and Tax, Subcommittee Hearing on Improving the SBA's Access to Capital Programs for Our Nation's Small Business, 110th Cong., 2nd sess., March 5, 2008, H.Hrg. 110-76 (Washington: GPO, 2008), p. 2.

[3] U.S. Small Business Administration, "Express and Pilot Programs," at http://www.sba. gov/content/express-programs. The SBA also administers four special purpose loan guaranty programs that address particular business needs: the Community Adjustment and Investment Program (CAIP), CAPLines Program, Employee Trusts Program, and Pollution Control Program (currently not funded). See U.S. Small Business Administration, "Special Purpose Loans Program," at http://www.sba.gov/category/navigation-structure/loans-grants/small-business-loans/sba-loan-programs/ 7a-loan-program/special-purpose-loans-program.

[4] 13 C.F.R. §120.120.

[5] U.S. Small Business Administration, "SBA Lending Statistics for Major Programs (as of 9/30/2012)," at http://www.sba.gov/about-sba-info/317721. The number of 7(a) loans approved annually is typically about 10% to 20% higher than the number of loans disbursed (e.g., some borrowers decide not to accept the loan or there is a change in business ownership). The amount of 7(a) loans approved annually is typically about 10% to 15% higher than the amount disbursed.

[6] U.S. Small Business Administration, Press Office, "Recovery Loan Incentives Spurred Continued Rebound in SBA Lending in FY2010," October 4, 2010, at http://www.sba. gov/about-sba-services/7367/5527; and U.S. Small Business Administration, "Jobs Act Supported More Than $12 Billion in SBA Lending to Small Businesses in Just Three Months," January 3, 2011, at http://www.sba.gov/content/jobs-act-supported-more-12-billion-sba-lending-smallbusinesses-just-three-months.

[7] P.L. 111-5, the American Recovery and Reinvestment Act of 2009 (ARRA), enacted on February 17, 2009, provided the SBA $375 million to temporarily reduce fees in the 7(a) and 504/CDC loan guaranty programs, and increase the 7(a) program's maximum loan guaranty percentage to 90% for all standard 7(a) loans through September 30, 2010, or until available funds were exhausted. Due to the increased demand for 7(a) loans, available funding was anticipated to be exhausted in early January 2010. P.L. 111-118, the Department of Defense Appropriations Act, 2010, provided the SBA $125 million to continue the fee subsidies and 90% maximum loan guaranty percentage through February 28, 2010. P.L. 111-144, the Temporary Extension Act

of 2010, provided the SBA $60 million to continue the fee subsidies and 90% maximum loan guaranty percentage through March 28, 2010. P.L. 111-150, an act to extend the Small Business Loan Guarantee Program, and for other purposes, provided the SBA authority to reprogram $40 million in previously appropriated funds to continue the fee subsidies and 90% maximum loan guaranty percentage through April 30, 2010. P.L. 111-157, the Continuing Extension Act of 2010, provided the SBA $80 million to continue the SBA's fee subsidies and 90% maximum loan guaranty percentage through May 31, 2010. The fee subsidies and 90% loan guaranty percentage expired on May 31, 2010. P.L. 111-240, the Small Business Jobs Act of 2010, enacted on September 27, 2010, provided the SBA $505 million (plus an additional $5 million for related administrative expenses) to reinstate the fee subsidies and 90% maximum loan guaranty percentage through December 31, 2010, or until available funds were exhausted. P.L. 111-322, the Continuing Appropriations and Surface Transportation Extensions Act, 2011, authorized the SBA to use any funds remaining from the Small Business Jobs Act of 2010 to continue the fee subsidies and the 7(a) program's 90% maximum loan guaranty percentage through March 4, 2011, or until the available funding was exhausted. The funds were exhausted on January 3, 2011.

[8] U.S. Government Accountability Office, Small Business Administration: 7(a) Loan Program Needs Additional Performance Measures, GAO-08-226T, November 1, 2007, pp. 3, 9-11, at http://www.gao.gov/new. items/d08226t.pdf; and Veronique de Rugy, Why the Small Business Administration's Loan Programs Should Be Abolished, American Enterprise Institute for Public Policy Research, AEI Working Paper #126, April 13, 2006. Proponents of federal funding for the SBA's loan guarantee programs also argue that small business can promote competitive markets. See, P.L. 83-163, §2(a), as amended; and 15 U.S.C. §631a.

[9] For further analysis, see CRS Report R40860, Small Business Size Standards: A Historical Analysis of Contemporary Issues, by Robert Jay Dilger.

[10] 13 C.F.R. §120.100; and 13 C.F.R. §120.101. A list of ineligible businesses, such as non-profit businesses, insurance companies, and businesses deriving more than one-third of gross annual revenue from legal gambling activities, are contained in 13 C.F.R. §120.110.

[11] 13 C.F.R. §120.150.

[12] 13 C.F.R. §120.120.

[13] 13 C.F.R. §120.130; and U.S. Small Business Administration, "Use of 7(a) Loan Proceeds," at http://www.sba.gov/ content/use-7a-loan-proceeds.

[14] U.S. Small Business Administration, "SBA Lending Statistics for Major Programs (as of 9/30/2012)," at http://www.sba.gov/about-sba-info/317721.

[15] 13 C.F.R. §120.212. A portion of a 7(a) loan used to acquire or improve real property may have a term of 25 years plus an additional period needed to complete the construction or improvements.

[16] 13 C.F.R. §120.213.

[17] For fixed interest rates, the SBA first calculates a fixed base rate using the 30 day London Interbank Offered Rate (LIBOR) in effect on the first business day of the month as published in a national financial newspaper published each business day, adds to that 300 basis points (3%) and the average of the 5-year and 10-year LIBOR swap rates in effect on the first business day of the month as published in a national financial newspaper published each business day. For 7(a) fixed loans with maturities of less than seven years, the SBA adds 2.25% to the fixed base rate to arrive at the maximum allowable fixed rate. For 7(a) fixed loans with maturities of seven years or longer, the SBA adds 2.75% to the fixed base rate to arrive at the maximum allowable fixed rate. Lenders may increase the maximum fixed interest rate allowed by an additional 1% if the fixed rate loan is over $25,000 but not exceeding $50,000, and by an additional 2% if the fixed rate loan is $25,000 or less. See, U.S. Small Business Administration, "Business Loan Program Maximum Allowable Fixed Rate," 74 Federal Register 50263, 50264, September 30, 2009.

[18] Colson Services Corp., "SBA Base Rates," New York, at http://www.colsonservices. com/ main/news.shtml.

[19] Ibid.

[20] U.S. Small Business Administration, "7(a) Loan Program: Terms and Conditions," at http://www.sba.gov/ content/7aterms-conditions.

[21] U.S. Small Business Administration, "SOP 50 10 5(E): Lender and Development Company Loan Programs," (effective June 1, 2012), pp. 188-189, at http://www.sba.gov/sites/ default/files/SOP% 2050% 2010%205(E)%20(5-16- 2012)%20clean.pdf. Liquidation value is the amount expected to be realized if the lender took possession after a loan default and sold the asset after conducting a reasonable search for a buyer and after deducting the costs of taking possession, preserving and marketing the asset, less the value of any existing liens.

[22] 13 C.F.R. §120.410.

[23] U.S. Small Business Administration, Fiscal Year 2013 Congressional Budget Justification and FY 2011 Annual Performance Report, p. 31.

[24] U.S. Small Business Administration, "7(a) Loan Program: How the Program Works," at http://archive.sba.gov/financialassistance/borrowers/guaranteed/7alp/FINANCIAL_GLP_7A_WORK.html.

[25] U.S. Small Business Administration, "SOP 50 10 5(E): Lender and Development Company Loan Programs," (effective June 1, 2012), p. 225, at http://www.sba.gov/sites/default/files/ SOP%2050%2010%205(E)%20(5-16- 2012)%20clean.pdf.

[26] U.S. Government Accountability Office, Small Business Administration: Opportunities Exist to Build on Leadership's Efforts to Improve Agency Performance and Employee Morale, GAO-08-995, September 24, 2008, p. 3, at http://www.gao.gov/new.items/d08995.pdf.

[27] U.S. Small Business Administration, "SOP 50 10 5(E): Lender and Development Company Loan Programs," (effective June 1, 2012), pp. 217-220, at http://www.sba.gov/sites/default/ files/SOP%2050%2010%205 (E)%20(5-16- 2012)%20clean.pdf.

[28] U.S. Congress, Senate Select Committee on Small Business, SBA Loan Oversight, hearing on SBA loan oversight, 96th Cong., 1st sess., September 18, 1997 (Washington: GPO, 1997), p. 31; and U.S. General Accounting Office, SBA's Pilot Programs to Improve Guaranty Loan Procedures Need Further Development, CED-81-25, February 2, 1981, p. 7, at http://www.gao.gov/assets/140/131789.pdf; and U.S. General Accounting Office, SBA's Certified Lenders Program Falls Short of Expectations, RCED-83-99, June 7, 1983, p. 1, at http://www.gao.gov/assets/150/140126.pdf.

[29] U.S. Small Business Administration, Office of Congressional and Legislative Affairs, correspondence with the author, September 17, 2012.

[30] U.S. Small Business Administration, "SOP 50 10 5(E): Lender and Development Company Loan Programs," (effective June 1, 2012), p. 221, at http://www.sba.gov/sites/default/files/ SOP%2050%2010%205(E)%20(5-16- 2012)%20clean.pdf. CLP lenders are expected to perform a complete analysis of the application and, in return, the SBA promises a faster loan decision. The SBA still makes the final credit and eligibility decision, but by completing a credit review instead of an independently conducted analysis, the SBA attempts to arrive at its decision in three working days. See, U.S. Small Business Administration, "The Certified Lenders Program (CLP)," at http://www.sba.gov/content/ steps-participating-clp.

[31] U.S. General Accounting Office, SBA's Certified Lenders Program Falls Short of Expectations, RCED-83-99, June 7, 1983, p. 3, at http://www.gao.gov/ assets/150/ 140126.pdf.

[32] U.S. General Accounting Office, Small Business: Analysis of SBA's Preferred Lenders Program, GAO/RCED-92- 124, May 15, 1992, pp. 1-4, http://www.gao.gov/ assets/220/ 216229.pdf.

[33] PLP lenders approved 12,496 7(a) loans amounting to $8.4 billion in FY2012, 15,167 7(a) loans amounting to $10.7 billion in FY2011, and 13,168 7(a) loans amounting to $6.9 billion in FY2010. See U.S. Small Business Administration, "SBA Lending Statistics for Major Programs (as of 9/30/2012)," at http://www.sba.gov/about-sba-info/ 317721.

[34] U.S. Small Business Administration, "SOP 50 10 5(E): Lender and Development Company Loan Programs," (effective June 1, 2012), p. 221, at http://www.sba.gov/ sites/default/files/SOP%2050%2010%205(E)%20(5-16- 2012)%20clean.pdf. Lenders are considered for PLP status based on their record with SBA, and must have demonstrated a proficiency in processing and servicing SBA-guaranteed loans. The SBA continues to review the submitted materials to check loan eligibility criteria. See U.S. Small Business Administration, "The Preferred Lenders Program (PLP)," at http://www.sba.gov /content/preferred-lenders-program-plp. Of the 3,537 active lenders in the 7(a) program in FY2011, 545 participated in the Preferred Lenders Program.

[35] U.S. Small Business Administration, "SOP 50 10 5(E): Lender and Development Company Loan Programs," (effective June 1, 2012), pp. 83, 163, at http://www.sba.gov/sites/ default/files/SOP%2050%2010%2 05(E)%20(5-16- 2012)%20clean.pdf. The fee is refundable if the loan application is withdrawn prior to SBA approval, the SBA declines to guarantee the loan, or the SBA substantially changes the loan terms and those terms are unacceptable to the lender. Also, because the SBA does not approve or decline the credit for PLP loans, PLP lenders are required to send the guaranty fee directly to the SBA Denver Finance Center within 10 business days from the date the loan number is assigned and before the lender signs the Authorization for SBA.

[36] 15 U.S.C. 636(a)(18)(a).

[37] U.S. Small Business Administration, "Small Business Jobs Act: Implementation of Conforming and Technical Amendments," 76 Federal Register 63544, 63545, October 13, 2011.

[38] U.S. Small Business Administration, "SOP 50 10 5(E): Lender and Development Company Loan Programs," (effective June 1, 2012), p. 163, at http://www.sba.gov/sites/default/files/ SOP%2050%2010%205(E)%20(5-16- 2012)%20clean.pdf.

Small Business Administration 7(a) Loan Guaranty Program   81

[39] 15 U.S.C. 636(a)(23)(a).

[40] U.S. Small Business Administration, "SBA Information Notice: 7(a) and 504 Fees Effective On October 1, 2012," at http://www.colsonservices.com/main/news/5000-1253%20-%207(a)%20and%20504%20Fees%20 Effective% 20On%20October%201%202012.pdf.

[41] 15 U.S.C. 636(a)(23)(b).

[42] 13 C.F.R. §120.221.

[43] Ibid.; and U.S. Small Business Administration, "SOP 50 10 5(E): Lender and Development Company Loan Programs," (effective June 1, 2012), p. 171, at http://www. sba.gov/sites/default/files/ SOP%2050% 2010%205(E)%20(5-16-2012)%20clean.pdf.

[44] 13 C.F.R. §120.222. A commitment fee may be charged for a loan made under the Export Working Capital Loan Program.

[45] 13 C.F.R. §120.221; and U.S. Small Business Administration, "SOP 50 10 5(E): Lender and Development Company Loan Programs," (effective June 1, 2012), p. 172, at http://www.sba.gov/sites/default/files/ SOP%2050%2010%205(E)%20(5-16-2012)% 20 clean.pdf.

[46] 13 C.F.R. §120.223; and U.S. Small Business Administration, "SOP 50 10 5(E): Lender and Development Company Loan Programs," (effective June 1, 2012), p. 172, at http://www.sba.gov/sites/ default/files/ SOP%2050%2010%205(E)%20(5-16-2012)% 20clean.pdf.

[47] U.S. Small Business Administration, Office of Congressional and Legislative Affairs, correspondence with the author, September 17, 2012. The SBA maintains selected disbursement data and will provide that data to congressional offices by request.

[48] U.S. Small Business Administration, "SBA Lending Report for Major Programs, Fiscal Year 2010," October 4, 2010, at http://archive.sba.gov/idc/groups/public/documents/ sba_homepage/serv_fa_lending_major_ progs. pdf; and U.S. Small Business Administration, Office of Congressional and Legislative Affairs, correspondence with the author, September 17, 2012.

[49] U.S. Small Business Administration, Press Office, "Recovery Loan Incentives Spurred Continued Rebound in SBA Lending in FY2010," October 4, 2010, at http://www.sba. gov/about-sba-services/7367/5527; and U.S. Small Business Administration, "Jobs Act Supported More Than $12 Billion in SBA Lending to Small Businesses in Just Three Months," January 3, 2011, at http://www.sba.gov/content/jobs-act-supported-more-12-billion-sba-lending-smallbusinesses-just-three-months.

[50] P.L. 111-5, the American Recovery and Reinvestment Act of 2009 (ARRA), enacted on February 17, 2009, provided the SBA $375 million to temporarily reduce fees in the 7(a) and 504/CDC loan guaranty programs, and increase the 7(a) program's maximum loan guaranty percentage to 90% for all standard 7(a) loans through September 30, 2010, or until available funds were exhausted. Due to the increased demand for 7(a) loans, available funding was anticipated to be exhausted in early January 2010. P.L. 111-118, the Department of Defense Appropriations Act, 2010, provided the SBA $125 million to continue the fee subsidies and 90% maximum loan guaranty percentage through February 28, 2010. P.L. 111-144, the Temporary Extension Act of 2010, provided the SBA $60 million to continue the fee subsidies and 90% maximum loan guaranty percentage through March 28, 2010. P.L. 111-150, an act to extend the Small Business Loan Guarantee Program, and for other purposes, provided the SBA authority to reprogram $40 million in previously appropriated funds to continue the fee subsidies and 90% maximum loan guaranty percentage through April 30, 2010. P.L. 111-157, the Continuing Extension Act of 2010, provided the SBA $80 million to continue the SBA's fee subsidies and 90% maximum loan guaranty percentage through May 31, 2010. The fee subsidies and 90% loan guaranty percentage expired on May 31, 2010. P.L. 111-240, the Small Business Jobs Act of 2010, enacted on September 27, 2010, provided the SBA $505 million (plus an additional $5 million for related administrative expenses) to reinstate the fee subsidies and 90% maximum loan guaranty percentage through December 31, 2010, or until available funds were exhausted. P.L. 111-322, the Continuing Appropriations and Surface Transportation Extensions Act, 2011, authorized the SBA to use any funds remaining from the Small Business Jobs Act of 2010 to continue the fee subsidies and the 7(a) program's 90% maximum loan guaranty percentage through March 4, 2011, or until the available funding was exhausted. The funds were exhausted on January 3, 2011.

[51] U.S. Small Business Administration, Office of Advocacy, "Frequently Asked Questions About Small Business Finance," September 2011, at http://www.sba.gov/sites/default/ files/Finance%20FAQ%208-25-11%20FINAL%20for%20web.pdf.

[52] U.S. Small Business Administration, FY 2008 Small Business Administration (SBA) Loss Report, p. 7, at http://archive.sba.gov/idc/groups/public/documents/ sba_program_office/ cfo_2008_loss_report.pdf. Loans include those made through the SBA's 7(a), 8(A), FIS 8a, Economic Opportunity, Small Business Energy,

Handicap Assistance, Veterans, Pollution Control, Import Export, Foreign Trade, USCAIP (NAFTA) and Reconstruction Finance Corporation Business programs.

[53] U.S. Small Business Administration, Office of Congressional and Legislative Affairs, correspondence with the author, September 17, 2012. 7(a) program loan loss was calculated by subtracting total 7(a) loan purchases from total 7(a) program disbursements, and then adding total 7(a) loan recoveries.

[54] U.S. Small Business Administration, FY 2013 Congressional Budget Justification and FY 2011 Annual Performance Report, p. 19, at http://www.sba.gov/sites/default/files/files/ FY%202013%20CBJ%20 FY%202011%20APR.pdf.

[55] U.S. Small Business Administration, Fiscal Year 2013 Congressional Budget Justification and FY 2011 Annual Performance Report, p. 21.

[56] Christopher Hayes, An Assessment of Small Business Administration Loan and Investment Performance: Survey of Assisted Businesses (Washington, DC: The Urban Institute, 2008), p. 3, at http://www.urban.org/ UploadedPDF/ 411599_assisted_business_survey.pdf. The percentage total exceeds 100 because recipients were allowed to name more than one use for the loan proceeds.

[57] Ibid., p. 5.

[58] Ibid.

[59] Kenneth Temkin, Brett Theodos, with Kerstin Gentsch, Competitive and Special Competitive Opportunity Gap Analysis of the 7(A) and 504 Programs (Washington, DC: The Urban Institute, 2008), p. 13, at http://www.urban.org/ UploadedPDF/411596_504_gap_ analysis.pdf.

[60] U.S. Small Business Administration, "SBA Lending Statistics for Major Programs (as of 9/30/2012)," at http://www.sba.gov/about-sba-info/317721.

[61] Kenneth Temkin, Brett Theodos, with Kerstin Gentsch, Competitive and Special Competitive Opportunity Gap Analysis of the 7(A) and 504 Programs (Washington, DC: The Urban Institute, 2008), p. 21, at http://www.urban.org/UploadedPDF/411596_504_gap_ analy sis.pdf.

[62] For further analysis, see CRS Report R40985, Small Business: Access to Capital and Job Creation, by Robert Jay Dilger.

[63] P.L. 110-343, the Emergency Economic Stabilization Act of 2008.

[64] U.S. Department of the Treasury, Troubled Assets Relief Program Monthly 105(a) Report – November 2010, December 10, 2010, pp. 2-4, at http://www.financialstability.gov/docs/ November%20105(a)%20FINAL.pdf. On March 16, 2009, President Obama announced that the Department of the Treasury would use TARP funds to purchase up to $15 billion of SBA-guaranteed loans to "immediately unfreeze the secondary market for SBA loans and increase the liquidity of community banks." The plan was deferred after it met resistance from lenders. Some lenders objected to TARP's requirement that participating lenders comply with executive compensation limits and issue warrants to the federal government. Smaller, community banks objected to the program's paperwork requirements, such as the provision of a small-business lending plan and quarterly reports. See The White House, "Remarks by the President to Small Business Owners, Community Leaders, and Members of Congress," March 16, 2009, at http://www.whitehouse.gov/the_press_office/Remarks-by-the-President-to-small-business-owners/.

[65] P.L. 111-240, the Small Business Jobs Act of 2010, §1111. Section 7(A) Business Loans. The Senate had adopted H.R. 4213, the American Workers, State, and Business Relief Act of 2010, on March 10, 2010, by a 62-36 vote. It would have provided $560 million to extend the fee reductions and 90% loan guarantee limit through December 31, 2010. The House approved an amended version of the bill, renamed the American Jobs and Closing Tax Loopholes Act of 2010, on May 28, 2010, by a 245-171 vote. It would have provided $505 million to extend the fee reductions and 90% loan guarantee limit through December 31, 2010. The extension provision was subsequently removed from the bill, which became P.L. 111-205, the Unemployment Compensation Extension Act of 2010.

[66] U.S. Small Business Administration, "Administration Announces New Small Business Commercial Real Estate and Working Capital Programs," February 5, 2010, at http://www.sba.gov/sites/default/files/ sba_rcvry_ factsheet_cre_refi.pdf.

[67] Susan Eckerly, "NFIB Responds to President's Small Business Lending Initiatives," Washington, DC, October 21, 2009, at http://www.nfib.com/newsroom/newsroom-item/cmsid/50080/; and NFIB, "Government Spending," Washington, DC, at http://www.nfib.com/issues-elections/issues-elections-item/cmsid/49051/.

[68] U.S. Small Business Administration, Office of Inspector General, "Semiannual Report to Congress, Fall 2009," p. 5, at http://www.sba.gov/office-of-inspector-general/867/12348.

[69] Ibid., p. 3.

[70] Ibid., p. 5.

[71] Ibid.

[72] U.S. Government Accountability Office, Small Business Administration: Actions Needed to Improve the Usefulness of the Agency's Lender Risk Rating System, GAO-1—53, November 6, 2009, p. i, at http://www.gao.gov/new.items/ d1053.pdf.

[73] Ibid., pp. i, 27-30.

[74] Ibid., p. 35.

[75] U.S. Government Accountability Office, Small Business Administration: Additional Guidance on Documenting Credit Elsewhere Decisions Could Improve 7(a) Program Oversight, GAO-09-228, February 12, 2009, p. 3, at http://www.gao.gov/new.items/d09228.pdf.

[76] 15 U.S.C. 636(a)(1)(A). The act defines credit elsewhere as "the availability of credit from non-Federal sources on reasonable terms and conditions taking into consideration the prevailing rates and terms in the community in or near where the concern transacts business, or the homeowner resides, for similar purposes and periods of time." See 15 U.S.C. 632(h).

[77] U.S. Small Business Administration, "SOP 50 10 5(E): Lender and Development Company Loan Programs," (effective June 1, 2012), p. 102, at http://www.sba.gov/sites/ default/files/SOP%2050%2010%205(E)%20(5-16- 2012)%20clean.pdf.

[78] U.S. Government Accountability Office, Small Business Administration: Additional Guidance on Documenting Credit Elsewhere Decisions Could Improve 7(a) Program Oversight, GAO-09-228, February 12, 2009, pp. 25-26, at http://www.gao.gov/new.items/d09228.pdf.

[79] Ibid., p. 26.

[80] U.S. Small Business Administration, Fiscal Year 2011 Congressional Budget Justification and FY 2009 Annual Performance Report, p. 6.

[81] Ibid., p. 43.

[82] Ibid.

[83] U.S. Small Business Administration, Fiscal Year 2012 Congressional Budget Justification and FY 2010 Annual Performance Report, p. 7.

[84] U.S. Government Accountability Office, Small Business Administration: 7(a) Loan Program Needs Additional Performance Measures, GAO-08-226T, November 1, 2007, p. 2, at http://www.gao.gov/new.items/ d08226t.pdf.

[85] U.S. Small Business Administration, Office of the Inspector General, SBA's Administration of the Microloan Program under the Recovery Act, December 28, 2009, p. 6, at http://www.sba.gov/sites/default/files/om10-10.pdf.

[86] Ibid.

[87] Ibid., p. 7.

88 U.S. Government Accountability Office, Small Business Administration: 7(a) Loan Program Needs Additional Performance Measures, GAO-08-226T, November 1, 2007, p. 8, at http://www.gao.gov/new.items/ d08226t.pdf.

[89] U.S. Small Business Administration, Office of the Inspector General, SBA's Administration of the Microloan Program under the Recovery Act, December 28, 2009, p. 9, at http://www.sba.gov/sites/default/files/om10-10.pdf.

[90] U.S. Small Business Administration, "Administration Announces New Small Business Commercial Real Estate and Working Capital Programs," February 5, 2010, at http://www. sba.gov/sites/default/files/ sba_rcvry_factsheet_cre_refi.pdf.

[91] Ibid.

[92] Ibid.

[93] Robb Mandelbaum, "Small Business Incentives Face a Hard Road in Congress," New York Times, February 12, 2010, at http://boss.blogs.nytimes.com/2010/02/12/small-business-incentives-face-a-hard-road-in-congress/; and U.S. Congress, House Committee on Small Business, House Committee on Small Business Views With Regard to the Fiscal Year (FY) 2010 Budget, Letter from Nydia Velázquez, Chair, House Committee on Small Business, to John M. Spratt, Jr., Chair, House Committee on the Budget, 111th Cong., 2nd sess., March 11, 2009, p. 3, at http://www.house.gov/ smbiz/democrats/Reports/FY%202010% 20Views %20and%20 Estimates%20v2.pdf.

[94] U.S. Congress, House Committee on Small Business, Small Business Financing and Investment Act Of 2009, report to accompany H.R. 3854, 111th Cong., 2nd sess., October 26, 2009, H.Rept. 111-315 (Washington: GPO, 2009), p. 1.

[95] Robb Mandelbaum, "Why Won't the S.B.A. Lend Directly to Small Businesses?" New York Times, March 10, 2010, at http://boss.blogs.nytimes.com/2010/03/10/why-wont-the-s-b-a-loan-directly-to-small-businesses/.

[96] Susan Eckerly, "NFIB Responds to President's Small Business Lending Initiatives," Washington, DC, October 21, 2009, at http://www.nfib.com/newsroom/newsroom-item/ cmsid/50080/; and NFIB, "Government Spending," Washington, DC, at http://www. nfib.com/issues-elections/issues-elections-item/cmsid/49051/.

[97] For further analysis, see CRS Report R40985, Small Business: Access to Capital and Job Creation, by Robert Jay Dilger.

[98] ARC's loan limit would be increased from $35,000 to $50,000, and to $75,000 in areas of high unemployment, and borrowers would be allowed to use ARC loans to refinance existing SBA loan debt. The ARC program ended on September 30, 2010.

[99] H.R. 3854, the Small Business Financing and Investment Act of 2009.

[100] Ibid. For further analysis, see CRS Report R40985, Small Business: Access to Capital and Job Creation, by Robert Jay Dilger.

[101] S. 2869, the Small Business Job Creation and Access to Capital Act of 2009; and H.R. 4213, the American Workers, State and Business Relief Act.

[102] P.L. 111-240, the Small Business Jobs Act of 2010, §1122. Low-Interest Refinancing Under the Local Development Business Loan Program.

[103] For further analysis of P.L. 111-240, the Small Business Jobs Act of 2010, see CRS Report R41385, Small Business Legislation During the 111th Congress, by Robert Jay Dilger and Gary Guenther. For further analysis of the Small Business Lending Fund, see CRS Report R42045, The Small Business Lending Fund, by Robert Jay Dilger. For further analysis of the State Small Business Credit Initiative, see CRS Report R42581, State Small Business Credit Initiative: Implementation and Funding Issues, by Robert Jay Dilger.

[104] Representative Nydia Velázquez, "Small Business Financing and Investment Act of 2009," House debate, Congressional Record, daily edition, vol. 155, no. 159 (October 29, 2009), pp. H12074, H12075; Senator Mary Landrieu, "Statements on Introduced Bills and Joint Resolutions," remarks in the Senate, Congressional Record, daily edition, vol. 155, no. 185 (December 10, 2009), p. S12910; and The White House, "Remarks by the President on Job Creation and Economic Growth," December 8, 2009, at http://www.whitehouse.gov/the-press-office/remarkspresident-job-creation-and-economic-growth.

[105] Susan Eckerly, "NFIB Responds to President's Small Business Lending Initiatives," Washington, DC, October 21, 2009, at http://www.nfib.com/newsroom/newsroom-item/cmsid/50080/; and NFIB, "Government Spending," Washington, DC, at http://www. nfib.com/issues-elections/issues-elections-item/cmsid/49051/.

[106] Shelli B. Rossman and Brett Theodos, with Rachel Brash, Megan Gallagher, Christopher Hayes, and Kenneth Temkin, Key Findings from the Evaluation of the Small Business Administration's Loan and Investment Programs: Executive Summary (Washington, DC: The Urban Institute, January 2008), p. 58, at http://www.urban.org/ Uploaded PDF/ 411602_executive_summary.pdf.

[107] Ibid.

[108] U.S. Government Accountability Office, Small Business Administration: 7(a) Loan Program Needs Additional Performance Measures, GAO-08-226T, November 1, 2007, p. 2, at http://www.gao.gov/new.items/ d08226t. pdf; and U.S. Small Business Administration, Office of the Inspector General, SBA's Administration of the Microloan Program under the Recovery Act, December 28, 2009, pp. 6-7, at http://www.sba.gov /sites/default/files/om10-10.pdf.

[109] U.S. Small Business Administration, "The SBA Express Pilot Program: Inspection Report," June 1998, p. 3, at http://archive.sba.gov/idc/groups/public/ documents/sba/ oig_ loarchive_980601.pdf.

[110] U.S. Small Business Administration, "SBA Lending Statistics for Major Programs (as of 9/30/2012)," at http://www.sba.gov/about-sba-info/317721.

[111] Ibid.

[112] U.S. Small Business Administration, "SBAExpress," at http://www.sba.gov/content/sba-express.

[113] Ibid.

[114] U.S. Small Business Administration, "SOP 50 10 5(E): Lender and Development Company Loan Programs," (effective June 1, 2012), p. 42, at http://www.sba.gov/sites/ default/files/SOP%2050%2010%205(E)%20(5-16-2012)%20clean.pdf.

[115] Ibid., pp. 83, 127.

[116] U.S. Small Business Administration, "Popular SBA Patriot Express Loan Initiative Renewed for Three More Years," December 10, 2010, at http://www.sba.gov/content/popular-sba-patriot-express-loan-initiative-renewed -threemore-years.

[117] U.S. Small Business Administration, "SOP 50 10 5(E): Lender and Development Company Loan Programs," (effective June 1, 2012), pp. 83, 146, 148-153, at http://www.sba. gov/sites/default/files/SOP%2050% 2010% 205(E)%20(5-16-2012)%20 clean.pdf.

[118] Ibid., pp. 84, 172-173.

Small Business Administration 7(a) Loan Guaranty Program

[119] U.S. Congress, Senate Committee on Small Business and Entrepreneurship, Assessing Federal Small Business Assistance Programs for Veterans and Reservists, hearing, 110th Cong., 1st sess., January 31, 2007, S.Hrg. 110-209 (Washington: GPO, 2007), p. 32.

[120] U.S. Congress, House Committee on Veterans' Affairs, Subcommittee on Economic Opportunity, Status of Veterans Small Business, hearing, 111th Cong., 2nd sess., April 29, 2010, House Committee on Veterans' Affairs Serial No. 111- 74 (Washington: GPO, 2010), p. 75.

[121] U.S. Small Business Administration, "Popular SBA Patriot Express Loan Initiative Renewed for Three More Years," December 10, 2010, at http://www.sba.gov/content/popular-sba-patriot-express-loan-initiative-renewed-threemore-years.

[122] U.S. Congress, House Committee on Veterans' Affairs, Subcommittee on Economic Opportunity, Status of Veterans Small Business, hearing, 111th Cong., 2nd sess., April 29, 2010, House Committee on Veterans' Affairs Serial No. 111- 74 (Washington: GPO, 2010), p. 17.

[123] Ibid.

[124] In FY2010, the SBA's Veterans Business Outreach Centers Program, which provides management and technical assistance training for veteran-owned small businesses, conducted its sixth annual "Customer Satisfaction Survey." The centers surveyed 1% of their total veteran customer population (408 of the 485 clients surveyed responded). The FY2010 survey found that 85% of the clients using the centers were satisfied or highly satisfied with the quality, relevance and timeliness of the assistance provided. Clients evaluating the centers gave 85% ratings for the training programs provided and 85% ratings for program evaluation. See U.S. Small Business Administration, "FY2012 Congressional Budget Justification and FY2010 Annual Performance Report," p. 73. In FY2011, the Veterans Business Outreach Centers Program conducted its seventh annual "Customer Satisfaction Survey." The FY2011 survey found that 91% of the clients using the centers were satisfied or highly satisfied with the quality, relevance, and timeliness of the assistance provided. See U.S. Small Business Administration, "FY2013 Congressional Budget Justification and FY2011 Annual Performance Report," 2012, p. 62.

[125] For further information and analysis, see CRS Report R41352, Small Business Management and Technical Assistance Training Programs, by Robert Jay Dilger; U.S. Small Business Administration, Office of Entrepreneurial Development, "Impact Study of Entrepreneurial Development Resources: Face to Face Counseling," November 9, 2011, at http://www. sba.gov/sites/default/files/ SBA%20ED%20Resources% 20Impact%20Study%20Nov %20 2011%20Final%20Report.pdf; and P.L. 96-302, the Small Business Development Center Act of 1980.

[126] U.S. Small Business Administration, "Small Loan Advantage," at http://www.sba.gov/ content/small-loan-advantage; and U.S. Small Business Administration, "SBA Announces New Initiatives Aimed at Increasing Lending in Underserved Communities," December 15, 2010, at http://www.sba.gov/content/sba-announces-new-initiatives-aimedincreasing-lending-underserved-communities.

[127] U.S. Congress, House Committee on Small Business, Small Business Financing and Investment Act Of 2009, report to accompany H.R. 3854, 111th Cong., 2nd sess., October 26, 2009, H.Rept. 111-315 (Washington: GPO, 2009), p. 7. The SBA indicated that the Community Express Pilot Program "has had mixed outcomes," providing loans "to new businesses, minority businesses and other underserved sectors" but with "significantly higher default rates (almost 40% of loans defaulted in certain cohorts) compared with other similarly sized 7(a) loans." See U.S. Small Business Administration, "Community Express Pilot Program," 75 Federal Register 80562, December 22, 2010.

[128] U.S. Small Business Administration, "Advantage Loan Initiatives," at http://www.sba. gov/advantage.

[129] U.S. Small Business Administration, "Small Loan Advantage," at http://www.sba.gov /content/small-loan-advantage.

[130] Ibid.

[131] Ibid.

[132] U.S. Small Business Administration, "Advantage Loan Initiatives," at http://www. sba. gov/advantage.

[133] Ibid.

[134] Ibid.

[135] Ibid.

[136] U.S. Small Business Administration, "Community Advantage Participant Guide," p. 18, at http://www.sba.gov/sites/ default/files/files/CA%20-%20Participants%20Guide.pdf; and U.S. Small Business Administration, "Community Advantage Pilot Program," 77 Federal Register 6619, February 8, 2012.

[137] U.S. Small Business Administration, "Community Advantage," at http://www.sba.gov/ content/community-advantage.

[138] U.S. Small Business Administration, "SBA Announces New Initiatives Aimed at Increasing Lending in Underserved Communities," December 15, 2010, at http://www.sba.gov/ content/sba-announces-new-initiatives-aimedincreasing-lending-underserved-communities. The SBA maintains a list of approved Community Advantage pilot program lenders on its website at http://www.sba.gov/content/community-advantage-approved-lenders.

In: Small Business Administration Programs
Editor: Walter Janikowski

ISBN: 978-1-62417-992-1
© 2013 Nova Science Publishers, Inc.

Chapter 4

SMALL BUSINESS ADMINISTRATION 504/CDC LOAN GUARANTY PROGRAM[*]

Robert Jay Dilger

SUMMARY

The Small Business Administration (SBA) administers programs to support small businesses, including several loan guaranty programs designed to encourage lenders to provide loans to small businesses "that might not otherwise obtain financing on reasonable terms and conditions."

The SBA's 504 Certified Development Company (504/CDC) loan guaranty program is administered through non-profit Certified Development Companies (CDC). It provides long-term fixed rate financing for major fixed assets, such as land, buildings, equipment, and machinery. Of the total project costs, a third-party lender must provide at least 50% of the financing, the CDC provides up to 40% of the financing through a 100% SBA-guaranteed debenture, and the applicant provides at least 10% of the financing.

It is named from Section 504 of the Small Business Investment Act of 1958 (P.L. 85-699, as amended), which authorized the program. In FY2012, the SBA approved 9,471 504/CDC loans amounting to about $6.7 billion.

Congressional interest in the SBA's 504/CDC program has increased in recent years because of concern that small businesses might be prevented from accessing sufficient capital to assist in the economic recovery. During the 111th Congress, P.L. 111-240, the Small Business Jobs Act of 2010, increased the 504/CDC program's loan guaranty limits from $1.5 million to $5 million for "regular" borrowers, from $2 million to $5 million if the loan proceeds are directed toward one or more specified public policy goals, and from $4 million to $5.5 million for manufacturers. It also temporarily expanded, for two years, the types of projects eligible for 504/CDC program refinancing of existing debt, created an alternative 504/CDC size standard to increase the number of businesses eligible for assistance, and provided $510 million to extend temporary fee subsidies for the 504/CDC and 7(a) loan guaranty programs and a temporary increase in the 7(a) program's maximum loan guaranty percentage to 90%.

---

[*] This is an edited, reformatted and augmented version of a Congressional Research Service publication, CRS Report for Congress R41184, prepared for Members and Committees of Congress, from www.crs.gov, dated October 9, 2012.

The temporary fee subsidies and 90% loan guaranty percentage ended on January 3, 2011, and the temporary expansion of the projects eligible for 504/CDC program refinancing of existing debt expired on September 27, 2012.

This report opens with a discussion of the rationale provided for the 504/CDC program, the program's borrower and lender eligibility standards, program requirements, and program statistics, including loan volume, loss rates, use of the proceeds, borrower satisfaction, and borrower demographics.

It then examines congressional action taken during the 111th Congress to help small businesses gain greater access to capital, including the enactment of P.L. 111-5, the American Recovery and Reinvestment Act of 2009 (ARRA), and P.L. 111-240, the Small Business Jobs Act of 2010. It also discusses congressional efforts during the 112th Congress to extend the temporary expansion of the projects eligible for 504/CDC program refinancing of existing debt, which expired on September 27, 2012.

For example, H.R. 2950, the Small Business Administration 504 Loan Refinancing Extension Act of 2011, would extend that expiration date another year and S. 3572, the Restoring Tax and Regulatory Certainty to Small Businesses Act of 2012, would extend that expiration date another year and a half. S. 1828, a bill to increase small business lending, and for other purposes, is also discussed. It would reinstate for a year following the date of its enactment the temporary fee subsidies for the 504/CDC and 7(a) programs and the 90% loan guaranty percentage for the 7(a) program, which ended on January 3, 2011. Issues raised concerning the SBA's administration of the program, including the oversight of 504/CDC lenders, are also discussed.

SMALL BUSINESS ADMINISTRATION LOAN GUARANTY PROGRAMS

The Small Business Administration (SBA) administers programs to support small businesses, including several loan guaranty programs designed to encourage lenders to provide loans to small businesses "that might not otherwise obtain financing on reasonable terms and conditions."[1]

The SBA's 504 Certified Development Company (504/CDC) loan guaranty program provides longterm fixed rate financing for major fixed assets, such as land, buildings, equipment, and machinery.

It is named from Section 504 of the Small Business Investment Act of 1958 (P.L. 85-699, as amended), which authorized the program.[2] It is administered through non-profit Certified Development Companies (CDCs). Of the total project costs, a third-party lender must provide at least 50% of the financing, the CDC provides up to 40% of the financing backed by a 100% SBA-guaranteed debenture, and the applicant provides at least 10% of the financing.

The SBA's debenture is backed with the full faith and credit of the United States and is sold to underwriters who form debenture pools. Investors purchase interests in the debenture pools and receive certificates representing ownership of all or part of the pool. The SBA and CDCs use various agents to facilitate the sale and service of the certificates and the orderly flow of funds among the parties.[3] After a 504/CDC loan is approved and disbursed, accounting for the loan is set up at the Central Servicing Agent (CSA, currently Colson Services Corporation), not the SBA.

The SBA guarantees the timely payment of the debenture. If the small business is behind in its loan payments, the SBA pays the difference to the investor on every semi-annual due date.[4] In FY2012, the SBA approved 9,471 504/CDC loans amounting to about $6.7 billion.[5]

Historically, one of the justifications presented for funding the SBA's loan guaranty programs has been that small businesses can be at a disadvantage, compared with other businesses, when trying to obtain access to sufficient capital and credit.[6] Congressional interest in small business access to capital, in general, and the 504/CDC program, in particular, has increased in recent years because of concern that small businesses might be prevented from accessing sufficient capital to enable them to assist in the economic recovery. For example, senior loan officers at private lending institutions have indicated in Federal Reserve Board surveys that they have tightened small business lending standards, largely in reaction to relatively high loan default rates and increased numbers of noncurrent (past due) loans.[7]

Congress authorized several changes to the 504/CDC program during the 111th Congress in an effort to increase the number, and amount, of 504/CDC loans. For example, P.L. 111-5, the American Recovery and Reinvestment Act of 2009 (ARRA), provided $375 million to temporarily reduce fees in the SBA's 7(a) and 504/CDC loan guaranty programs and to temporarily increase the 7(a) program's maximum loan guaranty percentage to 90%. Congress subsequently appropriated another $265 million, and authorized the SBA to reprogram another $40 million, to extend those subsidies and loan modification through May 31, 2010.

ARRA also authorized the SBA to allow, under specified circumstances, the use of 504/CDC program funds to refinance existing debt for business expansion.[8]

P.L. 111-240, the Small Business Jobs Act of 2010, increased the 504/CDC program's loan guaranty limits from $1.5 million to $5 million for "regular" borrowers, from $2 million to $5 million if the loan proceeds are directed toward one or more specified public policy goals, and from $4 million to $5.5 million for manufacturers. The act also temporarily expanded for two years after the date of enactment (until September 27, 2012) the types of projects eligible for refinancing of existing debt under the 504/CDC program; provided $510 million to continue the 504/CDC program's fee subsidies from its date of enactment through December 31, 2010; and established an alternative size standard that allows more companies to qualify for 504/CDC assistance. P.L. 111-322, the Continuing Appropriations and Surface Transportation Extensions Act, 2011, authorized the SBA to continue the fee subsidies and the 7(a) program's 90% maximum loan guaranty percentage through March 4, 2011, or until funding provided for these purposes in P.L. 111-240 was exhausted (which occurred on January 3, 2011).

This report examines the 504/CDC program's borrower and lender eligibility standards; program requirements; and program statistics, including loan volume, loss rates, use of the proceeds, borrower satisfaction, and borrower demographics. It then examines congressional action taken during the 111th Congress to help small businesses gain greater access to capital, including the enactment of ARRA and P.L. 111-240, the Small Business Jobs Act of 2010. It also discusses H.R. 2950, the Small Business Administration 504 Loan Refinancing Extension Act of 2011; S.Amdt. 1833, the INVEST in America Act of 2012 — an amendment in the nature of a substitute for H.R. 3606, the Jumpstart Our Business Startups Act; and S. 3572, the Restoring Tax and Regulatory Certainty to Small Businesses Act of 2012. They would extend the temporary expansion of the projects eligible for 504/CDC program refinancing of existing debt, which expired on September 27, 2012. S. 1828, a bill to increase small business lending, and for other purposes, is also discussed. It would reinstate for a year following the date of its enactment the temporary fee subsidies for the 504/CDC and 7(a) programs and the 90% loan guaranty percentage for the 7(a) program, which ended on January 3, 2011.

The report also examines issues raised concerning the SBA's administration of the program, including the oversight of 504/CDC lenders.

PROGRAM PARTICIPANTS
AND FINANCING CONTRIBUTION

As shown in *Table 1*, 504/CDC projects generally have three main participants: a third-party lender provides 50% or more of the financing; a CDC provides up to 40% of the financing through a 504/CDC debenture, which is guaranteed 100% by the SBA; and the borrower contributes at least 10% of the financing. No more than 50% of eligible costs can be from federal sources.

Table 1. 504/CDC Loan Structures and Contribution Requirements

Participant	Standard Loan	New Business or Limited or Special Purpose Property Loan	Both New Business and Limited or Special Purpose Property Loan
Third Party Lender	at least 50%	at least 50%	at least 50%
CDC/SBA	maximum 40%	maximum 35%	maximum 30%
Borrower	at least 10%	at least 15%	at least 20%

Source: U.S. Small Business Administration, "U.S. Small Business Administration, "SOP 50 10 5(E): Lender and Development Company Loan Programs," (effective June 1, 2012), p. 266, at http://www.sba.gov/sites/default/files/SOP% 2050%2010%205(E)%20(5-16-2012)%20clean.pdf.

The CDC's contribution, and the amount of the SBA's 100% guaranteed debenture, cannot exceed 40% of the financing for standard 504/CDC loans and 35% of the financing for new businesses (defined as "a business that is two years old or less at the time the loan is approved") or if the loan is for a limited-market property (defined as "a property with a unique physical design, special construction materials, or a layout that restricts its utility to the use for which it is designed") or for a special purpose property.

The SBA lists 27 limited or special purpose properties (e.g., dormitories, golf courses, hospitals, and bowling alleys).[9] The CDC's contribution cannot exceed 30% of the financing when the borrower is both a new businesses and the loan is for either a limited-market property or a special purpose property.

Borrowers must contribute at least 10% of the financing for standard 504/CDC loans and at least 15% of the financing if they are a new business or if the loan is for a limited-market property or for a special purpose property. They must contribute at least 20% of the financing if they are both a new businesses and the loan is for either a limited-market property or a special purpose property.

BORROWER ELIGIBILITY STANDARDS AND PROGRAM REQUIREMENTS

Borrower Eligibility Standards

To be eligible for an SBA business loan, a small business applicant must

- be located in the United States;
- be a for-profit operating business (except for loans to eligible passive companies);
- qualify as small;[10]
- demonstrate a need for the desired credit and that the funds are not available from alternative sources, including personal resources of the principals; and
- be certified by a lender that the desired credit is unavailable to the applicant on reasonable terms and conditions from non-federal sources without SBA assistance.[11]

Several types of businesses are prohibited from participating in the program. For example, financial businesses primarily engaged in the business of lending, such as banks and finance companies; life insurance companies; businesses located in a foreign country; businesses deriving more than one-third of gross annual revenue from legal gambling activities; businesses that present live performances of a prurient sexual nature; and businesses with an associate who is incarcerated, on probation, on parole, or has been indicted for a felony or a crime of moral turpitude are ineligible.[12] To qualify for a SBA business loan, applicants must be creditworthy and able to reasonably assure repayment. The SBA requires lenders to consider the applicant's

- character, reputation, and credit history;
- experience and depth of management;
- strength of the business;
- past earnings, projected cash flow, and future prospects;
- ability to repay the loan with earnings from the business;
- sufficient invested equity to operate on a sound financial basis;
- potential for long-term success;
- nature and value of collateral (although inadequate collateral will not be the sole reason for denial of a loan request); and
- affiliates' effect on the applicant's repayment ability.[13]

Borrower Program Requirements

Use of Proceeds
A 504/CDC loan can be used to

- purchase land and make necessary improvements to the land, such as adding streets, curbs, gutters, parking lots, utilities, and landscaping;

- finance short-term debt ("bridge financing") on the land as long as there is no building currently on the land and the financing term is three years or less;
- purchase buildings and make improvements to the buildings, such as altering the building's facade and updating its heating and electrical systems, plumbing, and roofing;
- purchase, transport, dismantle, or install machinery and equipment, provided the machinery and equipment have a useful life of at least 10 years;
- purchase essential furniture and fixtures;
- pay professional fees that are directly attributable and essential to the project, such as title insurance, title searches and abstract costs, surveys and zoning matters;
- pay interim financing costs, including points, fees, and interest;
- create a contingency fund, provided that the fund does not exceed 10% of the project's construction costs; and
- finance permissible debt refinancing related to business expansion.[14] A 504/CDC loan cannot be used for working capital or inventory.

Job Creation and Retention Requirement

All 504/CDC borrowers must meet one of two specified economic development objectives.

First, borrowers, other than small manufacturers, must create or retain at least one job for every $65,000 of project debenture. Borrowers who are small manufacturers (defined as a small business with its primary North American Industry Classification System Code in Sectors 31, 32, and 33, and all of its production facilities are located in the United States) must create or retain one job per $100,000 of project debenture.

The jobs created do not have to be at the project facility, but 75% of the jobs must be created in the community where the project is located. Using job retention to satisfy this requirement is allowed only if the CDC "can reasonably show that jobs would be lost to the community if the project was not done."[15]

Second, if the borrower does not meet the job creation or retention requirement, the borrower can retain eligibility by meeting any one of five community development goals or ten public policy goals, provided the CDC meets its required job opportunity average of at least one job opportunity created or retained for every $65,000 in project debenture, or for every $75,000 in project debenture for projects located in special geographic areas (Alaska, Hawaii, state-designated enterprise zones, empowerment zones, enterprise communities, and labor surplus areas). Loans to small manufacturers are excluded from the calculation of this average.[16] The five community development goals are

- improving, diversifying or stabilizing the economy of the locality;
- stimulating other business development;
- bringing new income into the community;
- assisting manufacturing firms; or
- assisting businesses in labor surplus areas as defined by the U.S. Department of Labor.

The ten public policy goals are

- revitalizing a business district of a community with a written revitalization or redevelopment plan;
- expansion of exports;
- expansion of small businesses owned and controlled by women;
- expansion of small businesses owned and controlled by veterans (especially service-disabled veterans);
- expansion of minority enterprise development;
- aiding rural development;
- increasing productivity and competitiveness (e.g., retooling, robotics, modernization, and competition with imports);
- modernizing or upgrading facilities to meet health, safety, and environmental requirements;
- assisting businesses in or moving to areas affected by federal budget reductions, including base closings, either because of the loss of federal contracts or the reduction in revenues in the area due to a decreased federal presence; or
- reducing unemployment rates in labor surplus areas, as determined by defined by the U.S. Department of Labor.[17]

Loan Amounts

The minimum 504/CDC debenture is $25,000. P.L. 111-240 increased the maximum gross debenture amount

- from $1.5 million for regular 504/CDC loans to $5 million,
- from $2 million if the loan proceeds are directed toward one or more of the public policy goals described above to $5 million,
- from $4 million for small manufacturers to $5.5 million,
- from $4 million for projects that reduce the borrower's energy consumption by at least 10% to $5.5 million, and
- from $4 million for projects for plant, equipment, and process upgrades of renewable energy sources, such as the small-scale production of energy for individual buildings or communities consumption (commonly known as micropower), or renewable fuel producers, including biodiesel and ethanol producers to $5.5 million.[18]

Loan Terms, Interest Rate, and Collateral

Loan Terms

The SBA determines the 504/CDC program's loan terms and publishes those terms in the *Federal Register*.[19] The current maturities for 504/CDC loans are

- 20 years for real estate,
- 10 years for machinery and equipment, and
- 10 or 20 years based upon a weighted average of the useful life of the assets being financed.[20]

The maturities for the first mortgage issued by the third-party lender must be at least seven years when the CDC/504 loan is for a term of 10 years, and 10 years when the loan is for 20 years.[21]

Interest Rate

The interest rate for 504/CDC debentures is set by the SBA and approved by the Secretary of the Treasury.[22] It is based on market conditions for long-term government debt at the time of sale, and pegged to an increment above the current market rate for 5-year and 10-year U.S. Treasury issues. The rate for October 2012 is 4.28%.[23] In addition, the SBA sets the maximum interest rate that can be charged by any third party lender for a commercial loan which funds any portion of the cost of a 504/CDC project. That rate "must be reasonable" and published in the *Federal Register*. The current maximum interest rate that a third-party lender is allowed to charge for a commercial loan that funds any portion of the cost of a 504/CDC project is 6% over the New York prime rate or the maximum interest rate permitted in that state, whichever is less.[24]

Collateral

The SBA usually takes a second lien position on the project property to secure the loan. The SBA's second lien position is considered adequate when the applicant meets all of the following criteria:

- strong, consistent cash flow that is sufficient to cover the debt;
- demonstrated, proven management;
- the applicant's business has been in operation for more than two years; and
- the proposed project is a logical extension of the applicant's current operations.[25]

If one or more of the above factors is not met, additional collateral or increased equity contributions may be required. All collateral must be insured against such hazards and risks as the SBA may require, with provisions for notice to the SBA and the CDC in the event of impending lapse of coverage.[26] However, for 504/CDC loans, the applicant's cash flow is the primary source of repayment, not the liquidation of collateral. Thus, "if the lender's financial analysis demonstrates that the applicant lacks reasonable assurance of repayment in a timely manner from the cash flow of the business, the loan request must be declined, regardless of the collateral available."[27]

LENDER ELIGIBILITY STANDARDS, OPERATING REQUIREMENTS, AND PROGRAM REQUIREMENTS

Lender Eligibility Standards

CDCs apply to the SBA for certification to participate in the 504/CDC program. A CDC must be a non-profit corporation and

- be in good standing in the state in which it is incorporated;

- be in compliance with all laws, including taxation requirements, in the state in which it is incorporated and any other state in which it conducts business;
- have satisfactory performance as determined by the SBA in its discretion. Examples of the factors that may be considered in determining satisfactory performance include the CDC's risk rating, on-site review and examination assessments, historical performance measures (like default rate, purchase rate and loss rate), loan volume to the extent that it impacts performance measures, and other performance related measurements and information (such as contribution toward SBA's mission); and
- provide the SBA a copy of its IRS tax exempt status.[28]

In addition, when applying for certification a CDC must

- indicate its area of operations, which is the state of the CDC's incorporation;[29]
- report its membership, which must include at least 25 members who actively support economic development in their area of operations and represent (1) government organizations, (2) financial institutions (lenders), (3) community organizations, such as chambers of commerce, trade associations, colleges, or small business development centers, and (4) businesses in the area of operations;
- meet other specified membership requirements, such as meeting at least annually, requiring a quorum to transact business, and prohibiting any person or entity from owning or controlling more than 10% of the CDC's voting membership; and
- have a board of directors which meet specified requirements, such as being chosen from the membership by the members and representing at least three of the four membership groups.[30]

If approved by the SBA, newly certified CDCs are on probation for two years. At the end of this time, the CDC must petition for either permanent CDC status or a single, one-year extension of probation. There are about 260 CDCs actively participating in the program.[31]

Lender Operating Requirements

The CDC's board of directors is allowed to establish a loan committee composed of members of the CDC who may or may not be on its board of directors. The loan committee reports to the board, and must meet specified requirements, such as having at least one member with commercial lending experience acceptable to the SBA, having all of its members live or work in the area of operations of the state where the 504/CDC project they are voting on is located, allowing CDC staff to serve on the committee, and requiring a quorum of at least five committee members authorized to vote in order to hold a meeting.[32] In addition, multi-state CDCs are required to have a separate loan committee "for each state into which the CDC expands."[33]

The SBA also has a number of requirements concerning CDC staff, such as requiring CDCs to "have qualified full-time professional staff to market, package, process, close and service loans" and "directly employ full-time professional management," typically including an executive director (or the equivalent) to manage daily operations.[34]

CDCs are also required to operate "in accordance with all SBA loan program requirements" and provide the SBA "current and accurate information about all certification and operational requirements."[35] CDCs with 504/CDC loan portfolio balances of $20 million or more are required to submit financial statements audited in accordance with Generally Accepted Accounting Principles (GAAP) by an independent Certified Public Accountant (CPA). CDCs with 504/CDC loan portfolio balances of less than $20 million must, at a minimum, submit a review of their loan portfolio balances by an independent CPA or independent accountant in accordance with GAAP. The auditor's opinion must state that the financial statements are in conformity with GAAP.[36]

Lender Program Requirements

The Application Process

CDCs must analyze each application in a commercially reasonable manner, consistent with prudent lending standards. The CDC's analysis must include

- a financial analysis of the applicant's pro forma balance sheet. The pro forma balance sheet must reflect the loan proceeds, use of the loan proceeds, and any other adjustments such as required equity injection or stand-by debt;
- a financial analysis of repayment ability based on historical income statements, tax returns (if an existing business) and projections, including the reasonableness of the supporting assumptions;
- a ratio analysis of the financial statements including comments on any trends and a comparison with industry averages;
- a discussion of the owners' and managers' relevant experience in the type of business, as well as their personal credit histories;
- an analysis of collateral adequacy, including an evaluation of the collateral and lien position offered as well as the liquidation value;
- a discussion of the applicant's credit experience, including a review of business credit reports and any experience the CDC may have with the applicant; and
- other relevant information (e.g., if the application involves a franchise and the success of the franchise).[37]

Lenders submit this information, using required SBA forms, to the Sacramento, CA, Loan Processing Center. The SBA's goal is to process all 504/CDC regular loans within six business days and all loans submitted by members of the Accredited Lender Program (ALP) within three business days.[38]

Accredited Lender Program Status

In 1991, the SBA established the Accredited Lenders Program (ALP) on a pilot basis to provide CDCs "which have developed a good partnership with their SBA field office in promoting local economic development and have demonstrated a good track record in the submission of documentation needed for making and servicing of sound loans" an expedited process for approving loan applications and servicing actions.[39] P.L. 103-403, the Small

Business Administration Reauthorization and Amendments Act of 1994, authorized the SBA to establish the ALP on a permanent basis.

CDCs may apply to the SBA for ALP status. Selection is based on several factors, including the CDC's experience as a CDC, the number of 504/CDC loans approved, the size of their portfolio, their record of compliance with SBA loan program requirements, and their record of cooperation with all SBA offices.[40] The SBA is able to process loan requests from ALP-CDCs more quickly than from regular CDCs because it relies on their credit analysis when making the decision to guarantee the debenture. About one-third of CDCs have ALP status and ALP CDCs approve about two-thirds of total 504/CDC loan amounts each year.[41]

Premier Certified Lenders Program Status

P.L. 103-403, the Small Business Administration Reauthorization and Amendments Act of 1994, authorized the SBA's Premier Certified Lenders Program (PCLP) on a pilot basis through October 1, 1997. The program's authorization was later extended through October 1, 2002, and given permanent statutory authorization by P.L. 106-554, the Consolidated Appropriations Act, 2001 (§1: H.R. 5667, the Small Business Reauthorization Act of 2000).[42]

ALP-CDCs must apply to the SBA for PCLP status. CDCs provided PCLP status have increased authority to process, close, service and liquidate 504/CDC loans. The loans are subject to the same terms and conditions as other 504/CDC loans, but the SBA delegates to the PCLP-CDC all loan approval decisions, except eligibility. Selection is based on several factors, including all of the factors used to assess ALP status plus evidence that the CDC is "in compliance with its Loan Loss Reserve Fund (LLRF) requirements [described below], has established a PCLP processing goal of 50%, and has a demonstrated ability to process, close, service and liquidate 504 and/or PCLP loans."[43]

PCLP-CDCs are required to establish and maintain a LLRF for its financings under the program. The LLRF is used to reimburse the SBA for 10% of any loss sustained by the SBA resulting from a default in the payment of principal or interest on a PCLP debenture. Each LLRF must equal 1% of the original principal amount of each PCLP debenture.[44]

About one out of every 14 CDCs have PCLP status.[45] In recent years, the number and amount of 504/CDC loans made through the PCLP program has declined. In FY2009, PCLP CDCs approved 441 504/CDC loans amounting to $238.0 million. Those figures declined to 129 504/CDC loans amounting to $69.8 million in FY2010, 37 504/CDC loans amounting to $16.1 million in FY2011, and 23 504/CDC loans amounting to $8.6 million in FY2012.[46]

Real Estate Appraisals

As part of its analysis of each application, CDCs are required to have an independent appraisal conducted of the real estate if the estimated value of the project property is greater than $250,000, or $250,000 or less "if such appraisal is necessary for appropriate evaluation of creditworthiness."[47] The appraiser must have no appearance of a conflict of interest and be either state-licensed or state-certified. When the project property's estimated value is over $1 million, the appraiser must be state-certified.[48]

Closing

The CDC closes the loan in time to meet a specific debenture funding date. At the time of closing, the project must be complete (except funds put into a construction escrow account to complete a minor portion of the project). The SBA's district counsel reviews the closing package and notifies the CSA (currently Colson Services Corporation) and the CDC via e-mail if the loan is approved for debenture funding. If the loan is approved, the CDC forwards specified documents needed for the debenture funding directly to the CSA using a transmittal letter or spreadsheet. Because the 504/CDC program provides permanent or "take-out" financing, an interim lender (either the third party lender or another lender) typically provides financing to cover the period between SBA approval of the project and the debenture sale. Proceeds from the debenture sale are used to repay the interim lender for the amount of the project costs that it advanced on an interim basis.[49]

Loan Guaranty and Servicing Fees

Borrowers are currently charged fees amounting to about 3.5% of the net debenture proceeds plus annual servicing and guaranty fees of about 1.5% of the unpaid debenture balance. Some of these fees are charged by the SBA to the CDC and others are charged by the CDC directly to the borrower.

SBA Fees
The SBA is authorized to charge CDCs five fees: a guaranty fee, servicing fee, funding fee, development company fee, and participation fee.

Guaranty Fee
The SBA is authorized to charge CDCs a one time, up-front guaranty fee of 0.5% of the debenture.[50] The SBA elected not to charge this fee in FY2009, FY2010, and FY2011. The SBA is charging this fee in FY2012.[51]

Servicing Fee
The SBA is authorized to charge CDCs an ongoing, annual servicing fee that is adjusted annually based on the date the loan was approved. By statute, the fee is the lesser of the amount necessary to cover the estimated cost of purchasing and guaranteeing debentures under the 504/CDC program or 0.9375% of the unpaid principal balance of the loan.[52] The SBA's annual servicing fee for FY2012 is the maximum fee permitted under law — 0.9375% of the unpaid principal balance.[53]

Funding Fee
The SBA charges CDCs a funding fee, not to exceed 0.25% of the debenture, to cover costs incurred by the trustee, fiscal agent, and transfer agent.[54]

Development Company Fee
For SBA loans approved after September 30, 1996, the SBA charges CDCs an annual development company fee of 0.125% of the debenture's outstanding principal balance. The fee must be paid from the servicing fees collected by the CDC and cannot be paid from any additional fees imposed on the borrower.[55]

Participation Fee

The SBA charges third-party lenders a one time participation fee of 0.5% of the senior mortgage loan if in a senior lien position to the SBA and the loan was approved after September 30, 1996.[56] The fee may be paid by the third party lender, CDC, or borrower.

CDC Fees

CDCs are allowed to charge borrowers a processing (or packaging) fee, closing fee, servicing fee, late fee, assumption fee, Central Servicing Agent (CSA) fee, other agent fees, and an underwriters' fee.

Processing (or Packaging) Fee

The CDC is allowed to charge borrowers a processing (or packaging) fee of up to 1.5% of the net debenture proceeds. Two-thirds of this fee is considered earned and may be collected by the CDC when the SBA issues an "Authorization for the Debenture." The portion of the processing fee paid by the borrower may be reimbursed from the debenture proceeds.[57]

Closing Fee

The CDC is also allowed to charge "a reasonable closing fee sufficient to reimburse it for the expenses of its in-house or outside legal counsel, and other miscellaneous closing costs."[58] Up to $2,500 in closing costs may be financed out of the debenture proceeds.[59]

Servicing Fee

CDCs can also charge a monthly servicing fee of at least 0.625% per annum and no more than 2% per annum on the unpaid balance of the loan as determined at five-year anniversary intervals. A servicing fee greater than 1.5% for rural areas and 1% elsewhere requires the SBA's prior written approval, based on evidence of substantial need. The servicing fee may be paid only from loan payments received. The fees may be accrued without interest and collected from the CSA when the payments are made. CSAs are entities that receive and disburse funds among the various parties involved in 504/CDC financing under a master servicing agent agreement with the SBA.[60]

Late Fee and Assumption Fee

Loan payments received after the 15th of each month may be subject to a late payment fee of 5% of the late payment or $100, whichever is greater. Late fees will be collected by the CSA on behalf of the CDC. Also, with the SBA's written approval, CDCs may charge an assumption fee not to exceed 1% of the outstanding principal balance of the loan being assumed.[61]

Central Servicing Agent Fee

CSAs are allowed to charge an initiation fee on each loan and an ongoing monthly servicing fee of 0.1% under the terms of the master servicing agreement (with the CSA receiving three sixty-fourths of the servicing fee and the remainder going to the SBA). Also, "agent fees and charges necessary to market and service debentures and certificates may be assessed to the borrower or the investor."[62] CDCs must review the agent's services and related fees "to determine if the fees are necessary and reasonable when there is an indication from a third party that an agent's fees might be excessive, or when an applicant complains about the fees charged by an agent."[63] In cases where fees appear to be unreasonable, CDCs "should contact" the SBA which, after conducting an investigation, can "reduce the fee to an amount SBA deems reasonable, refund any sum in excess of that amount to the applicant, and refrain from charging or collecting from the applicant any funds in excess of the amount SBA deems reasonable."[64]

Underwriters' Fee

Borrowers are also charged an up front underwriters' fee of 0.4% for 20-year loans and 0.375% for 10-year loans. The underwriters' fee is paid by the borrower to the underwriter.[65] As mentioned previously, underwriters are approved by the SBA to form debenture pools and arrange for the sale of certificates.

Fee Subsidies

As mentioned previously, the SBA was provided more than $1.1 billion in additional funding in 2009 and 2010 to subsidize the 504/CDC program's third party participation fee and CDC processing fee, subsidize the SBA's 7(a) program's guaranty fee, and increase the 7(a) program's maximum loan guaranty percentage from up to 85% of loans of $150,000 or less and up to 75% of loans exceeding $150,000 to 90% for all standard 7(a) loans.[66] The last extension, P.L. 111-322, the Continuing Appropriations and Surface Transportation Extensions Act, 2011, authorized the SBA to continue the fee subsidies and the 7(a) program's 90% maximum loan guaranty percentage through March 4, 2011, or until funding provided by the Small Business Jobs Act of 2010 for this purpose was exhausted (which occurred on January 3, 2011).[67]

The Obama Administration argued that additional funding for the SBA's loan guaranty programs, including the 504/CDC program's fee subsidies, improved the small business lending environment, increased both the number and amount of SBA guaranteed loans, and supported "the retention and creation of hundreds of thousands of jobs."[68] Critics argued that small business tax reduction, reform of financial credit market regulation, and federal fiscal restraint are a better means to assist small business economic growth and job creation.[69]

PROGRAM STATISTICS

Loan Volume

The SBA generally uses the number and amount of loans approved each fiscal year, as opposed to the number and amount of loans disbursed, for making comparisons of lending volume among its loan guaranty programs. Although loan disbursement data can be useful, loan disbursements in one fiscal year typically include significant amounts approved in previous fiscal years. For example, in FY2011, 67.0% of 504/CDC loan disbursements were from loans approved prior to FY2011.[70]

As shown in *Table 2*, the number and amount of 504/CDC loans approved by the SBA declined in FY2008 and FY2009. The most likely causes for the decline were decreased small business demand for capital during the recession; difficulties in secondary credit markets, especially from October 2008 to February 2009; and a tightening of small business credit

Small Business Administration 504/CDC Loan Guaranty Program 101

lending standards. The number and amount of 504/CDC loans increased during FY2010 and FY2011, and reached pre-recession levels in FY2012.

The SBA attributed the increased number and amount of 504/CDC loans approved in FY2010 and FY2011 to the continuation of 504/CDC fee subsidies, which were in place through most of FY2010 and the first quarter of FY2011.[71]

Table 2. 504/CDC Loans and Amounts Approved, FY2006 - FY2012
($ amounts in billions)

Fiscal Year	Number of Loans Approved	Amount of the Debentures Approved
2006	9,943	$5.7
2007	10,669	$6.3
2008	8,883	$5.3
2009	6,608	$3.8
2010	7,833	$4.4
2011	7,983	$4.8
2012	9,471	$6.7

Source: U.S. Small Business Administration, "SBA Lending Report for Major Programs, Fiscal Year 2010," October 4, 2010, at http://archive.sba.gov/idc/ groups/public/documents/sba_homepage/ serv_fa_lending_major_progs.pdf; and U.S. Small Business Administration, "SBA Lending Statistics for Major Programs (as of 9/30/2012)," at http://www.sba.gov/about-sba-info/317721.

Note: Based on previous experience, the number of loans approved is typically about 4% to 5% higher than the actual number of loans issued (e.g., some borrowers decide not to accept the loan or there is a change in ownership).

Loss Rate and Appropriations for Subsidy Costs

Since the program's inception in FY1958 through FY2008, the SBA experienced a 2.36% loss rate (ratio of actual losses to disbursements) on its 504/CDC business loans. The loss rate for 504/CDC guaranteed loans from FY1958 through FY2008 was 1.9%, and 26.9% for direct loans (last issued in FY1988).[72]

In recent years, the loss rate for 504/CDC guaranteed loans has increased. In FY2010, the loss rate was 4.2%. In FY2011, the loss rate was 6.0%.[73]

One of the SBA's goals is to achieve a zero subsidy rate for its loan guaranty programs. A zero subsidy rate means that the SBA's loan guaranty programs do not require annual appropriations of budget authority for the issuance of new loan guarantees. From 2005 to 2009, the SBA did not request appropriations to subsidize the cost of any of its loan guaranty programs, including the 504/CDC program. However, in recent years, loan guaranty fees and loan liquidation recoveries, especially in the 7(a) loan guaranty program, have not generated enough revenue to cover loan losses, resulting in the need for additional appropriations to account for the shortfall.

In FY2010 and FY2011, the SBA was provided $80.0 million to subsidize the cost of SBA guaranteed loans. In FY2012, the SBA was provided $207.1 million for that purpose, and P.L. 112-175, the Continuing Appropriations Resolution, 2013 (which provides appropriations through March 27, 2013), provided a projected $333.6 billion for the cost of

SBA loan guaranty program subsidies for FY2013. The SBA reports that most of the agency's loan losses have occurred in the SBA's 7(a) loan guaranty program. For example, there were no subsidy costs for the 504/CDC program in FY2011. However, the SBA anticipates subsidy costs of about $67.7 million for the 504/CDC program in FY2012, and $113.0 million in FY2013.[74]

Use of Proceeds and Borrower Satisfaction

In 2008, the Urban Institute released the results of a SBA-commissioned study of the SBA's loan guaranty programs. As part of its analysis, the Urban Institute surveyed a random sample of SBA loan guaranty borrowers. The survey indicated that borrowers used 504/CDC loan proceeds to

- build a new building (36%),
- purchase a new building (33%),
- purchase new land (16%),
- purchase or install new equipment (15%),
- acquire original business (8%),
- expand or renovate current building (7%),
- other (7%),
- improve land (6%),
- finance working capital (4%),
- refinance existing debt (3%), or
- hire additional staff (2%).[75]

The Urban Institute also reported that two-thirds the 504/CDC borrowers responding to their survey rated their overall satisfaction with their loan and loan terms as either excellent (21%) or good (45%). About one out of every four borrowers (23%) rated their overall satisfaction with their loan and loan terms as fair, 8% rated their overall satisfaction as poor, and 4% reported that they don't know or did not respond.[76]

In addition, 87% of the survey's respondents reported that the 504/CDC loan was either very important (53%) or somewhat important (34%) to their business success (4% reported somewhat unimportant, 4% reported very unimportant, and 6% reported that they don't know or did not respond).[77]

Borrower Demographics

The Urban Institute found that about 9.9% of private sector small business loans are issued to minority-owned small businesses and about 16% of those loans are issued to women-owned businesses.[78]

In FY2012, 19.4% of 504/CDC loan recipients were minority-owned businesses (11.9% Asian, 5.9% Hispanic, 1.4% African American, and 0.2% Native American) and 14.3% were women-owned businesses.[79]

Based on its comparative analysis of private sector small business loans and the SBA's loan guaranty programs, the Urban Institute concluded

> Overall, loans under the 7(a) and 504 programs were more likely to be made to minority-owned, women-owned, and start-up businesses (firms that have historically faced capital gaps) as compared to conventional small business loans. Moreover, the average amounts for loans made under the 7(a) and 504 programs to these types of firms were substantially greater than conventional small business loans to such firms. These findings suggest that the 7(a) and 504 programs are being used by lenders in a manner that is consistent with SBA's objective of making credit available to firms that face a capital opportunity gap.[80]

CONGRESSIONAL ISSUES

Fee Subsidies and the 7(a) Program's 90% Maximum Loan Guaranty Percentage

Congress included provisions in ARRA to encourage both lenders and small businesses to use the SBA's loan guaranty programs. For example, ARRA provided an additional $730 million for SBA programs.

As mentioned previously, included in that amount was $375 million to subsidize the 504/CDC program's third party participation fee and CDC processing fee, subsidize the SBA's 7(a) program's guaranty fee, and increase the 7(a) program's maximum loan guaranty percentage from up to 85% of loans of $150,000 or less and up to 75% of loans exceeding $150,000 to 90% for all standard 7(a) loans.[81]

ARRA's funding for the fee subsidies and 7(a) program's 90% loan guaranty percentage was exhausted on November 23, 2009. Congress subsequently approved an additional $305 million to extend the fee reductions and the 90% loan guaranty percentage through May 31, 2010.[82] P.L. 111-240, the Small Business Jobs Act of 2010, provided $505 million (plus an additional $5 million for related administrative expenses) to continue the fee subsidies and the 7(a) program's 90% loan guaranty percentage through December 31, 2010. P.L. 111-322, the Continuing Appropriations and Surface Transportation Extensions Act, 2011, authorized the SBA to continue the fee subsidies and the 90% loan guaranty percentage through March 4, 2011, or until the funding provided by the Small Business Jobs Act of 2010 for these purposes was exhausted (which occurred on January 3, 2011).[83]

The Obama Administration argued that additional funding for the SBA's loan guaranty programs, including the 504/CDC program, improved the small business lending environment, increased both the number and amount of SBA guaranteed loans, and supported "the retention and creation of hundreds of thousands of jobs."[84]

Critics argued that small business tax reduction, reform of financial credit market regulation, and federal fiscal restraint are a better means to assist small business economic growth and job creation.[85]

Program Administration

The SBA's Office of Inspector General (OIG) and the U.S. Government Accountability Office (GAO) have independently reviewed the administration of SBA's loan guaranty programs.

Both agencies have reported deficiencies which they argued needed to be addressed, including issues involving the oversight of 504/CDC lenders.

On March 23, 2010, the SBA's OIG released the results of an audit of "25 of 100 statistically selected CDC/504 loans approved under Premier Certified Lender (PCL) authority that were disbursed during fiscal year (FY) 2008."[86] The loans "had been approved by 3 of the most active of the 24 PCLs" operating in 2008.[87]

The audit was initiated "based on concerns that PCLs were engaging in risky underwriting practices and that five PCLs were paying their executives excessive compensation."[88] The OIG determined that

> PCLs may not have used prudent practices in approving and disbursing 68% of the sampled loans, totaling nearly $8.9 million, due to poor loan underwriting, and eligibility or loan closing issues. Specifically, 40% of the loans had faulty underwriting repayment analyses, and 52% of the loans had eligibility and/or loan closing issues.... Projecting our sample results to the universe of CDC/504 loans disbursed in 2008 by these three PCLs, we estimate with 90% confidence that at least 572 loans, totaling nearly $254.9 million in CDC/504 loan proceeds, had weaknesses in the underwriting process, eligibility determinations or loan closing. Of this amount, we estimate that a minimum of 183 loans, totaling $56.4 million or more, were made to borrowers based on faulty repayment analyses. We also estimate that lenders disbursed $209 million or more to borrowers who had eligibility and/or loan closing issues.[89]

In terms of dollars paid for CDC executive compensation, the OIG found that

> 4 of the 5 CDCs reviewed were among the top 10 highest for executive compensation.... In terms of percentage of gross receipts spent on executive compensation, 3 of the 5 questioned CDCs ranked among the top 10 highest of the 56 CDCs that had gross receipts over $1 million.[90]

The OIG made several recommendations to address these issues, including changing the SBA's Standard Operating Procedures (SOP) to require lenders to use

> (1) the actual cash flow method to determine borrower repayment ability for businesses using accrual accounting, (2) historical salary levels to estimate salaries of the borrower's officers, and (3) historical sales data to make sales projections.[91]

It also recommended that the SBA develop a process "to ensure that corrective actions are taken in response to the Agency's onsite reviews to ensure these conditions do not continue, and/or guidance for these reviews should be modified, as appropriate, to ensure that reviewers properly assess lender determination of borrower repayment ability and eligibility."[92]

The OIG reported that the SBA

> disagreed that SOP 50 10 should be revised to strengthen lender repayment analyses by requiring the use of the actual cash flow method and historical salary and sales data. The Agency also did not believe an additional process was needed to ensure that corrective actions are taken to improve lender performance, but acknowledged that better use of onsite review results are needed to make more informed lender decisions and programmatic determinations.[93]

In 2009, GAO released an analysis of the SBA's oversight of the lending and risk management activities of lenders that extend 7(a) and 504/CDC loans to small businesses. GAO recommended that the SBA strengthen its oversight of these lenders. GAO argued that although the SBA's "lender risk rating system has enabled the agency to conduct some off-site monitoring of lenders, the agency does not use the system to target lenders for on-site reviews or to inform the scope of the reviews."[94] It also noted that

> the SBA targets for review those lenders with the largest SBA-guaranteed loan portfolios. As a result of this approach, 97% of the lenders that SBA's risk rating system identified as high risk in 2008 were not reviewed. Further, GAO found that the scope of the on-site reviews that SBA performs is not informed by the lenders' risk ratings, and the reviews do not include an assessment of lenders' credit decisions.[95]

GAO argued that although the SBA "has made improvements to its off-site monitoring of lenders, the agency will not be able to substantially improve its lender oversight efforts unless it improves its on-site review process."[96]

As mentioned previously, in recent years, both the number and amount of 504/CDC loans made through the PCL program has declined. In FY2009, PCLP CDCs approved 441 504/CDC loans amounting to $238.0 million. Those figures declined to 129 504/CDC loans amounting to $69.8 million in FY2010, 37 504/CDC loans amounting to $16.1 million in FY2011, and 23 504/CDC loans amounting to $8.6 million in FY2012.[97]

LEGISLATIVE ACTIVITY DURING THE 111TH CONGRESS

Congress authorized several changes to the 504/CDC program during the 111th Congress in an effort to increase the number, and amount, of 504/CDC loans, including provisions contained in ARRA and the Small Business Jobs Act of 2010. Congress has not approved any changes to the program during the 112th Congress.

The Obama Administration's Proposals

The Obama Administration supported congressional efforts to temporarily subsidize fees for the 7(a) and 504/CDC loan guaranty programs and to increase the 7(a) program's loan guaranty percentage from up to 85% of loans of $150,000 or less and up to 75% of loans exceeding $150,000 to 90%. As mentioned previously, the latest extension of the fee subsidies and 7(a) program's 90% maximum loan guaranty percentage was authorized by the

Continuing Appropriations and Surface Transportation Extensions Act, 2011. The act authorized the SBA to continue the fee subsidies and the 7(a) program's 90% maximum loan guaranty percentage through March 4, 2011, or until the funding provided by the Small Business Jobs Act of 2010 for these purposes was exhausted (which occurred on January 3, 2011).[98]

In an effort to make the SBA's loan guaranty programs more attractive to small businesses, the Obama Administration also proposed the following modifications to several SBA programs, including the 504/CDC program:

- increase the maximum loan size for the 504/CDC program from $2 million to $5 million for regular projects and from $4 million to $5.5 million for manufacturing projects;
- temporarily allow in FY2010 and FY2011, with an option to extend into FY2012, the refinancing of owner-occupied commercial real estate loans within one year of maturity under the 504/CDC program;
- increase the maximum loan size for standard 7(a) loans from $2 million to $5 million;
- increase the maximum loan size for microloans to small business concerns from $35,000 to $50,000;
- increase the maximum loan limits for lenders in their first year of participation in the Microloan program, from $750,000 to $1 million, and from $3.5 million to $5 million in the subsequent years; and
- temporarily increase the cap on SBAExpress loans from $350,000 to $1 million.[99]

H.R. 3854, the Small Business Financing and Investment Act of 2009

H.R. 3854 would have authorized several new SBA programs and change several existing SBA programs, including the 504/CDC program, in an effort to enhance job creation by increasing the availability of credit to small businesses. The bill was passed by the House, 389-32, on October 29, 2009. The Senate did not take action on the bill.[100]

It would have

- increased the maximum loan size for 504/CDC loans from $1.5 million to $3 million for regular projects, from $2 million to $4 million for projects located in a low-income community, from $4 million to $8 million for manufacturers, and for up to $10 million for projects that constitute "a major source of employment" as determined by the Administration;
- extended ARRA's fee reductions and loan modifications through September 30, 2011;
- increased the maximum loan size for 7(a) loans from $2 million to $3 million;
- extended, with modifications, ARRA's America's Recovery Capital Loan Program (ARC), which temporarily provided small businesses loan assistance for debt relief, through the end of FY2011;[101] and

- provided a 100% loan guaranty for small business concerns owned and controlled by veterans, and expanded and made permanent the SBA's secondary market lending authority.[102]

The bill would have also created a temporary SBA direct lending program following enactment that would have been available to creditworthy small business borrowers that were unable to find credit elsewhere.[103]

S. 2869, the Small Business Job Creation and Access to Capital Act of 2009

S. 2869 was ordered to be reported by the Senate Committee on Small Business and Entrepreneurship on December 10, 2009. The Senate did not take further action on the bill, but several of its provisions were later included in the Small Business Jobs Act of 2010. It would have

- increased the maximum loan size for the 504/CDC loans from $1.5 million to $5 million for regular projects, from $2 million to $5 million for projects meeting one of the program's specified public policy goals, and from $4 million to $5.5 million for manufacturers;
- allowed 504/CDC loans to be used to refinance up to $4 billion in short-term commercial real estate debt each fiscal year for two years after enactment into long-term fixed rate loans;
- authorized the SBA to establish an alternative size standard for the 7(a) and 504/CDC programs that uses maximum tangible net worth and average net income as an alternative to the use of industry standards;
- extended ARRA's fee reductions and loan modifications through December 31, 2010;
- increased the maximum loan size for 7(a) loans from $2 million to $5 million; and
- increased the maximum loan size for the Microloan program from $35,000 to $50,000.[104]

P.L. 111-240, the Small Business Jobs Act of 2010

P.L. 111-240 was signed into law by President Obama on September 27, 2010. The act authorizes the Secretary of the Treasury to establish a $30 billion Small Business Lending Fund (SBLF) to encourage community banks to provide small business loans ($4 billion was issued), a $1.5 billion State Small Business Credit Initiative to provide funding to participating states with small business capital access programs, and about $12 billion in tax relief for small businesses.[105] It also contains revenue raising provisions to offset the act's cost, a number of changes to the SBA's loan and contracting programs, and establishes an alternative SBA small business eligibility size standard.[106]

As mentioned previously, the act also increased the 504/CDC program's loan limits from $1.5 million to $5 million for regular 504/CDC loans; from $2 million to $5 million if the loan proceeds are directed toward one or more of the program's specified public policy goals; from $4 million to $5.5 million for small manufacturers; from $4 million to $5.5 million for projects that reduce the borrower's energy consumption by at least 10%; and from $4 million to $5.5 million for projects for plant, equipment, and process upgrades of renewable energy sources, such as the small-scale production of energy for individual buildings or communities consumption (commonly known as micropower), or renewable fuel producers, including biodiesel and ethanol producers.[107]

P.L. 111-240 also provided $505 million (plus an additional $5 million for related administrative expenses) to continue the fee subsidies for the 7(a) and 504/CDC loan guaranty programs and the temporary increase in the 7(a) program's loan guaranty percentage from up to 85% of loans of $150,000 or less and up to 75% of loans exceeding $150,000 to 90% for all standard 7(a) loans from September 27, 2010, through December 31, 2010. The fee subsidies and 90% loan guaranty percentage had expired on May 31, 2010.

In addition, the act temporarily allowed, for two years from the date of enactment, 504/CDC loans to be used to refinance projects not involving expansions as long as the financing did not exceed 90% of the value of the collateral for the financing, "except that, if the appraised value of the eligible fixed assets serving as collateral for the financing is less than the amount equal to 125% of the amount of the financing, the borrower may provide additional cash or other collateral to eliminate any deficiency."[108] The refinancing could be used only for commercial indebtedness incurred not less than two years before the date of the application for assistance and only for eligible fixed assets (to acquire land, buildings, or equipment, or to construct a building). The refinancing could not be used for indebtedness subject to a federal guarantee, and it had to be collateralized by eligible fixed assets. The borrower also had to be current on all payments due on the existing debt for not less than one year before the date of the application. The act authorized the SBA to issue up to $7.5 billion in refinancing annually, for two fiscal years.[109] This temporary refinancing provision expired on September 27, 2012.

Finally, the act required the SBA to establish an alternative size standard for the 504/CDC and 7(a) loan programs that uses maximum tangible net worth and average net income as an alternative to the use of industry size standards.[110] At the time of passage, the 7(a) program used industry specific size standards and the 504/CDC program used maximum net worth of $8.5 million and maximum average net income of $3 million to determine program eligibility. The act establishes on an interim basis "until the date on which the alternative size standard [is] established" the following alternative size standard for both the 504/CDC and 7(a) programs: the business qualifies as small if it does not have a tangible net worth in excess of $15 million and does not have an average net income after federal taxes (excluding any carry-over losses) in excess of $5 million for two full fiscal years before the date of application.[111]

LEGISLATIVE ACTIVITY DURING THE 112ᵀᴴ CONGRESS

As mentioned previously, Congress has not approved any changes to the 504/CDC program during the 112th Congress. However, legislation has been introduced during the 112th Congress that would affect the 504/CDC program.

H.R. 2950, the Small Business Administration 504 Loan Refinancing Extension Act of 2011, was introduced on September 15, 2011, and referred to the House Committee on Small Business. The bill would allow 504/CDC loans to be used to refinance projects not involving expansions as long as the financing does not exceed 90% of the value of the collateral for the financing for an additional year beyond the two years from the date of enactment which was authorized by the Small Business Jobs Act of 2010.

S.Amdt. 1833, the INVEST in America Act of 2012—an amendment in the nature of a substitute for H.R. 3606, the Jumpstart Our Business Startups Act—was introduced on March 15, 2012. It would have allowed 504/CDC loans to be used to refinance projects not involving expansions for an additional year beyond the two years from the date of enactment authorized by the Small Business Jobs Act of 2010.[112] The amendment was ruled non-germane by the chair on March 21, 2012, and was not included in the final version of the bill which was approved by the Senate the following day.[113]

S. 3572, the Restoring Tax and Regulatory Certainty to Small Businesses Act of 2012, was introduced on September 19, 2012, and referred to the Senate Committee on Small Business and Entrepreneurship and the Senate Committee on Finance. It would, among other provisions, allow 504/CDC loans to be used to refinance projects not involving expansions for an additional year and a half beyond the two years from the date of enactment authorized by the Small Business Jobs Act of 2010.

S. 1828, a bill to increase small business lending, and for other purposes, was introduced on November 8, 2011, and referred to the Senate Committee on Small Business and Entrepreneurship. The bill would reinstate for a year following the date of its enactment the fee subsidies for the 504/CDC and 7(a) loan guaranty programs and the 90% loan guaranty percentage for the 7(a) program which were originally funded by ARRA.

CONCLUSION

During the 111th Congress, congressional debate concerning proposed changes to the SBA's loan guaranty programs, including the 504/CDC program, centered on the likely impact the changes would have on small business access to capital, job retention, and job creation. As a general proposition, some, including the chairs of the House and Senate Committees on Small Business and President Obama, argued that economic conditions made it imperative that the SBA be provided additional resources to assist small businesses in acquiring capital necessary to start, continue, or expand operations and create jobs.[114] Others worried about the long-term adverse economic effects of spending programs that increase the federal deficit. They advocated business tax reduction, reform of financial credit market regulation, and federal fiscal restraint as the best means to assist small business economic growth and job creation.[115]

In terms of specific program changes, continuing the 504/CDC program's temporary fee subsidies, increasing its loan limits, temporarily expanding its refinancing options, and requiring the SBA to establish an alterative size standard were designed to achieve the same goal: to enhance job creation and retention by increasing the ability of 504/CDC borrowers to obtain credit at affordable rates. For example, the Obama Administration argued that increasing the maximum loan limits for the 504/CDC, 7(a), Microloan, and SBAExpress programs will allow the SBA to "support larger projects" which will "allow the SBA to help America's small businesses drive long-term economic growth and the creation of jobs in communities across the country."[116] The Administration also argued that increasing the maximum loan limits for these programs will be "budget neutral" over the long run and "help improve the availability of smaller loans."[117]

Critics argued that increasing these loan limits might increase the risk of defaults and result in higher guaranty fees or the need to provide the SBA additional funding, especially for the SBAExpress program, which had experienced somewhat higher losses than other SBA loan guaranty programs.[118] Others advocated a more modest increase in the maximum loan limits to ensure that the programs focus on start-ups and early-stage small firms, "businesses that have historically encountered the greatest difficulties in accessing credit" and "avoids making small borrowers carry a disproportionate share of the risk associated with larger loans."[119]

During the 112th Congress, Congress focused on the SBA's administration of the program changes enacted during the 111th Congress, the impact of these changes on the SBA's lending, and ways to address and minimize increased costs associated with loan losses. Although there is widespread congressional support for providing assistance to small businesses, federal fiscal constraints may impede efforts to expand the 504/CDC program in the near future, especially given that the program is expected to continue to require federal assistance to cover the cost of loan losses. In addition, unless there is a change in law, the SBA faces a potential loss of about $75 million in federal funding in January 2013 (including $29 million of $359 million in the SBA's business loans program account) as part of the sequestration process under P.L. 112-25, the Budget Control Act of 2011.[120]

Given existing fiscal constraints, it is likely that Congress will, in the coming months, continue to focus on the SBA's administration of the 504/CDC program to ensure that the program is as efficient as possible, request information concerning the program's efficacy in job retention and creation, and explore ways to address and minimize costs associated with 504/CDC loan losses.

End Notes

[1] U.S. Small Business Administration, Fiscal Year 2010 Congressional Budget Justification, p. 30.

[2] The 504/CDC program was preceded by a 501 state development company program (1958-1982), a 502 local development company program (1958-1995), and a 503/CDC program (1980-1986). The 504/CDC program started in 1986. There are a small number of for-profit CDCs that participated in these predecessor programs that have been grandfathered into the current 504/CDC program. See U.S. Small Business Administration, "SOP 50 10 5(E): Lender and Development Company Loan Programs," (effective June 1, 2012), p. 49, at http://www.sba.gov/sites/default/files/SOP%2050%2010%205(E)%20(5-16-2012)%20 clean.pdf.

[3] 13 C.F.R. §120.801. 504/CDC debentures are normally sold and proceeds disbursed on the Wednesday after the second Sunday of each month. See U.S. Small Business Administration, "SOP 50 10 5(E): Lender and Development Company Loan Programs," (effective June 1, 2012), p. 348, at http://www.sba.gov/sites/default/files/SOP%2050% 20 10%205(E)%20(5-16-2012)%20clean.pdf.

[4] U.S. Small Business Administration, "Monthly Purchase of 504 Debentures for Accelerated Loans," at http://archive.sba.gov/aboutsba/sbaprograms/elending/notices/BANK_ 5000_ 602_MONTHLY_ PURC_504. html.

[5] U.S. Small Business Administration, "SBA Lending Statistics for Major Programs (as of 9/30/2012)," at http://www.sba.gov/about-sba-info/317721.

[6] U.S. Government Accountability Office, Small Business Administration: 7(a) Loan Program Needs Additional Performance Measures, GAO-08-226T, November 1, 2007, pp. 3, 9-11, at http://www.gao.gov/new.items/d08226t.pdf; and Veronique de Rugy, Why the Small Business Administration's Loan Programs Should Be Abolished, American Enterprise Institute for Public Policy Research, AEI Working Paper #126, April 13, 2006, at http://www.aei.org/ docLib/20060414_wp126.pdf. Proponents of federal funding for the SBA's loan guarantee programs also argue that small business can promote competitive markets. See P.L. 83-163, §2(a), as amended; and 15 U.S.C. §631a.

[7] Federal Reserve Board, "Senior Loan Officer Opinion Survey on Bank Lending Practices," at http://www.federalreserve.gov/boarddocs/SnLoanSurvey/.

[8] The specified circumstances include the following: the amount of existing indebtedness does not exceed 50% of the project cost of the expansion; the proceeds of the indebtedness were used to acquire land, including the building situated thereon, to construct a building thereon, or to purchase equipment; the existing indebtedness is collateralized by fixed assets; the existing indebtedness was incurred for the benefit of a small business; the financing is used only for refinancing existing indebtedness or costs related to the project being financed; the refinancing provides a substantial benefit to the borrower; the borrower has been current on all payments due on the existing debt for not less than one year preceding the date of refinancing; and the financing provided will have better terms or rate of interest than the existing indebtedness. See P.L. 111-5, the American Recovery and Reinvestment Act of 2009, Section 504. Stimulus for Community Development Lending.

[9] The SBA considers the following as a limited or special purpose property: amusement parks; bowling alleys; car wash properties; cemeteries; clubhouses; cold storage facilities where more than 50% of total square footage is equipped for refrigeration; dormitories; farms, including dairy facilities; funeral homes with crematoriums; gas stations; golf courses; hospitals, surgery centers, urgent care centers and other health medical facilities; hotels and motels; marinas; mines; museums; nursing homes, including assisted living facilities; oil wells; quarries, including gravel pits; railroads; sanitary landfills; service centers (e.g., oil and lube, brake or transmission centers) with pits; sports arenas; swimming pools; tennis clubs; theaters; and wineries. See U.S. Small Business Administration, "SOP 50 10 5(E): Lender and Development Company Loan Programs" (effective June 1, 2012), p. 269, at http://www.sba.gov/sites/default/files/ SOP%2050%2010%205(E)%20(5-16-2012)% 20 clean.pdf.

[10] P.L. 111-240, the Small Business Jobs Act of 2010, requires the SBA to establish an alternative size standard for the 504/CDC and 7(a) loan programs that uses maximum tangible net worth and average net income as an alternative to the use of industry standards. At the time of passage, the 7(a) program used industry specific size standards and the 504/CDC program used maximum net worth of $8.5 million and maximum average net income of $3 million to determine program eligibility. The act establishes the following alternative size standard for both the 504/CDC and 7(a) programs on an interim basis: the business qualifies as small if it does not have a tangible net worth in excess of $15 million and does not have an average net income after federal taxes (excluding any carry-over losses) in excess of $5 million for two full fiscal years before the date of application. For further analysis concerning SBA size standards see CRS Report R40860, Small Business Size Standards: A Historical Analysis of Contemporary Issues, by Robert Jay Dilger.

[11] 13 C.F.R. §120.100; and 13 C.F.R. §120.101.

[12] 13 C.F.R. §120.110. Nineteen types of businesses are ineligible for 504/CDC loans. Also, an associate is an officer, director, owner of more than 20% of the equity, or key employee of the small business; any entity in which one or more individuals referred to above owns or controls at least 20% of the equity; and any individual or entity in control of or controlled by the small business, except a Small Business Investment Company licensed by the SBA. See 13 C.F.R. §120.10.

[13] 13 C.F.R. §120.150.

[14] U.S. Small Business Administration, "SOP 50 10 5(E): Lender and Development Company Loan Programs," (effective June 1, 2012), pp. 309-313, at http://www.sba.gov/sites/default/ files/SOP%2050%2010%205 (E)%20(5-16- 2012)%20clean.pdf. Expansion "includes any project that involves the acquisition, construction or improvement of land, building or equipment for use by the small business applicant." See Ibid., p. 309.

[15] Ibid., p. 305.

[16] A job opportunity is defined as a full time (or equivalent) permanent job created within two years of receipt of 504/CDC funds, or retained in the community because of a 504/CDC loan. See Ibid., pp. 56, 264, 305-307.

[17] 13 C.F.R. §120.862.

[18] P.L. 111-240, the Small Business Jobs Act of 2010, §1112. Maximum Loan Amounts Under 504 Program.

[19] 13 C.F.R. §120.933.

[20] U.S. Small Business Administration, "SOP 50 10 5(E): Lender and Development Company Loan Programs," (effective June 1, 2012), p. 332, at http://www.sba.gov/sites/default/files /SOP%2050%2010%205(E)%20(5-16- 2012)%20clean.pdf.

[21] 13 C.F.R. §120.921.

[22] 13 C.F.R. §120.932.

[23] Capital Certified Development Corporation, "504/CDC Program Interest Rates," Austin, TX, at https://www.capitalcdc.com/loan-programs/the-sba-504-program. The interest rate for March 2012 was 4.59%

[24] 13 C.F.R. §120.921; and U.S. Small Business Administration, "Reporting and Recordkeeping Requirements Under OMB Review," 77 Federal Register 59447, September 27, 2012.

[25] U.S. Small Business Administration, "SOP 50 10 5(E): Lender and Development Company Loan Programs," (effective June 1, 2012), p. 316, at http://www.sba.gov/sites/ default/files/SOP%2050%2010%205(E)%20(5-16- 2012)%20clean.pdf.

[26] 13 C.F.R. §120.934.

[27] U.S. Small Business Administration, "SOP 50 10 5(E): Lender and Development Company Loan Programs," (effective June 1, 2012), p. 180, at http://www.sba.gov/sites/ default/files/ SOP%2050%2010%205(E)%20(5-16- 2012)%20clean.pdf.

[28] Ibid., p. 49.

[29] A CDC can apply to be a multi-state CDC "provided the State the CDC seeks to expand into is contiguous to the State of the CDC's incorporation; the CDC demonstrates that its membership meets the requirements in 13 CFR §120.822 separately for its State of incorporation and for each additional State in which it seeks to operate as a Multi-State CDC; and the CDC has a loan committee meeting the requirements of 13 CFR §120.823." See ibid., p. 77.

[30] Ibid., pp. 49-51.

[31] U.S. Small Business Administration, "CDC/504 Loan Program," at http://www.sba.gov/ content/cdc504-loan-program; and National Association of Development Companies, "504 Loan Approval Statistics," at http://www.nadco.org/i4a/pages/index.cfm?pageid=3558.

32 U.S. Small Business Administration, "SOP 50 10 5(E): Lender and Development Company Loan Programs," (effective June 1, 2012), pp. 50, 51, at http://www.sba.gov/sites/ default/files/SOP%2050% 2010%205 (E)%20(5-16- 2012)%20clean.pdf.

33 Ibid., p. 51.

[34] Ibid.

[35] Ibid., p. 53.

[36] Ibid.

[37] Ibid., pp. 180, 181.

[38] Ibid., pp. 328, 329.

[39] U.S. Small Business Administration, "Loans to State and Local Development Companies Accredited Lenders Program for Certified Development Companies," 60 Federal Register 20391, April 26, 1995.

[40] U.S. Small Business Administration, "SOP 50 10 5(E): Lender and Development Company Loan Programs," (effective June 1, 2012), pp. 68, 69, at http://www.sba.gov/sites/ default/files/SOP%2050%2010%205(E)% 20(5-16- 2012)%20clean.pdf.

[41] U.S. Small Business Administration, Office of Congressional and Legislative Affairs, correspondence with the author, April 7, 2010; and U.S. Small Business Administration, Office of Congressional and Legislative Affairs, correspondence with the author, September 17, 2012.

[42] P.L. 105-135, the Small Business Reauthorization Act of 1997, extended the program's authorization to October 1, 2002.

[43] U.S. Small Business Administration, "SOP 50 10 5(E): Lender and Development Company Loan Programs," (effective June 1, 2012), p. 70, at http://www.sba.gov/sites/ default/files/SOP%2050%2010%205(E)%20(5-16-2012)%20clean.pdf.

[44] Ibid., p. 71.

[45] U.S. Small Business Administration, Office of Congressional and Legislative Affairs, correspondence with the author, April 7, 2010. All PCLP-CDCs have ALP status as that is a requirement for being provided PCLP authority.

[46] U.S. Small Business Administration, "SBA Lending Statistics for Major Programs (as of 9/30/2011)," at http://www.sba.gov/about-sba-info/26641; and U.S. Small Business Administration, "SBA Lending Statistics for Major Programs (as of 9/30/2012)," at http://www.sba.gov/about-sba-info/317721.

47 U.S. Small Business Administration, "SOP 50 10 5(E): Lender and Development Company Loan Programs," (effective June 1, 2012), p. 318, at http://www.sba.gov/sites/ default/files/SOP%2050%2010%205(E)%20(5-16- 2012)%20clean.pdf.

48 Ibid.

49 Ibid., p. 267.

50 13 C.F.R. §120.971(d).

51 U.S. Small Business Administration, "SBA Information Notice: 7(a) and 504 Fees Effective On October 1, 2011," Washington, DC, September 30, 2011, http://www.sba.gov/sites/ default/files/5000-1223.pdf.

52 15 U.S.C. §697(b)(7)(A)(i); and 13 C.F.R. §120.971(d). The SBA's annual servicing fee was 0.749% in FY2011 and 0.389% in FY2010.

53 U.S. Small Business Administration, "SBA Information Notice: 7(a) and 504 Fees Effective On October 1, 2011," Washington, DC, September 30, 2011, at http://www.sba.gov/sites/ default/files/5000-1223.pdf.

54 13 C.F.R. §120.971(e).

55 13 C.F.R. §120.972.

56 Ibid. When there are different liens on a property, the senior lien must be satisfied before junior liens in the event of a default.

57 U.S. Small Business Administration, "SOP 50 10 5(E): Lender and Development Company Loan Programs," (effective June 1, 2012), p. 347, at http://www.sba.gov/sites/default/ files/SOP%2050%2010%205(E)%20(5-16- 2012)%20clean.pdf; and 13 C.F.R. §120.971(a)(1).

58 13 C.F.R. §120.971(a)(2).

59 U.S. Small Business Administration, "SOP 50 10 5(E): Lender and Development Company Loan Programs," (effective June 1, 2012), p. 356, at http://www.sba.gov/sites/default/ files/SOP%2050%2010%205(E)%20(5-16- 2012)%20clean.pdf; and 13 C.F.R. §120.883(e).

60 13 C.F.R. §120.971(a)(3); and U.S. Small Business Administration, "SOP 50 10 5(E): Lender and Development Company Loan Programs," (effective June 1, 2012), pp. 264, 350, at http://www.sba.gov/sites/ default/files/SOP%2050%2010%205(E)%20(5-16-2012)%20clean.pdf.

61 13 C.F.R. §120.971(a)(4); 13 C.F.R. §120.971(a)(5); and U.S. Small Business Administration, "SOP 50 10 5(E): Lender and Development Company Loan Programs," (effective June 1, 2012), p. 350, at http://www.sba.gov/ sites/ default/files/SOP%2050%2010%205(E)%20(5-16-2012)%20clean.pdf.

62 13 C.F.R. §120.971(c).

63 U.S. Small Business Administration, "SOP 50 10 5(E): Lender and Development Company Loan Programs," (effective June 1, 2012), p. 355, at http://www.sba.gov/sites/default/files/ SOP%2050%2010%205(E)%20(5-16- 2012)%20clean.pdf.

64 Ibid.

65 Ibid., p. 351.

66 P.L. 111-5, the American Recovery and Reinvestment Act of 2009, provided $375 million for fee subsidies and the 7(a) program's 90% guaranty for all standard 7(a) loans. ARRA's funding for these purposes was exhausted on November 23, 2009. P.L. 111-118, the Department of Defense Appropriations Act, 2010, enacted on December 19, 2009, provided $125 million to extend the fee subsidies and 90% guaranty through February 28, 2010. P.L. 111-144, the Temporary Extension Act of 2010, enacted on March 2, 2010, provided $60 million to extend the fee subsidies and 90% guaranty through March 28, 2010. P.L. 111-150, an act to extend the Small Business Loan Guarantee Program, enacted on March 26, 2010, authorized the use of $40 million in SBA appropriated funds to extend the fee subsidies and 90% guaranty through April 30, 2010. P.L. 111-157, the Continuing Extension Act of 2010, enacted on April 15, 2010, provided $80 million to extend the fee subsides and 90% guaranty through May 31, 2010. P.L. 111-240, the Small Business Jobs Act of 2010, enacted on September 27, 2010, provided $505 million (plus $5 million for related administrative expenses) to extend the fee subsidies and 90% guaranty through December 31, 2010. P.L. 111-322, the Continuing Appropriations and Surface Transportation Extensions Act, 2011, authorized the SBA to continue the fee subsidies and 90% guaranty through March 4, 2011, or until the funding provided by the Small Business Jobs Act of 2010 for these purposes was exhausted (which occurred on January 3, 2011).

67 On January 3, 2011, the SBA announced that it had formed a SBA Loan Queue for loan applicants should any funding with the enhancements should become available from loan cancellations. Typically, 7% to 10% of previously approved SBA loans are later cancelled by the borrower or lender and are not disbursed for a variety of reasons. See U.S. Small Business Administration, "Jobs Act Supported More Than $12 Billion in SBA Lending to Small Businesses in Just Three Months," Washington, DC, January 3, 2011, at http://www.sba.gov/content/jobs-act-supported-more-12- billion-sba-lending-small-businesses-just-three-months.

[68] U.S. Small Business Administration, "Administration Announces New Small Business Commercial Real Estate and Working Capital Programs," February 5, 2010, at http://www.sba.gov/sites/default/files/ sba_rcvry_ factsheet_cre_refi.pdf; and U.S. Small Business Administration, "SBA Recovery Lending Extended Through April 30," March 29, 2010, at http://www.sba.gov/about-sba-services/7367/5883.

[69] Susan Eckerly, "NFIB Responds to President's Small Business Lending Initiatives," Washington, DC, October 21, 2009, at http://www.nfib.com/newsroom/newsroom-item/cmsid/50080/; and NFIB, "Government Spending," Washington, DC, at http://www.nfib.com/issues-elections/issues-elections-item/cmsid/49051/.

[70] U.S. Small Business Administration, Office of Congressional and Legislative Affairs, correspondence with the author, September 17, 2012. The SBA maintains selected disbursement data and will provide that data to congressional offices by request.

[71] U.S. Small Business Administration, Press Office, "Recovery Loan Incentives Spurred Continued Rebound in SBA Lending in FY2010," October 4, 2010, at http://www.sba.gov/about-sba-services/7367/5527; and U.S. Small Business Administration, "Jobs Act Supported More Than $12 Billion in SBA Lending to Small Businesses in Just Three Months," January 3, 2011, at http://www.sba.gov/content/jobs-act-supported-more-12-billion-sba-lending-smallbusinesses-just-three-months.

[72] U.S. Small Business Administration, "2008 Loss Report," Washington, DC, p. 8, http://archive.sba.gov/ idc/groups/ public/documents/sba_program_office/cfo_2008_loss_report.pdf.

[73] U.S. Small Business Administration, "Agency Financial Report: Fiscal Year, 2010," p. 66, at http://www.sba.gov/ sites/default/files/afr_2010_final.pdf; and U.S. Small Business Administration, "Agency Financial Report: Fiscal Year, 2011," p. 71, at http://www. sba.gov/sites/default/files/Agency%20Financial%20Report%20FY% 202011_0.pdf.

[74] U.S. Small Business Administration, FY 2013 Congressional Budget Justification and FY 2011 Annual Performance Report, p. 19, at http://www.sba.gov/sites/default/files/ files/FY%202013%20CBJ%20FY% 202011%20APR.pdf.

[75] Christopher Hayes, An Assessment of Small Business Administration Loan and Investment Performance: Survey of Assisted Businesses (Washington, DC: The Urban Institute, 2008), p. 3, at http://www.urban.org/ UploadedPDF/ 411599_assisted_business_survey.pdf. The percentage total exceeds 100 because recipients were allowed to name more than one use for the loan proceeds.

[76] Ibid., p. 5.

[77] Ibid.

[78] Kenneth Temkin, Brett Theodos, with Kerstin Gentsch, Competitive and Special Competitive Opportunity Gap Analysis of the 7(A) and 504 Programs (Washington, DC: The Urban Institute, 2008), p. 13, at http://www.urban.org/ UploadedPDF/411596_504 _gap_ analysis.pdf.

[79] U.S. Small Business Administration, "SBA Lending Statistics for Major Programs (as of 9/30/2012)," at http://www.sba.gov/about-sba-info/317721.

[80] Kenneth Temkin, Brett Theodos, with Kerstin Gentsch, Competitive and Special Competitive Opportunity Gap Analysis of the 7(A) and 504 Programs (Washington, DC: The Urban Institute, 2008), p. 21, at http://www.urban.org/ UploadedPDF/411596_504_ gap_ analysis.pdf.

[81] P.L. 111-5, the American Recovery and Reinvestment Act of 2009, Section 501. Fee Reductions.

[82] P.L. 111-118, the Department of Defense Appropriations Act, 2010, enacted on December 19, 2009, provided $125 million to extend ARRA's "fee reductions and eliminations" for the SBA's 7(a) and 504/CDC programs and 90% maximum loan guarantee limit for the SBA's 7(a) program through February 28, 2010. P.L. 111-144, the Temporary Extension Act of 2010, enacted on March 2, 2010, provided $60 million to extend those fee reductions and loan modifications through March 28, 2010. P.L. 111-150, an act to extend the Small Business Loan Guarantee Program, enacted on March 26, 2010, authorized the use of $40 million in SBA appropriated funds to extend those fee reductions and loan modifications through April 30, 2010. P.L. 111-157, the Continuing Extension Act of 2010, enacted on April 15, 2010, provided $80 million to extend those fee reductions and loan modifications through May 31, 2010.

[83] On January 3, 2011, the SBA announced that it had formed a SBA Loan Queue for loan applicants should any funding with the enhancements should become available from loan cancellations. Typically, 7% to 10% of previously approved SBA loans are later cancelled by the borrower or lender and are not disbursed for a variety of reasons. See U.S. Small Business Administration, "Jobs Act Supported More Than $12 Billion in SBA Lending to Small Businesses in Just Three Months," January 3, 2011, at http://www.sba.gov/ content/jobs-act-supported-more-12-billion-sbalending-small-businesses-just-three-months.

[84] U.S. Small Business Administration, "Administration Announces New Small Business Commercial Real Estate and Working Capital Programs," February 5, 2010, at http://www.sba.gov/sites/default/files/ sba_rcvry_

factsheet_cre_refi.pdf; and U.S. Small Business Administration, "SBA Recovery Lending Extended Through April 30," March 29, 2010, at http://www.sba.gov/about-sba-services/7367/5883.

[85] Susan Eckerly, "NFIB Responds to President's Small Business Lending Initiatives," Washington, DC, October 21, 2009, at http://www.nfib.com/newsroom/newsroom-item/cmsid/50080/; and NFIB, "Government Spending," Washington, DC, at http://www. nfib.com/issues-elections/issues-elections-item/cmsid/49051/.

[86] U.S. Small Business Administration, Office of the Inspector General, "Report on Audit of Premier Certified Lenders in the Section 504 Loan Program," March 23, 2010, at p. 20, http://www.sba.gov/office-of-inspector-general/868/5032.

[87] Ibid.

[88] Ibid., p. 1.

[89] Ibid., pp. 3, 4.

[90] Ibid., p. 4.

[91] Ibid., pp. 4, 5.

[92] Ibid., p. 5.

[93] Ibid.

[94] U.S. Government Accountability Office, Small Business Administration: Actions Needed to Improve the Usefulness of the Agency's Lender Risk Rating System, GAO-1-53, November 6, 2009, p. i, at http://www.gao.gov/new.items/ d1053.pdf.

[95] Ibid., pp. i, 27-30.

[96] Ibid., p. 35.

[97] U.S. Small Business Administration, "SBA Lending Statistics for Major Programs (as of 9/30/2011)," at http://www.sba.gov/about-sba-info/26641; and U.S. Small Business Administration, "SBA Lending Statistics for Major Programs (as of 9/30/2012)," at http://www.sba.gov/about-sba-info/317721.

[98] U.S. Small Business Administration, "Jobs Act Supported More Than $12 Billion in SBA Lending to Small Businesses in Just Three Months," January 3, 2011, at http://www.sba.gov/content/jobs-act-supported-more-12-billionsba-lending-small-businesses-just-three-months.

[99] U.S. Small Business Administration, "Administration Announces New Small Business Commercial Real Estate and Working Capital Programs," February 5, 2010, http://www.sba.gov/sites/default/files/sba_rcvry_factsheet_cre_refi.pdf. For an analysis of the pros and cons associated with these actions see CRS Report R41146, Small Business Administration 7(a) Loan Guaranty Program, by Robert Jay Dilger.

[100] For further analysis see CRS Report R40985, Small Business: Access to Capital and Job Creation, by Robert Jay Dilger.

[101] ARC's loan limit would have been increased from $35,000 to $50,000, and to $75,000 in areas of high unemployment, and borrowers would be allowed to use ARC loans to refinance existing SBA loan debt. The ARC program ended on September 30, 2010.

[102] H.R. 3854, the Small Business Financing and Investment Act of 2009.

[103] Ibid. For further analysis see CRS Report R40985, Small Business: Access to Capital and Job Creation, by Robert Jay Dilger.

[104] S. 2869, the Small Business Job Creation and Access to Capital Act of 2009.

[105] For further analysis of P.L. 111-240, the Small Business Jobs Act of 2010, see CRS Report R41385, Small Business Legislation During the 111th Congress, by Robert Jay Dilger and Gary Guenther. For further analysis of the Small Business Lending Fund see CRS Report R42045, The Small Business Lending Fund, by Robert Jay Dilger. For further analysis of the State Small Business Credit Initiative see CRS Report R42581, State Small Business Credit Initiative: Implementation and Funding Issues, by Robert Jay Dilger.

[106] For further analysis of the SBA's size standards see CRS Report R40860, Small Business Size Standards: A Historical Analysis of Contemporary Issues, by Robert Jay Dilger.

[107] P.L. 111-240, the Small Business Jobs Act of 2010, §1112. Maximum Loan Amounts Under 504 Program.

[108] P.L. 111-240, the Small Business Jobs Act of 2010, §1122. Low-Interest Refinancing Under the Local Development Business Loan Program.

[109] Ibid. The House Committee on Small Business has indicated that it will examine the refinancing program for termination because it does not believe that the program's fees "will cover the subsidy costs of the program." U.S. Congress, House Committee on Small Business, Budget Views and Estimates, 112th Cong., 1st sess., March 17, 2011, p. 3, http://smbiz.house.gov/UploadedFiles/March_17_Views_and_Estimates_Letter.pdf.

[110] P.L. 111-240, the Small Business Jobs Act of 2010, §1116. Alternative Size Standards.

[111] Ibid.

[112] Senator Harry Reid, "Consideration of H.R. 3606, the Jumpstart our Business Startups Act," Text of Amendments, Congressional Record, vol. 158, part 43 (March 15, 2012), p. S1754.

[113] H.R. 3606, the Jumpstart Our Business Startups Act, was passed by the House on March 8, 2012. The bill did not contain a provision concerning 504/CDC refinancing. President Obama signed the bill, as amended, into law on April 5, 2012 (P.L. 112-106, the Jumpstart Our Business Startups).

[114] Representative Nydia Velázquez, "Small Business Financing and Investment Act of 2009," House debate, Congressional Record, daily edition, vol. 155, no. 159 (October 29, 2009), pp. H12074, H12075; Senator Mary Landrieu, "Statements on Introduced Bills and Joint Resolutions," remarks in the Senate, Congressional Record, daily edition, vol. 155, no. 185 (December 10, 2009), p. S12910; and The White House, "Remarks by the President on Job Creation and Economic Growth," December 8, 2009, at http://www.whitehouse.gov/the-press-office/remarkspresident-job-creation-and-economic-growth.

115 Susan Eckerly, "NFIB Responds to President's Small Business Lending Initiatives," Washington, DC, October 21, 2009, at http://www.nfib.com/newsroom/newsroom-item/cmsid/50080/; and NFIB, "Government Spending," Washington, DC, at http://www. nfib.com/issues-elections/issues-elections-item/cmsid/49051/.

[116] U.S. Small Business Administration, "Administration Announces New Small Business Commercial Real Estate and Working Capital Programs," February 5, 2010, at http://www. sba.gov/sites/default/files/ sba_rcvry_ factsheet_cre_refi.pdf.

[117] Ibid.

[118] Robb Mandelbaum, "Small Business Incentives Face a Hard Road in Congress," New York Times, February 12, 2010, at http://boss.blogs.nytimes.com/2010/02/12/small-business-incentives-face-a-hard-road-in-congress/; and U.S. Congress, House Committee on Small Business, House Committee on Small Business Views With Regard to the Fiscal Year (FY) 2010 Budget, Letter from Nydia Velázquez, Chair, House Committee on Small Business, to John M. Spratt, Jr., Chair, House Committee on the Budget, 111th Cong., 2nd sess., March 11, 2009, p. 3, at http://www.house.gov/ smbiz/democrats/Reports/FY%202010% 20Views%20and%20Estimates %20v2.pdf.

[119] U.S. Congress, House Committee on Small Business, Small Business Financing and Investment Act of 2009, report to accompany H.R. 3854, 111th Cong., 2nd sess., October 26, 2009, H.Rept. 111-315 (Washington: GPO, 2009), p. 1.

[120] U.S. Office of Management and Budget, "OMB Report Pursuant to the Sequestration Transparency Act of 2012 (P.L. 112-112–155)," p. 193, at http://www.whitehouse.gov/sites/ default/files/omb/assets/legislative_reports/ stareport.pdf.

In: Small Business Administration Programs
Editor: Walter Janikowski

ISBN: 978-1-62417-992-1
© 2013 Nova Science Publishers, Inc.

Chapter 5

SMALL BUSINESS ADMINISTRATION MICROLOAN PROGRAM[*]

Robert Jay Dilger

SUMMARY

The Small Business Administration's (SBA's) Microloan program provides direct loans to qualified non-profit intermediary Microloan lenders who, in turn, provide "microloans" of up to $50,000 to small business owners, entrepreneurs, and non-profit child care centers. It also provides marketing, management, and technical assistance to Microloan borrowers and potential borrowers. The program was authorized in 1991 as a five-year demonstration project and became operational in 1992. It was made permanent, subject to reauthorization, in 1997. The SBA's Microloan program is designed to assist women, low-income, veteran, and minority entrepreneurs and small business owners and other individuals possessing the capability to operate successful business concerns by providing them small-scale loans for working capital or the acquisition of materials, supplies, or equipment. In FY2012, Microloan intermediaries provided 3,973 Microloans amounting to $44.7 million. The average Microloan was $11,254 and had a 8.18% interest rate. Critics of the SBA's Microloan program argue that it is expensive relative to alternative programs, duplicative of the SBA's 7(a) loan guaranty program, and subject to administrative shortfalls. The program's advocates argue that it provides assistance that reaches many who otherwise would not be served by the private sector and is an important source of capital and training assistance for low-income women and minority business owners. Congressional interest in the Microloan program has increased in recent years, primarily because microloans are viewed as a means to assist very small businesses, especially women- and minority-owned startups, to get loans that enable them to create and retain jobs. Job creation, always a congressional interest, has taken on increased importance given the nation's current economic difficulties.

This report opens with a discussion of the rationale provided for having a Microloan program, describes the program's eligibility standards and operating requirements for lenders and borrowers, and examines the arguments presented by the program's critics and by its advocates. It concludes with an examination of changes to the program

---

[*] This is an edited, reformatted and augmented version of Congressional Research Service, Publication No. R41057, dated October 16, 2012.

authorized by P.L. 111-240, the Small Business Jobs Act of 2010. The Small Business Jobs Act increased the Microloan program's loan limit for borrowers from $35,000 to $50,000, and for intermediaries after their first year of participation in the program from $3.5 million to $5 million. It also authorized the SBA to waive, in whole or in part through FY2012, the non-federal share requirement for loans to the Microloan program's intermediaries and for grants made to Microloan intermediaries for small business marketing, management, and technical assistance for up to a fiscal year.

SMALL BUSINESS MICROLOANS AND TRAINING ASSISTANCE

The Small Business Administration (SBA) administers programs that support small businesses, including loan guarantees to lenders to encourage them to provide loans to small businesses "that might not otherwise obtain financing on reasonable terms and conditions" and grants to nonprofit organizations to provide marketing, management, and technical training assistance to small business owners.[1] Historically, one of the justifications presented for funding the SBA's loan guarantee programs has been that small businesses can be at a disadvantage, compared with other businesses, when trying to obtain access to sufficient capital and credit.[2] It has been argued that this disadvantage is particularly acute for startups and microbusinesses (firms with fewer than five employees):

> Traditional lending institutions, such as banks and investors, are unlikely to offer loans and investment capital to microfirms due to a variety of reasons. One barrier to microlending is a concern that startups and smaller enterprises are risky investments since growing businesses typically exhibit erratic bursts of growth and downturn. The perceived risk of these types of companies reduces the chances of a microbusiness to obtain financing. Another issue is that microbusinesses by and large require smaller amounts of capital, and thus banks or investment companies often believe that it is not efficient use of their time or resources, nor will they receive a substantive return on investment from such a small loan amount.[3]

An Urban Institute survey of SBA 7(a), 504/Certified Development Company (504/CDC), Small Business Investment Company (SBIC), and Microloan borrowers conducted in 2007 found that Microloan borrowers reported having the most difficulty in finding acceptable financing elsewhere. Less than one-third (31%) of Microloan borrowers reported that they would have been able to find acceptable financing elsewhere, compared with 35% of SBIC borrowers, 40% of 7(a) borrowers, and 48% of 504/CDC borrowers.[4]

The SBA has provided loan guarantees to encourage lenders to issue small businesses loans since the agency's inception in 1953.[5] Interest in creating a separate loan program to address the specific needs of startups and microbusinesses increased during the 1980s, primarily due to the growth and experience of microlending institutions abroad and evidence concerning private lending practices that led Congress to the conclusion that a new loan program was necessary "to reach very small businesses that were not being served by traditional lenders of SBA's credit programs."[6] To address the perceived disadvantages faced by very small businesses in gaining access to capital, Congress authorized the SBA's Microloan lending program in 1991 (P.L. 102-140, the Departments of Commerce, Justice, and State, the Judiciary, and Related Agencies Appropriations Act, 1992). The program became operational in 1992.

Its stated purpose is

> to assist women, low-income, veteran ... and minority entrepreneurs and business owners and other individuals possessing the capability to operate successful business concerns; to assist small business concerns in those areas suffering from a lack of credit due to economic downturns; ... to make loans to eligible intermediaries to enable such intermediaries to provide small-scale loans, particularly loans in amounts averaging not more than $10,000, to start-up, newly established, or growing small business concerns for working capital or the acquisition of materials, supplies, or equipment; [and] to make grants to eligible intermediaries that, together with non-Federal matching funds, will enable such intermediaries to provide intensive marketing, management, and technical assistance to microloan borrowers.[7]

The SBA's Microloan lending program was authorized initially as a five-year demonstration project. It was made permanent, subject to reauthorization, in 1997 (P.L. 105-135, the Small Business Reauthorization Act of 1997).

Congressional interest in the Microloan program has increased in recent years, primarily because microloans are viewed as a means to assist very small businesses, especially women- and minority-owned startups, obtain loans that enable them to create jobs. Job creation and preservation, always a congressional interest, has taken on increased importance given the nation's current economic difficulties.[8] This report describes the Microloan program's eligibility standards and operating requirements for lenders and borrowers, and examines the arguments presented by the program's critics and by its advocates. It concludes with an examination of changes to the program authorized by P.L. 111-240, the Small Business Jobs Act of 2010. P.L. 111-240 authorizes the Secretary of the Treasury to establish a $30 billion Small Business Lending Fund (SBLF) to encourage community banks to provide small business loans ($4.0 billion was issued), a $1.5 billion State Small Business Credit Initiative to provide funding to participating states with small business capital access programs, and about $12 billion in tax relief for small businesses.[9] It also authorizes changes to the SBA's loan guaranty programs, including increasing the Microloan program's loan limit for borrowers from $35,000 to $50,000, and for intermediaries after their first year of participation in the program from $3.5 million to $5 million. It also authorized the SBA to waive, in whole or in part through FY2012, the non-federal share requirement for loans to the Microloan program's intermediaries and for grants made to Microloan intermediaries for small business marketing, management, and technical assistance for up to a fiscal year.

THE SBA MICROLOAN PROGRAM: FUNDING, ELIGIBILITY

Standards, Program Requirements, and Statistics

Unlike the SBA's 7(a) and 504/CDC loan guarantee programs, the SBA Microloan program does not guarantee loans.[10] Instead, it provides direct loans to qualified non-profit intermediary Microloan lenders who, in turn, provide "microloans" of up to $50,000 to small business owners, entrepreneurs, and non-profit child care centers.[11] There are 181 intermediaries participating in the program, located in 48 states, the District of Columbia, and Puerto Rico.[12]

Funding

The program received an appropriation of $3.678 million in FY2012, which was expected to support about $25.0 million in lending to intermediaries.[13] The Obama Administration recommended that the program receive an appropriation of $2.844 million for FY2013, which was expected to support about $18.0 million in lending to intermediaries.[14] P.L. 112-175, the Continuing Appropriations Resolution, 2013, which provides appropriations for FY2013 through March 27, 2013, provided the program a projected $3,700,509 for FY2013 (the FY2012 appropriation amount plus 0.612%).

Microloan intermediaries and qualified "non-lending technical assistance providers" selected by the SBA also received $20.0 million in FY2012 to provide Microloan borrowers and prospective borrowers marketing, management, and technical training assistance.[15] The Obama Administration recommended that the Microloan technical assistance program receive $19.76 million in FY2013.[16] P.L. 112-175, the Continuing Appropriations Resolution, 2013, which provides appropriations through March 27, 2013, provided the program a projected $20.124 million for FY2013 (the FY2012 appropriation amount plus 0.612%).

The Microloan technical assistance program provided counseling services to 15,892 small businesses in FY2012.[17]

Intermediary Microloan Lender Eligibility Standards

To become a qualified intermediary Microloan lender, an applicant must be organized as a nonprofit organization, quasi-governmental economic development corporation, or an agency established by a Native American Tribal Government. It must also have made and serviced short-term, fixed rate loans of not more than $50,000 to newly established or growing small businesses for at least one year and have at least one year of experience providing technical assistance to its borrowers.[18] If accepted into the program by the SBA, it can borrow no more than $750,000 from the SBA during its first year of participation, and no more than an aggregate of $5 million in later years.[19]

Intermediary Microloan Lender Program Requirements

After receiving an SBA microloan, intermediaries are not required to make any interest payments on the loan during the first year, but interest accrues from the date that the SBA disburses the loan proceeds to the intermediary. After that, the SBA determines the schedule for periodic payments. Loans must be repaid within 10 years.[20]

The interest rate charged to the intermediary is based on the five-year Treasury rate, adjusted to the nearest one-eighth percent, less 1.25%. The SBA's interest rate is updated on a monthly basis. In addition, intermediaries that maintain an average loan size of $10,000 or less are charged an interest rate based on the five-year Treasury rate, adjusted to the nearest one-eighth percent, less 2.0%. Portfolios are evaluated annually to determine the applicable rate.[21]

Intermediaries are required to contribute not less than 15% of the loan amount in cash from nonfederal sources and, as security for repayment of the loan, must provide the SBA first lien position on all notes receivable from any microloans issued under the program.[22] Unlike the SBA's 7(a) and 504/CDC loan guarantee programs, the SBA does not charge intermediaries upfront or on-going service fees under the Microloan program.[23]

As mentioned previously, P.L. 111-240, the Small Business Jobs Act of 2010, temporarily allowed the SBA to waive, in whole or in part through FY2012, the intermediary's 15% non-federal share requirement under specified circumstances (e.g., the economic conditions affecting the intermediary and the intermediary's performance) for up to a fiscal year.[24]

Intermediaries are required to deposit the proceeds from the SBA's loans, their 15% contribution, and payments from their microloan borrowers into an interest-bearing Microloan Revolving Fund. Intermediaries may only withdraw from this account funds necessary to make microloans to borrowers, repay the SBA, and establish and maintain an interest-bearing Loan Loss Reserve Fund to pay any shortage in the Microloan Revolving Fund caused by delinquencies or losses on its microloans.[25] They are required, until they have been in the program for at least five years, to maintain a balance in the Loan Loss Reserve Fund equal to 15% of the outstanding balance of the notes receivable from their microloan borrowers.[26] After five years, if the intermediary's average annual loss rate during the preceding five years is less than 15% and no other factors exist that may impair the intermediary's ability to repay its obligations to the SBA, the SBA Administrator may reduce the required balance in the intermediary's Loan Loss Reserve Fund to the intermediary's average annual loss rate during the preceding five years, but not less than 10% of the portfolio.[27] Intermediaries are required to maintain their Loan Loss Reserve Fund until they have repaid all obligations owed to the SBA.

The borrower default rate for the Microloan program is about 12%.[28] Because the Loan Loss Reserve Fund is used to contribute toward the cost of borrower defaults, and is often sufficient to cover the entire cost of such defaults, the SBA's loss rate for intermediary repayment is typically less than 3%.[29]

An intermediary may be suspended or removed from the Microloan program if it fails to comply with a specified list of program performance standards. For example, intermediaries are required to close and fund a minimum of four microloans per year, cover the service territory assigned by the SBA, honor the SBA determined boundaries of neighboring intermediaries and non-lender technical assistance providers, fulfill reporting requirements, maintain a loan currency rate of 85% or more (where loans are no more than 30 days late in scheduled payments), maintain a default rate of 15% or less, and "satisfactorily provide" in-house technical assistance to microloan clients and prospective microloan clients.[30]

Intermediary Marketing, Management, and Technical Training Assistance

As mentioned previously, the SBA provided intermediaries and qualified "non-lending technical assistance providers" $20.0 million in FY2012 to provide Microloan borrowers and Microloan prospective borrowers marketing, management, and technical training assistance. P.L. 112-175, the Continuing Appropriations Resolution, 2013, which provides appropriations through March 27, 2013, provides the SBA a projected $20.124 million in FY2013 for this purpose.

Intermediaries are eligible to receive a Microloan technical assistance grant "of not more than 25% of the total outstanding balance of loans made to it under this subsection."[31] Grant funds may be used only to provide marketing, management, and technical assistance to microloan borrowers, except that up to 25% of the funds may be used to provide such assistance to prospective Microloan borrowers. Grant funds may also be used to attend training required by the SBA.[32] In most instances, intermediaries must contribute, solely from non-federal sources, an amount equal to 25% of the grant amount.[33] In addition to cash or other direct funding, the contribution may include indirect costs or in-kind contributions paid for under non-federal programs.[34] Intermediaries may expend no more than 25% of the grant funds on third-party contracts for the provision of technical assistance.[35]

Also, as mentioned earlier, P.L. 111-240, the Small Business Jobs Act of 2010, temporarily allowed the SBA to waive, in whole or in part through FY2012, the 25% non-federal share requirement for grants made to Microloan intermediaries for small business marketing, management, and technical assistance under specified circumstances (e.g., the economic conditions affecting the intermediary and the intermediary's performance) for up to a fiscal year.[36]

The SBA does not require Microloan borrowers to participate in the marketing, management, and technical assistance program. However, intermediaries typically require microloan borrowers to participate in the training program as a condition of the receipt of a microloan. Combining loan and intensive training assistance is one of the Microloan program's distinguishing features.

Intermediaries that make at least 25% of their loans to small businesses located in or owned by residents of an Economically Distressed Area (defined as having 40% or more of its residents with an annual income that is at or below the poverty level), or have a portfolio of loans made under the program "that averages not more than $10,000 during the period of the intermediary's participation in the program" are eligible to receive an additional training grant equal to 5% of "the total outstanding balance of loans made to the intermediary."[37] Intermediaries are not required to make a matching contribution as a condition of receiving these additional grant funds.

Non-lending Technical Assistance Providers

Each year, the SBA is authorized to select qualified non-profit, non-lending technical assistance providers to receive grant funds to provide marketing, management, and technical assistance to Microloan borrowers. Any non-profit entity that is not an intermediary may apply for these funds.[38]

The SBA may award up to 55 grants each year to qualified non-lending technical assistance providers to deliver marketing, management, and technical assistance to Microloan borrowers. The grants may be for terms of up to five years and may not exceed $200,000.[39] The nonprofit entity must contribute, solely from non-federal sources, an amount equal to 20% of the grant. In addition to cash or other direct funding, the contribution may include indirect costs or in-kind contributions paid for under non-federal programs.[40]

The SBA stopped awarding these grants at the beginning of FY2005. The SBA determined at that time that the non-lending technical assistance providers duplicated much of what was already being provided by Microloan intermediaries and other SBA entrepreneurial development programs.[41]

Microloan Borrower Eligibility Standards

With one exception, Microloan borrowers must be an eligible, for-profit small business as defined by the Small Business Act. P.L. 105-135, the Small Business Reauthorization Act of 1997, expanded the Microloan program's eligibility to include borrowers establishing a nonprofit childcare business.

Microloan Borrower Program Requirements

Intermediaries are directed by legislative language to provide borrowers "small-scale loans, particularly loans in amounts averaging not more than $10,000."[42] They are also directed, "to the extent practicable ... to maintain a microloan portfolio with an average loan size of not more than $15,000."[43] Microloans for more than $20,000 are allowed "only if such small business concern demonstrates that it is unable to obtain credit elsewhere at comparable interest rates and that it has good prospects for success."[44] The maximum loan amount is $50,000 and no borrower may owe an intermediary more than $50,000 at any one time.[45]

Microloan proceeds may be used only for working capital and acquisition of materials, supplies, furniture, fixtures, and equipment. Loans cannot be made to acquire land or property, and must be repaid within six years.[46] Within these parameters, loan terms vary depending on the loan's size, the planned use of funds, the requirements of the intermediary lender, and the needs of the small business borrower. On loans of more than $7,500, the maximum interest rate that can be charged to the borrower is the interest rate charged by the SBA on the loan to the intermediary, plus 7.75 percentage points. On loans of $7,500 or less, the maximum interest rate that can be charged to the borrower is the interest charged by the SBA on the loan to the intermediary, plus 8.5 percentage points.[47] Rates are negotiated between the borrower and the intermediary, and typically range from 8% to 10%.[48] Each intermediary establishes its own lending and credit requirements. However, borrowers are generally required to provide some type of collateral, and a personal guarantee to repay the loan. The SBA does not review the loan for creditworthiness.[49]

Microloan Program Statistics

In FY2012, the SBA provided 42 loans amounting to $23.9 million to intermediaries, and intermediaries provided 3,973 microloans amounting to $44.7 million to small businesses. The average loan to an intermediary was $568,238, and the average microloan to a small business was $11,255.[50]

The Microloan program is open to all small business entrepreneurs, but targets new and early-stage businesses in "underserved markets, including borrowers with little to no credit history, low-income borrowers, and women and minority entrepreneurs in both rural and urban areas who generally do not qualify for conventional loans, or other, larger SBA guaranteed loans."[51] An analysis conducted by the Urban Institute found that about 9.9% of conventional small business loans are issued to minority-owned small businesses and about 16% of conventional small business loans are issued to women-owned businesses.[52] In FY2012, more than half (57.4%) of the Microloan program's loans went to women-owned or -controlled firms and, of those reporting their race, 43.0% went to minority-owned or -controlled firms.[53]

More than three-quarters of all microloan borrowers (79.8%) in FY2012 were located in an urban area. Also, startup companies received about half (51.9%) of all microloans in FY2012.[54]

As mentioned previously, the borrower default rate for the Microloan program is about 12%.[55] Because the Loan Loss Reserve Fund is used to contribute toward the cost of borrower defaults, and is often sufficient to cover the entire cost of such defaults, the SBA's loss rate for intermediary repayment is typically less than 3%.[56]

Microloans are often used for more than one purpose. In FY2012, they were most commonly used to finance working capital (65.5%), purchase new equipment (26.0%), and purchase inventory (24.3%).[57]

CONGRESSIONAL ISSUES

Critics of the SBA's Microloan program argue that it is duplicative of other available programs, expensive relative to alternative programs, and subject to administrative shortfalls. The program's advocates argue that it provides assistance that "reaches many who otherwise would not be served by the private sector or even the SBA's 7(a) loan program" and "has provided an important source of capital for low-income women business owners and minority borrowers."[58]

Program Duplication

Critics of the SBA's Microloan program argue that its direct lending program is duplicative of the SBA's 7(a) loan guarantee program and its marketing, management, and technical training assistance grant program is duplicative of the SBA's training assistance provided through Small Business Development Centers, SCORE (Service Corps of Retired Executives), and Women Business Centers. For example, President George W. Bush proposed to eliminate all funding for the Microloan program in his FY2005, FY2006, and FY2007 budget requests to Congress, arguing that "the 7(a) program is capable of serving the same clientele through the Community Express programs for much lower cost to the Government."[59] President Bush also proposed to terminate the Microloan program's marketing, management, and technical assistance grant program in his FY2008 and FY2009 budget requests to Congress.[60]

Critics of the SBA's Microloan program argued in 2007 that about 44% of the SBA's 7(a) program's loan guarantees at that time were for loans under $35,000 (the Microloan program's former loan limit for borrowers), representing more than 17 times the number of loans issued through the SBA's Microloan program.[61] In their view, the 7(a) program had demonstrated that it can service the needs of small businesses targeted by the SBA's Microloan program.[62] They also argued that the SBA's Microloan program's marketing, management, and technical assistance grants program was not necessary because the SBA "already supports a nationwide network of resource partners who provide counseling and training to entrepreneurs, including Small Business Development Centers, Women's Business Centers, and SCORE."[63] They argued that about 94% of Microloan intermediaries are located within 20 miles of a Small Business Development Center, a Women's Business Center, or a SCORE partner.[64]

The program's advocates argue that the SBA's Microloan program is complementary, not duplicative of the SBA's 7(a) loan guarantee program. They assert that microloan borrowers are particularly disadvantaged when seeking access to capital, often having no credit history or lower credit scores than most applicants for the SBA's 7(a) loan guarantee program.[65] In their view, it is important that the SBA has a program whose sole focus is to assist microloan borrowers in starting a microbusiness and have in place intermediaries that "have essential expertise on the needs of this key demographic."[66]

They also argue that the SBA's Microloan marketing, management, and technical assistance grants program is "a crucial element which enables intermediaries to assist microbusiness owners step by step through their development and growth" and "not only increases the likelihood of full repayment of the loan, but augments business survival and success."[67] As mentioned previously, intermediaries typically require Microloan borrowers to participate in the training program as a condition of the receipt of the microloan.

Program Cost

Critics of the SBA's Microloan program argue that it is expensive relative to other SBA programs, costing about $9,685 per small business assisted in FY2011, compared to $1,882 per small business assisted in the SBA's 7(a) loan guarantee program.[68] President George W. Bush cited the program's higher expense when he recommended in his FY2005, FY2006, and FY2007 budget requests to Congress that the program be terminated and when he recommended in his FY2008 and FY2009 budget requests to Congress that the interest rate charged to Microloan intermediaries be increased to make the program "self-financing."[69]

The SBA's Microloan program's advocates argue that the program's higher cost per small business assisted is unavoidable given the relatively unique nature of the program and the special needs of its borrowers. They assert that intermediaries often have to spend a significant amount of time with Microloan borrowers because those borrowers tend to have less experience with the credit application process and a more difficult time documenting their qualifications for assistance than borrowers in the SBA's loan guaranty programs. Also, in their view, raising the interest rate charged to intermediaries to make the program self-financing would reduce the program's cost, but could also defeat the program's purpose. They assert that because microloans are small, it is difficult for intermediaries to generate enough interest income to cover their costs. As a result, if the interest rate charged to intermediaries is increased, they contend that intermediaries would have to pass the increase on to Microloan borrowers. In their view, increasing the program's cost to microloan borrowers "will create an economic hardship for them and make it more difficult for them to grow their businesses" and "lead to fewer jobs created and fewer tax dollars paid."[70]

Program Administration

On December 28, 2009, the SBA's Office of Inspector General released an analysis of the SBA's administration of the Microloan program. It reported a number of deficiencies that it argued needed to be addressed. The analysis was undertaken in response to language in P.L. 111-5, the American Recovery and Reinvestment Act of 2009 (ARRA), directing Offices of Inspector General to perform audits of their respective agencies to determine whether adequate safeguards exist concerning the use of ARRA funds.[71]

Program Oversight
The SBA's Office of Inspector General found that the SBA's oversight of the Microloan program "was not sufficient to ensure effective operation of the Microloan program":

> SBA's oversight is focused on the intermediaries' ability to repay their SBA loans and is limited to a cursory review of quarterly financial reports supported by only one monthly bank statement.... The bank statements are used to simply verify the outstanding balances reported on the intermediaries' quarterly reports. This review process does not allow SBA to analyze the sources and uses of funds ... which is necessary to detect inappropriate fund transfers between the intermediaries' [Microloan Revolving Funds and Loan Loss Reserve Funds] accounts.[72]

The Office of Inspector General's report noted that the SBA only conducts onsite reviews when an intermediary defaults on its SBA loan. It also argued that the program was inadequately staffed, operating at that time "with 6 analysts who oversee more than 160 intermediaries, 460 intermediary loans, and approximately 2,500 microloans per year."[73]

The SBA agreed with the Office of Inspector General that a more detailed review of the financial information provided by intermediaries was appropriate. It now collects three months of bank statements each quarter from intermediaries. It also hired three additional staff members to monitor the program's ARRA funding, and indicated that it will continue to reassess the program's overall staffing needs.[74]

Reliability of the Microloan Program's Performance Data
The SBA's Office of Inspector General found that the SBA's reported Microloan borrower default rate of 12% "appeared low given the high-risk nature of the program."[75] It found that one intermediary made 1,182 microloans valued at over $11 million since 1993 and only reported slightly more than a 1% historical default rate, and 39 other intermediaries that reported that none of their loans had defaulted. It also identified duplicate loan reporting; multiple loans to microloan borrowers in the same amount, indicating the use of revolving lines of credit, which is disallowed by program regulations; and 92 microloan borrowers with outstanding microloan balances exceeding the $35,000 limit. It noted that ARRA "makes clear the importance of data verification" yet "all of the data used by SBA to report on the Microloan program performance is based on unverified information that is self-reported by intermediaries."[76] It concluded that "as a result, SBA cannot ensure that the reported microloan default rates are accurate and comply with the statutory requirement."[77]

In response, the SBA agreed with the Office of Inspector General with the need for accurate program data and indicated that microloan data will be evaluated as part of a "data quality initiative to identify areas for improvement."[78] The SBA also indicated that it will revise its SOPs (standard operating procedures) to "include guidance on data review and procedures for following up with intermediaries to resolve data discrepancies."[79]

Outcome-Oriented Performance Measures

The SBA's Office of Inspector General found that the SBA's program performance is based on the number of microloans funded and small businesses assisted. It argued that these "performance metrics ... do not ensure the ultimate program beneficiaries, the microloan borrowers, are truly assisted by the program" and "without appropriate metrics, SBA cannot ensure the Microloan program is meeting policy goals."[80] It noted that the SBA does not track the number of microloan borrowers who remain in business after receiving a microloan to measure the extent to which the loans contributed to the success of borrowers and does not determine the effect that technical training assistance may have on the success of microloan borrowers and their ability to repay loans.[81] It recommended that the SBA "develop additional performance metrics to measure the program's achievement in assisting microloan borrowers in establishing and maintaining successful small businesses."[82]

In response, the SBA indicated that it has "contracted with the Aspen Institute to advise on appropriate program and performance metrics for both microloans and technical assistance grants."[83] It also indicated that the program metrics developed will be used to assist the agency in measuring the Microloan program's effectiveness.

LEGISLATION

Congress has not considered any bills during the 112th Congress that would affect the Microloan program. However, it did consider several bills during the 111th Congress that would have affected the SBA's Microloan program before passing the Small Business Jobs Act of 2010, which President Obama signed into law (P.L. 111-240) on September 27, 2010.

H.R. 3854, the Small Business Financing and Investment Act of 2009, was passed by the House by a vote of 389-32, on October 29, 2009.[84] The Senate did not act on the bill. It would have authorized several new SBA programs and changed several existing SBA programs, including the Microloan program. For example, it would have

- increased the Microloan program's loan funding to "such sums as may be necessary" to support $110 million in direct microloans in FY2010 and $110 million in FY2011.[85]
- increased the program's marketing, management, and technical assistance grant funding to $80 million in FY2010 and $80 million in FY2011.
- authorized $20 million ($10 million in FY2010 and $10 million in FY2012) for a new Microloan interest assistance grant program.[86]
- broadened the eligibility requirements for Microloan intermediaries to qualify for lower interest rates.[87]
- increased the program's maximum loan amount to intermediaries during their first year of participation in the program from $750,000 to $1 million, and in later years from an aggregate of $3.5 million to $7 million. The SBA's Administrator would

have been provided discretion to increase the limit to $10 million if such treatment was determined by the SBA Administrator to be appropriate.[88]

- broadened the eligibility requirements for Microloan intermediaries "to help expand access to the Microloan program."[89]
- required the SBA to establish a process under which Microloan intermediaries "provide to the major credit reporting agencies the information about the borrower, both positive and negative, that is relevant to credit reporting, such as the payment activity of the borrower on the loan."[90]
- provided lenders with the authority to offer more flexible loan terms to Microloan borrowers, particularly with longer-term loans or revolving lines of credit, by removing existing requirements that all microloans be "short-term."[91]
- increased the percentage of technical assistance grant funds that an intermediary can spend on prospective borrowers from 25% to 35%, and on the provision of technical assistance through third-party providers from 25% to 35%.[92]
- required the SBA to annually provide the House Committee on Small Business and the Senate Committee on Small Business and Entrepreneurship a detailed, comprehensive report on the Microloan program.[93]

S. 2869, the Small Business Job Creation and Access to Capital Act of 2009, was ordered to be reported by the Senate Committee on Small Business and Entrepreneurship on December 10, 2009. It would have authorized changes to several SBA programs, including the Microloan program. The Senate did not take further action on the bill, but several of its provisions, including those affecting the Microloan program, were later included in P.L. 111-240. For example, it would have

- increased the SBA's Microloan program's maximum loan amount to intermediaries after their first year of participation in the program from $3.5 million to $5 million.[94]
- increased the maximum loan amount to Microloan borrowers from $35,000 to $50,000.[95]

As mentioned previously, P.L. 111-240 the Small Business Jobs Act of 2010, authorizes the Secretary of the Treasury to create a $30 billion SBLF to encourage community banks to provide small business loans ($4 billion was issued), a $1.5 billion State Small Business Credit Initiative, and about $12 billion in tax relief for small businesses. It also includes revenue raising provisions to offset the act's cost, and authorizes a number of changes to the SBA's loan guaranty, export promotion, and contracting programs, including changes to the SBA's Microloan program. For example, it

- authorizes the SBA to increase the Microloan program's loan limit for borrowers from $35,000 to $50,000, and for Microloan intermediaries after their first year of participation in the program from $3.5 million to $5 million.[96]
- temporarily allowed the SBA to waive, in whole or in part through FY2012, the non-federal share requirement for loans to the Microloan program's intermediaries and for grants made to Microloan intermediaries for small business marketing, management, and technical assistance under specified circumstances (e.g., the

economic conditions affecting the intermediary and the intermediary's performance) for up to a fiscal year.[97]

CONCLUSION

During the 111th Congress, congressional debate concerning proposed changes to the SBA's loan guaranty programs, including the Microloan program, centered on the likely impact the changes would have on small business access to capital, job retention, and job creation. As a general proposition, some, including President Obama, argued that economic conditions made it imperative that the SBA be provided additional resources to assist small businesses in acquiring capital necessary to start, continue, or expand operations and create jobs.[98] Others worried about the long-term adverse economic effects of spending programs that increase the federal deficit. They advocated business tax reduction, reform of financial credit market regulation, and federal fiscal restraint as the best means to assist small business economic growth and job creation.[99]

In terms of specific program changes, the provisions considered in H.R. 3854 and S. 2869 and authorized by P.L. 111-240 (allowing the SBA to temporarily waive the Microloan program's non-federal share matching requirements, increasing its loan limit for borrowers from $35,000 to $50,000, and increasing its loan limit for intermediaries after their first year of participation in the program from $3.5 million to $5 million) were all designed to achieve the same goal: to enhance job creation by increasing the ability of Microloan borrowers to obtain credit at affordable rates. Determining how specific changes in federal policy are most likely to enhance job creation is a challenging question. For example, a 2008 Urban Institute study concluded that differences in the term, interest rate, and amount of SBA financing "was not significantly associated with increasing sales or employment among firms receiving SBA financing."[100] However, they also reported that their analysis accounted for less than 10% of the variation in firm performance. The Urban Institute suggested that local economic conditions, local zoning regulations, state and local tax rates, state and local business assistance programs, and the business owner's charisma or business acumen also "may play a role in determining how well a business performs after receipt of SBA financing."[101]

As the Urban Institute study suggests, given the many factors that influence business success, measuring the SBA's Microloan program's effect on job retention and creation is complicated. That task is made even more challenging by the absence of performance-oriented measures that could serve as a guide.

The SBA's Office of Inspector General has recommended that the SBA adopt performance-oriented measures, specifically recommending that the SBA track the number of Microloan borrowers who remain in business after receiving a microloan to measure the extent to which the Microloan program contributed to their ability to stay in business. It has also recommended that the SBA require intermediaries to report the technical assistance provided to each Microloan borrower and "use this data to analyze the effect technical assistance may have on the success of Microloan borrowers and their ability to repay microloans."[102] Other performance-oriented measures that Congress might also consider include requiring the SBA to survey Microloan borrowers to measure the difficulty they experienced in obtaining a loan from the private sector; the ease or difficulty of finding, applying, and obtaining a microloan from an intermediary; and the extent to which the microloan or technical assistance received contributed to their ability to create jobs or expand their scope of operations.

End Notes

[1] U.S. Small Business Administration, "Fiscal Year 2010 Congressional Budget Justification," pp. 29, 30.

[2] Veronique de Rugy, *Why the Small Business Administration's Loan Programs Should Be Abolished*, American Enterprise Institute for Public Policy Research, AEI Working Paper #126, April 13, 2006, at http://www.aei.org/files/ 2006/04/13/20060414_wp126.pdf. Also, see U.S. Government Accountability Office, *Small Business Administration: 7(a) Loan Program Needs Additional Performance Measures*, GAO-08-226T, November 1, 2007, pp. 3, 9-11, at http://www.gao.gov/new.items/d08226t.pdf.

[3] U.S. Congress, House Committee on Small Business, *Full Committee Legislative Hearing on the SBA's Microloan and Trade Programs*, 110th Cong., 1st sess., July 12, 2007, H.Hrg. 110-35 (Washington: GPO, 2007), p. 6.

[4] Christopher Hayes, *An Assessment of the Small Business Administration's Loan and Investment Programs: Survey of Assisted Businesses* (Washington: The Urban Institute, January 2008), p. 5, at http://www.urban.org/ UploadedPDF/ 411599_assisted_business_survey.pdf.

[5] The SBA also provided direct loans to small businesses until 1994. For further analysis, see CRS Report R40985, *Small Business: Access to Capital and Job Creation*, by Robert Jay Dilger.

[6] Robert Cull, Asli Demiriguc-Kunt, and Jonathan Morduch, "Microfinance Meets the Market," *Journal of Economic Perspectives*, vol. 23, no. 1 (Winter 2009), pp. 169-172; and U.S. Congress, Senate Committee on Small Business and Entrepreneurship, *Microloan Program Improvement Act of 2001*, report to accompany S. 174, 107th Cong., 1st sess., May 26, 2001, S.Rept. 107-18 (Washington: GPO, 2001). About 3.55 million firms in the United States in 2009 had fewer than five employees. See U.S. Census Bureau, *Statistics of U.S. Businesses: U.S. & States, Totals*, at http://www.census.gov/econ/susb/index.html.

[7] 15 U.S.C. §636 7(m)(1)(A).

[8] U.S. Small Business Administration, Office of Advocacy, *Small Business Economic Indicators for 2003*, August 2004, p. 3; and Brian Headd, "Small Businesses Most Likely to Lead Economic Recovery," *The Small Business Advocate*, vol. 28, no. 6 (July 2009), pp. 1, 2.

[9] For further information and analysis concerning the Small Business Lending Fund see CRS Report R42045, *The Small Business Lending Fund*, by Robert Jay Dilger. For further information and analysis concerning the State Small Business Credit Initiative see CRS Report R42581, *State Small Business Credit Initiative: Implementation and Funding Issues*, by Robert Jay Dilger.

[10] For information and analysis concerning the SBA's 7(a) and 504/CDC programs, see CRS Report R41146, *Small Business Administration 7(a) Loan Guaranty Program*, by Robert Jay Dilger and CRS Report R41184, *Small Business Administration 504/CDC Loan Guaranty Program*, by Robert Jay Dilger.

[11] P.L. 111-240, the Small Business Jobs Act of 2010, increased the loan limit for borrowers from $35,000 to $50,000.

[12] There are no Microloan intermediaries located in Alaska and Utah. U.S. Small Business Administration, "Microloan Program: Partner Identification & Management System Participating Intermediary Microlenders Report," at http://www.sba.gov/sites/default/files/ partner_by_subcat_report_20120705.pdf. An intermediary may not operate in more than one state unless the SBA determines that it would be in the best interests of the small business community for it to operate across state lines. For example, the microloan intermediary located in Washington, Pennsylvania is allowed to service ten West Virginia counties due to its proximity to these counties and the distance to the only other intermediary serving West Virginia, which is located in Charleston, West Virginia. Also, a microloan intermediary located in Laguna Nigel, California, which focuses on the capital needs of disabled veteran-owned businesses, serves many jurisdictions throughout the nation that lack a participating intermediary.

[13] The Obama Administration and the House Committee on Appropriations recommended that the Microloan program receive an appropriation of $3.765 million for FY2012, which was expected to support about $25.0 million in lending to intermediaries. The Senate Committee on Appropriations recommended that the Microloan program receive an appropriation of $3.678 million for FY2012, which was expected to support about $25.0 million in lending to intermediaries. See U.S. Office of Management and Budget, *FY2012, Budget of the United States Government, Appendix*, pp. 1161-1172; U.S. Congress, House Committee on

Small Business Administration Microloan Program

Appropriations, *Financial Services and General Government Appropriations Bill, 2012*, report to accompany H.R. 2434, 112th Cong., 1st sess., July 7, 2012, H.Rept. 112-136 (Washington: GPO, 2012), p. 67; and U.S. Congress, Senate Committee on Appropriations, *Financial Services and General Government Appropriations Bill, 2012*, report to accompany S. 1573, 112th Cong., 1st sess., September 15, 2011, S.Rept. 112-79 (Washington: GPO, 2011), p. 115.

[14] U.S. Office of Management and Budget, *FY2013, Budget of the United States Government, Appendix*, p. 1267. The House Committee on Appropriations recommended that the Microloan program receive an appropriation of $2.844 million for FY2013, which is expected to support about $18.0 million in lending to intermediaries. The Senate Committee on Appropriations recommended that the Microloan program receive an appropriation of $4.0 million for FY2013, which is expected to support about $25.0 million in lending to intermediaries. See U.S. Congress, House Committee on Appropriations, *Financial Services and General Government Appropriations Bill, 2013*, report to accompany H.R. 6020, 112th Cong., 2nd sess., June 26, 2012, H.Rept. 112-550 (Washington: GPO, 2012), p. 78; and U.S. Congress, Senate Committee on Appropriations, *Financial Services and General Government Appropriations Bill, 2013*, report to accompany S. 3301, 112th Cong., 2nd sess., June 14, 2012, S.Rept. 112-177 (Washington: GPO, 2012), p. 115.

[15] U.S. Small Business Administration, "Fiscal Year 2013 Congressional Budget Justification and Fiscal Year 2011 Annual Performance Report," p. 15; and P.L. 112-74, the Consolidated Appropriations Act, 2012.

[16] U.S. Office of Management and Budget, *FY2013, Budget of the United States Government, Appendix*, p. 1265. The House Committee on Appropriations recommended that the Microloan technical assistance program receive an appropriation of $20.0 million for FY2013. The Senate Committee on Appropriations recommended that the Microloan technical assistance program receive an appropriation of $24.0 million. See U.S. Congress, House Committee on Appropriations, Financial Services and General Government Appropriations Bill, 2013, report to accompany H.R. 6020, 112th Cong., 2nd sess., June 26, 2012, H.Rept. 112-550 (Washington: GPO, 2012), p. 76; and U.S. Congress, Senate Committee on Appropriations, *Financial Services and General Government Appropriations Bill, 2013*, report to accompany S. 3301, 112th Cong., 2nd sess., June 14, 2012, S.Rept. 112-177 (Washington: GPO, 2012), p. 111.

[17] U.S. Small Business Administration, Office of Congressional and Legislative Affairs, correspondence with the author, October 16, 2012. The Microloan technical assistance program provided counseling services to 15,900 small businesses in FY2011, 14,916 small businesses in FY2010, and 2,757 in FY2009. See U.S. Small Business Administration, "Fiscal Year 2013 Congressional Budget Justification and Fiscal Year 2011 Annual Performance Report," p. 34.

[18] 13 C.F.R §120.701; and 13 C.F.R §120.702. P.L. 111-240, the Small Business Jobs Act of 2010, increased the loan limit for borrowers from $35,000 to $50,000.

[19] 13 C.F.R §120.706. P.L. 111-240, the Small Business Jobs Act of 2010, increased the loan limit for intermediaries after their first year of participation in the program from $3.5 million to $5 million.

[20] 13 C.F.R §120.706.

[21] 15 U.S.C. §636 7(m)(3)(F)(iii). In August 2012, the SBA's interest rate to intermediaries was 0.0% if the average loan size in the intermediary's portfolio was under $10,000. The rate was also 0.0% if the average loan size was greater than $10,000. U.S. Small Business Administration, Office of Congressional and Legislative Affairs, correspondence with the author, August 2, 2012.

[22] 13 C.F.R §120.706. Note: The 15% contribution must be from non-federal sources and may not be borrowed. For purposes of this program, Community Development Block Grants are considered non-federal sources.

[23] Ibid.

[24] P.L. 111-240, the Small Business Jobs Act of 2010, §1401. Matching Requirements Under Small Business Programs.

[25] 13 C.F.R §120.709.

[26] 13 C.F.R §120.710. If the intermediary's average annual loss rate during the preceding five years is less than 15% and no other factors exist that may impair the intermediary's ability to repay its obligations to the SBA, the SBA Administrator may reduce the required balance in the intermediary's Loan Loss Reserve Fund to the intermediary's average annual loss rate during the preceding five years, but not less than 10% of the portfolio.

[27] Ibid.

[28] U.S. Congress, House Committee on Small Business, *Full Committee Hearings on the Small Business Administration's Microloan Program*, 110th Cong., 1st sess., June 14, 2007, H.Hrg. 110-30 (Washington: GPO, 2007), p. 15. Note: A study released on December 28, 2009 by the U.S. Small Business Administration, Office of the Inspector General, concluded that Microloan intermediaries may be under-reporting the default rate. See U.S. Small Business Administration, Office of the Inspector General, "SBA's Administration of the Microloan

Program under the Recovery Act," December 28, 2009, at http://www.sba.gov/office-of-inspector-general/868/12427.

[29] U.S. Small Business Administration, "2008 Loss Report," p. 10, at http://archive.sba.gov/idc/groups/public/ documents/sba_program_office/cfo_2008_loss_ report.pdf; and U.S. Small Business Administration, Office of Congressional and Legislative Affairs, correspondence with the author, August 2, 2012. In FY2011, the Microloan program's intermediary default rate was 2.15%. See U.S. Small Business Administration, "Agency Financial Report, Fiscal Year 2011," p. 8, at http://www.sba.gov/sites/default/files/ Agency%20 Financial%20Report%20 FY%20 2011_ 0.pdf. A total of 27 loans to intermediaries have been charged off over the life of the Microloan program, through August 2, 2012. The amount charged off on these 27 loans is $3,985,056.54. This represents 1.11% of total funds disbursed to intermediaries and 3.20% of the current outstanding principal balance of loans to intermediary lenders.

[30] 13 C.F.R §120.716.

[31] 15 U.S.C. §636(m)(4)(A). Note: The SBA's Program for Investment in Microentrepreneurs Act (PRIME) program also provides non-profit organizations grant funding to assist low-income entrepreneurs with training assistance. See, U.S. Small Business Administration, "PRIME Program," at http://www.sba.gov/content/ prime-program-0.

[32] 13 C.F.R §120.712.

[33] Ibid. Intermediaries who make at least 50% of their loans to small businesses located in or owned by residents of Economically Distressed Areas are not subject to the 25% contribution requirement. An economically distressed area is a county or equivalent division of local government in which, according to the most recent available data from the U.S. Census Bureau, 40% or more of the residents have an annual income that is at or below the poverty level. See 13 C.F.R §120.701.

[34] 13 C.F.R §120.712. Intermediaries may not borrow their contribution.

[35] Ibid.

[36] P.L. 111-240, the Small Business Jobs Act of 2010, §1401. Matching Requirements Under Small Business Programs.

[37] 13 C.F.R §120.712; and 15 U.S.C. §636(m)(4)(C)(i).

[38] 13 C.F.R §120.714.

[39] Ibid.

[40] Ibid.

[41] U.S. Small Business Administration, Office of Congressional and Legislative Affairs, correspondence with the author, August 2, 2012.

[42] 15 U.S.C. §636(m)(1)(A)(iii)(I).

[43] 15 U.S.C. §636(m)(6)(B).

[44] 15 U.S.C. §636(m)(3)(E).

[45] 13 C.F.R §120.707. P.L. 111-240, the Small Business Jobs Act of 2010, increased the loan limit for borrowers from $35,000 to $50,000.

[46] Ibid.

[47] 15 U.S.C. §636 7(m)(6)(C)(i); and 15 U.S.C. §636 7(m)(6)(C)(ii).

[48] In FY2012, Microloan borrowers were charged, on average, an interest rate of 8.18, compared to 8.45% in FY2011. U.S Small Business Administration, "Nationwide Loan Report, October 1, 2011 through September 30, 2012," October 15, 2012; and U.S Small Business Administration, "Nationwide Loan Report, October 1, 2010 through September 30, 2011," November 2, 2011.

[49] U.S. Small Business Administration, "Microloan Program," at http://www.sba.gov/ content/microloan-program.

[50] U.S. Small Business Administration, Office of Congressional and Legislative Affairs, correspondence with the author, October 16, 2012.

[51] U.S. Small Business Administration, "Microloans Help Small Businesses Start, Grow and Succeed," at http://archive.sba.gov/idc/groups/public/documents/sba_homepage/recovery_ act_microloans.pdf.

[52] Kenneth Temkin, Brett Theodos, with Kerstin Gentsch, *Competitive and Special Competitive Opportunity Gap Analysis of the 7(A) and 504 Programs* (Washington: The Urban Institute, 2008), p. 13, at http://www.urban.org/ UploadedPDF/411596_504_gap_analysis.pdf.

[53] U.S Small Business Administration, "Nationwide Loan Report, October 1, 2011 through September 30, 2012," October 15, 2012.

[54] Ibid.

[55] U.S. Congress, House Committee on Small Business, *Full Committee Hearings on the Small Business Administration's Microloan Program*, 110th Cong., 1st sess., June 14, 2007, H.Hrg. 110-30 (Washington: GPO,

2007), p. 15. Note: A study released on December 28, 2009 by the U.S. Small Business Administration, Office of the Inspector General, concluded that Microloan intermediaries may be under-reporting the default rate. See U.S. Small Business Administration, Office of the Inspector General, "SBA's Administration of the Microloan Program under the Recovery Act," December 28, 2009, at http://www.sba.gov/office-of-inspector-general/868/12427.

[56] U.S. Small Business Administration, "2008 Loss Report," p. 10, at http://archive.sba.gov/idc/groups/public/ documents/sba_program_office/cfo_2008_loss_report.pdf; and U.S. Small Business Administration, Office of Congressional and Legislative Affairs, correspondence with the author, August 2, 2012. In FY2011, the Microloan program's intermediary default rate was 2.15%. See U.S. Small Business Administration, "Agency Financial Report, Fiscal Year 2011," p. 8, at http://www.sba.gov/sites/default/files/ Agency%20Financial%20 Report%20 FY%202011_0.pdf. A total of 27 loans to intermediaries have been charged off over the life of the Microloan program, through August 2, 2012. The amount charged off on these 27 loans is $3,985,056.54. This represents 1.11% of total funds disbursed to intermediaries and 3.20% of the current outstanding principal balance of loans to intermediary lenders.

[57] U.S Small Business Administration, "Nationwide Loan Report, October 1, 2011 through September 30, 2012," October 15, 2012.

[58] U.S. Congress, House Committee on Small Business, *Full Committee Hearing on the Small Business Administration's Microloan Program*, 110th Cong., 1st sess., June 14, 2007, H.Hrg. 110-30 (Washington: GPO, 2007), pp. 1, 2.

[59] U.S. Office of Management and Budget, *Budget of the United States Government: Fiscal Year 2005*, p. 334, at http://www.gpoaccess.gov/usbudget/fy05/pdf/budget/sba.pdf; U.S. Office of Management and Budget, *Budget of the United States Government: Fiscal Year 2006*, p. 313, at http://www.gpoaccess.gov/usbudget/fy06/ pdf/budget/sba.pdf; and U.S. Office of Management and Budget, *Budget of the United States Government: Fiscal Year 2007*, p. 283, at http://www.gpoaccess.gov/usbudget/fy07/pdf/budget/sba.pdf.

[60] U.S. Office of Management and Budget, *Budget of the United States Government: Fiscal Year 2008*, pp. 139, 140, at http://www.gpoaccess.gov/usbudget/fy08/pdf/budget/sba.pdf; and U.S. Office of Management and Budget, *Budget of the United States Government: Fiscal Year 2009*, p. 130, at http://www.gpoaccess.gov/ usbudget/fy09/pdf/budget/sba.pdf. The Bush Administration also proposed to increase the interest rate charged to intermediaries.

[61] U.S. Congress, House Committee on Small Business, *Full Committee Legislative Hearing on the SBA's Microloan and Trade Programs*, 110th Cong., 1st sess., July 12, 2007, H.Hrg. 110-35 (Washington: GPO, 2007), p. 37.

[62] Ibid.

[63] Ibid., pp. 37, 38.

[64] U.S. Congress, House Committee on Small Business, *Full Committee Hearing on the Small Business Administration's Microloan Program*, 110th Cong., 1st sess., June 14, 2007, H.Hrg. 110-30 (Washington: GPO, 2007), p. 7.

[65] U.S. Congress, House Committee on Small Business, *Full Committee Legislative Hearing on the SBA's Microloan and Trade Programs*, 110th Cong., 1st sess., July 12, 2007, H.Hrg. 110-35 (Washington: GPO, 2007), p. 27.

[66] Ibid., p. 7.

[67] Ibid.

[68] U.S. Small Business Administration, "Fiscal Year 2013 Congressional Budget Justification and Fiscal Year 2011 Annual Performance Report," pp. 31, 34.

[69] U.S. Office of Management and Budget, *Budget of the United States Government: Fiscal Year 2008*, pp. 139, 140, at http://www.gpoaccess.gov/usbudget/fy08/pdf/budget/sba.pdf; U.S. Office of Management and Budget, *Budget of the United States Government: Fiscal Year 2009*, p. 130, at http://www.gpoaccess.gov/usbudget/ fy09/pdf/budget/sba.pdf; U.S. Congress, House Committee on Small Business, *Full Committee Legislative Hearing on the SBA's Microloan and Trade Programs*, 110th Cong., 1st sess., July 12, 2007, H.Hrg. 110-35 (Washington: GPO, 2007), p. 38; and U.S. Congress, House Committee on Small Business, Subcommittee on Finance and Tax, *Subcommittee Hearing on Improving the SBA's Access to Capital Programs for our Nation's Small Businesses*, 110th Cong., 2nd sess., March 5, 2008, H.Hrg. 110-76 (Washington: GPO, 2008), p. 33.

[70] U.S. Congress, House Committee on Small Business, Subcommittee on Finance and Tax, *Subcommittee Hearing on Improving the SBA's Access to Capital Programs for our Nation's Small Businesses*, 110th Cong., 2nd sess., March 5, 2008, H.Hrg. 110-76 (Washington: GPO, 2008), p. 46.

[71] U.S. Small Business Administration, Office of the Inspector General, "SBA's Administration of the Microloan Program under the Recovery Act," p. 1, at http://www.sba.gov/office-of-inspector-general/868/12427.

[72] Ibid., p. 4.

[73] Ibid.

[74] Ibid., p. 8.

[75] Ibid., p. 4.

[76] Ibid., p. 5.

[77] Ibid.

[78] Ibid., p. 8.

[79] Ibid., p. 9.

[80] Ibid., p. 6.

[81] Ibid.

[82] Ibid., p. 7.

[83] Ibid., p. 9.

[84] H.R. 3854 combined language from eight bills and would have authorized changes to several SBA programs and create several new programs. For further analysis, see CRS Report R41385, *Small Business Legislation During the 111th Congress*, by Robert Jay Dilger and Gary Guenther.

[85] H.R. 3854, the Small Business Financing and Investment Act of 2009, §310. Authorization of Appropriations.

[86] Ibid.

[87] H.R. 3854, the Small Business Financing and Investment Act of 2009, §307. Interest Rates and Loan Size. The interest rate charged to intermediaries is based on the five-year Treasury rate, adjusted to the nearest one-eighth percent, less 1.25%. However, intermediaries that maintain an average loan size of $7,500 or less are charged an interest rate based on the five-year Treasury rate, adjusted to the nearest one-eighth percent, less 2.0%. H.R. 3854 would have enabled more intermediaries to qualify for the lower rate by increasing the required average loan size from $7,500 to $10,000.

[88] U.S. Congress, House Committee on Small Business, Small Business Financing and Investment Act of 2009, report to accompany H.R. 3854, 111th Cong., 1st sess., October 26, 2009, H.Rept. 111-315 (Washington: GPO, 2009), p. 34; and H.R. 3854, the Small Business Financing and Investment Act of 2009, §304. Increased Limit on Intermediary Borrowing.

[89] U.S. Congress, House Committee on Small Business, Small Business Financing and Investment Act of 2009, report to accompany H.R. 3854, 111th Cong., 1st sess., October 26, 2009, H.Rept. 111-315 (Washington: GPO, 2009), p. 34. At that time, intermediaries must have made and serviced short-term, fixed rate loans of not more than $35,000 (now $50,000) to newly established or growing small businesses for at least one year and have at least one year of experience providing technical assistance to its borrowers. Under H.R. 3854, intermediaries would have been required to have at least one year of experience making microloans to startup, newly established, or growing small business concerns, or have a full-time employee who has not less than three years' experience in managing a portfolio of loans to startup, newly established, or growing small business concerns. They would have been required to also have at least one year of experience providing, as an integral part of its microloan program, intensive marketing, management, and technical assistance to its borrowers, or one full-time employee who has not less than one year experience providing, as an integral part of its microloan program, intensive marketing, management, and technical assistance to its borrowers. This change would have allowed an aspiring intermediary with no direct experience in microlending and technical assistance to hire trained employees with considerable, equivalent experience and still qualify to participate in the program.

[90] H.R. 3854, the Small Business Financing and Investment Act of 2009, §301. Microloan Credit Building Initiative. This change was designed to enhance Microloan borrowers' credit scores and their future access to capital. Intermediaries generally opposed the provision, viewing it as an administrative burden. U.S. Congress, House Committee on Small Business, *Small Business Financing and Investment Act of 2009*, report to accompany H.R. 3854, 111th Cong., 1st sess., October 26, 2009, H.Rept. 111-315 (Washington: GPO, 2009), p. 34.

[91] H.R. 3854, the Small Business Financing and Investment Act of 2009, §302. Flexible Credit Terms; and U.S. Congress, House Committee on Small Business, *Small Business Financing and Investment Act of 2009*, report to accompany H.R. 3854, 111th Cong., 1st sess., October 26, 2009, H.Rept. 111-315 (Washington: GPO, 2009), p. 34.

[92] U.S. Congress, House Committee on Small Business, *Small Business Financing and Investment Act of 2009*, report to accompany H.R. 3854, 111th Cong., 1st sess., October 26, 2009, H.Rept. 111-315 (Washington: GPO, 2009), p. 35.

[93] H.R. 3854, the Small Business Financing and Investment Act of 2009, §308. Reporting Requirement. The report was to include the following information: the names and locations of each intermediary participating in the program; the amounts of each loan and each grant provided to each intermediary during the fiscal year and in prior fiscal years; a description of the contributions from non-federal sources; the number and amounts of microloans made by intermediaries to all borrowers and to each of the following: women entrepreneurs and business owners, low-income entrepreneurs and business owners, veteran entrepreneurs and business owners, disabled entrepreneurs and business owners, and minority entrepreneurs and business owners; a description of the marketing, management, and technical assistance provided by each intermediary to all borrowers and to each of the following: women entrepreneurs and business owners, low-income entrepreneurs and business owners, veteran entrepreneurs and business owners, disabled entrepreneurs and business owners, and minority entrepreneurs and business owners; the number of jobs created and retained as a result of microloans and marketing, management, and technical assistance provided by each intermediary; the repayment history of each intermediary; and the number of businesses that achieved success after receipt of a microloan.

[94] S. 2869, the Small Business Job Creation and Access to Capital Act of 2009, §103. Maximum Loan Limits Under Microloan Program.

[95] Ibid.

[96] P.L. 111-240, the Small Business Jobs Act of 2010, §1113. Maximum Loan Limits Under Microloan Program.

[97] P.L. 111-240, the Small Business Jobs Act of 2010, §1401. Matching Requirements Under Small Business Programs.

[98] Representative Nydia Velázquez, Small Business Financing and Investment Act of 2009," House debate, *Congressional Record*, daily edition, vol. 155, no. 159 (October 29, 2009), pp. H12074, H12075; Senator Mary Landrieu, "Statements on Introduced Bills and Joint Resolutions," remarks in the Senate, *Congressional Record*, daily edition, vol. 155, no. 185 (December 10, 2009), p. S12910; and The White House, "Remarks by the President on Job Creation and Economic Growth," December 8, 2009, at http://www.whitehouse.gov/the-press-office/remarkspresident-job-creation-and-economic-growth.

[99] Susan Eckerly, "NFIB Responds to President's Small Business Lending Initiatives," Washington, DC, October 21, 2009, at http://www.nfib.com/press-media/press-media-item?cmsid=50080; and NFIB, "Government Spending," Washington, DC, at http://www.nfib.com/issues-elections/issues-elections-item/cmsid/49051/.

[100] Shelli B. Rossman and Brett Theodos, with Rachel Brash, Megan Gallagher, Christopher Hayes, and Kenneth Temkin, *Key Findings from the Evaluation of the Small Business Administration's Loan and Investment Programs: Executive Summary* (Washington, DC: The Urban Institute, January 2008), p. 58, at http://www.urban.org/ UploadedPDF/ 411602_executive_summary.pdf.

[101] Ibid.

[102] U.S. Small Business Administration, Office of the Inspector General, "SBA's Administration of the Microloan Program under the Recovery Act," pp. 6, 7, at http://www.sba.gov/office-of-inspector-general/868/12427.

In: Small Business Administration Programs
Editor: Walter Janikowski

ISBN: 978-1-62417-992-1
© 2013 Nova Science Publishers, Inc.

Chapter 6

SBA SMALL BUSINESS INVESTMENT COMPANY PROGRAM[*]

Robert Jay Dilger

SUMMARY

The Small Business Administration's (SBA's) Small Business Investment Company (SBIC) Program is designed to enhance small business access to venture capital by stimulating and supplementing "the flow of private equity capital and long term loan funds which small business concerns need for the sound financing of their business operations and for their growth, expansion, and modernization, and which are not available in adequate supply." Facilitating the flow of capital to small businesses to stimulate the national economy was, and remains, the SBIC program's primary objective.

At the end of FY2012, there were 301 privately owned and managed SBICs licensed by the SBA, providing financing to small businesses with private capital the SBIC has raised (called regulatory capital) and funds the SBIC borrows at favorable rates (called leverage) because the SBA guarantees the debenture (loan obligation). SBICs pursue investments in a broad range of industries, geographic areas, and stages of investment. Some SBICs specialize in a particular field or industry, while others invest more generally. Most SBICs concentrate on a particular stage of investment (i.e., startup, expansion, or turnaround) and geographic area.

The SBA is authorized to provide up to $3 billion in leverage to SBICs annually. The SBIC program has invested or committed about $18.2 billion in small businesses, with the SBA's share of capital at risk about $8.8 billion. In FY2012, the SBA committed to guarantee $1.9 billion in SBIC small business investments, and SBICs provided another $1.3 billion in investments from private capital, for a total of more than $3.2 billion in financing for 1,094 small businesses.

Some Members of Congress, the Obama Administration, and small business advocates argue that the program should be expanded as a means to stimulate economic activity, create jobs, and assist in the national economic recovery. For example, S. 3442, the SUCCESS Act of 2012, and S. 3572, the Restoring Tax and Regulatory Certainty to Small Businesses Act of 2012, would, among other provisions, increase the program's

---

[*] This is an edited, reformatted and augmented version of Congressional Research Service, Publication No. R41456, dated December 11, 2012.

authorization amount to $4 billion from $3 billion, increase the program's family of funds limit (the amount of outstanding leverage allowed for two or more SBIC licenses under common control) to $350 million from $225 million, and annually adjust the maximum outstanding leverage amount available to both individual SBICs and SBICs under common control to account for inflation. Also, H.R. 6504, the Small Business Investment Company Modernization Act of 2012, would increase the program's family of funds limit (the amount of outstanding leverage allowed for two or more SBIC licenses under common control) to $350 million from $225 million.

Others worry that an expanded SBIC program could result in loses and increase the federal deficit. In their view, the best means to assist small business, promote economic growth, and create jobs is to reduce business taxes and exercise federal fiscal restraint.

Some Members have also proposed that the program target additional assistance to startup and early stage small businesses, which are generally viewed as relatively risky investments but also as having a relatively high potential for job creation. In an effort to target additional assistance to newer businesses, the SBA has established, as part of the Obama Administration's Startup America Initiative, a $1 billion early stage debenture SBIC initiative (up to $150 million in leverage in FY2012, and up to $200 million in leverage per fiscal year thereafter until the limit is reached). Early stage debenture SBICs are required to invest at least 50% of their investments in early stage small businesses, defined as small businesses that have never achieved positive cash flow from operations in any fiscal year.

This report describes the SBIC program's structure and operations, including two recent SBA initiatives, one targeting early stage small businesses and one targeting underserved markets. It also examines several legislative proposals to increase the leverage available to SBICs and to increase the SBIC program's authorization amount to $4 billion.

SBIC PROGRAM OVERVIEW

The Small Business Administration (SBA) administers several programs to support small businesses, including loan guaranty programs to enhance small business access to capital; programs to increase small business opportunities in federal contracting; direct loans for businesses, homeowners, and renters to assist their recovery from natural disasters; and access to entrepreneurial education to assist with business formation and expansion.[1] It also administers the Small Business Investment Company (SBIC) Program.

Authorized by P.L. 85-699, the Small Business Investment Act of 1958, as amended, the SBIC program is designed to "improve and stimulate the national economy in general and the small business segment thereof in particular" by stimulating and supplementing "the flow of private equity capital and long term loan funds which small business concerns need for the sound financing of their business operations and for their growth, expansion, and modernization, and which are not available in adequate supply."[2]

The SBIC program was created to address concerns raised in a Federal Reserve Board report to Congress that concluded that a gap existed in the capital markets for long-term funding for growth-oriented small businesses. The report noted that the SBA's loan programs were "limited to providing short-term and intermediate-term credit when such loans are unavailable from private institutions," and the SBA "did not provide equity financing."[3] Equity financing (or equity capital) is money raised by a company in exchange for a share of ownership in the business. Ownership is represented by owning shares of stock outright or having the right to convert other financial instruments into stock. Equity financing allows a business to obtain funds without incurring debt, or without having to repay a specific amount of money at a particular time. The Federal Reserve Board's report concluded that there was a need for a federal government program to "stimulate the availability of capital funds to small business" to assist them in gaining access to long-term financing and equity financing.[4] Facilitating the flow of capital to small businesses to stimulate the national economy was, and remains, the SBIC program's primary objective.

The SBA does not make direct investments in small businesses. It partners with privately owned and managed SBICs licensed by the SBA to provide financing to small businesses with private capital the SBIC has raised (called regulatory capital) and with funds (called leverage) the SBIC borrows at favorable rates because the SBA guarantees the debenture (loan obligation). At the end of FY2012, there were 301 licensed SBICs participating in the SBIC program.[5]

The SBA is authorized to provide up to $3 billion in leverage to SBICs annually. In FY2012, the SBA provided $1.9 billion in leverage to SBICs.[6]

Some Members of Congress, the Obama Administration, and small business advocates have argued that the SBIC program should be expanded as a means to stimulate economic activity, create jobs, and assist in the national economic recovery. For example, S. 3442, the SUCCESS Act of 2012, and S. 3572, the Restoring Tax and Regulatory Certainty to Small Businesses Act of 2012, would, among other provisions, increase the program's authorization amount to $4 billion from $3 billion, increase the program's family of funds limit (the amount of outstanding SBA leverage allowed for two or more SBIC licenses under common control) to $350 million from $225 million, and annually adjust the maximum outstanding SBA leverage amount available to both individual SBICs and SBIC investments under common control to account for inflation.[7] Also, H.R. 6504, the Small Business Investment Company Modernization Act of 2012, would increase the program's family of funds limit to $350 million from $225 million.[8]

Others worry about the potential risk an expanded SBIC program has for increasing the federal deficit. In their view, the best means to assist small business, promote economic growth, and create jobs is to reduce business taxes and exercise federal fiscal restraint.

Some Members and small business advocates have also proposed that the program target additional assistance to startup and early stage small businesses, which are generally viewed as relatively risky investments but also as having a relatively high potential for job creation. The SBA, in an effort to target additional assistance to newer businesses, recently established, as part of the Administration's Startup America Initiative, a $1 billion early stage debenture SBIC initiative (up to $150 million in leverage in FY2012, and up to $200 million in leverage per fiscal year thereafter until the limit is reached). Early stage debenture SBICs are required to invest at least 50% of their investments in early stage small businesses, defined as small businesses that have never achieved positive cash flow from operations in any fiscal year.

This report examines the structure and operation of the SBIC program, focusing on SBIC eligibility requirements, investment activity, and program statistics. It includes information concerning the SBIC program's debenture SBIC program, participating securities SBIC program, $1 billion early stage debenture SBIC initiative (targeting early stage small businesses), and $1 billion impact investment SBIC initiative (targeting underserved markets and communities facing barriers to access to credit and capital).

This report also examines proposals and legislation considered during the 111th and 112th Congresses, including H.R. 3854, the Small Business Financing and Investment Act of 2009; H.R. 5554, the Small Business Assistance and Relief Act of 2010; P.L. 111-240, the Small Business Jobs Act of 2010; H.R. 6504, the Small Business Investment Company Modernization Act of 2012; S.Amdt. 1833, the INVEST in America Act of 2012; S. 3442, the SUCCESS Act of 2012, S. 3572, the Restoring Tax and Regulatory Certainty to Small Businesses Act of 2012, and the Obama Administration's Startup America Initiative. These proposals and legislation address the program's financing and/or the targeting of additional assistance to startup and early stage small businesses.

SBIC TYPES

There are two types of SBICs. Investment companies licensed under Section 301(c) of the Small Business Investment Act of 1958, as amended, are referred to as original, or regular, SBICs. Investment companies licensed under Section 301(d) of the act, called Specialized Small Business Investment Companies (SSBICs), focus on providing financing to small business entrepreneurs "whose participation in the free enterprise system is hampered because of social or economic disadvantage."[9] Section 301(d) was repealed by P.L. 104-208, the Omnibus Consolidated Appropriations Act, 1997 (Title II of Division D, the Small Business Programs Improvement Act of 1996). As a result, no new SSBIC licenses have been issued since October 1, 1996. However, existing SSBICs were "grandfathered" and remain in operation.

With few exceptions, SBICs and SSBICs are subject to the same eligibility requirements and operating rules and regulations. Therefore, the SBIC name is usually used to refer to both SBICs and SSBICs simultaneously.

There are five types of regular SBICs. *Debenture* SBICs, *impact investment debenture* SBICs, and *early stage debenture* SBICs receive leverage through the issuance of debentures.[10] Debentures are debt obligations issued by SBICs and held or guaranteed by the SBA.[11] *Participating securities* SBICs receive leverage through the issuance of participating securities. Participating securities are redeemable, preferred, equity-type securities, often in the form of limited partnership interests, preferred stock, or debentures with interest payable only to the extent of earnings.[12] *Bank-owned, non-leveraged* SBICs do not receive leverage.[13] This report focuses on the four types of regular SBICs that receive leverage from the SBA.

SBIC ELIGIBILITY REQUIREMENTS

An SBIC can be organized in any state, as either a corporation, limited partnership (LP), or a limited liability company (LLCs must be organized under Delaware law). Most SBICs are owned by relatively small groups of local investors, although many are partially owned, and some are wholly owned (44 of 301), by commercial banks. A few SBICs are corporations with publicly traded stock.[14]

One of the primary criteria for licensure as an SBIC is having qualified management. The SBA reviews and approves a prospective SBIC's management team based upon its professional capabilities and character. Specifically, the SBA examines the SBIC's management team looking for

- substantive and relevant principal investment experience;
- realized track record of superior returns, based on an overall evaluation of appropriate quantitative performance measures;
- evidence of a strong rate of business proposals and investment offers (deal flow) in the investment area proposed for the new fund;
- a cohesive management team, with complementary skills and history of working together;
- managerial, operational, or technical experience that can add value at the portfolio company level; and
- a demonstrated ability to manage cash flows so as to provide assurance the SBA will be repaid on a timely basis.[15]

SBIC APPLICATION PROCESS

Applying for an SBIC debenture license is a multi-step process, beginning with the submission of the SBA Management Assessment Questionnaire (MAQ). It includes, among others, questions concerning

- the fund's legal name, and the name and addresses of its principals and control persons;[16]
- the fund's finances and expenses;
- the management team's professional experience;
- the fund's expected investing focus (e.g., will the fund be primarily a sole investor, lead investor, or co-investor; its anticipated percentage of investments in technology, life sciences, health care, manufacturing, distribution, service, consumer products and retail, or other industries; and its anticipated percentage of investments by business life cycle—seed, early stage, expansion, later stage, change of control, or turnaround);
- the geographic areas where the investments are expected to be made;
- the anticipated holding periods for investments;
- the types and characteristics of the securities that will be used to make investments; and
- the extent to which "special groups of businesses" will be targeted for investment, such as "ethnic groups, women, rural, inner city, etc."[17]

After receiving the firm's application, a member of the SBA's Program Development Office reviews the MAQ; assesses the investment company's proposal in light of the program's minimum requirements and management qualifications; performs initial due diligence, including making reference telephone calls; and prepares a written recommendation to the SBA's Investment Division's Investment Committee (composed of senior members of the division).

If, after reviewing the MAQ and the SBA's Program Development Office's evaluation, the Investment Committee concludes, by majority vote at a regularly scheduled meeting, that the investment company's management team may be qualified for a license, the investment company's management team is invited to the SBA's headquarters in Washington, DC, for an interview. If, following the interview, the Investment Committee votes to proceed, the investment team is provided a "Green Light" letter, formally inviting the investment team to file a license application, along with a filing fee of $10,000, plus an additional $5,000 for partnerships or LLC SBICs. If the license is approved, all SBIC principals must complete the SBA's SBIC Regulations training classes. On average, obtaining an SBIC license takes about six months from the time of the initial submission of the MAQ to issuance of the license.[18]

As will be discussed, new applications for the participating securities program are no longer being accepted. Impact investment debenture SBIC applicants are required to submit the same documents, follow the same process, and meet the same standards as applicants seeking a debenture SBIC license. However, impact investment debenture SBICs are provided an expedited review process.[19]

The application process for an early stage debenture SBIC license is similar to the application process for a SBIC debenture license. Two major differences are that the SBA only accepts applications to the early stage innovation program during specific time periods published "from time to time" in the *Federal Register* (expected to be annually) and places "particular emphasis on managers' skills and experience in evaluating and investing in early stage companies."[20]

Also, early stage debenture SBIC applicants must pay a partnership licensee fee plus an additional $10,000, for a total application fee of $25,000.[21]

The eligibility requirements and application process for small businesses requesting financial assistance from an SBIC is provided in the Appendix.

SBIC CAPITAL INVESTMENT REQUIREMENTS

Debenture SBICs

P.L. 85-699, the Small Business Investment Act of 1958, authorized the SBA to select companies to participate in the SBIC program and to purchase debentures from those companies to provide them additional funds to invest in small businesses.

Initially, debenture SBICs were required to have a private capital investment of at least $300,000 to participate in the SBIC program.

Debenture SBICs are now required to have a private capital investment of at least $5 million (called regulatory capital).[22] The SBA has discretion to license an applicant with regulatory capital of $3 million if the applicant has satisfied all licensing standards and requirements, has a viable business plan reasonably projecting profitable operations, and has a reasonable timetable for achieving regulatory capital of at least $5 million.[23]

At least 30% of a debenture SBIC's regulatory and leverageable capital must come from three people unaffiliated with the fund's management and unaffiliated with each other.[24] Also, no more than 33% of a SBIC's regulatory capital may come from state or local government entities.[25]

Participating Securities SBICs

P.L. 102-366, the Small Business Credit and Business Opportunity Enhancement Act of 1992 (Title IV, the Small Business Equity Enhancement Act of 1992), authorized the SBA to guarantee participating securities. Participating securities are redeemable, preferred, equity-type securities issued by SBICs in the form of limited partnership interests, preferred stock, or debentures with interest payable only to the extent of earnings. In 1994, the SBA established the SBIC Participating Securities Program (SBIC PSP) to encourage the formation of participating securities SBICs that would make equity investments in startup and early stage small businesses. The SBA created the program to fill a perceived investment gap created by the SBIC debenture program's focus on mid- and later-stage small businesses. The SBA stopped issuing new commitments for participation securities on October 1, 2004, beginning a process to end the program, which continues.[26] The SBA stopped issuing new commitments for participating securities primarily because the program experienced a projected loss of $2.7 billion during the early 2000s as investments in technology startup and early stage small businesses lost much of their stock value at that time. The SBA found that "the fees payable by SBICs for participating securities leverage are not sufficient to cover the projected net losses in the participating securities program."[27] The SBA continued to honor its existing commitments to participating securities SBICs and they were allowed to continue operations. However, they were required to comply with special rules concerning minimum capital, liquidity, non-SBA borrowing, and equity investing.[28] In recent years, some Members have expressed interest in either revising the program or starting a new program modeled on certain aspects of the SBIC PSP to assist startup and early stage small businesses has increased.[29] Although the SBA is no longer issuing new commitments for participating securities, and each year several participating securities SBICs leave the program as their leverage commitments are retired, at the end of FY2012 there were still 86 participating securities SBICs in the SBIC program.[30] To participate in the SBIC program, a participating securities SBICs must have regulatory capital of at least $10 million. The SBA has discretion to require less than $10 million in regulatory capital if the licensee can demonstrate that it can be financially viable over the long term with a lower amount. In this circumstance, the regulatory amount required may not be lower than $5 million.[31] At least 30% of a participating securities SBIC's regulatory and leverageable capital must come from three people unaffiliated with the fund's management and unaffiliated with each other.[32] Also, no more than 33% of a SBIC's regulatory capital can come from state or local government entities.[33]

Impact Investment Debenture SBICs

On April 7, 2011, the SBA announced that it was establishing a $1 billion impact investment SBIC initiative (up to $150 million in leverage in FY2012, and up to $200 million in leverage per fiscal year thereafter until the limit is reached). Under this initiative, SBA-licensed impact investment debenture SBICs are required to invest at least 50% of their financings, "which target areas of critical national priority including underserved markets and communities facing barriers to access to credit and capital."[34] Impact investment debenture SBICs are required to have a minimum private capital investment of at least $5 million, subject to the same conditions as debenture SBICs concerning the source of the funds. At the end of FY2012, two impact investment SBICs had been licensed and four standard debenture SBICs had an impact focus. The SBA reported that these funds have over $200 million in private capital and close to $400 million of SBA-guaranteed leverage to make impact investments.[35]

Early Stage Debenture SBICs

On April 27, 2012, the SBA published a final rule in the *Federal Register* establishing a $1 billion early stage debenture SBIC initiative (up to $150 million in leverage in FY2012, and up to $200 million in leverage per fiscal year thereafter until the limit is reached).[36] Early stage debenture SBICs are required to invest at least 50% of their financings in early stage small businesses, defined as small businesses that have never achieved positive cash flow from operations in any fiscal year.[37] In recognition of the higher risk associated with investments in early stage small businesses, the initiative includes "several new regulatory provisions intended to reduce the risk that an early stage SBIC would default on its leverage and to improve SBA's recovery prospects should a default occur."[38] For example, early stage debenture SBICs are required to raise more regulatory capital (at least $20 million) than debenture SBICs and impact investment debenture SBICs (at least $5 million) and participating securities SBICs (at least $10 million). They are also subject to special distribution rules to require pro rata repayment of SBA leverage when making distributions of profits to their investors.

In addition, as will be discussed, early stage debenture SBICs are also provided less leverage (up to 100% of regulatory capital, $50 million maximum) than debenture SBICs and participating securities SBICs (up to 200% of regulatory capital, $150 million maximum per SBIC and $225 million for two or more SBICs under common control), and impact investment debenture SBICs (up to 200% of regulatory capital, $80 million maximum). On May 1, 2012, the SBA published a notice in the *Federal Register* inviting venture capital fund managers to submit an application to become a licensed early stage debenture SBIC. The application deadline for applicants with signed commitments for at least $15 million in regulatory capital and evidence of their ability to raise the remaining $5 million in regulatory capital was set as July 30, 2012.

The application deadline for all other applicants was set as May 15, 2013.[39] Thirty-three venture capital funds submitted preliminary application materials to participate in the program. After these materials were examined and interviews held, the SBA announced on October 23, 2012, that it had issued "green light" letters to six funds, formally inviting these funds to file a license application.[40]

KEY DIFFERENCES AMONG REGULAR SBIC TYPES

Table 1 provides a comparison of the key differences among the four types of regular SBICs that receive leverage from the SBA: debenture, participating securities, impact investment debenture, and early stage debenture SBICs.

SBA Small Business Investment Company Program 145

Table 1. Key Differences Among SBA's Debenture, Participating Securities, Impact Investment Debenture, and Early Stage Debenture SBICs

Program Requirement	Debenture SBICs	Participating Security SBICs (no longer accepting new investments)	Impact Investment Debenture SBICs	Early Stage Debenture SBICs
Private Capital SBA Leverage	$5 million minimum	$10 million minimum	$5 million minimum	$20 million minimum
	200% of private capital up to $150 million per SBIC or $225 million for two or more SBICs under common controla	200% of private capital up to $150 million per SBIC or $225 million for two or more SBICs under common control	200% of private capital up to $80 million; limited to 100% of private capital during the first year	100% of private capital up to $50 million
Investments	Broad range of equity investments, but generally later stage and mezzanine	Broad range of equity investments	Broad range of equity investments, but generally later stage and mezzanine; at least 50% in underserved markets and communities facing barriers to access to credit and capital	Broad range of equity investments; at least 50% in early stage small businesses (no positive cash flow in any fiscal year prior to first financing)
Leverage Description	Interest and SBA annual charge payable semi-annually through maturity	SBA paid interest to bond holders; SBICs only owed and repaid SBA out of profits	Interest and SBA annual charge payable semi-annually through maturity	Standard: 5 years interest reserve required, interest and SBA annual charge payable quarterly through maturity OR
				Discounted: interest and SBA annual charge discounted for first 5 years plus the "stub" period; interest and SBA annual charge payable quarterly thereafter through maturity
Profit Participation	None	SBA typically received about 8% of any profits	None	None

Source: U.S. Small Business Administration, Office of Investment and Innovation, "Early Stage Small Business Investment Companies," January 2012; and U.S. Small Business Administration, "Correspondence with the author," May 2, 2012.

a. A licensed debenture SBIC in good standing, with a demonstrated need for funds, may apply to the SBA for leverage of up to 300% of its private capital. However, the SBA has traditionally approved debenture SBICs for a maximum of 200% of their private capital. It is anticipated that the SBA will also limit impact investment debenture SBICs to a maximum of 200% of their private capital. Also, a debenture SBIC licensed on or after October 1, 2009, may elect to have a maximum leverage amount of $175 million per SBIC and $250 million for two or more licenses under common control if it has invested at least 50% of its financings in low-income geographic areas and certifies that at least 50% of its future investments will be in low-income geographic areas.

SBIC INVESTMENTS IN SMALL BUSINESSES

SBICs provide equity capital to small businesses in various ways, including by

- purchasing small business equity securities (e.g., stock, stock options, warrants, limited partnership interests, membership interests in a limited liability company, or joint venture interests);[41]
- making loans to small businesses, either independently or in cooperation with other private or public lenders, that have a maturity of no more than 20 years;[42]
- purchasing debt securities from small businesses, which may be convertible into, or have rights to purchase, equity in the small business;[43] and
- subject to limitations, providing small businesses a guarantee of their monetary obligations to creditors not associated with the SBIC.[44]

SBICs are subject to statutory and regulatory restrictions concerning the nature of their approved investments. For example, SBICs are not allowed to

- directly or indirectly provide financing to any of their associates (e.g., officers, directors, and employees);[45]
- control, either directly or indirectly, any small business on a permanent basis;[46]
- invest, without SBA approval, more than specified percentages of its private (regulatory) capital in securities, commitments, or guarantees in any one small business (e.g., SBICs are not allowed to invest more than 30% of their private capital in any one small business if their investment plan includes two or more tiers of SBA leverage);[47]
- invest in farm land, unimproved land, or any small business classified under Major Group 65 (Real Estate) of the Standard Industrial Classification (SIC) Manual, with the exception of title abstract companies, real estate agents, brokers, and managers;[48]
- provide funds for small businesses whose primary business activity involves directly or indirectly providing funds to others, purchasing debt obligations, factoring, or leasing equipment on a long-term basis with no provision for maintenance or repair;[49] or
- provide funds to a small business if the funds will be used substantially for a foreign operation.[50]

The SBA also regulates the interest rates and fees SBICs are allowed to charge small businesses on loans, debt securities, and equity financing.[51]

In 1999, the SBA introduced the low and moderate income investments (LMI) initiative to encourage SBICs to invest in small businesses located in inner cities and rural areas "that have severe shortages of equity capital" because investments in those areas "often are of a type that will not have the potential for yielding returns that are high enough to justify the use of participating securities."[52] This ongoing initiative provides incentives to SBICs that invest in small businesses that have at least 50% of their employees or tangible assets located in a low-tomoderate income area (LMI Zone) or have at least 35% of their full-time employees with their primary residence in an LMI Zone.[53] For example, unlike regular SBIC debentures that typically have a 10-year maturity, LMI debentures are available in two maturities, for 5 years and 10 years, plus the stub period. The stub period is the time between the debenture's issuance date and the next March 1 or September 1. The stub period allows all LMI debentures to have common March 1 or September 1 maturity dates to simplify administration of the program.

In addition, LMI debentures are issued at a discount so that the proceeds that a SBIC receives for the sale of a debenture is reduced by (1) the debenture's interest costs for the first five years, plus the stub period; (2) the SBA's annual fee for the debenture's first five years, plus the stub period; and (3) the SBA's 2% leverage fee. As a result, these interest costs and fees are effectively deferred, freeing SBICs from the requirement to make interest payments on LMI debentures, or pay the SBA's annual fees on LMI debentures, for the first five years of a debenture, plus the stub period between the debenture's issuance date and the next March 1 or September 1.[54]

In FY2012, SBICs made 356 investments in small businesses located in a LMI Zone, totaling $471.5 million—about 15% of the total amount invested.[55]

LEVERAGE

Leverage Drawdown

A SBIC applies to the SBA for financial assistance (leverage) to secure the "SBA's conditional commitment to reserve a specific amount of leverage" for the SBIC's future use.[56] If the application is approved, a SBIC draws down the leverage as it makes financial commitments.

The SBA accepts draw applications from SBICs twice a month. When the draw is approved by the SBA, it issues a payment voucher to a SBIC (called an approval notice). The payment voucher has a term of approximately 60 days and provides a SBIC with the ability to draw funds on a daily basis.

A debenture is executed in conjunction with each draw and is held by an agent of a bank selected by the SBA (Federal Home Loan Bank of Chicago), which provides interim funding to the SBIC until a "SBIC's debenture(s) can be pooled with others and sold to the public, a process that occurs every six months [each March and September]."[57] During the interim period, the bank charges a SBIC the London Interbank Offered Rate (LIBOR), plus a 30 basis point premium.[58]

The SBA determines the size of the debenture pool two weeks prior to each scheduled pooling date. All of "the debentures scheduled to be pooled are purchased and pooled together by an entity called the Investment Trust which is managed by the Bank of New York Mellon" and, as the pooling occurs, "the SBA signs an agreement with the Trust to guarantee all the interest and principal payments due on each of the debentures in the pool."[59] The trust then securitizes the pool of debentures and issues new securities called trust certificates. Underwriters are hired to sell the trust certificates to investors in the public market. An offering circular is issued to notify investors of the trust certificates' availability, the terms of the securities, and information concerning how they can be purchased.[60]

The SBA operates the SBIC program on a zero-subsidy basis. To recoup its expenses should defaults occur, the SBA is authorized to charge SBICs a 3% origination fee for each debenture and for each participating security issued (1% at commitment and 2% at draw), an annual fee (not to exceed 1.38% for debentures and 1.46% for participating securities) on the leverage drawn, which is fixed at the time of the leverage commitment, and other administrative and underwriting fees which are adjusted annually.[61]

Debenture SBIC Leverage Requirements

A licensed debenture SBIC in good standing, with a demonstrated need for funds, may apply to the SBA for financial assistance (leverage) of up to 300% of its private capital. However, the SBA has traditionally approved debenture SBICs for a maximum of 200% of their private capital and no fund management team may exceed the allowable maximum amount of leverage of $150 million per SBIC and $225 million for two or more licenses under common control.[62] A SBIC licensed on or after October 1, 2009, may elect to have a maximum leverage amount of $175 million per SBIC and $250 million for two or more licenses under common control if it has invested at least 50% of its financings in low-income geographic areas and certifies that at least 50% of its future investments will be in low-income geographic areas.[63]

Debenture SBICs obtain leverage from the sale of SBA-guaranteed debenture participation trust certificates. SBA-guaranteed debenture participation trust certificates may have a term of up to 15 years, although only one outstanding SBA-guaranteed debenture participation trust certificate has a term exceeding 10 years and all recent public offerings have specified a term of 10 years.[64] Debenture SBICs are required to make semi-annual payments on the interest due on the debenture, semi-annual payments on the SBA's annual charge, and a lump sum principal payment to investors at maturity.[65] SBICs are allowed to prepay SBA-guaranteed debentures without penalty. However, a SBA-guaranteed debenture must be prepaid in whole and not in part, and can only be prepaid on a semi-annual payment date. The debenture's coupon (interest) rate is determined by market conditions and the interest rate of 10-year treasury securities at the time of the sale.[66] Also, as mentioned previously, LMI debentures are available in two maturities, for five years and 10 years (plus the stub period).

Because the SBA guarantees the debenture, investors are more likely to purchase a debenture participation trust certificate as opposed to others available on the market. They are also more likely to accept a lower coupon (interest) rate than what would be expected without the SBA's guarantee.[67]

As a result, the SBIC program enhances a SBIC's access to venture capital, and reduces its cost of raising additional financial resources.

Because debenture SBICs are required to make semi-annual interest payments on the debenture and semi-annual payments on the SBA's annual charge, they tend to focus their investments on mid- and later-stage small businesses that have a positive cash flow. Businesses with a positive cash flow have resources available to make payments to the debenture SBIC, either in the form of interest payments or dividends. In many instances, small businesses with positive cash flow are seeking capital for expansion.[68]

Participating Securities SBIC Leverage Requirements

Although the SBA is no longer issuing new commitments for participating securities, the SBA is authorized to accept an application from a licensed participating securities SBIC for leverage of up to 200% of its private capital.[69] Also, no fund management team may exceed the allowable maximum amount of leverage of $150 million per SBIC and $225 million for two or more licenses under common control.

Participating securities SBICs obtained leverage by issuing SBA-guaranteed participating securities. The SBA pooled these participating securities and sold SBA-guaranteed participating securities certificates, representing an undivided interest in the pool, to investors through periodic public offerings. SBA participating securities may have a term of up to 15 years, but all recent public offerings had a specified a term of 10 years.

There were 35 public offerings of SBA-guaranteed participating securities certificates since the start of the participating securities program, amounting to just under $10.3 billion. The final SBA-guaranteed participating securities certificate, for $332 million, had a term of 10 years and was offered to investors on February 19, 2009, with delivery of the certificates on February 25, 2009.[70]

SBIC participating securities certificates provide for quarterly payments to investors from dividends on preferred stock, interest on an income bond, or a priority return on a preferred limited partnership equal to a specified interest rate on the principal amount and a lump sum principal payment at maturity. A participating securities SBIC is obligated to make these quarterly payments "only to the extent it has sufficient profits available to make such payments."[71] If a participating securities SBIC is unable to make any required payment, the SBA will make the payment on its behalf. Because startup and early stage small businesses often are not initially profitable, the SBA included language in its participating securities' offering circulars that it "anticipates that it will be called upon routinely to make such ... payments for the SBICs in the early years of the lives of such SBICs" and that it "expects to be reimbursed [by the SBIC] any amounts paid ... under its guarantee over the life of a participating security."[72]

Because the SBA guaranteed the certificate, investors were more likely to purchase a SBIC participating securities certificate as opposed to others available on the market. They were also more likely to accept a lower payment rate than what would be expected without the SBA's guarantee.[73]

In addition, participating securities SBICs are more likely than debenture SBICs to invest in startup and early stage small businesses because the SBA is willing to make a participating securities SBIC's required quarterly payments to investors, at least during the early years of the investment. Because participating securities SBICs are not required to make these quarterly payments, they are encouraged to focus on a small business's long-term prospects for growth and profitability, rather than on its prospects for having immediate, positive cash-flow.[74]

As of September 30, 2012, the SBA had a guarantee on an outstanding unpaid principal balance of $4.9 billion in SBIC debentures, $1.5 billion in SBIC participating securities, and $15.9 million in SSBIC financings.[75] The SBA also had an outstanding commitment on $2.4 billion in SBIC debentures and $24.8 million in outstanding SBIC participating securities.[76]

Impact Investment Debenture SBIC Leverage Requirements

On April 7, 2011, the SBA announced that it was establishing a $1 billion Impact Investment SBIC Initiative (up to $150 million in leverage in FY2012, and up to $200 million in leverage per fiscal year thereafter until the limit is reached). SBA licensed impact investment debenture SBICs are required to invest at least 50% of their investments, "which target areas of critical national priority including underserved markets and communities facing barriers to access to credit and capital."[77] On July 26, 2011, the SBA announced that the first impact investment debenture SBIC license was awarded to InvestMichigan! Mezzanine Fund.[78]

Licensed impact investment debenture SBICs may apply to the SBA for leverage of up to 300% of its private capital, limited to $80 million. In addition, they may receive leverage amounting to no more than 100% of their private capital during any fiscal year (subject to the $80 million limit and the availability of impact investment initiative financing). It is anticipated that the SBA will limit impact investment debenture SBICs to a maximum of 200% of their private capital, up to $80 million.[79]

Impact investment debenture SBICs obtain leverage in the same way that debenture SBICs obtain leverage — through the issuance of SBA-guaranteed debentures with a term of up to 10 years. They are also subject to the same terms and conditions as debenture SBICs, except they are provided an expedited application review process.

Early Stage Debenture SBIC Leverage Requirements

On April 27, 2012, the SBA published a final rule in the *Federal Register* establishing the $1 billion Early Stage Innovation SBIC Initiative (up to $150 million in SBA leverage in FY2012, and up to $200 million in SBA leverage per fiscal year thereafter until the limit is reached). A licensed early stage SBIC may apply to the SBA for leverage of up to 100% of its private capital, limited to $50 million. The SBA does not consider applications from an early stage SBIC applicant that is under common control with another early stage SBIC applicant or an existing early stage SBIC (unless the existing early stage SBIC has no outstanding leverage or leverage commitments and will not seek additional leverage in the future).[80]

Early stage debenture SBICs obtain leverage in the same way that debenture SBICs obtain leverage — through the issuance of SBA-guaranteed debentures with a term of up to 10 years. However, early stage debentures come in two forms: early stage standard debentures and early stage discounted debentures.

Early stage standard SBIC debentures are similar to standard SBIC debentures, but, instead of requiring semi-annual payments on the debenture's interest and on the SBA's annual charge, they require quarterly payments on the debenture's interest and on the SBA's annual charge. In addition, early stage SBICs must maintain a reserve sufficient to pay the interest on the debenture and on the SBA's annual charges for the first 21 payment dates following the date of issuance (five years plus the stub period —the length of time between the issue date and the next March 1, June 1, September 1, or December 1).[81] Because early stage standard debentures require early stage debenture SBICs to make quarterly payments, they are most appropriate for investments in small businesses that have established a positive cash flow that enables them to pay interest or dividends to the early stage debenture SBIC.

Early stage discounted debentures are issued at a discount (less than face value) equal to the first five years' of interest on the debenture and the first five years of annual SBA charges. The discount eliminates the need for early stage debenture SBICs to make interest payments on the debenture and to make payments on the SBA's annual charge for five years from the date of issuance, plus the stub period.[82] Early stage debenture SBICs make quarterly payments on the debenture's interest and on the SBA's annual charge during years six through 10. They are also responsible for paying the debenture's principal amount when the debenture reaches its maturity date.

Because early stage discounted debentures do not require interest payments or payments on the SBA's annual charge for five years, they are most appropriate for investments in small businesses that have not established a positive cash flow to pay interest or dividends to the early stage debenture SBIC. As a result, early stage discounted debentures are designed to encourage investments in early stage small businesses, which by definition have not established a positive cash flow.

REPORTING REQUIREMENTS

Once licensed, each SBIC is required to file with the SBA an annual financial report that includes an audit by an SBA-approved independent public accountant. SBICs are also subject to annual onsite regulatory compliance examinations.[83] SBICs are also required to provide the SBA:

- a portfolio financing report within 30 days of the closing date for each financing of a small business;[84]
- the value of its loans and investments within 90 days of the end of the fiscal year in the case of annual valuations, and within 30 days following the close of other reporting periods;[85]
- any material adverse changes in valuations at least quarterly (within 30 days following the close of the quarter);[86] and
- copies of reports provided to investors, documents filed with the Securities and Exchange Commission, and documents pertaining to litigation or other legal proceedings, including criminal charges against any person who was required by the SBA complete a personal history statement in connection with the SBIC's license.[87]

SBIC PROGRAM STATISTICS

At the end of FY2012, there were 301 licensed SBICs in operation (158 debenture SBICs, 86 participating securities SBICs, 44 bank-owned/non-leveraged SBICs, and 13 SSBICs).[88] In FY2012, 221 SBICs provided at least one new financing to a small business.[89] Until this year, the number of licensed SBICs had declined each year since FY2006, with most of the decline due to the planned phase-out of participating securities SBICs and SSBICs.[90] In FY2006, there were 396 licensed SBICs (132 debenture SBICs, 173 participating securities SBICs, 67 bank-owned/non-leveraged SBICs, and 24 SSBICs).[91]

There were 369 licensed SBICs in FY2007, 348 in FY2008, 315 in FY2009, 307 in FY2010, and 299 in FY2011. The SBA has made it a goal to increase the number of new SBIC licenses issued each year "to position the program for continued growth."[92] Overall, SBICs pursue investments in a broad range of industries, geographic areas, and stage of investment. Some individual SBICs specialize in a particular field or industry in which their management has expertise, while others invest more generally. Most SBICs concentrate on a particular stage of investment (i.e., start-up, expansion, or turnaround) and identify a geographic area in which to focus.

Total Financing

Since its inception, the SBIC program has provided more than $62.6 billion in financial assistance and made more than 164,000 investments in small businesses.[93] As mentioned previously, as of September 30, 2012, the SBA had a guarantee on an outstanding unpaid principal balance of $4.9 billion in SBIC debentures, $1.5 billion in SBIC participating securities, and $15.9 million in SSBIC financings.[94] The SBA also had an outstanding commitment on $2.4 billion in SBIC debentures and $24.8 million in outstanding SBIC participating securities.[95] Including private investment, the SBIC program has invested or committed about $18.2 billion in small businesses, with the SBA's share of capital at risk about $8.8 billion.[96]

In FY2012, SBICs made 1,907 financings (including 58 financings by SSBICs). The average financing amount was $1,692,412 ($1,741,923 for debenture SBICs, $285,257 for participating securities SBICs, $878,299 for bank-owned/non-leveraged SBICs, and $114,053 for SSBICs).[97] The funds were used primarily for acquiring an existing business (58.1%). Other uses were for operating capital (21.7%), refinancing or refunding debt (10.1%), a new building or plant construction (1.8%), purchasing equipment (1.6%), research and development (1.3%), marketing activities (0.6%), plant modernization (0.4%), and other uses (4.4%).[98]

As shown in Table 2, the total amount of SBIC financing declined during the recession (December 2007-June 2009), reached pre-recession levels in FY2011, and exceeded pre-recession levels in FY2012. In FY2012, the SBA committed to guarantee $1.9 billion in SBIC small business investments and SBICs provided another $1.3 billion in investments from private capital, for a total of more than $3.2 billion in financing for 1,094 small businesses.

In addition, as shown in Table 2, the amount of SBA leverage as a share of total financing provided has increased in recent years. For example, the SBA's leverage commitments accounted for 12.3% of total financing in FY2005, compared with 59.6% in FY2012.

The SBA has had congressional authorization to issue up to $3.0 billion in SBIC leverage each year since 2005. For comparative purposes, private venture capital firms invested $20.2 billion in 3,110 companies in 2009, $23.4 billion in 3,598 companies in 2010, and $29.5 billion in 3,838 companies in 2011. As of September 30, 2012, private venture capital firms were on pace to invest $26.7 billion in 3,556 companies in 2012.[99]

The SBA has indicated that one of its goals is "to enhance program acceptance in the marketplace and increase the number of funds licensed and the amount of leverage issued so as to improve capital access for small businesses."[100]

SBA Small Business Investment Company Program

Table 2. SBIC Investments, FY2005-FY2012 ($ in millions)

Year	SBA Leverage/Guarantee Commitments	Private-Sector Investment	Total Financing	# of Small Businesses Financed
FY2012	$1,924	$1,303	$3,227	1,094
FY2011	$1,828	$1,005	$2,833	1,339
FY2010	$1,165	$882	$2,047	1,331
FY2009	$788	$1,068	$1,856	1,481
FY2008	$1,029	$1,398	$2,427	1,905
FY2007	$708	$1,940	$2,648	2,057
FY2006	$477	$2,420	$2,897	2,121
FY2005	$355	$2,540	$2,895	2,298

Source: U.S. Small Business Administration, "Performance and Financial Highlights, FY2007," February 4, 2008, p. 4; U.S. Small Business Administration, "FY2008 Budget Request and Performance Plan," 2007, p. 23; U.S. Small Business Administration, Investment Division, "SBIC Program Overview," January 23, 2009; U.S. Small Business Administration, "SBIC Program Overview: Program Achievements & Success Stories," at http://www.sba.gov/ content/sbic-program-overview-2; and U.S. Small Business Administration, Investment Division, "SBIC Program Overview," September 30, 2012.

In 2008, the Urban Institute released an analysis comparing debenture SBIC investments made from 1997 to 2005 to private-sector venture capital investments made during that time period in second stage business loans, third stage business loans, and bridge loans "because these investments are likely to be of the same character (debt with equity features) as those made by debenture SBICs."[101] The Urban Institute found that debenture SBIC investments accounted for more than 62% of all venture capital financings in second stage business loans, third stage business loans, and bridge loans in the United States during that time period. However, because the average amount of an SBIC debenture investment was much smaller than the industry average, SBIC debenture investments accounted for "only 8% of total dollars invested."[102]

Financing to Specific Demographic Groups

As shown in Table 3, in FY2012, SBICs made 116 financings (6.1% of all financings) amounting to $128.1 million (4.0% of the total amount of financings) to minority-owned and -controlled small businesses.

In addition, in FY2012, SBICs made 50 financings (2.6% of all financings) amounting to $38.4 million (1.2% of the total amount of financings) to women-owned small businesses, and 9 financings (0.5% of all financings) amounting to $8.9 million (0.3% of the total amount of financings) to veteran-owned small businesses.[103] Research concerning private venture capital investment in minority-owned or women-owned small businesses is limited. As a result, it is difficult to find the data necessary to compare the SBIC program's investment in minority-owned or women-owned small businesses to the private sector's investment in these firms.[104] In 2007, the SBA acknowledged at a congressional hearing on the SBA's investment programs that "women and minority representation in [the SBIC program] is low" and has been low for many years.[105]

Table 3. SBIC Financing, Minority-Owned Small Businesses, FY2012

Small Business Ownership Demographic	# of Financings	% of Financings	$ Amount of Financings	% of Total $ Amount of Financings
Black-Owned	42	2.2%	$56,200,200	1.7%
Subcontinent Asian-Owned	39	2.0%	$3,418,560	0.1%
Hispanic-Owned	18	0.9%	$27,987,568	0.9%
Asian Pacific-Owned	17	0.9%	$40,490,376	1.3%
Native American-Owned	0	0.0%	$0	0.0%
Subtotal	116	6.1%	$128,096,704	4.0%
Other (non-minority)	1,791	93.9%	$3,099,333,671	96.0%
Total—All Financings	1,907	100.0%	$3,227,430,375	100.0%

Source: U.S. Small Business Administration, "SBIC Program Licensees Financing to Small Businesses Reported Between October 2011 and September 2012."

Notes: Ownership is defined as owning at least 50% of the small business.

The SBA reported at that time that it did not control the investments made by SBICs, but it has tried to increase women and minority representation in the SBIC program by reaching out to venture capital firms, trade organizations, and others to better understand why women and minority representation in the SBIC program is low, and by "finding debenture firms with minority representation on their investment committees and in senior management."[106] However, despite these efforts, in 2009, the Small Business Investor Alliance (then called the National Association of Small Business Investment Companies) asserted at a congressional hearing on the SBA's capital access programs that the SBA's SBIC licensing process "has done an abysmal job at attracting and licensing funds led by women and minorities."[107] During the 111th Congress, S. 1831, the Small Business Venture Capital Act of 2009, was introduced on October 21, 2009, and referred to the Senate Committee on Small Business and Entrepreneurship. No further action was taken on the bill. It would have encouraged SBIC investments in women-owned small businesses and socially and economically disadvantaged small business concerns by increasing the amount of leverage available to SBICs that invest at least 50% of their financings in small business concerns owned and controlled by women or socially and economically disadvantaged small business concerns.

Financing by State

As shown in Table 4, in FY2012, SBICs provided financing to small businesses located in 45 states, the District of Columbia, and Puerto Rico, with the most financings taking place in California (247 financings amounting to $480.1 million), New York (226 financings amounting to $261.8 million), and Texas (182 financings amounting to $348.6 million).

The previously mentioned 2008 Urban Institute comparative analysis of debenture SBIC financing from 1997 to 2005 found that the dollar volume of investments from debenture SBICs was more evenly distributed across the nation than from comparable private venture capital funds. For example, the Urban Institute found that California (45.8%) and Massachusetts (12.9%) received the largest share of the total dollar volume invested by private venture capital funds from 1997 to 2005.

The two states accounted for more than half (58.7%) of the total dollar volume invested by private venture capital funds. In contrast, New York (18.7%) and California (11.1%) received the largest share of the total dollar volume invested by debenture SBICs from 1997 to 2005. The two states accounted for less than one-third (29.8%) of the total dollar volume invested by debenture SBICs. Also, the top 10 states in terms of their share of the total dollar volume invested accounted nearly 84% of the total invested by private venture capital funds, compared with 64% for debenture SBICs.[108] A comparison of the state-by-state distribution of private-sector venture capital fund investments and SBIC financings in FY2012 (see Table 4) suggest that the Urban Institute's finding that SBICs investments were more evenly distributed across the nation than private-sector venture capital fund investments from 1997 to 2005 continue to be the case today.[109] For example, California (53.7%), Massachusetts (11.6%), New York (6.4%), and Texas (3.6%) received the largest share of the total dollar volume invested by private venture capital funds during the first three quarters of FY2012. The four states accounted for about three-quarters (75.3%) of the total dollar volume invested by private venture capital funds. In contrast, the four states with the largest share of the total volume invested by SBICs in FY2012 (California at 14.9%, Texas at 10.8%, New York at 8.1%, and Illinois at 5.9%) accounted for 39.7% of the total dollar volume invested by SBICs.

Table 4. SBIC Financing, by State, FY2012
($ in millions)

State	# of Financings	Amount of Financings	State	# of Financings	Amount of Financings
Alabama	5	$34.2	Montana	0	$0.0
Alaska	0	$0.0	Nebraska	0	$0.0
Arizona	14	$27.7	Nevada	2	$0.8
Arkansas	10	$2.4	New Hampshire	10	$1.4
California	247	$480.1	New Jersey	120	$149.1
Colorado	36	$62.6	New Mexico	13	$12.9
Connecticut	24	$50.8	New York	226	$261.8
Delaware	7	$1.4	North Carolina	33	$96.4
District of Columbia	9	$15.6	North Dakota	1	$1.5
Florida	100	$179.2	Ohio	36	$59.6
Georgia	46	$135.0	Oklahoma	20	$15.6
Hawaii	1	$2.5	Oregon	15	$36.4
Idaho	2	$.2	Pennsylvania	67	$156.1
Illinois	108	$189.9	Puerto Rico	3	$13.4
Indiana	18	$46.1	Rhode Island	3	$4.0
Iowa	9	$20.4	South Carolina	16	$10.9
Kansas	26	$17.3	South Dakota	0	$0.0
Kentucky	12	$48.1	Tennessee	36	$78.1
Louisiana	11	$24.3	Texas	182	$348.6
Maine	1	$9.7	Utah	72	$39.2
Maryland	15	$52.5	Vermont	5	$13.2
Massachusetts	143	$125.2	Virginia	65	$79.2
Michigan	24	$80.0	Washington	25	$22.9
Minnesota	35	$110.3	West Virginia	2	$10.8
Mississippi	17	$1.7	Wisconsin	19	$70.8
Missouri	16	$27.4	Wyoming	0	$0.0
Total				1,907	$3,227.4

Source: U.S. Small Business Administration, "SBIC Program Licensees Financing to Small Businesses Reported Between October 2011 and September 2012."

Financing by Industry

As shown on Table 5, in FY2012, SBIC financings were made in a variety of industries, led by investments in manufacturing; professional, scientific, and technical services; transportation and warehousing; and information.

Table 5. SBIC Financing, by Industry, FY2012

Industry	# of Financings	% of Financings	$ Amount of Financings	% of $ Amount of Financings
Manufacturing	537	28.2%	$884,493,305	27.4%
Professional, Scientific, and Technical Services	300	15.7%	$508,094,582	15.7%
Transportation and Warehousing	242	12.7%	$162,474,082	5.0%
Information	216	11.3%	$268,203,978	8.3%
Administrative and Support and Waste Management	108	5.7%	$224,893,219	7.0%
Retail Trade	93	4.9%	$161,415,213	5.0%
Wholesale Trade	91	4.8%	$214,011,523	6.6%
Accommodation and Food Services	74	3.9%	$127,083,453	3.9%
Health Care and Social Assistance	56	2.9%	$170,186,509	5.3%
Construction	44	2.3%	$133,990,273	4.2%
Real Estate and Rental Leasing	30	1.6%	$34,340,426	1.1%
Finance and Insurance	21	1.1%	$40,144,640	1.2%
Mining	20	1.0%	$61,968,243	1.9%
Educational Services	17	0.9%	$47,601,840	1.5%
Arts, Entertainment and Recreation	14	0.7%	$28,383,083	0.9%
Management of Companies and Enterprises	5	0.3%	$44,265,110	1.4%
Other Industries	39	2.0%	$115,880,896	3.6%
Total	1,907	100.0%	$3,227,430,375	100.0%

Source: U.S. Small Business Administration, "SBIC Program Licensees Financing to Small Businesses Reported Between October 2011 and September 2012."

The previously mentioned 2008 Urban Institute comparative analysis of SBIC financings from 1997 to 2005 found that "SBIC financing is less concentrated by industry than financing from private venture capital firms" and "total financings by SBICs are much less likely to be in high-tech industries" than comparable private-sector venture capital investment firms.[110] The Urban Institute found that unlike SBICs, "the value of investments by private venture capital firms is predominately directed towards information and finance," with computer and Internet firms receiving roughly half of all private-sector investments.[111]

LEGISLATIVE ACTIVITY

P.L. 111-5, the American Recovery and Reinvestment Act of 2009 (ARRA), included provisions designed to increase the amount of leverage issued under the SBIC program by increasing the maximum amount of leverage available to an individual SBIC to 300% of its private capital, or $150 million, whichever is less; and by increasing the maximum amount of leverage available for two or more licenses under common control to $225 million.[112] It also encouraged SBIC investment in smaller enterprises by requiring SBICs licensed on or after the date of its enactment (February 17, 2009) to certify that at least 25% of all future financing dollars are invested in smaller enterprises. ARRA defined smaller enterprises as firms having either a net worth of no more than $6 million and average after-tax net income for the preceding two years of no more than $2 million, or meeting the SBA's size standard for its industry classification.[113]

ARRA also encouraged SBIC investments in low-income areas by allowing a SBIC licensed on or after October 1, 2009, to elect to have a maximum leverage amount of $175 million, and $250 million for two or more licenses under common control, if the SBIC has invested at least 50% of its financings in low-income geographic areas and certified that at least 50% of its future investments will be in low-income geographic areas.[114]

As part of its Startup America Initiative, on January 31, 2012, the Obama Administration recommended that the SBIC program's annual authorization be increased to $4 billion from $3 billion and that the amount of SBA leverage available to licensees under common control be increased to $350 million from $225 million.[115]

As will be discussed, several bills were subsequently introduced during the 112th Congresses to either target additional leverage to startup companies or to expand the program.

Legislation to Target Additional Assistance to Startup and Early Stage Small Businesses

As mentioned previously, some Members and small business advocates have proposed that the SBIC program target additional assistance to startup and early stage small businesses, which are generally viewed as relatively risky investments but also as having a relatively high potential for job creation.

Advocates of targeting additional assistance to startup and early stage small businesses argue that the SBA's participating securities program was created to fill a perceived investment gap resulting from the SBA's debenture program's focus on mid- and later-stage small businesses. Because the SBA is no longer providing new licenses or leverage for participating securities SBICs, several Members have introduced legislation to create a new SBA program that would focus on the investment needs of startup and early stage small businesses.

For example, during the 111th Congress the House passed, by a vote of 241-182, H.R. 5297, the Small Business Jobs and Credit Act of 2010.[116] Among its provisions, as passed by the House, H.R. 5297 would have authorized a $1 billion Small Business Early Stage Investment Program.

The proposed program would have provided equity investment financing of up to $100 million in matching funds to each participating investment company. It would have required participating investment companies to invest in small businesses, with at least 50% of the financing in early stage small businesses, defined as those small businesses not having "gross annual sales revenues exceeding $15 million in any of the previous three years."[117] The proposed program emphasized venture capital investments in startup companies operating in nine targeted industries.[118]

H.R. 5297, as subsequently enacted by Congress and signed into law by President Obama on September 27, 2010 (P.L. 111-240, the Small Business Jobs Act of 2010) did not include legislative language authorizing a Small Business Early Stage Investment Program.[119] However, it authorized a three-year Intermediary Lending Pilot Program to provide direct loans to not more than 20 eligible nonprofit lending intermediaries each year, totaling not more than $20 million and $1 million per intermediary.

The intermediaries, in turn, may make loans to new or growing small businesses, not to exceed $200,000 per business.[120] On August 4, 2011, the SBA announced the selection of the first 20 lenders to participate in the program.[121]

Discussion

Advocates of efforts to encourage capital investment in startup and early stage small businesses, including Members of Congress who have served on the House or Senate Small Business Committees, have argued that the SBA's elimination of the SBIC participating securities program has created a gap "in the SBA's existing array of capital access programs, particularly in the provision of capital to early stage small businesses in capital-intensive industries."[122]

As Representative Nydia Velázquez argued on the House floor during congressional consideration of H.R. 5297

> This legislation, Mr. Chairman, also recognizes that capital markets are changing dramatically. Credit standards are stricter, and small businesses are now looking not only to loans and to credit cards to finance their operations, but they are also looking to equity investment to turn their ideas into reality. This has become even more pronounced as asset values have declined, leaving entrepreneurs with less collateral to borrow against. Unfortunately, small firms' access to venture capital and to equity investment has declined. Last year, such investments plummeted from $28 billion in 2008 to only $17 billion last year.
>
> This is due, in part, to the previous administration's decision to terminate the SBA's largest pure equity financing program—the Small Business Investment Company Participating Securities program. This has left many entrepreneurs who need equity investment to fulfill their business plans without a source of such financing.[123]

Opponents of efforts to encourage capital investment in startup and early stage small businesses have argued that such efforts could "pile unnecessary risk or costs onto taxpayers at a time when we're dealing with record debt and unsustainable deficit spending."[124] During consideration of the proposed Small Business Early Stage Investment Program, opponents argued that it was untested, would likely encourage risky investments, and the legislation required "only 50% of the funding ... to be invested" in early stage small businesses.[125]

Legislation to Increase SBIC Financing Levels

In 2009, the Small Business Investor Alliance characterized the SBIC program as "dramatically underused."[126] It argued that the program's financing levels would increase if (1) the SBA further improved its licensing processing procedures to make them more timely and objective, (2) the percentage of SBIC regulatory capital allowed from state or local government entities was increased from its present maximum of 33%, and (3) the SBIC program's family of funds limit ($225 million for two or more licenses under common control) was increased to allow SBICs to have a series of investment funds in place, where, for example, "one fund could be winding down, another could be at peak, and another could just be ramping up."[127]

During the 111th Congress, H.R. 3854, the Small Business Financing and Investment Act of 2009, which was passed by the House on October 29, 2009, and H.R. 5554, the Small Business Assistance and Relief Act of 2010, which was not reported after being referred to five committees for consideration, proposed to encourage greater use of the SBIC program by increasing the maximum percentage of SBIC regulatory capital allowed from state or local government entities to 45% from 33%.[128] Both measures would have also increased the SBIC program's family of funds limit to $350 million from $225 million; increased the SBIC program's limit of $250 million to $400 million for multiple funds under common control that were licensed after September 30, 2009, and invested 50% of their dollars in low-income geographic areas; and increased the SBIC program's authorization level from to $5.5 billion from $3 billion in FY2011.[129]

The Obama Administration also recommended, as part of its Startup America Initiative (which included the SBA's $1 billion early stage debenture SBIC initiative and $1 billion impact investment SBIC initiative), that the 112th Congress adopt legislation to increase the SBIC program's annual authorization to $4 billion from $3 billion. The Administration recommended as well that the 112th Congress adopt legislation to increase the amount of SBA leverage available to licensees under common control to $350 million from $225 million.[130]

During the 112th Congress, H.R. 3219, the Small Business Investment Company Modernization Act of 2011, was introduced on October 14, 2011, and referred to the House Committee on Small Business. No further action has, so far, taken place on the bill. It proposes to encourage greater utilization of the SBIC program by increasing the maximum amount of outstanding SBA leverage available to any single licensed SBIC from the lesser of 300% of its private capital or $150 million, to the lesser of 300% of its private capital or $200 million if a majority of the managers of the company are experienced in managing one or more SBIC licensed companies. It would also increase the maximum amount of outstanding SBA leverage available to two or more licenses under common control to $350 million from $225 million. S. 2136, a bill to increase the maximum amount of leverage permitted under title III of the Small Business Investment Act of 1958, was introduced on February 28, 2012, and referred to the Senate Committee on Small Business and Entrepreneurship. No further action has yet taken place on the bill. It proposes to encourage greater use of the SBIC program by increasing the maximum amount of outstanding SBA leverage available to two or more licenses under common control to $350 million from $225 million. It would also increase the SBIC program's authorization level to $4 billion from $3 billion. On March 15, 2012, S.Amdt. 1833, the INVEST in America Act of 2012, was offered on the Senate floor as an amendment in the nature of a substitute to H.R. 3606, the Jumpstart Our Business Startups

Act, which had previously passed the House. Two of the provisions in the amendment proposed to encourage greater use of the SBIC program by (1) increasing the maximum amount of outstanding SBA leverage available to two or more licenses under common control to $350 million from $225 million and (2) increasing the SBIC program's authorization level to $4 billion from $3 billion.

The Senate later passed H.R. 3606 with amendments, which did not address the SBIC program. The House accepted the Senate amendments and passed the bill, which President Obama signed into law (P.L. 112-106). S. 3442, the SUCCESS Act of 2012, which was introduced on July 25, 2012, and S. 3572, the Restoring Tax and Regulatory Certainty to Small Businesses Act of 2012, which was introduced on September 19, 2012, would, among other provisions, increase the program's authorization amount to $4 billion from $3 billion, increase the program's family of funds limit (the amount of outstanding leverage allowed for two or more SBIC licenses under common control) to $350 million from $225 million, and annually adjust the maximum outstanding leverage amount available to both individual SBICs and SBICs under common control to account for inflation. Both bills were referred to the Senate Committee on Finance.

No further action has yet taken place on the bills. Also, H.R. 6504, the Small Business Investment Company Modernization Act of 2012, was introduced on September 21, 2012 and referred to the House Committee on Small Business. It would increase the program's family of funds limit (the amount of outstanding leverage allowed for two or more SBIC licenses under common control) to $350 million from $225 million.

Discussion

In 2010, the SBA announced that one of its goals for the SBIC program was to increase its "acceptance in the marketplace and increase the number of funds licensed and the amount of leverage issued so as to improve capital access for small businesses."[131] The SBA asserted that ARRA's changes to the SBIC program would help it to achieve this goal. ARRA increased the maximum leverage available to SBICs to up "to three times the private capital raised by the SBIC, or $150 million, whichever is less, and $225 million for multiple licensees under common control" and increased "the maximum leverage amounts to $175 million for single funds and $250 million for multiple funds under common control who are licensed after September 30, 2009, and invest 50% of their dollars in low income geographic areas."[132]

As mentioned previously, advocates of increasing the SBIC program's leverage limits still further and to increase the SBIC program's authorization level to $4 billion from $3 billion have argued that these actions are necessary to help fill a perceived gap in the SBA's "array of capital access programs."[133] In addition, they argue that the demise of the SBIC participating securities program and the current "underutilization" of the SBIC debentures program is preventing many small firms from accessing the capital necessary to fully realize their economic potential and assist in the national economic recovery.[134] On the other hand, others worry about the potential risk that an expanded SBIC program has for the taxpayer, especially if investments are targeted at startup and early stage small businesses which, by definition, have a more limited credit history and a higher risk for default than businesses that have established positive cash flow.

Conclusion

Some, including President Obama, as most recently evidenced by his Startup America Initiative, have argued that the SBA should be provided additional resources to assist small businesses in acquiring capital necessary to start, continue, or expand operations and create jobs.[135] In their view, encouraging greater utilization of the SBIC program will increase small business access to capital, result in higher levels of job creation and retention, and promote economic growth. For example, on March 19, 2012, during Senate consideration of S.Amdt. 1833, the INVEST in America Act of 2012, Senator Olympia Snowe argued

> The amendment [S.Amdt. 1833] I and Senator Landrieu introduced would also help small companies access capital by modifying the Small Business Investment Company, SBIC, Program to raise the amount of SBIC debt the Small Business Administration, SBA, can guarantee from $3 billion to $4 billion. It would also increase the amount of SBA guaranteed debt a team of SBIC fund managers who operate multiple funds can borrow. The SBIC provisions in this amendment have bipartisan support, are noncontroversial, come at no cost to taxpayers and will create jobs. We do not get many bills of this kind in the Senate anymore. One of the most difficult challenges facing new small businesses today is access to capital. The SBIC Program has helped companies like Apple, FedEx, Callaway Golf, and Outback Steakhouse become household names. As entrepreneurs and other aspiring small business owners well know, it takes money to make money. This legislation ensures that our entrepreneurs and high-growth companies have access to the resources they need so they can continue to drive America's economic growth and job creation in these challenging times. There is no reason why Congress should not approve this amendment to ensure capital is getting into the hands of America's job creators.
>
> This amendment will spur investment in capital-starved startup small businesses, which will play a critical role in leading the Nation of the devastating economic down turn from which we have yet to emerge. For those who may be unfamiliar, despite significant entrepreneurial demand for small amounts of capital, because of their substantial size, most private investment funds cannot dedicate resources to transactions below $5 million. The Nation's SBICs are working to fill that gap, especially even during these challenging times.[136]

Others worry about the potential risk an expanded SBIC program may have for increasing the federal deficit. In their view, the best means to assist small business, promote economic growth, and create jobs is to reduce business taxes and exercise federal fiscal restraint.[137] For example, Representative Sam Graves, chair of the House Committee on Small Business, indicated in the Small Business Committee's FY2013 "views and estimates" letter to the House Budget Committee that the House Small Business Committee supported an increase in the SBIC program's authorization to $4 billion from $3 billion. However, he indicated that the committee opposed funding for the SBA's early stage debenture SBIC initiative and impact investment SBIC initiative because of their potential to generate losses that could lead to higher SBIC fees, or for the need to provide federal funds to subsidize the SBIC program. Representative Graves wrote in the FY2013 views and estimates letter that

> The debenture SBIC program is designed to provide equity injections to small businesses that have been operational and have a track record of cash-flow and profits. ... The program is financially sound because the structure of repayments ensures that the

government will not suffer significant losses. Thus, no changes are needed to the program and it operates on a zero subsidy basis without an appropriation. The SBA budget is fully supportive of this program and we concur in that recommendation, including raising the program level from $3 billion to $4 billion. Presumably, some of the additional program level (which will cost the federal government no money) will be used to support two new variations in the Debenture SBIC Program [the early stage debenture SBIC initiative and the impact investment SBIC initiative] ... Neither initiative has received authority from Congress nor had its operational principles assessed by the Committee prior to implementation. The Committee reiterates its recommendation from last year's views and estimates – no funds should be allocated from the additional debenture program levels for these two programs. The Committee on the Budget also should provide further protection to the existing debenture SBIC program by requiring any modifications to the program, whether a pilot program or not, be based on a new subsidy calculation that ensures the current debenture program will operate at zero subsidy without any increase in fees due to losses stemming from the Impact and Early Stage Innovation programs.[138]

As these quotations attest, congressional debate concerning the SBIC program has primarily involved assessments of the ability of small businesses to access capital from the private sector and evaluations of the program's risk, the effect of proposed changes on the program's risk, and the potential impact of the program's risk on the federal deficit. Empirical analysis of economic data can help inform debate concerning the ability of small businesses to access capital from the private sector and the extent of the program's risk, the effect of proposed changes on the program's risk, and the potential impact of the program's risk on the federal deficit. Additional data concerning SBIC investment impact on recipient job creation and firm survival might also prove useful.

APPENDIX. SMALL BUSINESS ELIGIBILITY REQUIREMENTS AND APPLICATION PROCESS

Small Business Eligibility Requirements

Only businesses that meet the SBA's definition of "small" may participate in the SBIC program. They must meet either the SBA's size standard for the industry in which they are primarily engaged, or a separate financial size standard that has been established for the SBIC program. SBICs use the size standard that is most likely to qualify the company, typically the financial size standard for the SBIC program. The SBIC alternative size standard is currently set as a maximum net worth of no more than $18 million and average after-tax net income for the preceding two years of not more than $6 million.[139] All of a company's subsidiaries, parent companies, and affiliates are considered in determining if it meets the size standard.

In addition, since 1997, the SBA has required SBICs to set aside a specified percentage of their financing for "businesses at the lower end of the permitted size range," primarily because "the financial size standards applicable to the SBIC program are considerably higher than those used in other SBA programs."[140] P.L. 111-5, the American Recovery and Reinvestment Act of 2009 (ARRA), requires SBICs licensed on or after the date of its enactment (February 17, 2009) to certify that at least 25% of their future financing is invested in smaller enterprises. A smaller enterprise is a company that, together with any affiliates,

SBA Small Business Investment Company Program

either has net worth of no more than $6 million and average after-tax net income for the preceding two years of no more than $2 million, or meets the SBA's size standard in the industry in which the applicant is primarily engaged.[141]

A SBIC licensed before February 17, 2009, that has not received any SBA leverage commitments after February 17, 2009, must have at least 20% of its aggregate financing dollars (plus 100% for leverage commitments over $90 million) invested in smaller enterprises.

A SBIC licensed before February 17, 2009, that has received an SBA leverage commitment after February 17, 2009, must meet the 20% threshold (plus 100% for leverage commitments over $90 million) for financing provided before the date of the first leverage commitment issued after February 17, 2009, and the 25% threshold for financing made on or after such date.[142]

SBICs are not allowed to invest in the following: other SBICs; finance and investment companies or finance-type leasing companies; unimproved real estate; companies with less than 51% of their assets and employees in the United States; passive or casual businesses (those not engaged in a regular and continuous business operation); or companies that will use the proceeds to acquire farmland.[143] In addition, SBICs may not provide funds for a small business whose primary business activity is deemed contrary to the public interest or if the funds will be used substantially for a foreign operation.[144]

Small Business Application Process

Small business owners interested in receiving SBIC financing can search for active SBICs using the SBA's SBIC directory.[145] The directory provides contact information for all licensed SBICs, sorted by state. It also includes the SBIC's preferred minimum and maximum financing size range, the type of capital provided (e.g., equity, mezzanine, subordinated debt, 1st and 2nd lien secured term, or preferred stock), funding stage preference (e.g., early stage, growing and expansion stage, or later stage), industry preference (e.g., business services, manufacturing, environmental services, or distribution), geographic preference (e.g., national, regional, or specific state or states), and a description of the firm's focus (e.g., equity capital to later stage companies for expansion and acquisition, or targeting companies with revenues of at least $5 million and profitability at the time of financing).[146]

After locating a suitable SBIC, the small business owner presents the SBIC a business plan that addresses the business's operations, management, financial condition, and funding requirements. The typical business plan includes the following information:

- the name of the business as it appears on the official records of the state or community in which it operates;
- the city, county, and state of the principal location and any branch offices or facilities;
- the form of business organization and, if a corporation, the date and state of incorporation;
- a description of the business, including the principal products sold or services rendered;

- a history of the general development of the products or services during the past five years (or since inception);
- information about the relative importance of each principal product or service to the volume of the business and to its profits;
- a description of business's real and physical property and adaptability to other business ventures;
- a description of technical attributes of its products and facilities;
- detailed information about the business's customer base, including potential customers;
- a marketing survey or economic feasibility study;
- a description of the distribution system for the business's products or services;
- a descriptive summary of the competitive conditions in the industry in which the business is engaged, including its competitive position relative to its largest and smallest competitors;
- a full explanation and summary of the business's pricing polices;
- brief resumes of the business's management personnel and principal owners, including their ages, education, and business experience;
- banking, business, and personal references for each member of management and for the principal owners;
- balance sheets and profit and loss statements for the last three fiscal years (or from inception);
- detailed projections of revenues, expenses, and net earnings for the coming year;
- a statement of the amount of funding requested and the time requirements for the funds;
- the reasons for the request for funds and a description of the proposed uses; and
- a description of the benefits the business expects to gain from the financing (e.g., expansion, improvement in financial position, expense reduction, or increase in efficiency).[147]

Because SBICs typically receive hundreds of business plans per year, the SBA recommends that small business owners seek a personal referral or introduction to the particular SBIC fund manager being targeted to increase "the likelihood that the business plan will be carefully considered."[148] According to the Small Business Investor Alliance, "a thorough study an SBIC must undertake before it can make a final decision could take several weeks or longer."[149]

End Notes

[1] U.S. Small Business Administration, "Fiscal Year 2013 Congressional Budget Justification and FY2011 Annual Performance Report," p. 1.

[2] 15 U.S.C. §661.

[3] U.S. Congress, House Committee on Banking and Currency, *Small Business Investment Act of 1958*, report to accompany S.3651, 85th Cong., 2nd sess., June 30, 1958, H.Rept. 85-2060 (Washington: GPO, 1958), pp. 4, 5.

[4] Ibid., p. 5.

[5] U.S. Small Business Administration, "SBIC Program Overview, as of September 30, 2012," at http://c.ymcdn.com/ sites/www.sbia.org/resource/resmgr/Docs/SBIC_Program_Overview.pdf.

[6] Ibid.

[7] S. 2136, a bill to increase the maximum amount of leverage permitted under title III of the Small Business Investment Act of 1958, and for other purposes, would increase the SBIC program's authorization amount to $4 billion from $3 billion, and increase the program's family of funds limit (the amount of outstanding leverage allowed for two or more SBIC licenses under common control) to $350 million from $225 million.

[8] H.R. 3219, the Small Business Investment Company Modernization Act of 2011, the processor bill to H.R. 6504, the Small Business Investment Company Modernization Act of 2012, also would increase the SBIC program's family of funds limit (the amount of outstanding leverage allowed for two or more SBIC licenses under common control) to $350 million from $225 million.

[9] P.L. 92-595, the Small Business Investment Act Amendments of 1972.

[10] A debenture SBIC may issue and have outstanding both guaranteed debentures and participating securities, provided that the total amount of participating securities outstanding does not exceed 200% of its private capital. See 13 CFR §107.1170. The SBA stopped issuing new commitments for participating securities on October 1, 2004.

[11] 13 CFR §107.50.

[12] Ibid.

[13] Commercial banks may invest up to 5% of their capital and surplus to partially or wholly own an SBIC. Bank investments in an SBIC are presumed by federal regulatory agencies to be a "qualified investment" for Community Reinvestment Act purposes. See P.L. 90-104, the Small Business Act Amendments of 1967; The Board of Governors of the Federal Reserve Board, "Small Business Investment Companies," 33 *Federal Register* 6967, May 9, 1968; and U.S. Small Business Administration, "Small Business Investment Companies (SBICs)," *Small Business Notes*, 2009, at http://www.smallbusinessnotes.com/financing/sbic.html.

[14] U.S. Small Business Administration, "For SBIC Applicants: Phase II: Licensing Review," at http://www.sba.gov/content/phase-ii-licensing-review.

[15] U.S. Small Business Administration, "For SBIC Applicants: Pre-Screening," at http://www.sba.gov/content/pre-screening.

[16] A control person is generally defined as someone with the power to direct corporate management and policies.

[17] U.S. Small Business Administration, "SBIC Management Assessment Questionnaire and License Application: Form 2181," p. 21, at http://www.sba.gov/sites/default/files/SBA%20Form%202181.pdf.

[18] U.S. Small Business Administration, "SBIC Program Statistics & Administrative Performance," at http://www.sba.gov/content/program-statistics-administrative-perfor mance#LicTimes; and U.S. Small Business Administration, Office of Congressional and Legislative Affairs, "Correspondence with the author," September 21, 2010.

[19] U.S. Small Business Administration, "Impact Investment Initiative," at http://www.sba.gov /content/small-businessinvestment-company-sbic-impact-investment-initiative-2.

[20] U.S. Small Business Administration, "Small Business Investment Companies - Early Stage SBICs," 77 *Federal Register* 25052, April 27, 2012.

[21] Ibid.

[22] 13 CFR §107.210.

[23] Ibid.

[24] 13 CFR §107.150.

[25] 13 CFR §107.230.

[26] U.S. Congress, House Committee on Small Business, *Private Equity for Small Firms: The Importance of the Participating Securities Program*, 109th Cong., 1st sess., April 13, 2005, Serial No. 109-10 (Washington: GPO, 2005), p. 5, 33; and U.S. Small Business Administration, "SBIC Program: FAQs 7. What is the status of the Participating Securities Program?" at http://www.sba.gov/content/faqs.

[27] U.S. Small Business Administration, "Offering Circular, Guaranteed 4.727% Participating Securities Participation Certificates, Series SBIC-PS 2009-10 A," February 19, 2009, at http://www.sba.gov/content/sbic-ps-2009-10-cusip831641-ep6.

[28] 13 CFR §107.1500. A SBIC that wishes to be eligible to issue participating securities must have regulatory capital of at least $10 million unless it can demonstrate to the SBA's satisfaction that it can be financially viable over the longterm with a lower amount, but not less than $5 million. See 13 CFR §107.210. It must also maintain sufficient liquidity to avoid a condition of "Liquidity Impairment," defined as a liquidity ratio (total current funds available divided by total current funds required) of less than 1.2. See 13 CFR §107.1505. The only type of debt, other than leverage, than a SBIC that has applied to issue participating securities or have outstanding participating securities is permitted to incur is temporary debt. Temporary debt is defined as short-

term borrowings from a regulated financial institution, a regulated credit company, or a non-regulated lender approved by the SBA for the purpose of maintaining the SBIC's operating liquidity or providing funds for a particular financing of a small business. The total outstanding borrowings, not including leverage, may not exceed 50% of a SBIC's leveraged capital and all such borrowings must be fully paid off for at least 30 consecutive days during a SBIC's fiscal year so that it has no outstanding third-party debt for 30 days. See 13 CFR §107.570. A SBIC issuing participating securities is required to invest an amount equal to the original issue price of such securities solely in equity capital investments (e.g., common or preferred stock, limited partnership interests, options, warrants, or similar equity instruments). See 13 CFR §107.1505.

[29] U.S. Congress, House Committee on Small Business, *Subcommittee Markup of Legislation Affecting the SBA Capital Access Programs*, 111th Cong., 1st sess., October 8, 2009, House Small Business Committee Document No. 111-050 (Washington: GPO, 2009), pp. 7, 10, 11, 187-194; U.S. Congress, House Committee on Small Business, *Full Committee Hearing on Increasing Capital for Small Business*, 111th Cong., 1st sess., October 14, 2009, House Small Business Committee Document No. 111-051 (Washington: GPO, 2009), pp. 1, 2, 40, 98; and U.S. Congress, House Committee on Small Business, *Small Business Financing and Investment Act of 2009*, report to accompany H.R. 3854, 111th Cong., 1st sess., October 26, 2009, H.Rept. 111-315 (Washington: GPO, 2009), pp. 3, 4, 10-12.

[30] U.S. Small Business Administration, "SBIC Program Overview, as of September 30, 2012," at http://c.ymcdn.com/ sites/www.sbia.org/resource/resmgr/Docs/SBIC_Program_Overview.pdf. There were 149 participating securities SBICs at the end of FY2008.

[31] 13 CFR §107.210.

[32] 13 CFR §107.150.

[33] 13 CFR §107.230.

[34] U.S. Small Business Administration, "Impact Investment Initiative," at http://www.sba.gov /content/small-businessinvestment-company-sbic-impact-investment-initiative-2. To receive an investment, a small business must meet at least one of the following criteria: (a) it must be located in, or have at least 35% of its full-time employees, at the time of the initial investment, residing in a low or moderate income area as defined in 13 CFR §107.50; or be located in an economically distressed area as defined by Section 3011 of the Public Works and Economic Development Act of 1965, as amended [per capita income of 80% or less of the national average or an unemployment rate that is, for the most recent 24-month period for which data are available, at least 1% greater than the national average unemployment rate]; or (b) be in an industrial sector that the SBA has identified as a national priority (currently clean energy and education). The SBA has announced that additional industrial sectors will be added over time in partnership with other mission-driven agencies.

[35] U.S. Small Business Administration, "The Small Business Investment Company (SBIC) Program: Annual Report FY2012," p. 19, at http://www.sba.gov/sites/default/files/files/SBIC%20Program%20FY%202012%20 Annual %20Report.pdf.

[36] U.S. Small Business Administration, "Small Business Investment Companies - Early Stage SBICs," 77 *Federal Register* 25043, 25050, April 27, 2012.

[37] Ibid., pp. 25051-25053.

[38] Ibid., p. 25043.

[39] U.S. Small Business Administration, "Small Business Investment Companies - Early Stage SBICs," 77 *Federal Register* 25775-25779, May 1, 2012.

[40] U.S. Small Business Administration, "SBA's Growth Capital Program Sets Record For Third Year in a Row $2.95 Billion in Financing for Small Businesses in FY12," at http://www.sba.gov/about-sba-services/7367/342171; and U.S. Small Business Administration, "The Small Business Investment Company (SBIC) Program: Annual Report FY2012," p. 20, at http://www.sba.gov/sites/default/files/files /SBIC%20 Program% 20FY%202012%20Annual%20Report.pdf.

[41] 13 CFR §107.800. A SBIC is not allowed to become a general partner in any unincorporated business or become jointly or severally liable for any obligations of an unincorporated business.

[42] 13 CFR §107.810; and 13 CFR §107.840.

[43] 13 CFR §107.815. Debt securities are instruments evidencing a loan with an option or any other right to acquire equity securities in a small business or its affiliates, or a loan which by its terms is convertible into an equity position, or a loan with a right to receive royalties that are excluded from the cost of money.

[44] 13 CFR §107.820.

[45] 13 CFR §107.730.

[46] 13 CFR §107.865. The period of time that a SBIC may exercise control over a small business for purposes connected with its investment through ownership of voting securities, management agreements, voting trusts,

majority representation on the board of directors, or otherwise, is "limited to the seventh anniversary of the date on which such control was initially acquired, or any earlier date specified by the terms of any investment agreement." With the SBA's prior written approval, an SBIC "may retain control for such additional period as may be reasonably necessary to complete divestiture of control or to ensure the financial stability of the portfolio company."

[47] A tier of SBA leverage equals the amount of a SBIC's private (regulatory) capital. A SBIC approved for less than two tiers of SBA leverage must not invest more than 20% of its private capital in any one small business if the SBIC's plan contemplates one tier of leverage and no more than 25% of its private capital if its plan contemplates 1.5 tiers of leverage. See 13 CFR §107.740; and U.S. Small Business Administration, "American Recovery and Reinvestment Act of 2009: Implementation of SBIC Program Changes," letter from Harry Haskins, Acting Associate Administrator for Investment, to All Small Business Investment Companies (SBICs) and Applicants, May 4, 2009, p. 2, at http://archive.sba.gov/idc/groups/public/documents/sba_program_office/inv_rcvry_act_sbic_changes.pdf.

[48] 13 CFR §107.720.

[49] Ibid.

[50] Ibid. A SBIC may provide venture capital financing to "disadvantaged concerns" engaged in relending or reinvesting activities (except agricultural credit companies and banking and savings and loan institutions not insured by a federal agency). Without SBA approval, these financings, at the end of the fiscal year, may not exceed a SBIC's regulatory capital. A disadvantaged concern is defined as a small business that is at least 50% owned, controlled, and managed, on a day-to-day basis, by a person or persons whose participation in the free enterprise system is hampered because of social or economic disadvantages.

[51] The SBA has a general interest rate ceiling of 19% for a loan and 14% for a debt security, with provisions for a higher interest rate under specified circumstances. See 13 CFR §107.855. A SBIC is allowed to collect a nonrefundable application fee of no more than 1% of the amount of financing requested from a small business to review its financing application, a closing fee of no more than 2% of the amount of financing requested from a small business concern for a loan, charged no earlier than the date of the first disbursement, and a closing fee of no more than 4% of the amount of financing requested from a small business concern for a debt security or equity security financing, charged no earlier than the date of the first disbursement. A SBIC is also allowed to charge a small business for reasonable out-of-pocket expenses, other than management expenses incurred to process the small business's financing application. See 13 CFR §107.860.

[52] U.S. Small Business Administration, "Small Business Investment Companies," 64 *Federal Register* 52645, September 30, 1999.

[53] U.S. Small Business Administration, "Small Business Investment Companies," 64 *Federal Register* 52641-52646, September 30, 1999. LMI Zones are areas located in a HUBZone; an Urban Empowerment Zone or Urban Enterprise Community designated by the Secretary of the U.S. Department of Housing and Urban Development; a Rural Empowerment Zone or Rural Enterprise Community as designated by the Secretary of the U.S. Department of Agriculture; an area of low income or moderate income as recognized by the Federal Financial Institutions Examination Council; or a county with persistent poverty as classified by the U.S. Department of Agriculture's Economic Research Service. See 13 CFR §107.50.

[54] U.S. Small Business Administration, "For SBICs: Background Information on Low or Moderate Income (LMI) Debentures," at http://www.sba.gov/content/low-or-moderate-income-lmi-debentures.

[55] U.S. Small Business Administration, "SBIC Program Licensees Financing to Small Businesses Reported Between October 2011 and September 2012."

[56] 13 CFR §107.1100.

[57] U.S. Small Business Administration, "Funding the SBIC Program: An Overview," at http://www.sba.gov/content/funding-sbic-program-overview. The SBA is required by statute to issue guarantees "at periodic intervals of not less than every 12 months and shall do so at such shorter intervals as it deems appropriate, taking into consideration the amount and number of such guarantees or trust certificates." See 15 U.S.C. §687m.

[58] U.S. Small Business Administration, "Funding the SBIC Program: An Overview," at http://www.sba.gov/content/funding-sbic-program-overview.

[59] Ibid.

[60] To view recent SBIC debenture offering circulars see U.S. Small Business Administration, "SBIC Debentures Offering Circulars," at http://www.sba.gov/category/lender-navigation/sba-loan-programs/sbic-program/program-dataperformance/information-tru-1.

[61] 13 CFR §107.1130; and 13 CFR §107.1210.

[62] 13 CFR §107.1120; 13 CFR §107.1150; and U.S. Small Business Administration, "American Recovery and Reinvestment Act of 2009: Implementation of SBIC Program Changes," letter from Harry Haskins, Acting Associate Administrator for Investment, to All Small Business Investment Companies (SBICs) and Applicants, May 4, 2009, p. 1, at http://archive.sba.gov/idc/groups/public/documents /sba_program_office /inv_rcvry_act_sbic_changes.pdf.

[63] 13 CFR §107.1150. A low-income area is (1) any population census tract that has a poverty rate that is not less than 20% or (a) if located within a metropolitan area, 50% or more of the households in that census tract have an income equal to less than 60% of the area median gross income; or (b) if not located within a metropolitan area, the median household income in that census tract does not exceed 80% of the statewide median household income; or (c) has been determined by the SBA Administrator to contain a substantial population of low-income individuals in residence, an inadequate access to investment capital, or other indications of economic distress; or (2) any area located within (i) a Historically Underutilized Business Zone; (ii) an Urban Empowerment Zone or Urban Enterprise Community (as designated by the Secretary of the United States Department of Housing and Urban Development); or (iii) a Rural Empowerment Zone or Rural Enterprise Community (as designated by the Secretary of the United States Department of Agriculture). See 13 CFR §108.50.

[64] One debenture has a term of 10 years and 29 weeks. See U.S. Small Business Administration, "Offering Circular, Guaranteed 2.245% Debenture Participating Securities, Series SBIC 2012-10B," September 11, 2012, at http://www.sba.gov/content/sbic-2012-10-b-cusip-831641-ex9.

[65] U.S. Small Business Administration, "Small Business Investment Companies (SBICs)," *Small Business Notes*, 2009, at http://www.smallbusinessnotes.com/business-finances/small-business-investment-companies-sbics.html; and U.S. Small Business Administration, "For SBIC Applicants: Financing Options Explained," at http://www.sba.gov/content/ financing-options-explained.

[66] Ibid.; 13 CFR §107.50; and 13 CFR §107.1150.

[67] The coupon (interest) rate on SBA debentures is based on the 10-year Treasury rate (adjusted to the nearest $1/8^{th}$ of one percent) plus a market-driven spread, currently about 70-90 basis points. See 13 CFR §107.50; and U.S. Small Business Administration, "Trust Certificate Rates: SBIC Debenture Pools," at http://www.sba.gov /content/trustcertificate-rates-sbic-debenture-poolsat http://archive.sba.gov/aboutsba/sbaprograms/inv/faq /index.html. The coupon rate for the most recent sale of a SBA debenture participating certificate, which took place on September 11, 2012, was 2.245%. See U.S. Small Business Administration, "Offering Circular, Guaranteed 2.245% Debenture Participating Securities, Series SBIC 2012-10B," September 11, 2012, at http://www.sba.gov/content/sbic-2012-10-b-cusip-831641- ex9.

[68] U.S. Congress, House Committee on Small Business, Small Business Financing and Investment Act of 2009, report to accompany H.R. 3854, 111th Cong., 1st sess., October 26, 2009, H.Rept. 111-315 (Washington: GPO, 2009), p. 11; and U.S. Small Business Administration, "SBIC Program: FAQs: 8. What investment styles and fund types fit best with the SBIC Program?" at http://www.sba.gov/content/faqs.

[69] 13 CFR §107.1170.

[70] 13 CFR §107.1500; and U.S. Small Business Administration, "Offering Circular, Guaranteed 4.727% Participating Securities Participation Certificates, Series SBIC-PS 2009-10 A," February 19, 2009, pp. 7, 14, at http://www.sba.gov/content/sbic-ps-2009-10-cusip-831641-ep6.

[71] U.S. Small Business Administration, "Offering Circular, Guaranteed 4.727% Participating Securities Participation Certificates, Series SBIC-PS 2009-10 A," February 19, 2009, p. 2, at http://www.sba.gov/content/sbic-ps-2009-10-cusip-831641-ep6.

[72] Ibid., pp. 2, 3. Also, see U.S. Congress, House Committee on Small Business, *Private Equity for Small Firms: The Importance of the Participating Securities Program*, 109th Cong., 1st sess., April 13, 2005, Serial No. 109-10 (Washington: GPO, 2005), p. 5.

[73] The coupon rate for most recent sale of a SBA guaranteed participating securities participation certificate, which took place on February 25, 2009, was 4.727%. U.S. Small Business Administration, "Offering Circular, Guaranteed 4.727% Participating Securities Participation Certificates, Series SBIC-PS 2009-10 A," February 19, 2009, p. 1, at http://www.sba.gov/content/sbic-ps-2009-10-cusip-831641-ep6.

[74] U.S. Congress, House Committee on Small Business, Small Business Financing and Investment Act of 2009, report to accompany H.R. 3854, 111th Cong., 1st sess., October 26, 2009, H.Rept. 111-315 (Washington: GPO, 2009), p. 11; and U.S. Small Business Administration, "SBIC Program: FAQs 7. What is the status of the Participating Securities Program?" at http://www.sba.gov/content/faqs.

[75] U.S. Small Business Administration, Investment Division, "SBIC Program Overview," September 30, 2012.

[76] Ibid.

[77] U.S. Small Business Administration, "Impact Investment Initiative," at http://www.sba.gov /content/small-businessinvestment-company-sbic-impact-investment-initiative-2.

[78] U.S. Small Business Administration, "SBA Licenses First Impact Investment Fund in Michigan," July 26, 2011, at http://www.sba.gov/content/sba-licenses-first-impact-investment-fund-michigan. Mezzanine financing is a hybrid of debt and equity financing and is typically used to finance the expansion of an existing business. It provides the lender the right to convert to an ownership or equity interest in the company if the loan is not paid back in time and in full. It is generally subordinated to debt provided by senior lenders such as banks and venture capital companies.

[79] U.S. Small Business Administration, "Impact Investment Initiative," at http://www.sba.gov /content/small-businessinvestment-company-sbic-impact-investment-initiative-2.

[80] U.S. Small Business Administration, "Small Business Investment Companies - Early Stage SBICs," 77 *Federal Register* 25052, April 27, 2012.

[81] 13 CFR §107.1181. The required reserve is reduced on each payment date upon payment of the required interest and charges.

[82] U.S. Small Business Administration, Office of Congressional and Legislative Affairs, "Correspondence with the author," May 2, 2012.

[83] 13 CFR §107.630; and 13 CFR §107.690.

[84] 13 CFR §107.640.

[85] 13 CFR §107.650.

[86] Ibid.

[87] 13 CFR §107.660.

[88] U.S. Small Business Administration, Investment Division, "SBIC Program Overview," September 30, 2012.

[89] U.S. Small Business Administration, "SBIC Program Licensees Financing to Small Businesses Reported Between October 2011 and September 2012."

[90] U.S. Small Business Administration, Investment Division, "SBIC Program Overview," September 29, 2010; and U.S. Small Business Administration, Investment Division, "SBIC Program Overview," September 30, 2012.

[91] U.S. Small Business Administration, Investment Division, "SBIC Program Overview," September 29, 2010.

[92] U.S. Small Business Administration, "FY 2012 Congressional Budget Justification and FY 2010 Annual Performance Report," p. 60, at http://www.sba.gov/sites/default/files/ FINAL%20FY%202012%20CBJ% 20FY%202010%20APR_0.pdf. The SBA issued six new SBIC licenses (five to debenture SBICs and one to a bank-owned/non-leveraged SBIC) in FY2008 and 11 new SBIC licenses (eight to debenture SBICs and three to bank-owned/non-leveraged SBICs) in FY2009. The SBA issued 23 new SBIC licenses (21 to debenture SBICs and 2 to bank-owned/non-leveraged SBICs) in FY2010 and 22 new SBIC licenses (18 to debenture SBICs and 4 to bank-owned/non-leveraged SBICs) in FY2011. In FY2012, the SBA issued 30 new SBIC licenses (27 to debenture SBICs and 3 to bank-owned/non-leveraged SBICs).

[93] U.S. Small Business Administration, "Offering Circular, Guaranteed 2.245% Debenture Participating Securities, Series SBIC 2012-10B," September 11, 2012, at http://www.sba.gov/content/sbic-2012-10-b-cusip-831641-ex9. The SBA has a selected list of firms that have received SBIC financing, including Apple Computer, Compaq Computer, Costco Wholesale Corporation, FedEx, Intel, Jenny Craig, Inc., Outback Steakhouse, Sports Authority, Staples, and Sun Microsystems, on its website. See U.S. Small Business Administration, "Investment Division," at http://archive.sba.gov/aboutsba/sbaprograms/inv /INV_SUCCESS_STORIES.html.

[94] U.S. Small Business Administration, Investment Division, "SBIC Program Overview," September 30, 2012.

[95] Ibid.

[96] Ibid.

[97] U.S. Small Business Administration, "SBIC Program Licensees Financing to Small Businesses Reported Between October 2011 and September 2012."

[98] Ibid.

[99] National Venture Capital Association, "Corporate VC Stats as of 9/30/2012," Arlington, VA, at http://www.nvca.org/index.php?option=com_docman&task=cat_view&gid=99& Itemid= 317.

[100] U.S. Small Business Administration, "Fiscal Year 2011 Congressional Budget Justification and FY2009 Annual Performance Report," p. 52.

[101] Kenneth Temkin and Brett Theodos, with Kerstin Gentsch, "The Debenture Small Business Investment Company Program: A Comparative Analysis of Investment Patterns with Private Venture Capital Equity," Washington, DC: The Urban Institute, January 2008, p. 3, at http://www.urban.org/UploadedPDF/411601_ sbic_gap_analysis.pdf.

[102] Ibid., p. 1.

[103] U.S. Small Business Administration, "SBIC Program Licensees Financing to Small Businesses Reported Between October 2011 and September 2012."

[104] Kenneth Temkin and Brett Theodos, with Kerstin Gentsch, "The Debenture Small Business Investment Company Program: A Comparative Analysis of Investment Patterns with Private Venture Capital Equity," Washington, DC: The Urban Institute, January 2008, pp. 2, 26, at http://www.urban.org/Uploaded PDF/411601_sbic_gap_analysis.pdf.

[105] U.S. Congress, House Committee on Small Business, *Full Committee Hearing on Legislation Updating and Improving the SBA's Investment and Surety Bond Programs*, 110th Cong., 1st sess., September 6, 2007, Serial Number 110-44 (Washington: GPO, 2007), p. 15.

[106] Ibid.

[107] U.S. Congress, House Committee on Small Business, *Full Committee Hearing On Increasing Capital For Small Business*, 111th Cong., 1st sess., October 14, 2009, House Small Business Committee Document No. 111-051 (Washington: GPO, 2009), p. 89.

[108] Kenneth Temkin and Brett Theodos, with Kerstin Gentsch, "The Debenture Small Business Investment Company Program: A Comparative Analysis of Investment Patterns with Private Venture Capital Equity," Washington, DC: The Urban Institute, January 2008, pp. 3, 18-24, at http://www.urban.org/Uploaded PDF/411601_sbic_gap_analysis.pdf.

[109] National Venture Capital Association, "Venture Capital Investments Q3-2012 – MoneyTree Results, Regional Data," Arlington, VA, at http://www.nvca.org/.

[110] Kenneth Temkin and Brett Theodos, with Kerstin Gentsch, "The Debenture Small Business Investment Company Program: A Comparative Analysis of Investment Patterns with Private Venture Capital Equity," Washington, DC: The Urban Institute, January 2008, pp. 3, 11-17, at http://www.urban.org/Uploaded PDF/411601_sbic_gap_analysis.pdf.

[111] Ibid., p. 11.

[112] 13 CFR §107.1120; 13 CFR §107.1150; and U.S. Small Business Administration, "American Recovery and Reinvestment Act of 2009: Implementation of SBIC Program Changes," letter from Harry Haskins, Acting Associate Administrator for Investment, to All Small Business Investment Companies (SBICs) and Applicants, May 4, 2009, p. 1, at http://archive.sba.gov/idc/groups/public /documents/sba_program_office /inv_rcvry_act_sbic_changes.pdf. Previously, "... the total principal amount of outstanding debentures and participating securities guaranteed by SBA and issued by any SBIC or group of commonly controlled SBICs may not, in general, exceed at any one time an amount equal to three times such SBIC's Private Capital or $130.6 million, whichever is less, of which no more than two times the SBIC's Private Capital may be represented by participating securities. Such dollar limit has been adjusted annually to reflect increases in the Consumer Price Index since March 31, 1993." See U.S. Small Business Administration, "Offering Circular, Guaranteed 5.725% Debenture Participation Certificates, Series SBIC 2008-10 B," September 18, 2008, at http://www.sba.gov/content/sbic-2008-10-b-cusip-831641-en1.

[113] 13 CFR §107.1150; and 13 CFR §107.710.

[114] 13 CFR §107.1150.

[115] The White House, "Startup America Legislative Agenda," January 31, 2012, at http://www.whitehouse.gov/sites /default/files/uploads/startup_america_legislative_ agenda. pdf.

[116] Representative Edward Perlmutter, "Providing for Further Consideration of H.R. 5297, Small Business Jobs and Credit Act of 2010, Roll No. 368," *Congressional Record*, daily edition, vol. 156, no. 91 (June 17, 2010), pp. H4608, H 4609.

[117] H.R. 5297, the Small Business Lending Fund Act of 2010, Section 399L. Definitions.

[118] Ibid. The nine targeted industries are: agricultural technology, energy technology, environmental technology, life science, information technology, digital media, clean technology, defense technology, and photonics technology. A similar $200 million Small Business Early Stage Investment Program was included in H.R. 3854, the Small Business Financing and Investment Act of 2009, which was passed by the House on October 29, 2009, by a vote of 389-32. It is awaiting action in the Senate.

[119] Senator Al Franken, "Small Business Lending Fund Act of 2010," Rollcall Vote No. 237 Leg., *Congressional Record*, daily edition, vol. 156, part 125 (September 16, 2010), p. S7158.

[120] P.L. 111-240, the Small Business Jobs Act of 2010, Section 1131. Small Business Intermediary Lending Pilot Program.

[121] U.S. Small Business Administration, "Small Businesses Have New Non-Profit Sources for SBA-financed Loans," August 4, 2011, at http://www.sba.gov/content/intermediary-lending-pilot-program-0.

[122] U.S. Congress, House Committee on Small Business, *Small Business Financing and Investment Act of 2009*, report to accompany H.R. 3854, 111th Cong., 1st sess., October 26, 2009, H.Rept. 111-315, p. 2. For the arguments presented by various organizations advocating programs to assist early stage small businesses and startups see U.S. Congress, House Committee on Small Business, *Subcommittee on Finance and Tax Hearing on Legislative Proposals to Reform the SBA's Capital Access Programs*, 111th Cong., 1st sess., July 23, 2009, House Small Business Committee Document No. 111-039 (Washington: GPO, 2009), pp. 10-12, 60-67; and U.S. Congress, House Committee on Small Business, *Full Committee Hearing on Increasing Access to Capital for Small Business*, 111th Cong., 1st sess., October 14, 2009, House Small Business Committee Document No. 111-051 (Washington: GPO, 2009), pp. 33-35, 50-54, 63-69, 86-99.

[123] Representative Nydia Velázquez, "Small Business Jobs and Credit Act of 2010," House debate, *Congressional Record*, daily edition, vol. 156, no. 90 (June 16, 2010), p. H4516.

[124] Representative Sam Graves, "Small Business Jobs and Credit Act of 2010," House debate, *Congressional Record*, vol. 156, no. 90 (June 16, 2010), p. H4516.

[125] Ibid; and Representative Jeff Flake, "Small Business Early Stage Investment Act of 2009," House debate, Congressional Record, vol. 155, no. 171 (November 18, 2009), p. H13083. Note: H.R. 3738, the Small Business Early-Stage Investment Act of 2009, was one of eight bills merged into H.R. 3854, the Small Business Financing and Investment Act of 2009, and was later added to H.R. 5297, Small Business Jobs and Credit Act of 2010, by H.Res. 1436.

[126] U.S. Congress, House Committee on Small Business, *Full Committee Hearing On Increasing Capital For Small Business*, 111th Cong., 1st sess., October 14, 2009, House Small Business Committee Document No. 111-051 (Washington: GPO, 2009), pp. 32, 87.

[127] Ibid., pp. 88, 89.

[128] H.R. 3854, the Small Business Financing and Investment Act of 2009, Section 401. Increased Investment from States; and H.R. 5554, the Small Business Assistance and Relief Act of 2010, Section 591. Increased Investment from States.

[129] H.R. 3854, the Small Business Financing and Investment Act of 2009, Section 401. Increased Investment From States, Section 403. Revised Leverage Limitations For Successful SBICs, and Section 408. Program Levels; and H.R. 5554, the Small Business Assistance and Relief Act of 2010, Section 591. Increased Investment from States, Section 593. Revised Leverage Limitations for Successful SBICs, and Section 598. Program Levels.

[130] The White House, "Startup America Legislative Agenda," at http://www.whitehouse.gov /sites/default/files/uploads/ startup_america_legislative_agenda.pdf.

[131] U.S. Small Business Administration, "Fiscal Year 2011 Congressional Budget Justification and FY2009 Annual Performance Report," p. 52.

[132] U.S. Small Business Administration, "SBA Project Plan, Section 505: SBIC Program Changes," June 16, 2010, at http://archive.sba.gov/idc/groups/public/documents /sba_ homepage/sba_sbic_plan.pdf.

[133] U.S. Congress, House Committee on Small Business, *Small Business Financing and Investment Act of 2009*, report to accompany H.R. 3854, 111th Cong., 1st sess., October 26, 2009, H.Rept. 111-315 (Washington: GPO, 2009), p. 3.

[134] U.S. Congress, House Committee on Small Business, *Full Committee Hearing on Increasing Capital for Small Business*, 111th Cong., 1st sess., October 14, 2009, House Small Business Committee Document No. 111-051 (Washington: GPO, 2009), pp. 88-91; and Representative Nydia Velázquez, "Small Business Jobs and Credit Act of 2010," House debate, *Congressional Record*, daily edition, vol. 156, no. 90 (June 16, 2010), p. H4516.

[135] Representative Nydia Velázquez, "Small Business Financing and Investment Act of 2009," House debate, *Congressional Record*, daily edition, vol. 155, no. 159 (October 29, 2009), pp. H12074, H12075; Senator Mary Landrieu, "Statements on Introduced Bills and Joint Resolutions," remarks in the Senate, *Congressional Record*, daily edition, vol. 155, no. 185 (December 10, 2009), p. S12910; The White House, "Remarks by the President on Job Creation and Economic Growth," December 8, 2009, at http://www.whitehouse.gov/the-press-office/remarkspresident-job-creation-and-economic-growth; and The White House, "Startup America Legislative Agenda," at http://www.whitehouse.gov/sites/default/files /uploads/startup_america_legislative_ agenda.pdf.

[136] Senator Olympia Snowe, "Jumpstart Our Business Startups Act," remarks in the Senate, *Congressional Record*, vol. 158, no. 45 (March 19, 2012), p. S15845.

[137] National Federation of Independent Business, "Payroll Tax Holiday," Washington, DC, at http://www.nfib.com/issues-elections/issues-elections-item/cmsid/49039/; and NFIB, "Government Spending," Washington, DC, at http://www.nfib.com/issues-elections/issues-elections-item/cmsid/49051/.

[138] Representative Sam Graves, "Views and Estimates of the Committee on Small Business on Matters to be set forth in the Concurrent Resolution on the Budget for Fiscal Year 2013," Washington, DC, pp. 4, 5, at http://smbiz.house.gov/ UploadedFiles/Views_and_Estimates_ FY_2013.pdf. Also, see Representative Sam Graves, "Views and Estimates of the Committee on Small Business on Matters to be set forth in the Concurrent Resolution on the Budget for Fiscal Year 2012," Washington, DC, pp. 4, 5, at http://smbiz.house.gov /UploadedFiles/ March_17_Views_and_Estimates_Letter.pdf.

[139] 13 CFR §107.700; 13 CFR §107.710; 13 CFR §301(c)(2); and 13 CFR §301(c)(1).

[140] U.S. Small Business Administration, "Small Business Investment Companies — Leverage Eligibility and Portfolio Diversification Requirements," 74 *Federal Register* 33912, July 14, 2009.

[141] 13 CFR §107.710.

[142] U.S. Small Business Administration, "Small Business Investment Companies — Leverage Eligibility and Portfolio Diversification Requirements," 74 *Federal Register* 33912, July 14, 2009.

[143] 13 CFR §107.720.

[144] Ibid.

[145] U.S. Small Business Administration, "All SBIC Licensees By State," at http://www.sba.gov /content/all-sbic-licensees-state.

[146] Ibid.

[147] Small Business Investor Alliance (formerly the National Association of Small Business Investment Companies), "SBIC Financing: Step-by-Step," Washington, DC, at http://www.nasbic.org/?page=SBIC_financing.

[148] U.S. Small Business Administration, "SBIC Program," at http://www.sba.gov/content/sbic-program-0.

[149] Small Business Investor Alliance (formerly the National Association of Small Business Investment Companies), "SBIC Financing: Step-by-Step," Washington, DC, at http://www.nasbic.org/?page=SBIC_financing.

In: Small Business Administration Programs
Editor: Walter Janikowski

ISBN: 978-1-62417-992-1
© 2013 Nova Science Publishers, Inc.

Chapter 7

SMALL BUSINESS MANAGEMENT AND TECHNICAL ASSISTANCE TRAINING PROGRAMS[*]

Robert Jay Dilger

SUMMARY

The Small Business Administration (SBA) has provided "technical and managerial aides to small-business concerns, by advising and counseling on matters in connection with government procurement and on policies, principles and practices of good management" since it began operations in 1953. Initially, the SBA provided its own small business management and technical assistance training programs. However, over time, the SBA has relied increasingly on third parties to provide that training. In FY2012, the SBA will provide nearly $170 million to about "14,000 resource partners," including more than 900 small business development centers, 108 women's business centers, and 364 chapters of the mentoring program, SCORE. The SBA reports that more than 1 million aspiring entrepreneurs and small business owners receive training from an SBA-supported resource partner each year. The SBA has argued that these programs contribute "to the long-term success of these businesses and their ability to grow and create jobs." The Department of Commerce also provides management and technical assistance training for small businesses. For example, its Minority Business Development Agency provides training to minority business owners to assist them in becoming suppliers to private corporations and the federal government.

A recurring theme at congressional hearings concerning the SBA's management and technical assistance training programs has been the perceived need to improve program efficiency by eliminating duplication of services and increasing cooperation and coordination both within and among SCORE, women's business centers (WBCs), and small business development centers (SBDCs). For example, on March 15, 2011, the House Committee on Small Business recommended that several SBA training programs be defunded "because they duplicate existing programs at the SBA or at other agencies." Congress has also explored ways to improve the SBA's measurement of the programs' effectiveness and to address the impact of national economic conditions on WBC and SBDC finances and their capacity to maintain client service levels and meet federal

---

[*] This is an edited, reformatted and augmented version of Congressional Research Service, Publication No. R41352, dated July 25, 2012.

matching requirements. This report examines the historical development of federal small business management and technical assistance training programs; describes their current structures, operations, and budgets; and assesses their administration and oversight, the measures used to determine their effectiveness, and WBC and SBDC finances and their capacity to maintain client service levels and meet federal matching requirements. This report also discusses P.L. 111-240, the Small Business Jobs Act of 2010. It authorized $50 million in additional funds for SBDCs to provide targeted technical assistance to small businesses for various specified activities, such as seeking access to capital or credit; guaranteed each state not less than $325,000 of these additional funds; and waived the non-federal matching requirement for these funds. The act also authorizes the SBA to temporarily waive, in whole or in part, for successive fiscal years, the non-federal share matching requirement relating to "technical assistance and counseling" for WBCs. Two bills introduced during the 111th Congress, H.R. 2352, the Job Creation Through Entrepreneurship Act of 2009, and S. 3967, the Small Business Investment and Innovation Act of 2010, are also examined. They would have authorized several changes to the SBA's management and technical assistance training programs in an effort to improve their performance and oversight.

FEDERAL MANAGEMENT AND TECHNICAL ASSISTANCE TRAINING PROGRAMS

The Small Business Administration (SBA) administers several programs to support small businesses, including loan guaranty programs to enhance small business access to capital; programs to increase small business opportunities in federal contracting; direct loans for businesses, homeowners, and renters to assist their recovery from natural disasters; and access to entrepreneurial education to assist with business formation and expansion. The SBA has provided "technical and managerial aides to small-business concerns, by advising and counseling on matters in connection with government procurement and on policies, principles and practices of good management" since it began operations in 1953.[1]

Initially, the SBA provided its own management and technical assistance training programs. However, over time, the SBA has relied increasingly on third parties to provide that training. As shown in Table 1, the SBA will spend nearly $170 million on management and technical assistance training programs in FY2012. The SBA reports that more than 1 million aspiring entrepreneurs and small business owners receive training from an SBA-supported resource partner each year.[2]

The SBA has argued that its support of management and technical assistance training for small businesses has contributed "to the long-term success of these businesses and their ability to grow and create jobs."[3] It currently provides financial support to about "14,000 resource partners," including more than 900 small business development centers (SBDCs), 108 women's business centers (WBCs), and 364 chapters of the mentoring program, SCORE.[4]

The Department of Commerce also provides management and technical assistance training for small businesses. For example, the Department of Commerce's Minority Business Development Agency provides training to minority business owners to assist them in becoming suppliers to private corporations and the federal government.[5] In addition, the Department of Commerce's Economic Development Administration's Local Technical

Assistance Program promotes efforts to build and expand local organizational capacity in economically distressed areas. As part of that effort, it funds projects that focus on technical or market feasibility studies of economic development projects or programs, which often include consultation with small businesses.[6]

Table 1. SBA Management and Technical Assistance Training Programs Funding, FY2012

Training Program	FY2012
Small Business Development Center Grants Program	$112,500,000
Microloan Technical Assistance Program	$20,000,000
Women's Business Center Grants Program	$14,000,000
SCORE (Service Corps of Retired Executives)	$7,000,000
Entrepreneurial Development Initiatives (clusters)	$5,000,000
PRIME Technical Assistance Program	$3,500,000
7(j) Technical Assistance Program	$3,100,000
Veterans Business Development Program	$2,500,000
Native American Outreach Program	$1,250,000
National Women's Business Council	$998,000
Total	$169,848,000

Source: H.Rept. 112-331, report to accompany the Consolidated Appropriations Act, 2012.

For many years, a recurring theme at congressional hearings concerning the SBA's management and technical assistance training programs has been the perceived need to improve program efficiency by eliminating duplication of services and increasing cooperation and coordination both within and among its training resource partners. For example, the Obama Administration recommended in its FY2012 and FY2103 budget recommendations that funding for the PRIME technical assistance program be ended, arguing that it overlaps and duplicates "the technical assistance provided by SBA's microlending intermediaries."[7] Also, on March 15, 2011, the House Committee on Small Business recommended to the House Committee on the Budget that several SBA management and technical assistance training programs be defunded, including funding for WBCs, "because they duplicate existing programs at the SBA or at other agencies."[8]

Congress has also explored ways to improve the SBA's measurement of the programs' effectiveness and to address the impact of national economic conditions on WBC and SBDC finances and their capacity to meet federal matching requirements and to maintain client service levels.

This report examines the historical development of federal small business management and technical assistance training programs; describes their current structures, operations, and budgets; and assesses their administration and oversight, the measures used to determine their effectiveness, and WBC and SBDC finances and their capacity to maintain client service levels and meet federal matching requirements.

This report also discusses P.L. 111-240, the Small Business Jobs Act of 2010. It authorizes $50 million in additional funds for SBDCs to provide targeted technical assistance to small businesses for various specified activities, such as seeking access to capital or credit, federal procurement opportunities, and opportunities to export products. The act also guarantees each state not less than $325,000 of these additional funds and waives the non-federal matching requirement for these additional funds.

This report also discusses two bills introduced during the 111th Congress: H.R. 2352, the Job Creation Through Entrepreneurship Act of 2009, and S. 3967, the Small Business Investment and Innovation Act of 2010. They would have authorized several changes to these programs in an effort to improve their performance and oversight.

SBA MANAGEMENT AND TECHNICAL ASSISTANCE TRAINING PROGRAMS

The SBA supports a number of management and technical assistance training programs, including the

- Small Business Development Center Grants Program,
- Women's Business Center Grants Program,
- Microloan Technical Assistance Program,
- SCORE (Service Corps of Retired Executives),
- PRIME Technical Assistance Program,
- Veterans Business Development Programs,
- 7(j) Technical Assistance Program, and
- Native American Outreach Program.

The legislative history and current operating structures, functions, and budget for each of these programs is presented. In addition, if the data are available, their performance based on outcome-based measures, such as their effect on small business formation, survivability, and expansion, and on job creation and retention, is also presented. Also, a brief description of each of these programs is provided in the Appendix.

The SBA Entrepreneurial Development Initiatives Program is not discussed in detail. It is designed to accelerate small business growth and job creation through clusters that leverage and align a region's economic, business and workforce assets."[9] Regional clusters are "geographic concentrations of firms and industries that do business with each other and have common needs for talent, technology, and infrastructure."[10] Regional cluster advocates argue that these networks "create a multiplier effect that increases efficiency, innovation, and ultimately produces conditions for high-growth, high-impact small businesses to prosper."[11] The SBA's Entrepreneurial Development Initiatives Program will provide 15 one-year grants of up to $600,000 each, with an option for an additional funding year, to local and regional business clusters to "provide business training, commercialization and technology transfer services, counseling, mentoring and other services that support the growth and development of small businesses in the cluster area and its industries."[12] The first 10 grant awards, selected from 173 applicants, were announced on September 20, 2010.[13] The clusters "will be assessed on the impact they will have on the region's economic growth, creation of sustainable jobs and the opportunities the cluster provides for small businesses."[14] In FY2011, SBA-funded regional clusters formed 308 collaborative projects, joint product development, joint sales

Small Business Management and Technical Assistance Training Programs   177

activities, information sourcing agreements, and joint ventures with other businesses; assisted in commercializing 28 new technologies; and assisted in creating 19 patents.[15]

Small Business Development Centers

In 1976, the SBA created the University Business Development Center pilot program to establish small business centers within universities to provide counseling and training for small businesses. The first center was founded at California State Polytechnic University at Pomona in December, 1976. Seven more centers were funded over the next six months at universities in seven different states. By 1979, 16 SBDCs received SBA funding and were providing management and technical training assistance to small businesses.[16]

The SBDC program was given statutory authorization by P.L. 96-302, the Small Business Development Center Act of 1980.[17] SBDCs were to "rely on the private sector primarily, and the university community, in partnership with the SBA and its other programs, to fill gaps in making quality management assistance available to the small business owner."[18] Although most SBDCs continued to be affiliated with universities, the legislation authorized the SBA to provide funding

> to any State government or any agency thereof, any regional entity, any State-chartered development, credit or finance corporation, any public or private institution of higher education, including but not limited to any land-grant college or university, any college or school of business, engineering, commerce, or agriculture, community college or junior college, or to any entity formed by two or more of the above entities.[19]

SBDC funding is allocated on a pro rata basis among the states (defined to include the District of Columbia, the Commonwealth of Puerto Rico, the Virgin Islands, Guam, and American Samoa) by a statutory formula "based on the percentage of the population of each State, as compared to the population of the United States."[20] If, as is currently the case, SBDC funding exceeds $90 million, the minimum funding level is "the sum of $500,000, plus a percentage of $500,000 equal to the percentage amount by which the amount made available exceeds $90 million."[21]

In 1984, P.L. 98-395, the Small Business Development Center Improvement Act of 1984, required SBDCs, as a condition of receiving SBA funding, to contribute a matching amount equal to the grant amount, and that the match must be provided by non-federal sources and be comprised of not less than 50% cash and not more than 50% of indirect costs and in-kind contributions.[22] It also required SBDCs to have an advisory board and a full-time director who has authority to make expenditures under the center's budget. It also required the SBA to implement a program of onsite evaluations for each SBDC and to make those evaluations at least once every two years.

Today, the SBA provides grants to SBDCs that are "hosted by leading universities, colleges, and state economic development agencies" to deliver management and technical assistance training "to small businesses and nascent entrepreneurs (pre-venture) in order to promote growth, expansion, innovation, increased productivity and management improvement."[23] These services are delivered, in most instances, on a non-fee, one-on-one confidential counseling basis and are administered by 63 lead service centers, one located in each state (four in Texas and six in California), the District of Columbia, Puerto Rico, the Virgin Islands, Guam, and American Samoa.[24] These lead centers manage more than 900 service centers located throughout the United States and the territories.[25]

The SBDC program assisted approximately 210,000 small business owners (102,000) and prospective owners (108,000) in FY2011.[26] It received an appropriation of $113.0 million in both FY2010 and FY2011, and $112.5 million for FY2012.[27] In addition, P.L. 111-240, the Small Business Jobs Act of 2010, appropriated $50 million in additional funds for SBDCs to provide targeted technical assistance to small businesses for various specified activities, such as seeking access to capital or credit, federal procurement opportunities, and opportunities to export products. The act guaranteed each state not less than $325,000 of these additional funds and waived the non-federal matching requirement for these additional funds.[28] About $16.2 million of these funds were awarded to SBDCs in FY2010, and the remainder was awarded to SBDCs during FY2011.[29]

The Obama Administration has recommended that the SBDC program receive an appropriation of $101.1 million in FY2013.[30]

Special areas of emphasis for the SBDC program in FY2012 include "facilitating innovation and high-growth companies small business innovation research (SBIR) grants, commercialization and technology transfer services, and export tools and guidance."[31] In FY2011, more than 13,600 new businesses were formed with assistance from SBDC counselors.[32]

As part of its legislative mandate to evaluate each SBDC, in 2003, the SBA's Office of Entrepreneurial Development designed "a multi-year time series study to assess the impact of the programs it offers to small businesses."[33] The survey has been administered annually by a private firm. The latest survey findings were released on November 9, 2011.

The latest survey was sent to 20,329 SBDC clients in 2010 to assess the "initial attitudinal impact" of their counseling experience in 2010, and "a follow-up study showing the financial impact on 2009 and 2008 clients."[34] A total of 5,113 surveys (25.2%) were completed.[35]

The 2010 survey of SBDC clients indicated that

- approximately 74% of SBDC respondents reported that the information they received from their counselor was valuable,
- 74% of SBDC respondents that received between three and five hours and 77% that received more than five hours of counseling rated SBDC usefulness as "high" as compared to 71% of respondents that received less than three hours of counseling,
- 33% of start-up clients and 37% of in-business clients reported that they were able to increase sales as a result of SBDC assistance, and
- 11% of start-up clients and 19% of in-business clients reported that they were able to hire new staff as a result of SBDC assistance.[36]

Women's Business Centers

The Women's Business Center (WBC) Renewable Grant Program was initially established by P.L. 100-533, the Women's Business Ownership Act of 1988, as the Women's Business Demonstration Pilot Program. The act directed the SBA to provide financial assistance to private, nonprofit organizations to conduct demonstration projects giving financial, management, and marketing assistance to small businesses, including start-up businesses, owned and controlled by women. Since its inception, the program has targeted the needs of socially and economically disadvantaged women.[37] The WBC program was expanded and provided permanent legislative status by P.L. 109-108, the Science, State, Justice, Commerce, and Related Agencies Appropriations Act, 2006.

Since the program's inception, the SBA has awarded WBCs a grant of up to $150,000 per year. Initially, the grant was awarded for one year, with the possibility of being renewed twice, for a total of up to three years. Also, as a condition of the receipt of funds, the WBC was required to raise at least one non-federal dollar for each two federal dollars during the grant's first year (1:2), one non-federal dollar for each federal dollar during year two (1:1), and two non-federal dollars for each federal dollar during year three (2:1).[38] Over the years, Congress has extended the length of the WBC program's grant award and reduced the program's matching requirement.

Today, WBC initial grants are awarded for up to five years, consisting of a base period of 12 months from the date of the award and four 12-month option periods.[39] The SBA determines if the option periods are exercised and makes that determination subject to the continuation of program authority, the availability of funds, and the recipient organization's compliance with federal law, SBA regulations, and the terms and conditions specified in a cooperative agreement. WBCs that successfully complete the initial five-year grant period may apply for an unlimited number of three-year funding intervals.[40]

During their initial five-year grant period, WBCs are now required to provide a non-federal match of one non-federal dollar for each two federal dollars in years one and two (1:2), and one nonfederal dollar for each federal dollar in years three, four and five (1:1).[41] After the initial five-year grant period, the matching requirement in subsequent three-year funding intervals is not more than 50% of federal funding (1:1).[42]

The non-federal match may consist of cash, in-kind and program income.[43] As will be discussed later, P.L. 111-240, the Small Business Jobs Act of 2010, provides the SBA temporary authority, through FY2012, to waive the WBC matching requirement under specified circumstances.

Today, there are 108 WBCs located throughout most of the United States and the territories.[44] In FY2011, they assisted 138,923 small business owners.[45] They also assisted in the formation of more than 500 new businesses in FY2011.[46] The WBC program received a $14.0 million appropriation in FY2010, FY2011, and FY2012.[47] The Obama Administration has recommended that the WBC program receive an appropriation of $12.6 million in FY2013.[48]

P.L. 105-135, the Small Business Reauthorization Act of 1997, required the SBA to "develop and implement an annual programmatic and financial examination of each" WBC.[49] As part of its legislative mandate to implement an annual programmatic and financial examination of each WBC, the SBA's Office of Entrepreneurial Development includes WBCs in its previously mentioned multi-year time series study of its programs.[50] The survey has been administered annually by a private firm. The latest survey findings were released on November 9, 2011.

The firm administering the 2010 survey of SBA management and training clients contacted 3,021 WBC clients and received 589 completed surveys (19.5%).[51]

The survey indicated that

- approximately 73% of WBC respondents reported that the information they received from their counselor was valuable,
- 76% of WBC respondents that received more than three hours of counseling rated WBC usefulness "high" as compared to 69% of respondents that received less than three hours of counseling, and
- 39% of start-up clients and 42% of in-business clients reported that they were able to increase sales as a result of WBC assistance, and
- 11% of start-up clients and 19% of in-business clients reported that they were able to hire new staff as a result of WBC assistance.[52]

Microloan Technical Assistance Program

Congress authorized the SBA's Microloan lending program in 1991 (P.L. 102-140, the Departments of Commerce, Justice, and State, the Judiciary, and Related Agencies Appropriations Act, 1992) to address the perceived disadvantages faced by women, low-income, and minority entrepreneurs and business owners gaining access to capital for starting or expanding their business. The program became operational in 1992. Its stated purpose is

> to assist women, low-income, veteran ... and minority entrepreneurs and business owners and other individuals possessing the capability to operate successful business concerns; to assist small business concerns in those areas suffering from a lack of credit due to economic downturns; ... to make loans to eligible intermediaries to enable such intermediaries to provide small-scale loans, particularly loans in amounts averaging not more than $10,000, to start-up, newly established, or growing small business concerns for working capital or the acquisition of materials, supplies, or equipment; [and] to make grants to eligible intermediaries that, together with non-Federal matching funds, will enable such intermediaries to provide intensive marketing, management, and technical assistance to microloan borrowers.[53]

Initially, the SBA's Microloan program was authorized as a five-year demonstration project. It was made permanent, subject to reauthorization, by P.L. 105-135.

The SBA's Microloan Technical Assistance Program, which is part of the SBA's Microloan program but receives a separate appropriation, provides grants to Microloan intermediaries to provide management and technical training assistance to Microloan program borrowers and prospective borrowers.[54] There are 181 intermediaries participating in the program, located in 48 states, the District of Columbia, and Puerto Rico.[55]

Intermediaries are eligible to receive a Microloan technical assistance grant "of not more than 25% of the total outstanding balance of loans made to it" under the Microloan program.[56] Grant funds may be used only to provide marketing, management, and technical assistance to Microloan borrowers, except that up to 25% of the funds may be used to provide such assistance to prospective Microloan borrowers. Grant funds may also be used to attend training required by the SBA.[57]

In most instances, intermediaries must contribute, solely from non-federal sources, an amount equal to 25% of the grant amount.[58] In addition to cash or other direct funding, the contribution may include indirect costs or in-kind contributions paid for under non-federal programs.[59] Intermediaries that make at least 50% of their loans to small businesses located in or owned by residents of an Economically Distressed Area are not subject to the 25% contribution requirement.[60] Intermediaries may expend no more than 25% of the grant funds on third-party contracts for the provision of management and technical assistance.[61]

The SBA does not require Microloan borrowers to participate in the Microloan Technical Assistance Program. However, intermediaries typically require Microloan borrowers to participate in the training program as a condition of the receipt of a microloan. Combining loan and intensive management and technical assistance training is one of the Microloan program's distinguishing features.[62]

The Microloan technical assistance program provided counseling services to 15,900 small businesses in FY2011.[63] The program was appropriated $46 million in FY2010, including $24 million in additional temporary funding provided by P.L. 111-5, the American Recovery and Reinvestment Act of 2009. It received a $22 million appropriation for FY2011, and $20 million for FY2012.[64] The Obama Administration has recommended that the Microloan technical assistance program receive an appropriation of $19.76 million in FY2013.[65]

SCORE (Service Corps of Retired Executives)

The SBA has partnered with various voluntary business and professional service organizations to provide management and technical assistance training to small businesses since the 1950s. On October 5, 1964, using authority under the Small Business Act to provide "technical and managerial aids to small business concerns" in cooperation with "educational and other nonprofit organizations, associations, and institutions," then-SBA Administrator Eugene P. Foley officially launched SCORE (Service Corps of Retired Executives) as a national, volunteer organization with 2,000 members, uniting over 50 independent nonprofit organizations into a single, national nonprofit organization.[66] Since then, the SBA has provided financial assistance to SCORE to provide training to small business owners and prospective owners.[67]

Over the years, Congress has authorized the SBA to take certain actions relating to SCORE. For example, P.L. 89-754, the Demonstration Cities and Metropolitan Development Act of 1966, authorized the SBA to permit members of nonprofit organizations use of the SBA's office facilities and services. P.L. 90-104, the Small Business Act Amendments of 1967, added the authority to pay travel and subsistence expenses "incurred at the request of the Administration in connection with travel to a point more than fifty miles distant from the home of that individual in providing gratuitous services to small businessmen" or "in connection with attendance at meetings sponsored by the Administration."[68] P.L. 93-113, the Domestic Volunteer Service Act of 1973, was the first statute to mention SCORE directly, providing the Director of ACTION authority to work with SCORE to "expand the application of their expertise beyond Small Business Administration clients."[69] P.L. 95-510, a bill to amend the Small Business Act, provided the SBA explicit statutory authorization to work with SCORE (Sec 8(b)(1)(A)). P.L. 106-554, the Consolidated Appropriations Act, 2001 (Section 1(a)(9)—the Small Business Reauthorization Act of 2000) authorized SCORE to solicit cash and in-kind contributions from the private sector to be used to carry out its functions.

The SBA currently provides grants to SCORE to provide in-person mentoring, online training, and "nearly 9,000 local training workshops annually" to small businesses.[70] SCORE's 364 chapters and more than 800 branch offices are located throughout the United States and partner with nearly 13,000 volunteer counselors, who are working or retired business owners, executives and corporate leaders, to provide management and training assistance to small businesses "at no charge or at very low cost."[71]

SCORE assisted 356,837 small business owners and prospective entrepreneurs in FY2011.[72] In FY2011, 816 new businesses were formed with assistance from SCORE counselors.[73] SCORE received a $7 million appropriation in FY2010, FY2011, and FY2012.[74] The Obama Administration has recommended that SCORE receive an appropriation of $6.3 million in FY2013.[75]

W. Kenneth Yancey, Jr., SCORE's chief executive officer, provided the following description at a congressional hearing of SCORE's efforts to assist small businesses as they deal with the nation's current economic environment:

> SCORE volunteers know things that only experience can teach. All across the country, SCORE is helping clients navigate the credit crunch. SCORE can mentor an aspiring entrepreneur through the business plan process to get them through the start-up phase. For in-business clients, SCORE can provide advice on handling cash flow problems and marketing to drive leads and sales. Many SCORE chapters offer team counseling, where a group of volunteers examine various aspects of the client's business and make recommendations.[76]

The SBA Office of Entrepreneurial Development includes SCORE in its multi-year time series study to assess its programs' effectiveness. The firm administering the 2010 survey of SBA management and training clients contacted 21,521 SCORE clients and received 4,444 completed surveys (20.6%).[77] The survey indicated that

- approximately 73% of SCORE respondents reported that the information they received from their counselor was valuable,
- 78% of SCORE respondents that received three or more hours of counseling rated SCORE usefulness as "high" compared to 68% of respondents that received less than three hours of counseling,
- 25% of start-up clients and 33% of in-business clients reported that they were able to increase sales as a result of SCORE assistance, and
- 8% of start-up clients and 16% of in-business clients reported that they were able to hire new staff as a result of SCORE assistance.[78]

Program for Investment in Micro-entrepreneurs

P.L. 106-102, the Gramm-Leach-Bliley Act (of 1999) (Subtitle C—Microenterprise Technical Assistance and Capacity Building Program) amended P.L. 103-325, the Riegle Community Development and Regulatory Improvement Act of 1994, to authorize the SBA to "establish a microenterprise technical assistance and capacity building grant program."[79] The program was to "provide assistance from the Administration in the form of grants" to

> nonprofit microenterprise development organizations or programs (or a group or collaborative thereof) that has a demonstrated record of delivering microenterprise services to disadvantaged entrepreneurs; an intermediary; a microenterprise development organization or program that is accountable to a local community, working in conjunction with a state or local government or Indian tribe; or an Indian tribe acting on its own, if the Indian tribe can certify that no private organization or program referred to in this paragraph exists within its jurisdiction."[80]

The SBA was directed "to ensure that not less than 50% of the grants ... are used to benefit very low-income persons, including those residing on Indian reservations."[81] It was also directed to

> (1) provide training and technical assistance to disadvantaged entrepreneurs; (2) provide training and capacity building services to microenterprise development organizations and programs and groups of such organizations to assist such organizations and programs in developing microenterprise training and services; (3) aid in researching and developing the best practices in the field of microenterprise and technical assistance programs for disadvantaged entrepreneurs; and (4) for such other activities as the Administrator determines are consistent with the purposes of this subtitle.[82]

The SBA's Program for Investment in Micro-entrepreneurs (PRIME) was designed to meet these legislative requirements by providing "assistance to organizations that help low-income entrepreneurs who lack sufficient training and education to gain access to capital to establish and expand their small businesses."[83] The program offers four types of grants:

- Technical Assistance Grants support training and technical assistance to disadvantaged micro-entrepreneurs,
- Capacity Building Grants support training and capacity building services to micro-enterprise development organizations and programs to assist them in developing micro-enterprise training and services,
- Research and Development Grants support the development and sharing of best practices in the field of micro-enterprise development and technical assistance programs for disadvantaged micro-entrepreneurs, and
- Discretionary Grants support other activities determined to be consistent with these purposes.[84]

Grants are awarded on an annual basis. Applicants may be approved for option year funding for up to four subsequent years. Award amounts vary depending on the availability of funds. However, no single grantee may receive more than $250,000 or 10% of the total funds made available for the program in a single fiscal year, whichever is less.[85]

Recipients must match 50% of the funding from non-federal sources. Revenue from fees, grants, and gifts; income from loan sources; and in-kind resources from non-federal public or private sources may be used to comply with the matching requirement.[86] SBA regulations indicate that "applicants or grantees with severe constraints on available sources of matching funds may request that the Administrator or designee reduce or eliminate the matching requirements."[87] Any reductions or eliminations must not exceed 10% of the aggregate of all PRIME grant funds made available by SBA in any fiscal year.[88]

The SBA awarded 100 PRIME grants to management and technical assistance service providers in FY2011, ranging from $33,500 to $227,500.[89] The number of clients served by this program during FY2011 is unavailable. The PRIME program received an $8 million appropriation in FY2010 and FY2011, and $3.5 million for FY2012.[90] As mentioned previously, the Obama Administration recommended in its FY2012 and FY2013 budget requests that funding for the program be eliminated, arguing that it overlaps and duplicates the SBA's Microloan Technical Assistance Program.[91]

Veterans Business Development Programs

The SBA has supported management and technical assistance training for veteran-owned small businesses since its formation as an agency. However, during the 1990s, some in Congress noted that a direct loan program for veterans was eliminated by the SBA in 1995 and that the "training and counseling for veterans dropped from 38,775 total counseling sessions for veterans in 1993 to 29,821 sessions in 1998."[92] Concerned that "the needs of veterans have been diminished systematically at the SBA," Congress adopted P.L. 106-50, the Veterans Entrepreneurship and Small Business Development Act of 1999.[93] It authorized the establishment of the federally chartered National Veterans Business Development Corporation (now also known as The Veterans Corporation) to

> (1) expand the provision of and improve access to technical assistance regarding entrepreneurship for the Nation's veterans; and (2) to assist veterans, including service-disabled veterans, with the formation and expansion of small business concerns by working with and organizing public and private resources, including those of the Small Business Administration, the Department of Veterans Affairs, the Department of Labor, the Department of Commerce, the Department of Defense, the Service Corps of Retired Executives ..., the Small Business Development Centers ..., and the business development staffs of each department and agency of the United States.[94]

The act re-emphasized the SBA's responsibility "to reach out to and include veterans in its programs providing financial and technical assistance."[95] It also included veterans as a target group for the SBA's 7(a), 504/CDC, and Microloan programs. It also required the SBA to enter into a memorandum of understanding with SCORE to, among other things, establish "a program to coordinate counseling and training regarding entrepreneurship to veterans through the chapters of SCORE throughout the United States."[96] It also directed the SBA to enter into a memorandum of understanding with small business development centers, the Department of Veteran Affairs, and the National Veterans Business Development Corporation "with respect to entrepreneurial assistance to veterans, including service-disabled veterans."[97] The act specified that the following services were to be provided:

> 1) Conducting of studies and research, and the distribution of information generated by such studies and research, on the formation, management, financing, marketing, and operation of small business concerns by veterans.

2) Provision of training and counseling to veterans concerning the formation, management, financing, marketing, and operation of small business concerns.
3) Provision of management and technical assistance to the owners and operators of small business concerns regarding international markets, the promotion of exports, and the transfer of technology.
4) Provision of assistance and information to veterans regarding procurement opportunities with Federal, State, and local agencies, especially such agencies funded in whole or in part with Federal funds.
5) Establishment of an information clearinghouse to collect and distribute information, including by electronic means, on the assistance programs of Federal, State, and local governments, and of the private sector, including information on office locations, key personnel, telephone numbers, mail and electronic addresses, and contracting and subcontracting opportunities.
6) Provision of Internet or other distance learning academic instruction for veterans in business subjects, including accounting, marketing, and business fundamentals.
7) Compilation of a list of small business concerns owned and controlled by service-disabled veterans that provide products or services that could be procured by the United States and delivery of such list to each department and agency of the United States. Such list shall be delivered in hard copy and electronic form and shall include the name and address of each such small business concern and the products or services that it provides.[98]

The SBA's Office of Veterans Business Development (OVBD) was established to address these statutory requirements by promoting "veterans' small business ownership by conducting comprehensive outreach, through program and policy development and implementation, ombudsman support, coordinated Agency initiatives, and direct assistance to veterans, service-disabled veterans, Reserve and National Guard members, and discharging active duty service members and their families."[99]

The OVBD provided, or supported third-parties to provide, management and technical assistance training services to 137,011 veterans during FY2011. These services were provided "through funded SBA district office outreach; OVBD-developed and distributed materials; websites; partnering with DOD [Department of Defense], DOL [Department of Labor] and universities; agreements with regional veterans business outreach centers; direct guidance, training and assistance to Agency veteran customers; and through enhancements to intra-agency programs used by the military and veteran communities."[100]

In FY2012, the OVBD launched the "Operation Boots to Business: From Service to Startup" initiative, "a comprehensive veteran entrepreneurship initiative for transitioning service members."[101] It also plans to continue its efforts to strengthen its outreach to women veterans and veterans with disabilities.[102]

The SBA received an appropriation of $2.5 million in FY2010, FY2011, and FY2012 to support veteran management and training activities.[103] The Obama Administration recommended that these activities receive an appropriation of $2.496 million in FY2013. The Obama Administration also recommended an additional appropriation of $7.0 million in FY2013 for the National Veterans Entrepreneurial Training (VET) Program initiative, Operation Boots to Business: From Service to Startup, "with the goal of ensuring robust, coordinated, and focused assistance for transitioning military members who are interested in pursuing entrepreneurship and/or business ownership."[104]

The OVBD's Veterans Business Outreach Centers Program is one of its larger and better known third-party provider management and technical assistance training programs. It was established by the SBA under the authority in Section 8(b)(17) of the Small Business Act. It is to "provide outreach, assessment, long term counseling, training, coordinated service delivery referrals, mentoring & network building, procurement assistance and E-based assistance to benefit Small Business concerns and potential concerns owned and controlled by Veterans, Service Disabled Veterans and Members of Reserve Components of the U.S. Military."[105]

There are currently 16 Veterans Business Outreach Centers.[106] Each center is funded on an annual basis, with funding not to exceed $150,000 each year. Awards "may vary, depending upon location, staff size, project objectives, performance and agency priorities, and additional special initiatives initiated by the Office of Veterans Business Development."[107] Existing centers may receive additional funding for special outreach or other initiatives. The initial grant award is for 12 months, with the possibility of four additional (option) years.

In FY2011, the Veterans Business Outreach Centers Program conducted its seventh annual "Customer Satisfaction Survey." The FY2011 survey found that 91% of the clients using the centers were satisfied or highly satisfied with the quality, relevance, and timeliness of the assistance provided.[108]

7(j) Management and Technical Assistance Program

Utilizing what it viewed as broad statutory powers granted under Section 8(a) of the Small Business Act of 1958, as amended, the SBA issued regulations in 1970 creating the 8(a) contracting program to "assist small concerns owned by disadvantaged persons to become self-sufficient, viable businesses capable of competing effectively in the market place."[109] Utilizing its statutory authority under Section 7(j) of the Small Business Act to provide management and technical assistance through contracts, grants, and cooperative agreement to qualified service providers, the regulations specified that "the SBA may provide technical and management assistance to assist in the performance of the subcontracts."[110]

On October 24, 1978, P.L. 95-507, to amend the Small Business Act and the Small Business Investment Act of 1958, provided the SBA explicit statutory authority to extend financial, management, technical, and other services to socially and economically disadvantaged small businesses. The SBA's current regulations indicate that the 7(j) Management and Technical Assistance Program, named after the section of the Small Business Act of 1958, as amended, authorizing the SBA to provide management and technical assistance training, will, "through its private sector service providers" deliver "a wide variety of management and technical assistance to eligible individuals or concerns to meet their specific needs, including: (a) counseling and training in the areas of financing, management, accounting, bookkeeping, marketing, and operation of small business concerns; and (b) the identification and development of new business opportunities."[111] Eligible individuals and businesses include "8(a) certified firms, small disadvantaged businesses, businesses operating in areas of high unemployment, or low income or firms owned by low income individuals."[112]

In FY2011, the 7(j) Management and Technical Assistance Program awarded 27 contracts to 23 service providers totaling more than $5 million, ranging from $141,000 to

$530,000.[113] The 7(j) program assisted 3,550 small business owners in FY2011.[114] It received a $3.4 million appropriation in FY2010 and FY2011, and $3.1 million for FY2012.[115] The Obama Administration has recommended that the 7(j) program receive an appropriation of $2.79 million in FY2013.[116]

Native American Outreach Program

The SBA established the Office of Native American Affairs in 1994 to "address the unique needs of America's First people."[117] It oversees the Native American Outreach Program, which provides management and technical educational assistance to American Indians, Alaska Natives, Native Hawaiians, and "the indigenous people of Guam and American Samoa ... to promote entity-owned and individual 8(a) certification, government contracting, entrepreneurial education, and capital access."[118] The program's management and technical assistance services are available to members of these groups living in most areas of the nation.[119] However, "for Native Americans living in much of Indian Country, actual reservations communities where the land is held in trust by the U.S. federal government, SBA loan guaranties and technical assistance services are not available."[120]

The SBA's Office of Native American Affairs has four goals:

- to increase financial literacy across a broad section of the community and to educate internally on the roles of tribal governments;
- to formulate an SBA-specific tribal consultation policy to engage with tribally run economic development branches;
- to conduct a Native American veterans' outreach initiative to increase the utilization of the SBA's counseling services and the Patriot Express loan guaranty program; and
- to conduct an in-depth market research analysis to fine tune marketing efforts ending in a comprehensive communications plan to reach the target market with the end goal being a measurable increase in the use of all SBA tools with particular emphasis on loans and contracting.[121]

The Native American Outreach Program assisted 3,116 small businesses in FY2010.[122] It received a $1.25 million appropriation in FY2010, FY2011, and FY2012.[123] The Obama Administration has recommended that the program receive an appropriation of $850,000 in FY2013.[124]

DEPARTMENT OF COMMERCE SMALL BUSINESS MANAGEMENT AND TECHNICAL ASSISTANCE TRAINING PROGRAMS

As mentioned previously, the Department of Commerce's Minority Business Development Agency provides training to minority business owners to assist them in becoming suppliers to private corporations and the federal government.[125] In addition, the Department of Commerce's Economic Development Administration's Local Technical Assistance Program promotes efforts to build and expand local organizational capacity in distressed areas. As part of that effort, it funds projects that focus on technical or market feasibility studies of economic development projects or programs, which often include consultation with small businesses.[126]

The Minority Business Development Agency

The Minority Business Development Agency (MBDA) was established by President Richard M. Nixon by Executive Order 11625, issued on October 13, 1971, and published in the *Federal Register* the next day. It clarified the authority of the Secretary of Commerce to:

- implement federal policy in support of the minority business enterprise program,
- provide additional technical and management assistance to disadvantaged businesses,
- assist in demonstration projects, and
- coordinate the participation of all federal departments and agencies in an increased minority enterprise effort.[127]

The MBDA received an appropriation of $31.5 million for FY2010, $30.4 million for FY2011, and $30.3 million for FY2012.[128] The Obama Administration has recommended that the program receive an appropriation of $28.689 million in FY2013.[129]

As part of its mission, the MBDA seeks to train minority business owners to become first- or second-tier suppliers to private corporations and the federal government. Progress is measured in the business's increased gross receipts, number of employees, and size and scale of the firms associated with minority business enterprises. According to the MBDA's annual report:

> In FY2010, the MBDA created 6,397 new jobs across the nation and saved tens of thousands of existing jobs by helping minority-owned and operated businesses obtain 964 contracts, totaling $1.688 billion, and 522 financial awards, totaling $2.264 billion.
>
> ... MBDA funded 28 MBECs [Minority Business Enterprise Centers] providing business development services in strategic locations with large concentrations of minority business enterprises. The centers provided one-on-one and group consulting in managerial, technical areas, and marketing, in addition to support in obtaining contracts and financial awards. MBDA funded eight MBOCs [Minority Business Opportunity Centers] which provided business facilitation brokerage services to minority business enterprises. MBOCs fostered contract and financial transactions between MBE clients and public/private sector entities. This program was originally designed to maximize referral and business brokering services while minimizing consulting services unlike the MBEC and NABEC programs. MBDA funded six NABECs [Native American Business Enterprise Centers] providing business development services to Native American firms and tribal entities. The centers provided one-on-one and group consulting services in managerial and technical areas and marketing, in addition to support in obtaining contracts and financial awards. MBDA funded centers are operated by a network of private and public organizations through cooperative agreements which provide multi-year funding. These entities compete under a public solicitation for an MBDA grant. The network of private and public organizations that operate MBDA funded centers are comprised of for-profit and non-profit entities, state and local governments, tribal entities and institutions of higher education, including minority serving institutions. The operators of an MBDA funded center hire business development professionals in local

communities to delivery program-specific services. The average annual funding for an MBDA center in FY 2010 was $260,000 for MBECs, $219,000 for NABECs and $219,000 for MBOCs.[130]

The EDA Local Technical Assistance Program

P.L. 89-186, the Public Works and Economic Development Act of 1965, authorized the Department of Commerce's Economic Development Administration (EDA) to provide financial assistance to economically distressed areas in the United States that are characterized by high levels of unemployment and low per-capita income. The EDA currently administers seven Economic Development Assistance Programs (EDAPs) that award matching grants for public works, economic adjustment, planning, technical assistance, research and evaluation, trade adjustment assistance, and global climate change mitigation.[131] Grants awarded under the EDA's Local Technical Assistance Program are designed to help solve specific economic development problems, respond to development opportunities, and build and expand local organizational capacity in distressed areas.[132] The majority of local technical assistance projects focus on technical or market feasibility studies of economic development projects or programs, including consultation with small businesses. The EDA's Local Technical Assistance Program received a $9.8 million appropriation for FY2010 and FY2011, and $12.0 million for FY2012.[133] The Obama Administration has recommended that the program receive an appropriation of $12.0 million in FY2013.[134]

CONGRESSIONAL ISSUES

For many years, a recurring theme at congressional hearings concerning the SBA's management and technical assistance training programs has been the perceived need to improve program efficiency by eliminating duplication of services and increasing cooperation and coordination both within and among SCORE, WBCs, and SBDCs.[135]

As mentioned previously, the Obama Administration has recommended that the PRIME program be eliminated, arguing that it overlaps and duplicates the SBA's Microloan Technical Assistance Program.[136] Also, on March 15, 2011, the House Committee on Small Business recommended to the House Committee on the Budget that several SBA management and technical assistance training programs be defunded "because they duplicate existing programs at the SBA or at other agencies."[137]

The committee recommended that funding for Women Development Centers, Veterans Business Outreach Centers, PRIME, HUBZone outreach, the Office of Native American Affairs, Regional Innovation Centers, the State Trade and Export Promotion Pilot Program, the Drug-Free Workplace Program, and the Emerging Leaders Program be ended.[138]

In recent years, Congress has also explored ways to improve the SBA's measurement of the programs' effectiveness. Congress has also paid increased attention to the impact of national economic conditions on WBC and SBDC finances and their capacity to meet federal matching requirements and to maintain client service levels.[139]

Program Administration

In 2007, the U.S. Government Accountability Office (GAO) was asked to assess the SBA's oversight of WBCs and the coordination and duplication of services among the SBA's management and technical training assistance programs. GAO found that

> As described in the terms of the SBA award, WBCs are required to coordinate with local SBDCs and SCORE chapters. In addition, SBA officials told us that they expected district offices to ensure that the programs did not duplicate each other. However, based on our review, WBCs lacked guidance and information from SBA on how to successfully carry out their coordination efforts. Most of the WBCs that we spoke with explained that in some situations they referred clients to an SBDC or SCORE counselor, and some WBCs also took steps to more actively coordinate with local SBDCs and SCORE chapters to avoid duplication and leverage resources. We learned that WBCs used a variety of approaches to facilitate coordination, such as memorandums of understanding, information-sharing meetings, and co-locating staff and services. However, some WBCs told us that they faced challenges in coordinating services with SBDC and SCORE, in part because the programs have similar performance measures, and this could result in competition among the service providers in some locations. We also found that on some occasions SBA encouraged WBCs to provide services that were similar to services already provided by SBDCs in their district. Such challenges thwart coordination efforts and could increase the risk of duplication in some geographic areas.[140]

Some organizations have argued that the SBA's management and technical assistance training programs should be merged. For example, the U.S. Women's Chamber of Commerce has argued that

> over the last 50 years, the SBA entrepreneurial development system has grown into a fragmented array of programs, which has resulted in a disorganized, overlapping, and [in] efficient delivery of service through a system that is ill-prepared to effectively address the challenges of our economy....
>
> if we are to serve the needs of American entrepreneurs, we must commit to a top to bottom restructuring of the delivery of the entrepreneurial services of the SBA. The myriad of entrepreneurial development programs should be unified into one centrally managed organization that has the flexibility to provide services when and where they are needed.[141]

These organizations argue that merging the SBA's management and technical assistance training programs would provide greater coordination of services and "one clear channel for assistance" that "is paramount to the average business owner seeking help."[142]

Advocates of merging the SBA's management and technical assistance training programs often mention merging them into the SBDC Program because, in their view, it has the advantage of having a broader connection to mainstream resources and its locations are "greater and more diverse" than other SBA management and technical assistance training programs.[143]

Others argue that providing separate management and training assistance programs for specific groups is the best means to ensure that those group's unique challenges are recognized and their unique needs are met.[144]

For example, when asked at a congressional hearing about the rationale for having separate management and technical assistance training programs for specific groups, a representative of the Association of Women's Business Centers stated:

> I think that there is tremendous rationale for having different programs.... The women's business center programs really target a very different kind of population than the SBDCs.... We serve very different clientele.... We create a very different culture at the women's business center. We really have made it a welcoming place where ... they feel comfortable.... And it's very important to me that the woman have a place where they feel comfortable ... and where they see other women like themselves who are aspiring to reach their dreams.[145]

At another congressional hearing, the Association of Women's Business Centers' executive director argued that "the new three-year funding arrangement" for WBCs had enabled them to "concentrate on better serving their clients and growing their programs" and that WBCs should be provided continued and expanded funding because they provide effective services:

> We know that when our program performance is measured against any other enterprise assistance program, we will meet or exceed any performance measures. Indeed, the SBA's own client-based performance reviews have shown our clients to be just as satisfied or in some cases more satisfied with the services they have received compared to the SBA's other entrepreneurial development efforts.[146]

Instead of merging programs, some argue that improved communication among the SBA's management and technical assistance training resource partners and enhanced SBA program oversight is needed. For example, during the 111th Congress, the House passed H.R. 2352, the Job Creation Through Entrepreneurship Act of 2009, on May 20, 2009, by a vote of 406–15. The Senate did not take action on the bill. In its committee report accompanying the bill, the House Committee on Small Business concluded that

> Each ED [Entrepreneurial Development] program has a unique mandate and service delivery approach that is customized to its particular clients. However, as a network, the programs have established local connections and resources that benefit entrepreneurs within a region. Enhanced coordination among this network is critical to make the most of scarce resources available for small firms. It can also ensure that best practices are shared amongst providers that have similar goals but work within different contexts.[147]

In an effort to enhance the oversight and coordination of the SBA's management and technical assistance training programs, the Job Creation Through Entrepreneurship Act of 2009 would have

- required the SBA to create a new online, multilingual distance training and education program that was fully integrated into the SBA's existing management and technical assistance training programs and "allows entrepreneurs and small business owners the opportunity to exchange technical assistance through the sharing of information."[148]

- required the SBA to coordinate its management and technical assistance training programs "with State and local economic development agencies and other federal agencies as appropriate."[149]
- required the SBA to "report annually to Congress, in consultation with other federal departments and agencies as appropriate, on opportunities to foster coordination, limit duplication, and improve program delivery for federal entrepreneurial development activities."[150]

There has also been some discussion of merging SBA's management and training programs with business management and training programs offered by other federal agencies, both as a means to improve program performance and to achieve savings. For example, P.L. 111-139, Increasing the Statutory Limit on the Public Debt, requires GAO to "conduct routine investigations to identify programs, agencies, offices, and initiatives with duplicative goals and activities within Departments and governmentwide and report annually to Congress on the findings."[151]

GAO identified 51 programmatic areas in its 2012 annual report on federal duplication "where programs may be able to achieve greater efficiencies or become more effective in providing government services."[152] GAO identified management and training assistance provided to businesses by the SBA and the Departments of Commerce, Housing and Urban Development, and Agriculture as one of these areas.[153] GAO identified 53 business management and technical assistance programs sponsored by the SBA and these three departments.

GAO reported that "the number of programs that support entrepreneurs – 53 – and the overlap among these programs raise questions about whether a fragmented system is the most effective way to support entrepreneurs. By exploring alternatives, agencies may be able to determine whether there are more efficient ways to continue to serve the unique needs of entrepreneurs, including consolidating various programs."[154]

Program Evaluation

GAO noted in its 2007 assessment of the SBA's management and technical assistance training programs that, in addition to its annual survey of WBC, SBDC, and SCORE participants, the SBA requires WBCs to provide quarterly performance reports that include "the WBCs' actual accomplishments, compared with their performance goals for the reporting period; actual budget expenditures, compared with an estimated budget; cost of client fees; success stories; and names of WBC personnel and board members."[155] GAO also noted that WBCs are also required to issue fourth quarter performance reports that "also include a summary of the year's activities and economic impact data that the WBCs collect from their clients, such as number of business startups, number of jobs created, and gross receipts."[156] SBDCs have similar reporting requirements.[157]

In recent years, Congress has considered requiring the SBA to expand its use of outcome-based measures to determine the effectiveness of its management and technical training assistance programs.

For example, the previously mentioned Job Creation Through Entrepreneurship Act of 2009 would have required the SBA to create "outcome-based measures of the amount of job creation or economic activity generated in the local community as a result of efforts made and services provided by each women's business center."[158]

It would also would have required the SBA to "develop and implement a consistent data collection process to cover all entrepreneurial development programs" including "data relating to job creation, performance, and any other data determined appropriate by the Administrator with respect to the Administration's entrepreneurial development programs."[159]

WBC and SBDC Finances

In recent years, Congress has provided increased attention to the impact of national economic conditions on WBC and SBDC finances and their capacity to meet federal matching requirements and to maintain client service levels.[160] For example, Donald Wilson, president, Association of Small Business Development Centers, testified before Congress that national economic conditions were making it more difficult for SBDCs to raise the funds necessary to meet federal matching requirements:

> One of the issues is the whole design of the program [where] the federal dollar would leverage the non-federal dollar. And so when you get states that match and the federal dollar never goes up, the states are not likely to go up. And now with this current economic downturn, all you have to do is look at foundations and you see where their stock portfolios are going. You see banks which have often been very helpful for us because we bring them high quality loan candidates. Their dollars are declining. States that are facing severe budget deficits which by law by their state constitution they cannot have. They are cutting back. And so the issue now is not the same rosy outlook in terms of getting matched that it was, say, three or four years ago, and quite frankly, we encounter all the time if the federal government does not believe in this program, you know, we are not going to start pouring a lot of money into it.[161]

P.L. 111-240, the Small Business Jobs Act of 2010, authorizes changes to several SBA programs, including the SBA's management and training programs.[162] For example, as mentioned previously, the act authorizes $50 million in additional funds for SBDCs to provide targeted technical assistance to small businesses for various specified activities, such as seeking access to capital or credit, federal procurement opportunities, and opportunities to export products. It also authorizes the SBA to temporarily waive, in whole or in part, for successive fiscal years, the nonfederal share matching requirement relating to "technical assistance and counseling" for WBCs under the following specified circumstances: the economic conditions affecting the center, the waiver's impact on the WBC program's credibility, the WBC's demonstrated ability to raise nonfederal funds, and the WBC's performance.[163] The non-federal share requirement can not be waived in FY2013, or any fiscal year thereafter.[164] In addition, S. 3967, the Small Business Investment and Innovation Act of 2010, which was introduced on November 18, 2010, would authorize changes to several SBA programs, including the SBA's training and technical assistance programs.[165] For example, the bill would have

- increased SCORE's funding to $13 million in FY2011, $15 million in FY2012, and $18 million in FY2013.

- increased WBC funding to $20 million in FY2011, $20.5 million in FY2012, and $21 million in FY2013.
- required the SBA Administrator to "maximize the transparency of the WBC financial assistance proposal process and the WBC programmatic and financial oversight process" by (1) providing public notice of announcements for financial assistance and grants not later than the end of the first quarter of each fiscal year; (2) providing in the announcements an outline of the award and program evaluation criteria used, including a description of the weighting of the criteria used; (3) minimizing paperwork and reporting requirements for applicants for and recipients of financial assistance; (4) standardizing the WBC program's oversight and review process; and (5) providing to each WBC, "not later than 60 days after the completion of a site visit (whether conducted for an audit, performance review, or other reason), a copy of site visit reports and evaluation reports prepared by district office technical representatives or officers or employees of the Administration."[166]
- directed the Comptroller General to study the unique economic issues facing WBCs located in predominately rural, urban, and insular areas, including the difficulties these centers face (1) raising non-federal funds; (2) competing for financial assistance, non-federal funds, or other types of assistance; (3) writing grant proposals; and (4) any other difficulty which may result from the economic circumstances of the area in which they are located. The Comptroller General would be required to submit to Congress a report regarding the results of the study within one year of the bill's enactment.
- increased Veteran Business Centers' funding to $8 million in FY2011, $8.5 million in FY2012, and $9 million in FY2013.
- established an Associate Administrator of the Office of Native American Affairs to implement training and technical assistance programs for the development of business enterprises by Native Americans and to establish Native American business centers which would be awarded funding for five-year projects that offer culturally tailored business development assistance to Native Americans.
- authorized $10 million in FY2011, $10 million in FY2012, and $10 million in FY2013 for the Native American business center program.

CONCLUSION

Congressional interest in the federal government's small business management and technical assistance training programs has increased in recent years. One of the reasons for the heightened level of interest in these programs is that small business has led job formation and retention during previous economic recoveries.[167] It has been argued that effective small business management and technical assistance training programs are needed if small businesses are to lead job creation and retention during the current economic recovery. As Representative Heath Shuler stated during a congressional hearing,

> We often talk about the role that small business plays in the creation of jobs and with good reason. Small firms generate between 60 and 80 percent of new positions. Following the recession in the mid-1990s, they created 3.8 million jobs.... we could use

that growth today. But unfortunately, many firms are struggling to make ends meet. Let's allow them to hire new workers. In the face of historic economic challenges, we should be investing in America's job creators.

SBA's Entrepreneurial Development Programs, or ED, do just that. Of all the tools in the small business toolbox, these are some of the most critical. They help small firms do everything from draft business plans to access capital.[168]

There is a general consensus that federal management and technical assistance training programs serve an important purpose and, for the most part, are providing needed services that are not available elsewhere. As Karen Mills, SBA Administrator, stated during a press interview:

> We find that our counseling operations are equally important as our credit operations because small businesses really need help and advice, and when they get it, they tend to have more sales and more profits and more longevity, and they hire more people. So we have looked forward and said, "How do we get all the tools small businesses need into their hands?" Maybe they want to export. Maybe they want to know how to use broadband. Maybe they are veterans who are coming back and want to start a business or grow their business.
>
> Our job is to make sure all that information and opportunity is accessible for small businesses so they can do what they do, which is keep our economy strong.[169]

There is also a general consensus that making federal management and technical assistance training programs more effective and responsive to the needs of small business would assist the national economic recovery. However, there are disagreements over how to achieve that goal. Some advocate increasing funding for existing programs to enable them to provide additional training opportunities for small businesses while, at the same time, maintaining separate training programs for specific demographic groups as a means to ensure that those groups' specific needs are met; require the SBA to make more extensive use of outcome-based measures to better determine the programs' effect on small business formation and retention, job creation and retention, and the generation of wealth; and temporarily reduce or eliminate federal matching requirements to enable SBA's management and technical assistance training resource partners to focus greater attention to service delivery and less to fund raising. Others argue for a merger of existing programs to reduce costs and improve program efficiency, to focus available resources on augmenting the capacity of SBDCs to meet the needs of all small business groups, and require the SBA to make more extensive use of outcome-based performance measures to determine program effectiveness.

There are no case studies or empirical data available concerning the efficiencies that might be gained by merging the SBA's management and technical assistance training programs. Advocates argue that merging the programs would improve communications, reduce confusion by business owners seeking assistance by ensuring that all small business management and technical assistance training centers serve all small business owners and aspiring entrepreneurs, lead to more sustainable and predictable funding for the programs from non-federal sources, and result in more consistent and standard operating procedures throughout the country.[170] Opponents argue that any gains in program efficiency that might be realized would be more than offset by the loss of targeted services for constituencies that often require different information and training to meet their unique challenges and needs.[171]

APPENDIX. BRIEF DESCRIPTIONS OF SBA MANAGEMENT AND TECHNICAL ASSISTANCE TRAINING PROGRAMS

Table A-1. Brief Descriptions of SBA Management and Technical Assistance Training Programs

Program Name	Authority	Brief Description	Number	Federal Matching Requirement
Small Business Development Center Grant Program	P.L. 96-302, 1980	Provides management and technical assistance training to small businesses through centers located in leading universities, colleges, and state economic development agencies.	63 lead centers and 900+ local centers	50% match from non-federal sources comprised of not less than 50% cash and not more than 50% of indirect costs.
Women Business Center Grant Program	P.L. 100-533, 1988	Provides long-term training, counseling, networking, and mentoring to women entrepreneurs, especially those who are socially and economically disadvantaged.	108	50% match from non-federal sources; not more than one-half of the non-federal matching assistance may be in the form of in-kind contributions, including office equipment and office space.
SCORE ((Service Corps of Retired Executives)	Section 8(b) of the Small Business Act; P.L. 89-754, 1966	Provides technical, managerial, and informational assistance to small business concerns through in-person mentoring by volunteer counselors who are working or, in most instances, retired business owners.	364 chapters and 800+ branch offices	none
7(j) Technical Assistance Program	Section 7(j) of the Small Business Act; Section 8(a) of the Small Business Act; P.L. 95-507, 1978	Provides management and technical assistance training to 8(a) certified firms, small disadvantaged businesses, businesses operating in areas of high unemployment or low-income and firms owned by low-income individuals.	23 service providers	none
Microloan Technical Assistance Program	P.L. 102-140, 1992	Provides management and technical assistance training to Microloan borrowers and, within specified limits, to prospective Microloan borrowers.	179 intermediaries	25% from non-federal sources; no matching requirement if the intermediary makes at least 50% of its loans in an Economically Distressed Area.

Program Name	Authority	Brief Description	Number	Federal Matching Requirement
Native American Outreach Program	Section 7(j) of the Small Business Act; SBA regulations, 1994	Provides management and technical assistance training to American Indians, Alaska Natives, Native Hawaiians and "the indigenous people of Guam and American Samoa … to promote entity-owned and individual 8(a) certification, government contracting, entrepreneurial education, and capital access."	NA	none
PRIME Technical Assistance Program	P.L. 106-102, 1999	Provides assistance in the form of grants to nonprofit microenterprise development organizations or programs that has a demonstrated record of delivering microenterprise services to disadvantaged entrepreneurs.	100 service providers	50% from non-federal sources; sources such as fees, grants, gifts, income from loan sources, and in-kind resources from non-federal public or private sources may be used to comply with the matching funds requirement
Veterans Business Development Programs	P.L. 106-50, 1999	The mission of the SBA's Office of Veterans Business Development is to (1) expand the provision of and improve access to technical assistance regarding entrepreneurship for the Nation's veterans; and (2) to assist veterans, including service-disabled veterans, with the formation and expansion of small business concerns by working with and organizing public and private resources, including those of the SBA.	NA	none

Source: Federal statutes, cited in table.

End Notes

[1] U.S. Congress, Senate Committee on Banking and Currency, *Extension of the Small Business Act of 1953*, report to accompany S. 2127, 84th Cong., 1st sess., July 22, 1955, S.Rept. 84-1350 (Washington: GPO, 1955), p. 17.

[2] U.S. Small Business Administration, *Agency Financial Report, Fiscal Year 2011* (Washington, DC: GPO, 2011), p. 5.

[3] U.S. Small Business Administration, "Fiscal Year 2011 Congressional Budget Justification and FY2009 Annual Performance Report," Washington, DC: GPO, 2010, p. 4.

[4] U.S. Small Business Administration, "FY2012 Congressional Budget Justification and FY2010 Annual Performance Report," Washington, DC: GPO, 2011, p. 4; and U.S. Small Business Administration, "Women's Business Centers Directory," Washington, DC, at http://www.sba.gov/about-offices-content /1/2895/resources/13729.

[5] U.S. Department of Commerce, Minority Business Development Agency, *Annual Performance Report, Fiscal Year 2008*, Washington, DC, 2009, p. 6, at http://www.mbda.gov /?section_ id=2&bucket_id=643&content_ id=3205&well=entire_page&portal_document_download=true&download_cid=3205&name=MBDA_ Annual_Performance_Report_2008.pdf&legacy_flag=false.

[6] 13 C.F.R. §306.

[7] U.S. Small Business Administration, "FY2012 Congressional Budget Justification and FY2010 Annual Performance Report," Washington, DC: GPO, 2011, p. 4.

[8] Representative Sam Graves, "Opening Statement for Views and Estimates Markup," Washington, DC, March 15, 2011, at http://www.smallbusiness.house.gov /Calendar/EventSingle.aspx?EventID=227626. Also, see U.S. Congress, House Committee on Small Business, "Views and Estimates of the Committee on Small Business on Matters to be set forth in the Concurrent Resolution on the Budget for FY2012, communication to the Chairman, House Committee on the Budget," 112th Cong., 1st sess., March 17, 2011, at http://smbiz.house.gov/UploadedFiles/ March_17_Views_and_Estimates_Letter.pdf. The management and technical assistance training programs recommended to be defunded include Women Development Centers, Veterans Business Outreach Centers, Program for Investment in Micro-entrepreneurs (PRIME), HUBZone outreach, Office of Native American Affairs, Regional Innovation Centers, State Trade and Export Promotion Pilot Program, the Drug-Free Workplace Program, and the Emerging Leaders Program.

[9] U.S. Small Business Administration, "SBA Announces Funding Available to Support Regional Clusters, Job Creation," Washington, DC, at http://www.sba.gov/content/sba-announces-funding-available-support-regional-clustersjob-creation 0.

[10] Ibid.

[11] Ibid.

[12] Ibid.; and U.S. Small Business Administration, Press Office, "SBA Announces Funding Available to Support Regional Clusters, Job Creation," Washington, DC, June 22, 2010, at http://www.sba.gov/about-sba-services/7367/ 5732.

[13] U.S. Small Business Administration, Press Office, "SBA Announces Support for 10 Regional 'Innovative Economies' Clusters, Local Job Creation," Washington, DC, September 20, 2010, at http://www.sba.gov/about-sbaservices/7367/5590; and U.S. Small Business Administration, "Innovative Economy Clusters," Washington, DC, at http://www.sba.gov /content/innovative-economy-clusters.

[14] U.S. Small Business Administration, Press Office, "SBA Announces Funding Available to Support Regional Clusters, Job Creation," Washington, DC, June 22, 2010, p. 2, at http://www.sba.gov/about-sba-services/7367/5732. In FY2011, SBA-funded regional cluster small businesses formed 308 collaborative projects, joint product development, joint sales activities, information sourcing agreements, and joint ventures with other businesses; assisted in the commercialization of 28 new technologies; and assisted in creating 19 patents.

[15] U.S. Small Business Administration, "FY2013 Congressional Budget Justification and FY2011 Annual Performance Report," Washington, DC, 2012, p. 58.

[16] Association of Small Business Development Centers, "A Brief History of America's Small Business Development Center Network," Burke, VA, at http://www.asbdc-us.org /About_Us/aboutus_history.html.

[17] Ibid.; and U.S. Congress, Senate Committee on Small Business, *Oversight of the Small Business Administration's Small Business Development Center Program*, 98th Cong., 1st sess., February 8, 1983, S.Hrg. 98-31 (Washington: GPO, 1983), p. 2.

Small Business Management and Technical Assistance Training Programs   199

[18] U.S. Congress, Senate Committee on Small Business, *Oversight of the Small Business Administration's Small Business Development Center Program*, 98th Cong., 1st sess., February 8, 1983, S.Hrg. 98-31 (Washington: GPO, 1983), p. 2.

[19] Ibid., p. 4.

[20] 15 U.S.C. 648(a)(4)(C).

[21] Ibid.; and P.L. 106-554, the Consolidated Appropriations Act, 2001.

[22] For American Samoa, Guam, and the U.S. Virgin Islands, the SBA is required to waive the matching requirements on awards less than $200,000 and has discretion to waive the match for awards exceeding $200,000. See 48 U.S.C. Section 1469a. Also, there is one exception to the disallowance of federal funds as a cash match. Community Development Block Grant (CDBG) funds received from the Department of Housing and Urban Development are allowed when: (1) the SBDC activities are consistent with the authorized CDBG activities for which the funds were granted; and (2) the CDBG activities are identified in the Consolidated Plan of the CDBG grantee or in the agreement between the CDBG grantee and the subrecipient of the funds.

[23] U.S. Small Business Administration, "Small Business Development Center Fy/Cy 2011 Program Announcement for Renewal of the Cooperative Agreement for Current Recipient Organizations," Washington, DC, p. 3, at http://archive.sba.gov/idc/groups/public /documents/sba_program_office/sbdc_2011_prgm_announce.pdf.

[24] Ibid.

[25] Association of Small Business Development Centers, "Welcome," Burke, Virginia, at http://www.asbdc-us.org/; and U.S. Small Business Administration, "FY2012 Congressional Budget Justification and FY2010 Annual Performance Report," Washington, DC, 2010, p. 45.

[26] U.S. Small Business Administration, "FY2013 Congressional Budget Justification and FY2011 Annual Performance Report," Washington, DC, 2012, p. 44.

[27] H.Rept. 111-366, The Departments of Transportation and Housing and Urban Development, and Related Agencies Appropriations Act, 2010; P.L. 111-117, the Consolidated Appropriations Act, 2010; P.L. 112-10, the Department of Defense and Full-Year Continuing Appropriations Act, 2011; and H.Rept. 112-331, the Consolidated Appropriations Act, 2012.

[28] P.L. 111-240, the Small Business Jobs Act of 2010, Section 1402. Grants for SBDCs. In addition, not less than 80% of the funding shall be used for counseling of small business concerns and not more than 20% may be used for classes and seminars. Total funding for SBDCs was $130 million in FY2010.

[29] U.S. Small Business Administration, "FY2011 Congressional Budget Justification and FY2009 Annual Performance Report," Washington, DC, 2010, p. 21; U.S. Small Business Administration, "FY2012 Congressional Budget Justification and FY2010 Annual Performance Report," Washington, DC, 2011, pp. 25, 47; and U.S. Small Business Administration, "FY2013 Congressional Budget Justification and FY2011 Annual Performance Report," Washington, DC, 2012, p. 45.

[30] U.S. Small Business Administration, "FY2013 Congressional Budget Justification and FY2011 Annual Performance Report," Washington, DC, 2012, p. 15.

[31] Ibid., p. 45.

[32] Ibid., p. 44.

[33] U.S. Small Business Administration, Office of Entrepreneurial Development, "Impact Study of Entrepreneurial Development Resources," Washington, DC, September 10, 2009, p. 2, at http://archive.sba.gov/idc/groups /public/documents/sba_program_office/ed_finalreport_2009.pdf.

[34] U.S. Small Business Administration, Office of Entrepreneurial Development, "Impact Study of Entrepreneurial Development Resources: Face-to-Face Counseling," Washington, DC, November 9, 2011, p. 5, at http://www.sba.gov/about-offices-content/1/2463 /resources /36721.

[35] Ibid.

[36] Ibid., pp. 46, 50.

[37] U.S. Congress, House Committee on Small Business, *Review of Women's Business Center Program*, 106th Cong., February 11, 1999, Serial No. 106-2 (Washington: GPO, 1999), p. 4.

[38] Matching contributions must come from non-federal sources such as state and local governments, private individuals, corporations and foundations, and program income. Community Development Block Grant funds, when permissible under the terms of that program, may also be used as a match. At least half of the non-federal match must be in the form of cash. U.S. Small Business Administration, "Women's Business Center (Initial Grant), FY2011" Washington, DC, at http://www.sba.gov/sites/default/files/files/Program% 20Announcement%20OWBO-2011-01-1%20- %20New%20WBC%20in%20Idaho.pdf.

[39] P.L. 105-135, the Small Business Reauthorization Act of 1997, authorized the SBA to award grants to WBCs for up to five years—one base year and four option years. P.L. 106-165, the Women's Business Centers

Sustainability Act of 1999, provided WBCs that had completed the initial five-year grant an opportunity to apply for an additional five-year sustainability grant. Thus, the act allowed successful WBCs to receive SBA funding for a total of 10 years. Because the program has permitted permanent three-year funding intervals since 2007, the sustainability grants will be phased out by FY2012, leaving the initial five-year grants with the continuous three-year option. See U.S. Small Business Administration, "FY2012 Congressional Budget Justification and FY2010 Annual Performance Report," Washington, DC, 2011, p. 49.

[40] P.L. 110-28, the U.S. Troop Readiness, Veterans' Care, Katrina Recovery, and Iraq Accountability Appropriations Act, 2007, allowed WBCs that successfully completed the initial five-year grant to apply for an unlimited number of three-year funding renewals.

[41] P.L. 105-135, the Small Business Reauthorization Act of 1997, reduced the program's matching to one non-federal dollar for each two federal dollars in years one through three rather than just during the first year (1:2), one non-federal dollar for each federal dollar in year four rather than during year two (1:1), and two non-federal dollars for each federal dollar in year five rather than in year three (2:1). P.L. 106-17, the Women's Business Center Amendments Act of 1999, reduced the program's matching requirement to one non-federal dollar for each two federal dollars in years one and two (1:2), and one non-federal dollar for each federal dollar in years three, four and five (1:1).

[42] P.L. 110-28, the U.S. Troop Readiness, Veterans' Care, Katrina Recovery, and Iraq Accountability Appropriations Act, 2007, reduced the federal share to not more than 50% for all grant years (1:1) following the initial five-year grant.

[43] P.L. 105-135, the Small Business Reauthorization Act of 1997, specified that not more than one-half of the non-federal sector matching assistance may be in the form of in-kind contributions that are budget line items only, including office equipment and office space.

[44] U.S. Small Business Administration, "Women's Business Centers Directory," Washington, DC, at http://www.sba.gov/about-offices-content/1/2895/resources/13729.

[45] U.S. Small Business Administration, "FY2013 Congressional Budget Justification and FY2011 Annual Performance Report," Washington, DC, 2011, p. 47.

[46] Ibid.

[47] H.Rept. 111-366, The Departments of Transportation and Housing and Urban Development, and Related Agencies Appropriations Act, 2010; P.L. 111-117, the Consolidated Appropriations Act, 2010; P.L. 112-10, the Department of Defense and Full-Year Continuing Appropriations Act, 2011; and H.Rept. 112-331, the Consolidated Appropriations Act, 2012.

[48] U.S. Small Business Administration, "FY2013 Congressional Budget Justification and FY2011 Annual Performance Report," Washington, DC, 2012, p. 15.

[49] P.L. 105-135, the Small Business Reauthorization Act of 1997, Section 29. Women's Business Center Program.

[50] U.S. Small Business Administration, Office of Entrepreneurial Development, "Impact Study of Entrepreneurial Development Resources: Face-to-Face Counseling," Washington, DC, November 9, 2011, p. 5, at http://www.sba.gov/ about-offices-content/1/2463/resources /36721.

[51] Ibid.

[52] Ibid., pp. 71, 74.

[53] 15 U.S.C. §636 7(m)(1)(A).

[54] For further analysis of the SBA's Microloan program see CRS Report R41057, *Small Business Administration Microloan Program*, by Robert Jay Dilger.

[55] There are no Microloan intermediaries located in Alaska and Utah. U.S. Small Business Administration, "Microloan Program: Partner Identification & Management System Participating Intermediary Microlenders Report," Washington, DC, at http://www.sba.gov /sites/default/files/partner_by_subcat_report_20120705.pdf. An intermediary may not operate in more than one state unless the SBA determines that it would be in the best interests of the small business community for it to operate across state lines. For example, the microloan intermediary located in Washington, Pennsylvania is allowed to service ten West Virginia counties due to its proximity to these counties and the distance to the only other intermediary serving West Virginia, which is located in Charleston, West Virginia. Also, a microloan intermediary located in Laguna Nigel, California, which focuses on the capital needs of disabled veteran-owned businesses, serves many jurisdictions throughout the nation that lack a participating intermediary.

[56] 15 U.S.C. §636(m)(4)(A).

[57] 13 C.F.R §120.712.

[58] Ibid.

[59] Ibid. Intermediaries may not borrow their contribution.

[60] An economically distressed area is a county or equivalent division of local government which, according to the most recent available data from the United States Bureau of the Census, 40% or more of the residents have an annual income that is at or below the poverty level. See 13 C.F.R §120.701.

[61] 13 C.F.R §120.712.

[62] Intermediaries that make at least 25% of their loans to small businesses located in or owned by residents of an Economically Distressed Area (defined as having 40% or more of its residents with an annual income that is at or below the poverty level), or have a portfolio of loans made under the program that averages not more than $10,000 during the period of the intermediary's participation in the program are eligible to receive an additional training grant equal to 5% of the total outstanding balance of loans made to the intermediary. Intermediaries are not required to make a matching contribution as a condition of receiving these additional grant funds. See 13 C.F.R §120.712; and 15 U.S.C. §636(m)(4)(C)(i).

[63] U.S. Small Business Administration, "FY2013 Congressional Budget Justification and FY2011 Annual Performance Report," Washington, DC, 2012, p. 34.

[64] H.Rept. 111-366, The Departments of Transportation and Housing and Urban Development, and Related Agencies Appropriations Act, 2010; P.L. 111-117, the Consolidated Appropriations Act, 2010; P.L. 112-10, the Department of Defense and Full-Year Continuing Appropriations Act, 2011; and H.Rept. 112-331, the Consolidated Appropriations Act, 2012.

[65] U.S. Small Business Administration, "FY2013 Congressional Budget Justification and FY2011 Annual Performance Report," Washington, DC, 2012, p. 15.

[66] P.L. 83-163, the Small Business Act of 1953; and U.S. Congress, Senate Select Committee on Small Business, *Small Business Administration - 1965*, 89th Cong., 1st sess., May 19, 1965 (Washington: GPO, 1965), pp. 21, 45; and SCORE (Service Corps of Retired Executives), "Milestones in SCORE History," Washington, DC, at http://www.score.org/ node/147953.

[67] U.S. Congress, Senate Select Committee on Small Business and House Select Committee on Small Business, *1966 Federal Handbook for Small Business: A Survey of Small Business Programs in the Federal Government Agencies*, committee print, 89th Cong., 3rd sess., January 31, 1966 (Washington: GPO, 1966), p. 5; and U.S. Congress, House Committee on Small Business, Subcommittee on Rural Development, Entrepreneurship, and Trade, *Subcommittee Hearing on Legislative Initiatives to Modernize SBA's Entrepreneurial Development Programs*, 111th Cong., 1st sess., April 2, 2009 (Washington: GPO, 2009), p. 6.

[68] U.S. Congress, Senate Select Committee on Small Business, *Small Business Act*, 90th Cong., 1st sess., November 22, 1967 (Washington: GPO, 1967), pp. 13, 14.

[69] P.L. 93-113, the Domestic Volunteer Service Act of 1973, Section 302. Authority to Establish, Coordinate, and Operate Programs. ACTION was created on July 1, 1971, by President Richard M. Nixon (Reorganization Plan Number One and Executive Order 11603) to oversee several federal volunteer agencies, including the Peace Corps, VISTA (Volunteers in Service to America); and SCORE. P.L. 103-82, the National and Community Service Trust Act of 1993, directed that ACTION be merged with the Commission on National and Community Service to form the Corporation for National and Community Service, which became operational in 1994. See Corporation for National and Community Service, "National Service Timeline," Washington, DC, at http://www.nationalservice.gov/about/ role_impact/history_timeline.asp.

[70] U.S. Small Business Administration, "FY2013 Congressional Budget Justification and FY2011 Annual Performance Report," Washington, DC, 2012, p. 45.

[71] SCORE (Service Corps of Retired Executives), "About SCORE," Washington, DC, at http://www.score.org/aboutscore.

[72] U.S. Small Business Administration, "FY2013 Congressional Budget Justification and FY2011 Annual Performance Report," Washington, DC, 2012, p. 46.

[73] Ibid.

[74] H.Rept. 111-366, The Departments of Transportation and Housing and Urban Development, and Related Agencies Appropriations Act, 2010; P.L. 111-117, the Consolidated Appropriations Act, 2010; P.L. 112-10, the Department of Defense and Full-Year Continuing Appropriations Act, 2011; and H.Rept. 112-331, the Consolidated Appropriations Act, 2012.

[75] U.S. Small Business Administration, "FY2013 Congressional Budget Justification and FY2011 Annual Performance Report," Washington, DC, 2012, p. 15.

[76] U.S. Congress, House Committee on Small Business, *Full Committee Hearing on Legislation to Reauthorize and Modernize SBA's Entrepreneurial Development Programs*, 111th Cong., 1st sess., May 6, 2009 (Washington: GPO, 2009), p. 53.

77 U.S. Small Business Administration, Office of Entrepreneurial Development, "Impact Study of Entrepreneurial Development Resources: Face-to-Face Counseling," Washington, DC, November 9, 2011, p. 5, at http://www.sba.gov/about-offices-content/1/2463 /resources /36721.

78 Ibid., pp. 59, 62.

79 P.L. 106-102, the Gramm-Leach-Bliley Act, Section 173. Establishment of Program.

80 P.L. 106-102, the Gramm-Leach-Bliley Act, Section 173. Establishment of Program and Section 175. Qualified Organizations.

81 P.L. 106-102, the Gramm-Leach-Bliley Act, Section 176. Allocation of Assistance; Subgrants.

82 P.L. 106-102, the Gramm-Leach-Bliley Act, Section 174. Uses of Assistance.

83 U.S. Small Business Administration, "PRIME Program," Washington, DC, at http://www.sba.gov/content/prime-program-0.

84 Ibid.

85 U.S. Small Business Administration, Office of Financial Assistance, "Program for Investment in Microentrepreneurs Act ("PRIME"): Microenterprise and Technical Assistance Programs to Disadvantaged Entrepreneurs, Fiscal Year 2010," June 2010, Washington, DC, p. 2, at http://archive.sba.gov/idc /groups/public/documents/sba_homepage/ serv_fa_2010_primetrack123.pdf.

86 Ibid., pp. 2, 8.

87 13 C.F.R §119.8.

88 Ibid.

89 U.S. Small Business Administration, "Non-profit Organizations Receive SBA PRIME Grants to Assist Micro Entrepreneurs," Washington, DC, September 8, 2011, at http://www.sba.gov/about-sba-services/7367/22711; and U.S. Small Business Administration, "PRIME 2011 Awardees," Washington, DC, at http://www.sba.gov/sites /default/files/ files/PRIME%20Grantees%202011.pdf.

90 H.Rept. 111-366, The Departments of Transportation and Housing and Urban Development, and Related Agencies Appropriations Act, 2010; P.L. 111-117, the Consolidated Appropriations Act, 2010; P.L. 112-10, the Department of Defense and Full-Year Continuing Appropriations Act, 2011; and H.Rept. 112-331, the Consolidated Appropriations Act, 2012.

91 U.S. Small Business Administration, "FY2012 Congressional Budget Justification and FY2010 Annual Performance Report," Washington, DC: GPO, 2011, p. 4; and U.S. Small Business Administration, "FY2013 Congressional Budget Justification and FY2011 Annual Performance Report," Washington, DC, 2012, pp. 8, 15.

92 U.S. Congress, House Committee on Small Business, *Veterans Entrepreneurship and Small Business Development Act of 1999*, report to accompany H.R. 1568, 106th Cong., 1st sess., June 29, 1999, H.Rept. 106-206 (Washington: GPO, 1999), pp. 14, 15.

93 Ibid.

94 P.L. 106-50, the Veterans Entrepreneurship and Small Business Development Act of 1999, Section 33. National Veterans Business Development Corporation.

95 U.S. Congress, House Committee on Small Business, *Veterans Entrepreneurship and Small Business Development Act of 1999*, report to accompany H.R. 1568, 106th Cong., 1st sess., June 29, 1999, H.Rept. 106-206 (Washington: GPO, 1999), p. 14.

96 P.L. 106-50, the Veterans Entrepreneurship and Small Business Development Act of 1999, Section 301. Score Program.

97 Ibid., Section 302. Entrepreneurial Assistance.

98 Ibid.

99 U.S. Small Business Administration, "FY2013 Congressional Budget Justification and FY2011 Annual Performance Report," Washington, DC, 2012, p. 62.

100 Ibid.

101 U.S. Small Business Administration, "FY2013 Congressional Budget Justification and FY2011 Annual Performance Report," Washington, DC, 2012, p. 62; and U.S. Small Business Administration, "Operation Boots to Business: From Service to Startup," Washington, DC, at http://www.sba.gov/bootstobusiness.

102 U.S. Small Business Administration, "FY2013 Congressional Budget Justification and FY2011 Annual Performance Report," Washington, DC, 2012, pp. 62, 63.

103 H.Rept. 111-366, The Departments of Transportation and Housing and Urban Development, and Related Agencies Appropriations Act, 2010; P.L. 111-117, the Consolidated Appropriations Act, 2010; P.L. 112-10, the Department of Defense and Full-Year Continuing Appropriations Act, 2011; and H.Rept. 112-331, the Consolidated Appropriations Act, 2012.

Small Business Management and Technical Assistance Training Programs   203

[104] U.S. Small Business Administration, "FY2013 Congressional Budget Justification and FY2011 Annual Performance Report," Washington, DC, 2012, pp. 3, 15.

[105] U.S. Small Business Administration, Office of Veterans Business Development, "Special Program Announcement: Veterans Business Outreach Center Program," Washington, DC, April 2010, p. 1, at http://archive.sba.gov/idc/groups/public/documents/sba_program_office   /ovbd_vboc_prgm_announce2010.pdf.

[106] U.S. Small Business Administration, "Veterans Business Outreach Centers," Washington, DC, at http://www.sba.gov/content/veterans-business-outreach-centers. There were eight veterans business outreach centers in FY2009.

[107] U.S. Small Business Administration, Office of Veterans Business Development, "Special Program Announcement: Veterans Business Outreach Center Program," Washington, DC, April 2010, p. 2, at http://archive.sba.gov/idc/groups/public/documents/sba_program_office   /ovbd_vboc_prgm_announce2010.pdf.

[108] U.S. Small Business Administration, "FY2013 Congressional Budget Justification and FY2011 Annual Performance Report," Washington, DC, 2012, p. 62.

[109] 13 C.F.R. §124.8-1(b) (1970); and Notes, "Minority Enterprise, Federal Contracting, and the SBA's 8(a) Program: A New Approach to an Old Problem," *Michigan Law Review*, vol. 71, no. 2 (December 1972), pp. 377, 378. For further analysis of the Minority Small Business and Capital Ownership Development Program, also known as the 8(a) program, see CRS Report R40744, *The "8(a) Program" for Small Businesses Owned and Controlled by the Socially and Economically Disadvantaged: Legal Requirements and Issues*, by Kate M. Manuel and John R. Luckey.

[110] 13 C.F.R. §124.8-1(d) (1970).

[111] 13 C.F.R. §124.702.

[112] U.S. Small Business Administration, "FY2012 Congressional Budget Justification and FY2010 Annual Performance Report," Washington, DC, 2011, p. 75.

[113] USASpending.gov, search terms: 59.007: 7(j) Technical Assistance, FY2011.

[114] U.S. Small Business Administration, "FY2013 Congressional Budget Justification and FY2011 Annual Performance Report," Washington, DC, 2012, p. 69.

[115] H.Rept. 111-366, The Departments of Transportation and Housing and Urban Development, and Related Agencies Appropriations Act, 2010; P.L. 111-117, the Consolidated Appropriations Act, 2010; P.L. 112-10, the Department of Defense and Full-Year Continuing Appropriations Act, 2011; and H.Rept. 112-331, the Consolidated Appropriations Act, 2012.

[116] U.S. Small Business Administration, "FY2013 Congressional Budget Justification and FY2011 Annual Performance Report," Washington, DC, 2012, p. 15.

[117] U.S. Congress, House Committee on Small Business, Subcommittee on Workforce, Empowerment, and Government Programs, *Oversight of the Small Business Administration's Entrepreneurial Development Programs*, 109th Cong., 2nd sess., March 2, 2006, Serial No. 109-40 (Washington: GPO, 2006), pp. 5, 37. H.R. 2352, the Job Creation Through Entrepreneurship Act of 2009, would provide statutory authorization for the Office of Native American Affairs. It was passed by the House on May 20, 2009.

[118] U.S. Small Business Administration, "FY2011 Congressional Budget Justification and FY2009 Annual Performance Report," Washington, DC, 2010, p. 65.

[119] Ibid.

[120] Ibid.

[121] Ibid.

[122] U.S. Small Business Administration, "FY2012 Congressional Budget Justification and FY2010 Annual Performance Report," Washington, DC, 2011, p. 69.

[123] H.Rept. 111-366, The Departments of Transportation and Housing and Urban Development, and Related Agencies Appropriations Act, 2010; P.L. 111-117, the Consolidated Appropriations Act, 2010; P.L. 112-10, the Department of Defense and Full-Year Continuing Appropriations Act, 2011; and H.Rept. 112-331, the Consolidated Appropriations Act, 2012.

[124] U.S. Small Business Administration, "FY2013 Congressional Budget Justification and FY2011 Annual Performance Report," Washington, DC, 2012, p. 15.

[125] U.S. Department of Commerce, Minority Business Development Agency, *Annual Performance Report, Fiscal Year 2008*, Washington, DC, 2009, p. 6, at http://www.mbda.gov/?section_id=2&bucket_id=643 &content_id=3205&well=   entire_page&portal_document_download=true&download_cid=3205&name= MBDA_Annual_Performance_Report_2008.pdf&legacy_flag=false.

[126] 13 C.F.R. §306.

[127] The Executive Office of the President, "Executive Order 11625," 36 *Federal Register* 11625, October 14, 1971; and 3 C.F.R., 1971-1975 Comp. 9. 616. The MBDA superseded the Office of Minority Business Enterprise, which was established by Executive Order 11458 signed by President Richard Nixon on March 5, 1969.

[128] P.L. 111-117, the Consolidated Appropriations Act, 2010; P.L. 112-10, the Department of Defense and Full-Year Continuing Appropriations Act, 2011; and P.L. 112-55, the Consolidated and Further Continuing Appropriations Act, 2012.

[129] U.S. Office of Management and Budget, *Budget of the United States Government, FY2013: Appendix, Department of Commerce*, Washington, DC, 2012, p. 216.

[130] U.S. Department of Commerce Minority Business Development Agency, *Annual Performance Report, Fiscal Year 2010*, Washington, DC, 2010, pp. 2, 14, at http://www.mbda.gov/sites/default/files/APR2010.pdf.

[131] In addition, since 1970, Congress has periodically allocated supplemental funds for EDA to assist with disaster mitigation and economic recovery. Also, EDA grant applicants must be designated by EDA as part of an EDD—a multijurisdictional consortium of county and local governments—to be eligible for EDA funding and grants. To be designated as an EDD, an area must meet the definition of economic distress, under 13 C.F.R 303.3: (i) An unemployment rate that is, for the most recent twenty-four (24) month period for which data are available, at least one (1) percentage point greater than the national average unemployment rate; (ii) Per capita income that is, for the most recent period for which data are available, eighty (80) percent or less of the national average per capita income; or (iii) A Special Need, as determined by Economic Development Administration (EDA).

[132] 13 C.F.R. §306.

[133] U.S. Department of Commerce Economic Development Administration, "FY2012 Congressional Budget Request," Washington, DC, p. 33, at http://www.osec.doc.gov/bmi /budget/12CJ/EDA_FY_2012_ Congressional_Submission.pdf; P.L. 111-117, the Consolidated Appropriations Act, 2010; P.L. 112-10, the Department of Defense and Full-Year Continuing Appropriations Act, 2011; and H.Rept. 112-284, Agriculture, Rural Development, Food and Drug Administration, and Related Agencies Programs for the Fiscal Year Ending September 30, 2012, and for other purposes.

[134] U.S. Office of Management and Budget, *Budget of the United States Government, FY2013: Appendix, Department of Commerce*, Washington, DC, 2012, p. 207.

[135] U.S. Congress, House Committee on Small Business, *Full Committee Markup of H.R. 2352 The Job Creation Through Entrepreneurship Act of 2009*, 111th Cong., 1st sess., May 13, 2009, Doc. No. 111-022 (Washington: GPO, 2009), pp. 2, 14; U.S. Congress, Senate Committee on Small Business, *SBA's Management and Assistance Programs*, Roundtable before the Committee on Small Business United States Senate, 106th Cong., 1st sess., May 20, 1999, S. Hrg. 106-337 (Washington: GPO, 1999), pp. 69, 74, 82, 92; U.S. Congress, House Committee on Small Business, *To Investigate the Legislation That Would Increase the Extent and Scope of the Services Provided By Small Business Development Centers*, 107th Cong., 1st sess., July 19, 2001, Serial No. 107-20 (Washington: GPO, 2001), pp. 13, 59, 60; and U.S. Congress, Senate Committee on Small Business, *Oversight on the Small Business Administration's Small Business Development Center Program*, 100th Cong., 1st sess., October 15, 1987, S. Hrg. 100-339 (Washington: GPO, 1987), pp. 6, 165, 168, 230.

[136] U.S. Small Business Administration, "FY2012 Congressional Budget Justification and FY2010 Annual Performance Report," Washington, DC: GPO, 2011, p. 4; and U.S. Small Business Administration, "FY2013 Congressional Budget Justification and FY2011 Annual Performance Report," Washington, DC, 2012, pp. 8, 15.

[137] Representative Sam Graves, "Opening Statement for Views and Estimates Markup," Washington, DC, March 15, 2011, at http://www.smallbusiness.house.gov /Calendar /EventSingle.aspx?EventID=227626.

[138] U.S. Congress, House Committee on Small Business, "Views and Estimates of the Committee on Small Business on Matters to be set forth in the Concurrent Resolution on the Budget for FY2012, communication to the Chairman, House Committee on the Budget," 112th Cong., 1st sess., March 17, 2011, at http://smbiz.house.gov/UploadedFiles/ March_17_Views_and_ Estimates_Letter.pdf.

[139] U.S. Congress, House Committee on Small Business, *Full Committee Hearing on Legislation to Reauthorize and Modernize SBA's Entrepreneurial Development Programs*, 111th Cong., 1st sess., May 6, 2009 (Washington: GPO, 2009), pp. 12, 13, 15, 18.

[140] U.S. Government Accountability Office, Small Business Administration: Opportunities Exist to Improve Oversight of Women's Business Centers and Coordination among SBA's Business Assistance Programs, GAO-08-49, November 2007, pp. 6, 24-31, at http://www.gao.gov/new.items/d0849.pdf.

[141] U.S. Congress, House Committee on Small Business, *Full Committee Hearing on the State of the SBA's Entrepreneurial Development Programs and Their Role in Promoting an Economic Recovery*, 111th Cong., 1st sess., February 11, 2009, Small Business Comm. Doc. No. 111-005 (Washington: GPO, 2009), p. 4.

[142] U.S. Congress, House Committee on Small Business, Subcommittee on Rural Development, Entrepreneurship, and Trade, *Subcommittee Hearing on Legislative Initiatives to Modernize SBA's Entrepreneurial Development Programs*, 111th Cong., 1st sess., April 2, 2009 (Washington: GPO, 2009), p. 29.

[143] U.S. Congress, House Committee on Small Business, *Full Committee Hearing on the State of the SBA's Entrepreneurial Development Programs and Their Role in Promoting an Economic Recovery*, 111th Cong., 1st sess., February 11, 2009, Small Business Committee Doc. No. 111-005 (Washington: GPO, 2009), p. 26.

[144] Ibid., pp. 15, 17, 26, 29, 58-65, 72; and U.S. Congress, House Committee on Small Business, *Women's Business Ownership Act of 1988*, report to accompany H.R. 5050, 100th Cong., 2nd sess., September 22, 1988, H.Rept. 100-955 (Washington: GPO, 1988), pp. 9, 10, 13, 14.

[145] U.S. Congress, House Committee on Small Business, *Full Committee Legislative Hearing on Energy, Veterans Entrepreneurship, and the SBA's Entrepreneurial Development Programs*, 110th Cong., 1st sess., May 16, 2007, Serial Number 110-22 (Washington: GPO, 2007), p. 20.

[146] U.S. Congress, House Committee on Small Business, *Full Committee Hearing on the State of the SBA's Entrepreneurial Development Programs and Their Role in Promoting an Economic Recovery*, 111th Cong., 1st sess., February 11, 2009, Small Business Committee Doc. No. 111-005 (Washington: GPO, 2009), pp. 45, 47.

[147] U.S. Congress, House Committee on Small Business, *Job Creation Through Entrepreneurship Act of 2009*, report to accompany H.R. 2352, 111th Cong., 1st sess., May 15, 2009, H.Rept. 111-112 (Washington: GPO, 2009), pp. 17, 18.

[148] H.R. 2352, the Job Creation Through Entrepreneurship Act of 2009, Section 201. Educating Entrepreneurs Through Technology; and H.R. 2352, the Job Creation Through Entrepreneurship Act of 2009, Section 601. Expanding Entrepreneurship.

[149] H.R. 2352, the Job Creation Through Entrepreneurship Act of 2009, Section 601. Expanding Entrepreneurship.

[150] Ibid.

[151] P.L. 111-139, Increasing the statutory limit on the public debt, Section 21. Identification, Consolidation, and Elimination of Duplicative Government Programs.

[152] U.S. Government Accountability Office, *2012 Annual Report: Opportunities to Reduce Duplication, Overlap and Fragmentation, Achieve Savings, and Enhance Results*, GAO-12-342SP, February 28, 2012, p. 1, http://www.gao.gov/ assets/590/588818.pdf

[153] Ibid., pp. 52-61.

[154] Ibid., p. 55.

[155] U.S. Government Accountability Office, Small Business Administration: Opportunities Exist to Improve Oversight of Women's Business Centers and Coordination among SBA's Business Assistance Programs, GAO-08-49, November 2007, p. 15, at http://www.gao.gov/new.items/d0849.pdf.

[156] Ibid.

[157] U.S. Small Business Administration, "FY/CY 2011, Program Announcement for Renewal of the Cooperative Agreement for Current Recipient Organizations," Washington, DC, pp. 27-38, at http://ohiosbdcrfp.com /Documents/ 12%20Program%20Announcement%20FFY2011 %20DRAFT%20.pdf.

[158] H.R. 2352, the Job Creation Through Entrepreneurship Act of 2009, Section 404. Performance and Planning.

[159] H.R. 2352, the Job Creation Through Entrepreneurship Act of 2009, Section 601. Expanding Entrepreneurship.

[160] U.S. Congress, House Committee on Small Business, Subcommittee on Rural Development, Entrepreneurship and Trade, *Subcommittee Hearing on Legislative Initiatives to Modernize SBA's Entrepreneurial Development Programs*, 111th Cong., 1st sess., April 2, 2009, H. Hrg. 111-015 (Washington: GPO, 2009), pp. 26, 27, 31.

[161] U.S. Congress, House Committee on Small Business, Subcommittee on Rural and Urban Entrepreneurship, *Subcommittee Hearing on Oversight of the Entrepreneurial Development Programs Implemented By the Small Business Administration and National Veterans Business Development Corporation*, 110th Cong., 2nd sess., March 12, 2008, House Serial No. 110-78 (Washington: GPO, 2008), pp. 17, 18.

[162] In addition to authorizing changes to the SBA's loan guaranty, training, and contracting programs, the Small Business Jobs Act of 2010 authorizes a $30 billion Small Business Lending Fund to encourage community banks to provide small business loans, a $1.5 billion State Small Business Credit Initiative to provide funding to participating states with small business capital access programs, and about $12 billion in tax relief for small businesses. It also includes revenue raising provisions to offset the act's cost. For further analysis see CRS Report R41385, *Small Business Legislation During the 111th Congress*, by Robert Jay Dilger and Gary Guenther.

[163] P.L. 111-240, the Small Business Jobs Act of 2010, Section 1401. Matching Requirements Under Small Business Programs. This provision was also included in S. 3165, Small Business Community Partner Relief Act of 2010; and a similar provision was included in S. 3103, the Small Business Job Creation Act of 2010.

[164] Ibid.

[165] The bill would also establish a Rural Small Business Technology Pilot Program, increase maximum loan limits for the SBA's home and business disaster loan programs, increase surety bond limits, and expand eligibility for the SBA's State Trade and Export Promotion Grant Program to cities and other major metropolitan areas.

[166] S. 3967, the Small Business Investment and Innovation Act of 2010, Section 241. Office of Women's Business Ownership.

[167] U.S. Small Business Administration, Office of Advocacy, *Small Business Economic Indicators for 2003*, Washington, DC, August 2004, p. 3; Brian Headd, "Small Businesses Most Likely to Lead Economic Recovery," *The Small Business Advocate*, vol. 28, no. 6 (July 2009), pp. 1, 2; and U.S. Small Business Administration, *Fiscal Year 2010 Congressional Budget Justification* (Washington: GPO, 2009), p. 1.

[168] U.S. Congress, House Committee on Small Business, Subcommittee on Rural Development, Entrepreneurship and Trade, *Subcommittee On Rural Development, Entrepreneurship And Trade Markup On Entrepreneurial Development Programs Legislation*, 111th Cong., 1st sess., April 30, 2009, Small Business Committee Document No. 111-118 [ERRATA – printing error, should be 111-018] (Washington: GPO, 2009), p. 1.

[169] David Port, "But Where Is the Money?" *Entrepreneur Magazine*, August 2010, at http://www.entrepreneur.com/magazine/entrepreneur/2010/august/207500.html.

[170] U.S. Congress, House Committee on Small Business, *Full Committee Hearing on the State of the SBA's Entrepreneurial Development Programs and Their Role in Promoting an Economic Recovery*, 111th Cong., 1st sess., February 11, 2009, Small Business Committee Doc. No. 111-005 (Washington: GPO, 2009), pp. 3-5, 24-27, 29; and U.S. Congress, House Committee on Small Business, *Full Committee Hearing on Legislation to Reauthorize and Modernize SBA's Entrepreneurial Development Programs*, 111th Cong., 1st sess., May 6, 2009 (Washington: GPO, 2009), pp. 3-5, 15, 27-34.

[171] U.S. Congress, House Committee on Small Business, *Full Committee Hearing on the State of the SBA's Entrepreneurial Development Programs and Their Role in Promoting an Economic Recovery*, 111th Cong., 1st sess., February 11, 2009, Small Business Committee Doc. No. 111-005 (Washington: GPO, 2009), pp. 44-49; U.S. Congress, House Committee on Small Business, *Job Creation Through Entrepreneurship Act of 2009*, report to accompany H.R. 2352, 111th Cong., 1st sess., May 15, 2009, H.Rept. 111-112 (Washington: GPO, 2009), pp. 16-31; and U.S. Congress, House Committee on Small Business, *Women's Business Ownership Act of 1988*, report to accompany H.R. 5050, 100th Cong., 2nd sess., September 22, 1988, H.Rept. 100-955 (Washington: GPO, 1988), pp. 9, 10, 13, 14.

In: Small Business Administration Programs
Editor: Walter Janikowski

ISBN: 978-1-62417-992-1
© 2013 Nova Science Publishers, Inc.

Chapter 8

THE "8(A) PROGRAM" FOR SMALL BUSINESSES OWNED AND CONTROLLED BY THE SOCIALLY AND ECONOMICALLY DISADVANTAGED: LEGAL REQUIREMENTS AND ISSUES[*]

Kate M. Manuel and John R. Luckey

SUMMARY

Commonly known as the "8(a) Program," the Minority Small Business and Capital Ownership Development Program is one of several federal contracting programs for small businesses. The 8(a) Program provides participating small businesses with training, technical assistance, and contracting opportunities in the form of set-asides and sole-source awards. A "set-aside" is an acquisition in which only certain contractors may compete, while a sole-source award is a contract awarded, or proposed for award, without competition. In FY2011, the federal government spent $16.7 billion on contracts and subcontracts with 8(a) firms. Other programs provide similar assistance to other types of small businesses (e.g., women-owned, HUBZone).

Eligibility for the 8(a) Program is generally limited to small businesses "unconditionally owned and controlled by one or more socially and economically disadvantaged individuals who are of good character and citizens of the United States" that demonstrate "potential for success." Each of these terms is further defined by the Small Business Act, regulations promulgated by the Small Business Administration (SBA), and judicial and administrative decisions.

A "business" is generally a for-profit entity that has a place of business located in the United States and operates primarily within the United States or makes a significant contribution to the U.S. economy by paying taxes or using American products, materials, or labor. A business is "small" if it is independently owned and operated; is not dominant in its field of operations; and meets any definitions or standards established by the Administrator of Small Business. Ownership is "unconditional" when it is not subject to any conditions precedent or subsequent, executory agreements, or similar limitations.

---

[*] This is an edited, reformatted and augmented version of Congressional Research Service, Publication No. R40744, dated October 12, 2012.

"Control" is not the same as ownership and includes both strategic policy setting and day-to-day administration of business operations.

Members of certain racial and ethnic groups are presumed to be socially disadvantaged, although individuals who do not belong to these groups may prove they are also socially disadvantaged. To be economically disadvantaged, an individual must have a net worth of less than $250,000 (excluding ownership in the 8(a) firm and equity in one's primary residence) at the time of entry into the 8(a) Program. This amount increases to $750,000 for continuing eligibility. In determining whether an applicant has good character, SBA looks for criminal conduct, violations of SBA regulations, or current debarment or suspension from federal contracting. For a firm to have demonstrated "potential for success," it generally must have been in business in the field of its primary industry classification for at least two years immediately prior to applying to the 8(a) Program. However, small businesses owned by Indian tribes, Alaska Native Corporations (ANCs), Native Hawaiian Organizations (NHOs), and Community Development Corporations (CDCs) are eligible for the 8(a) Program under somewhat different terms.

The 8(a) Program has periodically been challenged on the grounds that the presumption that members of certain racial and ethnic groups are disadvantaged violates the constitutional guarantee of equal protection. The outcomes in early challenges to the program varied, with some courts finding that plaintiffs lacked standing because they were not economically disadvantaged. Most recently, a federal district court found that the program is not unconstitutional on its face because "breaking down barriers to minority business development created by discrimination" constituted a compelling government interest, and the government had a strong basis in evidence for concluding that race-based action was necessary to further this interest. However, the court found that the program was unconstitutional as applied in the military simulation and training industry because there was no evidence of public- or private-sector discrimination in this industry.

INTRODUCTION

Commonly known as the "8(a) Program," the Minority Small Business and Capital Ownership Development Program is one of several federal contracting programs for small businesses.[1]

The 8(a) Program provides participating small businesses with training, technical assistance, and contracting opportunities in the form of set-asides and sole-source awards. A "set-aside" is an acquisition in which only certain contractors may compete, while a sole-source award is a contract awarded, or proposed for award, without competition. Eligibility for the 8(a) Program is generally limited to small businesses "unconditionally owned and controlled by one or more socially and economically disadvantaged individuals who are of good character and citizens of the United States" that demonstrate "potential for success." However, small businesses owned by Indian tribes, Alaska Native Corporations (ANCs), Native Hawaiian Organizations (NHOs), and Community Development Corporations (CDCs) are eligible for the 8(a) Program under somewhat different terms.

In FY2011, the federal government spent $16.7 billion on contracts and subcontracts with 8(a) firms.[2] Other programs provide similar assistance to other types of small businesses (e.g., women-owned, HUBZone).

The 8(a) and other programs for small businesses are of perennial interest to Congress, given that:

> It is the declared policy of the Congress that the Government should aid, counsel, assist, and protect, insofar as is possible, the interests of small-business concerns in order to preserve free competitive enterprise, to insure that a fair proportion of the total purchases and contracts or subcontracts for property and services for the Government (including but not limited to contracts or subcontracts for maintenance, repair, and construction) be placed with small-business enterprises, to insure that a fair proportion of the total sales of Government property be made to such enterprises, and to maintain and strengthen the overall economy of the Nation.[3]

However, recent Congresses have had particular interest in the 8(a) Program because of the recession of 2007-2009,[4] its effects on minority-owned small businesses,[5] and small businesses' role in job creation.[6]

This report provides a brief history of the 8(a) Program, summarizes key requirements, and discusses legal challenges alleging that the program's presumption that members of certain racial and ethnic groups are socially disadvantaged violates the constitutional guarantee of equal protection.

HISTORICAL DEVELOPMENT

Origins of the 8(a) Program

The current 8(a) Program resulted from the merger of two distinct types of federal programs: those seeking to assist small businesses in general and those seeking to assist racial and ethnic minorities. This merger first occurred, as a matter of executive branch practice, in 1967 and was given a statutory basis in 1978.

Federal Programs for Small Businesses

Congress first authorized a federal agency to enter into prime contracts with other agencies and subcontract with small businesses for the performance of these contracts in 1942. The agency was the Smaller War Plants Corporation (SWPC), which was created partly for this purpose, and Congress gave it these powers in order to ameliorate small businesses' financial difficulties while also "mobiliz[ing] the productive facilities of small business in the interest of successful prosecution of the war."[7] The SWPC's subcontracting authority expired along with the SWPC at the end of the World War II. However, in 1951, at the start of the Korean War, Congress created the Small Defense Plants Administration (SDPA), which was generally given the same powers that the SWPC had exercised.[8] Two years later, in 1953, Congress transferred the SDPA's subcontracting authorities, among others, to the newly created Small Business Administration,[9] with the intent that the SBA would exercise these powers in peacetime, as well as in wartime.[10] When the Small Business Act of 1958 transformed the SBA into a permanent independent agency, this subcontracting authority was included in Section 8(a) of the act.[11] At its inception, the SBA's subcontracting authority was not limited to small businesses owned and controlled by the socially and economically disadvantaged. Under the original Section 8(a), the SBA could contract with any "small-business concerns or others,"[12] but the SBA seldom, if ever, employed this subcontracting authority, focusing instead upon its loan and other programs.[13]

Federal Programs for Minorities

Federal programs for minorities began developing at approximately the same time as those for small businesses, although there was initially no explicit overlap between them. The earliest programs were created by executive orders, beginning with President Franklin Roosevelt's order on June 25, 1941, requiring that all federal agencies include a clause in defense-related contracts prohibiting contractors from discriminating on the basis of race, creed, color, or national origin.[14] Subsequent Presidents followed Roosevelt's example, issuing a number of executive orders seeking to improve the employment opportunities of "Negroes, Spanish-Americans, Orientals, Indians, Jews, Puerto Ricans, etc."[15] These executive branch initiatives took on new importance after the Kerner Commission's report on the causes of the urban riots of 1966 concluded that African Americans would need "special encouragement" to enter the economic mainstream.[16]

Presidents Lyndon Johnson and Richard Nixon laid the foundations for the present 8(a) Program in the hope of providing such "encouragement." Johnson created the President's Test Cities Program (PTCP), which involved a small-scale use of the SBA's authority under Section 8(a) to award contracts to firms willing to locate in urban areas and hire unemployed individuals, largely African Americans, or sponsor minority-owned businesses by providing capital or management assistance.[17] However, under the PTCP, small businesses did not have to be minority-owned to receive subcontracts under Section 8(a).[18] Nixon's program was larger and focused more specifically on minority-owned small businesses.[19] During the Nixon Administration, the SBA promulgated its earliest regulations for the 8(a) Program. In 1970, the first of these regulations articulated the SBA's policy of using Section 8(a) to "assist small concerns owned by disadvantaged persons to become self-sufficient, viable businesses capable of competing effectively in the market place."[20] A later regulation, promulgated in 1973, defined "disadvantaged persons" as including, but not limited to, "black Americans, Spanish-Americans, oriental Americans, Eskimos, and Aleuts."[21] However, the SBA lacked explicit statutory authority for focusing its 8(a) Program on minority-owned businesses until 1978,[22] although courts generally rejected challenges alleging that SBA's implementation of the program was unauthorized because it was "not specifically mentioned in statute."[23]

1978 Amendments to the Small Business Act and Subsequent Regulations

In 1978, Congress amended the Small Business Act to give the SBA statutory authority for its 8(a) Program for minority-owned businesses.[24] Under the 1978 amendments, SBA can only subcontract under Section 8(a) with "socially and economically disadvantaged small business concerns,"[25] or businesses which are least 51% owned by one or more socially and economically disadvantaged individuals and whose management and daily operations are controlled by such individual(s).[26]

The 1978 amendments established a basic definition of "socially disadvantaged individuals," which included those who have been "subjected to racial or ethnic prejudice or cultural bias because of their identity as a member of a group without regard to their individual qualities."[27] They also included congressional findings that "Black Americans, Hispanic Americans, Native Americans, and other minorities" are socially disadvantaged.[28]

Thus, if an individual was a member of one of these groups, he or she was presumed to be socially disadvantaged. Otherwise, the amendments granted the SBA broad discretion to recognize additional groups or individuals as socially disadvantaged based upon criteria promulgated in regulations.[29] Under these regulations, which include a three-part test for determining whether minority groups not mentioned in the amendment's findings are disadvantaged,[30] the SBA recognized the racial or ethnic groups listed in Table 1 as socially disadvantaged for purposes of the 8(a) Program.[31] The regulations also established standards of evidence to be met by individuals demonstrating personal disadvantage and procedures for rebutting the presumption of social disadvantage accorded to members of recognized minority groups.[32] The 1978 amendments also defined "economically disadvantaged individuals," for purposes of the 8(a) Program, as "those socially disadvantaged individuals whose ability to compete in the free enterprise system has been impaired ... as compared to others in the same business area who are not socially disadvantaged."[33] Later, the SBA established by regulation that personal net worth of less than $250,000 at the time of entry into the 8(a) Program ($750,000 for continuing eligibility) constitutes economic disadvantage.[34]

Table 1. Groups Presumed to Be Socially Disadvantaged

Group	Countries of Origin Included Within Group
Black Americans	n/a
Hispanic Americans	n/a
Native Americans (including American Indians, Eskimos, Aleuts, Native Hawaiians)	n/a
Asian Pacific Americans	Burma, Thailand, Malaysia, Indonesia, Singapore, Brunei, Japan, China (including Hong Kong), Taiwan, Laos, Cambodia, Vietnam, Korea, The Philippines, U.S. Trust Territory of the Pacific Islands (Republic of Palau), Republic of the Marshall Islands, Federated States of Micronesia, Commonwealth of the Northern Mariana Islands, Guam, Samoa, Macao, Fiji, Tonga, Kiribati, Tuvalu, Nauru
Subcontinent Asian Americans	India, Pakistan, Bangladesh, Sri Lanka, Bhutan, the Maldives Islands, Nepal

Source: Congressional Research Service, based on 13 C.F.R. §124.103(b).

Expansion of the 8(a) Program to Include "Disadvantaged" Groups

Although the 8(a) Program was originally established for the benefit of disadvantaged *individuals*, in the 1980s, Congress expanded the program to include small businesses owned by four "disadvantaged" *groups*. The first owner-group to be included was Community Development Corporations (CDCs). A CDC is:

> a nonprofit organization responsible to residents of the area it serves which is receiving financial assistance under part 1 [42 USCS §§9805 et seq.] and any organization more than 50 percent of which is owned by such an organization, or otherwise controlled by such an organization, or designated by such an organization for the purpose of this subchapter [42 USCS §§9801 et seq.].[35]

Congress created CDCs with the Community Development Act of 1981[36] and instructed the SBA to issue regulations ensuring that CDCs could participate in the 8(a) Program.[37]

In 1986, two additional owner-groups, Indian tribes and Alaska Native Corporations, became eligible for the 8(a) Program when Congress passed legislation providing that firms owned by Indian tribes, which included Alaskan Native Corporations (ANCs),[38] were to be deemed "socially disadvantaged" for purposes of the 8(a) Program.[39] In 1992, ANCs were further deemed to be "economically disadvantaged."[40]

The final owner-group, that of Native Hawaiian Organizations (NHOs), was recognized in 1988.[41] An NHO was defined as:

> any community service organization serving Native Hawaiians in the State of Hawaii which—(A) is a nonprofit corporation that has filed articles of incorporation with the director (or the designee thereof) of the Hawaii Department of Commerce and Consumer Affairs, or any successor agency, (B) is controlled by Native Hawaiians, and (C) whose business activities will principally benefit such Native Hawaiians.[42]

CURRENT REQUIREMENTS

Under the current 8(a) Program, participating firms are eligible for set-asides or sole-source awards of federal contracts, as well as training and technical assistance from SBA. Detailed statutory and regulatory requirements govern eligibility for the Program; set-asides and sole-source awards to 8(a) firms; and related issues. These requirements are generally the same for all participants in the 8(a) Program, although there are instances where there are "special rules" for 8(a) firms owned by groups.[43] An Appendix compares the requirements applicable to individual owners of 8(a) firms to those applicable to groups owning 8(a) firms (i.e., Alaska Native Corporations, Indian tribes, Native Hawaiian Organizations, and Community Development Corporations).[44]

Requirements in General

Eligibility for the 8(a) Program
Eligibility for the 8(a) Program is limited to "small business[es] which [are] unconditionally owned and controlled by one or more socially and economically disadvantaged individuals who are of good character and citizens of and residing in the United States, and which demonstrate[] potential for success."[45] Each of these terms is further defined by the Small Business Act; regulations that the SBA has promulgated to implement Section 8(a); and judicial and administrative decisions.[46] The eligibility requirements are the same at the time of entry into the 8(a) Program and throughout the Program unless otherwise noted.[47]

"Business"
Except for small agricultural cooperatives, a "business" is a for-profit entity that has a place of business located in the United States and operates primarily within the United States or makes a significant contribution to the U.S. economy by paying taxes or using American

products, materials, or labor.[48] For purposes of the 8(a) Program, businesses may take the form of individual proprietorships, partnerships, limited liability companies, corporations, joint ventures, associations, trusts, or cooperatives.[49]

"Small"

A business is "small" if it is independently owned and operated; is not dominant in its field of operations; and meets any definitions or standards established by the Administrator of the SBA.[50] These standards focus primarily upon the size of the business as measured by the number of employees or its gross income, but they also take into account the size of other businesses within the same industry.[51] For example, businesses in the field of "scheduled passenger air transportation" are "small" if they have fewer than 1,500 employees, while those in the data processing field are "small" if they have a gross income of less than $25 million.[52]

Affiliations between businesses, or relationships allowing one party control or the power of control over another,[53] generally count in size determinations, with the SBA considering "the receipts, employees, or other measure of size of the concern whose size is at issue and all of its domestic and foreign affiliates, regardless of whether the affiliates are organized for profit."[54] Businesses can thus be determined to be other than small because of their involvement in joint ventures,[55] subcontracting arrangements,[56] or franchise or license agreements,[57] among other things, provided that their income or personnel numbers, plus those of their affiliate(s), are over the pertinent size threshold.

"Unconditionally Owned and Controlled"

Participants in the 8(a) Program must be "at least 51% unconditionally and directly owned by one or more socially and economically disadvantaged individuals who are citizens of the United States" unless they are owned by an Indian tribe, Alaska Native Corporation (ANC), Native Hawaiian Organization (NHO), or Community Development Corporation (CDC).[58] Ownership is "unconditional" when it is not subject to any conditions precedent or subsequent, executory agreements, voting trusts, restrictions on assignment of voting rights, or other arrangements that could cause the benefits of ownership to go to another entity.[59] Ownership is "direct" when the disadvantaged individuals own the business in their own right and not through an intermediary (e.g., ownership by another business entity or by a trust that is owned and controlled by one or more disadvantaged individuals).[60] Non-disadvantaged individuals and non-participant businesses that own at least 10% of an 8(a) business may generally own no more than 10 to 20% of any other 8(a) firm.[61]

Non-participant businesses that earn the majority of their revenue in the same or similar line of business are likewise barred from owning more than 10 to 20% of another 8(a) firm.[62]

Participants must also be controlled by one or more disadvantaged individuals.[63] "Control is not the same as ownership" and includes both strategic policy setting and day-to-day management and administration of business operations.[64] Management and daily business operations must also be conducted by one or more disadvantaged individuals unless the 8(a) business is owned by an Indian tribe, ANC, NHO, or CDC.[65] These individuals must have managerial experience "of the extent and complexity needed to run the concern" and generally must devote themselves full-time to the business "during the normal working hours of firms in the same or similar line of business."[66]

A disadvantaged individual must hold the highest officer position within the business.[67] Non-disadvantaged individuals may otherwise be involved in the management of an 8(a) business, or may be stockholders, partners, limited liability members, officers, or directors of an 8(a) business.[68] However, they may not exercise actual control or have power to control, or receive compensation greater than that of the highest-paid officer without SBA approval.[69]

"Socially Disadvantaged Individual"

Socially disadvantaged individuals are "those who have been subjected to racial or ethnic prejudice or cultural bias within American society because of their identities as members of groups and without regard to their individual qualities."[70] Members of designated groups, listed in Table 1, are entitled to a rebuttable presumption of social disadvantage for purposes of the 8(a) Program,[71] although this presumption can be overcome with "credible evidence to the contrary."[72]

Individuals who are not members of designated groups must prove they are socially disadvantaged by a preponderance of the evidence.[73] Such individuals must show (1) at least one objective distinguishing feature that has contributed to social disadvantage (e.g., race, ethnic origin, gender, physical handicap, long-term residence in an environment isolated from mainstream American society); (2) personal experiences of substantial and chronic social disadvantage in American society; and (3) negative impact on entry into or advancement in the business world.[74]

In assessing the third factor, the SBA will consider all relevant evidence produced by the applicant, but must consider the applicant's education, employment, and business history to see if the totality of the circumstances shows disadvantage.[75] Groups not included in Table 1 may obtain listing by demonstrating disadvantage by a preponderance of the evidence.[76]

"Economically Disadvantaged Individual"

Economically disadvantaged individuals are "socially disadvantaged individuals whose ability to compete in the free enterprise system has been impaired due to diminished financial capital and credit opportunities as compared to others in the same or similar line of business who are not socially disadvantaged."[77]

Individuals claiming economic disadvantage must describe it in a personal statement and submit financial documentation.[78] The SBA will examine their personal income for the past three years, their personal net worth, and the fair market value of the assets they own.[79] However, principal ownership in a prospective or current 8(a) business is generally excluded when calculating net worth, as is equity in individuals' primary residence.[80] For initial eligibility, applicants to the 8(a) Program must have a net worth of less than $250,000.[81] For continued eligibility, net worth must be less than $750,000.[82]

"Good Character"

In determining whether an applicant to, or participant in, the 8(a) Program possesses "good character," the SBA looks for criminal conduct; violations of SBA regulations; current debarment or suspension from government contracting; managers or key employees who lack business integrity; and the knowing submission of false information to the SBA.[83]

"Demonstrated Potential for Success"

For a firm to have demonstrated potential for success, it generally must have been in business in the field of its primary industry classification for at least two full years immediately prior to the date of its application to the 8(a) Program.[84]

However, the SBA may grant a waiver allowing firms that have been in business for less than two years to enter the 8(a) Program when (1) the disadvantaged individuals upon whom eligibility is based have substantial business management experience; (2) the business has demonstrated the technical experience necessary to carry out its business plan with a substantial likelihood of success; (3) the firm has adequate capital to sustain its operations and carry out its business plan; (4) the firm has a record of successful performance on contracts in its primary field of operations; and (5) the firm presently has, or can demonstrate its ability to timely obtain, the personnel, facilities, equipment, and other resources necessary to perform contracts under Section 8(a).[85]

Set-Asides and Sole-Source Awards under Section 8(a)

Section 8(a) of the Small Business Act authorizes agencies to award contracts for goods or services, or to perform construction work, to the SBA for subcontracting to small businesses participating in the 8(a) Program.[86]

A "set-aside" is an acquisition in which only certain contractors may compete, while a sole-source award is a contract awarded, or proposed for award, without competition.[87] Although the Competition in Contracting Act (CICA) generally requires that agencies obtain "full and open competition through the use of competitive procedures" when procuring goods or services, set-asides and sole-source awards are both permissible under CICA.

In fact, an 8(a) set-aside is a recognized competitive procedure.[88] Agencies are effectively encouraged to subcontract through the 8(a) Program because there are government-wide and agency-specific goals regarding the percentage of procurement dollars awarded to "small disadvantaged businesses," among others.[89] Awards made via set-asides or on a sole-source basis count toward these goals,[90] and businesses participating in the 8(a) Program are considered small disadvantaged businesses.[91]

Discretion to Subcontract through the 8(a) Program

There are few limits on agency discretion to subcontract through the 8(a) Program.[92] However, the SBA is prohibited by regulation from accepting procurements for award under Section 8(a) when

1) the procuring agency issued a solicitation for or otherwise expressed publicly a clear intent to reserve the procurement as a set-aside for small businesses not participating in the 8(a) Program prior to offering the requirement to SBA for award as an 8(a) contract;[93]

2) the procuring agency competed the requirement among 8(a) firms prior to offering the requirement to SBA and receiving SBA's acceptance of it;[94] or

3) the SBA makes a written determination that "acceptance of the procurement for 8(a) award would have an adverse impact on an individual small business, a group of small businesses located in a specific geographical location, or other small business programs."[95]

Additionally, SBA is barred from awarding an 8(a) contract, either via a set-aside or on a sole-source basis, "if the price of the contract results in a cost to the contracting agency which exceeds a fair market price."[96]

Otherwise, agency officials may offer contracts to the SBA "in [their] discretion," and the SBA may accept requirements for the 8(a) Program "whenever it determines such action is necessary or appropriate."[97] The courts and the Government Accountability Office (GAO) will generally not hear protests of agencies' determinations regarding whether to procure specific requirements through the 8(a) Program unless it can be shown that government officials acted in bad faith or contrary to federal law.[98]

Monetary Thresholds and Subcontracting Mechanism under 8(a)

Once the SBA has accepted a contract for the 8(a) Program, the contract is awarded either through a set-aside or on a sole-source basis, with the amount of the contract generally determining the acquisition method used, as Figure 1 illustrates. When the anticipated total value of the contract, including any options, is less than $4 million ($6.5 million for manufacturing contracts), the contract is normally awarded without competition.[99]

In contrast, when the anticipated value of the contract exceeds $4 million ($6.5 million for manufacturing contracts), the contract generally must be awarded via a set-aside with competition limited to 8(a) firms so long as there is a reasonable expectation that at least two eligible and responsible 8(a) firms will submit offers and the award can be made at fair market price.[100]

Sole-source awards of contracts valued at $4 million ($6.5 million or more for manufacturing contracts) may only be made when (1) there is not a reasonable expectation that at least two eligible and responsible 8(a) firms will submit offers at a fair market price, or (2) the SBA accepts the requirement on behalf of an 8(a) firm owned by an Indian tribe, an ANC or, in the case of Department of Defense contracts, an NHO.[101] Requirements valued at more than $4 million ($6.5 million for manufacturing contracts) cannot be divided into several acquisitions at lesser amounts in order to make sole-source awards.[102]

Source: Congressional Research Service.

Figure 1. Acquisition Methods at Various Price Thresholds.

Other Requirements

Other key requirements of the 8(a) Program include the following:

- *Inability to protest an 8(a) firm's eligibility for an award*: When the SBA makes or proposes an award to an 8(a) firm, that firm's eligibility for the award cannot be challenged or protested as part of the solicitation or proposed contract award. Instead, information concerning a firm's eligibility for the 8(a) Program must be submitted to SBA in accordance with separate requirements contained in 13 C.F.R. §124.517.[103]

- *Maximum of nine years in the 8(a) Program*: Firms may participate in the 8(a) Program for no more than nine years from the date of their admission into the Program, although they may be terminated or graduate from the program before nine years have passed.[104]

- *One-time eligibility for the 8(a) Program*: Once a firm or a disadvantaged individual upon whom a firm's eligibility was based has exited the 8(a) Program after participating in it for any length of time, neither the firm nor the individual is generally eligible to participate in the 8(a) Program again.[105] When at least 50% of the assets of one firm are the same as those of another firm, the firms are considered identical for purposes of eligibility for the 8(a) Program.[106]

- *Limits on ownership of 8(a) firms by family members of current or former 8(a) firm owners*: Individuals generally may not use their disadvantaged status to qualify a firm for the 8(a) Program if the individual has an immediate family member who is using, or has used, his or her disadvantaged status to qualify a firm for the 8(a) Program.[107]

- *Limits on the amount of 8(a) contracts that a firm may receive*: 8(a) firms may generally not receive additional sole-source awards once they have received a combined total of competitive and sole-source awards "in excess of the dollar amount set forth in this section during its participation in the 8(a) ... program."[108] Additionally, 8(a) firms in the "transitional stage," or the last five years of participation, must achieve annual targets for the amount of revenues they receive from non-8(a) sources.[109]

  These targets increase over time, with firms required to attain 15% of their revenue from non-8(a) sources in the fifth year; 25% in the sixth year; 35% in the seventh year; 45% in the eight year; and 55% in the ninth year.[110] Firms that do not display the relevant percentages of revenue from non-8(a) sources are ineligible for sole-source 8(a) contracts "unless and until" they correct the situation.[111]

- *Limitations on subcontracting*: Although not only under the authority of Section 8(a) of the Small Business Act or applicable only to 8(a) businesses, limitations on subcontracting require that small businesses receiving contracts under a set-aside perform minimum percentages of the contract work.[112]

  These percentages vary depending upon the type of the contract, with employees of the small business required to perform (1) at least 50% of the personnel costs of service contracts; (2) at least 50% of the costs of manufacturing (excluding materials) in supply contacts; (3) at least 15% of the costs of construction (excluding materials) in general construction contracts; and (4) at least 25% of the costs of construction (excluding materials) in "special trade" construction contracts.[113]

Requirements for Tribally, ANC-, NHO-, and CDC-Owned Firms

Tribes, ANCs, NHOs or CDCs themselves generally do not participate in the 8(a) Program. Rather, businesses that are at least 51% owned by such entities participate in the 8(a) Program,[114] although the rules governing their participation are somewhat different from those for the 8(a) Program generally.[115]

Eligibility for the 8(a) Program "Small"

Firms owned by Indian tribes, ANCs, NHOs, and CDCs must be "small" under the SBA's size standards.[116]

However, certain affiliations with the owning entity or other business enterprises of that entity are excluded in size determinations *unless* the Administrator of Small Business determines that a small business owned by an Indian tribe, ANC, NHO, or CDC "[has] obtained, or [is] likely to obtain, a substantial unfair competitive advantage within an industry category" because of such exclusions.[117]

Other affiliations of small businesses owned by Indian tribes, ANCs, NHOs, or CDCs can count in size determinations, and ANC-owned firms, in particular, have been subjected to early graduation from the 8(a) Program because they exceeded the size standards.[118]

"Business"

Firms owned by Indian tribes, ANCs, NHOs, and CDCs must be "businesses" under the SBA's definition.[119] Although ANCs themselves may be for-profit or non-profit, ANC-owned businesses must be for-profit to participate in the 8(a) Program.[120]

"Unconditionally Owned and Controlled"

Firms owned by Indian tribes, ANCs, NHOs, and CDCs must be unconditionally owned and substantially controlled by the tribe, ANC, NHO, or CDC, respectively.[121] However, under SBA regulations, tribally or ANC-owned firms may be managed by individuals who are not members of the tribe or Alaska Natives if the firm can demonstrate:

> that the Tribe can hire and fire those individuals, that it will retain control of all management decisions common to boards of directors, including strategic planning, budget approval, and the employment and compensation of officers, and that a written management development plan exists which shows how Tribal members will develop managerial skills sufficient to manage the concern or similar Tribally-owned concerns in the future.[122]

The rules governing NHO-owned firms do not address management of NHO-owned firms by persons who are not Native Hawaiians,[123] and although the general rules apply where no "special rules" exist,[124] it seems unlikely that NHO-owned firms are treated differently from tribally or ANC-owned firms in this regard.

CDCs are to be managed and have their daily operations conducted by individuals with "managerial experience of an extent and complexity needed to run the [firm]."[125]

"Socially Disadvantaged"

As owners of prospective or current 8(a) firms, Indian tribes, ANCs, NHOs, and CDCs are all presumed to be socially disadvantaged.[126]

"Economically Disadvantaged"

By statute, ANCs are deemed to be economically disadvantaged,[127] and CDCs are similarly presumed to be economically disadvantaged.[128] Indian tribes and NHOs, in contrast, must establish economic disadvantage at least once.

Indian tribes must present data on, among other things, the number of tribe members; the tribal unemployment rate; the per capita income of tribe members; the percentage of the local

Indian population above the poverty level; the tribe's access to capital; the tribe's assets as disclosed in current financial statements; and all businesses wholly or partially owned by tribal enterprises or affiliates, as well as their primary industry classification.[129] However, once a tribe has established that it is economically disadvantaged for purposes of one 8(a) business, it need not reestablish economic disadvantage in order to have other businesses certified for the 8(a) Program *unless* the Director of the Office of Business Development requires it to do so.[130]

When determining whether an NHO is economically disadvantaged, SBA will consider "the individual economic status of NHO's members," the majority of whom "must meet the same initial eligibility economic disadvantaged thresholds as individually-owned 8(a) applicants."[131] Specifically:

> For the first 8(a) applicant owned by a particular NHO, individual NHO members must meet the same initial eligibility economic disadvantage thresholds as individually-owned 8(a) applicants.
> For any additional 8(a) applicant owned by the NHO, individual NHO members must meet the economic disadvantage thresholds for continued 8(a) eligibility.[132]

"Good Character"

When an organization owns an actual or prospective 8(a) firm, all members, officers, or employees of that organization are generally not required to show good character. The regulations governing tribally and ANC-owned firms explicitly address the issue, stating that the "good character" requirement applies only to officers or directors of the firm, or shareholders owning more than a 20% interest.[133]

NHO-owned firms may be subject to the same requirements in practice.[134] With CDC-owned firms, the firm itself and "all of its principals" must have good character.[135]

"Demonstrated Potential for Success"

Firms owned by ANCs, Indian tribes, NHOs, and CDCs may evidence "potential for success" in several ways, including by demonstrating that:

1) the firm has been in business for at least two years, as shown by individual or consolidated income tax returns for each of the two previous tax years showing operating revenues in the primary industry in which the firm seeks certification;
2) the individuals who will manage and control the daily operations of the firm have substantial technical and management experience; the firm has a record of successful performance on government or other contracts in its primary industry category; and the firm has adequate capital to sustain its operations and carry out its business plan; or
3) the owner-group has made a firm written commitment to support the operations of the firm and has the financial ability to do so.[136]

The first of these ways for demonstrating potential for success is the same for individually owned firms,[137] and the second arguably corresponds to the circumstances in which SBA may waive the requirement that individually owned firms have been in business for at least two years.[138]

There is no equivalent to the third way for individually owned firms, and some commentators have suggested that this provision could "benefit ANCs by allowing more expeditious and effortless access to 8(a) contracts for new concerns without having to staff new subsidiaries with experienced management."[139]

Report of Benefits for Firms Owned by ANCs, Indian Tribes, NHOs, and CDCs

Although implementation of this requirement has been delayed,[140] 8(a) firms owned by ANCs, Indian tribes, NHOs, and CDCs must submit information annually to the SBA showing:

> how the Tribe, ANC, NHO or CDC has provided benefits to the Tribal or native members and/or the Tribal, native or other community due to the Tribe's/ANC's/NHO's/CDC's participation in the 8(a) ... program through one or more firms.
> This data includes information relating to funding cultural programs, employment assistance, jobs, scholarships, internships, subsistence activities, and other services provided by the Tribe, ANC, NHO or CDC to the affected community.[141]

Set-Asides and Sole-Source Awards

Like other participants in the 8(a) Program, firms owned by Indian tribes, ANCs, NHOs, and CDCs are eligible for 8(a) set-asides and may receive sole-source awards valued at less than $4 million ($6.5 million for manufacturing contracts).

However, firms owned by Indian tribes and ANCs can also receive sole-source awards in excess of $4 million ($6.5 million for manufacturing contracts) even when contracting officers reasonably expect that that at least two eligible and responsible 8(a) firms will submit offers and the award can be made at fair market price.[142]

NHO-owned firms may receive sole-source awards from the Department of Defense under the same conditions.[143]

Other Requirements

Firms owned by Indian tribes, ANCs, NHOs, and CDCs are governed by the same regulations as other 8(a) firms where certain of the "other requirements" are involved, including (1) inability to protest an 8(a) firm's eligibility for an award;[144] (2) maximum of nine years in the 8(a) Program (for individual firms);[145] and (3) limits on subcontracting.[146] However, the requirements for such firms differ somewhat from those for other 8(a) firms where one-time eligibility for the 8(a) Program; limits on majority ownership of 8(a) firms; and limits on the amount of 8(a) contracts that a firm may receive are involved.

Firms owned by Indian tribes, ANCs, NHOs, and CDCs may participate in the 8(a) Program only one time.[147]

However, unlike the disadvantaged individuals upon whom other firms' eligibility for the 8(a) Program is based, Indian tribes, ANCs, NHOs, and CDCs may confer eligibility for the 8(a) Program upon firms on multiple occasions and for an indefinite period.[148]

Additionally, although Indian tribes, ANCs, NHOs, and CDCs may not own 51% or more of a firm obtaining the majority of its revenues from the same "primary" industry in which another firm they own or owned currently operates or has operated within the past two years, there are no limits on the number of firms they may own that operate in other primary industries.[149]

Moreover, Indian tribes, ANCs, NHOs, and CDCs may own multiple firms that earn less than 50% of their revenue in the same "secondary" industries.[150]

Finally, firms owned by Indian tribes, ANCs, and NHOs may continue to receive additional sole-source awards even after they have received a combined total of competitive and sole-source 8(a) contracts in excess of the dollar amount set forth in 13 C.F.R. Section 124.519, while individually owned firms may not.[151]

However, firms owned by any of these four types of entities are subject to the same requirements regarding the percentages of revenue received from non-8(a) sources at various stages of their participation in the 8(a) Program as other 8(a) firms.[152]

CONSTITUTIONALITY OF THE 8(A) PROGRAM

The 8(a) Program has periodically been challenged on the grounds that the presumption that members of certain racial and ethnic groups are disadvantaged violates the constitutional guarantee of equal protection.

The outcomes in early challenges to the program varied, with some courts finding that the plaintiffs lacked standing to bring such challenges because they were not economically disadvantaged, or were otherwise ineligible for the program;[153] and other courts finding that the program was unconstitutional as applied in specific cases.[154]

Most recently, in *DynaLantic Corporation v. U.S. Department of Defense*, the U.S. District Court for the District of Columbia found that the 8(a) Program was not unconstitutional on its face because "breaking down barriers to minority business development created by discrimination" constituted a compelling government interest, and the government had a strong basis in evidence for concluding that race-based action was necessary to further this interest.[155]

However, the court found that the program was unconstitutional as applied in the military simulation and training industry because the Department of Defense (DOD) conceded it had "no evidence of discrimination, either in the public or private sector, in the simulation and training industry."[156]

Particularly in its rejection of the facial challenge to the 8(a) Program, the court emphasized certain aspects of the program's history and requirements when finding that the government had articulated a compelling interest for the program and had a strong basis in evidence for its actions.

Specifically, the court rejected the plaintiff's assertion that the 8(a) Program was "not truly remedial," but rather favored "virtually all minority groups ... over the larger pool of citizens," because non-minority individuals may qualify for the program, and all 8(a) applicants must demonstrate economic disadvantage.[157]

The court also noted that the history of the 8(a) program prior to 1978 (when Congress expressly authorized set-asides for disadvantaged small businesses) had evidenced that race-neutral methods were insufficient to promote contracting with minority-owned small businesses.[158]

The court further noted that the 8(a) Program was intended to be a business development program, not a means to "channel contracts" to minority firms;[159] that Section 8(a) of the Small Business Act expressly provides that awards may be made through the 8(a) Program only when SBA determines that "such action is necessary and appropriate";[160] and that the act requires the President and SBA to report annually to Congress on the program, thereby ensuring that Congress has evidence as to whether there is a "continuing compelling need for the program."[161]

Similarly, in finding that the program was narrowly tailored to meet the government's interests, the court noted (1) that goals for contracting with small disadvantaged businesses are purely aspirational, and there are no penalties for failing to meet them;[162] (2) the nine-year limits on program participation for individual owners and firms;[163] and (3) that SBA may not accept a requirement for the 8(a) Program if it determines that doing so will have a adverse effect on another small business or group of small businesses.[164]

The court emphasized that the last two factors, in particular, helped ensure that race-conscious remedies do not "last longer than the discriminatory effects [they are] designed to eliminate,"[165] and "work the least harm possible to other innocent persons competing for the benefit."[166]

In contrast, in upholding the as-applied challenge, the court focused on the industry in which DOD had proposed using an 8(a) set-aside, rather than aspects of the 8(a) Program. The court characterized the military simulation and training industry as a "highly skilled" one,[167] and noted that the government had conceded there was no evidence of public or private sector discrimination in this industry.[168]

The court further suggested that, with the requisite evidence, the government could use the 8(a) Program to make awards in the military simulation and training industry.[169]

However, despite such caveats, the 8(a) Program would appear vulnerable to as applied challenges in the wake of the *DynaLantic* decision, particularly in other "highly skilled" industries where there could be questions about the availability of qualified minority contractors.[170] As-applied challenges to the 8(a) Program have succeed in the past, arguably without materially diminishing the efficacy of the program.[171]

The current situation could be different, though, in that competition for federal contracts seems likely to increase as federal procurement spending decreases due to budget cuts and, potentially, sequestration.[172]

At least one other challenge to the 8(a) Program is also pending in the federal district court for the District of Columbia,[173] and new challenges could potentially be filed in other jurisdictions, including the U.S. Court of Federal Claims.

Appeals from the Court of Federal Claims are heard by the U.S. Court of Appeals for the Federal Circuit, which, in its 2008 decision in *Rothe Development Corporation v. Department of Defense*, struck down a DOD contracting program that incorporated a similar presumption that minorities are disadvantaged.[174]

The *Rothe* court applied what is arguably a more stringent approach to equal protection analysis—and, particularly, the evidence compiled by Congress—than that applied by the *DynaLantic* court, and it is unclear how the 8(a) Program would fare if reviewed in light of *Rothe*.[175]

Requirements	8(a) Businesses Generally	Tribally Owned 8(a) Businesses	ANC-Owned 8(a) Businesses	NHO-Owned 8(a) Businesses	CDC-Owned 8(a) Businesses
"Small"	Independently owned and operated; not dominant in field of operation; meets size standards (15 U.S.C. §631(a)) All affiliations count (13 C.F.R. §121.103)	Independently owned and operated; not dominant in field of operation; meets size standards (15 U.S.C. §631(a)) Affiliations based on the tribe or tribal ownership, among others, do not count (15 U.S.C. §636(j)(10)(J)(ii); 13 C.F.R. §124.109(c)(2))	Independently owned and operated; not dominant in field of operation; meets size standards (15 U.S.C. §631(a)) Affiliations based on the ANC or ownership by the ANC, among others, do not count (15 U.S.C. §636(j)(10)(J)(ii); 13 C.F.R. §124.109(c)(2))	Independently owned and operated; not dominant in field of operation; meets size standards (15 U.S.C. §631(a)) Affiliations based on the NHO or ownership by the NHO, among others, do not count (15 U.S.C. §636(j)(10)(J)(ii); 13 C.F.R. §124.110(c))	Independently owned and operated; not dominant in field of operation; meets size standards (15 U.S.C. §631(a)) Affiliations based on the CDC or ownership by the CDC, among others, do not count (15 U.S.C. §636(j)(10)(J)(ii); 13 C.F.R. §124.111(c))
"Business"	For-profit entity with its place of business in the United States; operates primarily within the United States or makes a significant contribution to the U.S. economy	For-profit entity with its place of business in the United States; operates primarily within the United States or makes a significant contribution to the U.S. economy	For-profit entity with its place of business in the United States; operates primarily within the United States or makes a significant contribution to the U.S. economy (13 C.F.R. §121.105(a)(1))	For-profit entity with its place of business in the United States; operates primarily within the United States or makes a significant contribution to the U.S. economy	For-profit entity with its place of business in the United States;
	(13 C.F.R. §121.105(a)(1))	(13 C.F.R. §121.105(a)(1))	Although ANC may be non-profit, ANC-owned firms must be for-profit to be eligible for 8(a) Program (13 C.F.R. §124.109(a)(3))	(13 C.F.R. §121.105(a)(1))	operates primarily within the United States or makes a significant contribution to the U.S. economy (13 C.F.R. §121.105(a)(1))

Appendix (Continued)

Requirements	8(a) Businesses Generally	Tribally Owned 8(a) Businesses	ANC-Owned 8(a) Businesses	NHO-Owned 8(a) Businesses	CDC-Owned 8(a) Businesses
"Unconditionally owned and controlled"	At least 51% unconditionally and directly owned by one or more disadvantaged individuals who are U.S. citizens (13 C.F.R. §124.105) Management and daily business operations must be conducted by one or more disadvantaged individuals (13 C.F.R. §124.106)	At least 51% tribally owned (13 C.F.R. §124.109(b)) Management may be conducted by individuals who are not members of the tribe provided that the SBA determines that such management is necessary to assist the business's development, among other things (13 C.F.R. §124.109(c)(4)(B))	At least 51% ANC-owned (13 C.F.R. §124.109(a)(3)) Management may be conducted by individuals who are not Alaska Natives provided that the SBA determines that such management is necessary to assist the business's development, among other things (13 C.F.R. §124.109(c)(4)(B))	At least 51% NHO-owned (13 C.F.R. §124.110(a)) Not explicitly addressed in regulationa	At least 51% CDC-owned (13 C.F.R. §124.111(a)) Management and daily business operations to be conducted by individuals having managerial experience of an extent and complexity needed to run the firm (13 C.F.R. §124.111(b))
"Socially disadvantaged individual"	Members of designated groups presumed to be socially disadvantaged; other individuals may prove personal disadvantage by a preponderance of the evidence (13 C.F.R. §124.103)	Indian tribes presumed to be socially disadvantaged (43 U.S.C. §1626(e); 15 U.S.C. §637(a)(4)(A)-(B); 13 C.F.R. §124.109(b)(1))	ANCs presumed to be socially disadvantaged (43 U.S.C. §1626(e); 15 U.S.C. §637(a)(4)(A)-(B); 13 C.F.R. §124.109(b)(1))	NHOs presumed to be socially disadvantaged (43 U.S.C. §1626(e); 15 U.S.C. §637(a)(4)(A)-(B); 13 C.F.R. §124.109(b)(1))	CDCs presumed to be socially disadvantaged (42 U.S.C. §9815(a)(2))
"Economically disadvantaged individual"	Financial information (e.g., personal income, personal net worth, fair market value of assets) must show diminished financial capital and credit opportunities (13 C.F.R. §124.104)	Tribe must prove economic disadvantage the first time a tribally owned firm applies to the 8(a) Program; thereafter, a tribe need only prove economic disadvantage at the request of the SBA (13 C.F.R. §124.109(b)(2))	Deemed to be economically disadvantaged (43 U.S.C. §1626(e); 13 C.F.R. §124.109(a)(2))	For first applicant to 8(a) Program, NHO members must meet the same initial eligibility economic disadvantage thresholds as individually-owned 8(a) applicants; for later applicants, NHO members must meet the economic disadvantage thresholds for continued 8(a) eligibility (13 C.F.R. §124.110(c)(1)	CDCs presumed to be economically disadvantaged (42 U.S.C. §9815(a)(2))

Requirements	8(a) Businesses Generally	Tribally Owned 8(a) Businesses	ANC-Owned 8(a) Businesses	NHO-Owned 8(a) Businesses	CDC-Owned 8(a) Businesses
"Good character"	No criminal conduct or violations of SBA regulations; cannot be debarred or suspended from government contracting (13 C.F.R. §124.108(a))	No criminal conduct or violations of SBA regulations; cannot be debarred or suspended from government contracting (13 C.F.R. §124.108(a)) Requirement applies only to officers, directors, and shareholders owning more than a 20% interest in the business, not to all members of the tribe (13 C.F.R. §124.109(c)(7)(B)(ii))	No criminal conduct or violations of SBA regulations; cannot be debarred or suspended from government contracting (13 C.F.R. §124.108(a)) Requirement applies only to officers, directors, and shareholders owning more than a 20% interest in the business, not to all ANC shareholders (13 C.F.R. §124.109(c)(7)(B)(ii))	No criminal conduct or violations of SBA regulations; cannot be debarred or suspended from government contracting (13 C.F.R. §124.108(a)) Regulations do not address to whom requirements applya	No criminal conduct or violations of SBA regulations; cannot be debarred or suspended from government contracting (13 C.F.R. §124.108(a)) Requirements apply to the firm and "all its principals" (13 C.F.R. §124.111(g))
"Demonstrated potential for success"	Firm must generally have been in business in primary industry for at least two full years prior to date of application to 8(a) Program unless SBA grants a waiver; waiver based on 5 conditionsb (13 C.F.R. §124.107)	Firm must have been in business in primary industry for at least two full years prior to date of application to 8(a) Program; individuals who will manage firm must have substantial experience,	Firm must have been in business in primary industry for at least two full years prior to date of application to 8(a) Program; individuals who will manage firm must have substantial experience, and firm must have had successful performance and adequate capital; or ANC must have made written commitment to support the firm and have the financial ability to do so (13 C.F.R. §124.109(c)(6)(i)-(iii)	Firm must have been in business in primary industry for at least two full years prior to date of application to 8(a) Program; individuals who will manage firm must have substantial experience, and firm must have had successful performance and adequate capital; or	Firm must have been in business in primary industry for at least two full years prior to date of application to 8(a) Program;
		and firm must have had successful performance and adequate capital; or Tribe must have made written commitment to support the firm and have the financial ability to do so (13 C.F.R. §124.109(c)(6)(i)-(iii)		NHO must have made written commitment to support the firm and have the financial ability to do so (13 C.F.R. §124.110 (g)(1)-(3)	individuals who will manage firm must have substantial experience, and firm must have had successful performance and adequate capital;

Appendix (Continued)

Requirements	8(a) Businesses Generally	Tribally Owned 8(a) Businesses	ANC-Owned 8(a) Businesses	NHO-Owned 8(a) Businesses	CDC-Owned 8(a) Businesses
					or CDC must have made written commitment to support the firm and have the financial ability to do so (13 C.F.R. §124.111 (f)(1)-(3)
Sole-source awards	With contracts valued at over $4 million ($6.5 million for manufacturing contracts), sole-source awards permissible only if there is not a reasonable expectation that at least two	Can be made with contracts valued at over $4 million ($6.5 million for manufacturing contracts) even if there is a reasonable expectation that at least two eligible 8(a)	Can be made with contracts valued at over $4 million ($6.5 million for manufacturing contracts) even if there is a reasonable expectation that at least two eligible 8(a) firms will submit offers and the award can be made at fair market price	Can be made with Department of Defense contracts valued at over $4 million ($6.5 million for manufacturing contracts)	With contracts valued at over $4 million ($6.5 million for manufacturing)contracts, sole-source awards permissible only
	eligible 8(a) firms will submit offers and the award can be made at fair market price (48 C.F.R. §19.805-1(b)(1)-(2))	firms will submit offers and the award can be made at fair market price (15 U.S.C. §637(a)(1)(D)(i)-(ii); 48 C.F.R. §19.805-1(b)(1)-(2))	(15 U.S.C. §637(a)(1)(D)(i)-(ii); 48 C.F.R. §19.805-1(b)(1)-(2))	even if there is a reasonable expectation that at least two eligible 8(a) firms will submit offers and the award can be made at fair market price (48 C.F.R. §219.805-1(b)(2)(A)-(B)). Otherwise cannot be made unless there is not a reasonable expectation that at least two eligible 8(a) firms will submit offers and the award can be made at fair market price (48 C.F.R. §19.805-1(b)(1)-(2))	if there is not a reasonable expectation that at least two eligible 8(a) firms will submit offers and the award can be made at fair market price (48 C.F.R. §19.805-1(b)(1)-(2))

Requirements	Generally	Tribally Owned 8(a) Businesses	ANC-Owned 8(a) Businesses	NHO-Owned 8(a) Businesses	CDC-Owned 8(a) Businesses
Inability to protest eligibility for award	Firm's eligibility for award cannot be challenged or protested as part of the solicitation or proposed contract award (48 C.F.R. §19.805-2(d))	Firm's eligibility for award cannot be challenged or protested as part of the solicitation or proposed contract award (48 C.F.R. §19.805-2(d))	Firm's eligibility for award cannot be challenged or protested as part of the solicitation or proposed contract award (48 C.F.R. §19.805-2(d))	Firm's eligibility for award cannot be challenged or protested as part of the solicitation or proposed contract award (48 C.F.R. §19.805-2(d))	Firm's eligibility for award cannot be challenged or protested as part of the solicitation or proposed contract award (48 C.F.R. §19.805-2(d))
Maximum of nine years in the 8(a) Program	Firm receives "a program term of nine years" but could be terminated or graduated early (13 C.F.R. §124.2)	Firm receives "a program term of nine years" but could be terminated or graduated early (13 C.F.R. §124.2)	Firm receives "a program term of nine years" but could be terminated or graduated early (13 C.F.R. §124.2)	Firm receives "a program term of nine years" but could be terminated or graduated early (13 C.F.R. §124.2)	Firm receives "a program term of nine years" but could be terminated or graduated early (13 C.F.R. §124.2)
One-time eligibility for 8(a) Program	Applies to both disadvantaged owners and firms (13 C.F.R. §124.108(b))	Applies only to tribally owned firms, not tribes (15 U.S.C. §636(j)(11)(B)-(C))	Applies only to ANC-owned firms, not ANCs (15 U.S.C. §636(j)(11)(B)-(C))	Applies only to NHO-owned firms, not NHOs (15 U.S.C. §636(j)(11)(B)-(C))	Applies only to CDC-owned firms, not CDCs (15 U.S.C. §636(j)(11)(B)-(C))
Limits on the amount of 8(a) contracts that a firm may receive	No source awards possible once the firm has received combined total of competitive and sole-source 8(a) contracts in excess of the dollar amount set forth in 13 C.F.R. §124.519 (13 C.F.R. §124.519(a))	Can make sole-source awards even when a firm has received combined total of competitive and sole-source 8(a) contracts in excess of the dollar amount set forth in 13 C.F.R. §124.519 (13 C.F.R. §124.519(a))	Can make sole-source awards even when a firm has combined total of competitive and sole-source 8(a) contracts in excess of the dollar amount set forth in 13 C.F.R. §124.519 (13 C.F.R. §124.519(a)) Firms must receive an increasing percentage of revenue from non-8(a) sources throughout their participation in the 8(a) Program (13 C.F.R. §124.509(b))	Can make sole-source awards even when a firm has combined total of competitive and sole-source 8(a) contracts in excess of the dollar amount set forth in 13 C.F.R. §124.519 (13 C.F.R. §124.519(a))	Combined total of competitive and sole-source 8(a) contracts in excess of the dollar amount set forth in 13 C.F.R. §124.519 not explicitly addressed in regulation

Appendix (Continued)

Requirements	8(a) Businesses Generally	Tribally Owned 8(a) Businesses	ANC-Owned 8(a) Businesses	NHO-Owned 8(a) Businesses	CDC-Owned 8(a) Businesses
	Firms must receive an increasing percentage of revenue from non-8(a) sources throughout their participation in the 8(a) Program (13 C.F.R. §124.509(b))	Firms must receive an increasing percentage of revenue from non-8(a) sources throughout their participation in the 8(a) Program (13 C.F.R. §124.509(b))		Firms must receive an increasing percentage of revenue from non-8(a) sources throughout their participation in the 8(a) Program (13 C.F.R. §124.509(b))	Firms must receive an increasing percentage of revenue from non-8(a) sources throughout their participation in the 8(a) Program (13 C.F.R. §124.509(b))

Source: Congressional Research Service.

[a] The rules governing NHO- and/or CDC-owned firms do not address this issue, and although the general rules apply where no "special rules" exist, it seems unlikely that NHO- and/or CDC-owned firms are treated differently than tribally or ANC-owned firms in this regard.

[b] These criteria include (1) the management experience of the disadvantaged individual(s) upon whom eligibility is based; (2) the business's technical experience; (3) the firm's capital; (4) the firm's performance record on prior federal or other contracts in its primary field of operations; and (5) whether the firm presently has, or can demonstrate its ability to timely obtain, the personnel, facilities, equipment, and other resources necessary to perform contracts under Section 8(a).

End Notes

[1] See generally CRS Report R41945, *Small Business Set-Aside Programs: An Overview and Recent Developments in the Law*, by Kate M. Manuel and Erika K. Lunder. The 8(a) Program takes its name from one of the sections of the Small Business Act that authorizes it. The program is also governed by Section 7(j) of the act.

[2] *See* Small Business Goaling Report: Fiscal Year 2011, available at https://www.fpds.gov /downloads /top_requests/FPDSNG_SB_Goaling_FY_2011.pdf. The report on FY2012 has not yet been compiled.

[3] Small Business Act of 1958, P.L. 85-536, §2(a), 72 Stat. 384 (July 18, 1958) (codified at 15 U.S.C. §631(a)).

[4] *See, e.g.*, Phil Izzo, Recession Over in June 2009, *Wall Street J.*, September 20, 2010, available at http://blogs.wsj.com/ economics/2010/09/20/nber-recession-ended-in-june-2009/ (discussing the recession of 2007- 2009).

[5] *See, e.g.*, Small Bus. Admin., The Small Business Economy: A Report to the President 3 (2009), available at http://www.sba.gov/ADVO/research/sb_econ2009.pdf ("The credit freeze in the short-term funding market had a devastating effect on the economy and small firms."); John Rosenthal, Tough Times Often Even Tougher on Minority Biz, *Chicago Business*, November 30, 2009, available at http://www.chicagobusiness.com/cgibin/mag/article.pl? articleId=32738&seenIt=1.

[6] *See, e.g.*, Mark Trumbull, Why Obama Job Creation Plan Focuses on Small Business, *The Christian Science Monitor*, December 8, 2009, available at http://features.csmonitor.com /politics/2009/12/08/why-obama-job-creation-planfocuses-on-small-business (noting that small businesses are reported to have created 65% of all new jobs in the United States over the past 15 years).

[7] Small Business Mobilization Act, P.L. 77-603, §4(f), 56 Stat. 351 (June 11, 1942).

[8] Act of July 31, 1951, P.L. 82-96, §110, 65 Stat. 131.

[9] P.L. 83-163, §207(c)-(d), 67 Stat. 230 (July 30, 1953).

[10] *See, e.g.*, H.Rept. 494, 83rd Cong., 1st sess., at 2 (1953) (stating that the SBA would "continue many of the functions of the [SDPA] in the present mobilization period and in addition would be given powers and duties to encourage and assist small-business enterprises in peacetime as well as in any future war or mobilization period"); S.Rept. 1714, 85th Cong., 2nd sess., at 9-10 (1958) (stating that the act would "put[] the procurement assistance program on a peacetime basis").

[11] P.L. 85-536, §8(a)(1)-(2), 72 Stat. 384 (July 18, 1958).

[12] *Id.*

[13] Thomas Jefferson Hasty, III, Minority Business Enterprise Development and the Small Business Administration's 8(a) Program: Past, Present, and (Is There a) Future? 145 *Mil. L. Rev.* 1, 8 (1994) ("[B]ecause the SBA believed that the efforts to start and operate an 8(a) program would not be worthwhile in terms of developing small business, the SBA's power to contract with other government agencies essentially went unused. The program actually lay dormant for about fifteen years until the racial atmosphere of the 1960s provided the impetus to wrestle the SBA's 8(a) authority from its dormant state.").

[14] Exec. Order No. 8802, 6 *Federal Register* 3,109 (June 25, 1941). Similar requirements were later imposed on nondefense contracts. See Exec. Order No. 9346, 8 *Federal Register* 7,182 (May 29, 1943).

[15] *See, e.g.*, Exec. Order No. 10308, 16 *Federal Register* 12,303 (December 3, 1951) (Truman); Exec. Order No. 10557, 19 *Federal Register* 5,655 (September 3, 1954) (Eisenhower); Exec. Order No. 10925, 26 *Federal Register* 1,977 (March 6, 1961) (Kennedy); Exec. Order No. 11458, 34 *Federal Register* 4,937 (March 7, 1969) (Nixon).

[16] *Report of the National Advisory Commission on Civil Disorders* 21 (1968).

[17] *See, e.g.*, Hasty, *supra* note 13, at 11-12.

[18] *See, e.g.*, Jonathan J. Bean, *Big Government and Affirmative Action: The Scandalous History of the Small Business Administration* 66 (2001).

[19] *See* Exec. Order No. 1625, 36 *Federal Register* 19,967 (October 13, 1971).

[20] 13 C.F.R. §124.8-1(b) (1970).

[21] 13 C.F.R. §124.8(c) (1973).

[22] S. Rep. No. 95-1070, 95th Cong., 2nd sess., at 14 (1978) ("One of the underlying reasons for the failure of this effort is that the program has no legislative basis."); H.Rept. 95-949, 95th Cong., 2nd sess., at 4 (1978) ("Congress has never extended legislative control over the activities of the 8(a) program, save through indirect appropriations, thereby permitting program operations.... [The] program is not as successful as it could be.").

[23] *See, e.g.*, Ray Billie Trash Hauling, Inc. v. Kleppe, 477 F.2d 696, 703-04 (5th Cir. 1973). In this case, the court particularly noted that the SBA's program was supported by congressional and presidential mandates issued after enactment of the Small Business Act in 1958. *Id.* at 705.

[24] P.L. 95-507, 92 Stat. 1757 (October 24, 1978).

[25] *Id.* at §202.

[26] *Id.* (codified at 15 U.S.C. §637(a)(4)(A)-(B)). Firms that are owned and controlled by Indian tribes, ANCs, or NHOs were later included within the definition of a "socially and economically disadvantaged small business concern." *See infra* notes 36-43 and accompanying text.

[27] *Id.* (codified at 15 U.S.C. §637(a)(5)).

[28] *Id.* at §201 (codified at 15 U.S.C. §631(f)(1)(C)). The meaning of "socially disadvantaged individuals" was the subject of much debate at the time of the 1978 amendments. Some Members of Congress, perhaps focusing on the SBA's use of its authority under §8(a) in 1968-1970, viewed the 8(a) Program as a program for African Americans and would have defined "social disadvantage" accordingly. *See, e.g.*, Parren J. Mitchell, Federal Affirmative Action for MBE's: An Historical Analysis, 1 *Nat'l Bar Ass'n Mag.* 46 (1983). Mitchell was a Member of the U.S. House of Representatives and leader of the Black Caucus when the 1978 amendments were enacted. Others favored a somewhat broader view, including both African Americans and Native Americans on the grounds that only those who did not come to the United States seeking the "American dream" should be deemed socially disadvantaged. *See, e.g.*, Testimony Before the House Comm. on Small Bus., Subcomm. on General Oversight & Minority Enter., Task Force on Minority Enter., 96th Cong., at 21 (1979). Yet others suggested that groups that are not racial or ethnic minorities should be able to qualify as "socially disadvantaged," or that individuals ought to be able to prove they are personally socially disadvantaged even if they are not racial or ethnic minorities. *See, e.g.*, H.Rept. 95-949, 95th Cong., 2nd sess., at 9 (1978) ("[T]he committee intends that the SBA give most serious consideration to, among others, women business owners" when determining which groups are socially disadvantaged.... [T]he bill does recognize that persons falling outside of the racial and ethnic groups presumed to be disadvantaged, may nevertheless be disadvantaged."). The bill that passed the House defined "socially disadvantaged individuals," in part, by establishing a rebuttable presumption that African Americans and Hispanic Americans are socially disadvantaged, while the bill that passed the Senate did not reference any racial or ethnic groups in defining "social disadvantage." *See, e.g.*, H.R. Conf. Rep. No. 95-1714, 95th Cong., 2nd sess., at 20 (1978); S.Rept. 95-1070, 95th Cong., 2nd sess., at 13-16 (1978). The conference committee reconciling the House and Senate versions ultimately arrived at a definition of "socially disadvantaged individuals" that was broader than the definition used in the SBA's 1973 regulation and included "those who have been subjected to racial or ethic prejudice or cultural bias because of their identity as a member of a group." P.L. 95-507, at §202. This definition did not incorporate the rebuttable presumption that members of certain groups are socially disadvantaged included in the House bill. However, the conference bill included congressional findings that "Black Americans, Hispanic Americans, Native Americans, and other minorities" are socially disadvantaged, thereby arguably achieving similar effect. *Id.* at §201.

[29] P.L. 95-507, at §202 (granting the SBA's Associate Administrator for Minority Small Business and Capital Ownership Development authority to make determinations regarding which other groups are socially disadvantaged); H.Rept. 95-949, *supra* note 28, at 9 (expressing the view that Sections 201 and 202 of the bill provide "sufficient discretion ... to allow SBA to designate any other additional minority group or persons it believes should be afforded the presumption of social ... disadvantage").

[30] *See* 13 C.F.R. §124.103(d)(2)(i)-(iii)(1980).

[31] 13 C.F.R. §124.103(b). Different groups are sometimes recognized as socially disadvantaged for purposes of other programs, such as those of the Department of Commerce's Minority Business Development Agency (MBDA). *See* 15 C.F.R. §1400.1(a). The SBA has rejected petitions from certain groups, including Hasidic Jews, women, disabled veterans, and Iranian-Americans. *See, e.g.*, George R. La Noue & John C. Sullivan, Gross Presumptions: Determining Group Eligibility for Federal Procurement Preferences, 41 *Santa Clara L. Rev.* 103, 127-29 (2000). However, Hasidic Jews are eligible to receive assistance from the MBDA, while women are deemed to be disadvantaged for purposes of the Department of Transportation's Disadvantaged Business Enterprise (DBE) program. *See* 49 U.S.C. §47113(a)(2) (DBE program); 15 C.F.R. §1400.1(c) (MBDA program).

[32] 13 C.F.R. §124.103(c)(2) (standards of evidence for showing personal disadvantage); 13 C.F.R. §124.103(b)(3) (mechanisms for rebutting the presumption of social disadvantage).

[33] P.L. 95-507, §202.

[34] 13 C.F.R. §124.104(c)(2). Some commentators estimate that 80 to 90% of Americans are economically disadvantaged under the SBA's net-worth requirements. *See, e.g.*, La Noue & Sullivan, *supra* note 31, at 108.

[35] 42 U.S.C. §9802.

[36] P.L. 97-35, Ch. 8, Subch. A, 95 Stat. 489 (1981) (codified at 42 U.S.C. §§9801 et seq.).

The "8(a) Program" for Small Businesses Owned and Controlled ...   231

[37] *Id.* at §626, 95 Stat. 496 (codified at 42 U.S.C. §9815).

[38] P.L. 99-272, §18015, 100 Stat. 370 (1986) (codified at 15 U.S.C.§637(a)(13)) (defining "Indian tribe" to include "any Indian tribe, band, nation, or other organized group or community of Indians, including any Alaska Native village or regional or village corporation (within the meaning of the Alaska Native Claims Settlement Act (43 U.S.C.§1606)) which—(A) is recognized as eligible for the special programs and services provided by the United States to Indians because of their status as Indians, or (B) is recognized as such by the State in which such tribe, band, nation, group, or community resides."). An Alaska Native Corporation is "any Regional Corporation, Village Corporation, Urban Corporation or Group Corporation organized under laws of Alaska in accordance with the Alaska Native Claims Settlement Act." 13 C.F.R. §124.3. An Alaska Native is any "citizen of the United States who is a person of one-fourth degree or more Alaskan Indian ..., Eskimo, Aleut blood, or a combination of those bloodlines. The term includes, in the absence of proof of a minimum blood quantum, any citizen whom a Native village or Native group regards as an Alaska Native if their father or mother is regarded as an Alaska Native." 13 C.F.R. §124.3.

[39] P.L. 99-272, §18015, 100 Stat. 370 (codified at 15 U.S.C. §637(a)(4)).

[40] P.L. 102-415, §10, 106 Stat. 2115 (1992) (codified at 43 U.S.C. §1626(e)).

[41] P.L. 100-656, §207, 102 Stat. 3861 (1988) (codified at 15 U.S.C. §637(a)(4)).

[42] *Id.* (codified at 15 U.S.C. §637(a)(15)). A "Native Hawaiian" is "any individual whose ancestors were natives, prior to 1778, of the area which now comprises the state of Hawaii." 13 C.F.R. §124.3.

[43] *See, e.g.*, 13 C.F.R. §124.109(a) ("*Special rules for ANCs.* Small business concerns owned and controlled by ANCs are eligible for participation in the 8(a) program and must meet the eligibility criteria set forth in §124.112 to the extent the criteria are not inconsistent with this section.") (emphasis in original).

[44] *See also* CRS Report R40855, *Contracting Programs for Alaska Native Corporations: Historical Development and Legal Authorities*, by Kate M. Manuel, John R. Luckey, and Jane M. Smith (discussing contracting with ANC-owned firms through the 8(a) Program and other programs).

[45] 13 C.F.R. §124.101. The Office of Legal Counsel at the Department of Justice has opined that SBA regulations limiting eligibility for the 8(a) Program to citizens do not deprive resident aliens of due process in violation of the Fifth Amendment to the U.S. Constitution. *See* U.S. Dep't of Justice, Office of Legal Counsel, Constitutionality of 13 C.F.R. §124.103 Establishing Citizenship Requirement for Participation in 8(a) Program, March 4, 1996, available at http://www.justice.gov/olc/sba8.htm.

[46] The SBA's Office of Hearings and Appeals has, for example, developed a seven-part test for determining whether a small business is "unusually reliant" on a contractor that is used in determining affiliation. *See* Valenzuela Eng'g, Inc. & Curry Contracting Co., Inc., SBA-4151 (1996).

[47] *See* 13 C.F.R. §124.112 (a) ("In order for a concern ... to remain eligible for 8(a) ... program participation, it must continue to meet all eligibility criteria contained in [Section] 124.101 through [Section] 124.108.").

[48] 13 C.F.R. §121.105(a)(1). "Business" is separately defined for small agricultural cooperatives. *See* 13 C.F.R. §121.105(a)(2).

[49] 13 C.F.R. §121.105(b).

[50] 15 U.S.C. §632(a)(1)-(2)(A).

[51] 13 C.F.R. §§121.101-121.108. The number of employees is the average of each pay period for the preceding twelve calendar months. Gross income is based on the average for the last three completed fiscal years. It includes all revenues, not just those from the firm's primary industry. *See* IMDT, Inc., SBA-4121 (1995).

[52] 13 C.F.R. §121.201.

[53] 13 C.F.R. §121.103(a)(1). Control, or the power of control, need only exist. It need not be exercised for affiliation to be found.

[54] 13 C.F.R. §121.103(a)(6).

[55] 13 C.F.R. §121.103(h) ("[A] specific joint venture entity generally may not be awarded more than three contracts over a two year period, starting from the date of the award of the first contract, without the partners to the joint venture being deemed affiliated for all purposes.").

[56] 13 C.F.R. §121.103(h)(4) ("A contractor and its ostensible subcontractor are treated as joint venturers, and therefore affiliates, for size determination purposes. An ostensible subcontractor is a subcontractor that performs primary and vital requirements of a contract, or of an order under a multiple award schedule contract, or a subcontractor upon which the prime contractor is unusually reliant.").

[57] 13 C.F.R. §121.103(i) ("Affiliation may arise ... through ... common ownership, common management or excessive restrictions on the sale of the franchise interest.").

[58] 15 U.S.C. §637(a)(4)(A)(i)-(ii) (requiring at least 51% unconditional ownership); 13 C.F.R. §124.105.

[59] 13 C.F.R. §124.3.

[60] 13 C.F.R. §124.105(a).

[61] 13 C.F.R. §124.105(h)(1). Ownership is limited to 10% when the 8(a) firm in is the "developmental stage" of the 8(a) Program and 20% when it is in the "transitional stage." *Id*. For more on the developmental and transitional stages, see *infra* notes 109-111 and accompanying text.

[62] 13 C.F.R. §124.105(h)(2).

[63] 15 U.S.C. §637(a)(4)(A)(i)-(ii) (requiring control of management and daily business operations); 13 C.F.R. §124.106.

[64] 13 C.F.R. §124.106.

[65] *Id.*

[66] 13 C.F.R. §124.106(a)(3).

[67] 13 C.F.R. §124.106(a)(2).

[68] 13 C.F.R. §124.106(e).

[69] 13 C.F.R. §124.106(e)(1) & (3).

[70] 13 C.F.R. §124.103(a). *See also* 15 U.S.C. §637(a)(5).

[71] 13 C.F.R. §124.103(b)(1). If required by the SBA, individuals claiming membership in these groups must demonstrate that they held themselves out and are recognized by others as members of the designated group(s). 13 C.F.R. §124.103(b)(2).

[72] 13 C.F.R. §124.103(b)(3).

[73] 13 C.F.R. §124.103(c)(1).

[74] 13 C.F.R. §124.103(c)(2)(i)-(iii).

[75] 13 C.F.R. §124.103(c)(2)(iii).

[76] 13 C.F.R. §124.103(d)(4). Groups petitioning for recognition as socially disadvantaged do not always obtain it. Over the years, the SBA has rejected petitions from Hasidic Jews, women, disabled veterans, and Iranian-Americans. *See supra* note 31.

[77] 13 C.F.R. §124.104(a). *See also* 15 U.S.C. §637(a)(6)(A).

[78] 13 C.F.R. §124.104(b)(1).

[79] 13 C.F.R. §124.104(c). *See also* 15 U.S.C. §637(a)(6)(E)(i)-(ii).

[80] 13 C.F.R. §124.104(c)(2).

[81] *Id.*

[82] *Id.*

[83] 13 C.F.R. §124.108(a)(1)-(5). For more on debarment and suspension, see CRS Report RL34753, *Debarment and Suspension of Government Contractors: An Overview of the Law Including Recently Enacted and Proposed Amendments*, by Kate M. Manuel.

[84] 13 C.F.R. §124.107. Specifically, "[i]ncome tax returns for each of the two previous tax years must show operating revenues in the primary industry in which the applicant is seeking 8(a) ... certification." 13 C.F.R. §124.107(a).

[85] 15 U.S.C. §637(a)(7)(A) ("reasonable prospects for success"); 13 C.F.R. §124.107(b)(1)(i)-(v).

[86] SBA may delegate the function of executing contracts to the procuring agencies and often does so. *See* 13 C.F.R. §124.501(a).

[87] Set-asides may be total or partial. *See* 48 C.F.R. §19.502-3(a).

[88] 15 U.S.C. §644(a) (describing when set-asides for small businesses are permissible); 41 U.S.C. §3303(b) (CICA provision authorizing set-asides for small businesses); 48 C.F.R. §§6.203-6.206 (set-asides for small business generally, 8(a) small businesses, Historically Underutilized Business Zone (HUBZone) small businesses, and service-disabled veteran-owned small businesses). CICA authorizes competitions excluding all sources other than small businesses when such competitions assure that a "fair proportion of the total purchases and contracts for property and services for the Federal Government shall be placed with small business concerns." 41 U.S.C. §3104. CICA also permits sole-source awards when such awards are made pursuant to a procedure expressly authorized by statute, or when special circumstances exist (e.g., urgent and compelling circumstances). *See* 10 U.S.C. §2304(c)(1) (defense agency procurements) & 41 U.S.C. §§3301 & 3304(a)(3)(A) (civilian agency procurements). For more on competition in federal contracting, see CRS Report R40516, *Competition in Federal Contracting: An Overview of the Legal Requirements*, by Kate M. Manuel.

[89] 15 U.S.C. §644(g)(1)-(2).

[90] They also count toward a separate goal for the percentage of federal procurement dollars awarded to small businesses generally. Currently, the government-wide goal is that 5% of all federal contract and subcontract dollars be spent with small disadvantaged businesses, including 8(a) businesses. Most agencies also have a 5%

goal. *See* Small Business Goaling Report, *supra* note 7. The government-wide goal was met in FY2011, the most recent year for which information is available, when 7.67% of all federal procurement dollars was spent with small disadvantaged businesses. *Id.* Performance by the large procuring agencies varies, from 1.9% (Department of Energy) to 47.4% (SBA). *Id.*

[91] *See* 13 C.F.R. §124.1002 (defining "small disadvantaged business").

[92] *See, e.g.*, AHNTECH, Inc., B-401092 (April 22, 2009) ("The [Small Business] Act affords the SBA and contracting agencies broad discretion in selecting procurements for the 8(a) program.").

[93] Even in this situation, SBA may accept the requirement under "extraordinary circumstances." 13 C.F.R. §124.504(a); Madison Servs., Inc., B-400615 (December 11, 2008) (finding that extraordinary circumstances existed when the agency's initial small business set-aside was erroneous and did not reflect its intentions).

[94] However, offers of requirements below the simplified acquisition threshold (generally $150,000) are "assume[d]" to have been accepted at the time they are made, and the agency may proceed with the award if it does not receive a reply from SBA within two days of sending the offer. 13 C.F.R. §124.503(a)(4)(i). *See also* Eagle Collaborative Computing Servs., Inc., B-401043.3 (January 28, 2011) (finding that an agency properly awarded a sole-source contract valued below the simplified acquisition threshold even though SBA never accepted the requirements).

[95] 13 C.F.R. §124.504(a)-(c). The third provision applies only to preexisting requirements. It does not apply to new contracts, follow-on or renewal contracts, or procurements under $150,000. *Id.* Also, under its regulations, SBA must presume an adverse impact when:

a) The small business concern has performed the specific requirement for at least 24 months;

b) The small business is performing the requirement at the time it is offered to the 8(a) ... program, or its performance of the requirement ended within 30 days of the procuring activity's offer of the requirement to the 8(a) ... program; and

c) The dollar value of the requirement that the small business is or was performing is 25 percent or more of its most recent annual gross sales (including those of its affiliates).

13 C.F.R. §124.504(c)(1)(i)(A)-(C).

[96] 15 U.S.C. §637(a)(1)(A); 48 C.F.R. §19.806(b). Fair market price is estimated by looking at recent prices for similar items or work, in the case of repeat purchases, or by considering commercial prices for similar products or services, available in-house cost estimates, cost or pricing data submitted by the contractor, or data from other government agencies, in the case of new purchases. 15 U.S.C. §637(a)(3)(B)(i)-(iii); 48 C.F.R. §19.807(b) & (c).

[97] 15 U.S.C. §637(a)(1)(A). *See also* Totolo v. United States, 87 Fed. Cl. 680, 695 (2009) ("The manner in which [an agency] assesses its needs is a business judgment and lies within its own discretionary domain."); JT Constr. Co., B254257 (December 6, 1993) (stating that it is a business judgment, within the contracting officer's discretion, to decide not to set aside a competition for small businesses). For a time in 2008-2010, the federal courts and the Government Accountability Office (GAO) found that set-asides for Historically Underutilized Business Zone (HUBZone) small businesses had "precedence" over set-asides for 8(a) firms. *See generally* CRS Report R40591, *Set-Asides for Small Businesses: Recent Developments in the Law Regarding Precedence Among the Set-Aside Programs and Set-Asides Under Indefinite-Delivery/Indefinite-Quantity Contracts*, by Kate M. Manuel. However, the Small Business Act was amended on September 27, 2010, to remove the language that formed the basis for these decisions. Small Business Jobs Act of 2010, P.L. 111-240, §1347,124 Stat. 2546-47 (September 27, 2010).

[98] *See, e.g.*, Rothe Computer Solutions, LLC, B-299452 (May 9, 2007).

[99] 15 U.S.C. §637(a)(16)(A). A noncompetitive award may be made under this authority so long as (1) the firm is determined to be a responsible contractor for performance of the contract; (2) the award of the contract would be consistent with the firm's business plan; and (3) award of the contract would not result in the firm exceeding the percentage of revenue from 8(a) sources forecast in its annual business plan. 15 U.S.C. §637(a)(16)(A)(i)-(iii).

[100] 15 U.S.C. §637(a)(1)(D)(ii); 48 C.F.R. §19.805-1(d). However, competitive awards for contracts whose anticipated value is less than $4 million ($6.5 million for manufacturing contracts) can be made with the approval of the SBA's Associate Administrator for 8(a) Business Development. 15 U.S.C. §637(a)(1)(D)(i)(I)-(II); 48 C.F.R. §19.805-1(d).

[101] 48 C.F.R. §19.805-1(b)(1)-(2) (sole-source awards to tribally or ANC-owned firms); 48 C.F.R. §219.805-1(b)(2)(A)-(B) (sole-source awards to NHO-owned firms). Prior to enactment of the National Defense Authorization Act (NDAA) for FY2010, contracting officers making sole-source awards in reliance on the second exception did not have to justify such awards or obtain approval of them from higher-level agency

officials. The NDAA changed this by requiring justifications, approvals, and notices for sole-source contracts in excess of $20 million awarded under the authority of §8(a) similar to those required for sole-source contracts awarded under the general contracting authorities. *Compare* P.L. 111-84, §811, 123 Stat. 2405-06 (October 28, 2009) *with* 10 U.S.C. §2304(c) & (f) (procurements of defense agencies); 41 U.S.C. §3304(a) & (e) (procurements of civilian agencies).

[102] 48 C.F.R. §19.805-1(c).

[103] 48 C.F.R. §19.805-2(d).

[104] 15 U.S.C. §636(j)(10)(C)(i) (nine-year term); 15 U.S.C. §637(a)(9) (termination and early graduation); 13 C.F.R. §124.301 (exiting the 8(a) Program); 13 C.F.R. §124.302 (early graduation); 13 C.F.R. §124.303 (termination from the Program).

[105] 15 U.S.C. §636(j)(11)(B)-(C); 13 C.F.R. §124.108(b).

[106] 13 C.F.R. §124.108(b)(4).

[107] 13 C.F.R. §124.105(g)(1). SBA may waive this prohibition if the firms have no connections in terms of ownership, control, or contractual relationships. *Id.*

[108] 13 C.F.R. §124.519(a). Currently, this section does not specify an amount. However, prior to being amended in 2011, Subsections 124.519(a)(1) and (2) specified the applicable amounts as $100 million, in the case of firms whose size is based on their number of employees, or an amount equivalent to the lesser of (1) $100 million or (2) five times the size standard for the industry, in the case of firms whose size is based on their revenues. 13 C.F.R. §124.519(a)(1)- (2) (2010). The Administrator of the SBA may waive this requirement if the head of the procuring agency represents that a sole-source award to a firm is necessary "to achieve significant interests of the Government." 13 C.F.R. §124.519(e). Even after they have received a combined total of competitive and sole-source awards in excess of $100 million, or other applicable amount, firms may still receive competitive contracts under the 8(a) Program. 13 C.F.R. §124.519(b).

[109] 15 U.S.C. §636(j)(10)(I)(i)-(iii); 13 C.F.R. §124.509(b)(1).

[110] 13 C.F.R. §124.509(b)(2).

[111] 13 C.F.R. §124.509(d)(1). This prohibition may be waived when the Director of the Office of Business Development finds that denial of a sole-source contract would cause severe economic hardship for the firm, potentially jeopardizing its survival, or when extenuating circumstances beyond the firm's control caused it to miss its target. 13 C.F.R. §125.509(e).

[112] 15 U.S.C. 637(a)(14)(A)-(B); 15 U.S.C. §644(o); 13 C.F.R. §125.6; 48 C.F.R. §52.219-14.

[113] 13 C.F.R. §124.510 (limits on subcontracting for 8(a) firms); 13 C.F.R. §125.6(a)(1)-(4) (limits on subcontracting for small businesses generally).

[114] 13 C.F.R. §124.109(c)(3)(i) (tribally and ANC-owned firms); 13 C.F.R. §124.110 (b) (NHO-owned firms); 13 C.F.R. §124.111(c) (CDC-owned firms).

[115] 13 C.F.R. §§124.109-124.111.

[116] 13 C.F.R. §124.109(c)(2)(i) (tribally and ANC-owned firms); 13 C.F.R. §124.110(b) (NHO-owned firms); 13 C.F.R. §124.111(c) (CDC-owned firms).

[117] 13 C.F.R. §124.109(c)(2)(iii) (tribally and ANC-owned firms); 13 C.F.R. §124.110(b) (NHO-owned firms); 13 C.F.R. §124.111(c) (CDC-owned firms). It is unclear how the language here, stating that "any other business enterprise owned by [an organization]" shall be excluded from the size determination, is to be reconciled with that in 13 C.F.R. §121.103(b)(2)(ii), which suggests that businesses owned and controlled by organizations could be found to be affiliates of the organization for reasons other than common ownership or management, or performance of common administrative services.

[118] *See, e.g.,* Valenzuela Eng'g, Inc. & Curry Contracting Co., Inc., SBA-4151 (1996) (rejecting a challenge to the size of an ANC-owned firm because its subcontractor performed less than 25% of the work on the contract and was not its affiliate); Gov't Accountability Office, Increased Used of Alaska Native Corporations' Special 8(a) Provisions Calls for Tailored Oversight, GAO-06-399, at 29 (April 2006) (describing "early graduation" of ANC-owned 8(a) firms).

[119] 13 C.F.R. §124.109(a) & (b) (requiring tribally and ANC-owned firms to comply with the general eligibility requirements where they are not contrary to or inconsistent with the special requirements for these entities); 13 C.F.R. §124.110(a) (similar provision for NHO-owned firms); 13 C.F.R. §124.111(a) (similar provision for CDC-owned firms).

[120] 13 C.F.R. §124.109(a)(3).

[121] 13 C.F.R. §124.109(a) & (b) (requiring tribally and ANC-owned firms to comply with the general eligibility requirements where they are not contrary to or inconsistent with the special requirements for these entities); 13

The "8(a) Program" for Small Businesses Owned and Controlled ...   235

C.F.R. §124.110(a) (similar provision for NHO-owned firms); 13 C.F.R. §124.111(a) (similar provision for CDC-owned firms).

[122] 13 C.F.R. §124.109(c)(4)(B).

[123] *See* 13 C.F.R. §124.110(d) (stating only that "[a]n individual responsible for the day-to-day management of an NHO-owned firm need not establish personal social and economic disadvantage").

[124] 13 C.F.R. §124.110(a) ("Concerns owned by economically disadvantaged Native Hawaiian Organizations, as defined in [Section] 124.3, are eligible for participation in the 8(a) program and other federal programs requiring SBA to determine social and economic disadvantage as a condition of eligibility. Such concerns must meet all eligibility criteria set forth in [Section] 124.101 through 124.108 and [Section] 124.112 to the extent that they are not inconsistent with this section.").

[125] 13 C.F.R. §124.111(b).

[126] 13 C.F.R. §124.109(b)(1) (tribally and ANC-owned firms); 15 U.S.C. §637(a)(4)(A)(i)(II) (NHO-owned firms); Small Disadvantaged Business Certification Application: Community Development Corporation (CDC) Owned Concern, OMB Approval No. 3245-0317 ("A Community Development Corporation (CDC) is considered to be a socially and economically disadvantaged entity if the parent CDC is a nonprofit organization responsible to residents of the area it serves which has received financial assistance under 42 U.S.C. 9805, et seq."). SBA's authority to designate CDCs as socially and economically disadvantaged derives from 42 U.S.C. §9815(a)(2). *See* 42 U.S.C. §9815(a)(2) ("Not later than 90 days after August 13, 1981, the Administrator of the Small Business Administration, after consultation with the Secretary, shall promulgate regulations to ensure the availability to community development corporations of such programs as shall further the purposes of this subchapter, including programs under §637(a) of title 15.").

[127] 43 U.S.C. §1626(e)(1) ("For all purposes of Federal law, a Native Corporation shall be considered to be a corporation owned and controlled by Natives and a minority and economically disadvantaged business enterprise if the Settlement Common Stock of the corporation and other stock of the corporation held by holders of Settlement Common Stock and by Natives and descendants of Natives, represents a majority of both the total equity of the corporation and the total voting power of the corporation for the purposes of electing directors."); 13 C.F.R. §124.109(a)(2) (same).

[128] *See* Small Disadvantaged Business Certification Application, *supra* note 125.

[129] 15 U.S.C. §637(a)(6)(A); 13 C.F.R. §124.109(b)(2)(i)-(vii).

[130] 13 C.F.R. §124.109(b).

[131] 13 C.F.R. §124.110(c)(1).

[132] *Id.* If the NHO has no members, then a majority of the members of the board of directors must qualify as economically disadvantaged.

[133] 13 C.F.R. §124.109(c)(7)(ii).

[134] *See supra* note 120 and accompanying text.

[135] 13 C.F.R. §124.111(g).

[136] 13 C.F.R. §124.109(c)(6)(i)-(iii) (ANC- and tribally-owned firms); 13 C.F.R. §124.110(g)(1)-(3) (NHO-owned firms); 13 C.F.R. §124.111(f)(1)-(3) (CDC-owned firms).

[137] *See supra* note 84 and accompanying text.

[138] *See supra* note 85 and accompanying text.

[139] Daniel K. Oakes, Inching Toward Balance: Reaching Proper Reform of the Alaska Native Corporations' 8(a) Contracting Preferences, 40 *Pub. Cont. L.J.* 777 (2011).

[140] Regulations promulgated by SBA in February 2011 provided that this reporting requirement would be effective "as of September 9, 2011, unless SBA further delays implementation through a Notice in the Federal Register." Small Bus. Admin., Small Business Size Regulations; 8(a) Business Development/Small Disadvantaged Business Status Determinations: Final Rule, 76 *Federal Register* 8222 (February 11, 2011). SBA appears to have delayed reporting through three such notices, two announcing tribal consultations about the reporting requirements, and a third announcing SBA's intent to request approval of an information collection in accordance with the Paperwork Reduction Act of 1995. See Small Bus. Admin., 60 Day Notice and Request for Comments, 76 *Federal Register* 63983 (October 14, 2011); Small Bus. Admin., Notice of Tribal Consultations, 76 *Federal Register* 27859 (May 13, 2011); Small Bus. Admin., Notice of Tribal Consultations, 76 *Federal Register* 12273 (March 7, 2011).

[141] 13 C.F.R. §124.604.

[142] An Act To Amend the Small Business Act To Reform the Capital Ownership Development Program, and for Other Purposes; P.L. 100-656, §602(a), 102 Stat. 3887-88 (November 15, 1988) (codified at 15 U.S.C. §637 note); 48 C.F.R. §19.805-1(b)(2).

[143] The authority for DOD to make sole-source awards to NHO-owned firms of contracts valued at more than $4 million ($6.5 million for manufacturing contracts) even if contracting officers reasonably expect that offers will be received from at least two responsible small businesses existed on a temporary basis in 2004-2006 and became permanent in 2006. *See* Department of Defense, Emergency Supplemental Appropriations to Address Hurricanes in the Gulf of Mexico, and Pandemic Influenza Act of 2006, P.L. 109-148, §8020, 119 Stat. 2702-03 (December 30, 2005) ("[Provided] [t]hat, during the current fiscal year and hereafter, businesses certified as 8(a) by the Small Business Administration pursuant to section 8(a)(15) of Public Law 85-536, as amended, shall have the same status as other program participants under section 602 of P.L. 100-656 ... for purposes of contracting with agencies of the Department of Defense."); 48 C.F.R. §219.805-1(b)(2)(A)-(B).

[144] *See supra* note 102.

[145] 13 C.F.R. §124.109(a) & (b) (requiring tribally and ANC-owned firms to comply with the general eligibility requirements where they are not contrary to or inconsistent with special requirements for these entities); 13 C.F.R. §124.110(a) (similar provision for NHO-owned firms); 13 C.F.R. §124.111(a) (similar provision for CDC-owned firms).

[146] 15 U.S.C. §644(o); 13 C.F.R. §125.6; 48 C.F.R. §52.219-14.

[147] 13 C.F.R. §124.109(a) & (b) (ANC- and tribally-owned firms); 13 C.F.R. §124.110(a) (NHO-owned firms); 13 C.F.R. §124.111(a) (CDC-owned firms).

[148] *Id.*; 15 U.S.C. §636(j)(11)(B)-(C).

[149] 13 C.F.R. §124.109(c)(3)(ii) (tribally and ANC-owned firms); 13 C.F.R. §124.110(e) (NHO-owned firms); 13 C.F.R. §124.111(d) (CDC-owned firms). These regulations also provide that an 8(a) firm owned by an ANC, Indian tribe, NHO, or CDC may not, within its first two years in the 8(a) Program, receive a sole-source contract that is a follow-on to an 8(a) contract currently performed by an 8(a) firm owned by that entity, or previously performed by an 8(a) firm owned by that entity that left the program within the past two years. *Id.* In addition, there are restrictions on the percentage of work that may be performed by any non-8(a) venturer(s) in joint ventures involving 8(a) firms. *See generally* 13 C.F.R. §124.513.

[150] 13 C.F.R. §124.109(c)(3)(ii) (tribally and ANC-owned firms); 13 C.F.R. §124.110(e) (NHO-owned firms); 13 C.F.R. §124.111(d) (CDC-owned firms).

[151] 13 C.F.R. §124.519(a). *See supra* note 108.

[152] 13 C.F.R. §124.509.

[153] *See, e.g.*, *Ray Baillie Trash Hauling*, 477 F.3d at 710 ("The plaintiffs never applied for participation in the section 8(a) program. Furthermore, they do not even contend that they are socially or economically disadvantaged and therefore eligible for participation in the program."); SRS Techs., Inc. v. U.S. Dep't of Defense, No. 96-1484, 1997 U.S. App. LEXIS 10143 (4th Cir., May 6, 1997) ("SBA's requirement of economic disadvantage for entry into the 8(a) Program is a race-neutral criterion. It was by virtue of this race-neutral criterion that plaintiff failed to qualify for a contract award, and its standing to challenge the race-conscious criteria is therefore lacking."). *But see* C.S. McCrossan Constr. Co., Inc. v. Cook, No. 95-1345-HB, 1996 U.S. Dist. LEXIS 14721 (D.N.M., April 2, 1996) ("Although Defendants attempt to characterize this set-aside program as one based on size and economic status of the owner, the fact remains that 'economic disadvantage' requires a showing of 'social disadvantage' which then implicates the race-based challenge. ... Plaintiff is not seeking admission into the 8(a) program. It is challenging the government's preferential treatment towards 8(a) program participants in the bidding of the job order contract.").

[154] *See, e.g.*, Cortez III Service Corp. v. Nat'l Aeronautics & Space Admin., 950 F. Supp. 357, 361 (D.D.C. 1996) (finding that the 8(a) Program is facially constitutional, but that "agencies have a responsibility to decide whether there has been a history of discrimination in the particular industry at issue" prior to procuring requirements through the 8(a) Program); Fordice Constr. Co. v. Marsh, 773 F. Supp. 867 (S.D. Miss. 1990) ("The court ... finds that the United States Army Corps of Engineers failed to give consideration to the impact of a 100% set-aside upon non-§8(a) eligible contractors in the Vicksburg area.").

[155] No. 95-2301 (EGS), 2012 U.S. Dist. LEXIS 114807 (D.D.C., August 15, 2012), at *29, *90. If the 8(a) Program as it presently exists, with its presumption that minorities are socially disadvantaged, were ever found to be unconstitutional on its face, the program could potentially be reconstituted without the presumption. Such a program might require proof of actual social disadvantage from all applicants to the 8(a) Program, perhaps using the same three criteria currently used by individual applicants demonstrating personal social disadvantage. *See* 13 C.F.R. §124.103(c)(2) (standards of evidence for showing personal disadvantage). Alternatively, the 8(a) Program could potentially continue as a program for small businesses owned by Indian tribes, ANCs, NHOs, or CDCs because tribes and other entities are generally not seen as constituting racial groups. Morton v. Mancari, 417 U.S. 535, 548 (1973) (treating the category of "Native Americans" as a

The "8(a) Program" for Small Businesses Owned and Controlled ... 237

political class, not a racial one, and describing programs targeting Native Americans as "reasonably designed to further the cause of Indian self-government"). The presumption of social and/or economic disadvantage accorded to these groups would thus not implicate a racial classification and would probably be subject only to "rational basis" review. Rational basis review is characterized by deference to legislative judgment, and the party challenging a government program must show that it is not rationally related to a legitimate government interest. *See* Craig v. Boren, 429 U.S. 190, 197 (1976).

[156] *DynaLantic*, 2012 U.S. Dist. LEXIS 114807, at *72.

[157] *Id*. at *31-*32. The court also rejected DynaLantic's argument that the government may only seek to remedy discrimination by a government entity, or by private individuals directly using government funds to discriminate. The court viewed these arguments as foreclosed by prior decisions holding that, under the Fourteenth Amendment, the government may implement race-conscious programs "to prevent itself from acting as a 'passive participant' in private discrimination in the relevant industries or markets." *Id*. at 31 (quoting *City of Richmond v. J.A. Croson*, 488 U.S. 469, 492 (1989)).

[158] *Id*. at *40 ("Reports prepared by the GAO and investigations conducted by both the executive and legislative branches prior to the 1978 codification showed that the Section 8(a) program had fallen far short of its goal to develop businesses owned by disadvantaged individuals, and that one reason for this failure was that the program had no legislative basis.").

[159] *Id*. at *43 (quoting H.Rept. 1714, 95th Cong., 2nd sess., at 22-23 (1978)).

[160] *Id*. at *33-*34.

[161] *Id*. at *48. DynaLantic had asserted that post-enactment evidence of discrimination should not be considered. However, the court concluded that it was proper to consider such evidence, particularly where the "statute is over thirty years old and the evidence used to justify Section 8(a) [at the time of its enactment] is stale for purposes of determining a compelling interest in the present." *Id*.

[162] *Id*. at *132-*135.

[163] *Id*. at *137-*140.

[164] *Id*. at *144-*150.

[165] Adarand Constructors, Inc. v . Peña, 515 U.S. 200, 238 (1995).

[166] Grutter v. Bollinger, 539 U.S. 306, 341 (2003).

[167] *DynaLantic*, 2012 U.S. Dist. LEXIS 114807, at *120.

[168] *Id*. at *72. The government attempted to assert that, "as a matter of law, [it] need not tie evidence of discriminatory barriers to minority business formation and development to evidence of discrimination in any particular industry." *Id*. at *118. However, the court rejected this position as inconsistent with Supreme Court precedent, which it construed as making "clear that the government must provide evidence demonstrating there were *eligible minorities in the relevant market* ... that were denied entry or access notwithstanding their eligibility." *Id*.

[169] *Id*. at *154. DOD, however, has responded to the *DynaLantic* decision by prohibiting the award of contracts for "military simulators or any services in the military simulator industry," a prohibition that applies to "all future contract awards, including extensions of existing contracts or the exercise of options on existing contracts." Dep't of Defense, Office of the Under Secretary of Defense, Immediate Cessation of Small Business Development Program (8(a) Program) Procurement Contracts for Military Simulators or Services in the Military Simulator Industry, August 22, 2012, available at http://www.acq.osd.mil/dpap /policy/policyvault/USA004988-12-DPAP.pdf. Some commentators have criticized this decision, in part, on the grounds that it prohibits the procurement of goods or services in this industry, while the *DynaLantic* decision addressed only goods. *See, e.g.*, National Minority Organizations Respond to Federal *DynaLantic Corp*. Decision, *PR Newswire*, August 31, 2012, available at http://www.prnewswire.com /news-releases/national-minority-organizations-respond-to-federal-court-dynalantic-corp-decision-168192866.html.

[170] *See, e.g.*, Danielle Ivory, Minority Vendors Say Awards Program at Risk on U.S. Court Ruling, *Bloomberg Gov't*, September 13, 2012 (quoting Alan Chvotkin, counsel and executive vice president of the Professional Services Council, as saying that the *DynaLantic* ruling may "open the door to more lawsuits," and "[t]he implications across the government could be significant").

[171] *See supra* note 153 and accompanying text.

[172] *See, e.g.*, Federal Spending Cuts Mean Fiercer Competition for Contractors and Higher Need for Market Research, According to US Federal Contractor Registration, *SFGate*, September 22, 2011, available at http://www.sfgate.com/ business/article/Federal-Spending-Cuts-Mean-Fiercer-Competition-2304840.php.

[173] Rothe Dev., Inc. v. Dep't of Defense, No. 12-CV-744, Original Complaint (filed D.D.C., May 9, 2012).

[174] 545 F.3d 1023 (Fed. Cir. 2008). For more on the *Rothe* decision, see generally CRS Report R40440, *Rothe Development Corporation v. Department of Defense: The Constitutionality of Federal Contracting Programs for Minority-Owned and Other Small Businesses*, by Jody Feder and Kate M. Manuel.

[175] In particular, the *DynaLantic* court relied on the precedent of *United States v. Salerno* in requiring that a plaintiff in a facial challenge must establish "that no set of circumstances exists under which [Section 8(a)] would be valid." *DynaLantic*, 2012 U.S. Dist. LEXIS 114807, at *23 (quoting *Salerno*, 481 U.S. 739, 745 (1987)). The *Rothe* court, in contrast, declined to apply this requirement of *Salerno* to the facial challenge to the program it struck down. *See Rothe*, 545 F.3d at 1032.

In: Small Business Administration Programs
Editor: Walter Janikowski

ISBN: 978-1-62417-992-1
© 2013 Nova Science Publishers, Inc.

Chapter 9

SMALL BUSINESS ADMINISTRATION HUBZONE PROGRAM[*]

Robert Jay Dilger

SUMMARY

The Small Business Administration (SBA) administers several programs to support small businesses, including the Historically Underutilized Business Zone Empowerment Contracting (HUBZone) program. The HUBZone program is a small business federal contracting assistance program "whose primary objective is job creation and increasing capital investment in distressed communities." It provides participating small businesses located in areas with low income, high poverty rates, or high unemployment rates with contracting opportunities in the form of "set-asides," sole-source awards, and price-evaluation preferences. Firms must be certified by the SBA to participate in the HUBZone program. On December 4, 2012, there were 5,667 certified HUBZone small businesses.

In FY2011, the federal government awarded 91,864 contracts valued at $9.9 billion to HUBZonecertified businesses, with about $2.75 billion of that amount awarded through a HUBZone set-aside, sole source, or price-evaluation preference award. The program's FY2011 administrative cost was about $15.6 million. Its FY2013 appropriation is just over $2.5 million, with the additional cost of administering the program provided by the SBA's appropriation for general administrative expenses.

Congressional interest in the HUBZone program has increased in recent years, primarily due to reports of fraud in the program. Some Members have called for the program's termination. Others have recommended that the SBA continue its efforts to improve its administration of the program, especially its efforts to prevent fraud.

This report examines the arguments presented both for and against targeting assistance to geographic areas with specified characteristics, such as low income, high poverty, or high unemployment, as opposed to providing assistance to people or businesses with specified characteristics. It then assesses the arguments presented both for and against the continuation of the HUBZone program.

---

[*] This is an edited, reformatted and augmented version of Congressional Research Service, Publication No. R41268, dated December 13, 2012.

The report also discusses the HUBZone program's structure and operation, focusing on the definitions of HUBZone areas and HUBZone small businesses and the program's performance relative to federal contracting goals. The report includes an analysis of (1) the SBA's administration of the program, (2) the SBA's performance measures, and (3) the effect of the release of economic date from the 2010 decennial census on which areas qualify as a HUBZone.

This report also examines congressional action on P.L. 111-240, the Small Business Jobs Act of 2010, which amended the Small Business Act to remove certain language that had prompted federal courts and the Government Accountability Office (GAO) to find that HUBZone set-asides have "precedence" over other small business set-asides. It also discusses several bills introduced during the 112th Congress to extend the eligibility for firms that lost their HUBZone redesignated eligibility status due to the release of economic data from the 2010 decennial census, including H.R. 2131, the Protect HUBZones Act of 2011; S. 1756, the HUBZone Protection Act of 2011; S. 633, the Small Business Contracting Fraud Prevention Act of 2011; and S. 3572, the Restoring Tax and Regulatory Certainty to Small Businesses Act of 2012. S. 633 and S. 3572 would also require the SBA to implement several GAO recommendations designed to improve the SBA's administration of the program. Also, S. 3254, the National Defense Authorization Act for Fiscal Year 2013, as amended, would extend HUBZone eligibility for BRAC base closures for an additional five years.

THE HUBZONE PROGRAM

The Small Business Administration (SBA) administers several programs to support small businesses, including the Historically Underutilized Business Zone Empowerment Contracting (HUBZone) program. The HUBZone program is "a place-based contracting assistance program whose primary objective is job creation and increasing capital investment in distressed communities."[1] It provides participating small businesses located in areas with low income, high poverty rates, or high unemployment rates with contracting opportunities in the form of "set-asides," sole-source awards, and price-evaluation preferences.[2]

The Competition in Contracting Act of 1984 generally requires "full and open competition" for government procurement contracts.[3] However, procurement set-asides are permissible competitive procedures.

A set-aside restricts competition for a federal contract to specified contractors. Set-asides can be exclusive or partial, depending upon whether the entire procurement, or just part of it, is so restricted. In this case, the competition may be restricted to SBA-certified HUBZone businesses if there is a reasonable expectation of at least two SBA-certified HUBZone bidders and a fair market price. It is the most commonly used mechanism in the HUBZone program, accounting for about 93% of HUBZone program contract dollars ($2.57 billion) in FY2011.

A sole-source award is a federal contract awarded, or proposed for award, without competition. Sole-source awards account for about 3% of HUBZone program contract dollars ($82.8 million) in FY2011. Also, in any full and open competition for a federal contract "the price offered by a qualified HUBZone business shall be deemed as being lower than the price of another offeror if the HUBZone business price offer is not more than 10% higher than the other offer."[4] Price-evaluation preferences account for about 4% of HUBZone program contract dollars ($100.2 million) in FY2011.[5]

In FY2011, the federal government awarded 91,864 contracts valued at $9.9 billion to HUBZonecertified businesses, with about $2.75 billion of that amount awarded through a HUBZone set-aside, sole-source award, or price evaluation preference.[6] The program's FY2011 administrative cost was about $15.6 million.[7] It received an FY2013 appropriation of just over $2.5 million, with the additional cost of administering the program covered by the SBA's appropriation for general administrative expenses.[8]

Congressional interest in the HUBZone program has increased in recent years, primarily due to U.S. Government Accountability Office (GAO) reports of fraud in the program. Some Members have called for the program's termination. Others have recommended that the SBA continue its efforts to improve its administration of the program, especially its efforts to prevent fraud.[9]

This report examines the arguments presented both for and against targeting assistance to geographic areas with specified characteristics, such as low income, high poverty, or high unemployment, as opposed to providing assistance to people or businesses with specified characteristics. It then assesses the arguments presented both for and against the creation and continuation of the HUBZone program, starting with the arguments presented during consideration of P.L. 105-135, the HUBZone Act of 1997 (Title VI of the Small Business Reauthorization Act of 1997), which authorized the program.

The report also discusses the HUBZone program's structure and operation, focusing on the definitions of HUBZone areas and HUBZone small businesses and the program's performance relative to federal contracting goals. The report includes an analysis of (1) the SBA's administration of the program, (2) the SBA's performance measures, and (3) the effect of the release of economic data from the 2010 decennial census on which areas qualify as a HUBZone.

As will be discussed, Congress included a provision in P.L. 106-554, the HUBZones in Native America Act of 2000 (Title VI, the Consolidated Appropriations Act, 2001), which provided census tracts and non-metropolitan counties that lose HUBZone eligibility an automatic extension for three years. The act labeled these areas a HUBZone "redesignated area."[10] Subsequently, P.L. 108-447, the Consolidated Appropriations Act, 2005, effectively extended the eligibility of HUBZone redesignated areas by allowing them to retain eligibility for three years or until the public release of data from the 2010 decennial census, whichever is later. As a result, HUBZone redesignated areas that had passed the three-year mark, but retained eligibility under P.L. 108- 447, lost eligibility when economic data from the 2010 decennial census was released in 2011. Because the number of HUBZone redesignated areas declined, the number of HUBZone-certified businesses also declined, primarily because their principal office was no longer located in a HUBZone or at least 35% of its employees no longer resided in a HUBZone. The SBA estimated that about 31% of HUBZone-certified small businesses (about 2,600 firms) were proposed for decertification on October 1, 2011, due to the expiration of their area's redesignated status.[11]

This report also examines congressional action on P.L. 111-240, the Small Business Jobs Act of 2010, which amended the Small Business Act to remove certain language that had prompted federal courts and GAO to find that HUBZone set-asides have "precedence" over other small business set-asides. It also discusses four bills introduced during the 112th Congress that would extend HUBZone eligibility for firms that lost their HUBZone redesignated eligibility status due to the release of 2010 decennial census economic data for three years after the first date on which the SBA publishes a HUBZone map that is based on the results from the 2010 decennial census: H.R. 2131, the Protect HUBZones Act of 2011; S. 1756, the HUBZone Protection Act of 2011; S. 633, the Small Business Contracting Fraud Prevention Act of 2011; and S. 3572, the Restoring Tax and Regulatory Certainty to Small Businesses Act of 2012. S. 633 and S. 3572 would also require the SBA to implement several GAO recommendations designed to improve the SBA's administration of the program. Also, S. 3254, the National Defense Authorization Act for Fiscal Year 2013, as amended, would extend HUBZone eligibility for BRAC base closure for an additional five years.

TARGETING ASSISTANCE TO GEOGRAPHIC AREAS

The HUBZone program was authorized by P.L. 105-135, the HUBZone Act of 1997 (Title VI of the Small Business Reauthorization Act of 1997).[12] Senator Christopher S. "Kit" Bond, the legislation's sponsor, described it as a "jobs bill and a welfare-to-work bill" designed to "create realistic opportunities for moving people off of welfare and into meaningful jobs" in "inner cities and rural counties that have low household incomes, high unemployment, and whose communities have suffered from a lack of investment."[13] Its enactment was part of a broader debate that had been underway since the late 1970s concerning whether the federal government should target assistance to geographic areas with specified characteristics, such as low income, high poverty, or high unemployment, as opposed to providing assistance to people or businesses with specified characteristics.

Discussion

The idea of targeting government assistance to geographic areas with specified characteristics, as opposed to targeting government assistance to people or businesses with specified characteristics, has its origins in a British experiment in urban revitalization started during the late 1970s. In 1978, Sir Geoffrey Howe, a Conservative member of Parliament, argued for the establishment of market-based enterprise zones, which provide government regulatory and tax relief, in economically distressed areas as a means to encourage entrepreneurs "to pursue profit with minimum governmental restrictions."[14] With the support of Prime Minister Margaret Thatcher's Conservative government (1979-1990), by the mid-1980s, more than two dozen enterprise zones were operating in England. Evaluations of the British enterprise zones' potential for having a positive effect on the long-term economic growth of economically distressed areas suggested that providing tax incentives and regulatory relief in those areas were "useful but not decisive economic development tools for distressed communities."[15]

In the United States, the idea of targeting regulatory and tax relief to economically distressed places appealed to some liberals who had become frustrated by the lack of progress some economically distressed communities had experienced under conventional government assistance programs, such as federal grant-in-aid programs. They tended to view the idea as a supplement to existing government assistance programs. Some conservatives also supported the idea of providing additional regulatory and tax relief to geographic areas because it generally aligned with their views on reducing government regulation and taxes. They tended to view it as a replacement, as opposed to a supplement, for existing government assistance programs.[16] As a result, support for targeting federal assistance to economically distressed places came from a diverse group of individuals and organizations that were often on opposing sides in other issue areas.

Some of its leading proponents were the Congressional Black Caucus; the National Urban League; the National League of Cities; the National Association for the Advancement of Colored People; President Ronald Reagan; Republican Representative Jack Kemp, who introduced the first enterprise zone bill in Congress in May 1980 (H.R. 7240, the Urban Jobs and Enterprise Zone Act of 1980); and Democratic Representative Robert Garcia, who co-sponsored with Representative Kemp H.R. 3824, the Urban Jobs and Enterprise Zone Act of 1981.[17]

Opponents noted that targeting government assistance, in this case regulatory and tax relief, to economically distressed places would "provide incentives in designated areas, regardless of the nature of the industry which would benefit from the incentives."[18] They argued that it would be more efficient and cost effective to target federal assistance to businesses that offer primarily high-wage, full-time jobs with benefits and have relatively high multiplier effects on job creation than to offer the same benefits to all businesses, including those that offer primarily low-wage, part-time jobs with few or no benefits and have relatively low multiplier effects on job creation.[19]

Others opposed the idea because they viewed it as a partisan extension of supply-side economics.[20] Others, including the National Federation of Independent Businesses, an organization representing the interests of the nation's small businesses, were not convinced that providing "marginal rate reductions or marginal reductions in taxes" would "stimulate the entry of new businesses into depressed areas."[21]

Also, some economists argued that it would be more efficient to let the private market determine where businesses locate rather than have the government enact policies that encourage businesses to locate, or relocate, in areas they would otherwise avoid. In their view, "the locational diversion of economic activity reduces or may outweigh gains from the creation of economic activity."[22]

These disagreements may have had a role in delaying the enactment of the first, fully functional federal enterprise zone program until 1993 (P.L. 103-66, the Omnibus Budget Reconciliation Act of 1993).[23] In the meantime, 37 states and the District of Columbia had initiated their own enterprise zone programs.[24]

Evaluations of their effect on job creation and the economic status of the targeted distressed areas "provided conflicting conclusions, with some finding little or no program-related impacts, and others finding gains in the zones associated with the enterprise zone incentives."[25] Evaluations of federal enterprise zones would later reach similarly mixed findings.[26]

The Debate over HUBZones

The federal enterprise zone program's enactment in 1993 established a precedent for the enactment of other programs, such as the HUBZone program, that target federal assistance, in this case government contracts, to places with specified characteristics. For example, the Senate Committee on Small Business's report accompanying the HUBZone program's authorizing legislation in 1997 presented many of the same arguments for adopting the HUBZone program that had been presented for adopting the federal enterprise zone program:

> Creating new jobs in economically distressed areas has been the greatest challenge for many of our nation's governors, mayors, and community leaders. The trend is for business to locate in areas where there are customers and a skilled workforce. Asking a business to locate in a distressed area often seems counter to its potential to be successful. But without businesses in these communities, we don't create jobs, and without sources of new jobs, we are unlikely to have a successful revitalization effort.
>
> The HUBZone program attempts to utilize a valuable government resource, a government contract, and make it available to small businesses who agree in return to locate in an economically distressed area and employ people from these areas.... Contracts to small businesses in HUBZones can translate into thousands of job opportunities for persons who are unemployed or underemployed.[27]

HUBZone opponents expressed many of the same arguments that were raised in opposition to federal enterprise zones. For example, some Members opposed contract set-asides because they "unfairly discriminate against more efficient producers" and argued that "lower taxes, fewer mandates and freer markets are what stimulate the growth of small business."[28] Others argued that the experiences under enterprise zones suggested that HUBZones would have, at best, a limited impact on the targeted area's economic prospects:

> the record of enterprise zones demonstrates that businesses that locate in an area because of tax breaks or other artificial inducements (such as HUBZone contract preferences), instead of genuine competitive advantages, generally prove not to be sustainable.... Thus, the incentives generally go to businesses that would have located in and hired from the target area anyway.... Therefore, we should be realistic about the impact the HUBZone legislation will have on business relocation decisions.[29]

HUBZone critics also argued that it would compete with, and potentially diminish the effectiveness of, the SBA's Minority Small Business and Capital Ownership Development 8(a) program.[30] That program provides participating small businesses with training, technical assistance, and contracting opportunities in the form of set-asides and sole-source awards. Eligibility for the 8(a) program is generally limited to small businesses "unconditionally owned and controlled by one or more socially and economically disadvantaged individuals who are of good character and citizens of the United States" that demonstrate "potential for success."[31] Small businesses owned by Indian tribes, Alaska Native Corporations, Native Hawaiian Organizations, and Community Development Corporations are also eligible for the 8(a) program under somewhat different terms. In FY2010, more than 9,000 firms participated in the 8(a) program, and the federal government spent $18.4 billion on contracts and subcontracts with 8(a) firms.[32]

Others argued that the HUBZone self-certification process "while laudable in its effort to reduce certification costs and delays, invites inadvertent or deliberate abuses."[33] As will be discussed in greater detail later, in recent years, the SBA's administration of the HUBZone program and the program's effectiveness in assisting economically distressed areas have been criticized. For example, GAO has argued that the program is subject to fraud and abuse and has recommended that the SBA "take additional actions to certify and monitor HUBZone firms as well as to assess the results of the HUBZone program."[34] Also, several Members of

Congress have questioned the program's effectiveness. For example, Representative Nydia M. Velázquez has argued that

> When first introduced, the HUBZone program promised to create opportunities for small businesses in low-income communities. It was designed to do this by helping entrepreneurs access the Federal marketplace. In theory, the benefits will be twofold; HUBZones will not only bolster the small business community, but will also breathe new life into struggling neighborhoods. However, the program has been undermined by chronic underfunding, inherent program flaws and sloppy management. Instead of being incubators for growth and development, HUBZones have become breeding grounds for fraud and abuse.[35]

HUBZONE AREAS DEFINED

There are currently five HUBZone types (or classes):

- qualified census tracts (QCTs),
- qualified non-metropolitan counties,
- qualified Indian Reservations/Indian Country,
- military bases closed under the Base Realignment and Closure Act (BRAC), and
- difficult development areas (DDAs).[36]

In addition, QCTs and qualified non-metropolitan counties that lose their eligibility may temporarily retain their eligibility by becoming a redesignated area.

Qualified Census Tracts

P.L. 105-135, the HUBZone Act of 1997 (Title VI of the Small Business Reauthorization Act of 1997), specified that the term "qualified census tract" has the meaning given that term in Section 42(d)(5)(C)(ii)(I) of the Internal Revenue Code of 1986. That section of the IRS code refers to qualified census tracts as determined by the U.S. Housing and Urban Development (HUD) for its low-income housing tax credit program. The current criteria are any census tract that is designated by the Secretary of HUD and, for the most recent year for which census data are available on household income in such tract, has

- at least 50% of households with income below 60% of the median gross income of the metropolitan statistical area (in metropolitan census tracts) or the median gross income for all non-metropolitan areas of the state (in non-metropolitan census tracts) or
- a poverty rate of at least 25%.[37]

In addition, the number of qualified census tracts within a metropolitan statistical area "shall not exceed an area having 20% of the population of such metropolitan statistical area."[38] In areas where more than 20% of the population qualifies, HUD orders the census tracts in that metropolitan statistical area from the highest percentage of eligible households to the lowest. HUD then designates the census tracts with the highest percentage of eligible households as qualified until the 20% limit is exceeded. If a census tract is excluded because it raises the percentage above 20%, then subsequent census tracts are considered to determine if a census tract with a smaller population could be included without exceeding the 20% limit.[39]

About 18.5% of all census tracts (13,635 of 73,790) have QCT status.[40]

In the past, these economic data were only available from the decennial census. As a result, QCTs changed relatively infrequently, typically as new economic data from each decennial census became available or when the Census Bureau undertook a new delineation of census tracts. The Census Bureau reexamines its census tracts following each decennial census in an effort to keep them homogeneous with respect to population characteristics, economic status, and living conditions.[41] As a result of this delineation process, some census tracts may be enlarged and others may be split into two or more census tracts. This can cause a change in the census tract's QCT status. The typical census tract has between 1,500 and 8,000 persons.

Previously, QCT status was based on census tract economic data from the 2000 decennial census long form. However, for the 2010 decennial census, the long form was replaced by the American Community Survey (ACS), an ongoing mailed survey of about 250,000 households per month that gathers largely the same income data as the long-form. The ACS collects and produces population and housing information annually. ACS annual reports are based on data collected over a year for areas with a population of at least 65,000, over three years for areas with a population of at least 20,000, and over five years for all areas (including census tracts).[42] The ACS survey concerning census tracts for the 2006-2010 period was released in December 2011. HUD used that data to determine the eligibility status of census tracts for the low-income housing tax credit program and announced the changes on April 20, 2012, with an effective date for the low-income housing tax credit program of January 1, 2013.[43] The SBA applied the changes in QCT status to the HUBZone program on October 1, 2012.[44] HUD will subsequently update the eligibility status of census tracts based on the release of new ACS economic data every five years.[45]

Qualified Non-metropolitan Counties

A qualified non-metropolitan county is any county that "was not located in a metropolitan statistical area at the time of the most recent census taken for purposes of selecting qualified census tracts under Section 42(d)(5)(C)(ii) of the Internal Revenue Code of 1986," and in which

- the median household income is less than 80% of the non-metropolitan state median household income, based on the most recent data available from the Bureau of the Census of the Department of Commerce or
- the unemployment rate is not less than 140% of the average unemployment rate for the United States or for the state in which such county is located, whichever is less, based on the most recent data available from the Secretary of Labor.[46]

About 15.6% (506) of the nation's 3,243 counties have qualified non-metropolitan county status (24.4% of the nation's 2,075 non-metropolitan counties).[47]

Previously, non-metropolitan county median household income was derived from income data generated from the 2000 decennial census long form. If a county qualified on that basis, its HUBZone status based on median household income was "secure until publication of the data from the following census."[48] However, the Census Bureau now relies on the ACS to collect that data. ACS survey data concerning county median household income is collected over a five-year period and published on a rolling basis each year. The SBA used ACS data concerning median household income that were released in 2011 to update the eligibility status of non-metropolitan counties, effective October 1, 2011.[49] The SBA has indicated that it will update the eligibility status of non-metropolitan counties based on median household income at least once every five years.[50] Because the ACS now releases data concerning county median income annually, the SBA could update the eligibility status of non-metropolitan counties based on median household income on an annual basis.

The non-metropolitan county's unemployment rate is derived from data released annually by the Department of Labor's Bureau of Labor Statistics. These data are typically sent to the SBA during June or July. The SBA has traditionally updated the eligibility status of non-metropolitan counties based on these data by October 1, the beginning of the fiscal year.[51] As a result, if a county qualifies, or fails to qualify, on this basis, its HUBZone status can change annually as new unemployment data are released. As will be discussed, Congress created redesignated areas to delay the loss of HUBZone status for areas that lose HUBZone eligibility.

The qualified non-metropolitan county designation is the only type of HUBZone that is determined by the SBA. The formula is set in law and the data are derived from other agencies, but the designation is made by the SBA.[52]

Qualified Indian Reservation/Indian Country

P.L. 105-135, the HUBZone Act of 1997 (Title VI of the Small Business Reauthorization Act of 1997), provided HUBZone eligibility to "lands within the external boundaries of an Indian reservation." Since then, the term *Indian reservation* has been clarified and expanded to include

- Indian trust lands and other lands covered under the term *Indian Country* as used by the Bureau of Indian Affairs,
- portions of the state of Oklahoma designated as former Indian reservations by the Internal Revenue Service (Oklahoma tribal statistical areas), and
- Alaska Native village statistical areas.[53]

There are 819 qualified Indian reservations, Oklahoma tribal statistical areas, and Alaska Native village statistical areas.[54] A private firm's analysis of Indian reservation's economic characteristics conducted on behalf of the SBA indicated that

for the most part—and particularly in states where reservations are numerous and extensive—mean income of reservations is far below state levels, and unemployment rates and poverty rates are far above state levels. There are some interesting exceptions, however, where reservations are basically on a par with the states they are in. Examples include Osage reservation in Oklahoma and reservations in Connecticut, Rhode Island, and Michigan. The factors at work here may be casinos and oil.[55]

Military Bases Closed under BRAC

P.L. 108-447, the Consolidated Appropriations Act, 2005, provided HUBZone eligibility for five years to "lands within the external boundaries of a military installation closed through a privatization process" under the authority of P.L. 101-510, the Defense Base Closure and Realignment Act of 1990 (BRAC—Title XXIX of the National Defense Authorization Act for Fiscal Year 1991). The military base's HUBZone eligibility commences on the effective date of the law (December 8, 2004) if the military base was already closed at that time, or on the date of formal closure if the military base was still operational at that time.

There are 127 qualified base closure areas currently designated as a HUBZone.[56]

Difficult Development Areas

P.L. 109-59, the Safe, Accountable, Flexible, Efficient Transportation Equity Act: A Legacy for Users (SAFETEA), provided HUBZone eligibility to difficult development areas (DDAs) within "Alaska, Hawaii, or any territory or possession of the United States outside the 48 contiguous states."[57] These areas are designated annually, typically in September or October, by the Secretary of HUD "in accordance with Section 42(d)(5)(C)(iii) of the Internal Revenue Code" which applies to HUD's low-income housing tax credit program.[58] This section of the Internal Revenue Code defines a DDA "as areas designated by the Secretary of Housing and Urban Development as having high construction, land, and utility costs relative to area median gross income."[59] These areas may not exceed 20% of the population of a metropolitan statistical area or of a non-metropolitan area.

There are 49 non-metropolitan counties that have HUBZone DDA status. Of these 49 non-metropolitan counties, 26 are HUBZone eligible only due to their DDA status, 16 are HUBZone eligible based on unemployment, 2 are HUBZone eligible based on income, and 5 are HUBZone eligible based on both income and unemployment.[60]

Redesignated Areas

One of the implicit goals of the HUBZone program is to improve the economic standing of the geographic areas receiving assistance so that they are no longer an economically distressed area. As a result, it could be argued that it is a program success when a QCT or a qualified non-metropolitan county loses its qualification as a HUBZone area when new economic data are published. However, because "small business concerns that locate to a HUBZone may lose their eligibility in only one year due to changes in such data" and out of concern that some HUBZone areas could "shift in and out of eligibility year after year," Congress included a provision in P.L. 106-554, the HUBZones in Native America Act of

2000 (Title VI, the Consolidated Appropriations Act, 2001), to address this issue.[61] The provision provided census tracts and non-metropolitan counties that lose HUBZone eligibility an automatic extension "for the 3-year period following the date on which the census tract or nonmetropolitan county ceased to be so qualified."[62] The act labeled census tracts and non-metropolitan counties that receive an extension of HUBZone eligibility "redesignated areas."

Subsequently, P.L. 108-447, the Consolidated Appropriations Act, 2005, effectively extended the eligibility of HUBZone redesignated areas by allowing them to retain eligibility for three years or until the public release of data from the 2010 decennial census, whichever is later:

> Redesignated area means any census tract or any non-metropolitan county that ceases to be a qualified HUBZone, except that such census tracts or non-metropolitan counties may be "redesignated areas" only until the later of: (1) The date on which the Census Bureau publicly releases the first results from the 2010 decennial census; or (2) Three years after the date on which the census tract or non-metropolitan county ceased to be so qualified.
>
> The date on which the census tract or non-metropolitan county ceases to be qualified is the date that the official government data, which affects the eligibility of the HUBZone, is released to the public.[63]

In 2008, GAO compared the economic characteristics of QCTs and qualified non-metropolitan counties to redesignated areas. It reported that it "found a marked difference" in their economic characteristics. For example, GAO reported that approximately 60% of QCTs (excluding redesignated areas) had a poverty rate of 30% or more compared to approximately 4% of redesignated QCTs. Also, about 75% of QCTs (excluding redesignated areas) had a median household income that was less than 60% of the metropolitan area median household income compared to about 10% of redesignated QCTs.[64]

The SBA initially indicated that it would update the eligibility status of redesignated areas on June 1, 2011. However, the Census Bureau took longer than expected to release the first economic data from the 2010 decennial census to affect the eligibility of HUBZones (the median household income of non-metropolitan counties). The SBA subsequently pushed back the date for the update of redesignated areas to October 1, 2011.[65]

Prior to October 1, 2011, there were 3,760 redesignated HUBZone census tracts, 651 redesignated HUBZone non-metropolitan counties, and 20 redesignated HUBZone DDAs.[66] On October 1, 2011, all redesignated HUBZones that were provided an extended grandfathering period beyond the original three years lost their redesignated status.[67] For example, on October 1, 2011, the number of redesignated HUBZone non-metropolitan counties was reduced from 651 to 318.[68]

As will be discussed, several bills were introduced during the 112th Congress to extend the eligibility of redesignated areas that lost their redesignated status on October 1, 2011, due to the release of 2010 decennial census data.

HUBZONE BUSINESSES DEFINED

Firms must be certified by the SBA to participate in the HUBZone program. On December 4, 2012, there were 5,667 certified HUBZone small businesses.[69]

To become certified, firms complete and submit specified SBA HUBZone application forms to the SBA, either online or by mail. Firms must

- meet SBA size standards for the firm's primary industry classification;
- be at least 51% owned and controlled by U.S. citizens, or a Community Development Corporation, an agricultural cooperative, or an Indian tribe (including Alaska Native Corporations);
- maintain a principal office located in a HUBZone;
- ensure that at least 35% of its employees reside in a HUBZone;[70]
- represent, as provided in the application, that it will "attempt to maintain" having 35% of its employees reside in a HUBZone during the performance of any HUBZone contract it receives;
- represent, as provided in the application, that it will ensure that it will comply with certain contract performance requirements in connection with contracts awarded to it as a qualified HUBZone small business concern (such as spending at least 50% of the cost of the contract incurred for personnel on its own employees or employees of other qualified HUBZone small business concerns and meeting specified subcontracting limitations to nonqualified HUBZone small business concerns);
- provide an active up-to-date Dun and Bradstreet profile and Data Universal Numbering System (DUNS) number that represents the business; and
- provide an active Central Contractor Registration profile for the business.[71]

Until recently, the SBA's goal was to make its determination within 30 calendar days after receipt of a complete application package, subject to the need for additional information or clarification of information contained in the application.

As will be discussed, in response to reports of applicant fraud, the SBA reengineered its applicant review process and initially took, depending on the complexity of the application and the need for additional information, from 5 to 12 months to make its determination. The SBA has since decreased the average time to process HUBZone applications to about three months.[72]

If the SBA approves the application, it will send a written notice to the business and automatically enter it on a list of certified HUBZone businesses. A decision to deny eligibility must be in writing, and state the specific reasons for denial.[73]

In the past, the SBA's staff conducted random program examinations "to verify the accuracy of any certification made or information provided as part of the HUBZone application process, or in connection with a HUBZone contract."[74]

Examiners typically verified that the business met the program's eligibility requirements, and that it met such requirements at the time of its application for certification, its most recent recertification, or its certification in connection with a HUBZone contract.[75]

In response to reports of fraud, the SBA, in addition to reengineering its applicant review process, now conducts program examinations of all firms that received a HUBZone contract in the previous fiscal year.[76]

Certified HUBZone small business concerns must recertify every three years to the SBA that they meet the requirements for being a HUBZone business.[77] They must also immediately notify the SBA of any material change that could affect their eligibility, such as a change in the ownership, business structure, or principal office of the concern, or a failure to meet the 35% HUBZone residency requirement.[78]

HUBZONE FEDERAL CONTRACTING GOALS

Since 1978, federal agency heads have been required to establish federal procurement contracting goals, in consultation with the SBA, "that realistically reflect the potential of small business concerns" to participate in federal procurement. Each agency is required, at the conclusion of each fiscal year, to report their progress in meeting the goals to the SBA.[79]

In 1988, Congress authorized the President to annually establish government-wide minimum participation goals for procurement contracts awarded to small businesses and small businesses owned and controlled by socially and economically disadvantaged individuals. Congress required the government-wide minimum participation goal for small businesses to be "not less than 20% of the total value of all prime contract awards for each fiscal year" and "not less than 5% of the total value of all prime contract and subcontract awards for each fiscal year" for small businesses owned and controlled by socially and economically disadvantaged individuals.[80]

Each federal agency was also directed to "have an annual goal that presents, for that agency, the maximum practicable opportunity for small business concerns and small business concerns owned and controlled by socially and economically disadvantaged individuals to participate in the performance of contracts let by such agency."[81] The SBA was also required to report to the President annually on the attainment of the goals and to include the information in an annual report to the Congress.[82] The SBA negotiates the goals with each federal agency and establishes a "small business eligible" baseline for evaluating the agency's performance.

The small business eligible baseline excludes certain contracts that the SBA has determined do not realistically reflect the potential for small business participation in federal procurement (such as contracts awarded to mandatory and directed sources), contracts awarded and performed overseas, contracts funded predominately from agency-generated sources, contracts not covered by Federal Acquisition Regulations, and contracts not reported in the Federal Procurement Data System (such as contracts or government procurement card purchases valued less than $3,000).[83] These exclusions typically account for 18% to 20% of all federal prime contracts each year.

The SBA then evaluates the agencies' performance against their negotiated goals annually, using data from the Federal Procurement Data System—Next Generation, managed by the U.S. General Services Administration, to generate the small business eligible baseline. This information is compiled into the official Small Business Goaling Report, which the SBA releases annually.

Over the years, federal government-wide procurement contracting goals have been established for small businesses generally (P.L. 100-656, the Business Opportunity Development Reform Act of 1988, and P.L. 105-135, the HUBZone Act of 1997 — Title VI of the Small Business Reauthorization Act of 1997), small businesses owned and controlled by socially and economically disadvantaged individuals (P.L. 100-656, the Business Opportunity Development Reform Act of 1988), women (P.L. 103-355, the Federal

Acquisition Streamlining Act of 1994), small businesses located within a HUBZone (P.L. 105-135, the HUBZone Act of 1997 – Title VI of the Small Business Reauthorization Act of 1997), and small businesses owned and controlled by a service disabled veteran (P.L. 106-50, the Veterans Entrepreneurship and Small Business Development Act of 1999).

The current federal small business contracting goals are

- at least 23% of the total value of all small business eligible prime contract awards to small businesses for each fiscal year,
- 5% of the total value of all small business eligible prime contract awards and subcontract awards to small disadvantaged businesses for each fiscal year,
- 5% of the total value of all small business eligible prime contract awards and subcontract awards to women-owned small businesses,
- 3% of the total value of all small business eligible prime contract awards and subcontract awards to HUBZone small businesses, and
- 3% of the total value of all small business eligible prime contract awards and subcontract awards to service-disabled veteran-owned small businesses.[84]

Table 1. Federal Contracting Goals and Percentage of FY2011 Federal Contract Dollars Awarded to Small Businesses, by Type

Business Type	Federal Goal	Percentage of FY2011 Federal Contracts (small business eligible)	Percentage of FY2011 Federal Contracts (all reported contracts)
Small Businesses	23.0%	21.65%	17.0%
Small Disadvantaged Businesses	5.0%	7.67%	6.0%
Women-Owned Small Businesses	5.0%	3.98%	3.1%
HUBZone Small Businesses	3.0%	2.35%	1.8%
Service-Disabled Veteran- Owned Small Businesses	3.0%	2.65%	2.1%

Source: U.S. Small Business Administration, "Statutory Guidelines," at http://www.sba.gov/content /goalingguidelines-0 (federal goals); U.S. General Services Administration, Federal Procurement Data System—Next Generation, "Small Business Goaling Report: Fiscal Year 2011," at https://www.fpds.gov /downloads/ top_requests/FPDSNG_SB_ Goaling_FY_2011.pdf; and U.S. General Services Administration, Federal Procurement Data System—Next Generation, at https://www.fpds.gov/fpdsng/ (contract dollars).

Notes: The total amount of federal contracts awarded in FY2011, as reported in the FPDS, was $536.8 billion; $422.5 billion of this amount was deemed by the SBA to be small business eligible. Of the total amount reported, $91.5 billion was awarded to small businesses, $32.4 billion to small disadvantaged businesses, $16.8 billion to women owned small businesses, $9.9 billion to SBA-certified HUBZone small businesses, and $11.2 billion to service-disabled veteran-owned small businesses.

There are no punitive consequences for not meeting the small business procurement goals. However, the SBA's Small Business Goaling Report is distributed widely, receives media attention, and serves to heighten public awareness of the issue of small business contracting. For example, agency performance as reported in the SBA's Small Business Goaling Report is often cited by Members during their questioning of federal agency witnesses during congressional hearings.

As shown in Table 1, in FY2011, federal agencies met the federal contracting goal for small disadvantaged businesses, but not the other goals. Federal agencies awarded 21.65% of the value of their small business eligible contracts to small businesses, 7.67% to small disadvantaged businesses, 3.98% to women-owned small businesses, 2.35% to HUBZone small businesses, and 2.65% to service-disabled veteran-owned small businesses.[85] The percentage of total reported federal contracts (without exclusions) awarded to small businesses, small disadvantaged businesses, women-owned small businesses, HUBZone small businesses, and service-disabled veteran-owned small businesses in FY2011 is also provided in the table for comparative purposes.

CONGRESSIONAL ISSUES

As mentioned previously, congressional interest in the HUBZone program has increased in recent years, primarily due to reports of fraud in the program. GAO was asked by Congress to review the SBA's administration of the HUBZone program and it has issued several recommendations designed to strengthen the SBA's fraud control measures.[86] GAO has also argued that the SBA lacks adequate performance measures to determine the HUBZone program's effect on the economically distressed areas it is designed to assist.[87] Another issue of congressional interest was the effect of the release of 2010 decennial census data on HUBZone area eligibility.

As will be discussed, Congress is currently considering legislation that would require the SBA to implement GAO's recommendations concerning the SBA's administration of the program and to revise the SBA's HUBZone performance measures. Congress is also considering legislation that would extend HUBZone eligibility for those redesignated HUBZone areas that lost eligibility on October 1, 2011, due to the release of 2010 decennial census data.

In addition, Congress recently addressed the potential consequence of two Court of Federal Claims decisions that directed federal agencies to provide HUBZone set-asides preference when two or more set-aside programs could potentially be used.[88] Providing the HUBZone program preference over other small business contracting programs could have resulted in an increase in the percentage of federal contract dollars awarded to HUBZone small businesses and a decrease in the percentage of federal contract dollars awarded to other small businesses. P.L. 111-240, the Small Business Jobs Act of 2010, amended the Small Business Act (15 U.S.C. 657a(b)(2)(B)) to remove the language that the court relied upon in finding that HUBZone set-asides have "precedence." Specifically, P.L. 111-240 struck "a contract opportunity shall" and replaced it with "a contract opportunity may."[89] The court had ruled that the use of the word shall made the HUBZone program mandatory, whereas the use of the word may in the Section 8(a) contracting program for small businesses owned and controlled by the socially and economically disadvantaged made it a discretionary program, and mandatory programs took precedence over discretionary ones.[90]

Also, on October 1, 2010, the maximum contract award amounts that federal officials can set-aside for sole source awards under various small business contracting programs were increased to adjust for inflation.[91] For example, the maximum sole source contract award amounts for the HUBZone program were increased from not exceeding $5.5 million for manufacturing contracts or $3.5 million for other contract opportunities to not exceeding $6.5 million for manufacturing contracts or $4.0 million for other contract opportunities. It could be argued that these changes, along with the recent decline in the number of HUBZone-certified small businesses resulting from the expiration of the eligibility of HUBZone redesignated areas following the release of 2010 decennial census data, will make it difficult to compare the results of the federal government's small business procurement goaling program with previous year results and diminishes the goaling program's value as a tool to measure federal agency progress in awarding contracts to small businesses. It is possible that Congress may consider proposals to adjust the goals to account for these changes.

Program Administration

SBA's Office of Inspector General Audits

The SBA's administration of the HUBZone program has been criticized for a number of years. In 2003, the SBA's Office of Inspector General (OIG) completed an audit of 15 HUBZone firms operating in Idaho Falls, ID, after receiving a complaint that a relatively large number of certified HUBZone firms in that city may not be qualified to participate in the program.[92] At that time, HUBZone businesses self-certified in their application materials that they met the requirements for being a HUBZone business. Validating documentation, such as a copy of a business owner's birth certificate as proof of U.S. citizenship or a copy of the lease agreement to verify the business concern's principal office's location within a qualified HUBZone, were not required. The SBA OIG's audit found that

> over two-thirds of the 15 subject companies were either not in compliance with HUBZone eligibility requirements or had presumably gone out of business.
>
> We also found that the Office of HUBZone Empowerment's internal controls were inadequate to ensure that only eligible firms are certified and remain certified. Therefore, there is little assurance that the program will provide increased employment, investment and economic development for depressed areas. Since ineligible companies could receive HUBZone contracts, the program is also vulnerable to federal contracting fraud.[93]

As a result of that audit, the SBA revised its program examination and recertification processes to provide "a more careful review" of HUBZone applications and implemented an online application process that was designed to "prescreen" potential applicants, "resulting in only those most-qualified actually submitting a completed application."[94]

Citing the efficiencies brought about by the automation of HUBZone applications, the SBA reduced the number of staff in the Office of the HUBZone Program, which was responsible for program examinations, from 12 full-time equivalent employees in 2004 to 8 in 2006.[95]

In 2006, the SBA OIG reported that there was a two-year backlog in HUBZone program examinations. It reported that it was concerned "that workload resources had not been adequately devoted to eliminating this two-year backlog" and firms that should be decertified from the program remained on the list of certified HUBZone businesses and potentially were "inappropriately receiving HUBZone contracts between the time they are initially certified and subsequently examined/recertified."[96]

As a result of the SBA OIG's second, follow-up audit of the HUBZone program, the SBA committed to reviewing 5% of all certifications "through a full-scale program of examinations."[97]

The audit also resulted in heightened congressional attention to the issue of potential fraud within the HUBZone program.

GAO's Audits

In 2007, Representative Nydia M. Velázquez, then-chair of the House Committee on Small Business, asked GAO to review the HUBZone program, including the criteria and processes that the SBA uses to identify and map HUBZone areas, the mechanisms the SBA uses to ensure that only eligible small businesses participate in the program, and the actions the SBA has taken to assess the program's results.[98]

GAO conducted its audit of the SBA's administration of the HUBZone program from August 2007 through June 2008. It reported on June 17, 2008, that

- the map used by the SBA to publicize qualified HUBZone areas was inaccurate, resulting in ineligible small businesses participating in the program and excluding eligible businesses;
- the mechanisms used by the SBA to certify and monitor HUBZone firms provided limited assurance that only eligible firms participated in the program;
- the SBA had not complied with its own policy of recertifying HUBZone firms every three years (about 40% of those firms had not been recertified); and
- the SBA lacked formal guidance that would specify a time frame for processing HUBZone firm decertifications (1,400 of 3,600 firms proposed for decertification had not been processed within the SBA's self-imposed goal of 60 days).[99]

GAO released another report on the HUBZone program on July 17, 2008. It reported that it had "identified substantial vulnerabilities in SBA's application and monitoring process, clearly demonstrating that the HUBZone program is vulnerable to fraud and abuse."[100] Using fictitious employee information and fabricated documentation, GAO obtained HUBZone certification for four bogus firms.

In one of its applications, GAO claimed that its principal office was the same address as a coffee store that happened to be located in a HUBZone. GAO argued that if the SBA "had performed a simple Internet search on the address, it would have been alerted to this fact."[101] Two of GAO's applications used leased mailboxes from retail postal services centers.

GAO argued that "a post office box clearly does not meet SBA's principal office requirement."[102] In addition, it identified "10 firms from the Washington, D.C. metro area that were participating in the HUBZone program even though they clearly did not meet eligibility requirements."[103]

The SBA responded to GAO's findings by announcing that it would undertake "a complete re-engineering of the program" designed to

- ensure that its HUBZone maps were up-to-date, and
- minimize program risk by collecting additional supporting documentation of all HUBZone applicants to support program eligibility.[104]

In response to GAO's findings and the SBA's response to those findings, Representative Velázquez asked GAO to determine "whether cases of fraud and abuse in the HUBZone program exist outside of the Washington, D.C. metropolitan area" and to assess the SBA's efforts to establish an effective fraud prevention system for the HUBZone program.[105]

On March 25, 2009, GAO reported that, as of that date

- the SBA had updated its HUBZone map but had not implemented procedures to ensure that it remains accurate,
- had made little progress in ensuring the eligibility of firms in the HUBZone program, and
- had eliminated its backlog of recertifications but had not established a process or procedures to prevent future backlogs.[106]

GAO also reported that it had selected four geographical areas for analysis to determine whether cases of fraud and abuse exist for HUBZone businesses located outside of the Washington, DC, metropolitan area: Dallas, TX; Huntsville, AL; San Antonio, TX; and San Diego, CA. GAO conducted its analysis of HUBZone businesses in those four areas from September 2008 through March 2009. GAO reported that it found "fraud and abuse" in all four metropolitan areas, including 19 firms that "clearly are not eligible" and highlighted 10 firms that it "found to be egregiously out of compliance with HUBZone program requirements."[107]

The SBA responded to GAO's audits and congressional criticism of its administration of the HUBZone program by "reengineering business processes to reduce fraud and abuse within the program."[108] In 2009, it "moved from verifying a sample of HUBZone firms to verifications of 100% of HUBZone firms receiving contracts in the previous fiscal year."[109] In 2010, the SBA reported that its standard HUBZone business process

> now requires all firms to submit supporting documentation verifying the information and statements made in their application. Previous practice required firms only to submit an electronic application.
>
> In addition, the Program Office implemented a new business process for recertifying HUBZone firms which requires all firms that are due for recertification to certify via wet signature that they still conform to the eligibility requirements. Previous practice required firms to submit an electronic verification.[110]

Karen Mills, the SBA's Administrator, testified before the House Committee on Small Business on April 21, 2010, that the SBA is "working to ensure that only legitimate and eligible firms are benefiting from HUBZone" and has "made dramatic increases in the number of site visits to HUBZone firms—from less than 100 in 2008 to over 900 in 2009. We're on track to do more than 1,000 this year."[111]

The SBA's new, more labor intensive certification process, coupled with an increase in applications for HUBZone certifications, resulted in what the SBA described as "significant delays in the processing of new applications for certification."[112] Noting that individual applications "can vary greatly depending on the complexity of the case and the applicant's responsiveness to any requests for supporting information," the SBA reported in 2010 that the final HUBZone determination time frames "vary from 5 months to 12 months, with an average of 8 to 10 months."[113] The SBA has since reduced the average time to review HUBZone applications to about three months.[114]

On June 25, 2010, GAO released another report concerning the SBA's efforts to reduce fraud in the HUBZone program. GAO submitted applications for HUBZone certification for "four new bogus firms ... using false information and fabricated documents ... fictitious employee information and bogus principal office addresses" including "the addresses of the Alamo in Texas, a public storage facility in Florida, and a city hall in Texas as principal office locations."[115] The SBA certified three of the four bogus firms and lost GAO's documentation for its fourth application "on multiple occasions," forcing GAO to abandon that application.[116] GAO reported that "the SBA continues to struggle with reducing fraud risks in its HUBZone certification process despite reportedly taking steps to bolster its controls."[117] It reported that

> A simple Internet search by SBA could have revealed these as phony applications. While the agency has required more documentation in its application process since GAO's July 2008 report, GAO's testing shows that SBA does not adequately authenticate self-reported information and, for these cases, did not perform site visits to validate the addresses. Further, the changes have significantly increased the time it takes SBA to process applications. Specifically, SBA took 7 or more months to process each of the bogus applications—at least 6 months longer than for GAO's previous investigations.[118]

GAO also reported that in response to their test, SBA officials "stated that it was unreasonable to expect them to have identified our fictitious firms because of bogus documentation that we included in our applications," that "the submission of false affidavits would subject an applicant to prosecution," and that "competitors may identify fraudulent firms and likely protest if those firms were awarded a HUBZone contract."[119] GAO also reported that SBA officials stated that "because of resource constraints, they primarily conduct site visits on certified firms that receive large prime HUBZone contracts."[120] GAO argued that "while the threat of prosecution is an important deterrent, it does not help to identify firms that attempt to commit fraud, as our testing shows."[121] GAO also argued that "while competitors may identify some ineligible firms that were awarded contracts, SBA is responsible for ensuring that only eligible firms participate in the HUBZone program."[122] GAO also reported that "if the SBA had conducted site visits at the addresses of the firms represented in our applications, those applications would have been identified as fraudulent."[123]

Legislation

S. 633, the Small Business Contracting Fraud Prevention Act of 2011, was introduced on March 17, 2011. It was agreed to by the Senate, with amendment, by unanimous consent on September 21, 2011. The bill was referred to the House Committee on Small Business on September 22, 2011.

It would require the SBA to implement GAO's recommendations to

- maintain a correct, accurate, and updated map to identify HUBZone areas;
- implement policies that ensure only eligible firms participate in the program;
- employ appropriate technology to control costs and maximize efficiency;
- notify the Small Business Committees of any backlogs in applications or recertifications with plans and timetables for eliminating the back log;
- ensure small businesses meet the 35% HUBZone residency requirement at the time of bid as well as contract award; and
- extend the redesignated status of HUBZone areas that lose that status due to the release of economic data from the 2010 decennial census for three years after the first date on which the SBA publishes a HUBZone map that is based on the results from the 2010 decennial census.[124]

S. 3572, the Restoring Tax and Regulatory Certainty to Small Businesses Act of 2012, was introduced on September 19, 2012, and referred to the Senate Committee on Finance. It includes, among other provisions, the HUBZone provisions contained in S. 633.

The SBA has not formally responded to the legislation. It has argued at congressional hearings and in its FY2012 congressional budget justification report that it is taking steps to implement GAO's recommendations.[125]

Performance Measures

As part of its 2008 audit of the HUBZone program, GAO reported that the SBA had taken "limited steps" to assess the effectiveness of the HUBZone program.[126] It noted that the SBA's performance measures—the number of applications approved and recertifications processed, the annual value of federal contracts awarded to HUBZone firms, and the number of program examinations completed—provide data on program activity but "do not directly measure the program's effect on firms (such as growth in employment or changes in capital investment) or directly measure the program's effect on the communities in which the firms are located (for instance, changes in median household income or poverty levels)."[127] GAO recommended that the SBA "further develop measures and implement plans to assess the effectiveness of the HUBZone program that take into account factors such as the economic characteristics of the HUBZone area."[128]

The SBA responded to GAO's findings by announcing that it "would develop an assessment tool to measure the economic benefits that accrue to areas in the HUBZone program" and that they "would then issue periodic reports accompanied by the underlying data."[129]

On March 25, 2009, GAO reported that, as of that date, the SBA had not developed measures or implemented plans to assess the program's effectiveness.[130] GAO noted that the SBA did commission an independent review of the HUBZone program's economic impact. That study was released in May 2008. It concluded that the HUBZone program

has not generated enough HUBZone contract dollars to have an impact on a national scale. When spread over an eight-year period across 2,450 metropolitan areas and counties with qualified census tracts, qualified counties, and Indian reservations, $6 billion has a limited impact....

About two-thirds of HUBZone areas have HUBZone businesses; just under one-third have HUBZone vendors that have won HUBZone contracts; and about 4 percent of HUBZone areas have received annual-equivalent HUBZone contract revenues greater than $100 per capita, based on HUBZone population....

The program has a substantial impact in only a very small percentage of HUBZones. Where the impact is largest, there generally is at least one very successful vender in the HUBZone. Thus, the program can be effective. At present, however, the impact in two-thirds of all HUBZones is nil.[131]

GAO also noted that the SBA had issued a notice in the *Federal Register* on August 11, 2008, seeking public comment on a proposed methodology for measuring the economic impact of the HUBZone program.[132] The notice presented a two-step economic model that the SBA had developed to estimate the impact directly attributable to the HUBZone program, the SBA's nonHUBZone programs, and other related federal procurement programs on HUBZone areas. The notice indicated that economic impact "will be measured by the estimated growth in median household income and employment (or a reduction in unemployment) in a specific HUBZone area."[133]

GAO criticized the SBA for relying on public comments to refine the proposed methodology "rather than conducting a comprehensive effort" that considered relevant literature and input from experts in economics and performance measurement.[134] GAO concluded that "based on our review, we do not believe this effort was a sound process for developing measures to assess the effectiveness of the program" and reported that the SBA had abandoned that proposal and "had initiated a new effort to address this issue."[135]

The SBA indicated in its FY2011 budget justification report to Congress that it had developed "a methodology for measuring the economic impact of the HUBZone program" in order to "provide for the continuous study and monitoring of the program's effectiveness in terms of its economic goals."[136] However, it did not provide any details concerning the methodology and has continued to use its previous performance measures—the number of small businesses assisted (applications approved and recertifications processed), the annual value of federal contracts awarded to HUBZone firms, and the number of program examinations completed—to assess the program's performance.[137]

Legislation

S. 633, the Small Business Contracting Fraud Prevention Act of 2011, would require the SBA to implement GAO's recommendation to "develop measures and implement plans to assess the effectiveness of the HUBZone program."[138] It would also require the SBA to identify "a baseline point in time to allow the assessment of economic development under the HUBZone program, including creating additional jobs" and take into account "the economic characteristics of the HUBZone and contracts being counted under multiple socioeconomic subcategories."[139]

The SBA has not formally responded to the legislation. It has argued at congressional hearings and in its FY2012 congressional budget justification report that it is taking steps to implement GAO's recommendation.[140]

One possible option available to Congress to further evaluate the HUBZone program's impact on small businesses and economically distressed communities is to require the SBA to commission a multi-year time series study of the HUBZone program's impact on small businesses and economically distressed communities similar to the multi-year time series study currently underway for the SBA's education and training programs.[141] That ongoing study, started in 2003, includes an annual survey of small business owners who have received SBA education and training services. The study's latest report, released on September 13, 2010, "measures attitudinal assessments, perceptions of changes in management/marketing practices, and business growth for firms that utilized the SBA's Entrepreneurial Development Resources [Small Business Development Centers, SCORE, and Women Business Centers] during the late summer or early fall of 2007, 2008 or 2009."[142]

The 2010 Decennial Census

As mentioned previously, P.L. 108-447, the Consolidated Appropriations Act, 2005, effectively extended the eligibility of redesignated HUBZone areas by allowing them to retain eligibility for three years or until the public release of data from the 2010 decennial census, whichever is later. At that time, based on past practice, it was anticipated that the Census Bureau would take at least a year to release the economic data contained in the 2010 decennial census that would be used in the determination of HUBZone area status.[143] In the past, such data were derived from the decennial census long form. For the 2010 decennial census, the long form was replaced by the American Community Survey (ACS), an ongoing mailed survey of about 250,000 households per month that gathers largely the same income data as the long-form. The ACS collects and produces population and housing information annually. ACS annual reports are based on data collected over a year for areas with a population of at least 65,000, over three years for areas with a population of at least 20,000, and over five years for all areas (including all census tracts and counties).[144]

Because this is the first time that ACS data is being used to determine HUBZone area status it is possible that questions might be raised concerning the reliability of the survey data. However, the census long form was also a survey, with a 17% sample size in 2000.

It is also possible that questions might be raised concerning the impact of having economic data that was formerly available once every 10 years now being available more frequently. HUD has announced that it will update the eligibility of QCTs based on ACS economic data every five years and the SBA has indicated that it will update the eligibility of qualified non-metropolitan counties based on ACS county median income data at least once every five years (perhaps as frequently as once every year) instead of waiting for the release of the next decennial census data.[145] It could be argued that using ACS data to more frequently review program eligibility may increase the HUBZone program's effectiveness in targeting assistance to areas most in need. The counter-argument is that increasing the frequency of QCT and qualified non-metropolitan county determinations could limit the ability of at least some certified HUBZone businesses to benefit from the program.

As mentioned previously, all redesignated HUBZones that were provided an extended grandfathering period beyond the original three years lost their redesignated status on October 1, 2011.[146] The SBA estimated that as a result of this change about 31% of HUBZone-certified small businesses at that time (about 2,600 firms) were proposed for decertification.[147] Firms are provided 30 calendar days from the date they receive a proposed decertification letter to respond. After reviewing the firm's response, the SBA will either decertify the firm or continue its certification if the firm demonstrates that it meets the HUBZone eligibility criteria. Firms are also provided an opportunity to voluntarily decertify themselves from the program if they no longer meet the HUBZone eligibility criteria.[148]

The SBA has argued in 2011 that because "all of the redesignated areas have been allowed to stay in the program or [have been] reinstated since December 2004" and no small business "has been decertified because of an expired redesignation," it believed that "many small business concerns in these redesignated areas have been given ample time to recoup a return on their investment."[149] However, the SBA also argued that many of these small businesses may want to continue to utilize the program by moving their business into a HUBZone. As a result, effective July 21, 2011, the SBA reduced the one-year wait period for recertification to 90 days. The SBA argued that reducing the wait period to 90 days "would encourage the businesses to move into newly designated HUBZones and hire HUBZone residents, which are the two purposes of the statute."[150]

Legislation

H.R. 2131, the Protect HUBZones Act of 2011, S. 1756, the HUBZone Protection Act of 2011, S. 633, the Small Business Contracting Fraud Prevention Act of 2011, and S. 3572, the Restoring Tax and Regulatory Certainty to Small Businesses Act of 2012, would amend the Small Business Act to allow redesignated HUBZone areas to retain their HUBZone eligibility for three years or until three years after the first date on which the SBA publishes a HUBZone map that is based on the results from the 2010 decennial census, whichever is later.[151] Current law allows HUBZone redesignated areas to retain eligibility for three years or until the public release of data from the 2010 decennial census (determined by the SBA to be October 1, 2011), whichever is later. As mentioned previously, the SBA estimated that about 31% of HUBZone-certified small businesses (about 2,600 firms) were proposed for decertification because they were located in an area that lost its redesignated status on October 1, 2011.[152]

In a related development, S. 3254, the National Defense Authorization Act for Fiscal Year 2013, as amended and passed by the Senate on December 4, 2012, would extend HUBZone eligibility for areas located within a military base closed under BRAC for an additional five years from the date of enactment. The amendment's advocates argue that many small businesses located within these areas were HUBZone eligible for much less than five years for a variety of reasons, often outside their control (e.g., they are located within the BRAC HUBZone several years after the base closed, the SBA's certification process took longer than expected, the company started operations several years after the base closed). Given continuing economic difficulties, the amendment's advocates argue that extending the eligibility of all BRAC base closure areas is warranted. Others worry that extending the HUBZone eligibility of bases closed under BRAC could lead to efforts to extend eligibility for other HUBZone areas. They prefer that the HUBZone program operate under existing eligibility criteria.

CONCLUSION

Congressional interest in the SBA's HUBZone program has increased in recent years to levels not seen since the initial debate over whether the program should be authorized.

Debates over the program's effect on economically distressed communities, as reflected in GAO's recommendation for new SBA performance measures; concerns, which were addressed by P.L. 111-240, the Small Business Jobs Act of 2010, over the potential impact of the U.S. Court of Federal Claims ruling in *Mission Critical Solutions v. United States* providing the HUBZone program preference in federal contracting when two or more federal contract set-aside programs could be used; and the potential impact of the 2010 decennial census on which areas qualify as a HUBZone have all served to elevate congressional interest in the program. But perhaps the most influential reason for the increased level of congressional interest has been GAO's finding of fraud in the program.

The SBA has attempted to overhaul the program. It reported in its FY2011 congressional budget justification that it had "met its primary goal during FY2009" to reengineer its "business processes to reduce fraud and abuse with the program."[153] On April 21, 2010, SBA Administrator Karen Mills testified before the House Committee on Small Business that progress has been made but "we know there's more work to do."[154] She testified that "At the front-end, it means more upfront certification and eligibility. For small businesses already in the program, it means more efforts with compliance and site visits. And if they're found to be out of compliance, it means pursuing and removing bad actors."[155] Also, in its FY2013 congressional budget justification, the SBA indicated that

> To further reduce fraud, waste, and abuse, the HUBZone program began the systematic Legacy Portfolio Review of firms that were certified as a HUBZone prior to the FY 2009 policy of full document review for initial certification. During FY 2011, 2,040 firms completed the Legacy Portfolio Review. The SBA also conducted and received 987 site visit reports from its field staff conveying whether or not the firm appeared to be operating from the HUBZone principal office. This amount is in sharp contrast with the seven site visits that had been conducted in FY 2008. In FY 2012, the SBA will be rolling out a HUBZone recruitment initiative to target firms that may be HUBZone eligible and educate them on the benefits of the program.[156]

One of the immediate by-products of the SBA's new business processes was an increase in the processing time for new HUBZone certifications. In the past, the SBA had a self-imposed goal of making those certifications within 30 calendar days after receipt of a complete application package, subject to the need for additional information or clarification of information contained in the application. Now, depending on the complexity of the application and the need for additional information, the SBA takes, on average, about three months to make those certifications. It remains to be determined if the SBA's new processes will reduce the incidence of fraud within the program. The resolution of that question could determine the future of the HUBZone program.

End Notes

[1] U.S. Small Business Administration, "FY2012 Congressional Budget Justification and FY2010 Annual Performance Report," p. 29, at http://www.sba.gov/sites/default/files/FINAL% 20FY%202012%20CBJ %20FY%202010%20APR_0.pdf.

[2] Henry Beale and Nicola Deas, "The HUBZone Program Report," Washington, DC: Microeconomic Applications, Inc., prepared for the U.S. Small Business Administration, Office of Advocacy, May 2008, p. i, at http://www.sba.gov/ advo/research/rs325tot.pdf. Sole-source awards under the HUBZone program can be

made only if the anticipated award price of the contract will not exceed $6.5 million for manufacturing contracts or $4.0 million for other contract opportunities, and the contracting officer believes that the award can be made at a fair and reasonable price. See 13 C.F.R. §126.612; 15 U.S.C. §657a(b)(2)(A)(i)-(iii) (statutory requirements); 48 C.F.R. §19.1306(a)(1)-(6) (increasing the price thresholds, among other things); and Department of Defense, General Services Administration, and National Aeronautics and Space Administration, "Federal Acquisition Regulation: Inflation Adjustment of Acquisition-Related Thresholds," 75 *Federal Register* 53129, August 30, 2010.

[3] 41 U.S.C. §253(b)(1); and 41 U.S.C. §259(b). For more on competition in federal contracting, see CRS Report R40516, *Competition in Federal Contracting: An Overview of the Legal Requirements*, by Kate M. Manuel.

[4] Henry Beale and Nicola Deas, "The HUBZone Program Report," Washington, DC: Microeconomic Applications, Inc., prepared for the U.S. Small Business Administration, Office of Advocacy, May 2008, p. i, at http://www.sba.gov/ advo/research/rs325tot.pdf.

[5] Federal procurement data generated from the U.S. General Services Administration, Federal Procurement Data System—Next Generation, at https://www.fpds.gov/fpdsng/.

[6] Ibid; and U.S. General Services Administration, Federal Procurement Data System—Next Generation, "Small Business Goaling Report: Fiscal Year 2011," at https://www.fpds.gov/downloads/top_requests/ FPDSNG_SB_Goaling_FY_2011.pdf.

[7] U.S. Small Business Administration, "FY2013 Congressional Budget Justification and FY2011 Annual Performance Report," p. 21, at http://www.sba.gov/sites/default/files/files /FY%202013%20CBJ%20FY% 202011%20APR.pdf.

[8] Ibid., p. 15; and P.L. 112-175, the Continuing Appropriations Resolution, 2013. Congress provides an appropriation for the SBA's non-credit programs ($173.3 million in FY2013) and includes guidance in its accompanying committee report concerning funding for the HUBZone program. See H.Rept. 112-331, the Military Construction and Veterans Affairs and Related Agencies Appropriations Act, 2012.

[9] U.S. Congress, House Committee on Small Business, *Full Committee Hearing on Oversight of the Small Business Administration and Its Programs*, 111th Cong., 1st sess., March 25, 2009, Small Business Committee Doc. 111-012 (Washington: GPO, 2009), pp. 1-3, 28-31.

[10] P.L. 106-554, the HUBZones in Native America Act of 2000 (Title VI, the Consolidated Appropriations Act, 2001).

[11] U.S. Small Business Administration, Office of Congressional and Legislative Affairs, correspondence with CRS, October 13, 2011. The original estimate was 40%, see U.S. Small Business Administration, "Small Business HUBZone Program; Government Contracting Programs," 76 *Federal Register* 43573, July 21, 2011.

[12] The SBA officially established the HUBZone program on March 22, 1999, when it began to accept applications from businesses interested in participating in the program. The SBA certified its first HUBZone business on March 24, 1999. The first HUBZone contract was issued on April 8, 1999. See U.S. Congress, Senate Committee on Small Business, *Small Business Reauthorization Act of 2000*, report to accompany S. 3121, 106th Cong., 2nd sess., September 27, 2000, S.Rept. 106-422 (Washington: GPO, 2000), p. 20.

[13] U.S. Congress, Senate Committee on Small Business, *Small Business Reauthorization Act of 1997*, report to accompany S. 1139, 105th Cong., 1st sess., August 19, 1997, S.Rept. 105-62 (Washington: GPO, 1997), p. 25.

[14] Marilyn Marks Rubin, "Can Reorchestration of Historical Themes Reinvent Government? A Case Study of the Empowerment Zones and Enterprise Communities Act of 1993," *Public Administration Review*, vol. 54, no. 2 (March/April 1994), p. 162. Note: Sir Peter Geoffrey Hall, the Bartlett Professor of Planning and Regeneration at the Bartlett School of Architecture and Planning, University College London, is often credited for developing the concept of empowerment zones.

[15] Ibid.

[16] Stuart M. Butler, *Enterprise Zones: Greenlining the Inner Cities* (New York: Universe Books, 1981).

[17] Ibid; U.S. Congress, House Committee on Ways and Means, *The Enterprise Zone Tax Act of 1982*, Message from the President of the United States transmitting proposed legislation entitled, "The Enterprise Zone Tax Act of 1982", 97th Cong., 2nd sess., March 23, 1982, H.Doc. 97-157 (Washington: GPO, 1982), pp. 1-5; and U.S. Congress, House Committee on Banking, Finance, and Urban Affairs, Subcommittee on the City, *Urban Revitalization and Industrial Policy*, 96th Cong., 2nd sess., September 17, 1980, Serial No. 96-72 (Washington: GPO, 1980), pp. 205-224.

[18] U.S. Congress, House Committee on Banking, Finance, and Urban Affairs, Subcommittee on the City, *Urban Revitalization and Industrial Policy*, 96th Cong., 2nd sess., September 17, 1980, Serial No. 96-72 (Washington: GPO, 1980), p. 283.

[19] Ibid.

[20] Marilyn Marks Rubin, "Can Reorchestration of Historical Themes Reinvent Government? A Case Study of the Empowerment Zones and Enterprise Communities Act of 1993," *Public Administration Review*, vol. 54, no. 2 (March/April 1994), p. 163.

[21] U.S. Congress, House Committee on Small Business, Subcommittee on Tax, Access to Equity Capital and Business Opportunities, *Job Creation and the Revitalization of Small Business*, 97th Cong., 1st sess., September 15, 1981 (Washington: GPO, 1981), pp. 22, 23.

[22] Herbert Grubel, "Review of Enterprise Zones: Greenlining the Inner Cities, by Stuart M. Butler," *Journal of Economic Literature*, vol. XX (December 1982), p. 1616.

[23] In 1987, Title VII of P.L. 100-242, the Housing and Community Development Act, authorized the Department of Housing and Community Development (HUD) to coordinate the community development block grant, urban development action grant, and other HUD programs and to provide the waiver or modification of housing and community development rules in up to 100 HUD-designated enterprise zone communities. No enterprise zone designations were subsequently made. See Marilyn Marks Rubin, "Can Reorchestration of Historical Themes Reinvent Government? A Case Study of the Empowerment Zones and Enterprise Communities Act of 1993," *Public Administration Review*, vol. 54, no. 2 (March/April 1994), p. 162.

[24] Ibid.; and Sarah F. Liebschutz, "Empowerment Zones and Enterprise Communities: Reinventing Federalism for Distressed Communities," *Publius: The Journal of Federalism*, vol. 25, no. 3 (Summer 1995), p. 127.

[25] Marilyn Marks Rubin, "Can Reorchestration of Historical Themes Reinvent Government? A Case Study of the Empowerment Zones and Enterprise Communities Act of 1993," *Public Administration Review*, vol. 54, no. 2 (March/April 1994), p. 164. Also see Sarah F. Liebschutz, "Empowerment Zones and Enterprise Communities: Reinventing Federalism for Distressed Communities," *Publius: The Journal of Federalism*, vol. 25, no. 3 (summer 1995), p. 128; and Edward L. Glaeser and Joshua D. Gottlieb, "The Economics of Place-Making Policies," *Brookings Papers on Economic Activity* (spring 2008), p. 157.

[26] U.S. Government Accountability Office, *Community Development: Federal Revitalization Programs Are Being Implemented, but Data on the Use of Tax Benefits Are Limited*, GAO-04-306, March 5, 2004, at http://www.gao.gov/ new.items/d04306.pdf; U.S. Government Accountability Office, *Empowerment Zone and Enterprise Community Program: Improvements Occurred in Communities, but the Effect of the Program Is Unclear*, GAO-06-727, September 22, 2006, at http://www.gao.gov/new.items/d06727.pdf; and U.S. Government Accountability Office, *Revitalization Programs: Empowerment Zones, Enterprise Communities, and Renewal Communities*, GAO-10-464R, March 12, 2010, at http://www.gao.gov/new.items/d10464r.pdf.

[27] U.S. Congress, Senate Committee on Small Business, *Small Business Reauthorization Act of 1997*, report to accompany S. 1139, 105th Cong., 1st sess., August 19, 1997, S.Rept. 105-62 (Washington: GPO, 1997), p. 26.

[28] U.S. Congress, Senate Committee on Small Business, *S. 208, The HUBZone Act of 1997*, 105th Cong., 1st sess., February 27, 1997, S.Hrg. 105-64 (Washington: GPO, 1997), p. 68.

[29] Ibid., p. 36.

[30] U.S. Congress, Senate Committee on Small Business, *S. 1574, The HUBZone Act of 1996: Revitalizing Inner Cities and Rural America*, 104th Cong., 2nd sess., March 21, 1996, S.Hrg. 104-480 (Washington: GPO, 1996), p. 17; U.S. Congress, Senate Committee on Small Business, *S. 208, The HUBZone Act of 1997*, 105th Cong., 1st sess., February 27, 1997, S.Hrg. 105-64 (Washington: GPO, 1997), p. 15; and U.S. Congress, Senate Committee on Small Business, *S. 208, The HUBZone Act of 1997*, 105th Cong., 1st sess., April 10, 1997, S.Hrg. 105-103 (Washington: GPO, 1997), pp. 20, 23, 26, 27, 33, 35, 77, 147, 149, 153-157.

[31] 13 C.F.R. §124.101.

[32] For further analysis of the 8(a) program, see CRS Report R40744, *The "8(a) Program" for Small Businesses Owned and Controlled by the Socially and Economically Disadvantaged: Legal Requirements and Issues*, by Kate M. Manuel and John R. Luckey.

[33] U.S. Congress, Senate Committee on Small Business, *S. 208, The HUBZone Act of 1997*, 105th Cong., 1st sess., February 27, 1997, S.Hrg. 105-64 (Washington: GPO, 1997), p. 36.

[34] U.S. Government Accountability Office, *HUBZone Program: Fraud and Abuse Identified in Four Metropolitan Areas*, GAO-09-440, March 25, 2009, p. 5, at http://www.gao.gov /new.items/d09440.pdf. Also see U.S. Government Accountability Office, *Small Business Administration: Undercover Tests Show HUBZone Program Remains Vulnerable to Fraud and Abuse*, GAO-10-759, June 25, 2010, pp. 2, 4, 5, at http://www.gao.gov/new.items/ d10759.pdf; U.S. Government Accountability Office, *HUBZone Program: Fraud and Abuse Identified in Four Metropolitan Areas* (congressional testimony), GAO-09-519T, March 25, 2009, pp. 2-9, at http://www.gao.gov/ new.items/d09519t.pdf; and U.S. Government Accountability Office, *Small Business Administration: Status of Efforts to Address Previous Recommendations on the HUBZone*

Program (congressional testimony), GAO-09-532T, March 25, 2009, pp. 1-3, at http://www.gao.gov/new.items/d09532t.pdf.

[35] U.S. Congress, House Committee on Small Business, *Full Committee Hearing on Oversight of the Small Business Administration and Its Programs*, 111th Cong., 1st sess., March 25, 2009, Small Business Committee Doc. 111-012 (Washington: GPO, 2009), p. 1.

[36] P.L. 105-135, the HUBZone Act of 1997 (Title VI of the Small Business Reauthorization Act of 1997) designated qualified census tracts, qualified counties (originally only in non-metropolitan areas) and qualified Indian Reservation/Indian Country (originally lands within the external boundaries of an Indian reservation) as eligible. P.L. 108-447, the Consolidated Appropriations Act, 2005, provided HUBZone eligibility for five years to bases closed under the Base Realignment and Closure Act (BRAC). P.L. 109-59, the Safe, Accountable, Flexible, Efficient Transportation Equity Act: A Legacy for Users, provided eligibility to difficult development areas outside of the continental United States.

[37] 13 C.F.R. §126.103 and 26 U.S.C. §42(d)(5)(C)(i).

[38] 26 U.S.C. §42(d)(5)(C)(ii).

[39] U.S. Housing and Urban Development, "Qualified Census Tracts and Difficult Development Areas," at http://www.huduser.org/portal/datasets/qct/qct99home.html.

[40] U.S. Small Business Administration, "The HUBZone Maps," count as of November 5, 2012, at http://www.sba.gov/ content/hubzone-maps.

[41] U.S. Census Bureau, "Census Tracts and Block Numbering Areas," at http://www.census.gov /geo/www/cen_tract.html.

[42] U.S. Census Bureau, "About the ACS: What Is the Survey?" at http://www.census.gov/acs/www/about_the_survey/ american_community_survey/; and U.S. Census Bureau, "American Community Survey: When to use 1-year, 3-year, or 5-year estimates," at http://www.census.gov/acs/www /guidance_for_data_users/estimates/. For further analysis, see CRS Report R40551, *The 2010 Decennial Census: Background and Issues*, by Jennifer D. Williams.

[43] Department of Housing and Urban Development, "Statutorily Mandated Designation of Qualified Census Tracts for Section 42 of the Internal Revenue Code of 1986," 77 *Federal Register* 23735-23740, April 20, 2012.

[44] U.S. Small Business Administration, "The HUBZone Maps," at http://www.sba.gov/content /hubzone-maps.

[45] U.S. Small Business Administration, "Small Business HUBZone Program; Government Contracting Programs," 76 *Federal Register* 43572, July 21, 2011; and U.S. Department of Housing and Urban Development, "Statutorily Mandated Designation of Difficult Development Areas and Qualified Census Tracts for 2012," 76 *Federal Register* 66745, October 27, 2011. HUD also updates QCT status if metropolitan area definitions change.

[46] 13 C.F.R. §126.103.

[47] U.S. Small Business Administration, "The HUBZone Maps," count as of November 5, 2012, at http://www.sba.gov/ content/hubzone-maps.

[48] Henry Beale and Nicola Deas, "The HUBZone Program Report," Washington, DC: Microeconomic Applications, Inc., prepared for the U.S. Small Business Administration, Office of Advocacy, May 2008, p. 146, at http://www.sba.gov/advo/research/rs325tot.pdf.

[49] U.S. Small Business Administration, "Small Business HUBZone Program; Government Contracting Programs," 76 *Federal Register* 43573, July 21, 2011; and U.S. Small Business Administration, Office of Congressional and Legislative Affairs, correspondence with the author, October 19, 2011. HUBZone non-metropolitan counties, by state, can be accessed at http://map.sba.gov/hubzone/maps/.

[50] U.S. Small Business Administration, "Small Business HUBZone Program; Government Contracting Programs," 76 *Federal Register* 43573, July 21, 2011.

[51] U.S. Small Business Administration, Office of Congressional and Legislative Affairs, correspondence with the author, October 17, 2011.

[52] Henry Beale and Nicola Deas, "The HUBZone Program Report," Washington, DC: Microeconomic Applications, Inc., prepared for the U.S. Small Business Administration, Office of Advocacy, May 2008, p. 146, at http://www.sba.gov/advo/research/rs325tot.pdf. About 13% of qualified non-metropolitan counties were redesignated in 2003 as a metropolitan county due to a change in the criteria for determining metropolitan county status. Those counties were allowed to retain their HUBZone status pending the results of the 2010 decennial census.

[53] Ibid., p. 160.

[54] U.S. Small Business Administration, "The HUBZone Maps," count as of November 5, 2012, at http://www.sba.gov/ content/hubzone-maps. There were 659 qualified Indian reservations, Oklahoma tribal

statistical areas, and Alaska Native village statistical areas in May 2010. U.S. Small Business Administration, Office of Congressional and Legislative Affairs, correspondence with the author, May 4, 2010.

[55] Henry Beale and Nicola Deas, "The HUBZone Program Report," Washington, DC: Microeconomic Applications, Inc., prepared for the U.S. Small Business Administration, Office of Advocacy, May 2008, p. 163, at http://www.sba.gov/advo/research/rs325tot.pdf.

[56] U.S. Small Business Administration, "The HUBZone Maps," count as of November 5, 2012, at http://www.sba.gov/ content/hubzone-maps.

[57] P.L. 109-59, the Safe, Accountable, Flexible, Efficient Transportation Equity Act: A Legacy for Users.

[58] Ibid.

[59] U.S. Department of Housing and Urban Development, "Statutorily Mandated Designation of Difficult Development Areas and Qualified Census Tracts for 2010," 74 *Federal Register* 51305, October 6, 2009. Note: In making this determination, HUD calculates a ratio for each metropolitan area and non-metropolitan county of the fair market rent (based on the 40th-percentile gross rent paid by recent movers to live in a two-bedroom apartment) to the monthly low-income housing tax credit-based rent limit, which was calculated as three-twelfths of 30% of 120% of the area's very low-income households (which is based on 50% of area's median gross income).

[60] U.S. Small Business Administration, "The HUBZone Maps: Link to Comprehensive List," at http://www.sba.gov/ content/hubzone-maps.

[61] U.S. Small Business Administration, "Small Business Size Regulations; Government Contracting Programs; HUBZone Program," 67 *Federal Register* 3828, January 28, 2002.

[62] P.L. 106-554, the HUBZones in Native America Act of 2000 (Title VI, the Consolidated Appropriations Act, 2001).

[63] 13 C.F.R. §126.103.

[64] U.S. Government Accountability Office, *Small Business Administration: Additional Actions are Needed to Certify and Monitor HUBZone Businesses and Assess Program Results*, GAO-08-643, June 17, 2008, p. 18, at http://www.gao.gov/new.items/d08643.pdf.

[65] U.S. Small Business Administration, "HUBZone Area Changes—Information Briefing," at http://www.sba.gov/ content/notice-expiration-redesignated-hubzones-october-1-2011.

[66] U.S. Small Business Administration, Office of Congressional and Legislative Affairs, correspondence with the author, May 5, 2011.

[67] U.S. Small Business Administration, "HUBZones: Latest News and Articles," at http://www.sba.gov/content/ hubzone-latest-news-and-articles.

[68] U.S. Small Business Administration, "List of Non-Metropolitan Counties." Final figures for the number of redesignated QCTs and redesignated DDAs that changed status on October 1, 2011, are not publicly available.

[69] U.S. Small Business Administration, "Dynamic Small Business Search Database," at http://dsbs.sba.gov/dsbs/search/ dsp_dsbs.cfm. There were 5,828 certified HUBZone small businesses on October 24, 2012, 5,825 on August 30, 2012, 6,602 on July 5, 2012, 6,623 on March 29, 2012, 6,900 on December 21, 2011, 8,533 on May 5, 2011, and 7,567 in April 2010.

[70] Employees must live in a primary residence within that area for at least 180 days or be a currently registered voter in that area. The HUBZone definition of employee changed on May 3, 2010. Previously, the definition was based on full-time equivalency and only permanent positions were counted. Effective May 3, 2010, "employee means all individuals employed on a full-time, part-time, or other basis, so long as that individual works a minimum of 40 hours per month. This includes employees obtained from a temporary employee agency, leasing concern, or through a union agreement or co-employed pursuant to a professional employer organization agreement." See U.S. Small Business Administration, "HUBZone and Government Contracting," 74 *Federal Register* 56702, November 3, 2009.

[71] 13 C.F.R. §126.200.

[72] U.S. Small Business Administration, "FY2013 Congressional Budget Justification and FY2011 Annual Performance Report," p. 72, at http://www.sba.gov/sites/default/files/files/FY% 202013%20CBJ%20FY% 202011%20APR.pdf.

[73] 13 C.F.R. §126.306.

[74] 13 C.F.R. §126.401.

[75] Ibid.

[76] U.S. Small Business Administration, "FY2011 Congressional Budget Justification and FY2009 Annual Performance Report," pp. 72, 73, at http://www.sba.gov/idc/groups/public /documents/sba_homepage /fy_2011_cbj_09_apr.pdf.

[77] 13 C.F.R. §126.500.

[78] 13 C.F.R. §126.501.

[79] P.L. 95-507, a bill to amend the Small Business Act and the Small Business Investment Act of 1958.

[80] P.L. 100-656, the Business Opportunity Development Reform Act of 1988.

[81] Ibid.

[82] Ibid.

[83] See U.S. General Services Administration, Federal Procurement Data System—Next Generation, "Small Business Goaling Report: Fiscal Year 2011," at https://www.fpds.gov /downloads/top_requests/ FPDSNG_SB_Goaling_FY_2011.pdf.

[84] 15 U.S.C. §644(g)(1)-(2). The SBA

[85] U.S. General Services Administration, Federal Procurement Data System—Next Generation, "Small Business Goaling Report: Fiscal Year 2011," at https://www.fpds.gov/downloads /top_requests/ FPDSNG_SB_Goaling_FY_2011.pdf.

[86] U.S. Government Accountability Office, *HUBZone Program: Fraud and Abuse Identified in Four Metropolitan Areas*, GAO-09-519T, March 25, 2009, p. 2, at http://www.gao.gov/new.items/d09519t.pdf.

[87] U.S. Government Accountability Office, Small Business Administration: Additional Actions are Needed to Certify and Monitor HUBZone Businesses and Assess Program Results, GAO-08-643, June 17, 2008, pp. 3-5, 22-30, 33-37, at http://www.gao.gov/new.items /d08643.pdf; U.S. Government Accountability Office, Small Business Administration: Status of Efforts to Address Previous Recommendations on the HUBZone Program, GAO-09-532T, March 25, 2009, pp. 3, 8, 9, at http://www.gao.gov/new.items/d09532t.pdf; and U.S. Government Accountability Office, Small Business Administration: Undercover Tests Show HUBZone Program Remains Vulnerable to Fraud and Abuse, GAO-10-759, June 25, 2010, at http://www.gao.gov/new.items/d10759.pdf.

[88] *DGR Assocs., Inc. v. United States*, 2010 U.S. Claims LEXIS 588 (August 13, 2010); and *Mission Critical Solutions v. United States*, 2010 U.S. Claims LEXIS 36 (March 2, 2010).

[89] For further information and legal analysis, see CRS Report R40591, *Set-Asides for Small Businesses: Recent Developments in the Law Regarding Precedence Among the Set-Aside Programs and Set-Asides Under IndefiniteDelivery/Indefinite-Quantity Contracts*, by Kate M. Manuel. Also see U.S. Government Accountability Office, *Mission Critical Solutions*, B-401057, May 4, 2009, at http://www.gao.gov/decisions/bidpro/401057.pdf; and Office of Legal Counsel, Department of Justice, "Permissibility of Small Business Administration Regulations Implementing the Historically Underutilized Business Zone, 8(a) Business Development, and Service-Disabled Veteran-Owned Small Business Concern Programs," August 21, 2009, at http://www.justice.gov/olc/2009/sba-hubzone-opinion082109.pdf.

[90] For further analysis of the 8(a) program, see CRS Report R40744, *The "8(a) Program" for Small Businesses Owned and Controlled by the Socially and Economically Disadvantaged: Legal Requirements and Issues*, by Kate M. Manuel and John R. Luckey.

[91] P.L. 108-375, Ronald W. Reagan National Defense Authorization Act for Fiscal Year 2005, §807. Inflation adjustment of acquisition-related dollar thresholds requires an adjustment for inflation every five years of all acquisition-related thresholds. See Department of Defense, General Services Administration, and National Aeronautics and Space Administration, "Federal Acquisition Regulation: Inflation Adjustment of Acquisition-Related Thresholds," 75 *Federal Register* 53129, August 30, 2010.

[92] U.S. Small Business Administration, Office of the Inspector General, "Audit Report of the Eligibility of 15 HUBZone Companies and a Review of the HUBZone Empowerment Contracting Program's Internal Controls," January 22, 2003, at http://www.sba.gov /idc/groups/public/documents/sba/oig_gcbd_03-05.pdf.

[93] Ibid., p. 3.

[94] U.S. Small Business Administration, Office of the Inspector General, "HUBZone Program Examination and Recertification Processes," May 23, 2006, p. 5, at http://www.sba.gov/idc/groups/public /documents /sba/oig_gcbd_6- 23.pdf.

[95] U.S. Small Business Administration, "SBA Budget Request & Performance Plan: FY2004 Congressional Submission," p. 44, at http://www.sba.gov/idc/groups/public/documents/sba_homepage/serv_abt_ budget_ 3.pdf.

[96] U.S. Small Business Administration, Office of the Inspector General, "HUBZone Program Examination and Recertification Processes," May 23, 2006, pp. 3, 6, at http://www.sba.gov/idc/groups/public/documents/sba/ oig_gcbd_6-23.pdf.

[97] U.S. Congress, House Committee on Small Business, *Full Committee Hearing to Consider Legislation Updating and Improving the SBA's Contracting Programs*, 110th Cong., 1st sess., October 4, 2007, Serial Number 110-50 (Washington: GPO, 2007), p. 6.

[98] U.S. Government Accountability Office, *Small Business Administration: Additional Actions are Needed to Certify and Monitor HUBZone Businesses and Assess Program Results*, GAO-08-643, June 17, 2008, p. i, at http://www.gao.gov/new.items/d08643.pdf.

[99] Ibid., pp. 1-5.

[100] U.S. Government Accountability Office, *HUBZone Program: SBA's Control Weaknesses Exposed the Government to Fraud and Abuse*, GAO-08-964T, July 17, 2008, pp. i, 4, 5, 7-9, at http://www.gao.gov /new.items/d08964t.pdf.

[101] Ibid.

[102] Ibid.

[103] Ibid., pp. 5, 10-20.

[104] U.S. Small Business Administration, "Fiscal Year 2010 Congressional Budget Justification," p. 65, at http://www.sba.gov/sites/default/files/Congressional_Budget_Justification_ 2010.pdf.

[105] U.S. Government Accountability Office, *HUBZone Program: Fraud and Abuse Identified in Four Metropolitan Areas*, GAO-09-440, March 25, 2009, p. 2, at http://www.gao.gov/new.items/d09440.pdf.

[106] U.S. Government Accountability Office, *Small Business Administration: Status of Efforts to Address Previous Recommendations on the HUBZone Program*, GAO-09-532T, March 25, 2009, pp. 5-8, at http://www.gao.gov/ new.items/d09532t.pdf.

[107] U.S. Government Accountability Office, *HUBZone Program: Fraud and Abuse Identified in Four Metropolitan Areas*, GAO-09-440, March 25, 2009, p. 7, at http://www.gao.gov /new.items/d09440.pdf.

[108] U.S. Small Business Administration, "FY2011 Congressional Budget Justification and FY2009 Annual Performance Report," pp. 72, 73, at http://www.sba.gov/idc/groups/public /documents/sba_homepage/fy_ 2011_cbj_09_apr.pdf.

[109] Ibid., p. 76.

[110] Ibid., pp. 72, 73.

[111] Testimony of Karen G. Mills, SBA Administrator, before the U.S. House of Representatives Committee on Small Business, "Accountability Update," April 21, 2010, at http://www.house.gov/smbiz /democrats/hearings/hearing-04-21- 10-oversight/Mills.pdf.

[112] U.S. Small Business Administration, "Application processing times remain significant, but are now decreasing," at http://www.sbaonline.sba.gov/hubzone/new/index.html.

[113] U.S. Small Business Administration, Office of Congressional and Legislative Affairs, correspondence with the author, May 4, 2010.

[114] U.S. Small Business Administration, "FY2013 Congressional Budget Justification and FY2011 Annual Performance Report," p. 72, at http://www.sba.gov/sites/default/files/files /FY%202013%20CBJ%20FY% 202011%20APR.pdf.

[115] U.S. Government Accountability Office, *Small Business Administration: Undercover Tests Show HUBZone Program Remains Vulnerable to Fraud and Abuse*, GAO-10-759, June 25, 2010, Highlights section and p. 2, at http://www.gao.gov/new.items/d10759.pdf.

[116] Ibid., p. 4.

[117] Ibid.

[118] Ibid., Highlights section.

[119] U.S. Government Accountability Office, *Small Business Administration: Undercover Tests Show HUBZone Program Remains Vulnerable to Fraud and Abuse*, GAO-10-920T, July 28, 2010, p. 3, at http://www.gao.gov/ new.items/d10920t.pdf.

[120] Ibid.

[121] Ibid.

[122] Ibid.

[123] Ibid.

[124] The bill's sponsor, Senator Olympia Snowe, introduced similar legislation in 2010, S. 3020, the HUBZone Improvement Act of 2010. See Senator Olympia Snowe, "Statements on Introduced Bills and Joint Resolutions," remarks in the Senate, *Congressional Record*, daily edition, vol. 156 (February 23, 2010), p. S702.

[125] U.S. Congress, House Committee on Small Business, *Full Committee Hearing on Oversight of the Small Business Administration and its Programs*, 111th Cong., 1st sess., March 25, 2009, Small Business Committee

Small Business Administration HUBZone Program   269

Document Number 111-012 (Washington: GPO, 2009), pp. 4-27, 32-38; Testimony of Karen G. Mills, SBA Administrator, before the U.S. House of Representatives Committee on Small Business, "Accountability Update," April 21, 2010, at http://www.house.gov/smbiz/democrats/hearings/hearing-04-21-10-oversight/Mills.pdf; U.S. Small Business Administration, "FY2011 Congressional Budget Justification and FY2009 Annual Performance Report," pp. 72, 73, at http://www.sba.gov/idc/groups/public /documents/sba_homepage/fy_2011_cbj_09_apr.pdf; and U.S. Small Business Administration, "FY2012 Congressional Budget Justification and FY2010 Annual Performance Report," pp. 77-79, at http://www.sba.gov/sites/default/files/FINAL %20FY%202012%20CBJ%20FY%202010%20APR_0.pdf.

[126] U.S. Government Accountability Office, *Small Business Administration: Additional Actions are Needed to Certify and Monitor HUBZone Businesses and Assess Program Results*, GAO-08-643, June 17, 2008, p. 5, at http://www.gao.gov/new.items/d08643.pdf.

[127] Ibid., p. 34.

[128] Ibid., p. 45.

[129] Ibid., p. 46.

[130] U.S. Government Accountability Office, *Small Business Administration: Status of Efforts to Address Previous Recommendations on the HUBZone Program*, GAO-09-532T, March 25, 2009, p. 8, at http://www.gao.gov/new.items/ d09532t.pdf.

[131] Henry Beale and Nicola Deas, "The HUBZone Program Report," Washington, DC: Microeconomic Applications, Inc., prepared for the U.S. Small Business Administration, Office of Advocacy, May 2008, pp. i–iii, at http://www.sba.gov/advo/research/rs325tot.pdf.

[132] U.S. Small Business Administration, "Notice of methodology for measuring the economic impact of the HUBZone Program," 73 *Federal Register* 46698-46703, August 11, 2008.

[133] Ibid., p. 46701.

[134] U.S. Government Accountability Office, *Small Business Administration: Status of Efforts to Address Previous Recommendations on the HUBZone Program*, GAO-09-532T, March 25, 2009, p. 9, at http://www.gao.gov /new.items/d09532t.pdf.

[135] Ibid.

[136] U.S. Small Business Administration, "FY2011 Congressional Budget Justification and FY2009 Annual Performance Report," p. 73, at http://www.sba.gov/idc/groups/public /documents/sba_homepage/fy_2011_cbj_09_apr.pdf.

[137] Ibid.

[138] S. 633, the Small Business Contracting Fraud Prevention Act of 2011, §6. HUBZone Improvements.

[139] Ibid.

[140] U.S. Congress, House Committee on Small Business, *Full Committee Hearing on Oversight of the Small Business Administration and its Programs*, 111th Cong., 1st sess., March 25, 2009, Small Business Committee Document Number 111-012 (Washington: GPO, 2009), pp. 4-27, 32-38; U.S. Small Business Administration, "FY2011 Congressional Budget Justification and FY2009 Annual Performance Report," pp. 72, 73, at http://www.sba.gov/sites/ default/files/Congressional_Budget_Justification.pdf; and U.S. Small Business Administration, "FY2012 Congressional Budget Justification and FY2010 Annual Performance Report," pp. 77-79, at http://www.sba.gov/sites/ default/files/FINAL%20FY%202012%20CBJ%20FY% 202010%20 APR.pdf.

[141] U.S. Small Business Administration, Office of Entrepreneurial Development, "Impact Study of Entrepreneurial Development Resources," September 13, 2010, at http://www.sba.gov/sites/default/files/09- 10%20SBA%2 0ED%20Resources%20Impact%20Study%20Final%20Report.pdf.

[142] Ibid., p. 4.

[143] Henry Beale and Nicola Deas, "The HUBZone Program Report," Washington D.C., for the U.S. Small Business Administration, May 2008, p. 159, at http://www.sba.gov/advo /research/rs325tot.pdf.

[144] U.S. Census Bureau, "About the ACS: What Is the Survey?" at http://www.census.gov/acs /www/SBasics/What/ What1.htm; and U.S. Census Bureau, "American Community Survey: When to use 1-year, 3-year, or 5-year estimates," at http://www.census.gov/acs/www /guidance_for_data_users/estimates/. For further analysis, see CRS Report R40551, *The 2010 Decennial Census: Background and Issues*, by Jennifer D. Williams.

[145] U.S. Small Business Administration, "How often do QCTs HUBZone designations change?" at http://www.sba.gov/ content/how-often-do-qcts-hubzone-designations-change; and U.S. Small Business Administration, "Small Business HUBZone Program; Government Contracting Programs," 76 *Federal Register* 43573, July 21, 2011.

[146] Ibid.

[147] U.S. Small Business Administration, Office of Congressional and Legislative Affairs, correspondence with CRS, October 13, 2011. The original estimate was 40%, see U.S. Small Business Administration, "Small Business HUBZone Program; Government Contracting Programs," 76 *Federal Register* 43573, July 21, 2011.

[148] U.S. Small Business Administration, Office of Congressional and Legislative Affairs, correspondence with CRS, October 13, 2011. A firm must be qualified both at the time of its initial offer and at the time of award in order to be eligible for a HUBZone contract.

[149] U.S. Small Business Administration, "Small Business HUBZone Program; Government Contracting Programs," 76 *Federal Register* 43573, July 21, 2011.

[150] Ibid.

[151] H.R. 2416, the Monroe County HUBZone Extension Act of 2011, and S. 976, the Monroe County HUBZone Act of 2011, would extend the designation of Monroe County, Pennsylvania as a HUBZone until October 1, 2014. H.R. 2712, the Shuttle Workforce Revitalization Act of 2011, would extend the designation of Brevard County, Florida as a HUBZone until January 1, 2020.

[152] U.S. Small Business Administration, Office of Congressional and Legislative Affairs, correspondence with CRS, October 13, 2011. The original estimate was 40%, see U.S. Small Business Administration, "Small Business HUBZone Program; Government Contracting Programs," 76 *Federal Register* 43573, July 21, 2011.

[153] U.S. Small Business Administration, "FY2011 Congressional Budget Justification and FY 2009 Annual Performance Report," p. 72, at http://www.sba.gov/sites/default/files /Congressional_Budget_Justification.pdf.

[154] Testimony of Karen G. Mills, SBA Administrator, before the U.S. House of Representatives Committee on Small Business, "Accountability Update," Washington, DC, April 21, 2010, at http://www.house.gov/smbiz/democrats/ hearings/hearing-04-21-10-oversight/Mills.pdf.

[155] Ibid.

[156] U.S. Small Business Administration, "FY2013 Congressional Budget Justification and FY2011 Annual Performance Report," p. 72, at http://www.sba.gov/sites/default/files/files /FY%202013%20CBJ%20FY %202011%20APR.pdf.

In: Small Business Administration Programs
Editor: Walter Janikowski

ISBN: 978-1-62417-992-1
© 2013 Nova Science Publishers, Inc.

Chapter 10

SBA SURETY BOND GUARANTEE PROGRAM[*]

Robert Jay Dilger

SUMMARY

The Small Business Administration's (SBA's) Surety Bond Guarantee Program is designed to increase small businesses' access to federal, state, and local government contracting, as well as private-sector contracts, by guaranteeing bid, performance, and payment bonds for individual contracts of $2 million or less for small businesses that cannot obtain surety bonds through regular commercial channels. The SBA's guarantee ranges from 70% to 90% of the surety's loss if a default occurs. In FY2012, the SBA guaranteed 9,503 bid and final surety bonds with a total contract value of about $3.9 billion. A surety bond is a three-party instrument between a surety (who agrees to be responsible for the debt or obligation of another), a contractor, and a project owner. The agreement binds the contractor to comply with the contract's terms and conditions. If the contractor is unable to successfully perform the contract, the surety assumes the contractor's responsibilities and ensures that the project is completed. Surety bonds are viewed as a means to encourage project owners to contract with small businesses that may not have the credit history or prior experience of larger businesses and are considered to be at greater risk of failing to comply with the contract's terms and conditions. P.L. 111-5, the American Recovery and Reinvestment Act of 2009 (ARRA), temporarily increased, from February 17, 2009, through September 30, 2010, the program's bond limit to $5 million, and up to $10 million if a federal contracting officer certifies in writing that a guarantee over $5 million is necessary. The Obama Administration has recommended that the bond limit be increased to $5 million, most recently as part of its request for supplemental assistance for damages caused by Hurricane Sandy. During the 112th Congress, several bills were introduced to increase the program's bond limit, including S. 1334, the Expanding Opportunities for Main Street Act of 2011, and its companion bill in the House, H.R. 2424. They would reinstate and make permanent ARRA's higher limits. Also, H.R. 4310, the National Defense Authorization Act for Fiscal Year 2013, passed by the House on May 18, 2012, would increase the program's bond limit to $6.5 million, and up to $10 million if a federal contracting officer certifies that such a guarantee is necessary. Also, on December 12,

---

[*] This is an edited, reformatted and augmented version of Congressional Research Service, Publication No. R42037, dated December 14, 2012.

2012, the Senate Committee on Appropriations released its draft of the Hurricane Sandy Emergency Assistance Supplemental bill. It includes a provision to increase the program's bond limit to $5 million. Advocates of raising the program's bond limit argue that doing so would increase contracting opportunities for small businesses and bring the limit more in line with limits of other small business programs, such as the 8(a) Minority Small Business and Capital Ownership Development Program and the Historically Underutilized Business Zone (HUBZone) Program. Opponents argue that raising the limit could lead to higher amounts being guaranteed by the SBA and, as a result, an increase in the risk of program losses. This report examines the program's origin and development, including the decision to supplement the original Prior Approval Program with the Preferred Surety Bond Guarantee Program that provides a lower guarantee rate (70%) than the Prior Approval Program (80% or 90%) in exchange for allowing preferred sureties to issue SBA-guaranteed surety bonds without the SBA's prior approval. It also examines the program's eligibility standards and requirements, provides performance statistics, and concludes with a discussion of proposals to increase the program's $2 million bond limit and to merge the Prior Approval Program and the Preferred Surety Bond Guarantee Program while retaining the Preferred Program's more flexible operating requirements.

CONGRESSIONAL INTEREST IN SURETY BONDS

The Small Business Administration (SBA) administers several programs to support small businesses, including loan guaranty programs to enhance small business access to capital; contracting programs to increase small business opportunities in securing federal contracts; direct loan programs for businesses, homeowners, and renters to assist their recovery from natural disasters; and small business management and technical assistance training programs to assist business formation and expansion. Congressional interest in these programs has increased in recent years, primarily because assisting small business is viewed as a means to enhance economic growth.

The SBA's Surety Bond Guarantee Program has been operational since April 1971.[1] It is designed to increase small business's access to federal, state, and local government contracting, as well as private-sector contracting, by guaranteeing "bid, performance, and payment bonds for individual contracts of $2 million or less for small and emerging contractors who cannot obtain surety bonds through regular commercial channels."[2] In FY2012, the SBA guaranteed 9,503 bid and final surety bonds (a payment bond, performance bond, or both a payment and performance bond) with a total contract value of about $3.9 billion.[3] Although the surety industry does not report the total value of the bonds it issues each year, estimates based on the total amount of premiums collected by the private sector in recent years suggests that the SBA's Surety Bond Guarantee Program represents, by design, a relatively small percentage of the market for surety bonds (from 0.6% to 2.5% of the value of surety bonds issued by the private sector).[4]

A surety bond is a three-party instrument between a surety (who agrees to be responsible for the debt or obligation of another), a contractor, and a project owner. The agreement binds the contractor to comply with the contract's terms and conditions. If the contractor is unable to successfully perform the contract, the surety assumes the contractor's responsibilities and ensures that the project is completed. The surety bond reduces the risk of contracting.[5]

Surety bonds are viewed as a means to encourage project owners to contract with small businesses that may not have the credit history or prior experience of larger businesses and are considered to be at greater risk of failing to comply with the contract's terms and conditions.[6] The three general types of surety bonds are

- *bid bonds* guarantee that the bidder on a contract will enter into the contract and furnish the required payment and performance bonds if awarded the contract,
- *payment bonds* guarantee that suppliers and subcontractors will be paid for work performed under the contract, and
- *performance bonds* guarantee that the contractor will perform the contract in accordance with its terms and conditions.[7]

Surety bonds are important to small businesses interested in competing for a federal contract because the federal government requires prime contractors, prior to the award of a federal contract exceeding $150,000 for the construction, alteration, or repair of any building or public work of the United States, to furnish a performance bond issued by a surety satisfactory to the officer awarding the contract, and in an amount the contracting officer considers adequate, to protect the government.[8] Prime contractors are also required to post a payment bond with a surety satisfactory to the contracting officer for the protection of all persons supplying labor and material in carrying out the work provided for in the contract. Both bonds become legally binding upon award of the contract and their "penal amounts," or the maximum amount of the surety's obligation, must generally be 100% of the original contract price plus 100% of any price increases.[9] Most state and local governments have adopted similar legislation, often called "Little Miller Acts," referencing the Miller Act of 1935 that established the federal requirement.[10] Many private project owners also require contractors to furnish a surety bond before awarding them a contract.

P.L. 111-5, the American Recovery and Reinvestment Act of 2009 (ARRA), temporarily increased, from February 17, 2009, through September 30, 2010, the program's bond limit to $5 million, and up to $10 million if a federal contracting officer certifies in writing that a guarantee in excess of $5 million is necessary. There have been several legislative efforts during the 112th Congress to increase the program's bond limit.

S. 1334, the Expanding Opportunities for Main Street Act of 2011, and its companion bill in the House, H.R. 2424, would reinstate and make permanent ARRA's higher limits. S. 1660, the American Jobs Act of 2011, and its companion bill in the House, H.R. 12, would have provided $3 million to fund a temporary increase in the program's $2 million bond limit to $5 million until the end of FY2012. H.R. 4310, the National Defense Authorization Act for Fiscal Year 2013, which the House passed on May 18, 2012, would increase the program's bond limit to $6.5 million, and up to $10 million if a federal contracting officer certifies that such a guarantee is necessary.

Also, on December 12, 2012, the Senate Committee on Appropriations released its draft of the Hurricane Sandy Emergency Assistance Supplemental bill. It includes a provision to increase the program's bond limit to $5 million.[11] As will be discussed, the Obama Administration has recommended that the SBA's surety bond limit be increased to $5 million, most recently as part of its request for supplemental assistance for damages caused by Hurricane Sandy.[12]

This report opens with an examination of the SBA's Surety Bond Guarantee Program's legislative origin and provides a historical summary of the major issues that have influenced the program's development, including the decision to supplement the original Prior Approval Program with a Preferred Surety Bond Guarantee Program that provides SBA-approved sureties a lower guarantee rate (70%) than those participating in the Prior Approval Program (80% or 90%) in exchange for allowing preferred sureties to issue SBA-guaranteed bonds to small businesses without the SBA's prior approval. It then examines the program's current eligibility standards and requirements, and provides performance statistics, including the number and amount of bond guarantees issued annually.

The report concludes by examining proposals to increase the program's $2 million bond limit and to merge the Prior Approval Program and the Preferred Surety Bond Guarantee Program while retaining the Preferred Program's more flexible operating requirements.

In addition, data concerning the number and amount, in both nominal and inflation-adjusted dollars, of final bonds guaranteed from FY1971 through FY2012 (see Table A-1) and for bid and final bonds combined from FY2000 through FY2012 (see Table A-2) are provided.

LEGISLATIVE ORIGIN

P.L. 91-609, the Housing and Urban Development Act of 1970, authorized the SBA's Surety Bond Guarantee Program.[13] The act amended Title IV of the Small Business Investment Act of 1958 (P.L. 85-699, as amended) to provide the SBA authority to guarantee any surety against loss as the result of a breach of the terms of a bid bond, payment bond, or performance bond by a principal on any contract up to $500,000.[14] The act specified that (1) the principal of the bond is a small business, (2) the bond is required as a condition of bidding on the contract or serving as a prime contractor or subcontractor on the project, (3) the small business is not able to obtain such bond on reasonable terms and conditions without the guarantee, (4) the SBA determines that there is a reasonable expectation that the small business will perform the covenants and conditions of the contract, (5) the contact meets SBA requirements concerning the feasibility of the contract being completed successfully and at a reasonable cost, and (6) the bond's terms and conditions are reasonable in light of the risks involved and the extent of the surety's participation.[15] The act also required that the SBA's guarantee not exceed 90% of the loss incurred by the surety in the event of a breach of the bond's terms and conditions by the small business.[16]

The SBA was authorized to finance the program through the Leasing Guarantee Revolving Loan Fund within the Department of the Treasury, which renamed that fund the Lease and Surety Bond Guarantee Revolving Fund. The act authorized the transfer of $5 million from the SBA's Business Loan and Investment Revolving Fund to the Lease and Surety Bond Guarantee Revolving Fund, raising that fund's capital to $10 million available without fiscal year limitation, to support both the lease guarantee program and the surety bond guarantee program.[17] The act also recommended that the program be appropriated up to $1.5 million each fiscal year for three fiscal years after its date of enactment (December 31, 1970) if additional funding were needed to offset the program's expenses.[18]

The SBA was directed to administer the program "on a prudent and economically justifiable basis."[19] It was authorized to offset the program's administrative costs by charging a uniform annual fee, subject to periodic review to ensure that the fee is the "lowest fee that experience under the program shows to be justified," and uniform fees for the processing of applications for guarantees.[20] The SBA also was authorized to "obligate the surety to pay the Administration such portions of the bond fee as the Administration determines to be reasonable in light of the relative risks and costs involved."[21]

The program's sponsors argued in 1970 that "there is widespread evidence that a significant number of construction contracting organizations find varying degrees of difficulty in obtaining surety bonds" and that " the major share of these organizations are small businesses, and many of them are headed by minority groups."[22] They argued that the Surety Bond Guarantee Program would "facilitate the entry and advancement of small and minority contractors in the construction business."[23] At that time, witnesses at congressional hearings testified that surety bonds were not necessarily required for most private sector construction contracts, but they were required for most public sector construction contracts.[24]

INITIAL DEMAND AND COSTS EXCEED EXPECTATIONS

The SBA implemented the program on a pilot basis on April 5, 1971, in Kansas City. The program later was expanded to Los Angeles and became nationwide on September 2, 1971.[25] Initially, the SBA guaranteed 90% of the amount of all of the surety bonds in the program and charged sureties 10% of the bond premium paid to the surety company by the contractor.[26] It also charged small business applicants for payment and performance bonds 0.2% of the contract price upon their obtaining the contract. It did not charge for the processing of bid bonds, rejected applications, or applications that did not result in a contract award.[27] Contractors wishing to participate in the program were required to have less than $750,000 in gross annual receipts for the past fiscal year or to have averaged less than $750,000 in gross annual receipts over the past three fiscal years. This size standard was more stringent than for other SBA programs, and it was designed "to reach that segment of small business which was obviously intended to benefit from the legislation as evidenced by the limit of $500,000 on any one contract."[28]

Demand for the program exceeded the SBA's expectations. In 1971, the SBA estimated that it would guarantee about 8,000 contracts amounting to about $540 million from FY1972 through FY1974. Instead, it guaranteed 16,118 contracts amounting to nearly $1.1 billion (see Table A-1 in the Appendix).[29] Because the demand for the program exceeded expectations and the initial fees proved to be insufficient to recoup the program's expenses, in 1974, the SBA requested an additional $25 million for the program. The SBA argued that the additional funds were necessary to take into account the program's projected growth and to establish a reserve fund "to protect against having to suspend [the] program in the fact of more rapid growth than is projected."[30]

In response to the SBA's request for additional funding for the program, Congress held congressional hearings to reassess the need for the program and to explore options concerning how to finance the program's proposed expansion. The financing discussions focused on the relative merits of relying primarily on higher fees to increase the program's revenue, reductions in the guarantee percentage to reduce the program's expenses, or additional appropriations to finance the program's proposed expansion. Although the SBA has periodically increased the program's fees and later instituted a tiered system of guarantee percentages, historically, the SBA has tried to keep the program's fees as low as economically feasible and the guarantee percentage as high as economically feasible to encourage the program's use. As a SBA official testified before Congress in 1975:

> SBA's loss exposure could be reduced by a decrease in the guarantee extended to sureties from 90% to 80%. Before proceeding with this recommendation, a thorough analysis will have to be made of the adverse effect on the willingness of sureties to participate in the program which would result from the increase from 10% to 20% of the sureties' share of the loss potential.
>
> An increase in contractor's fees would obviously be beneficial to the operating income of the program, but would also increase the bids which small business-contractors would have to make, thus placing them at a competitive disadvantage with contractors with more ready access to bonding.[31]

Moreover, as mentioned previously, the SBA is required by statute to ensure that the fees are the lowest "that experience under the program shows to be justified."[32] Determining the program's appropriate size, and how to finance the program, soon became a recurring theme at congressional hearings, and it has continued to serve as a major issue of congressional interest in the program to the present day. For example, as part of its continuing effort to determine the program's appropriate size, Congress has regularly requested testimony from representatives of the surety bond industry and various construction organizations concerning the extent to which the program is necessary to assist small businesses generally, and minority-owned small businesses in particular, in gaining access to surety bonds. It has also periodically asked the Government Accountability Office (GAO) to examine the need for the SBA's surety bond guarantee program and to recommend ways to improve the program's management.[33]

That testimony and GAO's reports have supported a need for the program, but, as will be discussed, have had somewhat limited usefulness in helping Congress determine the program's appropriate size. In 1974, Congress responded to the SBA's request for additional funding for the program by passing P.L. 93-386, the Small Business Amendments of 1974. It established a separate Surety Bond Guarantees Revolving Fund account within the Department of the Treasury to support the program. The act also recommended that the program be appropriated $35 million in additional funding. It also increased the maximum dollar amount of the contract that could be provided a guarantee to $1 million from $500,000.[34] The Ford Administration objected to increasing the program's funding through appropriations. Instead, it recommended transferring $20 million from the SBA's Business Loan and Investment Revolving Fund to the Surety Bond Guarantee Revolving Fund. The transfer would provide the program access to additional capital without affecting the federal budget deficit. Congress approved the Administration's proposal.[35]

As shown on Table 1, Congress subsequently approved additional appropriations amounting to $130.5 million for FY1976 through FY1979 to support the program's continued growth. Congress also provided the program additional appropriations during the 1980s and 1990s, but as will be discussed, the appropriations were not sufficient to continue the program's growth.

Table 1. SBA Surety Bond Guarantee Program Appropriations, FY1976-FY2012

Fiscal Year	Appropriation	Fiscal Year	Appropriation
1976	$12,500,000	1995	$5,369,000
1977	$36,000,000	1996	$2,530,000
1978	$47,000,000	1997	$3,730,000
1979	$35,000,000	1998	$3,500,000
1980	$0	1999	$3,300,000
1981	$0	2000	$0
1982	$19,000,000	2001	$0
1983	$0	2002	$0
1984	$8,910,000	2003	$0
1985	$8,910,000	2004	$0
1986	$7,000,000	2005	$2,900,000
1987	$9,497,000	2006	$2,861,000
1988	$9,497,000	2007	$2,861,000
1989	$9,497,000	2008	$3,000,000
1990	$11,000,000	2009	$17,000,000
1991	$10,200,000	2010	$1,000,000
1992	$14,600,000	2011	$0
1993	$13,020,000	2012	$0
1994	$7,000,000	2013	$0

Source: P.L. 94-121, the Department of State, Justice, and Commerce, the Judiciary, and Related Agencies Appropriation Act, 1976; P.L. 94-362, the Departments of State, Justice, and Commerce, the Judiciary, and Related Agencies Appropriation Act, 1977; P.L. 95-86, the Departments of State, Justice, and Commerce, the Judiciary, and Related Agencies Appropriation Act, 1978; P.L. 95-431, the Departments of State, Justice, and Commerce, the Judiciary, and Related Agencies Appropriation Act, 1979; P.L. 97-92, A joint resolution making further continuing appropriations for the fiscal year 1982, and for other purposes; P.L. 98-166, the Departments of Commerce, Justice, and State, the Judiciary, and Related Agencies Appropriation Act, 1984; P.L. 98-411, the Departments of Commerce, Justice, and State, the Judiciary, and Related Agencies Appropriation Act, 1985; P.L. 99-180, the Departments of Commerce, Justice, and State, the Judiciary, and Related Agencies Appropriation Act, 1986; P.L. 99-591, A joint resolution making continuing appropriations for the fiscal year 1987, and for other purposes; P.L. 100-202; A joint resolution making further continuing appropriations for the fiscal year 1988, and for other purposes; P.L. 100-459, the Departments of Commerce, Justice, and State, the Judiciary, and Related Agencies Appropriations Act, 1989; P.L. 101-162, the Departments of Commerce, Justice, and State, the Judiciary, and Related Agencies Appropriations Act, 1990; P.L. 101-515, the Departments of Commerce, Justice, and State, the Judiciary, and Related Agencies Appropriations Act, 1991; P.L. 102-140, the Departments of Commerce, Justice, and State, the Judiciary, and Related Agencies Appropriations Act, 1992; P.L. 102-395, the Departments of Commerce, Justice, and State, the Judiciary, and Related Agencies Appropriations Act, 1993; P.L. 103-121, the Departments of Commerce, Justice, and State, the Judiciary, and Related Agencies Appropriations Act, 1994; P.L. 103-317, the Departments of Commerce, Justice, and State, the Judiciary and Related Agencies Appropriations Act, 1995; P.L. 104-134, the Omnibus Consolidated Rescissions and Appropriations Act of 1996; P.L. 104-208, the Omnibus Consolidated Appropriations Act, 1997; P.L. 105-119, the Departments of Commerce, Justice, and State, the Judiciary, and Related Agencies Appropriations Act, 1998; P.L. 105-277, the Omnibus Consolidated and Emergency Supplemental Appropriations Act, 1999; P.L. 108-447, the Consolidated Appropriations Act, 2005; P.L. 109-108, the Science, State, Justice, Commerce, and Related Agencies Appropriations Act, 2006; P.L. 109-289, Making Appropriations for the Department of Defense for the fiscal year ending September 30, 2007, and for other purposes; P.L. 110-161, the Consolidated Appropriations Act, 2008; P.L. 111-5, the American Recovery and Reinvestment Act of 2009; P.L. 111-8, the Omnibus Appropriations Act, 2009; P.L. 111-117, the Consolidated Appropriations Act, 2010; P.L. 112-10, the Department of Defense and Full-Year Continuing Appropriations Act, 2011; P.L. 112-74, the Consolidated Appropriations Act, 2012; and P.L. 112-175, the Continuing Appropriations Resolution, 2013.

Instead, both in terms of the number of final surety bonds guaranteed by the SBA and the amount guaranteed by the SBA, the program began to slowly diminish, a general trend that has generally continued for final bonds, but, as will be shown, not for bid bonds. As shown on Table 1, Congress did not appropriate any funding for the program from FY2000- FY2004, allowing the program to cover the cost of claim defaults through its reserve. Congress appropriated $2.9 million for the program in FY2005, $2.86 million in FY2006, $2.86 million in FY2007, and $3.0 million in FY2008. During the 111th Congress, P.L. 111-5, the American Recovery and Reinvestment Act of 2009, provided the program a separate appropriation of $15 million to support a temporary increase in the program's bond limit to $5 million, and up to $10 million if a federal contracting officer certifies in writing that a guarantee in excess of $5 million is necessary. Those funds were in addition to the $2 million that had already been appropriated for the program for FY2009. In FY2010, the program received $1 million, and in FY2011, FY2012, and FY2013, as part of an effort to contain costs, Congress did not provide the program additional funding, noting that the Obama Administration had estimated that there were sufficient funds in the program's reserve to cover the cost of anticipated claim defaults.[36] As mentioned previously, the SBA relied primarily on increased appropriations to finance the program's expansion during the 1970s, but it also increased the program's fees charged to applicants and sureties. For example, in 1976, the SBA increased its fees to sureties to 20% from 10% of the bond premium, instituted a deductible clause on bond claims, and generally limited its approval for bid, participation, and performance bonds to $250,000 unless specified circumstances were met.[37] In 1977, it increased the contractor applicant fee for payment and performance bonds to 0.5% from 0.2% of the contract price upon their obtaining the contract.[38] The program's current fee structure is discussed later in this report.

RAPID GROWTH IS NOT SUSTAINED

Both the number of final surety bonds guaranteed by the SBA each fiscal year and the amount guaranteed by the SBA increased relatively rapidly during the 1970s (see Table A-1 in the Appendix). The number of final surety bonds guaranteed by the SBA increased from 1,339 in FY1972 to 20,095 in FY1979, and the amount guaranteed by the SBA increased from $94.4 million in FY1972 to $1.39 billion in FY1979.

During the 1980s and 1990s, both the number of final surety bonds guaranteed by the SBA each fiscal year and the amount guaranteed by the SBA generally declined, in both nominal and inflation-adjusted dollars. A review of congressional testimony during the 1980s and 1990s suggests that there was no single, discernible factor to account for the program's slow contraction over that time period. Because the demand for surety bonds tends to fluctuate with changes in the economy, the program might have been expected to contract somewhat during recessions, but the economy experienced periods of both economic growth and decline during the 1980s and 1990s. There also was no indication that the ability of small businesses to access surety bonds in the private marketplace without the SBA's assistance had materially improved, which, if that had been the case, might have contributed to the decline by reducing the number of small businesses applying for assistance.

One possible contributing factor to the decline in the number of final surety bonds guaranteed by the SBA during the 1980s and 1990s was the continuing reluctance of many surety companies to participate in the program, either because they did not view the program as particularly profitable or because they "had developed alternative methods to the program, such as requiring collateral or funds controls and underwriting programs based in part on credit scores, in order to write small and emerging contractors."[39] Another possible contributing factor was a change in the way the program was perceived by congressional leaders and in their willingness to provide additional resources necessary to continue the program's expansion.

During the 1970s, the program was uniformly praised by witnesses at congressional hearings as a great success in helping small businesses access surety bonds and compete for government contracts. During the 1980s and 1990s, congressional hearings focused less on the program's successes and more on its shortcomings.

For example, in 1982, the chair of the Senate Committee on Small Business indicted that the program at that time was subject to "the most insidious types of fraud," including "evidence of involvement of organized crime figures."[40] In addition, reports by both GAO and the SBA's inspector general had called into question the SBA's management of the program, arguing, among other things, that the SBA lacked useful underwriting guidelines for surety companies and adequate procedures for verifying information provided by applicants.[41]

During the 1980s, the SBA guaranteed, on average, 11,840 final surety bonds each fiscal year, with the SBA's share of those bonds' value averaging $1.0 billion. During the 1990s, the SBA guaranteed, on average, 5,859 final surety bonds each fiscal year, with the SBA's share of those bonds' value averaging $823 million.

During the 2000s, the SBA guaranteed, on average, about 1,802 final surety bonds each fiscal year, with the SBA's share of those bonds' value averaging about $385 million.[42] In FY2012, the SBA guaranteed 2,323 final surety bonds. The SBA's share of those bonds' value was $625.3 million.[43]

THE PREFERRED SURETY BOND GUARANTEE PROGRAM

The surety bonding process begins when a contractor applies for a bond. As GAO has reported

> Surety companies are generally corporations that are licensed under various insurance laws and, under their charters, have legal power to act as a surety (making themselves responsible for another's obligations) for others. Most surety companies accept business only through independent agents and brokers. In screening a bond applicant, a surety attempts to measure the contractor's ability to undertake and complete the job. When the surety's evaluation of the contractor's acceptability to perform the contract is favorable, the surety underwrites the bond. If the surety does not provide a bond to the bond applicant, the appropriate forms are forwarded to SBA for consideration of a surety bond guarantee.[44]

Initially, the SBA surety guaranteed program's bonds were underwritten and issued by large, "standard" surety companies. However, the larger surety companies' participation in the program soon began to decline, reportedly because of the administrative burdens associated with the program, such as the SBA's requirement that sureties submit all bond applications to the SBA for its review and approval.[45] In addition, the administrative costs of dealing with relatively small bonds versus relatively large ones may have also played a role in the larger, standard surety companies leaving the program. As a congressional witness testified in 1976:

> you have a professional underwriter, who ... is going to be asked to spend 3 or 4 days looking into a $25,000 first-time application. There are many expenses involved. That same underwriter could very easily be writing four or five bonds for $10 million for contractors that everyone knows can perform. And it becomes a matter of how much time and resources can the surety industry devote to this type of business.[46]

Another contributing factor may have been the outbreak of the Israeli-Egyptian War in 1973, which was followed by a tripling of oil prices and double-digit inflation. This led to the failure of many smaller contracting companies. In response to the economic downturn, many surety companies enhanced their underwriting standards to protect themselves from rising defaults. As a result, many of the larger surety companies became increasing reluctant to participate in a program in which the profit margins were relatively small given the required paperwork and the program's limitation on the bond amount, and when the risk of defaults was at a historically high level.[47]

The void created by the departure of standard sureties from the program was filled by the expansion of "specialty" surety companies. Initially, specialty sureties devoted almost all their business exclusively to SBA-guaranteed surety bonds.[48] These companies later expanded their business into offering other high-risk bonds not normally handled by standard sureties. Specialty sureties typically required the contractor to provide collateral for the projects they bonded, and, in most cases, charged higher premiums than standard sureties.[49]

In 1982, the SBA invited officials from the Surety Association of America, representing the standard surety companies, to suggest ways to encourage their participation in the program.[50] As mentioned previously, at that time, some specialty surety companies had been accused of being associated with organized crime and GAO and the SBA's inspector general had reported the existence of fraud and mismanagement in the program. This may help to explain why the SBA was interested in encouraging the larger, more established surety companies to return to the program. The SBA also hoped that greater participation by the larger sureties would lead to lower premiums for small business contractors.

During this outreach period, representatives of the standard surety companies indicated a willingness to increase their participation in the program if the SBA would create a second special program, similar to the Preferred Lenders Program already in place for the SBA's 7(a) loan guarantee program.[51] Under the proposal, firms meeting specified qualification standards would be designed as a "preferred surety" and would not be required to seek the SBA's prior approval of each decision relating to the issuance and administration of a guaranteed bond. Instead, the SBA would only approve the firm's standards and procedures for bond underwriting and administration. The preferred surety's decisions would be subject to regular, annual audits and existing reporting and access to records requirements. As a measure of their confidence in their own underwriting standards and claims decisions, the standard surety firms indicated that they would accept a 70% guarantee against losses as opposed to the then allowed 80% or 90% guarantee against losses, as long as they would not be required to seek prior approval of their underwriting decisions, bond administration, and claims procedures from the SBA.[52]

Congress subsequently authorized the proposed Preferred Surety Bond Guarantee Program in P.L. 100-590, the Small Business Administration Reauthorization and Amendment Act of 1988 (Title II, the Preferred Surety Bond Guarantee Program Act of 1988). The program was initially authorized on a three year trial basis. The program was provided permanent statutory authority by P.L. 108-447, the Consolidated Appropriations Act, 2005.

Small Business Eligibility Standards and Program Requirements

The SBA is authorized to guarantee surety bonds issued to contractors or subcontractors when

- the business, together with its affiliates, meets the SBA's size standard for the primary industry in which it is engaged;[53]
- the bond is required;
- the applicant is not able to obtain such bond on reasonable terms and conditions without a guarantee; and
- there is a reasonable expectation that the applicant will perform the covenants and conditions of the contract, and the terms and conditions of the bond are reasonable in light of the risks involved and the extent of the surety's participation.[54]

The applicant must also "possess good character and reputation," as demonstrated by (1) not being under indictment, being convicted of a felony, or having a final civil judgment stating that the applicant has committed a breach of trust or has violated a law or regulation protecting the integrity of business transactions or business relationships; (2) not having a regulatory authority revoke, cancel, or suspend a license held by the applicant which is necessary to perform the contract, and (3) never having obtained a bond guarantee by fraud or material misrepresentation or failing to keep the surety informed of unbonded contracts or of a contract bonded by another surety.[55]

Applicants must also certify the percentage of work under the contract to be subcontracted. The SBA does not guarantee bonds for applicants that are primarily brokers or who have effectively transferred control over the project to one or more subcontractors.[56] The applicant must also certify that they are not presently debarred, suspended, proposed for debarment, declared ineligible, or voluntarily excluded from transactions with any federal department or agency.[57] Also, the SBA will not guarantee a bond issued by a particular surety if that surety, an affiliate of that surety, or a close relative or member of the household of that surety or affiliate owns, directly or indirectly, 10% or more of the business applying for the guarantee. This conflict of interest prohibition also applies to ownership interests in any of the applicant's affiliates.[58]

The SBA guarantees contracts up to $2 million. The SBA has also been provided authority, and has issued final rules, to guarantee within specified time frames (typically within 12 months following a major disaster declaration) contracts up to $5 million for non-federal contracts or orders if the product will be manufactured or the services will be performed in a major disaster area as identified in the Federal Emergency Management Administration's (FEMA's) website; and up to $5 million for federal contracts or orders under those circumstances or if the products will be manufactured or the services will be provided outside the major disaster area and the products or services will directly assist in the recovery efforts in the major disaster area. The SBA is also authorized to issue a guarantee of up to $10 million on a federal contract if the contract meets any of the conditions above and is requested by the head of the agency involved in disaster reconstruction efforts.[59] There is no limit to the number of bonds that can be guaranteed for any one contractor.[60]

The SBA may guarantee up to 70% of the loss incurred and paid by a surety issued under the Preferred Surety Bond Guarantee Program.[61] Under the SBA's original Prior Approval Program, the SBA may guarantee up to 90% of the loss incurred if the contract is $100,000 or less, or if the bond was issued on behalf of a small business owned and controlled by socially and economically disadvantaged individuals, a qualified HUBZone small business, a small business owned and controlled by veterans, or a small business owned and controlled by a service-disabled veteran. The guarantee rate is 80% under the Prior Approval Program if the contract is greater than $100,000, and the business is not owned and controlled by socially and economically disadvantaged individuals, a qualified HUBZone small business, a veteran-owned or a service-disabled veteran-owned small business.[62]

The SBA does not charge principals (small business applicants) application or bid bond guarantee fees. If the SBA guarantees a final bond, the principal must pay a guarantee fee equal to a percentage of the contract amount, which is determined by the SBA and published in notices in the *Federal Register*.[63] The current rate is 0.729% of the contract price for a final bond.[64] The principal's fee is rounded to the nearest dollar, paid to the surety, and the surety remits the fee to the SBA.[65]

Sureties also charge principals a premium for issuing and servicing the bond. Sureties are not allowed to charge principals a premium that is more than the amount permitted under applicable state law.[66] On average, a small business will pay around $19,000 for a $500,000 contract.[67]

SURETY ELIGIBILITY STANDARDS AND PROGRAM REQUIREMENTS

Sureties interested in participating in the Prior Approval Program or the Preferred Surety Bond Guarantee Program must apply in writing to the SBA. Each applicant must be a corporation listed by the U.S. Treasury as eligible to issue bonds in connection with federal procurement contracts.[68]

The SBA considers several factors when considering sureties for the Preferred Surety Bond Guarantee Program. For example,

- the surety must have an underwriting limitation of at least $2 million on the U.S. Treasury Department's list of acceptable sureties,
- the surety must agree that it will neither charge a bond premium in excess of that authorized by the appropriate state insurance department nor impose any non-premium fee unless such fee is permitted by applicable state law and approved by the SBA,

- the surety's premium income from contract bonds guaranteed by any government agency (federal, state, or local) can account for no more than one-quarter of the surety's total contract bond premium income, and
- the surety must vest the underwriting authority for SBA guaranteed bonds to its own employees, and it must vest final settlement authority for claims and recovery to employees in the surety's permanent claims department.[69]

The SBA will also take into consideration the surety's rating or ranking designation that is assigned to the surety by a recognized authority.[70] Sureties participating in the Preferred Surety Bond Guarantee Program are not eligible to participate in the Prior Approval Program. However, this prohibition does not apply to the surety's affiliates provided that the affiliate is not a participant in the Preferred Program and the relationship between the affiliate and the surety has been fully disclosed to the SBA and the affiliate has been approved by the SBA to participate in the Prior Approval Program.[71]

In the Prior Approval Program, the surety must obtain the SBA's approval before issuing a guaranteed bond. Sureties participating in the Preferred Surety Bond Guarantee Program may issue, monitor, and service SBA guaranteed bonds without SBA approval.[72] However, sureties participating in the Preferred Program must notify the SBA electronically of all bonds issued and, for final bonds, the surety must report and submit to the SBA on a monthly basis all contractor and surety fees that are due.[73] These sureties are also subject to a periodic maximum guarantee authority amount set by the SBA.[74]

The terms and conditions of the SBA's bond guarantee agreements with the surety, including the guarantee percentage, may vary from surety to surety, depending on past experience with the SBA. The SBA may take into consideration, among other things, the rating or ranking assigned to the surety by recognized authorities, the surety's loss rate, average contract amount, average bond penalty per guaranteed bond, and the ratio of bid bonds to final bonds, all in comparison with other sureties participating in the same SBA Surety Bond Guarantee Program (Prior Approval Program or Preferred Surety Bond Guarantee Program).[75]

Sureties are required, among other things, to

- evaluate the credit, capacity, and character of a principal using standards generally accepted by the surety industry and in accordance with the SBA's Standard Operating Procedures on underwriting and the surety's principles and practices on unguaranteed bonds;
- reasonably expect that the principal will successfully perform the contract to be bonded;
- provide bond terms and conditions that are reasonable in light of the risks involved and the extent of the surety's participation;
- be satisfied as to the reasonableness of cost and the feasibility of successful completion of the contract;
- ensure that the principal remains viable and eligible for the program;
- monitor the principal's progress on guaranteed contracts; and
- maintain documentation of job status requests;
- take all reasonable action to minimize risk of loss, including, but not limited to, obtaining from each principal a written indemnity agreement, secured by such

collateral as the surety or the SBA finds appropriate, which covers actual losses under the contract and imminent breach payments; and

- in the case of loss, the surety must pursue all possible sources of salvage and recovery.[76]

Sureties participating in the program are subject to audits by examiners selected and approved by the SBA. Sureties participating in the Prior Approval Program are audited at least once each year and sureties participating in the Preferred Surety Bond Guarantee Program are audited at least once every three years.[77]

The SBA does not charge sureties or small businesses application or bid bond guarantee fees. The surety pays the SBA a guarantee fee on each guaranteed bond (other than bid bonds) within 60 days calendar days after the SBA's approval of the prior approval payment or performance bond. The fee is equal to a percentage of the bond premium which is determined by the SBA and published in notices in the *Federal Register*.[78]

The current rate is 26% of the fee charged by the surety company to the small business.[79] The fee is rounded to the nearest dollar.[80] The SBA does not receive any portion of a surety's non-premium charges.

PROGRAM STATISTICS

As mentioned previously, the number of final bonds guaranteed, and the amount of final bonds guaranteed by the SBA has generally declined over the past two decades—both in nominal and in inflation-adjusted dollars. However, perhaps reflecting current economic conditions (in which many small businesses eager to secure additional work are seeking SBA surety bond assistance, but are not necessarily winning the contract), the number of bid bonds guaranteed by the SBA has increased in recent years.

The SBA guaranteed 4,192 bid bonds valued at $1.7 billion in FY2007, 4,479 bid bonds valued at $1.9 billion in FY2008, 4,915 bid bonds valued at $2.3 billion in FY2009, 6,760 bid bonds valued at $3.4 billion in FY2010, 6,775 bid bonds valued at $3.0 billion in FY2011, and 7,180 bid bonds valued at $3.1 billion in FY2012.[81]

Excluding program costs of about $6 million annually, the program has had a positive cash flow in each of the past five six years (see Table 2). For example, in FY2012, the program collected $10.5 million from fees and recoveries, paid out $8.0 million for claims, and had a net gain of $2.5 million.[82]

There is about $42 million in the Surety Bond Guarantee Program Revolving Fund.[83]

Historically, the program's default rate has averaged about 2%.[84] According to the SBA, on average, the default rate on larger contracts tend to be lower than for smaller contracts and the recovery rate for larger contract defaults tend to be greater than for smaller contract defaults.[85]

There are currently 16 sureties participating in the Prior Approval Program and five sureties participating in the Preferred Surety Bond Guarantee Program.[86] Agents empowered to represent a participating surety company are located, or licensed, in all 50 states, American Samoa, the District of Columbia, Guam, the Marshall Islands, Micronesia, the Northern Mariana Islands, Palau, Puerto Rico, and the Virgin Islands.[87]

Table 2. Surety Bond Guarantee Program, Net Cash Flow
(excluding program costs of about $6 million annually)

Fiscal Year	Fees and Recoveries Collected	Claims Paid	Net Cash Flow
2007	$8.3 million	$5.2 million	$3.1 million
2008	$7.3 million	$6.6 million	$0.7 million
2009	$7.8 million	$6.0 million	$1.8 million
2010	$9.2 million	$4.3 million	$4.9 million
2011	$8.9 million	$5.8 million	$3.1 million
2012	$10.5 million	$8.0 million	$2.5 million

Source: U.S. Small Business Administration, Office of Congressional and Legislative Affairs, correspondence with the author, March 24, 2011; Office of Congressional and Legislative Affairs, correspondence with the author, December 15, 2011; and Office of Congressional and Legislative Affairs, correspondence with the author, December 5, 2012.

CONGRESSIONAL ISSUES: BOND LIMITS

111th Congress

During the 111th Congress, P.L. 111-5, the American Recovery and Reinvestment Act of 2009 (ARRA), provided the program an additional appropriation of $15 million and temporarily increased, from February 17, 2009, through September 30, 2010, the maximum bond amount from $2 million to $5 million.[88] The act also authorized the SBA to guarantee a bond of up to $10 million if a federal contracting officer certified in writing that a guarantee in excess of $5 million was necessary.[89] It also revised the program's size standard to "the size standard for the primary industry in which such business concern, and the affiliates of such business concern, is engaged, as determined by the Administrator in accordance with the North American Industry Classification System."[90] The new size standard (e.g., up to $33.5 million in average annual receipts over the previous three years for general building and heavy construction contractors, and up to $14.0 million in average annual receipts over the previous three years for specialty trade contractors) increased the number of businesses that qualified for the program.[91] Using its rulemaking authority, the SBA made ARRA's temporary size standard permanent on August 11, 2010.[92]

Proponents argued that the increased bond limit and size were necessary to "ensure that small businesses are able to secure the surety bonds they need to compete for contracts, grow, and hire more employees."[93] They also argued that "in our current economic recession, small businesses are finding it even more difficult to secure the credit lines necessary to get bonds in the private sector."[94] In their view, the temporary changes would create "significant opportunities to create jobs now in which small businesses will participate and be the driving engine for creation of new jobs in our country."[95]

There was no apparent organized opposition to these specific temporary changes to the Surety Bond Guarantee Program. However, there was opposition to ARRA's package of program enhancements for the SBA as a whole, which among other things, provided the SBA $730 million in additional funding, including $255 million for a temporary, two-year small business stabilization program to guarantee loans of $35,000 or less to small businesses for qualified debt consolidation, later named the America's Recovery Capital (ARC) Loan program and $375 million to temporarily subsidize fees for the SBA's 7(a) and 504/CDC loan guaranty programs and increase the 7(a) program's maximum loan guaranty percentage to 90%. Instead of modifying the SBA's program requirements and increasing the SBA's appropriation, opponents advocated business tax reduction, reform of financial credit market regulation, and federal fiscal restraint as the best means to assist small businesses, generate economic growth, and create jobs.[96]

112th Congress

On September 12, 2011, the Obama Administration advocated, as part of its proposed American Jobs Act, a temporary increase in the SBA surety bond limit to $5 million until the end of FY2012. The Administration argued that raising the program's bond limit "will make it easier for small businesses to take advantage of contracting opportunities generated by the American Jobs Act's proposed infrastructure investments."[97]

On December 7, 2012, the Administration also recommended, as part of its request for an additional $60.4 billion in federal resources to address damage caused by Hurricane Sandy, that the SBA surety bond limit be increased to $5 million to enable "more small businesses to participate in the recovery efforts."[98] There have been several legislative efforts during the 112th Congress to increase the program's bond limit. S. 1334, the Expanding Opportunities for Main Street Act of 2011, and its companion bill in the House, H.R. 2424, would reinstate and make permanent ARRA's higher limits. The bills would increase the maximum bond amount to $5 million from $2 million and authorize the SBA to guarantee a bond of up to $10 million if a federal contracting officer certifies in writing that a guarantee in excess of $5 million is necessary. Neither of these bills has been reported by a committee, to date, for consideration by the House or the Senate.

S. 1660, the American Jobs Act of 2011, and its companion bill in the House, H.R. 12, would provide $3 million in additional funding to pay for the cost of temporarily increasing the program's bond limit to $5 million from $2 million until the end of FY2012. Cloture on a motion to proceed to S. 1660 was not invoked in the Senate on October 11, 2011, by a vote of 50 to 49. H.R. 12 has not, as of yet, been reported by a committee for consideration in the House. On May 18, 2012, the House passed H.R. 4310, the National Defense Authorization Act for Fiscal Year 2013. The bill would, among many other provisions, increase the SBA surety bond program's bond limit to $6.5 million, and up to $10 million if a federal contracting officer certifies that such a guarantee is necessary. Also, on December 12, 2012, the Senate Committee on Appropriations released its draft of the Hurricane Sandy Emergency Assistance Supplemental bill. It includes a provision to increase the program's bond limit to $5 million.[99]

Discussion

There is relatively little discussion in the legislative record concerning the reasons for increasing the surety bond program's bond limits, and even less discussion of the reasons for not increasing the limits.[100] There was no apparent organized opposition to raising the program's bond limits on a temporary basis under ARRA. Hearings have not been held on S. 1334 and H.R. 2424. Also, only one witness during hearings on H.R. 4310 addressed the SBA surety bond program. That witness supported an increase in the surety bond limit to $5 million, and up to $10 million if a federal contracting officer certifies that such a guarantee is necessary.[101]

Advocates of raising the program's bond limits argue that the current limits should be raised to bring them more in line with the contracting amounts for other small business programs, such as the 8(a) Minority Small Business and Capital Ownership Development Program, the Historically Underutilized Business Zone (HUBZone) Program, the Women-Owned Small Business Federal Contract program, and the Service-Disabled Veteran-Owned Small Business Concerns Program.[102] For example, under 8(a) Minority Small Business and Capital Ownership Development Program federal contracting officials may provide a sole source award to a 8(a) small business if the anticipated award price of the contract will not exceed $6.5 million for manufacturing contracts or $4.0 million for other contract opportunities, and the contracting officer believes that the award can be made at a fair and reasonable price.[103] Advocates argue that increasing the surety bond program's bond limit would provide more consistency across small business contracting programs and make it easier for some agencies that have experienced some difficulty issuing contracts in increments of $2 million or less (e.g., the Department of Defense, the General Services Administration, and the Department of State) to increase their participation in the program.[104]

Advocates also argue that small businesses awarded contracts under these other small business contracting programs that exceed the surety bond program's $2 million limit could be at risk of not being able to complete those contracts due to difficulties related to securing a surety bond. For example, the House Committee on Armed Services' Panel on Business Challenges in the Defense Industry has argued that the SBA surety bond program's limit should be increased to $6.5 million to match the 8(a) program's $6.5 million threshold for manufacturing contracts and to "increase the opportunities for small businesses to compete for federal contracts, especially in those departments, such as the Department of Defense, where the average size of construction contracts awarded to small businesses for FY2010 exceeded $5.9 million – nearly triple the size for which SBA can provide bonding support."[105]

Opponents of raising the program's bond limits might argue that raising the limit could lead to higher amounts being guaranteed by the SBA and, as a result, an increase in the risk of program losses. Advocates of raising the program's bond limits might argue that the SBA's experience with Recovery Act bonds (over $2 million) suggests that raising the limit might not lead to an increased risk of program losses. The SBA reported that the program's default rate on Recovery Act bonds was lower, in 2009 and 2010, than for its other bonds. The SBA guaranteed 166 Recovery Act bid bonds valued at $518.0 million and 52 Recovery Act final bonds valued at $145.4 million. There were two defaults, with a bond value of $2.7 million and $2.2 million, respectively.[106] Opponents might make the following three counter-arguments: (1) because of the differences in their sizes the default rate for larger bonds (over $2 million) would have to be significantly lower than for smaller bonds to prevent an increase in the risk of program losses, (2) the SBA's experience with Recovery Act bonds may be too limited to project future trends and, (3) given current federal budgetary conditions, some might argue that they oppose any possibility of increasing the program's risk of losses, no matter how small or how unlikely.

In addition, advocates might also argue that increasing the bond limit would not necessarily increase the risk of program losses because the businesses seeking the larger bonds tend to be somewhat larger and financially stronger than other program participants. As a result, if a default should occur on these larger bonds, the resources available to recover costs are generally greater than the resources that are available when recovering costs on smaller bond defaults. A similar argument was presented during consideration of the recent decision to increase the loan limits for the SBA's 7(a) loan guaranty program from $2 million to $5 million and for the SBA's 504/Certified Development Company loan guaranty program from $1.5 million to $5 million for "regular" borrowers, from $2 million to $5 million if the loan proceeds are directed toward one or more specified public policy goals, and from $4 million to $5.5 million for manufacturers.[107]

Opponents might argue that they could not support an increase in the program's bond limit without additional evidence that small businesses awarded contracts under the other small business contracting programs have not been able to access surety bonds in the private marketplace.

Opponents might also argue that even if small businesses awarded contracts under the other small business contracting programs had difficulty accessing surety bonds in the private marketplace, they would still oppose an increase in the program's bond limit because a higher limit could lead to higher amounts being guaranteed by the SBA and, as a result, increase the risk of program losses.

CONGRESSIONAL ISSUES: PROGRAM STRUCTURE

The SBA has reported that it is focusing on "strengthening relationships with individual surety companies and the large network of bond agents and producers across the country in order to reach more small businesses in need of bonding."[108] As part of this outreach effort, the SBA has reported that it will continue to emphasize "process improvements that will streamline the application requirements for small businesses and surety companies and their agents."[109] One of the proposed means to streamline the application requirements for surety companies and their agents that the SBA is considering is to combine the Prior Approval Program and Preferred Surety Bond Guarantee Program into a single program featuring the streamlined bond approval and monitoring processes under the Preferred Program. Several industry groups, including the National Association of Surety Bond Producers and The Surety & Fidelity Association of America, have recommended that the programs be merged, the emphasis on reduced regulatory burdens under the Preferred Program be maintained, and the program's fees kept as low as economically feasible as a means to encourage more sureties to participate in the program.[110]

Perhaps because the proposal has not been formally introduced as a bill, there are no public statements opposing the merger of the two programs. Opposition might come from those who are not convinced that the Surety Bond Guarantee Program is necessary to supplement the private market for surety bonds and would prefer that the program be eliminated rather than reformed, or from those who believe that a federal program is necessary to supplement the private market for surety bonds, but the existing program is sufficient to meet that need and does not require changes to encourage its expansion. Other opponents might argue that providing additional authority to sureties to approve and monitor bonds might increase the risk of defaults and program losses.

CONCLUSION

Throughout the program's history, both congressional testimony and GAO examinations have indicated that smaller contracting firms, and especially minority-owned and women-owned small business contracting firms, often have a more difficult time accessing surety bonds in the private marketplace than larger firms. For example, in 1995, GAO reported that "it is not unusual for a small construction company to have some difficulty in obtaining a surety bond."[111] GAO found that about one in three of the smallest contracting firms it surveyed at that time, compared with about one in six of the larger contracting firms it surveyed, reported that they were required to provide collateral.[112] GAO also reported

> The experiences of the minority-owned firms differed from those of the firms not owned by minorities in several areas. For example, these firms were more likely to be asked to provide certain types of financial documentation, as well as to provide collateral or to meet other conditions; were more likely to be denied a bond and to report losing an opportunity to bid because of delays in processing their request for a bond; and were more likely to depend on jobs requiring bonds for a higher proportion of their revenues.
>
> The women-owned firms differed from the firms not owned by women in a few key respects. For example, they ... were more likely to be asked to provide more types of financial or other documentation to obtain a bond.
>
> In addition, the minority-owned firms reported more often than the firms not owned by minorities that they had to (1) establish an escrow account controlled by the surety company, (2) hire a CPA or a management or consulting firm selected by the surety company to manage the contract, and (3) enter into an arrangement that allows the surety company to manage the job even when the firm is not in default.[113]

Although congressional testimony and GAO examinations have supported the need for a program like the SBA's Surety Bond Guarantee Program, that testimony and GAO's surveys of businesses have been somewhat less useful in helping Congress determine the appropriate size for the program. For example, a review of congressional hearings since the program's inception suggests that congressional witnesses representing the surety companies and various construction organizations, including minority-owned small contracting businesses, have focused their testimony on the need to reduce the SBA's paperwork requirements, which are designed to prevent fraud but increase the sureties' costs, keep the program's fees as low as possible, and keep the program's guarantee rates as high as possible. The SBA's testimony has tended to focus on the need to attract more sureties to the program so that it can reverse the slow downward trajectory the program has experienced over the past two decades in the number and amount of final bonds guaranteed. There has been relatively little testimony provided concerning the broader issue of how large the program should be relative to the private sector and what measures or metrics might be used to help make that determination.

One possible starting point for determining how large the program should be relative to the private sector is to examine congressional testimony concerning the supply and demand for sureties in the private sector. That testimony suggests that the supply and demand for sureties tends to fluctuate with changes in the overall economy, with the supply of sureties contracting during economic recessions and expanding during economic expansions and the demand for sureties slowing during economic recessions and increasing during economic expansions.[114] It could be argued that federal policies could take these fluctuations into account—enacting policies that expand federal support for surety guarantees when supply is tight and reducing federal support for surety guarantees when supplies are more plentiful. Of course, when making these determinations it is necessary to first establish measures or metrics to determine current market conditions. Also, this line of reasoning assumes that having a federal presence in the surety marketplace is desirable, an assumption not held by all. Ultimately, while having established measures or metrics concerning the supply and demand for surety bonds might be helpful in determining the appropriate size for the SBA's Surety Bond Guarantee Program, that decision will largely rest on personal views concerning the role of the federal government in the private marketplace and the level of acceptable risk in assisting small businesses gain greater access to surety bonds.

APPENDIX. SBA SURETY BOND GUARANTEE PROGRAM STATISTICS

Table A-1. SBA Surety Bond Guarantee Program Volume, Final Bonds, FY1971-FY2012

Fiscal Year	Final Bonds Guaranteed	Contract Value (SBA Share)	Contract Value Adjusted for Inflation (2012 dollars)
1971	7	$312,252	$1,783,436
1972	1,339	$94,434,157	$522,589,136
1973	5,597	$351,189,011	$1,829,639,379
1974	9,182	$633,229,829	$2,971,132,339
1975	11,595	$706,152,366	$3,036,153,287
1976	7,831	$503,607,938	$2,047,330,006
1977	15,485	$886,500,000	$3,383,869,975
1978	19,044	$1,177,500,000	$4,177,542,446
1979	20,095	$1,390,900,000	$4,431,664,122
1980	19,928	$1,534,400,000	$4,307,436,951
1981	17,821	$1,400,000,000	$3,562,638,063
1982	10,306	$763,800,000	$1,830,880,047
1983	7,703	$567,400,000	$1,317,763,712
1984	7,262	$571,000,000	$1,271,241,645
1985	10,778	$959,100,000	$2,061,859,987
1986	11,200	$1,043,900,000	$2,203,210,002
1987	11,128	$957,400,000	$1,949,497,322
1988	11,097	$1,051,000,000	$2,055,064,809
1989	11,183	$1,151,600,000	$2,148,263,364
1990	9,943	$1,071,200,000	$1,895,843,690
1991	7,544	$896,300,000	$1,522,242,489
1992	7,262	$848,300,000	$1,398,618,753
1993	6,478	$944,000,000	$1,511,164,346
1994	6,591	$1,090,000,000	$1,701,319,365
1995	6,807	$1,200,000,000	$1,821,393,700

SBA Surety Bond Guarantee Program

Fiscal Year	Final Bonds Guaranteed	Contract Value (SBA Share)	Contract Value Adjusted for Inflation (2012 dollars)
1996	4,684	$724,596,082	$1,068,268,909
1997	4,021	$615,000,000	$886,354,859
1998	2,860	$414,000,000	$587,516,797
1999	2,399	$426,000,000	$591,482,845
2000	1,774	$242,784,741	$326,133,785
2001	1,703	$254,295,891	$332,333,122
2002	2,123	$350,782,086	$451,038,686
2003	2,400	$459,331,071	$577,451,550
2004	2,230	$475,347,150	$582,085,106
2005	1,680	$387,401,149	$458,845,220
2006	1,706	$427,666,723	$490,707,258
2007	1,617	$444,852,668	$496,291,077
2008	1,576	$429,437,158	$461,378,220
2009	1,220	$377,896,791	$407,453,968
2010	1,588	$487,550,613	$517,203,206
2011	1,863	$488,102,579	$501,942,412
2012	2,323	$625,301,882	$625,301,882
Total	290,973	$29,423,572,137	NA

Source: U.S. Congress, Senate Committee on Banking, Housing, and Urban Affairs, *Oversight of SBA Set-Aside, Lease Guaranty, and Surety Bond Programs*, 94th Cong., 2nd sess., March 8, 1976 (Washington: GPO, 1976), p. 28; U.S. Congress, House Committee on Small Business, Subcommittee on General Oversight and Minority Enterprise, *Overview of SBA's Activities*, 96th Cong., 1st sess., February 28, 1979 (Washington: GPO, 1979), p. 108; U.S. Congress, House Committee on Appropriations, Subcommittee on the Departments of State, Justice, and Commerce, The Judiciary, and Related Agencies, *Departments of State, Justice, and Commerce, The Judiciary, and Related Agencies Appropriations for 1980, Part 6*, 96th Cong., 1st sess., March 27, 1979 (Washington: GPO, 1979), p. 603; U.S. Congress, House Committee on Appropriations, Subcommittee on the Departments of State, Justice, and Commerce, The Judiciary, and Related Agencies, *Departments of State, Justice, and Commerce, The Judiciary, and Related Agencies Appropriations for 1981, Part 4*, 96th Cong., 2nd sess., March 10, 1980 (Washington: GPO, 1980), p. 532; U.S. Congress, House Committee on Appropriations, Subcommittee on the Departments of Commerce, Justice, and State, The Judiciary, and Related Agencies, *Departments of Commerce, Justice, and State, The Judiciary, and Related Agencies Appropriations for 1982, Part 7*, 97th Cong., 1st sess., March 16, 1981 (Washington: GPO, 1981), p. 15; U.S. Congress, House Committee on Appropriations, Subcommittee on the Departments of Commerce, Justice, and State, The Judiciary, and Related Agencies, *Departments of Commerce, Justice, and State, The Judiciary, and Related Agencies Appropriations for 1983, Part 5*, 97th Cong., 2nd sess., March 22, 1982 (Washington: GPO, 1982), p. 162; U.S. Congress, House Committee on Appropriations, Subcommittee on the Departments of Commerce, Justice, and State, The Judiciary, and Related Agencies, *Departments of Commerce, Justice, and State, The Judiciary, and Related Agencies Appropriations for1984, Part 4*, 98th Cong., 1st sess., March 9, 1983 (Washington: GPO, 1983), p. 625; U.S. Congress, House Committee on Appropriations, Subcommittee on the Departments of Commerce, Justice, and State, The Judiciary, and Related Agencies, *Departments of Commerce, Justice, and State, The Judiciary, and Related Agencies Appropriations for1985, Part 5*, 98th Cong., 2nd sess., March 26, 1984 (Washington: GPO, 1984), p. 573; U.S. Congress, House Committee on Appropriations, Subcommittee on the Departments of Commerce, Justice, and State, The Judiciary, and Related Agencies, *Departments of Commerce, Justice, and State, The Judiciary, and Related Agencies Appropriations for1986, Part 4*, 99th Cong., 1st sess., March 14, 1985 (Washington: GPO, 1985), p. 716; ; U.S. Congress, House Committee on Appropriations, Subcommittee on the Departments of Commerce, Justice, and State, The Judiciary, and Related Agencies, *Departments of Commerce,*

Justice, and State, The Judiciary, and Related Agencies Appropriations for1987, Part 5, 99th Cong., 2nd sess., March 24, 1986 (Washington: GPO, 1986), p. 305; U.S. Congress, House Committee on Appropriations, Subcommittee on the Departments of Commerce, Justice, and State, The Judiciary, and Related Agencies, *Departments of Commerce, Justice, and State, The Judiciary, and Related Agencies Appropriations for1988, Part 3, 100th* Cong., 1st sess., March 4, 1987 (Washington: GPO, 1987), pp. 289, 323; U.S. Congress, House Committee on Appropriations, Subcommittee on the Departments of Commerce, Justice, and State, The Judiciary, and Related Agencies, *Departments of Commerce, Justice, and State, The Judiciary, and Related Agencies Appropriations for1989, Part 1, 100th* Cong., 2nd sess., March 3, 1988 (Washington: GPO, 1988), pp. 278; U.S. Congress, House Committee on Appropriations, Subcommittee on the Departments of Commerce, Justice, and State, The Judiciary, and Related Agencies, *Departments of Commerce, Justice, and State, The Judiciary, and Related Agencies Appropriations for!990, Part 6, !0!st* Cong., 1st sess., March 15, 1989 (Washington: GPO, 1989), p. 406; U.S. General Accounting Office, *Small Business: Information on and Improvements Needed to Surety Bond Guarantee Programs,* GA)/RCED-91-99, April 23, 1991, p. 19, at http://archive.gao.gov/d20t9/143966.pdf; U.S. Congress, House Committee on Appropriations, Subcommittee on the Departments of Commerce, Justice, and State, The Judiciary, and Related Agencies, *Departments of Commerce, Justice, and State, The Judiciary, and Related Agencies Appropriations for!99!, Part 6, !0!st* Cong., 2nd sess., March 21, 1990 (Washington: GPO, 1990), p. 810; U.S. Congress, House Committee on Appropriations, Subcommittee on the Departments of Commerce, Justice, and State, The Judiciary, and Related Agencies, *Departments of Commerce, Justice, and State, The Judiciary, and Related Agencies Appropriations for!992, Part 6, !02nd* Cong., 1st sess., March 14, 1991 (Washington: GPO, 1991), p. 233; U.S. Congress, House Committee on Appropriations, Subcommittee on the Departments of Commerce, Justice, and State, The Judiciary, and Related Agencies, *Departments of Commerce, Justice, and State, The Judiciary, and Related Agencies Appropriations for!993, Part 5, !02nd* Cong., 2nd sess., February 19, 1992 (Washington: GPO, 1992), p. 131; U.S. Congress, House Committee on Appropriations, Subcommittee on the Departments of Commerce, Justice, and State, The Judiciary, and Related Agencies, *Departments of Commerce, Justice, and State, The Judiciary, and Related Agencies Appropriations for!994, Part 5, !03rd* Cong., 1st sess., March 24, 1993 (Washington: GPO, 1993), pp. 960, 1122; U.S. Congress, House Committee on Small Business, *Small Business Reauthorization and Amendment Act of !994*, report to accompany H.R. 4801, 103rd Cong., 2nd sess., July 21, 1994, H. Rept. 103-616 (Washington: GPO, 1994); U.S. Congress, House Committee on Appropriations, Subcommittee on the Departments of Commerce, Justice, and State, The Judiciary, and Related Agencies, *Departments of Commerce, Justice, and State, The Judiciary, and Related Agencies Appropriations for!995, Part 5, !03ʳd* Cong., 2nd sess., March 4, 1994 (Washington: GPO, 1994), pp. 716; U.S. Congress, House Committee on Appropriations, Subcommittee on the Departments of Commerce, Justice, and State, The Judiciary, and Related Agencies, *Departments of Commerce, Justice, and State, The Judiciary, and Related Agencies Appropriations for!996, Part 6, !04th* Cong., 1st sess., March 30, 1995 (Washington: GPO, 1995), p. 529; U.S. Congress, House Committee on Small Business, Subcommittee on Procurement, Exports and Business Opportunities, *Small Business Administration's Surety Bond Guarantee Program,* 104th Cong., 1st sess., April 5, 1995, Serial No. 104-24 (Washington: GPO, 1995), p. 98; U.S. Congress, House Committee on Appropriations, Subcommittee on the Departments of Commerce, Justice, and State, The Judiciary, and Related Agencies, *Departments of Commerce, Justice, and State, The Judiciary, and Related Agencies Appropriations for!997, Part 5, !04th* Cong., 2nd sess., April 33, 1996 (Washington: GPO, 1996), p. 733; U.S. Small Business Administration, Office of the Chief Financial Officer, *Annual Report, !997*, p. 27; U.S. Small Business Administration, Office of the Chief Financial Officer, *Annual Report, !998*, p. 27; U.S. Small Business Administration, *FY !999 Performance and Accountability Report*, p. 29; and U.S. Small Business Administration, *FY 2002 Performance and Accountability Report*, p. 78.

Notes: The number of final bonds guaranteed in FYs 1990-1992, 1996, and 2000-2004, and the contract values for FYs 1996 and 2000-2010 were provided by the U.S. Small Business Administration, Office of Congressional and Legislative Affairs, correspondence with the author, September 29,

2011. The number of final bonds guaranteed in FY2011, and the contract value for FY2011 were provided by the U.S. Small Business Administration, Office of Congressional and Legislative Affairs, correspondence with the author, December 15, 2011. The number of final bonds guaranteed in FY2012, and the contract value for FY2012 were provided by the U.S. Small Business Administration, Office of Congressional and Legislative Affairs, correspondence with the author, December 11, 2012.

Table A-2. SBA Surety Bond Guarantee Program Volume, Bid and Final Bonds Combined, FY2000-FY2012

Fiscal Year	Bid and Final Bonds Approved	Contract Value	Contract Value Adjusted for Inflation (2012 dollars)
2000	7,034	$1,672,000,000	$2,246,004,785
2001	6,320	$1,400,000,000	$1,829,625,988
2002	7,372	$461,001,775	$592,760,131
2003	8,974	$593,572,000	$746,213,556
2004	7,803	$594,669,000	$728,200,365
2005	5,678	$907,674,000	$1,075,066,188
2006	5,214	$1,730,000,000	$1,985,011,954
2007	5,809	$2,250,000,000	$2,510,167,983
2008	6,055	$2,450,000,000	$2,632,228,301
2009	6,135	$2,760,000,000	$2,975,873,252
2010	8,348	$4,000,000,000	$4,243,278,072
2011	8,638	$3,607,069,163	$3,709,345,278
2012	9,503	$3,917,114,158	$3,917,114,158

Source: U.S. Small Business Administration, "FY 2000 Performance and Accountability Report," p. 37; U.S. Small Business Administration, "FY 2001 Performance and Accountability Report," p. 16; U.S. Small Business Administration, "FY 2002 Performance and Accountability Report," p. 78; U.S. Small Business Administration, "FY2002 Budget Request and Performance Plan," p. 34; U.S. Small Business Administration, "FY2003 Budget Request and Performance Plan," pp. 17, 19; U.S. Small Business Administration, "SBA Budget Request & Performance Plan, FY2004," pp. 3, 4; U.S. Small Business Administration, "Congressional Submission Fiscal Year 2005," p. 15; U.S. Small Business Administration, "Congressional Submission Fiscal Year 2006," pp. 19, 78; U.S. Small Business Administration, "FY2007 Congressional Budget Request and Performance Plan," pp. 25, 71; U.S. Small Business Administration, "FY2009 Congressional Budget Justification and FY207 Annual Performance Report," p. 65; U.S. Small Business Administration, "FY2012 Congressional Budget Justification and FY2010 Annual Performance Report," p. 40; U.S. Small Business Administration, Office of Congressional and Legislative Affairs, correspondence with the author, December 15, 2011; and U.S. Small Business Administration, Office of Congressional and Legislative Affairs, correspondence with the author, December 11, 2012.

End Notes

[1] U.S. Congress, Senate Committee on Banking, Housing, and Urban Affairs, *Small Business Legislation - 1974*, hearing on S. 3137 and S. 3138, 93rd Cong., 2nd sess., March 13, 1974 (Washington: GPO, 1974), p. 19.

[2] U.S. Small Business Administration, "About Office of Surety Bond Guarantees," at http://www.sba.gov/about-offices-content/1/2891/about-us. Ancillary bonds are also eligible if they are incidental and essential to a contract for which SBA has guaranteed a final bond. A reclamation bond is eligible if it is issued to reclaim an abandoned mine site and for a project undertaken for a specific period of time.

[3] U.S. Small Business Administration, Office of Congressional and Legislative Affairs, correspondence with the author, December 5, 2012.

[4] Surety bonds range in price from 0.5% to 2% of the contract price. By dividing the total amount of premiums issued each year by the private sector (about $3.1 billion annually in recent years) by .005 and .02 provides a range for the value of those contracts ($155 billion to $620 billion). Premium data from Surety Information Office, "Contract Surety Bonds, Understanding Today's Market, 2010," Washington, DC, at http://www.sio.org/ppt /pptfiles.html.

[5] U.S. Small Business Administration, "Surety Bonds," at http://www.sba.gov/category /navigation-structure/loans-grants/bonds/surety-bonds.

[6] Ibid.

[7] U.S. Small Business Administration, "Surety Bonds: Explained," at http://www.sba.gov/content /surety-bonds-explained.

[8] The threshold amount was originally set at $2,000 in 1935 under P.L. 74-321, An Act Requiring Contracts for the Construction, Alteration, and Repair of Any Public Building or Public Work of the United States to be Accompanied by a Performance Bond Protecting the United States and an Additional Bond for the Protection of Persons Furnishing Material or Labor for the Construction, Alteration, or Repair of Said Public Buildings or Public Work [the Miller Act of 1935], 49 Stat. 793 (August 24, 1935) (codified at 40 U.S.C. §3133(b)(1)). For further information and analysis of federal requirements concerning surety bonds, see CRS Report R41230, Legal Protections for Subcontractors on Federal Prime Contracts, by Kate M. Manuel.

[9] Performance bonds may be less than 100% provided that the contracting officer determines that a smaller amount will adequately protect the government. 40 U.S.C. §3133(b)(2).

[10] U.S. Small Business Administration, "Standard Operating Procedure: Surety Bond Guarantee Program," SOP 50 45 2, effective March 8, 1999, p. 7, at http://www.sba.gov /sites/default/files/sop5045.pdf.

[11] U.S. Senate, Committee on Appropriations, "Text of Hurricane Sandy Supplemental," December 12, 2012, at http://www.appropriations.senate.gov/news.cfm?method =news.view&id=0f718f5d-c9e1-49a1-9b5a-33a313 bb423d.

[12] Jeffrey D. Zients, Deputy Director for Management, U.S. Office of Management and Budget, "Letter sent to the Homnorable Harry Reid, Majority Leader of the Senate," December 7, 2012, p. 59.

[13] The SBA's Surety Bond Guarantee Program was authorized in this particular act because the program, as introduced in the House (H.R. 19436), would have been administered by the Department of Housing and Urban Development to provide or guarantee surety bonds for construction contractors and subcontractors. The program's administration was shifted to the SBA in the conference agreement accompanying the bill. See U.S. Congress, House Committee of Conference, Housing and Urban Development Act of 1970, report to accompany H.R. 19436, 91st Cong., 2nd sess., December 17, 1970, H.Rept. 91-1784 (Washington: GPO, 1970), p. 65.

[14] P.L. 91-609, the Housing and Urban Development Act of 1970, Section 411. Authority of the Administration.

[15] Ibid. At that time, the SBA considered contractors small if the company's average annual receipts over three years did not exceed $2 million, or $1 million for most special trade contractors. See U.S. Congress, Senate Select Committee on Small Business, Surety Bond Guarantee Program of the Small Business Administration, 94th Cong., 1st sess., November 19, 1975 (Washington: GPO, 1975), p. 14.

[16] P.L. 91-609, the Housing and Urban Development Act of 1970, Section 411. Authority of the Administration.

[17] U.S. Office of Management and Budget, Budget of the U.S. Government, FY1974, Appendix, p. 944.

[18] P.L. 91-609, the Housing and Urban Development Act of 1970, Section 411. Authority of the Administration.

[19] Ibid.

[20] Ibid.

[21] Ibid.

[22] U.S. Congress, House Banking and Currency, Housing and Urban Development Legislation - 1970, 91st Cong., 2nd sess., June 5, 1970 (Washington: GPO, 1970), p. 351.

[23] Ibid.

[24] U.S. Congress, House Committee on Small Business, Subcommittee on SBA Oversight and Minority Experience, Selected Small Business Administration Programs and Activities, 94th Cong., 2nd sess., February 24, 1976, H. Rept. 94- 840 (Washington: GPO, 1976), p. 4.

[25] U.S. Congress, Senate Committee on Banking, Housing, and Urban Affairs, Oversight of SBA Set-Aside, Lease Guaranty, and Surety Bond Programs, 94th Cong., 2nd sess., March 8, 1976 (Washington: GPO, 1976), pp. 26, 28.

[26] The SBA reported to the Government Accounting Office in 1975 that the surety bond industry initially insisted that the SBA guarantee "90% of any loss for no more than 10% of the premiums collected" as a condition of participating in the program. The SBA also reported that the industry indicated a willingness to "reassess the

SBA Surety Bond Guarantee Program

adequacy of SBA's 10% share after two years of experience." See U.S. General Accounting Office, *Use Of Surety Bonds In Federal Construction Should be Improved*, LCD-74-319, January 17, 1975, p. 35, at http://archive.gao.gov/d46t13/094722.pdf.

[27] U.S. Congress, Senate Select Committee on Small Business, *Surety Bond Guarantee Program of the Small Business Administration*, 94th Cong., 1st sess., November 19, 1975 (Washington: GPO, 1975), p. 14.

[28] U.S. Congress, Senate Select Committee on Small Business, *Review of Small Business Administration's Programs and Policies - 1971*, 92nd Cong., 1st sess., October 5, 1971 (Washington: GPO, 1971), p. 46.

[29] U.S. Congress, Senate Committee on Banking, Housing, and Urban Affairs, *Small Business Legislation - 1974*, hearing on S. 3137 and S. 3138, 93rd Cong., 2nd sess., March 13, 1974 (Washington: GPO, 1974), pp. 4, 19.

[30] U.S. Congress, Senate Committee on Banking, Housing, and Urban Affairs, *Small Business Legislation - 1974*, hearing on S. 3137 and S. 3138, 93rd Cong., 2nd sess., March 13, 1974 (Washington: GPO, 1974), p. 20. As of 1974, the SBA reportedly took in $3 million in surety bond premiums and paid out more than $12 million in claims. See Representative William Cotter, "Providing for Consideration of H.R. 15578, Small Business Amendments of 1974," House Debate, *Congressional Record*, vol. 120, part 20 (August 1, 1974), p. 26398.

[31] Testimony of John T. Wettach, SBA Associate Administrator for Finance and Investment, in U.S. Congress, Senate Select Committee on Small Business, *Surety Bond Guarantee Program of the Small Business Administration*, 94th Cong., 1st sess., November 19, 1975 (Washington: GPO, 1975), p. 3.

[32] P.L. 91-609, the Housing and Urban Development Act of 1970.

[33] U.S. General Accounting Office, *Use Of Surety Bonds In Federal Construction Should be Improved*, LCD-74-319, January 17, 1975, at http://archive.gao.gov/d46t13/094722.pdf; U.S. General Accounting Office, *The Surety Bond Guarantee Program: Significant Changes Are Needed In Its Management*, CED-80-34, December 27, 1979, at http://archive.gao.gov/f0202/111534.pdf; U.S. General Accounting Office, *Surety Bond Guarantee Program: Small Business Administration's Actions on Prior Program Recommendations*, GAO/RCED-86-183BR, September 18, 1986, at http://archive.gao.gov/d4t4/131018.pdf; U.S. General Accounting Office, *Small Business: Information on and Improvements Needed to Surety Bond Guarantee Programs*, GAO/RCED-91-99, April 23, 1991, at http://archive.gao.gov/d20t9/143966.pdf; U.S. General Accounting Office, *Small Business: Construction Firms' Access to Surety Bonds*, GAO/RCED-95-173FS, June 26, 1995, at http://www.gao.gov/archive/1995/rc95173f.pdf; and U.S. General Accounting Office, *Minority-Owned Firms' Access to Surety Bonds*, GAO/RCED-95244R, July 14, 1995, at http://archive.gao.gov/paprpdf1/154722.pdf.

[34] P.L. 93-386, the Small Business Amendments of 1974, Section 411. Authority of the Administration.

[35] S.Doc. 93-116, Supplemental Appropriations for FY75 for Department of Commerce and Small Business Administration, Communication from the President, October 2, 1974; and P.L. 93-554, the Supplemental Appropriations Act, 1975.

[36] U.S. Office of Management and Budget, *Budget of the U.S. Government, FY2012: Appendix, Small Business Administration*, p. 1163; and U.S. Congress, House Committee on Small Business, *Views and Estimates of the Committee on Small Business on Matters to be set forth in the Concurrent Resolution on the Budget for Fiscal Year 2012*, 112th Cong., 1st sess., March 17, 2011 (Washington: GPO, 2011), pp. 5, 6, at http://smbiz.house.gov/ UploadedFiles/March_17_Views_and_Estimates_Letter.pdf.

[37] U.S. Small Business Administration, "Title 13 Business Credit and Assistance, Chapter 1 Small Business Administration, Part 115 - Surety Bond Guarantee Policy and Guarantee Fees," 41 *Federal Register* 16549-16550, April 20, 1976.

[38] U.S. Small Business Administration, "Guarantee Fees," 42 *Federal Register* 9397, February 16, 1977.

[39] U.S. Congress, House Committee on Small Business, *Full Committee Hearing on Legislation Updating and Improving the SBA's Investment and Surety Bond Programs*, 110th Cong., 1st sess., September 6, 2007, Serial No. 110- 44 (Washington: GPO, 2007), p. 64.

[40] U.S. Congress, Senate Committee on Small Business, *Small Business Administration's Surety Bond Guarantee Program*, 97th Cong., 2nd sess., March 11, 1982 (Washington: GPO, 1982), pp. 1, 257, 258.

[41] U.S. General Accounting Office, *The Surety Bond Guarantee Program: Significant Changes Are Needed In Its Management*, CED-80-34, December 27, 1979, at http://archive.gao.gov/f0202/111534.pdf; U.S. General Accounting Office, *Surety Bond Guarantee Program: Small Business Administration's Actions on Prior Program Recommendations*, GAO/RCED-86-183BR, September 18, 1986, at http://archive.gao.gov /d4t4/131018.pdf; U.S. General Accounting Office, *Small Business: Information on and Improvements Needed to Surety Bond Guarantee Programs*, GAO/RCED-91-99, April 23, 1991, at http://archive.gao.gov/d20t9/143966.pdf; U.S. Congress, House Committee on Small Business, Subcommittee

on Procurement, Exports and Business Opportunities, *Small Business Administration's Surety Bond Guarantee Program*, 104th Cong., 1st sess., April 5, 1995, Serial No. 104-24 (Washington: GPO, 1995), pp. 252-307.

[42] U.S. Small Business Administration, "FY2003 Budget Request and Performance Plan," pp. 17, 19; U.S. Small Business Administration, "SBA Budget Request & Performance Plan, FY2004," pp. 3, 4; U.S. Small Business Administration, "Congressional Submission Fiscal Year 2005," p. 15; U.S. Small Business Administration, "Congressional Submission Fiscal Year 2006," pp. 19, 78; U.S. Small Business Administration, "FY2007 Congressional Budget Request and Performance Plan," pp. 25, 71; U.S. Small Business Administration, "FY2009 Congressional Budget Justification and FY207 Annual Performance Report," p. 65; U.S. Small Business Administration, "Fiscal Year 2010 Congressional Budget Justification," p. 46; U.S. Small Business Administration, "FY2011 Congressional Budget Justification and FY2009 Annual Performance Report," p. 46; and U.S. Small Business Administration, Office of Congressional and Legislative Affairs, correspondence with the author, September 29, 2011.

[43] U.S. Small Business Administration, Office of Congressional and Legislative Affairs, correspondence with the author, December 11, 2012. In FY2011, the SBA guaranteed 1,863 final surety bonds. The SBA's share of those bonds' value was $488.1 million.

[44] U.S. General Accounting Office, *Small Business: Information on and Improvements Needed to Surety Bond Guarantee Programs*, GAO/RCED-91-99, April 23, 1991, p. 10, at http://archive.gao.gov/d20t9/143966.pdf.

[45] Ibid., p. 11; U.S. Congress, Senate Select Committee on Small Business, *SBA Surety Bond Guarantee Program*, 96th Cong., 2nd sess., June 30, 1980 (Washington: GPO, 1980), p. 24; and S.Rept. 100-416, Small Business Administration Reauthorization and Amendments Act of 1988, p. 24.

[46] U.S. Congress, Senate Select Committee on Small Business, *Surety Bond and Lease Guarantee Programs of the Small Business Administration*, 94th Cong., 2nd sess., May 7, 1976 (Washington: GPO, 1976), pp. 15, 16.

[47] U.S. Congress, House Committee on Small Business, Subcommittee on SBA and SBIC Authority, Minority Enterprise, and General Small Business, *Surety Bond Guarantee Program*, 98th Cong., 1st sess., May 17, 1983 (Washington: GPO, 1983), p. 58.

[48] U.S. General Accounting Office, *Small Business: Information on and Improvements Needed to Surety Bond Guarantee Programs*, GAO/RCED-91-99, April 23, 1991, p. 10, at http://archive.gao.gov/d20t9/143966.pdf.

[49] Ibid., pp. 11, 12.

[50] S.Rept. 100-416, Small Business Administration Reauthorization and Amendments Act of 1988, p. 24; and U.S. Congress, Senate Committee on Small Business, *S. 2259, The Preferred Surety Bond Guarantee Program Act of 1988*, 100th Cong., 2nd sess., April 12, 1988, S.Hrg. 100-692 (Washington: GPO, 1988), pp. 2, 101, 103, 125-127.

[51] For information concerning the Preferred Lenders Program see CRS Report R41146, *Small Business Administration 7(a) Loan Guaranty Program*, by Robert Jay Dilger.

[52] U.S. General Accounting Office, *Small Business: Information on and Improvements Needed to Surety Bond Guarantee Programs*, GAO/RCED-91-99, April 23, 1991, p. 12, at http://archive.gao.gov/d20t9/143966.pdf; and S.Rept. 100-416, Small Business Administration Reauthorization and Amendments Act of 1988, pp. 24-25.

[53] U.S. Small Business Administration, "Surety Bond Guarantee Program; Size Standards," 76 Federal Register 48549, August 11, 2010. In addition, for any contract or subcontract, public or private, to be performed in the Presidentially-declared disaster areas resulting from the 2005 Hurricanes Katrina, Rita or Wilma, a construction (general or special trade) concern or concern performing a contract for services is small if it meets the size standard set forth in paragraph (d)(1) of this section, or the average annual receipts of the concern, together with its affiliates, do not exceed $7.0 million, whichever is higher. 13 C.F.R. §121.301(d)(2).

[54] 15 U.S.C. §694b(a)(4).

[55] 13 C.F.R. §115.13(a)(2).

[56] 13 C.F.R. §115.13(a)(5).

[57] 13 C.F.R. §115.13(a)(6).

[58] 13 C.F.R. §115.13(a)(6)(b).

[59] U.S. Small Business Administration, "Surety Bond Guarantee Program; Disaster and Miscellaneous Amendments," 76 *Federal Register* 2571, January 14, 2011; and P.L. 110-246, the Food, Conservation, and Energy Act of 2008, SEC. 12079. Small Business Bonding Threshold.

[60] The SBA reports that there is currently no funding available to implement the provisions related to disaster areas.

[61] 13 C.F.R. §115.68.

[62] 13 C.F.R. §115.31. Under the Prior Approval Program, if the contract amount increases to more than $100,000 after execution of the bond, the guarantee percentage decreases by one percentage point for each $5,000 of

increase or part thereof, but it does not decrease below 80%. If the contact or order is increased above the statutory limit after execution of the bond, the SBA's share of the loss is limited to that percentage of the increased contract or order amount that the applicable statutory limit represents multiplied by the guarantee percentage approved by the SBA. For example, if a contract amount increases to $2.1 million, the SBA's share of the loss under an 80% guarantee is limited to 76.1% [2,000,000/2,100,000=95.2%X80%=76.1%]. If the contract or order amount decreases to $100,000, or less, after execution of the bond, the SBA's guarantee increases to 90% if the surety provides the SBA with evidence supporting the decrease.

[63] C.F.R. §115.32.

[64] U.S. Small Business Administration, "Surety Bond Guarantee Program Fee," 76 *Federal Register* 9632, February 24, 2006.

[65] 13 C.F.R. §115.32.

[66] U.S. Small Business Administration, "Surety Bond Guarantee Program-Preferred Surety Qualification, Increased Guarantee for Veteran and Service-Disabled Veteran-Owned Business," 72 *Federal Register* 34598, June 25, 2007.

[67] U.S. Small Business Administration, "Surety Bonds: Insurance and Reassurance for the Construction Industry," May 6, 2011, at http://www.sba.gov/content/surety-bonds-insurance-and-reassurance-construction-industry.

[68] 13 C.F.R. §115.11.

[69] 13 C.F.R. §115.60.

[70] Ibid.

[71] 13 C.F.R. §115.62.

[72] 13 C.F.R. §115.12.

[73] U.S. Small Business Administration, "Bond Guarantee Application – Surety Company/Agent," at http://www.sba.gov/content/bond-guarantee-application%E2%80%93-surety-company agent.

[74] 13 C.F.R. §115.63.

[75] 13 C.F.R. §115.12.

[76] 13 C.F.R. §115.15; and 13 C.F.R. §115.17. Imminent breach is a threat to the successful completion of a bonded contract which, unless remedied by the surety, makes a default under the bond appear to be inevitable. 13 C.F.R. §115.10.

[77] 13 C.F.R. §115.21.

[78] C.F.R. §115.32.

[79] U.S. Small Business Administration, "Surety Bond Guarantee Program Fee," 76 *Federal Register* 9632, February 24, 2006.

[80] 13 C.F.R. §115.32.

[81] U.S. Small Business Administration, Office of Congressional and Legislative Affairs, correspondence with the author, March 24, 2011; U.S. Small Business Administration, Office of Congressional and Legislative Affairs, correspondence with the author, December 15, 2011; and U.S. Small Business Administration, Office of Congressional and Legislative Affairs, correspondence with the author, December 5, 2012.

[82] U.S. Small Business Administration, Office of Congressional and Legislative Affairs, correspondence with the author, December 5, 2012.

[83] U.S. Small Business Administration, Office of Congressional and Legislative Affairs, correspondence with the author, December 15, 2011.

[84] The default rate was 3.7% in FY2011 and 3.1% in FY2012. U.S. Small Business Administration, Office of Congressional and Legislative Affairs, correspondence with the author, September 29, 2011; and U.S. Small Business Administration, Office of Congressional and Legislative Affairs, correspondence with the author, December 11, 2012.

[85] Ibid; and U.S. Small Business Administration, Office of Congressional and Legislative Affairs, correspondence with the author, December 5, 2012.

[86] U.S. Small Business Administration, "Prior Approval Surety Companies," at http://www.sba. gov/content/prior-approval-surety-companies; and U.S. Small Business Administration, "Preferred Surety Bond Companies," at http://www.sba.gov/content/preferred-surety-bond-participants.

[87] U.S. Small Business Administration, "Participating Surety Company/Agent Search," at http://web.sba.gov/orasbgpub/dsp_welcome.cfm.

[88] The temporary higher maximum limit did not apply if the statement of work involved, directly or indirectly, construction, operation, renovation or improvement of a casino or other gambling establishment, aquarium, zoo, golf course, or swimming pool. 13 C.F.R. §115.12.

[89] The contracting officer's certification had to include a statement that the small business was experiencing difficulty obtaining a bond and that an SBA bond guarantee would be in the best interests of the government. 13 C.F.R. §115.13.

[90] P.L. 111-5, Section 508. Surety Bonds. The program's size standard at that time had three parts: up to $7 million in average annual receipts for any construction (general or special trade) business, together with its affiliates; any other business had to meet the size standard for the primary industry in which it, combined with its affiliates, was engaged; and for any contract or subcontract, public or private, to be performed in the presidentially-declared disaster areas resulting from the 2005 Hurricanes Katrina, Rita or Wilma, a construction (general or special trade) business performing a contract for services was small if it met either of the above conditions, whichever was higher. 13 C.F.R. §121.301.

[91] U.S. Small Business Administration, "Table of Small Business Size Standards," at http://www.sba.gov/content/tablesmall-business-size-standards. Land subdivision contractors may have up to $7 million in average annual receipts over the previous three years and dredging and surface cleanup contractors may have up to $20 million in average annual receipts over the previous three years.

[92] U.S. Small Business Administration, "Surety Bond Guarantee Program; Size Standards," 76 *Federal Register* 48549, August 11, 2010. In addition, for any contract or subcontract, public or private, to be performed in the presidentially declared disaster areas resulting from the 2005 Hurricanes Katrina, Rita or Wilma, a construction (general or special trade) concern or concern performing a contract for services is small if it meets the size standard set forth in paragraph (d)(1) of this section, or the average annual receipts of the concern, together with its affiliates, do not exceed $7.0 million, whichever is higher. 13 C.F.R. §121.301(d)(2).

[93] Senator Olympia Snowe, "Consideration of H.R. 1 American Recovery and Reinvestment Act of 2009," Senate debate, *Congressional Record*, vol. 155, no. 22 (February 4, 2009), p. S1485.

[94] Ibid.

[95] Senator Benjamin Cardin, "Stimulus Package Report," Senate debate, *Congressional Record*, vol. 155, no. 30 (February 13, 2009), p. S2283.

[96] For further information and analysis of the small business provisions in P.L. 111-5, see CRS Report R40985, *Small Business: Access to Capital and Job Creation*, by Robert Jay Dilger.

[97] The White House, "Section-by-Section Analysis and Explanation of the American Jobs Act of 2011," September 12, 2011, at http://www.whitehouse.gov/blog/2011/09/12/president-obama-sends-american-jobs-act-congress.

[98] Jeffrey D. Zients, Deputy Director for Management, U.S. Office of Management and Budget, "Letter sent to the Honorable Harry Reid, Majority Leader of the Senate," December 7, 2012, p. 59.

[99] U.S. Senate, Committee on Appropriations, "Text of Hurricane Sandy Supplemental," December 12, 2012, Sec. 5501, p. 24, at http://www.appropriations.senate.gov /news.cfm?method=news.view&id=0f718f5d-c9e1-49a1-9b5a33a313bb423d.

[100] See U.S. Congress, House Committee on Armed Services, Panel on Business Challenges Within the Defense Industry, *Doing Business With DOD: Unique Challenges Faced by Small and Mid-Sized Businesses*, 112th Cong., 2nd sess., January 17, 2012, HASC No. 112-94 (Washington: GPO, 2012), pp. 48-55. In 2007, the SBA supported a legislative effort to increase the program's bond limit to $3 million as a means to increase the program's use. U.S. Congress, House Committee on Small Business, *Full Committee Hearing on Legislation Updating and Improving the SBA's Investment and Surety Bond Programs*, 110th Cong., 1st sess., September 6, 2007, Serial No. 110-44 (Washington: GPO, 2007), p. 55.

[101] U.S. Congress, House Committee on Armed Services, Panel on Business Challenges Within the Defense Industry, *Doing Business With DOD: Unique Challenges Faced by Small and Mid-Sized Businesses*, 112th Cong., 2nd sess., January 17, 2012, HASC No. 112-94 (Washington: GPO, 2012), p. 52.

[102] For further information and analysis of small business contracting programs see CRS Report R41945, *Small Business Set-Aside Programs: An Overview and Recent Developments in the Law*, by Kate M. Manuel and Erika K. Lunder, CRS Report R40744, *The "8(a) Program" for Small Businesses Owned and Controlled by the Socially and Economically Disadvantaged: Legal Requirements and Issues*, by Kate M. Manuel and John R. Luckey, and CRS Report R41268, *Small Business Administration HUBZone Program*, by Robert Jay Dilger.

[103] 13 C.F.R. §124.506; 48 C.F.R. §19.1306(a)(1)-(6) (increasing the price thresholds, among other things); and Department of Defense, General Services Administration, and National Aeronautics and Space Administration, "Federal Acquisition Regulation: Inflation Adjustment of Acquisition-Related Thresholds," 75 *Federal Register* 53129, August 30, 2010.

[104] U.S. Small Business Administration, Office of Congressional and Legislative Affairs, correspondence with the author, March 31, 2011.

[105] U.S. Congress, House Committee on Armed Services, Panel on Business Challenges Within the Defense Industry, *Challenges to Doing Business with the Department for Defense*, Findings of the Panel on Business Challenges in the Defense Industry, 112th Cong., 2nd sess., March 19, 2012 (Washington: GPO, 2012), pp. 18-19.

[106] U.S. Small Business Administration, Office of Congressional and Legislative Affairs, correspondence with the author, December 5, 2012.

[107] For further information and analysis concerning the 7(a) program see CRS Report R41146, *Small Business Administration 7(a) Loan Guaranty Program*, by Robert Jay Dilger. For further information and analysis concerning the 504/Certified Development Company program see CRS Report R41184, *Small Business Administration 504/CDC Loan Guaranty Program*, by Robert Jay Dilger.

[108] U.S. Small Business Administration, "FY2012 Congressional Budget Justification and FY2010 Annual Performance Report," p. 40, at http://www.sba.gov/sites/default/files/FINAL%20FY%202012%20 CBJ%20 FY%202010%20APR_0.pdf.

[109] Ibid.

[110] National Association of Surety Bond Producers and The Surety & Fidelity Association of America, "Revitalizing the SBA Bond Guarantee Program," Washington, DC, May 24, 2010.

[111] U.S. General Accounting Office, *Small Business: Construction Firms' Access to Surety Bonds*, GAO/RCED-95-173FS, June 26, 1995, p. 1, at http://www.gao.gov/archive /1995/rc95173f.pdf.

[112] Ibid., p. 27.

[113] Ibid., pp. 19, 20, 29.

[114] U.S. Congress, House Committee on Small Business, *Full Committee Hearing on Legislation Updating and Improving the SBA's Investment and Surety Bond Programs*, 110th Cong., 1st sess., September 6, 2007, Serial No. 110- 44 (Washington: GPO, 2007), p. 64.

In: Small Business Administration Programs
Editor: Walter Janikowski

ISBN: 978-1-62417-992-1
© 2013 Nova Science Publishers, Inc.

Chapter 11

SMALL BUSINESS INNOVATION RESEARCH (SBIR) PROGRAM[*]

Wendy H. Schacht

SUMMARY

In 1982, the Small Business Innovation Development Act (P.L. 97-219) established Small Business Innovation Research (SBIR) programs within the major federal research and development (R&D) agencies designed to increase participation of small innovative companies in federally funded R&D. Government agencies with R&D budgets of $100 million or more are required to set aside a portion of these funds to finance the SBIR activity. Through FY2009, over 112,500 awards have been made totaling more than $26.9 billion.

Reauthorized several times over the years, the SBIR program was scheduled to terminate on September 30, 2008. A companion pilot activity, the Small Business Technology Transfer (STTR) program, was scheduled to end the following year. A series of temporary extensions kept both programs in operation until the SBIR/STTR Reauthorization Act of 2011 was enacted as Title LI of the National Defense Authorization Act for Fiscal Year 2012, P.L. 112-81.

In general, the new legislation reauthorizes the SBIR and STTR programs through September 30, 2017; incrementally increases the set aside for the SBIR effort to 3.2% by FY2017 and beyond; incrementally expands the set aside for the STTR activity to 0.45% in FY2016 and beyond; increases the amount of Phase I and Phase II awards; allows the National Institutes of Health, the Department of Energy, and the National Science Foundation to award up to 25% of SBIR funds to small businesses that are majority-owned by venture capital companies, hedge funds, or private equity firms and other agencies to award up to 15% of SBIR funds to such firms; creates commercialization pilot programs; and expands oversight activities, among other things.

---

[*] This is an edited, reformatted and augmented version of a Congressional Research Service publication, CRS Report *for Congress* 96-402, *from* www.crs.gov, *prepared* for Members and Committees of Congress, *dated* November 14, 2012.

PROGRAM DESCRIPTION

The Small Business Innovation Research (SBIR) program is designed to increase the participation of small, high technology firms in the federal R&D endeavor. Congressional support for the initiative was predicated upon the belief that while technology-based companies under 500 employees tended to be highly innovative, and innovation is essential to the economic well-being of the United States, these businesses were underrepresented in government R&D activities. Agency SBIR programs guarantee this sector a portion of the government's R&D budget to compensate for what was viewed as a preference for contracting with large firms.

The law requires that every federal department with an R&D budget of $100 million or more establish and operate an SBIR program. A set percentage of that agency's applicable extramural research and development budget is to be used to support mission-related work in small companies.

The objectives of the SBIR program include stimulation of technological innovation in the small business sector, increased use of this community to meet the government's R&D needs, additional involvement of minority and disadvantaged individuals in the process, and expanded commercialization of the results of federally funded R&D. To achieve this, agency SBIR efforts involve a three-phase activity. Until 2010, first phase awards of up to $100,000 for six months were provided to evaluate a concept's scientific or technical merit and feasibility. As of March 30, 2010, the Small Business Administration (SBA) issued a Policy Directive that increased the amount of Phase I awards to $150,000.[1] The project must be of interest to and coincide with the mission of the supporting organization. Projects that demonstrate potential after the initial endeavor could compete for Phase II awards of originally up to $750,000, now up to $1 million per the above Policy Directive, and lasting one to two years. Phase II awards are for the performance of the principal R&D by the small firm. Phase III funding, directed at the commercialization of the product or process, is expected to be generated in the private sector. Federal dollars may be used if the government perceives that the final technology or technique will meet public needs. P.L. 102-564 directed agencies to weigh commercial potential as an additional factor in evaluating SBIR proposals.

Eleven departments currently have SBIR programs including the Departments of Agriculture, Commerce, Defense (DOD), Education, Energy, Health and Human Services, Homeland Security, and Transportation; the Environmental Protection Agency; the National Aeronautics and Space Administration (NASA); and the National Science Foundation (NSF). Each agency's SBIR activity reflects that organization's management style. Individual departments select R&D interests, administer program operations, and control financial support. Funding can be disbursed in the form of contracts, grants, or cooperative agreements. Separate agency solicitations are issued at established times.

The Small Business Administration is responsible for establishing the broad policy and guidelines under which individual departments operate SBIR programs. The agency monitors and reports to Congress on the conduct of the separate departmental activities. Prior to the December 2011 reauthorization legislation, criteria for eligibility in the SBIR program included companies that are independently owned and operated; not dominant in the field of research proposed; for profit; the employer of 500 or less people; the primary employer of the principal investigator; and at least 51% owned by one or more U.S. citizens or lawfully admitted permanent resident aliens. A rule change, effective January 3, 2005, permitted subsidiaries of SBIR-eligible companies to participate as long as the parent company meets all SBIR requirements.

A related activity, the Small Business Technology Transfer (STTR) program, was created by P.L. 102-564 and reauthorized several times through FY2009. Designed to encourage the commercialization of university and federal laboratory R&D by small companies, the STTR program provides funding for research proposals that are developed and executed cooperatively between a small firm and a scientist in a research organization and fall under the mission requirements of the federal funding agency. Until passage of P.L. 112-81, up to $100,000 in Phase I financing was available for one year; Phase II awards of up to $750,000 could be made for two years. Previously funded by a set-aside of 0.3% of the extramural R&D budget of departments that spend over $1 billion per year on this effort, the Departments of Energy, Defense, and Health and Human Services, NASA, and NSF participate in the STTR activity.

LEGISLATIVE CHANGES

In December 2011, Congress enacted the SBIR/STTR Reauthorization Act of 2011 as Title LI of the National Defense Authorization Act for Fiscal Year 2012, P.L. 112-81. This legislation extends both the SBIR and STTR programs through September 30, 2017.

The new law also makes several major changes to the existing programs. The SBIR set-aside is increased by 0.1% per year from 2.5% in FY2011 up to 3.0% in FY2016, and to 3.2% in FY2017 and beyond. The set-aside for the STTR activity is increased from 0.3% in FY2011 to 0.35% in FY2012 and FY2013; to 0.40% in FY2014 and FY2015; and to 0.45% in FY2016 and beyond.

Phase I SBIR and STTR awards are increased from $100,000 to $150,000 and Phase II SBIR and STTR awards are increased from $750,000 to $1,000,000. Awards cannot exceed the amount guidelines by more than 50% unless an exception is made for one topic to meet agency research requirements.

A recipient of a Phase I grant from one federal agency is permitted to apply for a Phase II award from another agency to pursue the original work. A small business is allowed to switch between the SBIR and STTR programs. Duplicative awards are not permitted.

A new pilot program is created in DOD, the Department of Education, and the National Institutes of Health (NIH) to permit the award of a Phase II grant without the small business receiving a prior Phase I grant.

Also at NIH, a new "Phase 0 proof of concept partnership program" is established to "accelerate the creation of small businesses and the commercialization of research innovations" from universities or other research institutions that participate in the NIH STTR program.

Phase III awards are to go to companies that developed the technologies in Phase I and Phase II and all grants are to be made on a competitive and merit-based basis.

Perhaps the most contentious issue was that of permitting majority venture capital owned small companies to receive grants under the SBIR and STTR programs. In what might be considered a compromise position, the new law permits NIH, DOE, and NSF to award not more than 25% of SBIR funds to "small business concerns that are owned in majority part by multiple venture capital operating companies, hedge funds, or private equity firms through competitive, merit-based procedures that are open to all eligible small business concerns." Other federal agencies may not award more than 15% of SBIR funds to "small business concerns that are owned in majority part by multiple venture capital operating companies, hedge funds, or private equity firms through competitive, merit-based procedures that are open to all eligible small business concerns."

In order to promote the use of federally funded research and development, the legislation provides for commercialization pilot programs for Phase II SBIR and STTR technologies in DOD and the civilian agencies. It also encourages the award of SBIR and STTR grants to small businesses that work with federal laboratories or are involved in cooperative research and development agreements (CRADAs). Agencies are required to establish minimum performance standards (benchmarks) to measure the commercialization success of awardees.

A pilot program is created to permit no more than 3% of SBIR program funds to be used for administrative activities, oversight, and contract processing. As part of this pilot program, a portion of these funds is to be used to increase participation of states which have traditionally received low levels of SBIR awards.

To ensure additional program oversight, the legislation provides for an interagency policy committee and agencies are to report on advanced manufacturing activities in the SBIR program. Also mandated are the creation and maintenance of data bases collecting relevant information on the SBIR and STTR programs for use by both the government and the public sector. Tracking of multiple Phase I awardees that do not receive Phase II grants is also required.

The Comptroller General is to audit agency calculation of extramural research and GAO is mandated to undertake a study on venture capital operating company, hedge fund, and private equity firm involvement in the program.

Provisions to prevent "waste, fraud, and abuse" in the SBIR program are included and the law limits new pilot programs created under this legislation to three years of operation.

The Small Business Administration was required to publish a revised policy directive incorporating the changes within six months of the passage of the legislation. This policy directive was issued in the Federal Register on August 6, 2012. The final rule for venture capital participation is expected to be finalized at the beginning of 2013.

IMPLEMENTATION

The Government Accountability Office (GAO; formerly the General Accounting Office) is legislatively directed to assess the implementation of the Small Business Innovation Development Act, as amended, and has issued a series of reports documenting its findings. A 1987 study found that both the evaluation and selection processes were sufficient to "reasonably" insure awards were based on technical merit. It was also determined that the majority of agencies were not awarding Phase I grants and contracts within the six-month time frame required by the SBA guidelines. Another GAO report the following month surveyed the participants and noted that most were "generally satisfied" with the administration of SBIR programs.

In 1989, GAO reported that agency heads found the SBIR effort to be beneficial and met the organization's R&D needs. Most indicated that the "SBIR programs had developed new research areas, placed more emphasis on the application of research results, and led to wider use of small businesses as research performers." The study concluded that projects were, for the most part, of high quality. At DOD and NASA, however, SBIR efforts stressed R&D to meet agency mission requirements in contrast to other SBIR programs that focused on commercialization for private sector markets. All of the departments stated that SBIR projects, when compared with other research activities, had greater potential to result in new products and processes.

Testimony presented by GAO in 1991 stated that the program "clearly is doing what Congress asked it to do in achieving commercial sales and developmental funding from the private sector." An SBA study found that approximately one in four SBIR projects will result in the sale of new commercial products or processes. Another GAO report issued in May 1992 noted that despite a short time frame and the fact that many SBIR projects had not had sufficient time to mature into marketable technologies and techniques, "the program is showing success in Phase III activity." As of July 1991, almost two-thirds of the projects already had sales or received additional funding (primarily from the private sector) totaling approximately $1.1 billion.

The 1992 study also identified several issues for possible further congressional exploration. According to GAO, DOD placed less emphasis on commercialization than other agencies and utilized the SBIR program primarily to address the department's R&D needs. Questions were raised about the requirements for competitive bidding when companies looked to federal departments for Phase III contracts after successfully completing Phases I and II. GAO noted that clarification of the Competition in Contracting Act of 1984 (as amended) might be necessary. In addition, there was disagreement over whether the federal agency or the small firm should continue to work on technology development after the cessation of SBIR project funding. GAO also concluded that firms receiving multiple Phase II awards tended to have lower Phase III sales and less additional developmental support. The reasons for this remained unclear, but the suggestion was made that these companies may have focused on securing funds through SBIR awards rather than through commercialization of their R&D results.

A March 1995 GAO report found that multiple Phase II funding had become a problem, particularly at NSF, NASA, and DOD. Among the reasons cited were the failure of companies to identify identical proposals made elsewhere in violation of the mandatory certification procedure; uncertainty in definitions and guidelines concerning "similar" research; and lack of interagency mechanisms to exchange information on projects. Several recommendations were made to address duplication. GAO testimony presented in March 1996 indicated that the SBA had taken steps to implement these suggestions. The study also determined that the quality of research appeared to have "kept pace" with the program's expansion, although it was still too early to make a definitive judgment. Factors supporting this assessment included the substantive level of competition, more proposals deemed meritorious than could be funded by agencies, and appraisals by departmental SBIR personnel indicating the high quality of submissions.

Another GAO study, released in April 1998, noted that between 35% and 50% of SBIR projects had resulted in sales or additional private sector investment. Despite earlier indications of problems associated with multiple award winners, this report found that such firms have similar commercialization rates as single awardees. Critical technology lists were being used to determine agency solicitations and there was little evidence of participation by foreign firms. While several agencies had new programs to assure continuity in funding, there were indications of possible inaccuracies in defining the extramural R&D budgets upon which the set-aside is based.

The June 1999 GAO analysis reported that SBIR awards tend to be concentrated both geographically and by firm despite widespread participation in the program. "The 25 most frequent winners, which represent fewer than 1 percent of the companies in the program, received about 11 percent of the program's awards from fiscal year 1983 through fiscal year 1997." Businesses in a small number of states, particularly California and Massachusetts, were awarded the most number of projects. The study also noted that while commercial potential is considered by all agencies, each has developed different evaluation approaches. Other goals, including innovation and responsiveness to agency mission, still remain important in determining awards.

A later report by GAO (June 2005) found that it is still difficult to adequately "assess the performance of the SBIR program" although the effort appears to be achieving its goal of "enhanced" participation of small business in the R&D enterprise. Utilizing "commercialization" as a measure may not be sufficient because other agency goals were being met such as research needs or expanded innovation. Success in the commercial market did not take into account the R&D requirements of departments like DOD or NASA. In a report the following year (October 2006), GAO noted that the agencies reporting to the SBA did not always provide the necessary data in the format required by SBA. GAO concluded that the "agencies need to strengthen [their] efforts to improve the completeness, consistency, and accuracy of awards data."

Data collection remains an issue according to several recent reports. An August 2009 GAO study reiterated past GAO findings of deficiencies in the SBA Tech-Net system designed to collect information from agency SBIR programs. This report noted that "Although SBA did not meet its statutorily mandated deadline of June 2001, the database has been operational since October 2008, and contains limited new information but may also contain inaccurate historical data."[2] A November 2010 report issued by the Office of the Inspector General, U.S. Small Business Administration noted that "limited progress" had been made on Tech-Net and that

> Participating agencies were still experiencing difficulty in searching the database for duplicative awards and other indicators of fraud because information in the Tech-Net database was incomplete, and the search capabilities of the system were limited.... Additionally, SBA had not developed the government-use component of Tech-Net to capture information on the commercialization of SBIR research and development projects. However, SBA recently allocated $1.25 million and has begun the acquisition process to enhance and expand the Tech-Net database.[3]

The ability to assess the commercialization success of SBIR awardees was addressed by GAO in a November 2010 report as well as an August 2011 study. The earlier report found that "DOD lacks complete commercialization data to determine the effectiveness of the program in transitioning space-related technologies into acquisition program for the commercial sector" and that "there are inconsistencies in recording and defining commercialization." The later study indicated that "Comparable data are not available across participating agencies to evaluate progress in increasing commercialization of SBIR technologies." The report goes on to state that, "with the exception of DOD, agencies that GAO reviewed did not generally take steps to verify commercialization data they collected from award recipients, so the accuracy of the data is largely unknown."

The STTR program also has been evaluated by GAO. A January 1996 report found that, in general, federal agencies favorably rated the quality of winning proposals (in the first year) and that most projects had commercial potential, although the costs might be high. The government had taken steps to avoid potential conflicts of interest between federal laboratories and departmental headquarters. There was no indication that this pilot effort was competing for proposals with the established SBIR activity or "reducing the quality of the agencies' R&D in general." Instead it was credited for encouraging collaborative work. Yet, GAO noted that because the programs are so similar, there are questions whether or not a separate activity is necessary. Any real evaluation of success in technology transfer, however, could not be accomplished for several years because of the time needed to bring the results of R&D to the commercial marketplace. These findings were reiterated in testimony given by GAO in May and September 1997.

A June 2001 GAO study of all companies which received STTR awards between FY1995 and FY1997 noted the participant's belief that both the firms and the research institutions contributed to expanded R&D although the private sector was more influential in determining the direction of the research. The companies "reported about $132 million in total sales and about $53 million in additional developmental funding." They identified 41 new patents and the creation of 12 new spin-off firms. Further, the awardees preferred that the STTR program remain separate from the SBIR activity.

Awards

According to the SBA's 2010 report to the President on *The Small Business Economy*, from its inception in FY1983 through FY2009, over 112,500 awards have been made totaling more than $26.9 billion.[4] *Table 1* summarizes the funding and the number of projects selected for the SBIR program. Information on the STTR program is contained in *Table 2* and is compiled from data provided by the SBA Office of Technology.

Issues for Consideration

Much of the debate over the reauthorization of the SBIR and STTR programs revolved around the regulations that require at least 51% ownership by an individual or individuals. Some experts argued participation by small firms that are majority-owned by venture capital companies should be permitted.

Proponents of this change maintain that, particularly in the biotechnology sector, the most innovative companies are not able to use the SBIR program because they do not meet these ownership criteria. Opponents of altering the eligibility requirements argued that the program is designed to provide financial assistance where venture capital is not available.

Table 1. SBIR Program: Dollars Awarded and Projects Funded

Fiscal Year	Number of Phase I Awards	Number of Phase II Awards	Total Number of Awards	Total Dollars Awarded (millions of dollars)
FY1983	686	74	760	44.5
FY1984	999	338	1,337	108.4
FY1985	1,397	407	1,804	199.1
FY1986	1,945	564	2,509	297.9
FY1987	2,189	768	2,957	350.5
FY1988	2,013	711	2,724	389.1
FY1989	2,137	749	2,886	431.9
FY1990	2,346	837	3,183	460.7
FY1991	2,553	788	3,341	483.1
FY1992	2,559	916	3,475	508.4
FY1993	2,898	1,141	4,039	698.0
FY1994	3,102	928	4,030	717.6
FY1995	3,085	1,263	4,348	981.7
FY1996	2,841	1,191	4,032	916.3
FY1997	3,371	1,404	4,775	1,066.7
FY1998	3,022	1,320	4,342	1,100.0
FY1999	3,334	1,256	4,590	1,096.5
FY2000	3,172	1,335	4,507	1,190.2
FY2001	3,215	1,533	4,748	1,294.4
FY2002	4,243	1,577	5,820	1,434.8
FY2003	4,465	1,759	6,224	1,670.1
FY2004	4,638	2,013	6,651	1,867.4
FY2005	4,300	1,871	6,171	2,029.8
FY2006	3,836	2,026	5,862	2,113.9
FY2007	3,909	1,615	5,356	1,777.6
FY2008	3,832	1,851	5,683	1,785.7
FY2009	4,008	1,801	5,809	1,937.7

Source: U.S. Small Business Administration, The Small Business Economy 2010, A Report to the President, available at http://www.sba.gov/sites/default/files /sb_econ2010.pdf.

They assert that the program's objective is to bring new concepts to the point where private sector investment is feasible. While the new law permits limited participation by majority venture capital owned companies, it remains to be determined how this will affect the goals of the two programs.

As the new legislation is implemented, the Congress may wish to explore how the new provisions impact program operation. Additional issues that might be addressed include whether the problems identified by GAO associated with the duplication of awards have been adequately resolved. Some experts question whether the SBIR and STTR programs are meeting their different mandated objectives and assert that they are serving identical purposes. Other critics maintain that the government has no role in directly supporting

Small Business Innovation Research (SBIR) Program

industrial research and development. These and other issues may be debated as the SBIR and STTR programs continue to function through September 30, 2017.

Table 2. STTR Program: Dollars Awarded and Projects Funded

Fiscal Year	Dollars Awarded (millions)				Awards		
	Phase I	Phase II	Total		Phase I	Phase II	Total
FY1994	18.9	—	18.9		198	—	198
FY1995	23	10.7	33.7		238	22	260
FY1996	22.7	41.8	64.5		238	88	326
FY1997	24.2	44.9	69.1		260	89	349
FY1998	19.7	45.1	64.8		208	109	317
FY1999	24.3	40.6	64.9		251	78	329
FY2000	23.9	45.9	69.8		233	95	328
FY2001	24.2	53.2	77.4		224	113	337
FY2002	36.4	55.4	91.8		356	114	470
FY2003	41.1	50.7	91.8		397	111	508
FY2004	79.7	110.3	190		674	195	869
FY2005	73.9	146.4	220.3		611	221	832
FY2006	74.0	152.3	226.3		644	234	878
FY2007	83.5	159.4	242.9		634	213	847
FY2008	61.2	178.4	239.6		483	251	734
FY2009	72.1	186.9	259.0		592	251	843

Source: Small Business Administration data and http://www.sbir.gov/awards/annual-reports.

End Notes

[1] See the Federal Register, Vol. 75, No. 60, Tuesday, March 30, 2010, 15756, available at http://www.acq. osd.mil/osbp/ sbir/overview/SBA%20Increase%20in%20Award%20Thresholds%20- %20Federal%20Register %20(30%20March%202010).pdf.

[2] Government Accountability Office, Small Business Innovation Research: Observations on Agencies' Data Collection and Eligibility Determination Efforts, GAO-09-956T, August 6, 2009, 11.

[3] Small Business Administration, Office of the Inspector General, Usefulness of the Small Business Innovation Research Tech-Net Database, Report Number 11-02, November 12, 2010, 3, available at http://www.sba. gov/sites/ default/files/oig_report_11_02.pdf.

[4] Small Business Administration, The Small Business Economy 2010, A Report to the President, 51-52, available at http://www.sba.gov/sites/default/files/sb_econ2010.pdf and http://www.sbir.gov.

In: Small Business Administration Programs
Editor: Walter Janikowski

ISBN: 978-1-62417-992-1
© 2013 Nova Science Publishers, Inc.

Chapter 12

SBA NEW MARKETS VENTURE CAPITAL PROGRAM[*]

Robert Jay Dilger

SUMMARY

Authorized by P.L. 106-554, the Consolidated Appropriations Act, 2001 (Appendix H — the New Markets Venture Capital Program Act of 2000), the New Markets Venture Capital (NMVC) program is designed to promote economic development and the creation of wealth and job opportunities in low-income geographic areas by addressing the unmet equity investments needs of small businesses located in those areas. Modeled on the SBA's Small Business Investment Company (SBIC) program, SBA-selected, privately owned and managed NMVC companies provide funding and operational training assistance to small businesses using private capital the NMVC company has raised (called regulatory capital) and up to 150% of that amount (called leverage) from the sale of SBA-guaranteed 10-year debentures (loan obligations) to third parties, subject to the availability of funds. Because the SBA guarantees the debenture, the SBA is able to obtain favorable interest rates. NMVC companies are responsible for meeting the terms and conditions set forth in the debenture. At least 80% of the investments must be in small businesses located in a low-income area.

Specialized Small Business Investment Companies (SSBICs) established under the SBIC program are also eligible for NMVC operational assistance training grants, which are awarded on a dollar-to-dollar matching basis. There are currently six NMVC companies participating in the program.

The NMVC program was appropriated $21.952 million in FY2001 to support up to $150 million in SBA guaranteed debentures and $30 million for operational assistance training grants for FY2001 through FY2006. The funds were provided in a lump sum in FY2001 and were to remain available until expended. In 2003, the unobligated balances of $10.5 million for the NMVC debenture subsidies and $13.75 million for operational assistance grants were rescinded. The program continues to operate, with the number and amount of financing declining in recent years as the program's initial investments expire

---

[*] This is an edited, reformatted and augmented version of a Congressional Research Service publication, CRS Report for Congress R42565, prepared for Members and Committees of Congress, from www.crs.gov, dated June 12, 2012.

and NMVC companies engage only in additional follow-on financings with the small businesses in their portfolio.

More than 30 bills have been introduced in recent Congresses to either expand or amend the NMVC program. Many of these bills would increase the program's funding. For example, during the 112th Congress, H.R. 2872, the Job Creation and Urban Revitalization Act of 2011, was introduced on September 8, 2011. The bill would provide the NMVC program such subsidy budget authority as may be necessary to guarantee $75 million of debentures and $15 million for operational assistance training grants for FY2012 through FY2013. The bill was referred to the House Committee on Small Business on September 8, 2011, and is awaiting further action.

This report examines the NMVC program's legislative origins and describes the program's eligibility and performance requirements for NMVC companies, eligibility requirements for small businesses seeking financing, and the definition of low-income areas. It also reviews regulations governing the SBA's financial assistance to NMVC companies and provides program statistics. The report concludes with an examination of (1) efforts to eliminate the program based on concerns that it duplicates other SBA programs and is relatively expensive, (2) the rescission of the program's unobligated funding in 2003, and (3) recent congressional efforts to provide the program additional funds.

NEW MARKETS VENTURE CAPITAL PROGRAM OVERVIEW

The Small Business Administration (SBA) administers several programs to support small businesses, including loan guaranty programs to enhance small business access to capital; programs to increase small business opportunities in federal contracting; direct loans for businesses, homeowners, and renters to assist their recovery from natural disasters; and access to entrepreneurial education to assist with business formation and expansion.1 It also administers the New Markets Venture Capital (NMVC) Program.

Authorized by P.L. 106-554, the Consolidated Appropriations Act, 2001 (Appendix H — the New Markets Venture Capital Program Act of 2000), the NMVC program is designed to

- promote economic development and the creation of wealth and job opportunities in low-income geographic areas and among individuals living in such areas by encouraging developmental venture capital investments in smaller enterprises primarily located in such areas; and
- address the unmet equity investment needs of small enterprises located in low-income geographic areas.[2]

Modeled on the SBA's Small Business Investment Company (SBIC) program, SBA-selected, privately owned and managed NMVC companies provide funding and operational training assistance to small businesses using private capital the NMVC company has raised (called regulatory capital) and up to 150% of that amount (called leverage) from the sale of SBA-guaranteed 10-year debentures (loan obligations) to third parties, subject to the availability of funds.[3] Because the SBA guarantees the debenture, the SBA is able obtain favorable interest rates. NMVC companies are responsible for meeting the terms and conditions set forth in the debenture. At least 80% of the investments must be in small businesses located in a low-income area, as defined in the statute.

Specialized Small Business Investment Companies (SSBICs) established under the SBIC program are also eligible for NMVC operational assistance training grants, which are awarded on a dollar-to-dollar matching basis. There are currently six NMVC companies participating in the program.

The NMVC program was appropriated $21.952 million in FY2001 to support up to $150 million in SBA guaranteed debentures and up to $30 million for operational assistance training grants for FY2001 through FY2006.[4] The funds were provided in a lump sum in FY2001 and were to remain available until expended. The SBA subsequently provided $72.0 million in leverage to NMVC companies in FY2002 and FY2003 ($12.5 million in FY2002 and $59.5 million in FY2003) and $14.4 million for operational assistance grants ($3.75 million in FY2002 and $10.65 million in FY2003).[5] In 2003, the unobligated balances of $10.5 million for the NMVC debenture subsidies and $13.75 million for operational assistance grants were rescinded.[6] The program continues to operate, with the number and amount of financing declining in recent years as the program's initial investments expire and NMVC companies engage only in additional follow-on financings with the small businesses in their portfolio.

As will be discussed, more than 30 bills have been introduced in recent Congresses to amend the NMVC program. Many of these bills would provide the program additional funding (a list and summary of bills introduced, by Congress, to provide the program additional funding is provided in the *Appendix*). For example, during the 112th Congress, H.R. 2872, the Job Creation and Urban Revitalization Act of 2011, was introduced on September 8, 2011. The bill would provide the NMVC program such subsidy budget authority as may be necessary to guarantee $75 million of debentures and $15 million for operational assistance training grants for FY2012 through FY2013. The bill was referred to the House Committee on Small Business on September 8, 2011, and is awaiting further action.

This report examines the NMVC program's legislative origins and describes the program's eligibility and performance requirements for NMVC companies, eligibility requirements for small businesses seeking financing, and the definition of low-income areas. It also reviews regulations governing the SBA's financial assistance to NMVC companies and provides program statistics. The report concludes with an examination of (1) efforts to eliminate the program based on concerns that it duplicates other SBA programs and is relatively expensive, (2) the rescission of the program's unobligated funding in 2003, and (3) recent congressional efforts to provide the program additional funds.

LEGISLATIVE ORIGINS

105th Congress

On September 15, 1998, the Senate Committee on Small Business conducted a markup of several bills pending before the committee, including H.R. 3412, the Small Business Investment Company Technical Corrections Act of 1998, which the House had passed.[7] Senator Christopher Bond, chair of the Senate Committee on Small Business, proposed an amendment in the nature of a substitute to H.R. 3412 incorporating the full texts of S. 2372, the Year 2000 Readiness Act; and S. 2407, the Small Business Programs Restructuring and Reform Act of 1998; and provisions from S. 2448, the Small Business Loan Enhancement Act.[8] The committee also debated and approved by unanimous voice votes seven amendments to the substitute amendment. One of the seven approved amendments was a precursor of the NMVC program.

The Community Development Venture Capital Demonstration Program

The amendment, offered by Senator Paul Wellstone, would have authorized a $20 million, four-year technical assistance program—the Community Development Venture Capital Demonstration Program—to provide grants, on a matching dollar-to-dollar basis, to experienced community development venture capital (CDVC) firms that invest in small businesses located in economically distressed areas, such as inner cities and poor rural counties. The grants would be used to provide technical expertise and operating assistance to new, emerging, less experienced CDVC organizations.[9] The program's stated purpose was "to develop and expand a new but growing field of organizations that use the tools of venture capital to create good jobs, productive wealth, and entrepreneurial capacity that benefit disadvantaged people and economically distressed communities."[10] The program's advocates argued that despite difficulties associated with making investments in economically distressed areas some successful CDVCs had produced "a 'double bottom line' of not only financial returns, but also social benefits in the form of good jobs and healthier communities."[11]

On September 15, 1998, the committee reported H.R. 3412, as amended, by a vote of 18-0. On September 30, 1998, the Senate passed the bill, with an amendment, by unanimous consent. The House did not act on the bill.

106th Congress

On January 19, 1999, President Bill Clinton announced during his State of the Union Address support for what was later called the "New Markets Investment Initiative."[12] The proposed initiative was comprised of several programs, including a New Markets Tax Credit program and a New Markets Venture Capital program, to encourage economic development in economically distressed areas.[13] President Clinton subsequently drew attention to the initiative by taking three separate trips to "underserved" inner city and rural communities, visiting the Pine Ridge Indian Reservation in South Dakota and Phoenix, AZ, on July 7, 1999, and Los Angeles, CA, and Anaheim, CA, on July 8, 1999 (trip 1); Newark, NJ, and Hartford, CT, on November 4, 1999 (trip 2); and Hermitage, AR, and Chicago, IL, on November 5, 1999 (trip 3).14 During his remarks in Chicago, President Clinton announced that he had reached an agreement with House Speaker Dennis Hastert (who was present) to develop a bipartisan legislative initiative on developing new market investments as a means to revitalize impoverished communities.[15]

SBA's LMI Initiative

In a related development, on February 9, 1999, the SBA proposed several incentives to encourage companies participating in its SBIC program to "expand their investment activity into economically distressed inner cities and rural areas."[16] After receiving public comments on several proposed incentives, the SBA issued a final rule, on September 30, 1999, implementing the SBIC low and moderate investments (LMI) initiative.[17]

The ongoing LMI initiative is designed to encourage SBICs to invest in small businesses located in inner cities and rural areas "that have severe shortages of equity capital" because investments in those areas "often are of a type that will not have the potential for yielding returns that are high enough to justify the use of participating securities."[18] SBICs that invest in small businesses that have at least 50% of their employees or tangible assets located in a low-to-moderate income area (LMI Zone), or have at least 35% of their full-time employees with their primary residence in an LMI Zone are eligible for the incentives.[19] For example, unlike regular SBIC debentures that typically have a 10-year maturity, LMI debentures are available in two maturities, 5 years and 10 years, plus the stub period. The stub period is the time between the debenture's issuance date and the next March 1 or September 1. The stub period allows all LMI debentures to have common March 1 or September 1 maturity dates to simplify administration of the program.

In addition, LMI debentures are issued at a discount so that the proceeds that an SBIC receives for the sale of a debenture are reduced by (1) the debenture's interest costs for the first five years, plus the stub period; (2) the SBA's annual fee for the debenture's first five years, plus the stub period; and (3) the SBA's 2% leverage fee. As a result, these interest costs and fees are effectively deferred, freeing SBICs from the requirement to make interest payments on LMI debentures, or pay the SBA's annual fees on LMI debentures, for the first five years of a debenture, plus the stub period between the debenture's issuance date and the next March 1 or September 1.[20]

The Community Development and Venture Capital Act of 2000

On September 16, 1999, Senator John Kerry introduced S. 1594, the Community Development and Venture Capital Act of 2000.[21] The bill included several provisions in President Clinton's New Markets Investment Initiative. The bill had three main parts: a New Markets Venture Capital Program, very similar to the present program, to encourage investment in economically distressed communities; a Community Development Venture Capital Assistance Program to expand the number of community development venture capital firms and professionals devoted to investing in economically distressed communities; and BusinessLINC, a mentoring program to link established, successful businesses with small business owners in economically stagnant or deteriorating communities to facilitate the development of small businesses in those communities.[22]

After conducting two hearings and sponsoring a roundtable discussion on the Community Development and Venture Capital Act of 2000, the Senate Committee on Small Business reported the bill, as amended, by a vote of 16-1, on July 26, 2000.

In the report accompanying the bill, Senator Christopher Bond, chair of the Senate Committee on Small Business, argued that the SBIC program had "proven to be an extremely successful public-private sector partnership with the government" and mentioned the SBA's LMI initiative as a new means to encourage SBICs to make investments in low-to-moderate income areas.[23] However, he argued that "as successful as the SBIC program is, it does not sufficiently reach areas of our country that need economic development the most."[24]

He added that SBICs invested $771 million in low-to-moderate income areas in 1999, but "the vast majority of those investments were very large and not at all comparable to the type of investments [NMVC] funds would make."[25] Senator Bond argued that the committee was approving the bill because it was necessary

> to expand the number of smaller investments being made to small businesses in the poorest areas, low-income geographic areas, and to fill another gap in access to capital that small businesses face. Investments for NMVC funds typically will range from $50,000 to $300,000 versus the $300,000 to $5 million range found in the Agency's SBIC program."[26]

The Senate did not take further action on the bill.

The New Markets Venture Capital Program Act of 2000

On December 14, 2000, Representative (later Senator) Jim Talent, chair of the House Committee on Small Business, introduced H.R. 5663, the New Markets Venture Capital Program Act of 2000.[27] The bill had two parts: the current New Markets Venture Capital Program and BusinessLINC. The next day, the bill was incorporated by reference in the conference report accompanying H.R. 4577, the Consolidated Appropriations Act, 2001, which became law (P.L. 106-554) on December 21, 2000.[28]

On January 22, 2001, the SBA published an interim final rule in the *Federal Register* to establish the NMVC program. Comments on the proposed rule were due by March 23, 2001. The SBA also published a notice in the *Federal Register* on January 22, 2001, inviting applications from venture capital firms and Specialized Small Business Investment Companies (SSBICs) established under the SBIC program to participate in the program.[29] The SBA published a final rule formally establishing the NMVC program on May 23, 2001.[30]

NMVC COMPANY ELIGIBILITY
AND PERFORMANCE REQUIREMENTS

P.L. 106-554 specified that venture capital companies interested in participating in the program must submit

- a detailed application to the SBA that includes, among other items, a business plan describing how the company intends to make successful developmental venture capital investments in identified low-income geographic areas, and
- information regarding the community development finance or relevant venture capital qualifications and general reputation of the company's management.[31]

In addition, an NMVC company must

- be a newly formed for-profit entity or a newly formed for-profit subsidiary of an existing entity;
- be organized under state law solely for the purpose of performing the functions and conducting the activities contemplated under the act;
- be organized either as a corporation, a limited partnership, or a limited liability company;

- show, to the SBA's satisfaction, that its current or proposed management team is qualified and has the knowledge, experience, and capability in community development finance or relevant venture capital finance necessary for investing in the types of businesses contemplated by the act; and
- have a primary objective of economic development of low-income areas.[32]

On January 22, 2001, the SBA solicited applications from venture capital companies and SSBICs to participate in the NMVC program. The SBA had planned to offer another round of applications for the program during the first quarter of 2003.

However, the second round of applications was canceled because, as mentioned previously, P.L. 108-7, the Consolidated Appropriations Resolution, 2003, which became law on February 20, 2003, rescinded the program's unobligated funding.[33]

The SBA received 23 applicants during its initial solicitation from companies interested in participating in the NMVC program, and conditionally approved 7 of them.[34] Final approval is subject to the applicant meeting several conditions. For example, applicants are required to raise, within 18 months of being conditionally approved, at least $5 million in private capital or in binding capital commitments from one or more investors (other than federal agencies or departments) who meet criteria established by the administrator (the private funds are called regulatory capital). Applicants also must have in place binding commitments from sources other than the SBA that are payable or available over a multiyear period not to exceed 10 years that amount to not less than 30% of the total amount of regulatory capital and commitments raised (30% of $5 million = $1.5 million).[35] This additional funding is required to guarantee the applicant's ability to meet the required dollar-to-dollar matching contribution for operational assistance training grants.[36]

Six of the seven companies granted conditional approval subsequently met all of the program requirements (one in April 2002, three in March 2003, one in April 2003, and one in August 2003) and were accepted into the program after signing a formal participation agreement with the SBA.[37] The six NMVC companies, which continue to participate in the program, initially raised $48 million in private capital and were subsequently provided $72 million in leverage.[38]

The companies are

- Adena Ventures, L.P., Athens, OH, approved on April 24, 2002, with targeted low-income areas in Ohio, West Virginia, and Maryland;
- New Markets Venture Partners, College Park, MD, approved on March 5, 2003, with targeted low-income areas in Maryland, Virginia, and the District of Columbia;
- CEI Community Ventures Fund, LLC, Portland, ME, approved on March 21, 2003, with targeted low-income areas in Maine, New Hampshire, and Vermont;
- Murex Investments I, L.P., Philadelphia, PA, approved on March 31, 2003, with targeted low-income areas in Pennsylvania, New Jersey, and Delaware;
- Penn Venture Partners, LP, Harrisburg, PA, approved on April 23, 2003, with targeted low-income areas in Pennsylvania;
- Southern Appalachian Fund, L.P., London, KY, approved on August 8, 2003, with targeted low-income areas in Kentucky, Tennessee, Georgia, Alabama, and Mississippi.[39]

NMVC companies are subject to various reporting requirements. For example, for each fiscal year, NMVC companies must file an annual financial statement with the SBA that has been audited by an independent public accountant acceptable to the SBA.[40]

The annual financial statement must include an assessment of the social, economic, or community development impact of each financing; the number of fulltime equivalent jobs created as a result of the financing; the impact on the revenues and profits of the business being financed; the impact on the taxes paid by the business being financed and by its employees; and a listing of the number and percentage of the business's employees that reside in a low-income area.[41]

NMVC companies are also required to submit to the SBA a portfolio financing report for each financing made within 30 days of the closing date.[42]

ELIGIBILITY OF SMALL BUSINESSES AND LOW-INCOME GEOGRAPHIC AREAS

NMVC companies are required to provide financial assistance and operational assistance training only to small businesses as defined under the SBA's SBIC program. The business must meet either the SBA's size standard for the industry in which it is primarily engaged or have a maximum net worth of no more than $18 million and average after-tax net income for the preceding two years of not more than $6 million.[43]

All of the company's subsidiaries, parent companies, and affiliates are considered in the size standard determination.[44] In addition, at the close of each NMVC company's fiscal year, at least 80% of the company's total financings (in total dollars) and 80% of the total number of concerns in that company's portfolio must be small businesses that, at the time of the financing, had their principal offices located in a low-income area (low-income enterprises).[45] NMVC companies that fail to reach these required percentages at the end of any fiscal year must be in compliance by the end of the following fiscal year.

They are not eligible for additional leverage from the SBA until such time as they reach the required percentages.[46] A low-income area is defined in the act as any census tract, or equivalent county division as defined by the Bureau of the Census, that meets any of the following criteria:

- a poverty rate of 20% or more;
- if located in a metropolitan area, at least 50% of its households have an income that is below 60% of the area median gross income;
- if not located in a metropolitan area, has a median household income that does not exceed 80% of the statewide median household income;
- is located within a HUBZone;
- is located in an urban empowerment zone or urban enterprise community as designated by the Department of Housing and Urban Development; or
- is located in a rural empowerment zone or rural enterprise community as designated by the Department of Agriculture.

NMVC LEVERAGE

NMVC companies invest funds that they have raised themselves (regulatory capital) in small businesses and, in addition, can receive up to 150% of that amount from the SBA, subject to the availability of funds. NMVC companies follow essentially the same process for obtaining SBA funding as prescribed under the SBIC program. The SBA's funding (leverage) comes from the sale of 10-year securities (debentures) to third parties which are backed by the full faith and credit of the United States.[47] Because the SBA guarantees the timely payment of the principal and interest due on the securities, the SBA is able to obtain favorable interest rates. NMVC companies are responsible for meeting the terms and conditions set forth in the debenture.

NMVC debentures are deferred interest debentures issued at a discount (less than face value) equal to the first five years' interest to eliminate the need for NMVC companies to make interest payments during that period. As a result, NMVC companies make no payments on the debenture for five years from the date of issuance, plus the length of time between the issue date and the next March 1 or September 1, whichever comes first.[48] The SBA refers to this period of time as the "stub" period and employs its use so that all NMVC debentures have common prepayment and maturity dates of either March 1 or September 1.[49] NMVC companies make semi-annual interest payment on the face amount of the debenture during years 6 to 10, and are responsible for paying the debenture's principal amount when the debenture reaches its maturity date.

NMVC companies receive funding (leverage) from the SBA in a two-step process. First, they submit a request to the SBA for a conditional commitment to reserve a specific amount of leverage for future use.[50]

This request authorizes the SBA to sell the requested debenture amount to a third party at an interest rate approved by the SBA or to pool the requested debenture amount with other requests, providing each request with the same maturity date, interest rates, and conditions. The NMVC companies then apply to the SBA to draw against the SBA's leverage commitment. These requests may come at any time during the term of the SBA's leverage commitment.[51]

Although the SBA is authorized to pool NMVC debentures, the Federal Home Loan Bank of Chicago (FHLB) has an agreement with the SBA to purchase all NMVC debentures and hold them until maturity.

The interest rate on the debentures is determined by FHLB using a spread over the FHLB's cost of funds as determined on each draw date.[52]

The SBA does not allow NMVC companies to prepay their draws for a period of 12 months (plus the stub period) after issuance. Prepayments are allowed after that waiting period, but only on March 1 or September 1 of each year. The cost of prepayment is the present value of the NMVC debenture on the semi-annual date chosen for prepayment.[53]

After receiving funds, NMVC companies make equity investments in small businesses of their choice. Equity investments typically are in the form of common or preferred stock, and sometimes in subordinated debt with equity features (provided that the debt is not amortized and provides for interest payments contingent upon and limited to the extent of earnings) or in limited partnership interests, options, warrants, and similar equity investment instruments.[54]

OPERATIONAL ASSISTANCE TRAINING GRANTS

The SBA awards grants to NMVC companies and to SSBICs to provide free operational assistance training to small businesses financed, or expected to be financed, under the program.[55] The grants have a dollar-to-dollar matching requirement and cannot be used for general and administrative expenses, including overhead.[56] Matching resources may be in the form of (1) cash; (2) in-kind contributions; (3) binding commitments for cash or in-kind contributions that are payable or available over a multiyear period acceptable to the SBA, but not to exceed 10 years; or (4) an annuity, purchased with funds other than regulatory capital, from an insurance company acceptable to the SBA that may be payable over a multiyear period acceptable to the SBA, but not to exceed 10 years.[57] NMVC companies and SSBICs are eligible for an operational assistance training grant award equal to the amount of matching resources the company has raised, subject to the availability of funds.[58]NMVC companies must use at least 80% of both the grant funds awarded by the SBA and its matching resources to provide free operational assistance training to small businesses located in a low-income area. SSBICs must use both the grant funds awarded by the SBA and its matching resources to provide free operational assistance training to small businesses "in connection with a low-income investment made by the SSBIC with regulatory capital raised after September 21, 2000."[59] Operational assistance includes management, marketing, and other technical assistance training that assists a small business with its development.[60]

PROGRAM STATISTICS

Table 1. New Markets Venture Capital Program Statistics, FY2002-FY2012

Fiscal Year	Operational Assistance Training Grant Awards	NMVC Financings	Number of Small Businesses Financed
2002	$3,750,000	$500,000	1
2003	$10,650,000	$2,694,164	6
2004	$0	$9,667,145	19
2005	$0	$8,603,678	22
2006	$0	$16,279,591	35
2007	$0	$14,015,821	32
2008	$0	$13,351,779	36
2009	$0	$4,241,016	24
2010	$0	$3,424,407	16
2011	$0	$2,506,576	18
2012 (to June 5)	$0	$368,472	5
Total	$14,400,000	$75,652,649	67[a]

Source: U.S. Small Business Administration, Congressional Budget Justification, Washington, DC, various years; U.S. Small Business Administration, Performance and Accountability Report, Washington, DC, various years; U.S. Small Business Administration, Office of Congressional and Legislative Affairs, "Correspondence with the author," Washington, DC, June 5, 2012.

[a] The total number of small businesses financed is fewer than the sum of small businesses financed each year because NMVC companies may make multiple financings into any one of their "portfolio companies" over the life of the fund.

As shown in *Table 1*, NMVC companies received operational assistance training grant awards in FY2002 and FY2003, and started making equity investments in small businesses in FY2002. As mentioned previously, the six NMVC companies, which continue to participate in the program, initially raised $48 million in private capital and were subsequently provided $72 million in leverage.[61] Since the program's inception through June 5, 2012, NMVC companies have invested more than $75.6 million in 67 different small businesses. The program reached its peak, in terms of the amount of financings, in FY2007, investing nearly $16.3 million in 35 different small businesses that year. Since then, the amount of financings has declined as the program's initial investments expire and NMVC companies engage only in additional follow-on financings with the small businesses in their portfolios.

CONGRESSIONAL ISSUES

As mentioned previously, the NMVC program has not received any additional funding since 2001. Opposition to the program within Congress began to gain momentum when President George W. Bush recommended in his FY2002 budget request that the NMVC program be eliminated, arguing that the program is relatively expensive and duplicative of other federal programs.[62]

> The Administration supports the objectives of the New Markets Venture Capital (NMVC) program but believes those objectives can be achieved more efficiently and at a lower cost through other existing programs. Several vehicles and incentives to direct investment into economically distressed communities already exist. Communities targeted by NMVC have access to a wide range of private for-profit and economic development programs, including the federally supported community development financial institutions administered through the Department of Treasury. In addition, SBA's SBIC program, which has 412 licensed venture capital companies with total capital resources amounting to $17.7 billion, is implementing incentives to encourage investment in economically distressed areas.
>
> The NMVC program is also expensive relative to the impact that it is expected to have. The total cost of the program in FY2001 is $52 million, not including administrative cost of running the program. Since the program is expected to generate $150-$200 million of investment activity, it will yield only $3.00-$4.00 of investment for every taxpayer dollar spent. In comparison, under the Small Business Investment Company (SBIC) program, there is no cost associated with the debenture portion of the program.[63]

Others argued that the NMVC program's targeted clientele of small businesses located in economically distressed areas is inherently too risky for government involvement. In their view, NMVC companies are "designed and chartered to operate (as profit-making firms) in a market niche that mainstream venture capital firms will not touch."[64]

The program's advocates argued that the NMVC program is necessary precisely because mainstream venture capital firms generally avoided investments in small businesses located in economically distressed areas. In their view, the NMVC program is an essential part of a larger federal effort, which includes tax incentives, to fill a market niche in private sector venture capital investments and, in the process, help to revitalize areas experiencing long-term economic difficulties. They also objected to the Bush Administration's argument that the program is duplicative of other federal programs. In their view, the NMVC program is targeted at a clientele that is not being adequately served by other federal programs.[65]

The Bush Administration continued to recommend the program's elimination in each of its subsequent budget requests. As mentioned previously, during congressional consideration of the FY2003 budget the unobligated balances of $10.5 million for NMVC debenture subsidies and $13.75 million for operational assistance training grants were rescinded.[66]

Since then, more than 30 bills have been introduced to amend the NMVC program, including bills to

- reduce the amount of capital NMVC companies must raise to become eligible for operational assistance training grants,
- eliminate the matching requirement for operational assistance training grants,
- create an Office of New Markets Venture Capital within the SBA,
- require the SBA to provide conditionally approved NMVC companies a full two years to meet all program requirements,
- provide increased financing to small manufacturers, and
- amend the program's definition for low-income area to correspond with the definition used by the New Market Tax Credits program (§45D(e) of the Internal Revenue Code of 1986) (26 U.S.C. 45D(e)).

Many of these bills also include provisions to provide the NMVC program additional funding.[67]

LEGISLATIVE EFFORTS TO PROVIDE ADDITIONAL NMVC FUNDING

As shown in *Table A-1* in the *Appendix*, during the 108th Congress, two bills were introduced, one in the House and one in the Senate, to provide the NMVC program "such subsidy budget authority as may be necessary to guarantee $75 million of debentures" and $15 million for operational assistance training grants over FY2004 and FY2005.[68] Neither bill was enacted.[69]

During the 109th Congress, an amendment was offered during the House during floor debate on H.R. 2862, the Science, State, Justice, Commerce, and Related Agencies Appropriations Act, 2006, to provide "$30 million in debenture guarantees and $5 million for operational assistance grants to fund the creation of a fresh round of New Market Venture Capital companies ... paid for by using funds from the Small Business Administration's salary and expense account."[70] The amendment failed by voice vote.[71] Also, a bill introduced in the House would have authorized an expansion of the NMVC program to include the selection of an NMVC company whose primary objective was the economic development of small businesses located in Hurricane Katrina-affected areas. The bill would have authorized "such subsidy budget authority as may be necessary to guarantee ... $50 million of debentures issued by the Gulf Region New Markets Venture Capital Company ... and $10 million for grants to the Gulf Region New Markets Venture Capital Company."[72] Another House bill would have provided the NMVC program "such subsidy budget authority as may be necessary to guarantee $100 million of debentures and $25 million for operational assistance training grants for FY2006 through FY2008."[73] Neither bill was enacted.[74]

During the 110th Congress, four bills were introduced, two in the House and two in the Senate, to provide the NMVC program additional funding. One of the House bills would have provided the NMVC program such subsidy budget authority as may be necessary to guarantee $100 million of debentures and $25 million for operational assistance training grants for FY2007 through FY2009.[75] The other House bill would have provided the NMVC program such subsidy budget authority as may be necessary to guarantee $30 million of debentures and $5 million for operational assistance training grants for FY2008 through FY2010.[76] The two Senate bills would have provided the NMVC program $20 million for operational assistance training grants.[77] None of these bills was enacted.

During the 111th Congress, two bills were introduced in the House to provide the NMVC program additional funding. One of the bills would have provided the NMVC program such subsidy budget authority as may be necessary to guarantee $100 million of debentures and $25 million for operational assistance training grants for FY2009 through FY2011.[78] The other bill would have provided the NMVC program such subsidy budget authority as may be necessary to guarantee $100 million of debentures and $20 million for operational assistance training grants for FY2010 through FY2011.[79]

During the 112th Congress, one bill, to date, has been introduced to provide additional funding for the NMVC program. H.R. 2872, the Job Creation and Urban Revitalization Act of 2011, was introduced by Representative Nydia Velázquez on September 8, 2011. The bill would provide the NMVC program such subsidy budget authority as may be necessary to guarantee $75 million of debentures and $15 million for operational assistance training grants for FY2012 through FY2013. The bill was referred to the House Committee on Small Business on September 8, 2011, and is awaiting further action.

RELATED SBIC PROGRAM DEVELOPMENTS

P.L. 111-5, the American Recovery and Reinvestment Act of 2009 (ARRA), included provisions designed to encourage SBIC investments in low-income areas. The act allows an SBIC licensed on or after October 1, 2009, to elect to have a maximum leverage amount of $175 million, instead of $150 million, if the SBIC has invested at least 50% of its financings in low-income geographic areas, as defined under the NMVC program, and certified that at least 50% of its future investments will be in low-income geographic areas.[80] ARRA also increased the maximum amount of leverage available for two or more licenses under common control to $250 million from $225 million if these requirements are met.

In addition, on April 7, 2011, the SBA announced a $1 billion impact investment SBIC initiative (up to $150 million in leverage in FY2012, and up to $200 million in leverage per fiscal year thereafter until the limit is reached). Under this initiative, SBA-licensed impact investment debenture SBICs are required to invest at least 50% of their financings "which target areas of critical national priority including underserved markets and communities facing barriers to access to credit and capital."[81] To receive an impact investment, a small business must meet at least one of the following criteria: (1) it must be located in, or have at least 35% of its full-time employees, at the time of the initial investment, residing in a low or moderate income area as defined in 13 CFR Section 107.50;[82] or be located in an economically distressed area as defined by Section 3011 of the Public Works and Economic Development Act of 1965, as amended (per capita income of 80% or less of the national average or an unemployment rate that is, for the most recent 24-month period for which data are available, at least 1% greater than the national average unemployment rate); or (2) be in an industrial sector that the SBA has identified as a national priority (currently clean energy and education).

CONCLUSION

The NMVC program continues to operate, but the amount and number of its financings remain lower than anticipated by its original sponsors and below levels desired by its advocates. In recent years, the amount of SBIC program investments in low-to-moderate income areas has increased—from $372.7 million in FY2009 (20.1% of total SBIC financing), to $444.5 million in FY2010 (21.1% of total SBIC financing), and to $687.1 million in FY2011 (24.3% of total SBIC financing).[83] In addition, the SBA's LMI and impact investment initiatives are designed to encourage SBIC investments in low-to-moderate income areas. It could be argued that the increased levels of SBIC investments in low-to-moderate income areas in recent years, coupled with the SBA's efforts to encourage SBIC investments in low-to-moderate income areas, may diminish the need for the NMVC program. NMVC advocates disagree. In FY2011, SBICs provided 553 financings amounting to $687.1 million to small businesses located in a low-tomoderate income area, an average investment of $1.24 million.[84] NMVC advocates argue, as Senator Bond did when the NMVC program was proposed, that the NMVC program targets small businesses seeking much smaller investments.[85]

The debate over the NMVC program's future, particularly whether the program should be provided additional funding, is, in many ways, reflective of broader disagreements about the role of government, and the SBA, in private enterprise. Some believe that the federal government, and the SBA, should take an active role in assisting small businesses to access capital—through the provision of loan guarantees, equity financing, and management training—to assist the economic recovery. In their view, the SBA's programs fill a market niche by providing loans to small businesses unable to get credit elsewhere, equity financings to small businesses often overlooked by private investors, and training for new and aspiring entrepreneurs unable to find affordable training elsewhere. They assert that increasing funding for the NMVC program is an investment that will create jobs by making capital available to entrepreneurs unable to find it in the private marketplace.

Others worry about the long-term adverse economic effects of the federal deficit. Instead of advocating increased funding for federal spending programs, they advocate business tax reduction, reform of financial credit market regulation, and federal fiscal restraint as the best means to assist small businesses, generate economic growth, and create jobs. They are particularly interested in achieving greater government efficiency by eliminating federal spending programs, such as the NMVC program, which they perceive are duplicative of others.

APPENDIX. LEGISLATIVE EFFORTS TO PROVIDE ADDITIONAL FUNDING FOR THE NMVC PROGRAM

Table A-1. Legislative Efforts to Provide Additional NMVC Funding

Congress	Legislation and Sponsor	Funding Necessary to Support NMVC Debenture Guarantee of	Funding for Operational Assistance Training Grants	Legislative Action
108th	H.R. 2802, the Small Business Reauthorization and Manufacturing Revitalization Act of 2003 (Representative Donald Manzullo) S. 1886, the MADE in America Act (by Senator Tom Daschle on behalf of Senator John Kerry)	$75 million $75 million	$15 million $15 million	Introduced on July 21, 2003, and referred to the House Committee on Small Business; reported by the House Committee on Small Business on October 21, 2003; and placed on the Union Calendar on March 8, 2004. No further action. Introduced on November 18, 2003, and referred to the Senate Committee on Small Business and Entrepreneurship. No further action.
109th	H.Amdt. 268, to H.R. 2862, the Science, State, Justice, Commerce, and Related Agencies Appropriations Act, 2006, to provide the NMVC program $30 million in debenture guarantees and $5 million for operational assistance (Representative Gwen Moore)	$30 million	$5 million	Offered on June 15, 2005. Failed by voice vote.
	H.R. 4234, the Small Business Gulf Coast Revitalization Act of 2005 (Representative Nydia Velázquez)	$50 million	$10 million	Introduced on November 5, 2005, and referred to the House Committee on Small Business. No further action.
	H.R. 4303, the Securing Equity for the Economic Development of Low Income Areas Act of 2005 (Representative Gwen Moore)	$100 million	$25 million	Introduced on November 10, 2005, and referred to the House Committee on Small Business. No further action.

Table A-1. (Continued)

Congress	Legislation and Sponsor	Funding Necessary to Support NMVC Debenture Guarantee of	Funding for Operational Assistance Training Grants	Legislative Action
110th	H.R. 1719, the Securing Equity for the Economic Development of Low Income Areas Act of 2007 (Representative Gwen Moore)	$100 million	$25 million	Introduced on March 27, 2007, and referred to the House Committee on Small Business. No further action.
	H.R. 3567, the Small Business Investment Expansion Act of 2007 (Representative Jason Altmire)	$30 million	$5 million	Introduced on September 18, 2007, and referred to the House Committee on Small Business; reported by the House Committee on Small Business on September 25, 2007;
				passed by the House on September 27, 2007, by a vote of 325-72; received in the Senate on September 28, 2007, and referred to the Senate Committee on Small Business and Entrepreneurship. No further action.
	S. 1663, the Securing Equity for the Economic Development of Low Income Areas Act of 2007 (Senator John Kerry)	NA	$20 million	Introduced on June 19, 2007, and referred to the Senate Committee on Small Business and Entrepreneurship; incorporated into S. 1662, the Small Business Venture Capital Act of 2007, which addressed the Small Business Administration's SBIC program; that bill, as amended, was reported by the Senate Committee on Small Business and Entrepreneurship on October 16, 2007. No further action.

SBA New Markets Venture Capital Program

Congress	Legislation and Sponsor	Funding Necessary to Support NMVC Debenture Guarantee of	Funding for Operational Assistance Training Grants	Legislative Action
	S. 2920, the SBA Reauthorization and Improvement Act of 2008 (Senator John Kerry)	NA	$20 million	Introduced on April 24, 2008, and placed on the Senate Legislative Calendar under General Orders under Read the First Time on September 24, 2008; placed on the Senate Legislative Calendar under General Orders under Read the Second Time on September 28, 2008. No further action.
111th	H.R. 1491, the Securing Equity for the Economic Development of Low Income Areas Act of 2009 (Representative Gwen Moore)	$100 million	$25 million	Introduced on March 12, 2009, and referred to the House Committee on Small Business. No further action.
111th	H.R. 3722, the Enhanced New Markets and Expanded Investment in Renewable Energy for Small Manufacturers Act of 2009 (Representative Ann Kirkpatrick)	$100 million	$20 million	Introduced on October 6, 2009, and referred to the House Committee on Small Business; incorporated into H.R. 3854, the Small Business Financing and Investment Act of 2009, introduced by Representative Kurt Schrader on October 20, 2009; that bill was reported by the House Committee on Small Business on October 26, 2009, and passed by the House, by a
				vote of 389-32, on October 29, 2009; received in the Senate and referred to the Senate Committee on Small Business and Entrepreneurship on November 2, 2009. No further action.
112th	H.R. 2872, the Job Creation and Urban Revitalization Act of 2011 (Representative Nydia Velázquez)	$75 million	$15 million	Introduced on September 8, 2011, and referred to the House Committee on Small Business. No further action to date.

Source: Legislative Information Service database, CRS.

End Notes

[1] U.S. Small Business Administration, "Fiscal Year 2013 Congressional Budget Justification and FY2011 Annual Performance Report," Washington, DC, 2012, p. 1.

[2] 15 U.S.C. §689(a).

[3] For further information and analysis concerning the SBA's Small Business Investment Company program, see CRS Report R41456, SBA Small Business Investment Company Program, by Robert Jay Dilger. The SBA is authorized to issue debentures with a term of up to 15 years. The SBA has opted to limit the term for NMVC debentures to 10 years.

[4] Because the SBA's NMVC debentures are discounted to guarantee the payment of interest during the first five years of the debenture, the funding provided was estimated to be sufficient to raise about $100 million in available capital for investment. Also, the appropriation was for FY2001 through FY2006, but was provided as a lump sum payment in FY2001.

[5] U.S. Small Business Administration, Office of Congressional and Legislative Affairs, "Correspondence with the author," Washington, DC, June 5, 2012.

[6] P.L. 108-7, the Consolidated Appropriations Resolution, 2003; and U.S. Congress, Committee of Conference, Making Further Continuing Appropriations for the Fiscal Year 2003, and for Other Purposes, report to accompany H.J.Res. 2, 108th Cong., 1st sess., February 13, 2003, H.Rept. 108-10 (Washington: GPO, 2003), p. 787.

[7] H.R. 3412, the Small Business Investment Company Technical Corrections Act of 1998, was introduced by Representative (later Senator) Jim Talent, chair of the House Committee on Small Business, on March 10, 1998. The bill would have authorized several technical corrections to the Small Business Administration's SBIC program. The House Committee on Small Business reported the bill on March 17, 1998, and the House passed it (on motion to suspend the rules and pass the bill, as amended), 407-0, on March 24, 1998.

[8] U.S. Congress, Senate Committee on Small Business, Year 2000 Readiness and Small Business Programs Restructuring and Reform Act of 1998, 105th Cong., 2nd sess., September 25, 1998, S.Rept. 105-347 (Washington: GPO, 1998).

[9] Ibid., pp. 18, 23; and Pherabe Kolb, "Senate Small Business Markup: Year 2000 Assistance, Drug-Free Workplace," CQ Markup and Vote Coverage, Washington, DC, September 15, 1998, http://www.cq.com/doc/committeesCOMM159517?print=true.

[10] U.S. Congress, Senate Committee on Small Business, Year 2000 Readiness and Small Business Programs Restructuring and Reform Act of 1998, 105th Cong., 2nd sess., September 25, 1998, S.Rept. 105-347 (Washington: GPO, 1998), p. 18.

[11] Ibid.

[12] U.S. President (Clinton), "Address Before a Joint Session of the Congress on the State of the Union," Weekly Compilation of Presidential Documents, vol. 35 (January 19, 1999), p. 83.

[13] U.S. President (Clinton), "Remarks on the New Markets Initiative," Weekly Compilation of Presidential Documents, vol. 35 (May 11, 1999), pp. 860-861.

[14] U.S. President (Clinton), "Remarks to the Community at Pine Ridge Indian Reservation, South Dakota," Weekly Compilation of Presidential Documents, vol. 35 (July 7, 1999), pp. 1298-1302; U.S. President (Clinton), "Remarks in a Roundtable Discussion on Small Business Development in Phoenix, Arizona," Weekly Compilation of Presidential Documents, vol. 35 (July 7, 1999), pp. 1303-1308; U.S. President (Clinton), "Remarks in a Discussion on Youth Opportunities in Los Angeles, California," Weekly Compilation of Presidential Documents, vol. 35 (July 8, 1999), pp. 1318-1321; U.S. President (Clinton), "Remarks to the National Academy Foundation Conference in Anaheim, California," Weekly Compilation of Presidential Documents, vol. 35 (July 8, 1999), pp. 1322-1327; U.S. President (Clinton), "Remarks to the Community in Newark," Weekly Compilation of Presidential Documents, vol. 35 (November 4, 1999), pp. 2246-2249; U.S. President (Clinton), "Remarks to the North End Community in Hartford, Connecticut," Weekly Compilation of Presidential Documents, vol. 35 (November 4, 1999), pp. 2257-2259; The White House, Office of the Press Secretary, "Remarks by the President to the people of Bradley County: Hermitage Tomato Cooperative, Hermitage, Arkansas," Washington, DC, November 5, 1999, at http://clinton3.nara.gov/WH/New/New_Markets_Nov/remarks/1105-1045a.html; and U.S. President (Clinton)," Remarks to the Englewood Community in Chicago, Illinois," Weekly Compilation of Presidential Documents, vol. 35 (November 4, 1999), pp. 2271-2275.

[15] U.S. President (Clinton)," Remarks to the Englewood Community in Chicago, Illinois," Weekly Compilation of Presidential Documents, vol. 35 (November 4, 1999), pp. 2273.

[16] U.S. Small Business Administration, "Small Business Investment Companies," 64 Federal Register 6256, February 9, 1999.

[17] U.S. Small Business Administration, "Small Business Investment Companies," 64 Federal Register 52641-52646, September 30, 1999.

[18] U.S. Small Business Administration, "Small Business Investment Companies," 64 Federal Register 52645, September 30, 1999.

[19] U.S. Small Business Administration, "Small Business Investment Companies," 64 Federal Register 52641-52646, September 30, 1999. LMI Zones are areas located in a HUBZone; an Urban Empowerment Zone or Urban Enterprise Community designated by the Secretary of the U.S. Department of Housing and Urban Development; a Rural Empowerment Zone or Rural Enterprise Community as designated by the Secretary of the U.S. Department of Agriculture; an area of low income or moderate income as recognized by the Federal Financial Institutions Examination Council; or a county with persistent poverty as classified by the U.S. Department of Agriculture's Economic Research Service. See 13 CFR §107.50.

[20] U.S. Small Business Administration, "For SBICs: Background Information on Low or Moderate Income (LMI) Debentures," Washington, DC, at http://www.sba.gov/content/low-or-moderate-income-lmi-debentures. In FY2011, SBICs made 553 investments in small businesses located in a LMI Zone, totaling $687.1 million—about 24% of the total amount invested. See U.S. Small Business Administration, "SBIC Program Licensees Financing to Small Businesses Reported Between October 2010 and September 2011," Washington, DC.

[21] The bill's five original co-sponsors were Senators Jeff Bingaman, Max Cleland, Carl Levin, Paul Sarbanes, and Paul Wellstone.

[22] U.S. Congress, Senate Committee on Small Business, Community Development and Venture Capital Act of 1999, report to accompany S. 1594, 106th Cong., 2nd sess., August 25, 2000, S.Rept. 106-383 (Washington: GPO, 2000), p. 4.

[23] Ibid., p. 3.

[24] Ibid.

[25] Ibid.

[26] Ibid.

[27] The bill was co-sponsored by Representative Nydia Velázquez.

[28] U.S. Congress, Committee of Conference, Making Omnibus Consolidated and Emergency Supplemental Appropriations for Fiscal Year 2001, report to accompany H.R. 4577, 106th Cong., 2nd sess., December 15, 2000, H.Rept. 106-1033 (Washington: GPO, 2000), pp. 1041-1054.

[29] U.S. Small Business Administration, "13 CFR Part 108: New Markets Venture Capital Program, Interim Final Rule" 66 Federal Register 7218-7246, January 22, 2001; and U.S. Small Business Administration, "New Markets Venture Capital Program; Notice of Funds Availability (NOFA) Inviting Applications for the New Markets Venture Capital Program," 66 Federal Register 7247, January 22, 2001.

[30] U.S. Small Business Administration, "New Markets Venture Capital Program: Final Rule," 66 Federal Register 28601-28632, May 23, 2001.

[31] In addition to these two items, NMVC applicants must also submit a description of how the company intends to work with community organizations and to seek to address the unmet capital needs of the communities served; a proposal describing how the company intends to use the grant funds provided under this part to provide operational assistance to smaller enterprises financed by the company, including information regarding whether the company intends to use licensed professionals, when necessary, on the company's staff or from an outside entity; with respect to binding commitments to be made to the company under this part, an estimate of the ratio of cash to in-kind contributions; a description of the criteria to be used to evaluate whether and to what extent the company meets the objectives of the program established under this part; information regarding the management and financial strength of any parent firm, affiliated firm, or any other firm essential to the success of the company's business plan; and such other information as the Administrator may require. See U.S. Congress, Committee of Conference, Making Omnibus Consolidated and Emergency Supplemental Appropriations for Fiscal Year 2001, report to accompany H.R. 4577, 106th Cong., 2nd sess., December 15, 2000, H.Rept. 106-1033 (Washington: GPO, 2000), p. 1044.

[32] 13 C.F.R. §108.100; 13 C.F.R. §108.110; and 13 C.F.R. §108.120.

[33] P.L. 108-7, the Consolidated Appropriations Resolution, 2003; and U.S. Congress, Committee of Conference, Making Further Continuing Appropriations for the Fiscal Year 2003, and for Other Purposes, report to accompany H.J.Res. 2, 108th Cong., 1st sess., February 13, 2003, H.Rept. 108-10 (Washington: GPO, 2003), p.787.

[34] The initial application deadline was April 19, 2001, and was later extended twice: first, to May 21, 2001; and second, to May 29, 2001. See U.S. Small Business Administration, "New Markets Venture Capital Program;

Extension of Application Deadline," 66 *Federal Register* 18993, April 12, 2001; and U.S. Small Business Administration, "New Markets Venture Capital Program; Extension of Application Deadline," 66 *Federal Register* 27721, May 18, 2001.

[35] The SBA may accept binding commitments for operational assistance matching resources equal to at least 20% of the required minimum if the company has a viable plan to raise the balance. In no case, however, will the SBA disburse grant funds for operational assistance in excess of the amount actually raised, including in-kind contributions. See 13 C.F.R. §108.380.

[36] P.L. 106-554 authorized the SBA to provide conditionally approved applicants a period of time, not to exceed two years, to satisfy all program requirements necessary to participate in the program. The SBA provided applicants 18 months. See U.S. Small Business Administration, Off ice of New Markets Venture Capital, "New Markets Venture Capital (MNVC) Program, FAQs: How much time does a conditionally approved NMVCC have to raise its capital and grant matching resources?" Washington, DC, at http://www.sba.gov/content/how-much-time-does-conditionallyapproved-nmvcc-have-raise-its-capital-and-grant-matching-resources.

[37] U.S. Small Business Administration, Off ice of New Markets Venture Capital, "New Markets Venture Capital (MNVC) Program," Washington, DC, June 2010, p. 13, at http://www.slideshare.net/Freddy56/new-markets-venturecapital-nmvc-program; and U.S. Small Business Administration, "NMVC Companies," Washington, DC, at http://www.sba.gov/content/nmvc-companies.

[38] The Community Development Venture Capital Alliance, "The New Markets Venture Capital Program," Washington, DC, pp. 6, 18, at http://www.community-wealth.org/_pdfs/articles-publications/cdfis/paper-cdvca.pdf; and U.S. Small Business Administration, Office of Congressional and Legislative Affairs, "Correspondence with the author," Washington, DC, June 5, 2012.

[39] U.S. Small Business Administration, "NMVC Companies," Washington, DC, at http://www.sba.gov/content/nmvc companies.

[40] 13 C.F.R. §108.630.

[41] Ibid.

[42] 13 C.F.R. §108.640.

[43] When the NMVC program started, to be deemed small, a business had to meet either the SBA's size standard for the industry in which it was primarily engaged, or had a maximum net worth of no more than $6 million and average after-tax net income for the preceding two years of not more than $2 million.

[44] 13 C.F.R. §121.301(c)(1) and 13 C.F.R. §121.301(c)(2). NMVC companies are not permitted to invest in passive businesses or real estate businesses, or to invest in project financings, farm land purchases, the financing of NMVC companies or SBICs, or projects that will be used substantially for a foreign operation or when more than 49% of the employees or tangible assets of the small business are located outside of the United States. See 13 C.F.R. §108.720.

[45] 13 C.F.R. §108.710.

[46] Ibid.

[47] P.L. 106-554 authorizes the SBA to sale debentures with a maturity of up to 15 years. The SBA has opted to sell debentures with a maturity of up to 10 years.

[48] The SBA does not charge a fee for the issuance of debentures by a NMVC company. See 13 C.F.R. §108.1130. In contrast, the SBA is authorized to charge SBICs a 3% origination fee for each debenture and participating security issued (1% at commitment and 2% at draw), an annual fee (not to exceed 1.38% for debentures and 1.46% for participating securities) on the leverage drawn which is fixed at the time of the leverage commitment, and other administrative and underwriting fees which are adjusted annually. See 13 CFR §107.1130; and 13 CFR §107.1210.

[49] U.S. Small Business Administration, "Debenture Calculator," Washington, DC, at http:// www.sba.gov/content/debenture-calculator.

[50] 13 C.F.R. §108.1230; and 13 C.F.R. §108.1240.

[51] 13 C.F.R. §108.1230.

[52] U.S. Small Business Administration, "Debenture Calculator," Washington, DC, at http://www. sba.gov/content/debenture-calculator; and Federal Home Loan Bank of Chicago, "New Markets Debenture Calculator," Chicago, Illinois, at http://www.fhlbc.com/sba/ newmarketcalculatorpage.htm. The interest rate was 5.494% on June 6, 2012.

[53] U.S. Small Business Administration, "Debenture Calculator," Washington, DC, at http://www. sba.gov/content/debenture-calculator; and 13 C.F.R. §108.1610.

[54] Subordinated debt (also known as subordinated debenture or junior debt) ranks after other debts should a company fall into liquidation or bankruptcy. Because subordinated debt is repayable after other debts have been paid, they are considered to carry a higher level of risk to the lender.

[55] The SBA disbursed operational assistance training grants over a 4.5 year period. See U.S. Small Business Administration, Off ice of New Markets Venture Capital, "New Markets Venture Capital (MNVC) Program," Washington, DC, June 2010, p. 7, at http://www. slideshare.net/Freddy56/new-markets-venture-capital-nmvc-program.

[56] 13 C.F.R. §108.2010; and 13 C.F.R. §108.2030.

[57] 13 C.F.R. §108.2040.

[58] 13 C.F.R. §108.2030.

[59] 13 C.F.R. §108.2010.

[60] 13 C.F.R. §108.10. Some examples of operational assistance training include writing or assisting in the preparation of a business plan, legal assistance relating to business formation or reorganization (but not litigation), recruitment of executives, creation of Internet capability, engineering or other technical services to create or enhance production or distribution of products or services, creation of marketing materials, creation of customized accounting or information systems, and active participation in negotiation with financial institutions (debt). See Adena Ventures, L.P., "Operational Assistance," Athens, Ohio, at http://www.adenaventures.com/serviceprograms/opsassist.aspx.

[61] The Community Development Venture Capital Alliance, "The New Markets Venture Capital Program," Washington, DC, pp. 6, 18, at http://www.community-wealth.org/_pdfs/articles-publications/cdfis/paper-cdvca.pdf; and U.S. Small Business Administration, Office of Congressional and Legislative Affairs, "Correspondence with the author," Washington, DC, June 5, 2012.

[62] U.S. Small Business Administration, "FY 2002 Budget Request and Performance Plan," Washington, DC, p. 15, at http://archive.sba.gov/idc/groups/public/documents/ sba_ homepage/serv_abt_budget_5.pdf.

[63] U.S. Congress, Senate Committee on Small Business and Entrepreneurship, SBA's Funding Priorities for Fiscal Year 2002, 107th Cong., 1st sess., May 1, 2002, S.Hrg. 107-237 (Washington: GPO, 2002), p. 45.

[64] Timothy Bates, "Government as Venture Capital Catalyst: Pitfalls and Promising Approaches," Economic Development Quarterly, vol. 16, no. 49 (2002): 58, at http://www. uk.sagepub.com/chaston/ Chaston% 20Web%20readings%20chapters%201-12/Chapter% 204%20-%2045%20Bates.pdf.

[65] U.S. Congress, Senate Committee on Small Business, The President's Fiscal Year 2000 Budget Request for the Small Business Administration, 106th Cong., 1st sess., March 16, 1999, S.Hrg. 106-118 (Washington: GPO, 1999), pp. 125, 126; U.S. Congress, Senate Committee on Small Business and Entrepreneurship, SBA's Funding Priorities for Fiscal Year 2002, 107th Cong., 1st sess., May 1, 2001, S.Hrg. 107-237 (Washington: GPO, 2002), pp. 14, 15, 20, 26, 91-93; U.S. Congress, House Committee on Small Business, Small Business Investment Expansion Act of 2007 , report to accompany H.R. 3567, 110th Cong., 1st sess., September 25, 2007, H.Rept. 110-110 (Washington: GPO, 2007), pp. 5, 6; and U.S. Congress, Senate Committee on Small Business and Entrepreneurship, Small Business Venture Capital Act of 2007' , 110th Cong., 1st sess., October 16, 2007, S.Rept. 110-199 (Washington: GPO, 2007), pp. 5, 6, 9-11.

[66] P.L. 108-7, the Consolidated Appropriations Resolution, 2003; and U.S. Congress, Committee of Conference, Making Further Continuing Appropriations for the Fiscal Year 2003, and for Other Purposes, report to accompany H.J.Res. 2, 108th Cong., 1st sess., February 13, 2003, H.Rept. 108-10 (Washington: GPO, 2003), p. 787.

[67] During the 111th Congress, P.L. 111-240, the Small Business Jobs Act of 2010, Sec. 1115. New Markets Venture Capital Company Investment Limitations, included the following language: "Except to the extent approved by the Administrator, a covered New Markets Venture Capital company may not acquire or issue commitments for securities under this title for any single enterprise in an aggregate amount equal to more than 10 percent of the sum of—"(A) the regulatory capital of the covered New Markets Venture Capital company; and "(B) the total amount of leverage projected in the participation agreement of the covered New Markets Venture Capital."

[68] H.R. 2802, the Small Business Reauthorization and Manufacturing Revitalization Act of 2003, was introduced by Representative Donald Manzullo on July 21, 2003. It would have provided the NMVC program the additional funding over FY2004 and FY2005. S. 1886, the MADE in America Act, was introduced by Senator Tom Daschle on behalf of Senator John Kerry on November 18, 2003. It would have provided the NMVC program the additional funding over FY2005 and FY2006.

[69] H.R. 2802, the Small Business Reauthorization and Manufacturing Revitalization Act of 2003, was reported by the House Committee on Small Business on October 21, 2003; and placed on the Union Calendar on March 8,

2004. The House took no further action on the bill. S. 1886, the MADE in America Act, was referred to the Senate Committee on Small Business and Entrepreneurship. No further action took place on the bill.

[70] Representative Gwen Moore, "Consideration of H.R. 2862, the Science, State, Justice, Commerce, and Related Agencies Appropriations Act, 2006," House debate, Congressional Record, vol. 151, part 79 (June 15, 2005), p. H4511.

[71] Ibid., p. H4512.

[72] H.R. 4234, the Small Business Gulf Coast Revitalization Act of 2005, Sec. 104. Gulf Region New Markets Venture Capital Company. The bill was introduced by Representative Nydia Velázquez on November 5, 2005.

[73] H.R. 4303, the Securing Equity for the Economic Development of Low Income Areas Act of 2005, was introduced by Representative Gwen Moore on November 10, 2005.

[74] H.R. 4303, the Securing Equity for the Economic Development of Low Income Areas Act of 2005, was referred to the House Committee on Small Business. The House took no further action on the bill. H.R. 4234, the Small Business Gulf Coast Revitalization Act of 2005, was referred to the House Committee on Small Business. The House took no further action on the bill.

[75] H.R. 1719, the Securing Equity for the Economic Development of Low Income Areas Act of 2007, was introduced by Representative Gwen Moore on March 27, 2007. The bill was referred to the House Committee on Small Business. The House took no further action on the bill.

[76] H.R. 3567, the Small Business Investment Expansion Act of 2007, was introduced by Representative Jason Altmire on September 18, 2007. The bill was referred to the House Committee on Small Business and reported on September 25, 2007. The House passed it on September 27, 2007, by a vote of 325-72. The bill was received in the Senate on September 28, 2007, and referred to the Senate Committee on Small Business and Entrepreneurship. The Senate took no further action on the bill.

[77] S. 1663, the Securing Equity for the Economic Development of Low Income Areas Act of 2007, was introduced by Senator John Kerry on June 19, 2007 and referred to the Senate Committee on Small Business and Entrepreneurship. The additional funding for operational assistance training grants would have been available over FY2007 through FY2010. The bill was incorporated into S. 1662, the Small Business Venture Capital Act of 2007, which addressed the Small Business Administration's SBIC program. That bill, as amended, was reported by the Senate Committee on Small Business and Entrepreneurship on October 16, 2007. The Senate took no further action on the bill. S. 2920, the SBA Reauthorization and Improvement Act of 2008, was introduced by Senator John Kerry on April 24, 2008. The additional funding for operational assistance training grants would have been available over FY2008 through FY2010. The bill was placed on the Senate Legislative Calendar under General Orders under Read the First Time on September 24, 2008 and was placed on the Senate Legislative Calendar under General Orders under Read the Second Time on September 28, 2008. The Senate took no further action on the bill.

[78] H.R. 1491, the Securing Equity for the Economic Development of Low Income Areas Act of 2009, was introduced by Representative Gwen Moore on March 12, 2009, and referred to the House Committee on Small Business. The House took no further action on the bill.

[79] H.R. 3722, the Enhanced New Markets and Expanded Investment in Renewable Energy for Small Manufacturers Act of 2009, was introduced by Representative Ann Kirkpatrick on October 6, 2009, and referred to the House Committee on Small Business. The bill's provisions were incorporated into H.R. 3854, the Small Business Financing and Investment Act of 2009, which was introduced by Representative Kurt Schrader on October 20, 2009. That bill was reported by the House Committee on Small Business on October 26, 2009, and passed by the House, by a vote of 389- 32, on October 29, 2009. The bill was received in the Senate and referred to the Senate Committee on Small Business and Entrepreneurship on November 2, 2009. The Senate took no further action on the bill.

[80] 13 CFR §107.1150.

[81] U.S. Small Business Administration, "Impact Investment Initiative," Washington, DC, at http://www.sba.gov/content/small-business-investment-company-sbic-impact-investment-initiative-2. For further analysis and information concerning the SBA's impact investment initiative see CRS Report R41456, SBA Small Business Investment Company Program, by Robert Jay Dilger.

[82] A low or moderate income area (LMI Zone) means any area located within a HUBZone (as defined in 13 CFR 126.103), an Urban Empowerment Zone or Urban Enterprise Community (as designated by the Secretary of the Department of Housing and Urban Development), a Rural Empowerment Zone or Rural Enterprise Community (as designated by the Secretary of the Department of Agriculture), an area of Low Income or Moderate Income (as recognized by the Federal Financial Institutions Examination Council), or a county with Persistent Poverty (as classified by the Economic Research Service of the Department of Agriculture). See 13 CFR §107.50.

[83] U.S. Small Business Administration, "All SBIC Program Licensees: Financing to Small Businesses Reported Between October 2008 and September 2009," Washington, DC; U.S. Small Business Administration, "All SBIC Program Licensees: Financing to Small Businesses Reported Between October 2009 and September 2010," Washington, DC; and U.S. Small Business Administration, "All SBIC Program Licensees: Financing to Small Businesses Reported Between October 2010 and September 2011," Washington, DC.

[84] U.S. Small Business Administration, "All SBIC Program Licensees: Financing to Small Businesses Reported Between October 2010 and September 2011," Washington, DC.

[85] U.S. Congress, Senate Committee on Small Business, Community Development and Venture Capital Act of 1999, report to accompany S. 1594, 106th Cong., 2nd sess., August 25, 2000, S.Rept. 106-383 (Washington: GPO, 2000), p. 3.

In: Small Business Administration Programs
Editor: Walter Janikowski

ISBN: 978-1-62417-992-1
© 2013 Nova Science Publishers, Inc.

Chapter 13

SBA VETERANS ASSISTANCE PROGRAMS: AN ANALYSIS OF CONTEMPORARY ISSUES[*]

Robert Jay Dilger and Sean Lowry

SUMMARY

Several federal agencies, including the Small Business Administration (SBA), provide training and other assistance to veterans seeking civilian employment. For example, the Department of Labor, in cooperation with the Department of Defense and the Department of Veterans Affairs, operates the Transition Assistance Program (TAP) and the Disabled Transition Assistance Program (DTAP). Both programs provide employment information and training to service members within 180 days of their separation from military service, or retirement, to assist them in transitioning from the military to the civilian labor force.

In recent years, the SBA has focused increased attention on meeting the needs of veteran small business owners and veterans interested in starting a small business, especially veterans who are transitioning from military to civilian life. In FY2011, the SBA provided management and technical assistance services to more than 100,000 veterans through its various management and technical assistance training partners (e.g., Small Business Development Centers, Women Business Centers, Service Corps of Retired Executives (SCORE), and Veteran Business Outreach Centers). The SBA also responded to more than 85,000 veteran inquires through its SBA district offices. In addition, the SBA's Office of Veterans Business Development administers several programs to assist veteran-owned small businesses.

Congressional interest in the SBA's veterans assistance programs has increased in recent years primarily due to reports by veterans organizations that veterans were experiencing difficulty accessing the SBA's programs, especially the SBA's Patriot Express loan guarantee program. There is also a continuing congressional interest in assisting veterans, especially those returning from overseas in recent years, in their transition from military into civilian life. Although the unemployment rate (as of September 2012) among veterans as a whole (6.7%) was lower than for non-veterans 18

---

[*] This is an edited, reformatted and augmented version of a Congressional Research Service publication, CRS Report for Congress R42695, prepared for Members and Committees of Congress, from www.crs.gov, dated October 18, 2012.

years and older (7.4%), the unemployment rate of veterans who have left the military since September 2001 (9.7%) was higher than the unemployment rate for non-veterans 18 years and older.

The expansion of federal employment training programs targeted at specific populations, such as women and veterans, has also led some Members and organizations to ask if these programs should be consolidated. In their view, eliminating program duplication among federal business assistance programs across federal agencies, and within the SBA, would result in lower costs and improved services. Others argue that keeping these business assistance programs separate enables them to offer services that match the unique needs of various underserved populations, such as veterans. In their view, instead of considering program consolidation as a policy option, the focus should be on improving communication and cooperation among the federal agencies providing assistance to entrepreneurs.

This report opens with an examination of the current economic circumstances of veteran-owned businesses drawn from the Bureau of the Census 2007 Survey of Business Owners, which was administered in 2008 and 2009, and released on the Internet on May 17, 2011. It then provides a brief overview of veteran employment experiences, comparing unemployment and labor force participation rates for veterans, veterans who have left the military since September 2001, and non-veterans. The report then describes the employment assistance programs offered by several federal agencies to assist veterans in their transition from the military to the civilian labor force, and examines, in greater detail, the SBA's veteran business development programs, the SBA's Patriot Express loan guarantee program, and veteran contracting programs. The SBA's Military Reservist Economic Injury Disaster Loan program is also discussed.

SBA ASSISTANCE FOR VETERANS

The Small Business Administration (SBA) administers several programs to support small business owners and prospective entrepreneurs. For example, it provides access to entrepreneurial education programs to assist with business formation and expansion; loan guaranty programs, such as the Patriot Express loan guaranty program that targets the needs of veteran small business owners, to enhance small business owners' access to capital; and programs to increase small business opportunities in federal contracting, including oversight of the service-disabled veteran-owned small business federal procurement goaling program.[1]

The SBA also provides direct loans for owners of businesses of all sizes, homeowners, and renters to assist their recovery from natural disasters. One of the SBA's disaster loan programs, the Military Reservist Economic Injury Disaster Loan Program (MREIDL program), is of particular interest to veterans.

The MREIDL program provides disaster assistance in the form of direct loans of up to $2 million to help small business owners who are not able to obtain credit elsewhere to meet ordinary and necessary operating expenses that they could have met, but are not able to meet because an essential employee has been called-up to active duty in their role as a military reservist or member of the National Guard due to a period of military conflict.[2]

In FY2011, the SBA provided management and technical assistance services to more than 100,000 veterans through its various management and technical assistance training partners (e.g., Small Business Development Centers, Women Business Centers, SCORE, and Veteran Business Outreach Centers). The SBA also responded to more than 85,000 veteran inquires through its SBA district offices. In addition, the SBA's Office of Veterans Business Development administers several programs to assist veteran-owned small businesses.

In recent years, the SBA has focused increased attention on meeting the needs of veteran small business owners and veterans interested in starting a business, especially veterans who are transitioning from military to civilian life.

For example, in FY2012, the SBA's Office of Veterans Business Development launched the "Operation Boots to Business: From Service to Startup" initiative, "a comprehensive veteran entrepreneurship initiative for transitioning service members."[3] The SBA has also announced that it plans to continue its efforts to strengthen its outreach to women veterans and service-disabled veterans.[4]

Congressional interest in the SBA's veterans assistance programs has increased in recent years primarily due to reports by veterans organizations that veterans were experiencing difficulty accessing the SBA's programs, especially the SBA's Patriot Express loan guarantee program. There is also a continuing congressional interest in assisting veterans, especially those returning from overseas in recent years, transition from military to civilian life.

Although the unemployment rate (as of September 2012) among veterans as a whole (6.7%) was lower than for non-veterans 18 years and older (7.4%), the unemployment rate of veterans who have left the military since September 2001 (9.7%) was higher than the unemployment rate for non-veterans 18 years and older.[5]

The expansion of federal employment training programs targeted at specific populations, such as women and veterans, has also led some Members and organizations to ask if these programs should be consolidated. In their view, eliminating program duplication among federal business assistance programs across federal agencies, and within the SBA, would result in lower costs and improved services.

Others argue that keeping these business assistance programs separate enables them to offer services that match the unique needs of various underserved populations, such as veterans. In their view, instead of considering program consolidation as a policy option, the focus should be on improving communication and cooperation among the federal agencies providing assistance to entrepreneurs.

This report examines the current economic circumstances of veteran-owned businesses drawn from the Bureau of the Census 2007 Survey of Business Owners, which was administered in 2008 and 2009, and released on May 17, 2011.[6] It provides a brief overview of veteran employment experiences, comparing unemployment and labor force participation rates for veterans, veterans who have left the military since September 2001, and non-veterans. The report also describes the employment assistance programs offered by several federal agencies to assist veterans transition from the military to the civilian labor force, and examines, in greater detail, the SBA's veterans business development programs, the SBA's Patriot Express loan guarantee program, and veteran contracting programs.

The SBA's Military Reservist Economic Injury Disaster Loan program is also discussed.

AN ECONOMIC PROFILE OF VETERAN-OWNED BUSINESSES

Every five years since 1972, for years ending in "2" and "7", the U.S. Bureau of the Census has sent a questionnaire to a stratified random sample of nonfarm businesses in the

United States that file Internal Revenue Service tax forms as individual proprietorships, partnerships, or any type of corporation, and with receipts of $1,000 or more.[7]

The questionnaire asks for information about the characteristics of the businesses and their owners. Approximately 2.3 million businesses received the 2007 Survey of Business Owners (SBO) and about 62% of these businesses responded to the survey.[8]

The SBO provides "the only comprehensive, regularly collected source of information on selected economic and demographic characteristics for businesses and business owners by gender, ethnicity, race, and veteran status."[9]

The Bureau of the Census uses information from the SBO to provide estimates of the number of employer and nonemployer firms and their sales and receipts, annual payroll, and employment. Data aggregates are provided by gender, ethnicity, race, and veteran status for the United States by 2007 North American Industry Classification System (NAICS) classification, the kind of business, and by state, metropolitan and micropolitan statistical area, and county.

The information obtained from the SBO was combined with data collected through the Bureau of the Census's main economic census and administrative records to provide a variety of searchable data products on their website, http://www.census.gov/econ/sbo/, including the most detailed economic information available on veterans and veteran-owned firms.

Demographics

The Bureau of the Census estimates that in 2007 about 9.0% of nonfarm firms in the United States (2,447,608 of 27,092,908) were owned by veterans.10 Four states had more than 100,000 veteran-owned firms: California (239,422), Texas (199,476), New York (127,156), and Florida (176,727). Of the nearly 2.45 million veteran-owned firms in 2007,

- 79.9% (1,956,259) had no paid employees and 20.1% (491,349) had paid employees. This ratio is very similar to comparable national figures for 2007, which are 78.8% had no paid employees (21,357,346) and 21.2% had paid employees (5,735,562).[11]
- 99.8% (490,560) had less than 500 employees and 0.2% (789) had at least 500 employees. This ratio is very similar to comparable national figures for 2007, which are 99.7% (5,717,830) had less than 500 employees and 0.3% (17,732) had at least 500 employees.[12]
- 94.8% (2,320,291) were owned by a male, 4.0% were owned by a female (97,114), and 1.2% (29,593) were owned equally by a male and a female. Veteran-owned firms were more likely than other firms in 2007 to be owned by a male. The comparable national figures for 2007 are 52.9% (13,900,554) were owned by a male, 29.6% were owned by a female (7,792,115), and 17.5% (4,602,192) were owned equally by a male and a female.[13]
- 90.7% (2,219,385) were owned by a Caucasian, 7.7% (188,820) were owned by an African-American, 1.3% (32,732) were owned by an Asian, 1.1% (27,111) were owned by an American Indian or Alaska Indian, 0.2% (4,123) were owned by a Native Hawaiian or other Pacific Islander, and 0.1% (3,096) were owned by "some other race." Veteran-owned firms were somewhat more likely than other firms in

2007 to be owned by a Caucasian and somewhat less likely to be owned by an Asian. The comparable national figures for 2007 are 83.4% (22,595,146) were owned by a Caucasian, 7.1% (1,921,864) were owned by an African-American, 5.7% (1,549,559) were owned by an Asian, 0.9% (236,691) were owned by an American Indian or Alaska Indian, 0.1% (37,687) were owned by a Native Hawaiian or other Pacific Islander, and 0.3% (80,777) were owned by "some other race."[14]

- 2.8% (68,891) were owned by an individual under the age of 35, 22.1% (543,359) were owned by an individual 35 to 54 years old, and 75.1% (1,841,809) were owned by an individual 55 years or older. Veteran-owned firms were more likely than other firms in 2007 to be 55 years or older. The comparable national figures for 2007 are 12.6% (2,535,187) were owned by an individual under the age of 35; 50.8% (10,196,376) were owned by an individual 35 to 54 years old; and 36.5% (7,332,182) were owned by an individual 55 years or older.[15]
- 8.3% (196,760) were owned by an individual who reported that he or she had a service-connected disability.[16]

Employment, Payroll, and Receipts

In 2007, veteran-owned employer firms

- employed 5.8 million persons (about 4.9% of total U.S. employment), had a total payroll of $210.0 billion (about 4.4% of total U.S. payroll), and generated $1.125 trillion in total receipts (about 4.1% of total U.S. receipts); and
- had average receipts of $2.3 million.17 In 2007, veteran-owned nonemployer firms:
- generated 7.7% ($93.8 billion) of the total receipts generated by veteran-owned firms; and
- had average receipts of $47,931.

The comparable national figures for receipts in 2007 were $45,544 for all nonemployer firms and $5.1 million for all employer firms.[18]

Access to Capital

As shown in *Table 1*, the most frequently used source of capital used by veterans to start or acquire a business in 2007 was personal or family savings (811,388 veterans or 61.7% of respondents), followed by a business loan from a bank or financial institution (128,895 veterans or 9.8% of respondents), a personal or business credit card (114,012 veterans or 8.7% of respondents), and personal or family assets other than the owner's savings (98,113 veterans or 7.5% of respondents).

As shown in *Table 2*, the most frequently used source of capital by veterans to expand or make capital improvements to an existing business in 2007 was personal or family savings (384,517 veterans or 30.0% of respondents), followed by a personal or business credit card (139,260 veterans or 10.9% of respondents), business profits or assets (138,440 veterans or

10.8% of respondents), and a business loan from a bank or financial institution (107,614 veterans or 8.4% of respondents).

VETERANS' EMPLOYMENT DATA

The Department of Labor's Bureau of Labor Statistics (BLS) provides monthly updates of the employment status of the nation's veterans. The BLS reports that as of September 2012, there were about 21.1 million veterans.[19]

Table 1. Source of Capital for Veteran-Owned Businesses Starting or Acquiring Their Business, 2007

Source of Capital	Number of Veteran Respondents	% of Veteran Respondents
personal or family savings	811,388	61.7%
business loan from a bank or financial institution	128,895	9.8%
personal or business credit card	114,012	8.7%
personal or family assets other than the owner's savings	98,113	7.5%
personal or family home equity loan	55,736	4.2%
business loan or investment from family or friends	25,038	1.9%
government guaranteed business loan from a bank or financial institution	8,305	0.6%
business loan from a federal, state, or local government	8,001	0.6%
investment from venture capitalists	3,664	0.3%
grant	1,364	0.1%
other source(s) of capital	23,825	1.8%
did not need any capital to start or acquire their business	284,505	21.6%
did not recall where they received the capital to start or acquire their business	40,390	3.1%

Source: U.S. Bureau of the Census, "American Fact Finder: Statistics for All U.S. Firms by Sources of Capital Used to Start or Acquire the Business by Industry, Gender, Ethnicity, Race, and Veteran Status for the U.S.: 2007," at http://factfinder2.census.gov/faces/tableservices/jsf/ pages/ productview.xhtml?pid= SBO_2007_00CSCB13&prodType=table.

Note: The total percentage exceeds 100 because each owner had the option of selecting more than one source of capital.

A little over 11.0 million veterans were in the civilian labor force (i.e., they were either employed or unemployed and available for work, except for temporary illness, and had made specific efforts to find employment sometime during the four-week period ending with the reference week). Of those in the civilian labor force, more than 10.3 million veterans were employed and about 735,000 veterans were unemployed.[20]

Veterans, as group, as of September 2012, had a lower unemployment rate (6.7%) than nonveterans 18 years and over (7.4%), but also had a lower labor force participation rate (the percentage of the available work force that is employed or actively seeking employment) than nonveterans 18 years and older (52.3% compared with 66.5%).[21]

Table 2. Source of Capital for Veteran-Owned Businesses Expanding or Making Capital Improvements to Their Business, 2007

Source of Capital	Number of Veteran Respondents	% of Veteran Respondents
personal or family savings	384,517	30.0%
personal or business credit card	139,260	10.9%
business profits or assets	138,440	10.8%
business loan from a bank or financial institution	107,614	8.4%
personal or family assets other than the owner's savings	54,479	4.3%
personal or family home equity loan	50,793	4.0%
business loan or investment from family or friends	9,720	0.8%
business loan from a federal, state, or local government	4,938	0.4%
government guaranteed business loan from a bank or financial institution	4,511	0.4%
investment from venture capitalists	1,591	0.1%
grant	1,438	0.1%
other source(s) of capital	9,200	0.7%
did not expand or make capital improvements in 2007	631,242	49.3%
did not recall where they received the capital to expand or make capital improvements to their business	18,,692	3.7%

Source: U.S. Bureau of the Census, "American Fact Finder: Statistics for All U.S. Firms by Sources Used to Finance Expansion or Capital Improvements by Industry, Gender, Ethnicity, Race, and Veteran Status for the U.S.: 2007," at http://factfinder2.census.gov/faces/tableservices/jsf/pages/productview. xhtml? pid=SBO_2007_00CSCB28&prodType=table.

Note: The total percentage exceeds 100 because each owner had the option of selecting more than one source of capital.

A recent report by the Council of Economic Advisers and the National Economic Council attributed the lower labor force participation rate for veterans to several factors, including the difficulty many civilian employers have in understanding a military resume and how military job titles translate into civilian jobs skills, the presence of a service-connected disability, especially among the post-9/11 veteran population, and the number of post-9/11 veterans (about 217,000) who have been diagnosed with post-traumatic stress disorder.[22]

The employment experiences of veterans who left the military since September 2001 differ somewhat from the employment experiences of veterans who left the military before September 2001. Veterans who left the military since September 2001, as of September 2012, had both higher levels of unemployment (9.7% compared with 5.9%) and higher levels of labor force participation (82.1% compared with 48.2%) than veterans who left the military before September 2001.

The higher labor force participation rate for veterans who left the military since September 2001 was not wholly unexpected. They entered the civilian workforce more recently and have had less time to develop a reason (e.g., health issue, family responsibility, discouragement, retirement) to withdraw from the civilian workforce than veterans who left the military before September 2001.

VETERANS' EMPLOYMENT AND BUSINESS DEVELOPMENT PROGRAMS

Several federal agencies, including the SBA, sponsor employment and business development programs to assist veterans in their transition from the military into the civilian labor force. As will be discussed, the expansion of federal employment and business development training programs targeted at specific populations, such as women and veterans, has led some Members and organizations to ask if these programs should be consolidated. Others question if the level of communication and coordination among federal agencies administering these programs has been sufficient to ensure that the programs are being administered in the most efficient and effective manner.

The SBA's Veterans Business Development Programs

In an effort to assist veteran entrepreneurs, the SBA has either provided or supported management and technical assistance training for veteran-owned small businesses since its formation as an agency.[23] In recent years, the SBA has provided management and technical assistance training services to more than 100,000 veterans annually through its various management and technical assistance training partners (e.g., Small Business Development Centers, Women Business Centers, Service Corps of Retired Executives [SCORE], and Veteran Business Outreach Centers) and has responded to more than 85,000 veteran inquires annually through its SBA district offices.[24] In addition, the SBA's Office of Veterans Business Development administers several programs to assist veteran-owned businesses, including

- the Entrepreneurial Boot Camp for Veterans with Disabilities Consortium of Universities, which provides "experiential training in entrepreneurship and small business management to post-9/11 veterans with disabilities" at eight universities;[25]
- the Veteran Women Igniting the Spirit of Entrepreneurship (V-WISE) program, at Syracuse University, which offers women veterans a 15-day, online course focused "on the basic skills of entrepreneurship and the 'language of business,'" followed by a three-day conference where participants "are exposed to accomplished entrepreneurs and entrepreneurship educators from across the United States" and participate in "courses on business planning, marketing, accounting/finance, operations/production, human resources and work life balance";[26]
- the Operation Endure and Grow Program, at Syracuse University, which is an eight-week online training program "focused on the fundamentals of launching and/or growing a small business" and is available to National Guard and Reservists and their family members;[27] and
- the Veterans Business Outreach Center program, which provides veterans and their spouses management and technical assistance training at 16 locations, including assistance with the development and maintenance of a five-year business plan and referrals to other SBA resource partners when appropriate for additional training or mentoring services.[28]

SBA Veterans Assistance Programs: An Analysis of Contemporary Issues 343

The SBA indicated in its FY2013 congressional budget justification document that "thousands of veterans are returning home with the skills, experience, and leadership to pursue entrepreneurship and create jobs ... yet veteran unemployment rates remain high. This requires strong action to encourage transitioning veterans to explore entrepreneurship and then to equip them with tools to start a business, creating jobs for themselves and other veterans."[29] To help meet veteran entrepreneurs' needs, the SBA indicated that it will

- continue its emphasis on identifying and meeting veterans' needs for management and technical assistance training;[30]
- work closely with the Interagency Task Force for Veterans Small Business Development, which was established by executive order on April 26, 2010, held its first meeting on September 15, 2010, and issued its first report on November 1, 2011, to identify "gaps in ensuring that transitioning military members who are interested in owning a small business get needed assistance and training;"[31] and
- seek $7 million in funding for a National Veterans Entrepreneurship Training (VET) program, which would, among other activities, expand several existing SBA supported management and technical assistance training programs for veterans and include "an 8-week online training program for up to 3,000 veterans to explore the fundamentals of small business ownership."[32]

Congressional Issues: Duplication of Services

The SBA's Office of Veterans Business Development, which serves as the SBA's focal point for its veteran assistance programs, was created by P.L. 106-50, the Veterans Entrepreneurship and Small Business Development Act of 1999. The act addressed congressional concerns that the United States generally, and the SBA in particular, was not, at that time, doing enough to meet the needs of veteran entrepreneurs, especially service-disabled veteran entrepreneurs.[33]

At that time, several Members of Congress argued that "the needs of veterans have been diminished systematically at the SBA" as evidenced by the SBA's elimination of direct loans, including direct loans to veterans, in 1995; and a decline in the SBA's "training and counseling for veterans ... from 38,775 total counseling sessions for veterans in 1993 to 29,821 sessions in 1998."[34]

To address these concerns, the act authorized the establishment of the federally chartered National Veterans Business Development Corporation (known as The Veterans Corporation and reconstituted, without a federal charter, in 2012 as Veteranscorp.org).[35] Its mission is to

> (1) expand the provision of and improve access to technical assistance regarding entrepreneurship for the Nation's veterans; and (2) to assist veterans, including service-disabled veterans, with the formation and expansion of small business concerns by working with and organizing public and private resources, including those of the Small Business Administration, the Department of Veterans Affairs, the Department of Labor, the Department of Commerce, the Department of Defense, the Service Corps of Retired Executives ..., the Small Business Development Centers ..., and the business development staffs of each department and agency of the United States.[36]

P.L. 106-50 re-emphasized the SBA's responsibility "to reach out to and include veterans in its programs providing financial and technical assistance."[37] It included veterans as a target group for the SBA's 7(a), 504/CDC, and Microloan lending programs. It also required the SBA to enter into a memorandum of understanding with SCORE to, among other things, establish "a program to coordinate counseling and training regarding entrepreneurship to veterans through the chapters of SCORE throughout the United States."[38] It also directed the SBA to enter into a memorandum of understanding with small business development centers, the Department of Veteran Affairs, and the National Veterans Business Development Corporation "with respect to entrepreneurial assistance to veterans, including service-disabled veterans."[39]

The act specified that the following services were to be provided:

1) Conducting of studies and research, and the distribution of information generated by such studies and research, on the formation, management, financing, marketing, and operation of small business concerns by veterans.

2) Provision of training and counseling to veterans concerning the formation, management, financing, marketing, and operation of small business concerns.

3) Provision of management and technical assistance to the owners and operators of small business concerns regarding international markets, the promotion of exports, and the transfer of technology.

4) Provision of assistance and information to veterans regarding procurement opportunities with Federal, State, and local agencies, especially such agencies funded in whole or in part with Federal funds.

5) Establishment of an information clearinghouse to collect and distribute information, including by electronic means, on the assistance programs of Federal, State, and local governments, and of the private sector, including information on office locations, key personnel, telephone numbers, mail and electronic addresses, and contracting and subcontracting opportunities.

6) Provision of Internet or other distance learning academic instruction for veterans in business subjects, including accounting, marketing, and business fundamentals.

7) Compilation of a list of small business concerns owned and controlled by service-disabled veterans that provide products or services that could be procured by the United States and delivery of such list to each department and agency of the United States. Such list shall be delivered in hard copy and electronic form and shall include the name and address of each such small business concern and the products or services that it provides.[40]

The SBA's Office of Veterans Business Development (OVBD) was established to address these statutory requirements by promoting "veterans' small business ownership by conducting comprehensive outreach, through program and policy development and implementation, ombudsman support, coordinated agency initiatives, and direct assistance to veterans, service-disabled veterans, Reserve and National Guard members, and discharging active duty service members and their families."[41]

The OVBD provided, or supported third-parties to provide, management and technical assistance training services to 137,011 veterans during FY2011. These services were provided "through funded SBA district office outreach; OVBD-developed and distributed materials; websites; partnering with DOD [Department of Defense], DOL [Department of Labor] and universities; agreements with regional veterans business outreach centers; direct guidance, training and assistance to Agency veteran customers; and through enhancements to intra-agency programs used by the military and veteran communities."[42]

The expansion of the SBA's outreach efforts to veterans has led some Members and organizations to ask if the nation's veterans might be better served if some of the veteran employment and business development programs offered by federal agencies were consolidated. For example, the Department of Labor (DOL), in cooperation with the Department of Defense and the Department of Veterans Affairs, operates the Transition Assistance Program (TAP) and the Disabled Transition Assistance Program (DTAP). Both programs provide employment information and training to service members within 180 days of their separation from military service or retirement to assist them in transitioning from the military into the civilian labor force.[43] In addition, the DOL's Jobs for Veterans State Grants program provides states funding for Disabled Veterans' Outreach Program specialists and Local Veterans' Employment Representatives to provide outreach and assistance to veterans, and their spouses, seeking employment.[44] The DOL also administers the Veterans Workforce Investment Program, which provides grants to fund programs operated by eligible state and local government workforce investment boards, state and local government agencies, and private non-profit organizations, to provide various services designed to assist veterans transition into the civilian labor force.[45] It also administers the Homeless Veterans Reintegration Program, which provides grants to fund programs operated by eligible state and local government workforce investment boards, state and local government agencies, and private non-profit organizations, that provide various services designed to assist homeless veterans to achieve meaningful employment and to assist in the development of a service delivery system to address problems facing homeless veterans.[46]

Advocates of consolidating veteran employment and business development programs argue that eliminating program duplication among federal agencies would result in lower costs and improved services. For example, H.R. 4072, the Consolidating Veteran Employment Services for Improved Performance Act of 2012, which was introduced during the 112th Congress and ordered to be reported by the House Committee on Veterans' Affairs on April 27, 2012, would transfer several veteran employment training programs from the Department of Labor to the Department of Veterans Affairs.[47] Also, in 2011 and 2012, the House Committee on Small Business, in its "Views and Estimates" letter to the House Committee on the Budget recommended that funding for the SBA's Veterans Business Outreach Centers (VBOCs) be eliminated (saving approximately $6.3 million) because "the SBA already provides significant assistance to veterans who are seeking to start or already operate small businesses. The VBOCs duplicate services already available from the SBA, other entrepreneurial development partners and programs available from the Department of Veterans Affairs."[48]

Advocates of consolidating federal veteran employment and business development programs point to various U.S. Government Accountability Office (GAO) reports which have generally characterized the broader category of federal support for entrepreneurs, including veteran entrepreneurs, as fragmented and having overlapping missions. For example, in 2012, GAO identified 53 programs within the SBA and the Departments of Commerce, Housing and Urban Development, and Agriculture that are designed to support entrepreneurs, including 36 programs that provide entrepreneurs technical assistance, such as business training, counseling, and research and development support. GAO found that "the overlap among these programs raise questions about whether a fragmented system is the most effective way to support entrepreneurs" and suggested that agencies should "determine whether there are more efficient ways to continue to serve the unique needs of entrepreneurs, including consolidating programs."[49]

Instead of consolidating programs, some argue that improved communication and cooperation among the federal agencies providing entrepreneur support programs, and among the SBA's management and technical assistance training resource partners, would enhance program efficiencies while preserving the ability of these programs to offer services that match the unique needs of various underserved populations, such as veterans. For example, during the 111th Congress, the House passed H.R. 2352, the Job Creation Through Entrepreneurship Act of 2009, on May 20, 2009, by a vote of 406–15. The Senate did not take action on the bill. In its committee report accompanying the bill, the House Committee on Small Business concluded at that time that

> Each ED [Entrepreneurial Development] program has a unique mandate and service delivery approach that is customized to its particular clients. However, as a network, the programs have established local connections and resources that benefit entrepreneurs within a region. Enhanced coordination among this network is critical to make the most of scarce resources available for small firms. It can also ensure that best practices are shared amongst providers that have similar goals but work within different contexts.[50]

The bill was designed to enhance the oversight and coordination of the SBA's management and technical assistance training programs by requiring the SBA to coordinate its management and technical assistance training programs "with State and local economic development agencies and other federal agencies as appropriate" and to "report annually to Congress, in consultation with other federal departments and agencies as appropriate, on opportunities to foster coordination, limit duplication, and improve program delivery for federal entrepreneurial development activities." [51]

In a related development, as mentioned previously, the Obama Administration formed the Interagency Task Force for Veterans Small Business Development by executive order on April 26, 2010. The SBA's representative (SBA Deputy Director Marie C. Johns) chairs the Task Force, which is composed of senior representatives from seven federal agencies and four representatives from veterans' organizations.[52]

One of the Task Force's goals is to improve "collaboration, integration and focus across federal agencies, key programs (e.g., Transition Assistance Program), veterans' service organizations, states, and academia."[53]

On November 1, 2011, the Task Force issued its first set of recommendations, which included several recommendations designed to increase and augment federal entrepreneurial training and technical assistance programs offered to veterans. For example, the Task Force recommended the development of a "standardized, national entrepreneurship training program specifically for veterans" that "could utilize expert local instructors, including academics and successful small business owners, to provide training in skills used to create and grow entrepreneurial ventures and small business. The national program could provide engaging training modules and workshops dedicated to the basics of launching a business."[54] The Task Force also recommended the development of a web portal "that allows veterans to access entrepreneurship resources from across the government."[55]

SBA's Patriot Express Pilot Loan Guaranty Program

In 2007, the SBA created the Patriot Express Pilot Loan Guaranty Program, within the broader framework of its 7(a) loan guaranty program, "to support the entrepreneur segment of the Nation's military community (including spouses)."[56] The SBA argued that this special loan guaranty program, which features an expedited approval process, was necessary to ensure that veterans "have the tools to rebuild their businesses or to start-up new businesses in order to provide themselves and their families with a livelihood after their service is done."[57]

Eligible businesses must be owned and controlled (51% or more) by one or more of the following groups: veteran (other than dishonorably discharged), service-disabled veteran, active duty military participating in the military's Transition Assistance Program, reservist or national guard member or a spouse of any of these groups, a widowed spouse of a service member who died while in service, or a widowed spouse of a veteran who died of a service-connected disability.[58]

The SBA announced on December 10, 2010, that it will continue to operate the program for at least three more years.[59]

The Patriot Express program provides the same loan guaranty to SBA-approved lenders as the 7(a) program on loan amounts up to $500,000 (up to 85% of loans of $150,000 or less and up to 75% of loans exceeding $150,000). The loan proceeds can be used for the same purposes as the 7(a) program (expansion, renovation, new construction, the purchase of land or buildings, the purchase of equipment, fixtures, and lease-hold improvements, working capital, to refinance debt for compelling reasons, seasonal line of credit, and inventory) except participant debt restructure cannot exceed 15%-25% of the project and may be used for revolving lines of credit.

The Patriot Express program loan terms are the same as the 7(a) program (e.g., the loan maturity for working capital, machinery, and equipment—not to exceed the life of the equipment—is typically 5 to 10 years, and the loan maturity for real estate is up to 25 years), except that the term for a revolving line of credit cannot exceed seven years. Also, collateral is not required for loans of $25,000 or less. Lenders are allowed to use their own established collateral policy for loans over $25,000 and up to $350,000. For loans exceeding $350,000, lenders must follow the SBA's regulations on collateral for standard 7(a) loans.[60]

Under the 7(a) program, lenders are required to collateralize the loan to the maximum extent possible up to the loan amount. If business assets do not fully secure the loan, the lender must take available personal assets of the principals as collateral. Loans are considered "fully secured" if the lender has taken security interests in all available assets with a combined "liquidation value" up to the loan amount.[61]

The Patriot Express program features streamlined documentation and processing features, with a targeted SBA processing time of one business day. The program's interest rates are negotiable with the lender, subject to the same maximum rate limitations as the 7(a) program, which vary depending upon the size and maturity of the loan.[62] It also has the same fees as the 7(a) program, which also vary depending on the size and maturity of the loan.[63]

Congressional Issues: Access

The SBA has indicated in both testimony at congressional hearings and in press releases that it views the Patriot Express program as a success. For example, in 2007, William Elmore, Associate Director of the SBA's Office of Veterans Business Development, testified at a congressional hearing shortly after the Patriot Express program's rollout that "so far, the results have been good.

The number of loans made to veterans increased from 4,800 in fiscal year 2000 to approximately 8,000 loans in fiscal year 2006."[64]

In 2010, Joseph Jordan, SBA's Associate Administrator for Contracting and Business Development, testified at a congressional hearing that

> SBA is committed to assisting veteran-owned small businesses access the capital they need. All of SBA's loan programs are available to veterans. In FY2009, veteran-owned small businesses received 8.00% of all 7(a) loans, totaling approximately $523 million, and 4.56% of all 504 development company loans, or $176 million. Additionally, veteran-owned small businesses received 4.33% of all microloans, totaling approximately $1.9 million. In total, SBA has supported more than $2 billion in recovery lending to veteran-owned small businesses. SBA also has a loan program dedicated to the military community—Patriot Express.... It features our lowest interest rates and fastest turnaround times, often within days.... In FY2009, we approved more than 2,300 Patriot Express loans and are on track to increase those numbers in FY2010.[65]

More recently, when the SBA announced in a December 10, 2010, press release that it was extending the Patriot Express program for another three years, the SBA characterized the program as "a very popular initiative that in just three-and-a-half years has provided more than $560 million in loan guarantees to nearly 7,000 veterans to start or expand their small businesses."[66]

Congressional testimony provided by various veteran service organizations provides a somewhat different perspective. The SBA's focus in its evaluation of the success of the Patriot Express Program has been on the SBA's application approval process (e.g., minimizing paperwork requirements and expediting the time necessary for the SBA to review and approve applications submitted by local lenders) and aggregate lending amounts (e.g., number of loans approved and the amount of loans approved). In contrast, veteran service organizations have focused on the program's outcomes, especially the likelihood of a veteran being approved for a Patriot Express loan by a local lender. For example, a representative of the American Legion testified at a congressional hearing in 2010 that being turned down for a SBA Patriot Express loan by a private lender "is probably the largest, most frequent complaint that we receive from our business owners."[67] At that same congressional hearing, a representative of the Vietnam Veterans of America testified in response to that statement that "I would have to concur ... in talking with some of the veterans with regard to the Patriot Express Loan, they are having difficulties also to acquire that capital. The rationale seems to be ... the banks in general seem to be tightening the credit, their lending practices, so that is ... what we are hearing."[68]

There are no empirical assessments of veterans' experiences with the SBA Patriot Express Loan program that would be useful for determining the relative ease or difficulty of veteran-owned small business owners accessing capital through the program. Since 2010, many lenders report that they have eased their credit standards, at least somewhat, for small business loans, suggesting that the experiences of veterans seeking a Patriot Express loan guaranty today may be different than it was in 2010. The SBA could survey veterans who have received a Patriot Express loan guaranty to obtain their views on the program, including the application process, but obtaining a list of veterans who have been turned down for a Patriot Express loan by a private lender would be difficult given privacy concerns.

FEDERAL CONTRACTING GOALS FOR SERVICE-DISABLED VETERAN-OWNED SMALL BUSINESSES

Since 1978, federal agency heads have been required to establish federal procurement contracting goals, in consultation with the SBA, "that realistically reflect the potential of small business concerns" to participate in federal procurement. Each agency is required, at the conclusion of each fiscal year, to report their progress in meeting the goals to the SBA.[69] The SBA negotiates the goals with each federal agency, and establishes a "small business eligible" baseline for evaluating the agency's performance.

The small business eligible baseline excludes certain contracts that the SBA has determined do not realistically reflect the potential for small business participation in federal procurement (such as contracts awarded to mandatory and directed sources), contracts awarded and performed overseas, contracts funded predominately from agency-generated sources, contracts not covered by Federal Acquisition Regulations, and contracts not reported in the Federal Procurement Data System (such as contracts or government procurement card purchases valued less than $3,000).[70] These exclusions typically account for 18% to 20% of all federal prime contracts each year.

The SBA then evaluates the agencies' performance against their negotiated goals annually, using data from the Federal Procurement Data System—Next Generation, managed by the U.S. General Services Administration, to generate the small business eligible baseline. This information is compiled into the official Small Business Goaling Report, which the SBA releases annually.

Over the years, federal government-wide procurement contracting goals have been established for small businesses generally (P.L. 100-656, the Business Opportunity Development Reform Act of 1988, and P.L. 105-135, the HUBZone Act of 1997 —Title VI of the Small Business Reauthorization Act of 1997), small businesses owned and controlled by socially and economically disadvantaged individuals (P.L. 100-656, the Business Opportunity Development Reform Act of 1988), women (P.L. 103-355, the Federal Acquisition Streamlining Act of 1994), small businesses located within a HUBZone (P.L. 105-135, the HUBZone Act of 1997 —Title VI of the Small Business Reauthorization Act of 1997), and small businesses owned and controlled by a service disabled veteran (P.L. 106-50, the Veterans Entrepreneurship and Small Business Development Act of 1999).

The current federal small business contracting goals are

- at least 23% of the total value of all small business eligible prime contract awards to small businesses for each fiscal year;

- 5% of the total value of all small business eligible prime contract awards and subcontract awards to small disadvantaged businesses for each fiscal year;
- 5% of the total value of all small business eligible prime contract awards and subcontract awards to women-owned small businesses;
- 3% of the total value of all small business eligible prime contract awards and subcontract awards to HUBZone small businesses; and
- 3% of the total value of all small business eligible prime contract awards and subcontract awards to service-disabled veteran-owned small businesses.[71]

There are no punitive consequences for not meeting the small business procurement goals. However, the SBA's Small Business Goaling Report is distributed widely, receives media attention, and serves to heighten public awareness of the issue of small business contracting. For example, agency performance as reported in the SBA's Small Business Goaling Report is often cited by Members during their questioning of federal agency witnesses during congressional hearings.

Table 3. Federal Contracting Goals and Percentage of FY2011 Federal Contract Dollars Awarded to Small Businesses, by Type

Business Type	Federal Goal	Percentage of FY2011 Federal Contracts (small business eligible)	Percentage of FY2011 Federal Contracts (all reported contracts)
Small Businesses	23.0%	21.65%	17.0%
Small Disadvantaged Businesses	5.0%	7.67%	6.0%
Women-Owned Small Businesses	5.0%	3.98%	3.1%
HUBZone Small Businesses	3.0%	2.35%	1.8%
Service-Disabled Veteran-Owned Small Businesses	3.0%	2.65%	2.1%

Source: U.S. Small Business Administration, "Statutory Guidelines," at http://www.sba.gov /content/goalingguidelines-0 (federal goals); U.S. General Services Administration, Federal Procurement Data System—Next Generation, "Small Business Goaling Report: Fiscal Year 2011," at https://www.fpds.gov/ downloads/ top_requests/FPDSNG_ SB_Goaling_FY_2011.pdf; and U.S. General Services Administration, Federal Procurement Data System—Next Generation, at https://www.fpds.gov/fpdsng/ (contract dollars).

Notes: The total amount of federal contracts awarded in FY2011, as reported in the FPDS, was $536.8 billion; $422.5 billion of this amount was deemed by the SBA to be small business eligible. Of the total amount reported, $91.5 billion was awarded to small businesses, $32.4 billion to small disadvantaged businesses, $16.8 billion to women owned small businesses, $9.9 billion to SBA-certified HUBZone small businesses, and $11.2 billion to service-disabled veteran-owned small businesses.

As shown in *Table 3*, in FY2011, federal agencies met the federal contracting goal for small disadvantaged businesses, but not the other goals. Federal agencies awarded 21.65% of the value of their small business eligible contracts to small businesses, 7.67% to small disadvantaged businesses, 3.98% to women-owned small businesses, 2.35% to HUBZone small businesses, and 2.65% to service-disabled veteran-owned small businesses.[72] The percentage of total reported federal contracts (without exclusions) awarded to small businesses, small disadvantaged businesses, women-owned small businesses, HUBZone small businesses, and service-disabled veteran-owned small businesses in FY2011 is also provided in the table for comparative purposes.

Congressional Issues: Contracting Fraud[73]

The prevention of fraud in federal small business contracting programs, and in the SBA's loan programs as well, has been a priority for both Congress and the SBA for many years, primarily because reports of fraud in these programs emerge with some regularity.[74] Of particular interest to veterans, GAO has found that "the lack of an effective government-wide fraud-prevention program" has left the service-disabled veteran owned small business program "vulnerable to fraud and abuse."[75]

Under the Small Business Act, a small business owned and controlled by a service-disabled veteran can qualify for a federal government procurement set-aside (a procurement in which only certain businesses may compete) or a sole source award (awards proposed or made after soliciting and negotiating with only one source) if the small businesses is at least 51% unconditionally and directly owned and controlled by one or more service-disabled veterans.[76] A veteran is defined as a person who has served "in the active military, naval, or air service, and who was discharged or released under conditions other than dishonorable."[77] A disability is service-related when it "was incurred or aggravated ... in [the] line of duty in the active military, naval, or air service."[78]

Federal agencies may set aside procurements for service-disabled veteran-owned small businesses only if the contracting officer reasonably expects that offers will be received from at least two responsible small businesses, and the award will be made at a fair market price (commonly known as the "rule of two" because of the focus on there being at least two small businesses involved).[79]

Federal agencies may award sole contracts to service-disabled veteran-owned small businesses when (1) the contracting officer does not reasonably expect that two or more service-disabled veteran-owned small businesses will submit offers; (2) the anticipated award will not exceed $3.5 million ($6 million for manufacturing contracts); and (3) the award can be made at a fair and reasonable price.[80] Otherwise, sole-source awards may only be made to service-disabled veteran-owned small businesses under other authority, such as the Competition in Contracting Act.[81] Service-disabled veteran-owned small businesses are not eligible for price evaluation preferences in unrestricted competitions.

In addition, the Department of Veterans Affairs (VA) is statutorily required to establish annual goals for the awarding of VA contracts to both service-disabled veteran-owned small businesses and to small businesses owned by other veterans.[82] VA is authorized to use "other than competitive procedures" in meeting these goals. For example, VA may award any contract whose value is below the simplified acquisition threshold (generally $150,000) to a veteran-owned business on a sole-source basis, and it may also make sole-source awards of contracts whose value (including options) is between $150,000 and $5 million, provided that certain conditions are met. When these conditions are not met, VA is generally required to set aside the contract for service-disabled or other veteran-owned small businesses.[83]

Service-disabled veteran-owned small businesses can generally self-certify as to their eligibility for contracting preferences available under the Small Business Act.[84] However, in an effort to address fraud in VA contracting, veteran-owned and service-disabled veteran-owned small businesses must be listed in VA's VetBiz database, and have their eligibility verified by the VA, in order to be eligible for preferences in certain VA contracts.[85]

Firms that fraudulently misrepresent their size or status have long been subject to civil and/or criminal penalties under Section 16 of the Small Business Act; SBA regulations implementing Section 16; and other provisions of law, such as the False Claims Act, Fraud and False Statements Act, Program Fraud Civil Remedies Act, and Contract Disputes Act.[86]

Several bills have been introduced during the 112th Congress to address fraud in small business contracting programs in various ways. Of particular interest to veterans, S. 633, the Small Business Contracting Fraud Prevention Act of 2011, would, among other changes, amend Section 16 of the Small Business Act to expressly include service-disabled veteran-owned small businesses among the types of small businesses subject to penalties for fraud under that section.[87] The bill would also require service-disabled veteran-owned small businesses to register in the VA's VetBiz database, or any successor database, and have their status verified by the VA in order to be eligible for contracting preferences for service-disabled veteran-owned small businesses under the Small Business Act.

Advocates of requiring service-disabled veteran-owned small businesses to register in the VetBiz database and have their status verified by the VA to be eligible for contracting preferences under the Small Business Act argue that doing so would reduce fraud.[88]

As Senator Snowe stated on the Senate floor when she introduced S. 633, "Our legislation attempts to remedy the spate of illegitimate firms siphoning away contracts from the rightful businesses trying to compete within the SBA's contracting programs"[89]

Others worry that requiring service-disabled veteran-owned small businesses to register in the VetBiz database and have their status verified by the VA to be eligible for contracting preferences under the Small Business Act may add to the paperwork burdens of small businesses. They seek alternative ways to address the need to reduce fraud in federal small business procurement programs that do not increase the paperwork requirements of small businesses.[90]

Still others note that the effectiveness of any change to prevent fraud in veteran owned and service-disabled veteran owned small business procurement programs largely depends upon how the change is implemented by the SBA and VA. For example, in July 2011, VA's Inspector General Office concluded that VA's implementation of its veteran owned and service-disabled veteran owned small business procurement fraud prevention programs needed improvement:

> We project that VA awarded ineligible businesses at least 1,400 VOSB [Veteran Owned Small Business] and SDVOSB [Service-Disabled Veteran Owned Small Business] contracts valued at $500 million annually and that it will award about $2.5 billion in VOSB and SDVOSB contracts to ineligible businesses over the next 5 years if it does not strengthen oversight and verification procedures. VA and the Office of Small and Disadvantaged Business Utilization (OSDBU) need to improve contracting officer oversight, document reviews, completion of site visits for "high-risk" businesses, and the accuracy of VetBiz Vendor Information Pages information.[91]

THE MILITARY RESERVIST ECONOMIC INJURY DISASTER LOAN PROGRAM

P.L. 106-50, the Veterans Entrepreneurship and Small Business Development Act of 1999, signed into law on August 17, 1999, authorized the SBA's Military Reservist Economic Injury Disaster Loan (MREIDL) Program. The SBA published the final rule establishing the program in the *Federal Register* on July 25, 2001, with an effective date of August 24, 2001.[92]

The Senate Committee on Small Business provided, in its committee report on the Veterans Entrepreneurship and Small Business Development Act of 1999, the following reasons for supporting the authorization of the MREIDL Program:

> During and after the Persian Gulf War in the early 1990's, the Committee heard from reservists whose businesses were harmed, severely crippled, or even lost, by their absence. Problems faced by reservists called to active duty and their small businesses were of a varied nature and included cash-flow problems, difficulties with training an appropriate alternate manager on very short notice to run the business during the period of service, lost clientele upon return, and on occasion, bankruptcy. These hardships can occur during a period of national emergency or during a period of contingency operation when troops are deployed overseas.
>
> To help such reservists and their small businesses, the Committee seeks to provide credit and management assistance to small businesses when an essential employee (i.e., an owner, manager or vital member of the business' staff) is a reservist called to active duty. The Committee believes that financial assistance in the form of loans, loan deferrals and managerial guidance are effective ways to minimize the adverse financial demands of the call to active duty. They not only ameliorate financial difficulties but also strengthen small businesses.[93]

The House Committee on Small Business also supported the program's authorization, indicating in its committee report that the program

> will also fulfill a long unmet need to assist our military reservists who are small business owners. Often these individuals, called to service at short notice, come back from fighting to protect our freedoms only to find their businesses in shambles. H.R. 1568 will establish loan deferrals, technical and managerial assistance, and loan programs for these citizen soldiers so that while they risk their lives they need not risk their livelihoods.[94]

As mentioned previously, the SBA provides direct loans for owners of businesses of all sizes, homeowners, and renters to assist their recovery from natural disasters. The SBA's MREIDL Program provides disaster assistance in the form of direct loans of up to $2 million to help small business owners who are not able to obtain credit elsewhere to (1) meet ordinary and necessary operating expenses that they could have met, but are not able to meet; or (2) to enable them to market, produce or provide products or services ordinarily marketed, produced, or provided by the business which cannot be done because an essential employee has been called-up to active duty in their role as a military reservist or member of the National Guard due to a period of military conflict.[95] Under specified circumstances, the SBA may waive the $2 million limit (e.g., the small business is in immediate danger of going out of business, is a major source of employment, employs 10% of more of the work force within the commuting area in which the business is located).[96]

P.L. 106-50 defines an essential employee as "an individual who is employed by a small business concern and whose managerial or technical expertise is critical to the successful day-to-day operations of that small business concern."[97] The act defines a military conflict as (1) a period of war declared by Congress; or (2) a period of national emergency declared by Congress or the President; or (3) a period of contingency operation. A contingency operation is designated by the Secretary of Defense as an operation in which our military may become involved in military actions, operations, or hostilities (peacekeeping operations).[98]

The SBA is authorized to make such disaster loans either directly, or in cooperation with banks or other lending institutions through agreements to participate on an immediate or deferred basis. The loan term may be up to a maximum of 30 years, and is determined by the SBA in accordance with the borrower's ability to repay the loan. The loan's interest rate is the SBA's published interest rate for an Economic Injury Disaster Loan at the time the application for assistance is approved by the SBA. Economic Injury Disaster Loan interest rates may not exceed 4%.

The SBA is not required by law to require collateral on disaster loans. However, the SBA has established collateral requirements for disaster loans based on "a balance between protection of the Agency's interest as a creditor and as a provider of disaster assistance."[99] The SBA generally does not require collateral to secure a MREIDL loan of $50,000 or less. Larger loan amounts require collateral, but the SBA will not decline a request for a MREIDL loan for a lack of collateral if the SBA is reasonably certain that the borrower can repay the loan.[100]

In FY2011, the SBA disbursed 10 MREIDL loans amounting to $1,152,400. Since the MREIDL's inception through July 31, 2012, the SBA has disbursed 340 MREIDL loans amounting to $32,184,050.[101] Of these 340 loans, 57 loans (16.8% of the total number of MREIDL loans disbursed), amounting to $5,658,310 (17.6% of the total amount of MREIDL loans disbursed), have been charged off (a declaration that the debt is unlikely to be collected) by the SBA.

Because the MREIDL program is relatively small and non-controversial, a discussion of the congressional issues affecting the program is not presented.

CONCLUSION

Congressional interest in federal programs designed to assist veterans in their transition from military into civilian life has increased in recent years for a variety of reasons, especially because of the relatively high rate of unemployment experienced by veterans who have left the military since 2001. The SBA's veterans assistance programs have also experienced a heightened level of congressional interest and scrutiny in recent Congresses. For example, the SBA's veteran business development programs, Patriot Express loan guaranty program, and federal procurement programs for small businesses generally, including service-disabled veteran-owned small businesses, have all been subject to congressional hearings during the past two Congresses. Also, as has been discussed, several bills have been introduced in recent Congresses to address the SBA's management of these programs and fraud.

SBA Veterans Assistance Programs: An Analysis of Contemporary Issues   355

Given the many factors that influence business success, measuring the effectiveness of the SBA's veterans assistance programs, especially the programs' effect on veteran job retention and creation, is both complicated and challenging. For example, it is difficult to determine with any degree of precision or certainty the extent to which any changes in the success of a small business result primarily from their participation in the SBA's programs or from changes in the broader economy. That task is made even more challenging by the absence of performance outcome measures that could serve as a guide. In most instances, the SBA uses program's performance measures that focus on indicators that are primarily output related, such as the number of Patriot Express loans approved and funded and the number and amount of federal contracts awarded to service-disabled veteran-owned small businesses.

Both GAO and the SBA's Office of Inspector General have recommended that the SBA adopt more outcome related performance measures for the SBA's loan guaranty programs, such as tracking the number of borrowers who remain in business after receiving a SBA guaranteed loan to measure the extent to which the SBA contributed to their ability to stay in business.[102] Other performance-oriented measures that Congress might also consider include requiring the SBA to survey veterans who participate in their business development programs or in the Patriot Express loan guaranty program to measure the difficulty they experienced in obtaining a loan from the private sector. The SBA could also survey service-disabled veteran-owned small businesses that were awarded a federal contract to determine the extent to which the SBA was instrumental in their receiving the award and the extent to which the award contributed to their ability to create jobs or expand their scope of operations.

End Notes

[1] For further information and analysis concerning the Small Business Administration's (SBA's) entrepreneurial education programs, see CRS Report R41352, Small Business Management and Technical Assistance Training Programs, by Robert Jay Dilger; for further information and analysis concerning the SBA's access to capital programs, see CRS Report R41146, Small Business Administration 7(a) Loan Guaranty Program, by Robert Jay Dilger and CRS Report R41184, Small Business Administration 504/CDC Loan Guaranty Program, by Robert Jay Dilger; and for further information and analysis of the SBA's federal contracting programs, see CRS Report R41945, Small Business Set-Aside Programs: An Overview and Recent Developments in the Law, by Kate M. Manuel and Erika K. Lunder and CRS Report R42390, Federal Contracting and Subcontracting with Small Businesses: Issues in the 112th Congress, by Kate M. Manuel and Erika K. Lunder.

[2] U.S. Small Business Administration, "Disaster Assistance Program: SOP 50-30-7," May 13, 2011, p. 48, at http://www.sba.gov/sites/default/files/SOP %2050%2030%207.pdf; and 13 C.F.R. §123.508. For further information and analysis concerning the SBA's disaster assistance loan program, see CRS Report R41309, The SBA Disaster Loan Program: Overview and Possible Issues for Congress, by Bruce R. Lindsay.

[3] U.S. Small Business Administration, "FY2013 Congressional Budget Justification and FY2011 Annual Performance Report," 2012, p. 62, at http://www.sba.gov/sites/ default/files /files/FY%202013%20CBJ% 20FY%202011%20APR.pdf; and U.S. Small Business Administration, "Operation Boots to Business: From Service to Startup," at http://www.sba.gov /bootstobusiness.

[4] U.S. Small Business Administration, "FY2013 Congressional Budget Justification and FY2011 Annual Performance Report," 2012, pp. 62-63, at http://www. sba. gov/sites/ default/files/files/ FY%202013%20CBJ% 20FY%202011%20APR.pdf.

[5] U.S. Department of Labor, Bureau of Labor Statistics, "Table A-5. Employment status of the civilian population 18 years and over by veteran status, period of service, and sex, not seasonally adjusted," at http://www.bls.gov/ news.release/empsit.t05.htm. Media reports typically cite national employment and unemployment statistics for adults 16 and older. Discussions of the employment and unemployment experiences of veterans usually use the employment and unemployment experiences of adults 18 years and older.

[6] U.S. Bureau of the Census, "Survey of Business Owners," at http://www. census.gov/econ/sbo/index.html.

[7] U.S. Bureau of the Census, "Survey of Business Owners: About the Survey," at http://www. census.gov/econ/sbo/about.html.

[8] U.S. Bureau of the Census, "Survey of Business Owners: 2007 Methodology," at http://www. census.gov/econ/sbo/ methodology.html.

[9] U.S. Bureau of the Census, "Survey of Business Owners," at http://www.census. gov/ econ/sbo/about.html.

[10] An additional 1.2 million nonfarm U.S. firms (about 4.5% of all nonfarm U.S. firms) were owned equally (50%-50%) by veterans and nonveterans. See U.S. Bureau of the Census, "Statistics for All U.S. Firms by Industry, Veteran Status, and Receipts Size of Firm for the U.S. and States: 2007," at http://factfinder2. census.gov/faces/tableservices/jsf/ pages/ productview. xhtml?pid=SBO_2007_00CSA08&prodType=table. Veteran status was based on self-identification. Respondents were asked to report if a business owner is a veteran of the U.S. military service including the Coast Guard. Businesses could be categorized either as: veteran-owned (U.S. military service veterans own 51% or more of the equity, interest, or stock of the business); equally veteran/nonveteran-owned (a 50% veteran and 50% nonveteran ownership of the equity, interest, or stock of the business); or nonveteran-owned (nonveterans own 51% or more of the equity, interest, or stock of the business).

[11] U.S. Bureau of the Census, "American Fact Finder: Statistics for All U.S. Firms by Industry, Veteran Status, and Race for the U.S., States, Metro Areas, Counties, and Places: 2007," at http://factfinder2.census.gov/faces/tableservices/jsf/pages/productview.xhtml?pid=SBO_2007_00CSA04&prodType=table.

[12] Of veteran-owned firms, 90.3% (443,495) had less than 20 employees, 8.2% (40,406) had 20 to 99 employees, and 1.4% (6,659) had 100 to 499 employees. See U.S. Bureau of the Census, "American Fact Finder: Statistics for All U.S. Firms With Paid Employees by Industry, Veteran Status, and Employment Size of Firm for the U.S. and States: 2007," at http://factfinder2.census.gov/faces/tableservices/jsf/pages/ productview. xhtml?pid=SBO_2007_00CSA12& prodType=table.

[13] U.S. Bureau of the Census, "American Fact Finder: Statistics for All U.S. Firms by Industry, Veteran Status, and Gender for the U.S., States, Metro Areas, Counties, and Places: 2007," at http://factfinder2.census.gov/faces/tableservices/jsf/pages/ productview.xhtml?pid =SBO_2007_00CSA02&prodType=table14 The total percentage exceeds 100 because each owner had the option of selecting more than one race and was included in each race selected. See U.S. Bureau of the Census, "American Fact Finder: Statistics for All U.S. Firms by Industry, Veteran Status, and Race for the U.S., States, Metro Areas, Counties, and Places: 2007," at http://factfinder2.census.gov/faces/tableservices/jsf/pages/productview.xhtml?pid=SBO_2007_00CSA04&prodType= table.

[15] U.S. Bureau of the Census, "American Fact Finder: Statistics for Owners of Respondent Firms by Owner's Age by Gender, Ethnicity, Race, and Veteran Status for the U.S.: 2007," at http://factfinder2.census.gov /faces/tableservices/jsf/pages/productview.xhtml?pid =SBO_2007_00CSCBO08&prodType=table.

[16] U.S. Bureau of the Census, "American Fact Finder: Statistics for Veteran Owners of Respondent Firms by Owner's Service-Disabled Veteran Status and Gender for the U.S.: 2007," at http://factfinder2. census. gov/ faces/tableservices/jsf/pages/productview. xhtml?pid=SBO_2007_00CSCBO10&prodType=table.

[17] U.S. Bureau of the Census, "American Fact Finder: Statistics for All U.S. Firms With Paid Employees by Veteran Status and Number of States in Which They Operate: 2007," at http://factfinder2.census.gov/ faces /tableservices/jsf/pages/productview.xhtml? pid= SBO_2007_00CSA20&prodType=table.

[18] Ibid.

[19] U.S. Department of Labor, Bureau of Labor Statistics, "Table A-5. Employment status of the civilian population 18 years and over by veteran status, period of service, and sex, not seasonally adjusted," at http://www.bls.gov/ news.release/empsit.t05.htm.

[20] Ibid.

[21] Ibid.

[22] Executive Office of the President, Council of Economic Advisers and the National Economic Council, "Military Skills for America's Future: Leveraging Military Service and Experience to Put Veterans and Military Spouses Back to Work," May 31, 2012, pp. 4-6, at http://www. whitehouse.gov/sites/default/ files/docs/veterans_ report_5-31-2012.pdf. The report also indicated that military spouses also face a number of employment barriers. For example, military spouses are "ten times more likely to have moved across state lines in the last year compared to their civilian counterparts," affecting job tenure, advancement opportunities, and, for those in occupations requiring a state specific occupational license or certification, the need to re-qualify for their license or certification after moving across state lines. See Ibid., pp. 8-10.

[23] U.S. Congress, Senate Committee on Banking and Currency, Extension of the Small Business Act of 1953, report to accompany S. 2127, 84th Cong., 1st sess., July 22, 1955, S.Rept. 84-1350 (Washington: GPO, 1955), p. 17.

SBA Veterans Assistance Programs: An Analysis of Contemporary Issues 357

[24] Interagency Task Force on Veterans Small Business Development, "Report to the President: Empowering Veterans Through Entrepreneurship," November 1, 2011, p. 15, at http://www.sba.gov/sites/default/files/FY2012-Final%20Veterans%20TF%20Report% 20to %20President. pdf.

[25] Syracuse University, "About the EBV," Syracuse, NY, at http://whitman.syr.edu/ebv/.

[26] Syracuse University, "Women Veterans Igniting the Spirit of Entrepreneurship (V-WISE)," Syracuse, NY, at http://www. whitman.syr. edu/vwise/index.asp.

[27] Syracuse University, "About Operation Endure and Grow," Syracuse, NY, at http:// www.whitman.syr.edu/EndureAndGrow/About/.

[28] U.S. Small Business Administration, "Veterans Business Outreach Centers," at http://www.sba.gov/content/veteransbusiness-outreach-centers/. Each Veterans Business Outreach Center is funded on an annual basis, with funding not to exceed $150,000 each year. Awards "may vary, depending upon location, staff size, project objectives, performance and agency priorities, and additional special initiatives initiated by the Office of Veterans Business Development." See U.S. Small Business Administration, Office of Veterans Business Development, "Special Program Announcement: Veterans Business Outreach Center Program," April 2010, p. 2, at http://archive.sba.gov/ idc/groups /public/documents/ sba_program_office/ovbd_ vboc_ prgm_announce2010.pdf. Also, existing centers may receive additional funding for special outreach or other initiatives. The initial grant award is for 12 months, with the possibility of four additional (option) years. In FY2011, the Veterans Business Outreach Centers Program conducted its seventh annual "Customer Satisfaction Survey." The FY2011 survey found that 91% of the clients using the centers were satisfied or highly satisfied with the quality, relevance, and timeliness of the assistance provided. See U.S. Small Business Administration, "FY2013 Congressional Budget Justification and FY2011 Annual Performance Report," 2012, p. 62, at http://www.sba.gov/sites/default/files/files/FY%202013%20CBJ%20FY%202011%20APR.pdf.

[29] U.S. Small Business Administration, "FY2013 Congressional Budget Justification and FY2011 Annual Performance Report," p. 48, at http://www.sba.gov/sites/ default/files/files/ FY%202013%20CBJ%20FY% 202011%20APR.pdf.

[30] Ibid., p. 49.

[31] Ibid.

[32] Ibid. The Interagency Task Force on Veterans Small Business Development includes senior level representatives of the U.S. Small Business Administration, the Departments of Defense, Labor, Treasury, and Veterans Affairs, the General Services Administration, the Office of Management and Budget, and four representatives from veterans' service or military organizations appointed by the SBA Administrator. The SBA's Deputy Administrator, Marie Johns, serves as its chair. See Executive Order 13540, "Interagency Task Force on Veterans Small Business Development," 75 Federal Register 22497-22498, April 29, 2010. U.S Small Business Administration, "Inter-Agency Task Force on Veterans Small Business Development: Kick Off Meeting Wednesday, September 15, 2010," at http://www.sba.gov/ about-sba-info/14368.

[33] P.L. 106-50, the Veterans Entrepreneurship and Small Business Development Act of 1999, Section 101. Findings.

[34] U.S. Congress, House Committee on Small Business, Veterans Entrepreneurship and Small Business Development Act of 1999, report to accompany H.R. 1568, 106th Cong., 1st sess., June 29, 1999, H.Rept. 106-206 (Washington: GPO, 1999), pp. 14-15.

[35] Veteranscorp, "About Us," Oxford, MD at http://www.veteranscorp.org/2012/01/a-new-veteranscorp-org-gets-thechance-to-help-veteran-entrepreneurs-2/.

[36] P.L. 106-50, the Veterans Entrepreneurship and Small Business Development Act of 1999, Section 33. National Veterans Business Development Corporation. Also, see 15 U.S.C. §657c.

[37] U.S. Congress, House Committee on Small Business, Veterans Entrepreneurship and Small Business Development Act of 1999, report to accompany H.R. 1568, 106th Cong., 1st sess., June 29, 1999, H.Rept. 106-206 (Washington: GPO, 1999), p. 14.

[38] P.L. 106-50, the Veterans Entrepreneurship and Small Business Development Act of 1999, Section 301. Score Program.

[39] Ibid., Section 302. Entrepreneurial Assistance.

[40] Ibid.

[41] U.S. Small Business Administration, "FY2013 Congressional Budget Justification and FY2011 Annual Performance Report," 2012, p. 62, at http://www.sba.gov/ sites/default/files/files/ FY%202013%20CBJ% 20FY%202011%20APR.pdf.

[42] Ibid.

[43] Both programs are offered as a three-day workshop conducted at military installations that include sessions on how to choose a career, how to look for a job, current occupational and labor market conditions, how to prepare job search materials, including resumes and cover letters, and interviewing techniques. DTAP adds

additional hours to the three-day program that focus on the special needs of disabled veterans. See Ibid.; and U.S. Department of Labor, "VETS Fact Sheet: 1: Transition Assistance Program," at http://www.dol.gov/vets /programs/tap/tap_fs.htm.

[44] For information on the Disabled Veterans' Outreach Program and Local Veterans' Employment Representatives Program see U.S. Department of Labor, "Jobs for Veterans State Grants," at http://www.dol.gov/vets /grants/state/ jvsg.htm.

[45] For further information and analysis of federal programs outside of the SBA which are designed to assist veterans seeking civilian employment, see CRS Report RS22666, Veterans Benefits: Federal Employment Assistance, by Christine Scott.

[46] For further information and analysis concerning the Homeless Veterans Reintegration Program, see CRS Report RL34024, Veterans and Homelessness, by Libby Perl.

[47] U.S. House of Representatives, Committee on Veterans' Affairs, "Debunking the Myths: H.R. 4072," at http://veterans.house.gov/4072.

[48] U.S. House of Representatives, Committee on Small Business, "Views and Estimates of the Committee on Small Business on Matters to be set forth in the Concurrent Resolution on the Budget for Fiscal Year 2013," March 17, 2011, at http://smallbusiness.house.gov/ uploadedfiles/march_17_views_and_estimates_letter.pdf; and U.S. House of Representatives, Committee on Small Business, "Views and Estimates of the Committee on Small Business on Matters to be set forth in the Concurrent Resolution on the Budget for Fiscal Year 2013,"March 7, 2012, at http://smallbusiness.house.gov/ uploadedfiles/ views_and_estimates_fy_2013.pdf.

[49] U.S. Government Accountability Office, 2012 Annual Report: Opportunities to Reduce Duplication, Overlap and Fragmentation, Achieve Savings, and Enhance Revenue, GAO-12-342SP, February 28, 2012, p. 55, at http://www.gao.gov/assets/590/588818.pdf. Also see U.S. Government Accountability Office, Entrepreneurial Assistance: Opportunities Exist to Improve Programs' Collaboration, Data-Tracking, and Performance Management, GAO-12-819, August 23, 2012, p. 55, at http://www.gao.gov/assets/650/647267.pdf.

[50] U.S. Congress, House Committee on Small Business, Job Creation Through Entrepreneurship Act of 2009, report to accompany H.R. 2352, 111th Cong., 1st sess., May 15, 2009, H.Rept. 111-112 (Washington: GPO, 2009), pp. 17-18.

[51] H.R. 2352, the Job Creation Through Entrepreneurship Act of 2009, Section 601. Expanding Entrepreneurship.

[52] The seven federal agencies are: the SBA, U.S. General Services Administration, U.S. Office of Management and Budget, and the Departments of Defense, Labor, Treasury, and Veterans Affairs. The four veterans organizations are: Association of State Directors of Veterans Affairs, Student Veterans of America, The American Legion, and VET-Force.

[53] Interagency Task Force on Veterans Small Business Development, "Report to the President: Empowering Veterans Through Entrepreneurship," November 1, 2011, p. 6, at http://www.sba.gov/sites/default/f iles/FY2012-Final%20Veterans%20TF%20Report% 20to %20President.pdf.

[54] Ibid., p. 15.

[55] Ibid., p. 8.

[56] U.S. Small Business Administration, "SOP 50 10 5(E): Lender and Development Company Loan Programs," (effective June 1, 2012), p. 42, at http://www.sba.gov/sites/default/files/ SOP%2050%2010%205(E)%20(5-16-2012)%20clean.pdf.

[57] U.S. Small Business Administration, "SBA Patriot Express Pilot Loan Initiative: Talking Points," June 13, 2007, at http://archive.sba.gov/idc/groups/public/ documents/sba_ program_office/sba_patriot_loan_initiative_ta.pdf.

[58] U.S. Small Business Administration, "SOP 50 10 5(E): Lender and Development Company Loan Programs," (effective June 1, 2012), p. 83, 127, at http://www.sba.gov /sites/default/files/SOP%2050% 2010%205(E)%20(5-16- 2012)%20clean.pdf.

[59] U.S. Small Business Administration, "Popular SBA Patriot Express Loan Initiative Renewed for Three More Years," December 10, 2010, http://www.sba.gov/content/popular-sba-patriot-express-loan-initiative-renewed-three-more-years. S. 532, the Patriot Express Authorization Act of 2011, would provide the program statutory authorization and increase the program's maximum loan amount from $500,000 to $1million.

[60] U.S. Small Business Administration, "SOP 50 10 5(E): Lender and Development Company Loan Programs," (effective June 1, 2012), p. 83, 84, 146, 148, 152, 153, 156, 157, at http:// www.sba.gov/sites/default /files/SOP%2050%2010%205(E)%20(5-16-2012)%20clean.pdf.

[61] Ibid., pp. 188-189.

[62] Under the 7(a) loan guaranty program, lenders may charge borrowers "a reasonable fixed interest rate" or, with the SBA's approval, a variable interest rate. The SBA uses a multi-step formula to determine the maximum allowable fixed interest rate and periodically publishes that rate and the maximum allowable variable interest rate in the Federal Register. For fixed interest rates, the SBA first calculates a fixed base rate using the 30 day

London Interbank Offered Rate (LIBOR) in effect on the first business day of the month as published in a national financial newspaper published each business day, adds to that 300 basis points (3%) and the average of the 5-year and 10-year LIBOR swap rates in effect on the first business day of the month as published in a national financial newspaper published each business day. For 7(a) fixed loans with maturities of less than seven years, the SBA adds 2.25% to the fixed base rate to arrive at the maximum allowable fixed rate. For 7(a) fixed loans with maturities of seven years or longer, the SBA adds 2.75% to the fixed base rate to arrive at the maximum allowable fixed rate. Lenders may increase the maximum fixed interest rate allowed by an additional 1% if the fixed rate loan is over $25,000 but not exceeding $50,000, and by an additional 2% if the fixed rate loan is $25,000 or less. See, U.S. Small Business Administration, "Business Loan Program Maximum Allowable Fixed Rate," 74 Federal Register 50263, 50264, September 30, 2009. The 7(a) program's maximum allowable variable interest rate may be pegged to the lowest prime rate, the 30 day LIBOR rate plus 300 basis points, or the SBA optional peg rate. The optional peg rate is a weighted average of rates the federal government pays for loans with maturities similar to the average SBA loan.

[63] Under the 7(a) loan guaranty program, the SBA charges lenders a guaranty fee and a servicing fee for each loan approved and disbursed. The maximum guaranty fee for 7(a) loans with maturities exceeding 12 months is set by statute. For loans with a maturity of 12 months or less, the SBA charges the lender a 0.25% guaranty fee, which the lender is required to submit with the application. The lender may charge the borrower for the fee when the loan is approved by the SBA. For loans with a maturity exceeding 12 months, the SBA charges the lender a 2% guaranty fee for the SBA guaranteed portion of loans of $150,000 or less, a 3% guaranty fee for the SBA guaranteed portion of loans exceeding $150,000 but not more than $700,000, and a 3.5% guaranty fee for the SBA guaranteed portion of loans exceeding $700,000. Loans with an SBA guaranteed portion in excess of $1 million are charged an additional 0.25% guaranty fee on the guaranteed amount in excess of $1 million. These fees are the maximum allowed by law. The lender must pay the SBA guaranty fee within 90 days of the date of loan's approval and may charge the borrower for the fee after the lender has made the first disbursement of the loan. Lenders are permitted to retain 25% of the upfront guaranty fee on loans with a gross amount of $150,000 or less. Also, the servicing fee cannot exceed 0.55% per year of the outstanding balance of the SBA's share of the loan.

[64] U.S. Congress, Senate Committee on Small Business and Entrepreneurship, Assessing Federal Small Business Assistance Programs for Veterans and Reservists, hearing, 110th Cong., 1st sess., January 31, 2007, S.Hrg. 110-209 (Washington: GPO, 2007), p. 32.

[65] U.S. Congress, House Committee on Veterans' Affairs, Subcommittee on Economic Opportunity, Status of Veterans Small Business, hearing, 111th Cong., 2nd sess., April 29, 2010, House Committee on Veterans' Affairs Serial No. 111- 74 (Washington: GPO, 2010), p. 75.

[66] U.S. Small Business Administration, "Popular SBA Patriot Express Loan Initiative Renewed for Three More Years," December 10, 2010, at http://www.sba.gov/content/popular-sba-patriot-express-loan-initiative-renewed-three-moreyears.

[67] U.S. Congress, House Committee on Veterans' Affairs, Subcommittee on Economic Opportunity, Status of Veterans Small Business, hearing, 111th Cong., 2nd sess., April 29, 2010, House Committee on Veterans' Affairs Serial No. 111- 74 (Washington: GPO, 2010), p. 17.

[68] Ibid.

[69] P.L. 95-507, a bill to amend the Small Business Act and the Small Business Investment Act of 1958.

[70] See U.S. General Services Administration, Federal Procurement Data System—Next Generation, "Small Business Goaling Report: Fiscal Year 2011," at https://www.fpds.gov/ downloads/top_requests/ FPDSNG_SB_Goaling_FY_2011.pdf.

[71] 15 U.S.C. §644(g)(1)-(2).

[72] U.S. General Services Administration, Federal Procurement Data System—Next Generation, "Small Business Goaling Report: Fiscal Year 2011," at https://www.fpds.gov/ downloads/ top_requests/ FPDSNG_SB_Goaling_FY_2011.pdf.

[73] For additional information and analysis concerning federal procurement small business issues see CRS Report R41945, Small Business Set-Aside Programs: An Overview and Recent Developments in the Law, by Kate M. Manuel and Erika K. Lunder; and CRS Report R42390, Federal Contracting and Subcontracting with Small Businesses: Issues in the 112th Congress, by Kate M. Manuel and Erika K. Lunder.

[74] For example, see U.S. Government Accountability Office, Small Business Administration: Undercover Tests Show HUBZone Program Remains Vulnerable to Fraud and Abuse, GAO-10-920T, July 28, 2010, at http://www.gao.gov/ assets/130/125130.pdf; U.S. Government Accountability Office, 8(a) Program: Fourteen Ineligible Firms Received $325 Million in Sole-Source and Set-Aside Contracts, GAO-10-425, March 30, 2010, at http://www.gao.gov/assets/ 310/302472.pdf; U.S. Government Accountability Office, Service-

Disabled Veteran-Owned Small Business Program: Case Studies Show Fraud and Abuse Allowed Ineligible Firms to Obtain Millions of Dollars in Contracts, GAO-10- 108, October 23, 2009, at http://www.gao.gov/products/GAO-10-108; and U.S. Government Accountability Office, Service-Disabled Veteran-Owned Small Business Program: Vulnerability to Fraud and Abuse Remains, GAO-12-697, August 1, 2012, at http://www.gao.gov/assets/600/593238.pdf.

[75] U.S. Government Accountability Office, Service-Disabled Veteran-Owned Small Business Program: Preliminary Information on Actions Taken by Agencies to Address Fraud and Abuse and Remaining Vulnerabilities, GAO-11-589T, July 28, 2011, p. 3, at http://www.gao.gov/products/GAO-11-589T.

[76] 15 U.S.C. §632(q)(1) & (4); P.L. 108-183, the Veterans Benefits Act of 2003; and P.L. 109-461, the Veterans Benefits, Health Care, and Information Technology Act of 2006.

[77] 38 U.S.C. §101(2).

[78] 38 U.S.C. §101(16).

[79] 15 U.S.C. §657f(b).

[80] 15 U.S.C. §657f(a)(1)-(3) (statutory requirements); and 48 C.F.R. §19.1406(a) (increasing the price thresholds).

[81] 10 U.S.C. §2304(c)(1)-(7) (procurements of defense agencies); and 41 U.S.C. §3304(a)(1)-(7) (procurements of civilian agencies). See also 48 C.F.R. §§6.302-1 to 6.302-7; and CRS Report R40516, Competition in Federal Contracting: An Overview of the Legal Requirements, by Kate M. Manuel.

[82] P.L. 109-461. the Veterans Benefits, Health Care, and Information Technology Act of 2006; and P.L. 110-389, the Veterans' Benefits Improvements Act of 2008.

[83] For further information and analysis of federal contracting legal authorities generally and affecting the Department of Veterans Affairs see CRS Report R42391, Legal Authorities Governing Federal Contracting and Subcontracting with Small Businesses, by Kate M. Manuel and Erika K. Lunder.

[84] 13 C.F.R. §125.15.

[85] 38 U.S.C. §8127(a)(1)(A). P.L. 109-461, the Veterans Benefits, Health Care, and Information Technology Act of 2006, requires the Secretary of Veterans Affairs to "establish a goal for each fiscal year for participation in Department contracts (including subcontracts)" by veteran-owned small businesses. The Secretary is also required to establish a separate goal for the participation of service-disabled veteran-owned small businesses in agency contracts and subcontracts. 38 U.S.C. §8127(a)(1)(A). However, the latter goal can be no less than the government-wide goal for the percentage of contract and subcontract dollars awarded to service-disabled veteran-owned small businesses given in Section 15(g)(1) of the Small Business Act (currently 3%), while the former goal is within the Secretary's discretion. See 38 U.S.C. §8127(a)(2)-(3).

[86] See 15 U.S.C. §645; and 13 C.F.R. §125.29.

[87] Currently, Section 36 of the Small Business Act, which governs set-asides and sole-source awards for service-disabled veteran-owned small businesses, provides that "[r]ules similar to the rules of paragraphs (5) and (6) of Section 637(m) of this title shall apply for purposes of this section." Section 8(m) governs set-asides for women-owned small businesses, and itself provides that such businesses are subject to penalties for fraud under Section 16. Thus, an argument could potentially be made that service-disabled veteran-owned small businesses are currently subject to penalties under Section 16 even if they are not expressly included there. See CRS Report R42390, Federal Contracting and Subcontracting with Small Businesses: Issues in the 112th Congress, by Kate M. Manuel and Erika K. Lunder.

[88] See 13 C.F.R. §§125.9-125.13.

[89] Senator Olympia Snowe, "Statements on Introduced Bills and Joint Resolutions," remarks in the Senate, Congressional Record, vol. 157, part no. 41 (March 17, 2011), p. S1843.

[90] U.S. Congress, House Committee on Oversight and Government Reform, Subcommittee on Technology, Information Policy, Intergovernmental Relations and Procurement Reform, Jobs for Wounded Warriors: Increasing Access to Contracts for Service Disabled Veterans, 112th Cong., 2nd sess., February 7, 2012, Serial No. 112-143 (Washington: GPO, 2012), pp. 86-90.

[91] U.S. Department of Veterans Affairs, Office of the Inspector General, "Audit of Veteran-Owned and Service-Disabled Veteran-Owned Small Business Programs," July 25, 2011, p. i, at http://www.va.gov /oig/52/reports/2011/ VAOIG-10-02436-234.pdf.

[92] U.S. Small Business Administration, "Military Reservist Economic Injury Disaster Loans," 66 Federal Register 38528-38531, July 25, 2001.

[93] U.S. Congress, Senate Committee on Small Business, Veterans Entrepreneurship and Small Business Development Act of 1999, report to accompany H.R. 1568, 106th Cong., 1st sess., August 4, 1999, S.Rept. 106-136 (Washington: GPO, 1999), p. 4.

[94] U.S. Congress, House Committee on Small Business, Veterans Entrepreneurship and Small Business Development Act of 1999, report to accompany H.R. 1568, 106th Cong., 1st sess., August 4, 1999, H.Rept. 106-206, Part 1 (Washington: GPO, 1999), p. 15.

[95] U.S. Small Business Administration, "Disaster Assistance Program: SOP 50-30-7," May 13, 2011, p. 48, at http://www.sba.gov/sites/default/files/SOP%2050%2030%207.pdf; and 13 C.F.R. §123.508. For further information and analysis concerning the SBA's disaster assistance loan program see CRS Report R41309, The SBA Disaster Loan Program: Overview and Possible Issues for Congress, by Bruce R. Lindsay.

[96] 13 C.F.R. §123.507.

[97] P.L. 106-50, the Veterans Entrepreneurship and Small Business Development Act of 1999, Section 402. Assistance To Active Duty Military Reservists; and 15 U.S.C. §636(b). The SBA's Military Reservist Economic Injury Disaster Loan Program applies to economic injury suffered or likely to be suffered as the result of a period of military conflict occurring or ending on or after March 24, 1999.

[98] P.L. 106-50, the Veterans Entrepreneurship and Small Business Development Act of 1999, Section 402. Assistance To Active Duty Military Reservists; and 15 U.S.C. §636(c).

[99] U.S. Small Business Administration, "Disaster Assistance Program: SOP 50-30-7," May 13, 2011, p. 152, at http://www.sba.gov/sites/default/files/SOP%2050%2030%207.pdf.

[100] 13 C.F.R. §123.513.

[101] U.S. Small Business Administration, Office of Congressional and Legislative Affairs, "Correspondence with Robert Dilger," August 27, 2012. In FY2012 (through July 31, 2012), the SBA has disbursed 6 MREIDL loans amounting to $788,100.

[102] U.S. Government Accountability Office, Small Business Administration: 7(a) Loan Program Needs Additional Performance Measures, GAO-08-226T, November 1, 2007, p. 2, http://www.gao.gov/new.items/d08226t.pdf; and U.S. Small Business Administration, Office of the Inspector General, SBA's Administration of the Microloan Program under the Recovery Act, December 28, 2009, pp. 6, 7, http://www.gao.gov/new.items/d08226t.pdf.

INDEX

A

abuse, 19, 40, 66, 244, 245, 255, 256, 262, 304, 351

accounting, 13, 20, 88, 104, 185, 186, 240, 331, 342, 344

acquisitions, 216

adaptability, 164

adjustment, 8, 189, 267

adults, 355

advancement, 214, 275, 356

advocacy, 26

African Americans, 210, 230

African-American, 65, 338

age, 59, 339

agency initiatives, 344

agriculture, 5, 177

Alaska, xiv, 13, 92, 130, 155, 187, 197, 200, 208, 212, 213, 218, 224, 231, 234, 235, 244, 247, 248, 250, 266, 338

Alaska Natives, 13, 187, 197, 218, 224

American Recovery and Reinvestment Act, vii, ix, x, xv, 1, 2, 21, 27, 50, 54, 55, 78, 81, 88, 89, 111, 113, 114, 126, 157, 162, 167, 168, 170, 181, 271, 273, 277, 278, 285, 298, 323

American Recovery and Reinvestment Act of 2009, vii, ix, x, xv, 1, 2, 21, 27, 50, 54, 55, 78, 81, 88, 89, 111, 113, 114, 126, 157, 162, 167, 168, 170, 181, 271, 273, 277, 278, 285, 298, 323

American Samoa, 13, 177, 178, 187, 197, 199, 284

ANC, 213, 216, 217, 218, 219, 220, 223, 224, 225, 226, 227, 228, 231, 233, 234, 235, 236

ancestors, 231

appraisals, 62, 305

appraised value, 108

appropriate technology, 258

appropriations, 3, 7, 21, 27, 50, 64, 101, 120, 121, 229, 276, 277, 294, 298

Appropriations Act, 27, 78, 81, 113, 114, 118, 179, 180, 199, 200, 201, 202, 203, 204, 241, 263, 277, 295, 322, 325, 332

aquarium, 297

ARC, 21, 50, 71, 84, 106, 115, 286

Asian Americans, 211

assessment, 13, 38, 67, 68, 105, 186, 192, 258, 259, 305, 318

assets, ix, 8, 9, 10, 21, 25, 27, 54, 57, 58, 59, 66, 80, 87, 88, 93, 108, 111, 116, 146, 163, 176, 205, 214, 217, 219, 224, 315, 330, 339, 340, 341, 347, 358, 359

asthma, 41

atmosphere, 229

Attorney General, 19

audit, 19, 69, 104, 151, 194, 254, 255, 258, 304

audits, 19, 20, 126, 256, 280, 284

authorities, 209, 234, 283, 360

automation, 254

automobiles, 4, 31

B

balance sheet, 59, 60, 96, 164

Bangladesh, 211

banking, 164, 167

bankruptcy, 331, 353

banks, 7, 21, 66, 72, 77, 82, 91, 107, 118, 119, 128, 165, 169, 193, 205, 348, 354

barriers, xiv, 24, 50, 139, 143, 145, 150, 208, 221, 237, 323, 356

base, xv, 75, 79, 93, 164, 179, 199, 240, 242, 248, 261, 358

base rate, 79, 358

base year, 199

basis points, 58, 79, 168, 359

364 Index

behaviors, 46
benchmarks, 6, 304
beneficiaries, 69, 127
benefits, 46, 54, 60, 164, 213, 220, 243, 245, 258, 262
Bhutan, 211
bias, 210, 214, 230
biodiesel, 93, 108
biotechnology, 307
blogs, 83, 116, 229
blood, 231
board members, 192
bonding, 276, 279, 287, 288
bonds, xv, 17, 26, 271, 272, 273, 274, 275, 276, 278, 279, 280, 281, 282, 283, 284, 285, 287, 288, 289, 290, 292, 293, 294, 296, 297
breakdown, 60
breeding, 245
bronchitis, 41
Budget Committee, 161
budget cuts, 222
budget deficit, 193, 276
budget line, 200
building code, 4, 31
Bureau of Indian Affairs, 247
Bureau of Labor Statistics, 247, 340, 355, 356
Burma, 211
business formation, vii, 1, 2, 138, 174, 176, 195, 237, 272, 312, 331, 336
business management, vii, xii, xiii, 1, 2, 173, 174, 175, 192, 194, 195, 215, 272, 342
business processes, 256, 262
business strategy, 13
buyer, 79
by-products, 262

C

Cambodia, 211
candidates, 193
capacity building, 183
capital markets, 16, 138, 158
capital programs, 355
case studies, 195
cash, xii, 56, 59, 91, 94, 104, 105, 108, 120, 122, 138, 139, 141, 144, 145, 148, 149, 150, 151, 160, 161, 177, 179, 180, 182, 196, 199, 284, 320, 329, 353
cash flow, xii, 56, 59, 91, 94, 104, 105, 138, 139, 141, 144, 145, 148, 150, 151, 160, 182, 284
casinos, 248

Census, xviii, 25, 130, 132, 201, 245, 246, 247, 249, 260, 265, 266, 269, 318, 336, 337, 338, 340, 341, 356
certificate, 12, 148, 149, 168, 254
certification, 33, 60, 68, 94, 95, 96, 187, 197, 219, 232, 244, 250, 255, 257, 261, 262, 298, 305, 356
CFR, 25, 112, 165, 166, 167, 168, 169, 170, 172, 324, 329, 330, 332
challenges, xiv, 161, 190, 195, 208, 209, 210, 221, 222
Chamber of Commerce, 190
charitable organizations, 7
Chicago, 147, 229, 314, 319, 328, 330
childcare, 24, 25, 123
children, 41, 59
China, 40, 41, 211
cities, 146, 206, 242, 314, 315
citizens, xiii, 46, 207, 208, 212, 213, 224, 231, 244, 302
citizenship, 254
City, 237, 263, 275
civil disorder, 4, 32
classes, 142, 199, 245
classification, xiv, 157, 208, 215, 219, 237, 250, 338
clean energy, 166, 324
clean technology, 170
cleanup, 298
clients, 27, 85, 121, 178, 179, 180, 181, 182, 184, 186, 188, 190, 191, 192, 346, 357
closure, 32, 242, 248, 261
clothing, vii, 4, 29, 31
clusters, 175, 176, 198
Coast Guard, 356
Code of Federal Regulations, 24, 25, 49, 50
coffee, 255
collaboration, 346
collateral, 7, 25, 57, 58, 59, 62, 67, 75, 76, 91, 94, 96, 108, 109, 123, 158, 279, 280, 284, 289, 347, 354
colleges, 95, 177, 196
color, 59, 210
commerce, vii, 29, 95, 177
commercial, xv, 5, 9, 10, 17, 18, 33, 70, 72, 94, 95, 106, 107, 108, 140, 233, 271, 272, 302, 305, 306, 307
commercial bank, 140
Commonwealth of the Northern Mariana Islands, 211
communication, xviii, 19, 191, 198, 204, 336, 337, 342, 346

communities, xiv, 9, 49, 70, 77, 85, 86, 92, 93, 108, 110, 139, 143, 145, 150, 185, 187, 189, 239, 240, 242, 244, 245, 258, 259, 262, 264, 314, 315, 321, 323, 329, 345
community service, 212
comparative analysis, 65, 103, 154, 156
compensation, 24, 82, 104, 214, 218
competition, xiii, 2, 6, 93, 190, 207, 208, 215, 216, 222, 232, 233, 240, 263, 305
competitive advantage, 218, 244
competitive conditions, 164
competitive markets, 79, 111
competitiveness, 93
competitors, 164, 257
complexity, 213, 218, 224, 250, 257, 262
compliance, 19, 20, 30, 47, 62, 67, 95, 97, 151, 179, 254, 256, 262, 318
composition, 49
computer, 156
conditioning, 41
conference, 20, 230, 294, 316, 342
conflict, 97, 281, 336, 353, 354, 361
conflict of interest, 97, 281
conformity, 96
congress, 83, 116, 298
congressional budget, 2, 68, 258, 259, 262, 343
congressional hearings, xii, 15, 76, 173, 175, 189, 253, 258, 259, 275, 276, 279, 289, 348, 350, 354
congressional offices, 81, 114
consensus, 195
consent, 257, 314
Consolidated Appropriations Act, xvi, 8, 27, 28, 74, 97, 131, 140, 175, 181, 199, 200, 201, 202, 203, 204, 241, 248, 249, 260, 263, 265, 266, 277, 281, 311, 312, 316
consolidation, xviii, 21, 286, 336, 337
Constitution, 231
construction, 2, 6, 59, 62, 75, 77, 78, 79, 90, 92, 97, 111, 152, 209, 215, 217, 248, 273, 275, 276, 285, 287, 289, 294, 296, 297, 298, 347
consulting, 188, 289
Consumer Price Index, 170
consumption, 93, 108
contamination, 32
contingency, 92, 353, 354
contracting programs, vii, xiii, xviii, 1, 2, 13, 16, 21, 72, 107, 128, 205, 207, 208, 253, 254, 272, 287, 288, 298, 336, 337, 351, 352, 355
control measures, 253
controversial, 354
cooperation, xii, xvii, xviii, 11, 39, 97, 146, 173, 175, 181, 189, 335, 336, 337, 345, 346, 354

cooperative agreements, 18, 188, 302
coordination, xii, 37, 39, 47, 173, 175, 189, 190, 191, 192, 342, 346
copper, 41
cost, xiv, 7, 12, 13, 24, 25, 40, 43, 46, 59, 60, 61, 64, 69, 72, 94, 98, 101, 107, 110, 111, 121, 124, 125, 128, 148, 161, 162, 166, 182, 192, 205, 216, 233, 239, 241, 243, 250, 274, 278, 283, 286, 319, 321
costs of manufacturing, 217
counsel, 2, 20, 97, 99, 209, 237
counseling, xii, xiii, 13, 50, 120, 125, 131, 173, 174, 176, 177, 178, 180, 181, 182, 184, 185, 186, 187, 193, 195, 196, 199, 343, 344, 345
Court of Appeals, 222
covering, viii, 30
credit history, xv, 10, 17, 42, 56, 91, 123, 125, 160, 271, 273
credit market, ix, 53, 55, 63, 66, 70, 73, 100, 103, 109, 129, 286, 324
creditors, 11, 12, 146
creditworthiness, 97, 123
criticism, 37, 256
CSA, 88, 98, 99
culture, 191
currency, 121
current limit, 287
customer service, 39
customers, 164, 185, 244, 345

D

damages, xv, 5, 271, 273
danger, 353
data collection, 193
data processing, 213
database, 306, 327, 352
debentures, xvii, 12, 94, 98, 99, 110, 140, 142, 143, 146, 147, 148, 149, 150, 151, 152, 160, 165, 167, 168, 170, 311, 312, 313, 315, 319, 322, 323, 328, 329, 330
debts, 55, 57, 331
deficiencies, 66, 104, 126, 306
deficiency, 108
deficit, viii, xii, 53, 55, 73, 109, 129, 138, 139, 158, 161, 162, 324
delegates, 97
democrats, 83, 116, 268, 269, 270
demographic characteristics, 338
denial, 57, 91, 234, 250
Department of Agriculture, 167, 168, 318, 329, 332

Department of Commerce, xii, 173, 174, 184, 187, 189, 204, 212, 230, 246, 295, 343
Department of Defense, xvii, 27, 78, 81, 113, 114, 184, 185, 199, 200, 201, 202, 203, 204, 216, 220, 221, 222, 226, 236, 238, 263, 267, 277, 287, 298, 335, 343, 344, 345
Department of Education, 303
Department of Energy, xvi, 233, 301
Department of Justice, 231, 267
Department of Labor, xvii, 9, 184, 185, 247, 335, 340, 343, 344, 345
Department of the Treasury, 9, 66, 82, 274, 276
Department of Transportation, 230
Departments of Agriculture, 17, 302
depth, 56, 91, 187
development assistance, 194
direct investment, 139, 321
directors, 59, 95, 146, 167, 214, 218, 219, 225, 235
disability, 59, 75, 339, 341, 347, 351
disaster, vii, viii, 1, 2, 3, 4, 5, 23, 24, 29, 30, 31, 32, 33, 35, 36, 37, 38, 39, 40, 41, 42, 43, 44, 45, 46, 47, 48, 49, 50, 51, 204, 206, 282, 296, 298, 336, 353, 354, 355, 361
disaster area, viii, 3, 4, 29, 31, 32, 282, 296, 298
disaster assistance, 2, 3, 31, 37, 38, 39, 42, 46, 51, 336, 353, 354, 355, 361
disaster relief, 42
disbursement, 50, 60, 61, 62, 81, 100, 114, 167, 359
discrimination, xiv, 59, 208, 221, 222, 236, 237
displacement, 32
distance learning, 185, 344
distress, 168, 204
distribution, 141, 144, 155, 163, 164, 184, 331, 344
District of Columbia, 119, 154, 155, 177, 178, 180, 221, 222, 243, 284, 317
divestiture, 167
DOL, 185, 344, 345
draft, xvi, 20, 60, 195, 272, 273, 286
dream, 230
due process, 231

E

earnings, 56, 91, 140, 143, 164, 319
economic activity, vii, xi, 1, 2, 137, 139, 193, 243
economic assistance, 30, 41
economic damage(s), vii, 29, 47
economic development, xvi, 9, 92, 95, 96, 120, 175, 177, 187, 188, 189, 192, 196, 242, 254, 259, 311, 312, 314, 315, 317, 321, 322, 346

economic disadvantage, 140, 167, 211, 214, 218, 219, 221, 224, 235, 236, 237
economic downturn, 119, 180, 193, 280
economic growth, ix, xii, 53, 55, 66, 70, 73, 100, 103, 109, 110, 129, 138, 139, 161, 176, 242, 272, 278, 286, 324
Economic Injury Disaster Loans (EIDL), vii, 29, 30
economic losses, vii, 29, 32
economic mainstream, 210
Economic Research Service, 167, 329, 332
economic status, 219, 236, 243, 246
economic well-being, 302
economics, 229, 243, 259
education, 138, 164, 166, 174, 183, 187, 191, 197, 214, 260, 312, 324, 336, 355
educators, 20, 342
eligibility criteria, 80, 231, 235, 261
emergency, 33, 42, 47, 48, 50
Emergency Assistance, xvi, 4, 33, 272, 273, 286
Emergency Economic Stabilization Act, 66, 82
employees, 6, 14, 32, 37, 39, 118, 130, 134, 146, 163, 166, 188, 194, 213, 214, 217, 219, 231, 234, 241, 250, 254, 266, 283, 285, 302, 315, 318, 323, 330, 338, 356
employers, 341
employment, xvii, xviii, 6, 18, 71, 74, 106, 129, 210, 214, 218, 220, 254, 258, 259, 335, 336, 337, 338, 339, 340, 341, 342, 345, 354, 355, 356, 358
employment opportunities, 18, 210
employment status, 340
empowerment, 92, 263, 318
encouragement, 210
energy, 93, 108, 170
energy consumption, 93, 108
enforcement, 20
engineering, 13, 177, 256, 331
England, 242
entrepreneurs, x, xii, xviii, 10, 13, 18, 20, 117, 119, 123, 125, 132, 135, 140, 158, 161, 173, 174, 177, 180, 182, 183, 190, 191, 192, 195, 196, 197, 198, 242, 245, 324, 336, 337, 342, 343, 345, 346, 357
entrepreneurship, 20, 184, 185, 197, 337, 342, 343, 344, 346
environment, 66, 100, 103, 182, 214
environmental impact, 62
Environmental Protection Agency, 17, 51, 302
environmental services, 163
environmental technology, 170
equipment, ix, x, 4, 8, 9, 10, 11, 32, 58, 59, 64, 75, 76, 77, 78, 87, 88, 92, 93, 102, 108, 111,

117, 119, 123, 124, 146, 152, 180, 196, 200, 215, 228, 347

equity, xi, xiv, xvi, 9, 10, 11, 12, 18, 25, 56, 57, 60, 91, 94, 96, 111, 137, 138, 140, 143, 145, 146, 153, 158, 161, 163, 166, 167, 169, 208, 214, 235, 301, 304, 311, 312, 315, 319, 321, 324, 340, 341, 356

erosion, 32

ethanol, 93, 108

ethnic groups, xiii, xiv, 141, 208, 209, 211, 221, 230

ethnicity, 338

evidence, xiv, 39, 43, 67, 97, 99, 118, 141, 144, 208, 211, 214, 219, 221, 222, 224, 230, 236, 237, 275, 279, 288, 297, 306

examinations, 18, 151, 250, 254, 255, 258, 259, 289

execution, 296

executive branch, 209, 210

Executive Order, 47, 188, 201, 204, 357

executive orders, 210

exercise, xii, 47, 138, 139, 161, 166, 209, 214, 237

expenditures, 43, 177, 192

expertise, 78, 125, 152, 181, 314, 354

export promotion, 128

exports, 93, 185, 344

exposure, 8, 276

F

faith, 88, 216, 319

families, 50, 185, 344, 347

family members, 20, 217, 342

farm land, 146, 163, 330

farms, 5, 111

federal advisory, 20

federal agency, 14, 15, 18, 19, 20, 167, 209, 251, 253, 254, 303, 305, 349, 350

federal assistance, 43, 110, 243

federal courts, xv, 233, 240, 241

Federal Emergency Management Administration, 282

Federal Emergency Management Agency, 5, 47, 51

federal employment, xviii, 336, 337, 342

federal funds, 9, 161, 185, 194, 199, 344

federal government, xii, xiii, xiv, 1, 3, 8, 15, 19, 31, 43, 46, 58, 73, 82, 139, 162, 173, 174, 187, 188, 193, 194, 207, 208, 239, 241, 242, 244, 251, 254, 273, 290, 324, 349, 351, 359

Federal Government, 201, 232

federal law, 179, 216

Federal Register, 24, 26, 50, 58, 75, 79, 80, 85, 93, 94, 112, 142, 144, 150, 165, 166, 167, 169, 172, 188, 204, 229, 235, 259, 263, 265, 266, 267, 269, 270, 282, 284, 295, 296, 297, 298, 304, 309, 316, 329, 330, 353, 357, 358, 360

Federal Reserve, 89, 111, 138, 165

Federal Reserve Board, 89, 111, 138, 165

FEMA, viii, 5, 24, 30, 33, 37, 39, 41, 47, 49, 50, 282

Fifth Amendment, 231

Fiji, 211

financial capital, 214, 224

financial condition, 42, 163

financial oversight, 194

financial reports, 126

financial resources, 148

financial stability, 167

financial support, 18, 174, 302

financial system, 66

fire hazard, 41

firm size, 24, 50

fishing, 32

fixed rate, ix, 30, 72, 79, 87, 88, 107, 120, 134, 359

flaws, 245

flexibility, 190

floods, 4, 32

fluctuations, 290

food, 32

Food and Drug Administration, 204

Food, Conservation, and Energy Act of 2008, 50, 296

force, xviii, 336, 337, 340, 341, 345, 354

Ford, 276

foreign firms, 306

formation, vii, 1, 2, 47, 138, 143, 174, 176, 179, 184, 185, 194, 195, 197, 237, 272, 312, 331, 336, 342, 343, 344

formula, 58, 177, 247, 358

foundations, 193, 199, 210

Fourteenth Amendment, 237

franchise, 23, 96, 213, 231

fraud, xiv, 18, 19, 21, 40, 66, 239, 241, 244, 245, 250, 253, 254, 255, 256, 257, 262, 279, 280, 281, 289, 304, 306, 351, 352, 354, 360

fund transfers, 126

G

gambling, 7, 79, 91, 297

General Accounting Office, 80, 292, 295, 296, 299, 304

General Services Administration, 15, 16, 26, 251, 252, 263, 267, 287, 298, 349, 350, 357, 358, 359
Generally Accepted Accounting Principles, 96
Georgia, 155, 317
global climate change, 189
goods and services, 62
government funds, 237
government procurement, xii, 15, 173, 174, 240, 251, 349
governments, 187
governor, 4, 33
grading, 54, 57
Gramm-Leach-Bliley Act, 182, 202
grants, xi, xvii, 3, 5, 13, 18, 26, 31, 37, 69, 78, 118, 119, 122, 125, 127, 128, 176, 177, 178, 179, 180, 182, 183, 184, 186, 189, 194, 197, 199, 204, 225, 302, 303, 304, 311, 312, 313, 314, 317, 320, 322, 323, 331, 332, 345, 358
Great Depression, 1
gross domestic product, 6
growth, xi, 11, 19, 84, 116, 118, 125, 135, 137, 138, 149, 152, 161, 171, 176, 177, 178, 195, 244, 245, 258, 259, 260, 275, 276
guidance, 67, 104, 127, 178, 185, 190, 255, 263, 265, 269, 345, 353
guidelines, 16, 18, 38, 59, 279, 302, 303, 304, 305
Gulf Coast, 30, 36, 37, 39, 40, 42, 43, 44, 45, 48, 51, 325, 332
Gulf of Mexico, 236

H

Hawaii, 92, 155, 212, 231, 248
hazards, 46, 94
health, 41, 93, 111, 141, 341
Health and Human Services, 17, 18, 302, 303
health care, 141
higher education, 177, 188
historical data, 306
history, 27, 59, 123, 135, 141, 164, 176, 198, 201, 209, 214, 221, 236, 289
homeowners, vii, viii, 1, 2, 30, 31, 33, 37, 41, 43, 44, 138, 174, 272, 312, 336, 353
homes, vii, 3, 4, 29, 41, 43, 49, 50, 111
Hong Kong, 211
hostilities, 354
hotels, 111
House of Representatives, 230, 268, 269, 270, 358
household income, 168, 242, 245, 246, 247, 249, 258, 259, 318

housing, 50, 245, 246, 248, 260, 264, 266
Housing and Urban Development (HUD), 167, 168, 192, 199, 200, 201, 202, 203, 245, 246, 248, 260, 264, 265, 266, 274, 294, 295, 318, 329, 332, 345
human, vii, 20, 29, 38, 342
human resources, 20, 38, 342
Hurricane Katrina, 43, 46, 47, 322
hurricanes, 30, 36, 37, 39, 40, 42, 43, 44, 45
hybrid, 169

I

identification, 68, 186, 356
identity, 210, 230
imports, 93
improvements, 4, 5, 32, 39, 57, 67, 75, 76, 77, 78, 79, 91, 92, 105, 288, 339, 341, 347
in transition, xvii, 306, 335, 345
incidence, 262
income tax, 219
India, 211
Indian reservation, 183, 247, 259, 265
Indians, 13, 187, 197, 210, 211, 231
Indonesia, 211
industrial sectors, 166
industries, xi, 6, 14, 137, 141, 152, 156, 158, 170, 176, 220, 221, 222, 237
inflation, xii, 138, 139, 160, 254, 267, 274, 278, 280, 284
information technology, 38, 170
infrastructure, 50, 176, 286
initiation, 99
injections, 161
injury, viii, 3, 5, 24, 29, 30, 32, 33, 49, 361
inspections, 62
institutions, 77, 78, 89, 118, 138, 167, 181, 188, 354
integration, 68, 346
integrity, 214, 281
interagency coordination, 47
interest rates, viii, xvii, 7, 30, 31, 37, 58, 75, 76, 77, 79, 123, 127, 146, 311, 312, 319, 347, 348, 354, 358
intermediaries, x, xi, 11, 22, 68, 77, 117, 118, 119, 120, 121, 122, 123, 125, 126, 127, 128, 129, 130, 131, 132, 133, 134, 135, 158, 175, 180, 181, 196, 200
internal controls, 254
Internal Revenue Service, 39, 60, 247, 338
international trade, 2
investment capital, 118, 168

Index

investment(s), xi, xii, xvi, xvii, 12, 18, 118, 137, 138, 139, 141, 143, 144, 145, 146, 147, 148, 150, 151, 152, 153, 154, 155, 156, 157, 158, 160, 165, 166, 286, 311, 312, 313, 314, 315, 316, 319, 321, 323, 324, 329
investors, 12, 118, 140, 144, 147, 148, 149, 151, 317, 324
Iowa, 155
Iraq, 200
issues, viii, ix, 19, 20, 30, 33, 37, 38, 53, 55, 61, 66, 82, 84, 90, 94, 99, 104, 114, 115, 116, 135, 147, 171, 193, 194, 212, 272, 305, 308, 354, 359

J

Japan, 211
Jews, 210, 230, 232
job creation, ix, xii, xiv, 8, 10, 11, 12, 53, 55, 66, 70, 71, 73, 92, 100, 103, 106, 109, 129, 138, 139, 157, 161, 162, 176, 193, 194, 195, 209, 239, 240, 243
joint ventures, 177, 198, 213, 236
Jordan, 76, 348
jurisdiction, 183
justification, 2, 60, 258, 259, 262, 343

K

Korea, 211

L

labor force, xvii, xviii, 335, 336, 337, 340, 341, 342, 345
labor force participation, xviii, 336, 337, 340, 341
labor market, 357
lakes, 32
landfills, 111
Laos, 211
large-scale disasters, 51
laws, 21, 59, 65, 73, 95, 231, 279
lead, xvi, 59, 125, 141, 161, 177, 194, 195, 196, 261, 272, 280, 287, 288
leadership, 343
legislation, xvi, 8, 19, 22, 23, 47, 55, 63, 74, 108, 140, 157, 158, 159, 161, 177, 212, 242, 244, 253, 258, 259, 263, 268, 273, 275, 301, 302, 303, 304, 308, 352
legislative proposals, xii, 138
life cycle, 141
life sciences, 141

light, 141, 144, 222, 274, 275, 281, 283
limited liability, 11, 140, 146, 213, 214, 316
liquidate, 58, 97
liquidity, 66, 67, 82, 143, 165
liquidity ratio, 165
literacy, 187
litigation, 151, 331
living conditions, 246
loan guarantee programs, vii, 1, 2, 3, 7, 8, 79, 111, 118, 119, 121
loan guarantees, 7, 21, 64, 76, 101, 118, 124, 324, 348
loan principal, 50
local community, 183, 193
local conditions, 13
local government, xv, 17, 50, 132, 142, 143, 159, 183, 185, 188, 199, 201, 204, 271, 272, 273, 340, 341, 344, 345
longevity, 195
Louisiana, 40, 41, 44, 45, 155

M

machinery, ix, 4, 9, 32, 50, 59, 75, 76, 87, 88, 92, 93, 347
major disaster declaration, 4, 32, 33, 281
major issues, 274
majority, vii, xvi, 29, 142, 159, 167, 189, 213, 219, 220, 235, 301, 303, 304, 307, 308, 315
Malaysia, 211
manufacturing, 6, 13, 32, 70, 92, 106, 141, 156, 163, 216, 220, 226, 233, 236, 254, 263, 287, 304, 351
marital status, 59
market failure, 46
marketing, x, xi, 10, 13, 20, 38, 79, 117, 118, 119, 120, 121, 122, 124, 125, 127, 128, 134, 135, 152, 164, 179, 180, 182, 184, 185, 186, 187, 188, 260, 320, 331, 342, 344
marketplace, 2, 152, 160, 245, 278, 288, 289, 290, 307, 324
Marshall Islands, 211, 284
Maryland, 155, 317
materials, x, xiii, 6, 11, 80, 90, 117, 119, 123, 144, 180, 185, 207, 213, 217, 254, 331, 344, 357
matter, 41, 77, 209, 237, 280, 287
measurement(s), xiii, 63, 95, 173, 175, 189
media, 3, 15, 40, 135, 170, 253, 350
median, 168, 245, 246, 247, 248, 249, 258, 259, 260, 266, 318
medical, 111
membership, 11, 95, 112, 146, 232

memorandums of understanding, 190
mentor, 182
mentoring, xii, 13, 20, 173, 174, 176, 182, 186, 196, 315, 342
mentoring program, xii, 173, 174, 315
methodology, 51, 259, 269, 356
metropolitan areas, 206, 245, 256, 258, 265
Mexico, 155
microloan, 68, 69, 119, 121, 122, 123, 124, 125, 126, 127, 129, 130, 134, 180, 200
military, xiv, xvii, xviii, 24, 75, 76, 185, 208, 221, 222, 237, 245, 248, 261, 335, 336, 337, 341, 342, 343, 345, 347, 348, 351, 353, 354, 356, 357, 361
minorities, 154, 209, 210, 222, 230, 236, 237, 289
minority groups, 211, 221, 275
mission(s), 2, 17, 18, 19, 20, 26, 47, 77, 95, 166, 188, 197, 302, 303, 305, 306, 343, 345
Missouri, 155
modernization, xi, 11, 93, 137, 138, 152
modifications, 22, 70, 71, 106, 107, 114, 162
modules, 346
momentum, 321
Montana, 155
motels, 111
multiplier, 176, 243
multiplier effect, 176, 243
museums, 111

N

NAFTA, 9, 82
National Aeronautics and Space Administration, 17, 263, 267, 298, 302
National Defense Authorization Act, xv, xvi, 26, 233, 240, 242, 248, 261, 267, 271, 273, 286, 301, 303
National Economic Council, 341, 356
national emergency, 353, 354
National Institutes of Health, xvi, 301, 303
national origin, 59, 210
Native Americans, 13, 187, 194, 210, 211, 230, 236
natural disaster(s), vii, 1, 2, 33, 138, 174, 272, 312, 336, 353
Nauru, 211
negotiating, 351
negotiation, 331
Nepal, 211
networking, 196
neutral, 70, 110, 221, 236

New Markets Venture Capital (NMVC), xvi, 311, 312, 321
NHOs, xiv, 208, 212, 217, 218, 219, 220, 221, 224, 227, 230, 236
non-citizens, 60
non-governmental entities, 19
nonprofit organizations, viii, 3, 4, 12, 24, 29, 30, 32, 33, 50, 118, 179, 181
North America, 6, 9, 24, 92, 285, 338
North American Free Trade Agreement, 9
nursing, 111
nursing home, 111

O

Obama, xi, xii, xv, 23, 66, 69, 70, 100, 103, 105, 106, 109, 120, 130, 137, 138, 139, 140, 157, 159, 175, 178, 179, 181, 182, 184, 185, 187, 188, 189, 229, 271, 273, 278, 286, 346
Obama Administration, xi, xii, xv, 23, 66, 69, 70, 100, 103, 105, 106, 109, 120, 130, 137, 138, 139, 140, 157, 159, 175, 178, 179, 181, 182, 184, 185, 187, 188, 189, 271, 273, 278, 286, 346
Office of Disaster Assistance (ODA), vii, 29
Office of Management and Budget, 25, 27, 28, 47, 51, 116, 130, 131, 133, 204, 294, 295, 298, 357, 358
Office of the Inspector General, 26, 83, 84, 115, 131, 133, 134, 135, 267, 306, 309, 360, 361
officials, 19, 38, 40, 61, 190, 216, 234, 254, 257, 280, 287
oil, 4, 32, 40, 111, 248, 280
oil spill, 4, 32, 40
Oklahoma, 155, 247, 248, 265
OMB, 27, 42, 47, 51, 112, 116, 235
Omnibus Appropriations Act,, 277
operating revenues, 219, 232
opportunities, vii, xiii, xiv, xvi, 1, 2, 17, 42, 138, 174, 175, 176, 178, 185, 186, 189, 192, 193, 195, 207, 208, 214, 224, 239, 240, 242, 244, 245, 254, 263, 272, 285, 286, 287, 311, 312, 336, 344, 346, 356
outreach, 13, 25, 27, 38, 185, 186, 187, 189, 198, 203, 280, 288, 337, 344, 345, 357
overlap, 192, 210, 345
oversight, ix, x, xiii, xvi, 19, 21, 39, 40, 48, 50, 54, 55, 64, 66, 67, 68, 80, 88, 90, 104, 105, 126, 174, 175, 176, 190, 191, 194, 268, 269, 270, 301, 304, 336, 346, 352
ownership, xiii, xiv, 50, 57, 60, 61, 62, 63, 78, 88, 101, 138, 166, 169, 185, 208, 213, 214,

Index

217, 220, 223, 231, 234, 251, 281, 307, 343, 344, 356

P

Pacific, 154, 211, 338
Pakistan, 211
Pandemic Influenza Act, 236
Parliament, 242
parole, 91
participants, 10, 14, 18, 90, 192, 212, 220, 236, 288, 297, 304, 342
patents, 177, 198, 307
Patriot Express Authorization Act, ix, 54, 56, 73, 75, 358
payroll, 6, 338, 339
peace, 354
peacekeeping, 354
penalties, 20, 222, 352, 360
per capita income, 166, 204, 218, 324
percentile, 266
performance measurement, 259
performers, 305
permit, 57, 181, 303, 304
Persian Gulf, 353
Persian Gulf War, 353
personal history, 151
personal views, 290
personnel costs, 217
Philadelphia, 317
Philippines, 211
photonics, 170
PLP, 61, 80
pneumonia, 41
policy, xiii, xviii, 2, 18, 40, 41, 46, 62, 67, 68, 69, 73, 75, 76, 127, 129, 185, 187, 188, 208, 209, 210, 213, 237, 255, 262, 302, 304, 336, 337, 344, 347
policymakers, 19
politics, 229
pollution, 9, 23
pools, 88, 100, 111
population, 85, 168, 177, 191, 219, 245, 246, 248, 259, 260, 341, 355, 356
portfolio, xvii, 47, 51, 68, 78, 96, 97, 121, 122, 123, 131, 134, 141, 151, 167, 201, 312, 313, 318, 320
portfolio management, 68
postal service, 255
post-traumatic stress disorder, 341
poverty, xiv, 122, 132, 167, 168, 201, 219, 239, 240, 241, 242, 245, 248, 249, 258, 318, 329
power generation, 6

precedent, xiii, 207, 213, 237, 238, 243
preferential treatment, 236
prejudice, 210, 214, 230
preparation, 331
preparedness, 46
present value, 319
preservation, 119
president, 193, 237, 298
President Clinton, 314, 315
President Obama, viii, 53, 55, 72, 73, 82, 107, 109, 116, 127, 129, 158, 160, 161
prevention, 256, 351, 352
prime rate, 8, 58, 75, 94, 359
principles, xii, 47, 162, 173, 174, 283
private insurance, viii, 30, 42, 43, 46
private investment, 152, 161
private sector, xi, 6, 17, 18, 20, 74, 102, 117, 124, 129, 153, 162, 177, 182, 185, 186, 188, 221, 222, 272, 275, 285, 289, 294, 302, 305, 307, 308, 315, 321, 344, 355
private sector investment, 305, 308
privatization, 46, 248
probability, 51
procurement, 13, 14, 15, 16, 175, 178, 185, 186, 193, 215, 222, 229, 232, 237, 240, 251, 253, 254, 259, 263, 282, 336, 344, 349, 350, 351, 352, 354, 359
producers, 93, 108, 244, 288
professional management, 95
professionals, 188, 315, 329
profit, ix, x, xiii, 6, 10, 56, 59, 79, 87, 88, 91, 94, 110, 117, 119, 122, 123, 132, 164, 188, 202, 207, 212, 213, 218, 223, 242, 280, 302, 316, 321, 345
profit margin, 280
profitability, 50, 149, 163
program features, 347
project, ix, x, xv, 8, 10, 17, 26, 27, 75, 76, 87, 88, 92, 94, 95, 97, 111, 117, 119, 180, 186, 271, 272, 273, 274, 281, 287, 293, 302, 305, 330, 347, 352, 357
proposition, 73, 109, 129
protection, xiv, 162, 208, 209, 221, 222, 273, 354
public awareness, 15, 253, 350
public debt, 205
public interest, 163
public policy, x, 18, 72, 87, 89, 92, 93, 107, 108, 288
public safety, 50
public sector, 275, 304
public-private partnerships, 18
Puerto Rico, 119, 154, 155, 177, 178, 180, 284

372 Index

Q

qualifications, 125, 141, 316
questioning, 15, 253, 350
questionnaire, 60, 337, 338

R

race, xiv, 59, 124, 208, 210, 214, 221, 222, 236,
   237, 338, 356
radio, 37
ratio analysis, 96
raw materials, 55, 57
real estate, 7, 8, 10, 58, 60, 70, 72, 75, 76, 93, 97,
   106, 107, 146, 163, 330, 347
real property, 4, 31, 32, 50, 79
reality, 158
reasoning, 290
recall, 340, 341
recession, 55, 63, 100, 152, 194, 209, 229, 285
recognition, 144, 232
recommendations, xv, 19, 38, 39, 68, 104, 175,
   182, 240, 242, 253, 258, 305, 346
reconciliation, 59
reconstruction, 282
recovery, vii, viii, x, xi, 1, 2, 30, 38, 43, 44, 46,
   48, 53, 55, 65, 76, 87, 89, 132, 137, 138, 139,
   144, 160, 174, 194, 195, 204, 272, 282, 283,
   284, 286, 312, 324, 336, 348, 353
recovery plan, 38
recreational, 4, 31
redevelopment, 93
reengineering, 250, 256
reform(s), ix, 15, 26, 27, 37, 38, 39, 42, 53, 55,
   66, 70, 73, 100, 103, 109, 129, 171, 235, 251,
   267, 286, 314, 324, 328, 349, 360
regional clusters, 176
regulations, vii, xiii, xiv, xvii, 5, 9, 19, 25, 29, 32,
   49, 59, 74, 76, 126, 129, 140, 179, 183, 186,
   197, 207, 208, 210, 211, 212, 214, 218, 219,
   220, 225, 231, 233, 235, 236, 307, 312, 313,
   347, 352
regulatory agencies, 165
regulatory requirements, 212
reimburse, 59, 97, 99
rejection, 221
relevance, 27, 85, 186, 357
reliability, 260
relief, 21, 50, 71, 72, 106, 107, 119, 128, 205,
   242, 243
religion, 59
renewable energy, 93, 108
renewable fuel, 93, 108

rent, 266
repair, vii, 2, 3, 4, 29, 30, 31, 32, 40, 41, 43, 50,
   146, 209, 273
reputation, 56, 58, 91, 281, 316
resale, 41
research institutions, 303, 307
Reservations, 245
resistance, 82
resolution, 262, 277
resources, viii, 40, 46, 47, 53, 55, 70, 73, 91, 109,
   118, 129, 148, 161, 183, 184, 190, 191, 195,
   197, 198, 199, 200, 202, 215, 228, 255, 279,
   280, 286, 288, 320, 321, 330, 343, 346
respiratory problems, 41
response, 37, 38, 39, 40, 47, 48, 49, 51, 69, 77,
   104, 126, 127, 250, 256, 257, 260, 275, 280,
   348
responsiveness, 257, 306
restoration, vii, 29
restrictions, 30, 146, 213, 231, 236, 242
restructuring, 8, 190
retail, 6, 32, 141, 255
retaliation, 20
retirement, xvii, 335, 341, 345
revenue, 7, 64, 72, 79, 91, 101, 107, 128, 205,
   213, 217, 221, 227, 228, 233, 275
rights, 11, 59, 146, 213
risk(s), xi, xv, 7, 17, 46, 67, 68, 70, 94, 95, 105,
   110, 118, 126, 137, 139, 144, 152, 158, 160,
   161, 162, 190, 256, 257, 271, 272, 273, 274,
   275, 280, 281, 283, 287, 288, 289, 290, 331,
   352, 353
risk factors, 68
risk management, 105
robotics, 93
rules, 24, 140, 143, 144, 212, 217, 218, 228, 231,
   264, 281, 328, 360
rural areas, 99, 146, 314, 315
rural counties, 242
rural development, 93

S

safety, 59, 93
sales activities, 177, 198
Samoa, 211
savings, 167, 192, 339, 340, 341
SBA disaster loans, vii, viii, 1, 2, 3, 4, 30, 37, 40,
   41, 44
scarce resources, 191, 346
school, 41, 177
science, 170
scope, 46, 67, 74, 105, 130, 355

Index

373

search terms, 203
Secretary of Agriculture, 4, 5, 33, 34
Secretary of Commerce, 4, 33, 34, 188
Secretary of Defense, 237, 354
Secretary of the Treasury, 21, 72, 94, 107, 119, 128
securities, 11, 12, 25, 66, 139, 140, 141, 142, 143, 144, 146, 147, 148, 149, 151, 152, 157, 158, 160, 165, 166, 168, 170, 315, 319, 330, 331
security, 58, 120, 148, 149, 167, 330, 347
seed, 141
seller, 60
seminars, 199
September 11, 37, 168, 169
service organizations, 76, 181, 346, 348
service provider, 184, 186, 190, 196, 197
sex, 59, 355, 356
shareholders, 219, 225
shoreline, 32
shortage, 121
shortfall, 7, 64, 101
showing, 178, 219, 220, 230, 236, 305
SIC, 146
signs, 80, 147
simulation, xiv, 208, 221, 222
Singapore, 211
small business development centers (SBDCs), xii, 173, 174
small firms, 70, 110, 158, 160, 191, 195, 229, 307, 346
social benefits, 314
society, 214
sole proprietor, 6
South Dakota, 155, 314, 328
specialists, 345
speculation, 7
spending, viii, 30, 37, 38, 42, 53, 55, 73, 109, 129, 158, 222, 250, 324
spin, 307
Sri Lanka, 211
stability, 66
stabilization, 21, 285
staff members, 126
staffing, 126
Stafford Act, 4, 33, 43, 48, 50, 51
stakeholders, 19
states, 13, 21, 44, 48, 72, 107, 119, 154, 155, 163, 177, 180, 193, 205, 243, 247, 248, 284, 304, 306, 338, 345, 346
statistics, ix, x, xvi, xvii, 53, 55, 88, 89, 139, 165, 272, 274, 312, 313, 355
statutes, 14, 24, 197

statutory authority, 186, 210, 281
stimulation, 302
stock, 11, 138, 143, 146, 193, 235, 356
stock value, 143
stockholders, 214
storage, 111, 257
strategic planning, 218
structure, xii, xv, 26, 78, 138, 139, 161, 240, 241, 251, 278, 294
style, 17, 302
subgroups, 68
Subsidies, 100, 103
subsidy(ies), xvii, 5, 7, 62, 64, 100, 101, 103, 115, 148, 162, 312, 313, 322, 323
subsistence, 181, 220
sulfur, 41
sulfuric acid, 40
Sun, 169
suppliers, xii, 173, 174, 187, 188, 273
Supreme Court, 237
surety bond, xv, 2, 17, 21, 206, 271, 272, 273, 274, 275, 276, 278, 279, 280, 281, 284, 285, 286, 287, 288, 289, 290, 294, 295, 296
surplus, 92, 93, 165
survival, 125, 162, 234
survivors, 35, 39, 40
sustainability, 200

T

Taiwan, 211
talent, 176
TAP, xvii, 335, 345
target, xii, 67, 105, 138, 139, 143, 150, 157, 184, 187, 191, 234, 242, 243, 244, 262, 323, 344
Task Force, 27, 51, 230, 343, 346, 357, 358
tax breaks, 244
tax incentive, 242, 321
tax rates, 74, 129
taxation, 95
taxes, xii, xiii, 6, 57, 71, 72, 108, 111, 138, 139, 161, 207, 212, 242, 243, 244, 318
taxpayers, 158, 161
teams, 68
techniques, 305, 357
technology(ies0, 13, 16, 17, 18, 141, 143, 170, 176, 178, 185, 302, 303, 304, 305, 306, 307, 344
technology transfer, 13, 176, 178, 307
telecommunications, 38
telephone, 141, 185, 344
telephone numbers, 185, 344
tenure, 356

374 Index

territory, 9, 13, 121, 248
terrorist attack, 37
testing, 257
Thailand, 211
threats, 20
time frame, 255, 257, 281, 304, 305
time periods, 142
time series, 178, 179, 182, 260
Title I, 140, 143, 274, 281
Title II, 140, 281
Title IV, 143, 274
Title V, 15, 241, 242, 245, 247, 249, 251, 263, 264, 265, 266, 349
Tonga, 211
trade, 6, 32, 95, 154, 189, 217, 285, 294, 296, 298
training programs, vii, xii, xviii, 1, 2, 77, 85, 173, 174, 175, 176, 186, 189, 190, 191, 192, 193, 194, 195, 198, 260, 272, 336, 337, 342, 343, 345, 346
trajectory, 289
transactions, 66, 161, 188, 281
transmission, 111
transparency, 68, 194
transport, 92
transportation, 156, 213
Treasury, 10, 11, 66, 120, 134, 168, 321, 357, 358
treatment, 128
trial, 281
triggers, 68
Tuvalu, 211

U

U.S. Department of Agriculture, 167, 329
U.S. Department of Commerce, 198, 203, 204
U.S. Department of Labor, 92, 93, 355, 356, 358
U.S. Department of the Treasury, 66, 82
U.S. economy, xiii, 6, 207, 212, 223
U.S. Treasury, 94, 282
underwriting, 12, 59, 104, 148, 279, 280, 282, 283, 330
unemployed individuals, 210
unemployment rate, xiv, xviii, 93, 166, 204, 218, 239, 240, 246, 247, 248, 324, 335, 337, 340, 343
uniform, 275
uninsured, 4, 31, 50
universe, 104
universities, 20, 177, 185, 196, 303, 342, 345
updating, 68, 92

urban, 10, 82, 84, 114, 123, 124, 130, 132, 135, 169, 170, 194, 210, 242, 264, 318
urban areas, 10, 123, 210
Urban Institute, 64, 65, 73, 74, 82, 84, 102, 114, 118, 124, 129, 130, 132, 135, 153, 154, 155, 156, 169, 170
utility costs, 248

V

valuation, 60, 61
variations, 162
vehicles, 4, 31, 321
venture capital, xi, xvi, 2, 10, 18, 137, 144, 148, 152, 153, 154, 155, 156, 158, 167, 169, 301, 303, 304, 307, 308, 312, 314, 315, 316, 317, 321, 340, 341
victims, viii, 4, 30, 32, 36, 44, 46, 47, 48, 49
Vietnam, 77, 211, 348
Volunteers, 201
vote, 75, 82, 95, 127, 142, 157, 170, 191, 286, 314, 315, 322, 325, 326, 327, 332, 346
voting, 95, 166, 213, 235

W

waiver, 41, 193, 215, 225, 264
war, 1, 209, 229, 354
waste, 66, 262, 304
water, 32, 50
wealth, xvi, 18, 195, 311, 312, 314, 330, 331
web, 297, 346
websites, 185, 344
welfare, 242
wells, 111
White House, 82, 84, 116, 135, 170, 171, 298, 328
wholesale, 6
Wisconsin, 155
witnesses, 15, 253, 275, 279, 289, 350
workers, 195
workforce, 78, 176, 244, 341, 345
working hours, 213
workload, 255
World War I, 1, 209
worry, viii, xii, 53, 55, 138, 139, 160, 161, 261, 324, 352

Y

yield, 321